MAP USE

Reading, Analysis, and Interpretation

Fourth Edition

MAP USE

Reading, Analysis, and Interpretation

Fourth Edition

Phillip C. Muehrcke
Professor of Geography
University of Wisconsin
Madison, Wisconsin

&

Juliana O. Muehrcke
Managing Editor, *Nonprofit World* Journal
Madison, Wisconsin

JP Publications
P.O. Box 44173
Madison, WIsconsin 53744-4173

To our families,
who gave so generously.

JP Publications
Post Office Box 44173
Madison, WI 53744-4173

Phone: (608) 231-2373

Fourth Edition

Library of Congress Catalog Card Number: 97-073803
ISBN 0-9602978-4-7

ACKNOWLEDGMENTS

In previous editions of *Map Use*, we acknowledged the importance of contributions made by special teachers and colleagues, teaching assistants, students at the Universities of Washington and Wisconsin, and the staff of the University of Wisconsin Cartography Laboratory, particularly Onno Brouwer and Mary Galneder. We continue to be grateful for the inspiration and assistance provided by these people.

To our delight, hundreds of people have taken the time to comment on these earlier editions. Some of these people were merely lovers of maps; others were professors responsible for teaching introductory courses in map reading, analysis, and interpretation; and a number were students who had occasion to use the book in their studies. We were especially moved by letters from people who stumbled upon *Map Use* by accident at a friend's house or library and felt compelled to let us know how pleased they were with their discovery.

All these responses were gratefully received, and many were useful in making revisions for this fourth edition. We alone, of course, bear full responsibility for errors in the text and controversial statements. This work reflects our deep love of maps and a desire to help others bring maps into their lives.

P.C. and J.O. Muehrcke
Madison, Wisconsin

My object in living is to unite

My avocation and my vocation

As my two eyes make one in sight.

—Robert Frost

PREFACE

Readers of earlier editions of *Map Use* will notice some major differences in this fourth edition. Electronic technology is having a profound impact on the way maps are used, and we've addressed this issue directly throughout this book. We've updated chapters devoted to computer mapping software and added chapters on Internet map resources and satellite positioning. We've revised the text and illustrations to incorporate changes that have occurred since the third edition was published.

In recent years, electronic aids for map use have become widely available at prices most people can afford. GPS receivers vastly simplify position and route-finding, while computers loaded with mapping software and databases let us use maps interactively. Such innovations are rapidly transforming the way we use maps. They also provide the focus for this revised edition.

And yet, we have retained much information from earlier editions because it is still useful today. Most of what you need to know about using maps isn't new.

The philosophy behind *Map Use* also remains the same. As in earlier editions, we stress that a good map user must understand what goes into the making of a map. From map makers, we ask for little less than a miracle. We want the overwhelming detail, complexity, and size of our confusing surroundings reduced to a simple representation which is convenient to carry around. We also want that abstract map to provide us with a meaningful basis for relating to the environment.

It's fair to say that cartographers have given us what we asked for. They have mapped a vast array of subjects in a variety of clever, even ingenious, ways. Maps not only cover almost any topic of interest for all parts of the world, but they're also remarkably low in cost.

This is no surprise to the many people who love maps and are intrigued with all aspects of the mapping process. Those falling in this group constantly find themselves surrounded by maps, collecting more maps, or daydreaming with a map in hand. If you're one of those people, our aim is to get you to think about maps in still new ways, to broaden your total mapping experience so that you get more pleasure from less activity.

But sadly, many of us have acquired neither the interest nor the basic skills necessary to take full advantage of the broad range of available maps. Too often we blunder through the environment, not appreciating what it has to offer, causing hardship for ourselves and others, and relating to our surroundings in a destructive way. This need not be the case. Learning to use a map is a relatively easy and painless process, with an immense payoff.

Many books have been written on map making. But since map use isn't the simple reverse of map making, most of these books are of limited value to you as a map user. In contrast, this book has been written strictly for the person who wants to use maps. Academics have tended to treat maps as indoor things, rarely including in their textbooks the fact that one of the most exciting ways to use maps is in the field. Conversely, military manuals and field guides to map and compass use have focused narrowly on way finding, virtually ignoring the role maps play in the way we think about and communicate environmental information. In this book, we bridge the gap between these two extremes, pulling fragments of information from many fields into a coherent view of the environment. We offer a comprehensive, philosophical, and practical treatment of map appreciation. To do so, we've had to deviate in several ways from approaches taken in previous cartographic literature.

First, we define a map as a graphical representation of the environment that shows relations between geographical features. This encompassing definition lets us include a variety of important map forms which are otherwise awkward to categorize. Our definition should also accommodate any new cartographic forms which might be developed in the future. Throughout this book, we have integrated discussions of standard planimetric maps, perspective diagrams, environmental photographs, and satellite images, rather than partitioning each into a separate category.

Second, we have made a clear distinction between the tangible cartographic map and the mental or cognitive map of the environment which we hold in our heads. Ultimately, it is the map in our minds, not the map in our hands, with which we make decisions. Throughout the text, we stress the point that cartographic maps are valuable aids for developing better mental maps. We should strive to become so familiar with the environment that we can move through it freely in both a physical and mental sense. Ideally, our cartographic and mental maps should merge into one.

In a third departure from tradition, we have, where appropriate, made extensive reference to commercial products of special interest to the map user. A few years ago this would have seemed strange, since most mapping was done by large government agencies. But times have changed. The field of mapping is rapidly being commercialized. Computer software and digital data for mapping are being developed and sold by private industry. What you do with maps in the future will be strongly influenced by the nature of these commercial products.

Our fourth break from established procedure has been to shift attention away from global map projections. Traditionally, a treatment of map use was almost synonymous with a discussion of map projections. Yet the use of a projection is only one of a multitude of ways in which reality is distorted and transformed when a map is made. Global map projections may be dramatic and mathematically elegant, but their impact on our everyday use of maps is relatively minor. Many people have been turned off to maps because they were forced to learn the names and characteristics of a long list of projections—information which had little to do with their lives. By devoting a smaller amount of space to projections, we've been able to explore topics more crucial to the general map user.

Finally, this book is not written in traditional textbook style. Only sparing reference is made within the text to the professional cartographic literature, and the selected readings at the end of each chapter are chosen as much for their general accessibility as their content. Whenever possible, examples and illustrations have been taken from popular sources. Maps touch so many aspects of our daily lives that it is simple and natural to make points and reinforce ideas with advertisements, cartoons, and quotations from everyday communications. These illustrations and examples are included to demonstrate and reinforce basic mapping and map use principles. They are thus an integral part of the book and should be given as much consideration as the text.

The book was designed for both the specialized and the general map user. It could be used as a basic reference work or as the textbook for a beginning map appreciation course in any of the environmental sciences. It has been specifically designed and tested for use in a three-credit semester course of 15 weeks at the college freshman level. Material is presented at the upper high school to intermediate college level.

Our aim has been to cut through the plethora of confusing terms and details that characterize so many cartographic texts. Readers can obtain an overview of the most important concepts and how they fit together by glancing through the beginning outline included for each chapter.

We have structured the material into three main sections under the headings *Map Reading* (Part I), *Map Analysis* (Part II), and *Map Interpretation* (Part III). In most books, these terms have not had more than vague definitions and are often used interchangeably. Here they have been defined precisely, and the relationship of each to the others has been made clear.

In *Part I, Map Reading*, we discuss the geographical data which make up a map, the process required to transform that information from environment to map, mapping techniques (image mapping, landform portrayal, attribute mapping, and statistical mapping), the temporal aspect of maps, software for map retrieval, and access to map resources on the Internet. The goal in this section is to give the reader an appreciation of how the cartographer represents the environment in the reduced, abstract form of a map. In map reading, in a sense, we're trying to "undo" the mapping process in our minds.

Once we grasp the degree to which cartographic procedures can influence the appearance and form of a map, we're in a position to use maps to analyze the spatial structure and relations of the mapped environment. *Part II, Map Analysis*, includes chapters on reference systems, direction, distance, map and compass use, GPS, cartometrics, form and structure, pattern comparison, software for map analysis, and map accuracy. With each of these topics, the concern is on estimating, counting, measuring, data manipulation, and pattern-seeking activities.

Map analysis in itself serves some engineering functions but intellectually is rather sterile. The results of map analysis come alive when we try to explain why the environment takes on one spatial character over another. This is the subject of *Map Interpretation (Part III)*. The material has been divided into five chapters: Interpreting the Physical Environment, Interpreting the Human Environment, Interpreting Environmental Interactions, Image Map Interpretation, and Maps and Reality. The emphasis in this final section is on environmental comprehension and understanding, for it is our surroundings, not the map, which is the real subject of map use.

These three parts are followed by a series of appendices. Topics include map scale, remote sensing of the environment, projections, navigational aids, and useful mathematical tables. Each appendix is designed to complement material presented in the main body of the text.

Although a systematic development of subject matter is followed throughout this book, each section and chapter is autonomous from, and cross-referenced to, the rest of the material. Therefore, it isn't necessary to read the book in order from cover to cover. The strategy most appropriate for you depends on your background and interests. Generally, the book is organized to provide inexperienced readers with a logical development of concepts. There is a progressive building of skills from beginning to end. More experienced map users may wish to focus initially on sections or chapters of special interest and then refer to other parts to refresh their memories or clarify terms, concepts, and methods.

This book will have served its purpose if readers finish it with a greater appreciation of maps than when they began. In even the simplest map, there is much to respect. Cartographers have managed to shape the jumble of reality into compact, usable form. They have done a commendable job. Now it is up to us.

MAP

It tells the truth by lying, like a poem

With bold hyperbole of shape and line—

A masterpiece of false simplicity.

Its secret meanings must be mulled upon,

Yet all the world is open to a glance.

With colors to fire the mind, a song of names,

A painting that is not at home on walls

But crumpled on a station wagon floor,

Worn through at folds, tape patched and chocolate smudged

(What other work of art can lead you home?)

—A map was made to use.

—JULIANA O. MUEHRCKE

CONTENTS

INTRODUCTION

TUCKER

Map me no maps, sir, my head
is a map of the whole world.
—Henry Fielding

INTRODUCTION

It should be easier to read a map than to read this book. After all, we know that a picture is worth a thousand words. Everyone from poets to the Internal Revenue (with its pamphlet entitled "Road Map to Form 1040A") works from the assumption that nothing could be easier to understand than a map. The very term "map" is ingrained in our thinking pattern. We use it to suggest clarification, as in "Map out your plan" or "Do I have to draw you a map?" How ironical, then, to write a book using language that is, supposedly, more complicated than the thing we're trying to explain!

The problem is that maps aren't nearly as straightforward as they seem. Using a map to represent our detailed and complexly interrelated surroundings can be quite deceptive. This isn't to say that maps themselves are unclear. But it's the mapped world, not the map, that we're trying to understand.

Making maps simple doesn't change the world; it only lets us treat it, for certain purposes, as if it were less complicated. There are advantages in such a treatment, but there's also the danger that we'll end up with an unrealistic view of reality. All too often, in fact, such warped views of the environment are held by people who manage critical natural and human resources.

In this book, we'll define a map as a **spatial representation of the environment**. By "representation," we mean something that stands for the environment, that portrays it, and is both a likeness and a simplified model. With this definition, we can encompass such diverse maps as those on walls and those held solely in the mind's eye. To appreciate why it's important to think of maps in such an all-encompassing sense, let's take a closer look at how you come to know the environment around you.

KNOWING YOUR SURROUNDINGS

What you know about the environment is tied closely to the way you think and communicate. You don't gain environmental knowledge passively. It comes through an active process of information gathering, structuring, and association. You can better understand this process if you look at the stages involved, with emphasis on seeing.

Sensory Data

The most natural way you learn about your environment is through direct sensory data. You receive this information through your senses of sight, sound, smell, taste, and touch.

For instance, you see things when cells in your retinas pick up light energy reflected from different locations in your field of view (**Figure I.1**). Consider how different your conception of the environment might be if you could use X-ray, infrared, or microwave energy to see rather than depending exclusively on visible light.

Obviously, relying solely on direct sensory data limits the scope of what you experience. It also requires direct contact. You must experience everything first-hand.

Categorization

But you don't limit yourself to raw sensory data, of course. Seeing involves more than recording light energy on the sensory cells in your retinas. Your brain organizes this information into meaningful categories (**see Figure I.1**). You see features such as trees, not tiny spots of color as recorded by the individual retina cells. Such categories enormously simplify your view of the environment.

Representation

Categorization is just one component of thinking abstractly. Rather than pointing at actual features, we need something to stand for these features. For this purpose we invented symbols (see Figure I.1).

Symbols are the basis for indirect forms of communication (**Figure I.2**). These indirect communication vehicles include: (1) **natural languages** (such as English) (2) **artificial languages** (branches of mathematics), and (3) **pictures**, both graphics and images.

Each of these indirect means of environmental thought and communication is limited in scope and sensitivity. No single method best serves all purposes. In fact, words, numbers, and

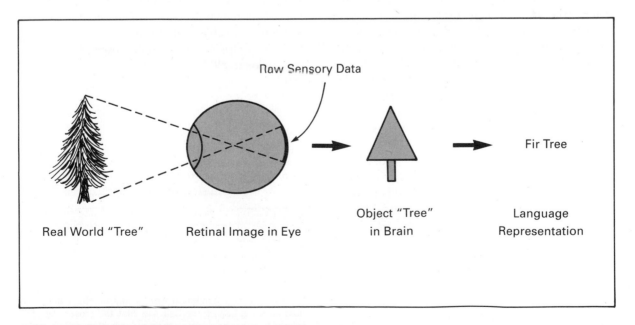

Raw Sensory Data

Real World "Tree"   Retinal Image in Eye   Object "Tree" in Brain   Fir Tree / Language Representation

I.1 The process of seeing begins with light rays reflected from environmental features falling on the retina in your eye and ends with the conception and representation of objects in your brain.

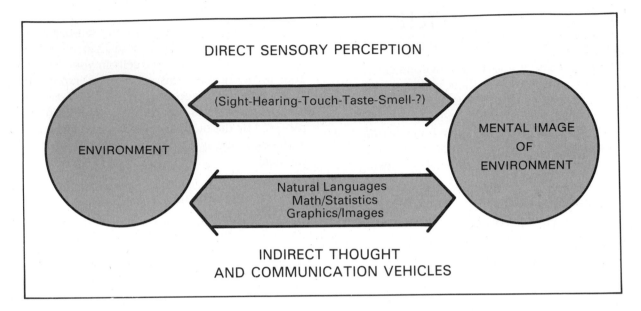

I.2 Humans are unique in learning to know their environment by supplementing raw sense data with indirect vehicles of thought and communication.

pictures occupy complementary positions along an abstraction gradient (**Figure I.3**).

You can use these abstractions in two ways when thinking about the environment: (1) You may see your surroundings in holistic, spatial terms, with everything occurring at once and in complete interrelation. This is the view of the visual arts and Eastern philosophy. Graphics serve this function well. (2) You may conceive of the environment in analytical terms, with the whole made up of parts which can be identified, isolated, and manipulated separately. This is the view of Western scientific thought. The formal logic of mathematics serves this function well.

Many people prefer one or the other of these approaches to environmental understanding. In this book we'll stress a flexible use of both. Such a mix accentuates the strengths while minimizing the limitations of each alone. The ability to shift back and forth between these different strategies is a valuable skill to master.

ENVIRONMENTAL VISUALIZATION

Your use of categorization and representation may take several forms. You may envision the environment by using physical maps, or you can use maps that are strictly in your mind.

The maps in your mind, known as **cognitive** or **mental maps**, are often slighted in map definitions. Yet they are really the ultimate maps, because they're the ones you use to make decisions about the environment.

Unfortunately, however, mental maps are restricted in scope and often fail. When this happens, it's helpful to rely on **cartographic maps**. Let's take a closer look at these two types of maps.

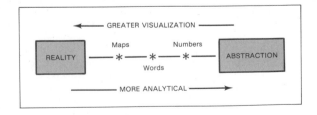

I.3 If we arrange graphics, words, and numbers along an abstraction gradient, we can see that the closer they fall toward reality the greater their visualization power, while greater abstraction better serves analytical purposes.

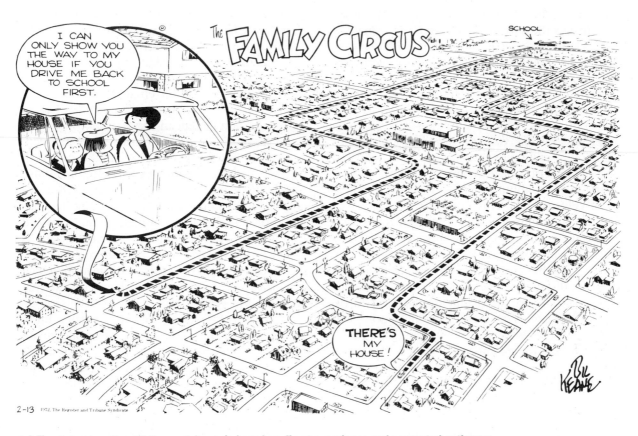

I.4 The geometry of a child's mental map is based on direct experience and connected pathways.

Mental Maps

As a child, your mental map was probably based on direct experience, connected paths, and egocentricism (in which you related everything to your own position). This view is summarized by the cartoon in **Figure I.4**. As an adult, you can appreciate this cartoon because you see how inefficient these primitive mental maps can be. But the truth is that you still resort to this way of structuring your environment when thrown into unfamiliar settings. If you go for a walk in a strange city, you will remember how to get back to your hotel by putting connective information together into a pathway. Your mental map will be narrow and striplike, resembling a ribbon with a few landmarks like beads strung along it.

Most of your mental maps are more complicated than this, however. For one thing, you take advantage of **indirect** as well as direct experience. You acquire information through TV, conversations, photographs, reading, and other secondary sources. You can transcend your physical limitations and conceptualize distant environments, even those at the other side of the planet. Your mental map becomes incredibly complex as it encompasses places you have never seen.

At the same time, your egocentricism is replaced by a **geocentric** point of view. Rather than relating everything to your own location, you learn to orient yourself with respect to the external environment. Thus, you can assume yourself to be at a distant position, even when you haven't moved physically. The feat might be called the geographical "What if....?"

Once you learn to separate yourself from your environment, you no longer need to structure your mental maps in terms of connected pathways. You can have a mental map of a scene without being part of it. You can visualize how to get from one place to another "as the crow flies"—the way you would go if you weren't restricted to roads. It's your ability to see the "big

6

picture," to have a comprehensive mental map, that makes the cartoon in Figure I.4 amusing.

Your geocentric viewpoint, with its freedom from the constraints of sequential pathways, is given a boost when you use a frame of spatial reference you can share with others. The system of **cardinal directions** (north, south, east, and west) provides just such a framework. Using this reference system, you can pinpoint something's location by stating its distance and direction from something else. You can say, for example, that a plane crashed about five kilometers northeast of here (**Figure I.5**). This conception of space is based on **Euclidean geometry**. You're familiar with Euclidean geometry, because it's the geometry taught in most schools. It's the same geometry which says that parallel lines never meet, that the shortest distance between two points is a straight line, that there are three dimensions, and so forth.

Your ability to view your surroundings in terms of these distance, direction, and dimensional relations is the essence of your geocentric perspective. It will serve you well when your surroundings are familiar, but it may fail you when you're thrown into a strange setting. In unfamiliar environments, most people revert to the more primitive pathway structuring. If they don't, they risk getting lost. Thus, while Euclidean geometry provides you with a conceptual framework, you probably don't adhere to it in all your mental maps.

Even when you view the world from a Euclidean perspective, your mental maps may not be Euclidean, because they must consider the routes you have to follow. Your environment is full of barriers which keep you from traveling along straight lines or taking what in Euclidean terms would be the shortest route. Planners who try to predict behavior often go wrong by assuming that people's mental maps are identical to maps based on Euclidean space.

If you think about your own mental map, you should now be able to pick out those parts of it which are based on direct experience and those which reflect indirect experience. But there will still be something—some images, some feelings about places—left unaccounted for, unexplained by either direct or indirect experience. This is because your mental maps are also influenced by **extrasensory perception**—information which originates in your mind rather than with external stimuli.

The major source of extrasensory information is thinking. You constantly ponder and modify the information you gather through experience. Much of what you *think* you know about your surroundings, therefore, is conjecture.

Extrasensory perception also encompasses information gained through your imagination, fantasies, dreams, and hallucinations. You have little control over these sources of information, and you're usually not conscious of the impact they have on your mental maps. Yet they shape your view of the world in the same way as do other information sources.

Although extrasensory input is the least reliable, there are problems with direct and indirect information, too. We like to believe that we take in environmental information in all the detail that our senses permit. In truth, however, perception is an active and highly selective process. You rarely see things as they are but, rather, as you expect or would like to see them. You bring much of yourself—past experience, biases, and limitations—to the perceptual process.

The problem is compounded when you rely on indirect experience, such as TV, books, or conversations. In this case, you are depending on the mental maps of other people, who have their own twisted notions of reality. In addition, their ability to communicate information, and your ability to decipher it, distort what you learn.

As an adult, then, your mental maps are a potpourri of fact and fiction, gleaned through a

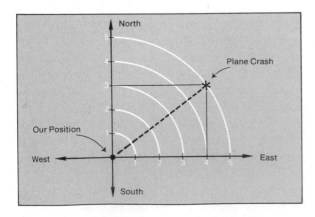

I.5 An adult's conception of space is based primarily on the principles of Euclidean geometry.

haphazard combination of direct, indirect, and extrasensory experience. Some parts of your mental maps are egocentric and based on connected paths, while others are geocentric and based on Euclidean distance-direction relations. You have forgotten some things and seen others incorrectly. Your fears and prejudices and longings all have biased your way of looking at the world. It is understandable that a combination of these factors may badly warp your image of the environment.

Try drawing, from memory, a map of the area in which you live. The resulting picture will tell you a great deal about your mental map.* Not

The accuracy of a drawn mental map is largely a reflection of a person's drawing skill. Those few with a flair for drawing may successfully convey on paper the true character of their mental maps. But for the vast majority of us lacking drawing ability, the resulting pictures on paper won't do justice to the maps held in our minds. Researchers have struggled unsuccessfully for decades to overcome this problem.

only will you draw the places you know best with the greatest spatial detail and accuracy, but you will likely draw those things which are important in your life and leave off those you don't care about. Many of your attitudes will be reflected by the map you draw. Whether you show Joe's Bar or the corner church, the library or the football stadium, says something about your lifestyle and values.

Few people's mental maps correspond perfectly with cartographic maps. **Figure I.6** shows the distorted image which a person from Michigan's Upper Peninsula might have of the country. Tongue in cheek though this map may be, it captures the fact that people view their own region as far more important than the rest of the world. In the same way, your mental maps emphasize your own neighborhood, with distant environments assuming less significance.

The study of people's mental maps is a growing area for research and gives us many insights into the way we view the world. In one

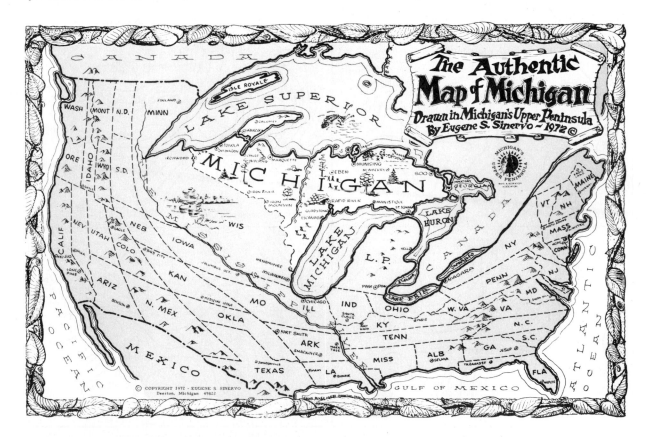

I.6 The United States as seen through the eyes of a resident of Michigan's Upper Peninsula.

8

study, done in the 1960s, students at four universities—Minnesota, Alabama, Pennsylvania State, and California at Berkeley—were asked to rank the 48 contiguous states from most to least desirable as places to live. The results are shown in **Figure I.7**, with high values indicating most desirable and low values least desirable.

A comparison of these four maps reveals some interesting patterns. Note that more than 100 years after the Civil War, there's still a definite Mason-Dixon line separating North and South. Northern students aren't eager to live in the Deep South, while Southern students see the North as an unattractive place to live. In their mental maps, it seems, the states are still not "united."

Also, while Northerners lump the southern states into one undesirable area, Alabama students see great variety in the South. Students from the North and West, for instance, make no distinction between Alabama and Mississippi, but those from Alabama see a distinct difference between the two states. They view Alabama as a favorite area but definitely don't want to live in Mississippi!

The four maps also show some correspondence of feeling by all students about certain areas. California and Colorado are highly rated by everyone. Similarly, there are interesting "sinkholes" in the preference surface, such as the Dakotas, where practically no one wants to live.

Notice, too, how all the students rank their own area high in desirability. As such results show, most people are guilty of some egocentricism in their mental maps. They can't help thinking of their state or city or school as the best.

It's important to recognize these biases in your environmental images. The quality of your mental maps is crucial, because the logic of your environmental behavior depends on it. You relate to your surroundings as you perceive them, not as they really are. If the discrepancy between your perceived world and the real world is great, you may act in self-defeating or even disastrous ways.

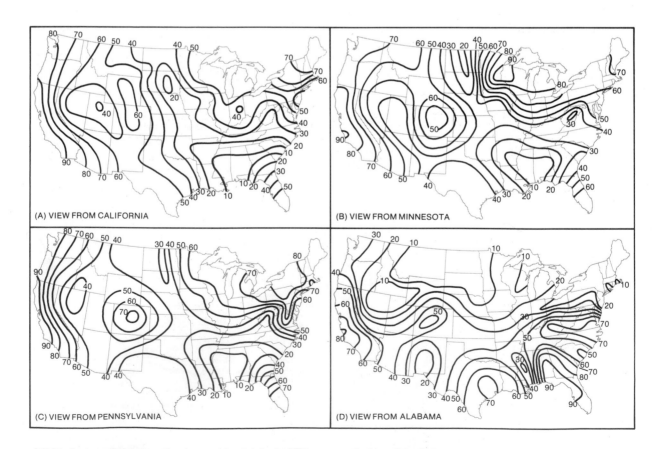

(A) VIEW FROM CALIFORNIA

(B) VIEW FROM MINNESOTA

(C) VIEW FROM PENNSYLVANIA

(D) VIEW FROM ALABAMA

I.7 Student mental maps, showing residential desirability on a scale from 0 to 100.

Luckily, you don't have to rely solely on your mental maps. To be sure, those who do so lead sadly limited lives. It is dangerous to put too much faith in the kaleidoscope of environmental images—some accurate, some not—in your head. You can sort out these images if you turn to external aids, especially cartographic maps.

Cartographic Maps

The cartographer's map is a physical representation of the environment. It is a graphic or image that you can view directly. Physical maps come in many forms. We have globes, physical models, line drawings, photographs taken from airplanes, and imagery of the earth taken from spacecraft. Such maps usually have a lasting, tangible form, as when they are printed on paper. But they also may be ephemeral and intangible, as when displayed on television or projected onto a screen.

The more you use cartographic maps, the better your mental map will become. One of the most important things you can learn is to keep changing those parts of your mental map which are irrational and self-defeating.

This process of continually editing your mental map will be most effective if you under-stand the **cartographic process**—the process of making and using maps. You can start by dividing the cartographic process into map making and map use, as in **Figure I.8. Map making** refers to the activities which lead to the creation of a physical map. It involves applying the principles of cartographic abstraction to available environmental data to produce a readable and useful graphic representation. (See Chapter 3: *Map Abstraction Process.*) The term **mapping** is used here synonymously with map making, with one exception. In mapping, a physical map need not be produced. Thus, the formation of a mental map is properly thought of as mapping.

Map use is the process of transcribing the physical map back into a mental picture of reality. Map use consists of three main activities—reading, analysis, and interpretation. In **map reading**, you determine just what the map makers have depicted and how they have gone about it. If you read the maps in **Figure I.9**, for instance, you can conclude that cancer deaths in the white population from 1950 to 1969 have been displayed by county. Information for males and females has been broken down into five frequency classes and mapped separately. The darkest tone has been assigned to the "well above average" class; a medium tone has been assigned to the intermediate class; and the lightest tone has been given to the "well below average" class. *Part I* of this book explores these and other issues of map reading.

Reading a map is only the first step; your curiosity may be aroused to look further. Your second step is **map analysis** (explored in *Part II* of this book). In this stage of map use, you look for spatial patterns. Analysis of the maps in Figure I.9 is particularly thought-provoking. While people may find comfort in believing that cancer is unpredictable, analysis of these maps shows that's not true.

If you focus on the patterns in these maps, you find that cancer deaths are far from random. Regional clustering occurs for both males and females. It's unlikely that this clustering of deaths occurred by chance.

If you next focus on spatial relations between the two maps, you find that the northeastern United States is highest in cancer deaths for both men and women. The Midwest is next highest for both sexes. But males in the

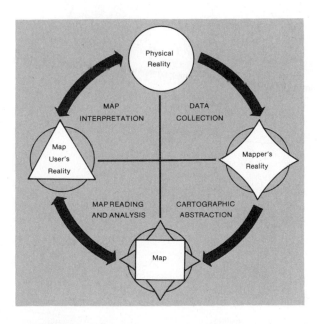

I.8 A diagram of the cartographic communication process. (The material in this book stresses the left side of the illustration).

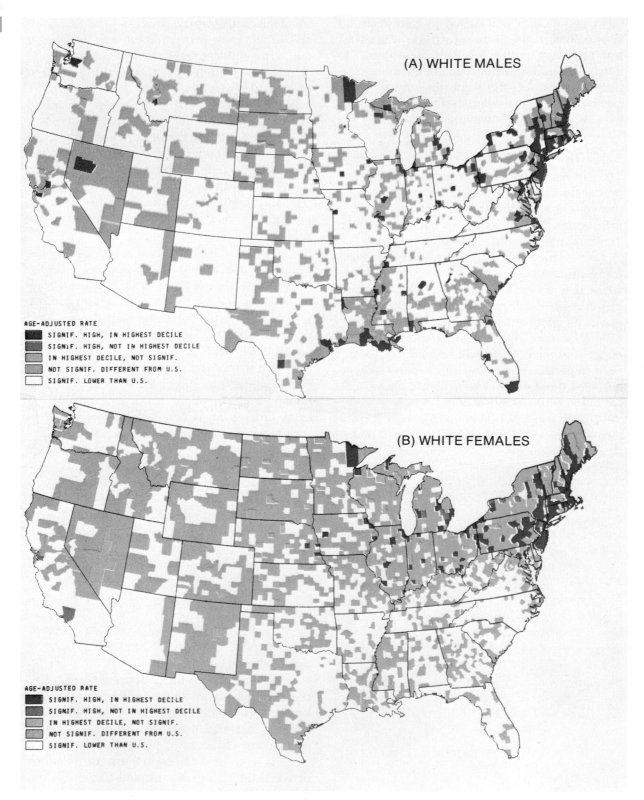

I.9 Cancer mortality in the United States by county, 1950-1969, for white males (A) and white females (B). (The original maps were printed in color).

Mississippi Delta region show a high incidence of cancer deaths while females don't. Many counties show high or low death rates for both sexes. Other counties show high death rates for one sex but low for the other sex.

Your curiosity may now be aroused still further. You may wonder how to explain these patterns and the relations between the two maps. Such explanations take you into the realm of map **interpretation**. To find answers, you have to search beyond the map. To do so, you may draw on your personal knowledge, field work, or other maps. In your search, you will find that cancer deaths are associated with many factors, including industrialized environments, mining activities, chemical plants, urban areas, ethnic backgrounds, and habits of eating and drinking. You will find that people die because of contaminants in the air, water, food, clothing, and building materials. Some local concentrations, however, don't seem to fit this pattern, suggesting that your search for causes is just beginning. We'll delve into map interpretation issues in *Part III* of this book.

The terms **reading, analysis, and interpretation** are merely convenient categories, of course. Map use activities aren't always simply defined. Also, the cartographer must take the map user's needs into consideration. To use a map, then, you must understand map making, map use, and the **communication** that exists between the two.

MAP COMMUNICATION

As we saw in the previous section, maps don't just happen. They are designed with communication between their maker and user in mind. Their nature is determined by cartographic rules and design constraints. But their communication essence is governed by the function they were designed to serve. Figure out this purpose, and you have taken the biggest step toward understanding the map.

Remember, however, that map understanding is not your ultimate goal. You want to use this knowledge to improve your life in the real world. With this important point in mind, let's look more closely at the map as a form of communication, beginning with the nature of mapping.

The Nature of Mapping

What makes a map so useful is its genius of omission. It is reality uncluttered, pared to its essence, stripped of all but the essentials. Maps, when well done, are a handsome blend of science and art.

A map's advantage is convenience. It is easier to manipulate symbols than to study the real world in every authentic detail.

At the same time, maps let you see a whole scene simultaneously in natural form. Thus, more than any other communication device, they capture the spatial character of your surroundings, helping you understand geographical relations. Imagine trying to communicate your city's layout to a stranger using only verbal or mathematical description—or even both! Now think how much simpler your task would be if you could include a map in your description.

Another advantage of maps is that they can provide many views of the environment. Maps let you see the environment anew, in fresh ways, and enhance your potential for creative thought.

This transformational character of maps also has a negative side. Sometimes extraneous details appear on the map. These unwanted byproducts of mapping are called **cartographic artifacts**.

Obvious artifacts, such as a jog in a road where separate map sheets come together, are little cause for concern. But some artifacts are more subtle. For instance, faulty film processing may cause light streaks on an aerial photograph. You could mistake these streaks for real features in the environment.

Computer mapping, in particular, is fraught with artifacts, due to technique, that are difficult to detect. We will investigate artifact problems in Chapter 25: *Maps and Reality*.

Design Logic

There are two types of maps, based on design logic. Maps designed to show the position of environmental details accurately are called **general-purpose** or **reference maps**. Maps designed to show variation in spatial patterns are called **special-purpose** or **thematic maps**.

As a map user, you need to know what type of map you're using. You will use each type differently. So let's look at each type more closely.

12

Reference Maps

The earliest known maps, dating back several thousand years, are of the reference type. On reference maps, symbols are used to locate and identify prominent landmarks and other pertinent features. An attempt is made to be as detailed and spatially truthful as possible so that accurate metric data can later be extracted with confidence. These maps have a basic "Here is found...." character and are useful for looking up the location of specific geographical features. On reference maps, no particular things are emphasized over the others; all features are given fairly equal visual importance.

A conventional aerial photograph, with its rather indiscriminate representation of environmental features, provides a good example of reference mapping. Standard line and symbol maps also commonly serve a reference function, particularly when they show a variety of phenomena with about the same emphasis given to each. On these maps, no symbols stand out boldly above the rest to attract our first glance.

Reference maps are often produced in national mapping series, such as the United States Geological Survey (USGS) topographic quadrangle and the navigational (nautical and aeronautical) map programs. They are also found in atlases, serve as wall maps in schools, and are distributed by *National Geographic* magazine as map supplements. The ubiquitous road map falls into the class of reference maps as well.

Thematic Maps

Unlike reference maps, which show many features but emphasize no particular one over the others, thematic maps stress just a few variables. Frequently, they show only one variable, as on the cancer death map in Figure I.9.

Also, while reference maps focus on the location of features, thematic maps stress spatial variation in the form of geographical distributions. A climate map, showing how climate changes across the country, is a good example. Vegetation and geology maps likewise show changing distributions.

Many thematic maps show concepts that don't physically exist in the real world. One example is a map showing population density by country. Another example is the cancer death map in Figure I.9. You couldn't go into the environment and see population density or cancer death rates. But maps showing such concepts can be very useful.

Thematic maps ask, "What if we were willing to look at the world this way?" Figure I.9, for example, asks, "What if we were willing to add up cancer deaths from 1950 to 1969 by county and group them into five classes?"

Take another look at the map in Figure I.9. Note how its "theme" (cancer deaths) is superimposed on a base or background of state outlines. Most thematic maps have similar background information to give a locational reference. Be careful not to rely on such spatial reference information to find specific locations or make precise measurements. Remember, that's not the intent of thematic mapping; it's what reference maps are for.

It's crucial to use a map as it was designed to be used. With reference maps, focus on locations and on distance and direction relations. When using thematic maps, focus on the changing distribution in space.

MAPPING CONSTRAINTS

To understand why maps vary so much in function, appearance, and form, put yourself in the cartographer's place. In making a map, the cartographer faces many influences or pressures, which we call mapping constraints. Before you use a map, it's a good idea to run through a mental checklist of the **mapping constraints** that probably were working when the map was made. Those constraints include map purpose, geographical reality, available data, scale, policy, technical limits, audience, and conditions of use. Let's take a closer look at each one.

Map Purpose

The overriding determinant of a map's final character is the purpose for which it is to be used. Thus, a map's purpose is the first mapping constraint you should consider when studying a map. The problem is that maps serve many roles. They're used as a computational device by engineers and a mobility aid by navigators. They may be used to summarize volumes of statistics or explore data for clusters, trends, or correlations. Sometimes we want a map to help us visualize what otherwise would be invisible. Maps are also used as triggers to stimulate thought.

Considering these many roles, it's clear that one design can't serve all needs equally well. Unfortunately, we often find ourselves with a map inappropriate for our needs. Another problem is that map makers sometimes try to serve too many masters and, as a consequence, serve none well. The breadth of purpose incorporated into the map design can greatly affect your ability to use it effectively. Attempts to combine too many purposes lead to design conflicts and visual confusion.

Note also that the purpose for which a map has been made may be unrealistic, unsupported by data, or otherwise rendered meaningless by the impact of the other mapping constraints in effect when it was created. It may help to remember that cartographers have no code of ethics which they violate at the risk of losing their professional certification (they are not certified!) Thus, you can't expect that map makers have always given map purpose first priority when making their design decisions. Stated bluntly, you may sometimes have to deal with poorly conceived maps.

Geographical Reality

Sometimes a map's purpose conflicts with geographical reality. Some places are easier to map than others. This we call **mappability**. Because there is such contrast in the geographical character of different regions, no set design formula will be equally effective from place to place. This can lead to variable generalization of features from location to location on even a single map.

Available Data

Assume for a moment that there's no conflict between map purpose and geographical reality. You still can't be sure the map will be useful until you consider the available data. Different sources of data require different design strategies. Enough information must be available, and it must be accurate and up-to-date enough to serve the map's purpose.

A key factor to consider before using any map is how the nature of available data has been handled cartographically. Maps that give an impression of accuracy or completeness greater than warranted by the source material are dangerous. You must try to gain a sense of the data's character before leaping to map-based conclusions about the environment. Has the map been sufficiently generalized (poor data should be mapped in less detail and at smaller scales)?

Scale

The scale at which the environment is depicted has such a strong influence on a map's character that it is one of the methods (others being subject matter and map function) commonly used to classify maps. (See Appendix A for a detailed discussion of scale). The smaller a map's scale, the less detail that can be shown, and the more aggregation that's likely to have occurred. Locational concerns tend to give way to emphasis on overall spatial structure as the scale decreases. Conversely, larger map scales facilitate greater feature detail and disaggregation and have a locational rather than a structural emphasis.

When you choose a map, be sure to note the scale. Check that the features of interest to you are at the right scale for your purposes. If you want to see many small details, you'll want a large-scale map. If you're more interested in regional patterns, you'll want a small-scale map.

Policy

A "code of conduct" guides everyone's private and public life. Certain things are O.K. to do, while others are not. Likewise, elaborate sets of rules govern the activities of agencies, firms, and individuals making maps. Sometimes the operating policy is official and written. But often it's a subtle and even unspoken aspect of accepted cultural behavior.

This implies that important environmental features may be left off maps purely for policy reasons. Taxpayer-supported government maps may show public sites such as museums or parks but not private or commercial ones. Similarly, fault lines, floodplains, and abandoned landfills don't appear on U.S. topographic quadrangles. It's not that these features aren't of interest and importance to many map users. Rather, their absence from certain official maps is largely a policy matter.

14

Technical Limitations

A map's appearance also reflects technical limitations at the time it was created. For instance, what materials were available to the cartographers? How skilled were the cartographers in using these materials? How much time and money were available to complete the map?

Technical constraints can influence the character of a map in several ways. For one thing, they can affect basic design decisions. Thus, the map maker may have been guided by practical concerns that bear no direct relevance to your needs as a map user. For another thing, execution failures in map reproduction may occur because the map design asked too much of the technical facilities available. Newspaper maps, for example, are often unreadable because the artwork was reduced too much or the paper was too rough and absorbent to hold fine graphic distinctions. It hardly matters whether the fault rests with the cartographer who designed a map to be reproduced on high-quality paper or with the newspaper editor who decided to reduce the map from three columns to one in order to save space. The effect on the map reader is the same.

Audience

It should be the map user who guides the cartographer through the mapping process. It would be useful for the cartographer to know, for instance, the age, physical condition, educational level, and map-reading skill of the map user. Yet cartographers rarely have such information. Instead, they have only a general idea of who might use a map.

Thus, your success in using a map depends on how well you fit into the intended map audience. The greater the mismatch between you and the intended audience, the harder it will be for you to use the map. Maps designed for general audiences tend to serve nobody well.

Conditions of Use

The circumstances of map use vary greatly. Maps may be used in the field or laboratory, at normal reading distance or as wall displays, under sunlight or artificial light, and in stable or unstable viewing environments. Map designers try to anticipate these conditions and create their maps accordingly. But they have little control over how a map will actually be used.

You may have problems if you use a map under conditions for which it wasn't designed. The success of map navigation displays in automobiles may prove to be a case in point. Several companies which supply such equipment have merely videotaped existing ink-on-paper road maps, which were by no means intended for electronic display. It will be interesting to see what happens when we attempt to use these maps under extreme driving conditions (poor light, vehicle vibration, etc.), especially under stress (heavy traffic in unfamiliar settings).

MAP APPRECIATION

An appreciation of maps' strengths and weaknesses will help you move with confidence through your environment. It will also help you make decisions about the best ways to use the earth's limited resources.

Those who lack this appreciation fall victim to realtors, tourist traps, wilderness guides, and con artists who prey on people's environmental ignorance. Inept map users also erode the quality of life for everyone. It's expensive and time-consuming to rescue people who get lost. A poor understanding of the knowledge coded into maps may result in inefficient agricultural, industrial, and recreational practices, even though the price to people and environment is intolerably high.

In contrast, maps teach you to view your surroundings in a perceptive way. They help keep you from getting lost. They help you see interrelations of resources, people, and activities. Few things can add more to your self-assurance than the study of maps. How is it, then, that so many otherwise competent people have never learned to use maps effectively?

First of all, probably, because they never had to. "I don't use maps," you hear people say. "I just follow the signs." You may be able to function without maps, but it's like cooking without a recipe—often inspired, perhaps, but limited.

There's an even simpler reason why many people never learned to read maps. They were never taught. There should be courses in map use in the early grades, but there rarely are. Instead of training people to use maps, educators tend to treat maps as if they were intuitively meaningful.

Thus, people gain the impression that knowing your way around is some kind of sixth sense that you either do or don't have. "I have no sense of direction," people say. But you're not born with a sense of direction, any more than a sense of algebra or economics. An orientation ability isn't something you mysteriously acquire but something you can learn, just as you learn English or math.

The most fundamental step in becoming comfortable with a map is to relate it to the landscape. The key is to assume a **bird's-eye vantage point** high above the region covered on the map. You must imagine what features would look like if viewed from above and at some distance.

The problem is that you rarely find yourself in the position of a bird. Therefore, maps show things in ways foreign to your everyday experience. Your usual location is the ground, where you see things from a side view. When you see these same things on a map, from a top (or plan) view, you may have trouble recognizing them. Relating a map to the earth, then, isn't a natural, intuitive process but a skill which you must learn and improve upon with practice.

Maps may make you nervous because you confront them only in emergency situations. Typically, you turn to maps when you're lost, late, and close to panic. This, obviously, isn't the ideal time to nurture a love for maps. The best time is when you're free from pressure. You must practice with maps both indoors (laboratory work) and outdoors (field work) before you find yourself in a stressful situation. Then when the time comes, you will have the confidence you need.

Since maps can reflect all aspects of environmental knowledge, their use is intertwined with many disciplines. It is impossible to appreciate them in isolation. The more different fields you study, the better you will be at using maps. Map appreciation grows naturally out of an appreciation of other subjects. The reverse is also true. An appreciation of maps leads to a greater appreciation of the world around you, for the subject of maps, after all, is the world itself.

This brings us to a final, important point. As you gain an appreciation for maps, be careful not to confuse the mapped world with the real world. Remember, the reason you're using maps is to understand reality. The ultimate aim of map appreciation is to stimulate you to interact with your environment and to experience more while you do.

SELECTED READINGS

Arnheim, R., *Visual Thinking* (Berkeley: University of California Press, 1969).

Balchin, W.G.V., "Graphicacy," *The American Cartographer*, Vol. 3, No. 1 (April 1976), pp. 33-38.

Castner, H.W., *Seeking New Horizons: A Perceptual Approach to Geographic Education* (Montreal: McGill-Queen's University Press, 1990).

Dent, B.D., *Cartography: Thematic Map Design*, 2nd ed. (Dubuque: Wm. C. Brown, 1990).

Downs, R.M., and Stea, D., *Maps in Mind: Reflections on Cognitive Mapping* (New York: Harper & Row Publishers, 1977).

Edwards, B., *Drawing on the Right Side of the Brain*, 2nd ed. (Los Angeles: J.P. Tarcher, Inc., 1989.)

Gersmehl, J.J., and Andrews, S.K., "Teaching the Language of Maps," *Journal of Geography*, Vol. 85, No. 6 (November-December 1986), pp. 267-270.

Hall, S.S., *Mapping the Next Millennium: The Discovery of New Geographies* (New York: Random House, 1991).

Head, C.G., "The Map as Natural Language: A Paradigm for Understanding," *Cartographica*, Vol. 21 (1984), pp. 1-32.

Keates, J.S., *Understanding Maps*, 2nd ed. (Essex: Addison Wesley Longman Ltd., 1996).

Kitchin, R.M., "Cognitive Maps: What They Are and Why Study Them?", *Journal of Environmental Psychology*, Vol. 14 (1994), pp. 1-19.

Liben, L.S., Patterson, A.H., and Newcombe, N., eds., *Spatial Representation and Behavior Across the Life Span: Theory and Applications* (New York: Academic Press, 1981).

Lloyd, R., *Spatial Cognition: Geographical Environments* (Boston: Kluwer Academic Publishers, 1997).

MacEachren, A.M., *How Maps Work: Representation, Visualization and Design* (New York: The Guilford Press, 1995).

McKim, R.H., *Experiences in Visual Thinking*, 2nd ed. (Monterey, CA: Brooks/Cole Publishing Co., 1980).

Monmonier, M., *How to Lie with Maps* (Chicago: The University of Chicago Press, 1991).

Monmonier, M., and Schnell, G.A., *Map Appreciation* (Englewood Cliffs, NJ: Prentice Hall, 1988).

Muehrcke, P.C., and Muehrcke, J.O., "Maps in Literature," *The Geographical Review*, Vol. 64, No. 3 (July 1974), pp. 317-338.

Potegal, M., ed., *Spatial Abilities: Development and Physiological Foundations* (New York: Academic Press, 1982).

Robinson, A.H., "The Potential Contribution of Cartography in Liberal Arts Education," *The Cartographer*, Vol. 3, No. 1 (June 1966), pp. 1-8.

Robinson, A.H., and Bartz-Petchenik, B., *The Nature of Maps: Essays Toward Understanding Maps and Mapping* (Chicago: University of Chicago Press, 1976).

Stein, H.F., and Niederland, W.G., *Maps from the Mind: Readings in Psychogeography* (Norman: University of Oklahoma Press, 1989).

16

Thompson, M.M., *Maps for America: Cartographic Products of the U.S. Geological Survey and Others*, 3rd ed. (Washington, DC: U.S. Geological Survey, 1988).

Tufte, E.R., *Visual Explanations: Images and Quantities, Evidence and Narrative* (Cheshire, CT: Graphics Press, 1997).

Tyner, J., *Introduction to Thematic Cartography* (Englewood Cliffs, NJ: Prentice-Hall, 1992).

Wilford, J.N., *The Map Makers: The Story of Great Pioneers in Cartography from Antiquity to the Space Age* (New York: Vintage Books, A Division of Random House, 1982).

PART ONE

MAP READING

Art, said Picasso, is a lie which makes us realize the truth. So is a map. We don't usually associate the precise craft of the cartographer with the fanciful realm of art. Yet a map has many ingredients of a painting or a poem. It is truth compressed in a symbolic way, holding meanings it doesn't express on the surface. And like any work of art, it requires imaginative reading.

To read a map, you translate its features into a mental image of the environment. The first step is to identify map symbols. This process is usually quite intuitive, especially if the symbols are self-evident and if the map is well designed. Obvious as this step may seem, however, you should look first at the map legend, both to confirm the intent of familiar symbols and to make sure of the cartographic logic underlying unfamiliar or poorly designed ones. Too many people look to the legend only after becoming confused. Such a habit is not only inefficient but potentially dangerous.

In addition to clarifying symbols, the map legend contains other information, such as scale, orientation, and data sources, important to map reading, and sometimes includes unexpectedly revealing facts. But the legend is still only a starting point. The map reader must make a creative effort to translate the world of the map into an image of the real world, for there is a large gap between the two. Much of what exists in the environment has been left off the map, while many things on the map do not occur in reality.

18

Thus, map and reality are not, cannot, be identical. No aspect of map use is so obvious yet so often overlooked. Most map reading mistakes occur because the user forgets this vital fact and expects a one-to-one correspondence between map and reality.

Since the exact duplication of a geographical setting is impossible, a map is actually a metaphor. The map maker asks the map reader to believe that an arrangement of points, lines, and areas on a flat sheet of paper is equivalent to a multi-dimensional world in space and time. For full meaning, the map reader must go beyond the paper-and-ink representation to the real-world referents of the symbols.

A map, like a painting, is just one special version of reality. To understand a painting, you must have some idea of the medium used by the artist. You wouldn't expect a water color to look anything like an acrylic painting or a charcoal drawing, even if the subject matter of all three were identical. In the same way, the techniques used to create maps will drastically influence the final portrayal. As a map reader, you should always be aware of the invisible hand of the map maker. Never use a map without asking yourself how it has been biased by the methods used to make it.

If the entire cartographic process operates at its full potential, communication takes place between map maker and user. The map maker translates reality into the clearest possible picture under the circumstances, and the map reader converts this picture back into an impression of the environment. For such communication to occur, the map reader as well as the maker must know something about how maps are created.

The best way to improve your map reading ability, therefore, is to become familiar with the basics of map making. The complex mapping procedure is easier to study if we break it up into simpler parts. Thus, we have divided this section into 10 chapters, each dealing with a different aspect of mapping. (Keep in mind, however, that these topics, although treated separately, are all interdependent.) Chapter 1 provides a look at the nature of the environment which is mapped. Chapter 2 considers the environmental data available for mapping. Chapter 3 explains how the incredibly complex world can be reduced to one piece of paper. The next four chapters cover the broad categories of image (Chapter 4), landform (Chapter 5), distribution (Chapter 6), and statistical (Chapter 7) mapping. Chapter 8 deals with the relation between time and maps. Chapter 9 explores some of the computer software available for map retrieval and viewing, and Chapter 10 introduces map resources on the Internet.

These 10 chapters should combine to give you an appreciation of all that goes into the making of a map. As a result, you'll better understand the large and varied amount of spatial information that you can glean from a map. In addition, once you realize how intricate the cartographic process is, you can't help but view even the crudest map with more respect, and your map reading skill will naturally grow.

CHAPTER ONE

THE ENVIRONMENT TO BE MAPPED

INTRODUCTION

GEOMETRICAL CHARACTERISTICS

Idea of Feature
Form of Feature
Type of Feature
Discrete Features
Dispersed/Discontinuous Features
Continuous Phenomena
Mosaic Surfaces
Stepped Surfaces
Smooth Surfaces

DIMENSIONALITY OF ENVIRONMENT

ENVIRONMENTAL CHANGE

The Nature of Time
Environmental Temporality
Change in Place
Rate of Change
Pattern of Change
Movement Through Space

CONCLUSION

SELECTED READINGS

Not chaos-like, together crushed and bruised,
But, as the world harmoniously confused:
Where order in variety we see,
And where, though all things differ, all agree.
—Alexander Pope, *Windsor Forest*

1

CHAPTER ONE

THE ENVIRONMENT TO BE MAPPED

In Eastern philosophy the world just "is." People and their surroundings are one. They form a single, integrated whole. Everything is related to everything else, often in complex and subtle ways. It isn't clear where something begins or ends. For us, this is the primitive realm of senses, feelings, and instincts. Our interaction with the environment is intuitive and unconscious. We just exist. We just "are."

However natural or ideal the integrated whole idea might be, people long ago learned to think and communicate about their existence in an alternative, more analytical way. As we saw in the *Introduction*, analytical thinking calls for decomposing the whole into parts, separating into object classes, and labeling. This distancing of people from the environment, and the further split of the environment into component parts, is at the core of Western philosophy. There's no question that this analytical perspective is both insightful and convenient. It has served as the very foundation of our abstract Western science.

But viewing our surroundings in simplified terms doesn't make the world less complex. It only leaves us with a simplified view of things. The haunting question is the degree to which we can truly know the environment and our relation to it through analytics. After all the parts have been identified, analyzed, and organized into conceptual structures, do we then know the whole? Can we, in humpty-dumpty fashion, put the knowledge of many professions back together in a meaningful way? Or is the whole really more than the sum of its parts? These "big questions" have intrigued philosophers for centuries.

Our task is to understand maps. As you've probably guessed, maps personify the analytical perspective. The genius of mapping is to ignore most of what could be mapped. This is done by applying cartographic abstraction principles that reduce the rich variety and detail of our surroundings. This focus cuts through the fog of reality and lets us see a few things clearly at any one time.

So how well do our maps do? That depends on their ability to capture the essence of our surroundings. Distortion will occur, of course, as it does with all methods of representation (words, numbers, pictures). To overcome this problem with each of our thought and communication tools, we must learn to compensate. To do so in the case of maps, we first must detect potentially distorting aspects of the mapping process.

At issue is the relation between map symbols and the mapped environment. To determine the potential for distortion in map symbols, we must first know something about the nature of the environment being mapped.

Understanding the environment, then, is the essential first step of using maps. That is the subject of this chapter. In subsequent chapters, we'll explore the mapping process. With that background, you'll be able to assess the relation between environment and map.

GEOMETRICAL CHARACTERISTICS

Let's begin by taking the "geography as geometry" point of view. From this perspective, the spatial whole is made up of simple **geometrical elements**.

To fathom the magnitude of the task of mapping the world around us, it's helpful to think analytically about the spatio-temporal nature of environmental phenomena. It's traditional to begin by thinking of geographical features in terms of Euclidean geometry—classing them as being more or less point-like, linear, areal, or volumetric. If we add a temporal context, we can say that these geometrical entities move through space along linear paths, over areas, or through volumes.

These time and space conceptions are just that, of course—abstract conceptions. They're more a matter of cognitive emphasis than a meaningful aspect of reality. Such a classification scheme simplifies the environment, serving many useful purposes in terms of human thought, communication, resource management, and spatial

behavior. There's always the chance, however, that more will be lost than gained by such simplification. To understand the ramifications of this geometric conception, it's necessary to look in more detail at what such a class scheme entails.

Idea of Feature

The most obvious geographical features are recognizable physical entities, such as bridges, railroads, and parking lots. Such features have a strong subject matter character, but don't have to be tangible objects. Thus, a cold air mass or a soil type count as topical features.

More abstract features are a consequence of our ability to recognize form and pattern. In this category of features are corners, centroids, edges, nodes, surfaces, and so on. In a sense, these form/pattern features are derived, since they represent aspects of topical features.

Finally, some features are defined by processes that manipulate form/pattern features. Toxic waste plumes, ocean currents, and air mass flows fall in this category. Characteristically, these features have a strong temporal component.

As this brief discussion suggests, the idea of feature is rather complex. Why, then, are people so willing to take it for granted? Apparently we're dealing with something basic to the way we think and communicate about our surroundings. For now, let us too accept the idea of feature at face value so that we can move on to consider what we mean by feature form.

Form of Feature

It's natural for us to classify geographical phenomena in terms of their geometrical **form**. For example, springs, mountain peaks, and river confluences tend toward the point-like. Rivers, coastlines, and faults tend toward linearity. Geologic outcrops, forests, and grass fires tend toward the areal. And stream discharge, mineral deposits, and biomass are volumetric in nature.

Perspective also enters into our assignment of phenomena to class. A river is essentially linear because length is its primary geometrical characteristic. Although it also has width and depth, these are, in strictly geometrical terms, considered to be secondary characteristics. Likewise, a lake is a point feature to someone describing its distance from a nearby town, a linear feature to a hiker walking around its shoreline, an areal feature to someone in a speedboat, and a volumetric feature to a scuba diver.

What this means is that environmental features don't fall neatly into inherent geometrical classes. Into which class they do fall depends to some degree on how we want to view them at the time. As our thinking grows more abstract, the assignment of feature to class becomes more figurative than literal.

Type of Feature

To say that a feature is point-like, linear, areal, or volumetric isn't enough distinction, however, since different **types** of features can be associated with each category. Some features are discrete, others are discontinuous, and still others are continuous. Let's look at each in turn.

Discrete Features

The most obvious geographical features (and usually, therefore, the easiest to map) are sharply defined **discrete** entities. Using hydrographic fea-

tures as an illustration, we have springs (point-like), rivers (linear), watersheds (areal), and reservoirs (volumetric). Because the attributes and locations of these discrete features are relatively well defined, we can count them, measure them, pinpoint their location, and define their shape.

Of course, to some degree discreteness is a matter of definition. For example, the topographic definition of a watershed may overestimate or underestimate the extent of the true (functional) watershed, which takes into consideration the underground configuration of the geologic structure and ground water movement (**Figure 1.1**).

In addition, few features stand alone in their environment. Thus, where a feature begins or ends may, upon closer inspection, be different from what it seems. Springs, for instance, depend on ground water supplies, which in turn depend on the nature of the subsurface strata and recharge from precipitation. Rivers and lakes depend on springs and surface runoff. These

1.1 The topographic definition of a watershed may overestimate the functional extent of the watershed in some areas and underestimate it in others.

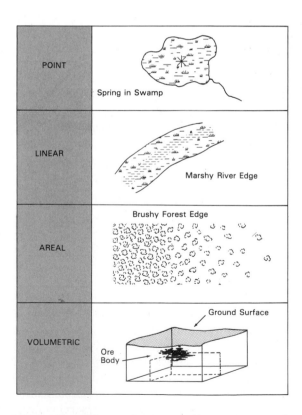

1.2 The edge of discrete features of all dimensions may be transitional rather than sharply defined.

interdependencies suggest that isolating discrete entities may be more a matter of conceptualization than a meaningful environmental characteristic. Treating the environment in a simplistic way can't help but lead to conflicts in inventory, use, and management of environmental resources.

So far we've treated environmental features as if they had abrupt, sharply defined edges. Some features—especially those of human origin such as buildings and roads—do have this trait. But many others—especially those of natural origin—are only thought of as discrete when in reality they have ill-defined edges. Yet, despite their fuzzy, transitional borders, their interiors are homogeneous enough to give them a distinct identity.

Discrete features of all dimensions may have transitional edges (**Figure 1.2**). The "shoreline" of a river which runs through a swamp, for example, exists only by definition. Likewise, we might speak of a forested region even though its boundary isn't obvious to an observer. The boundary between forested and non-forested land

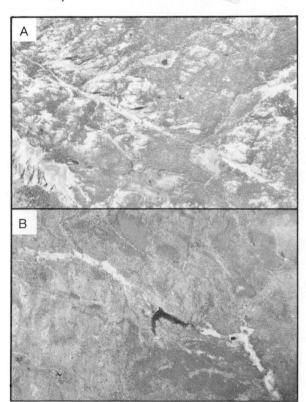

1.3 Dispersed, discontinuous phenomena include such features as rock outcrops along a linear fault (A) and an areal grouping of beaver meadows in a valley (B).

is more likely to fall in a transitional zone of mixed classes than along a sharp discontinuity between classes. The bounding surface of volumetric features, such as smoke plumes or cold air masses, is equally elusive upon inspection.

A discrete feature needn't be a physical entity. It may be an abstract concept such as a territory, range, or zone of influence. Although such conceptual entities tend to have a core/periphery nature, we commonly think of them as possessing a clearly defined edge. This is an example of conceptual abstraction.

Dispersed/Discontinuous Features

Sometimes we think of discrete features as being fragmented into a number of parts. Or, we can think of several discrete features located together. In both cases, we call them **dispersed** or **discontinuous** features. Thus, a series of outcrops of a particular rock strata may be found along a faultline (**Figure 1.3A**). Several beaver meadows may be found in an otherwise forested alpine valley (**Figure 1.3B**). Or a number of parcels of public land may be situated along a scenic river. We may find many seams of coal interlaced between beds of shale and limestone. The edge definition of these features may vary from distinct to transitional, as Figure 1.3 shows.

It's crucial to our definition of dispersed/discontinuous features that we think of them as being related to one another. There must be some sense that the composite of individual items forms a whole, as in the concept of an oil slick. Again, however, it's largely a matter of perspective. If we increase the detail of analysis (thus taking a more local perspective), any of the individual areal units may become the object of attention. Conversely, if we decrease the detail of analysis (thus taking a more regional perspective), we may find that the individual components merge into a whole.

Continuous Phenomena

When environmental phenomena simultaneously exist everywhere within the spatial domain of study, we think of them as being spatially **continuous.*** We can identify several types of continu-

---

Once again, the **scope of analysis is critical in any discussion of spatial continuity. What appears to be continuous at a local level may be clearly discrete when analysis shifts to the regional or global level.*

24

ous distributions. Since each type involves special considerations for environmental planners and decision makers, we'll discuss each in some detail.

Mosaic Surfaces. It's often convenient to think of a region as being exhaustively partitioned into zones of homogeneity which are separated by borders of discontinuity. The spatial units thus formed share some common trait within their borders but differ from each other in some qualitative way. In other words, like features are grouped together, while unlike features are mapped into different units.

The areal patches making up these mosaic surfaces may have distinct borders, similar to those of sharply defined discrete features. The patchwork arrangement of forest and agricultural fields in **Figure 1.4** contains many such distinct borders. Though this mosaic type of natural distribution is rare due to the melding, smoothing action of physical processes, local examples can be found. For instance, when wind, water, or ice have scoured away loose surface debris, the result may be a mosaic of different rock outcrops. The spatial pattern of forest communities (deciduous and coniferous) in Figure 1.3B is another example.

The edge definition of continuous mosaics is different from that of discrete/discontinuous features. The reason is that adjacent areal patches share a common border. Thus, if the border is indistinct, a transition must occur between adjacent features in the mosaic. The boundary between soil types, landform units, climate

1.5 Mosaic-like continuous distributions may exhibit smooth transitions from class to class, as in the case of soils shown here.

1.4 Farming in Wisconsin's "driftless area" is concentrated on the relatively flat ridge tops and in the valley bottoms where equipment mobility is facilitated and soil erosion risk is minimized.

1.6 Landforms may take a stepped form in regions in which erosion of the bedrock structure produces natural terraces. Photo taken in central Australia.

zones, and vegetation classes represent transitions from one type, unit, zone, or class to another (**Figure 1.5**).

Stepped Surfaces. Continuous distributions may also be characterized by phenomena that vary in intensity or magnitude "steps" from place to place in mosaic-like fashion. A region may be partitioned, for example, so that areal units have a constant intensity, with abrupt changes at the borders. Spatial distributions of human origin, such as tax rates by state, commonly have a pronounced stepped character. To a lesser extent, natural distributions can also exhibit steps. If we use elevation as an example, a region of mesas, buttes, or plateaus might have a tendency toward this form. Horizontal beds of alternating soft (easily eroded) and resistant (difficult to erode) rock also may take on a naturally terraced appearance (**Figure 1.6**). But, for the most part, naturally-occurring stepped surfaces aren't common. You can usually consider them anomalous, representing extreme situations.

As with areal mosaics, physical processes are ruthless in their attack on abrupt magnitude breaks. The borders separating stepped values tend to be gradients rather than cliffs. The edges of naturally terraced landforms are likely to be rounded. The more advanced the erosional process, the more transitional the edges become.

Smooth Surfaces. A third type of continuous surface is the smooth surface. It is like a stepped surface in that it is defined by the changing intensity of some phenomenon from one place to another. It differs from stepped surfaces in that the changes are gradual rather than abrupt. Atmospheric temperature, barometric pressure, humidity, and landform elevation fall into this category of surfaces that change gradually from place to place (**Figure 1.7**). We can measure their intensity at all locations on the earth's surface.

We can also create surfaces that are conceptually smooth using environmental data. Average annual precipitation is an example. Density distributions also fall into this category. Thus, rather than think of trees as discrete entities, we can count how many are found per unit area (say a square kilometer) and assign that figure to the center of the areal unit. If we then shift the unit area a bit east (or any other direction) and repeat the counting and locating processes, we obtain a second figure very similar to the first. By performing this operation many times, we derive a continuous density surface (**Figure 1.8**).

1.7 Natural landscape surfaces take a smooth form in their variation from place to place. Photo taken in California (courtesy of Tom Vale).

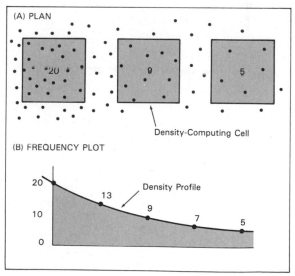

1.8 We can derive a smooth density surface from a scatter of discrete point features.

26

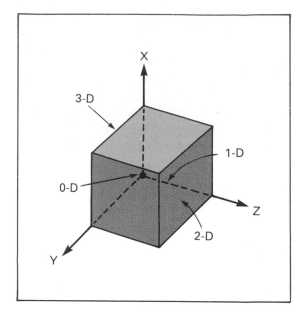

1.9 People seem comfortable with a three-dimensional conception of space, in which we characterize objects as having zero, one, two, or three dimensions.

DIMENSIONALITY OF ENVIRONMENT

We find it convenient to view the environment in dimensional terms. Indeed, dimensionality seems deeply rooted in the way we think. We express it most rigidly through mathematics—our ultimate achievement in formal logic.

We learn early that objects have three dimensions: length, width, and height (**Figure 1.9**). If all three dimensions are 0, we have a 0-dimensional (point) feature. If two dimensions are 0, we have a one-dimensional (linear) feature. If only one dimension is 0, we have a two-dimensional (areal) feature. If an object exhibits all three dimensions, we have a three-dimensional solid (volumetric) feature. In geographical terms, length and width become area or region, and height becomes elevation or magnitude.

Although people have lived for centuries with this formal three-dimensional conception of things, it's important to realize that this dimensionality scheme is of our own making. It is a mental tool we use to analyze our surroundings. This is easy to forget for two reasons.

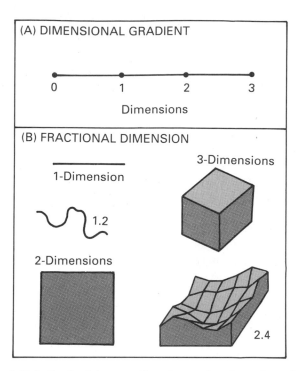

1.10 In the fractal conception of geometry, dimensions of one, two, or three are viewed as special cases along a gradient of continuous dimensionality.

First, this concept is firmly embedded in the geometry we learned in school. We can trace this geometry back to Euclid in classical Greece (thus the term Euclidean geometry).

The second reason we accept three-dimensional geometry so readily is its believability. It is supported by everyday experience. This doesn't mean all the rules of Euclidean geometry are intuitive, however. Faith is also required, as in the case of parallel lines. We learned they extend to infinity without meeting. Our experience, as when we look down a railroad track, suggests otherwise.

The important thing about Euclidean geometry is that for most of us it works fine most of the time. But this isn't true for everyone. People with special needs, such as scientists studying the behavior of objects in atomic or cosmic space, have had to devise other geometries to deal with extremes of scale and motion. The existence of these alternative geometries tailored to special uses reinforces the artificiality of three-dimensional geometry.

Is there room for a new geometry in our lives? Apparently yes, if the recent excitement created by **fractals** is any indication. Fractals, which stands for **fractional dimensionality**, is a concept put forth by Mandelbrot. He proposes that dimensionality is continuous, that our familiar three dimensions represent a degenerate whole-integer (0, 1, 2, 3) approximation of the true **geometry of nature (Figure 1.10A)**.

In a fractal conception, a straight line is one-dimensional, but as the line becomes more irregular it moves fractionally closer to the limit of two dimensions. Similarly, a flat surface is two-dimensional, but the more irregular the surface, the closer it moves in fractional steps toward the limit of three dimensions. In other words, two and three dimensions are the limiting cases of line and surface irregularity (**Figure 1.10B**).

In many ways, this idea goes against everything we've come to believe about the geometry of environmental features. But if convincingly challenged, beliefs do change. Fractals have already captured the imagination of people in many fields and now appear in numerous applications. Maybe it's time for you to reconsider your notion of environmental dimensionality as well.

The special geometries mentioned previously do something important that is lacking in our three-dimensional conception of the environment. They integrate time with three-dimensional space, producing a four-dimensional conception. Our problem is that it is difficult to understand a world of four dimensions when we are only able to visualize three dimensions at a time!* If you don't believe this, try drawing a four-dimensional figure.

To get around this problem, we think of three-dimensional objects moving or changing through time. In this abstraction, we have conveniently separated time from space. This is bound to have implications—especially in the case of maps which use two-dimensional media to represent our four-dimensional world. So, in the next section, let's take a closer look at the temporal aspect of the environment.

A delightful account of this problem is found in Abbott, Flatland (Dover).

ENVIRONMENTAL CHANGE

Environmental features exist in a spatio-temporal context. Within this framework, some features are essentially static, while others are in constant flux. Still others may be either static or dynamic, depending on the time and place.

Whether we think of a feature as static or dynamic depends on the time span used as a reference. Since we are making the judgment, the human life span provides our standard. This human bias can lead to environmental conflicts, particularly when we think only of our behavior's short-term impact. Soil erosion may seem insignificant in one farmer's lifetime, for example, but be catastrophic over several generations of farmers.

Temporal change can occur with both the character and position of environmental features. Let's first discuss the nature of time and then consider temporality as shown in changes in environmental features.

The Nature of Time

Time can be defined only in reference to some ongoing process. There's no absolute thing called "time"; it can be interpreted in many different ways. One way to think of time, for instance, is in terms of earth relations, or **natural time**. The natural rhythmic relations between the earth and other heavenly bodies have been used as external time keepers by even the most primitive societies. The diurnal cycle of light and dark, the monthly cycle of the moon, and the annual progression of the seasons all have been used to structure human behavior.

Or we may think of **biological time**, for all living things are also linked with the rhythms of the earth, sun, and stars by delicate and precise biological clocks. These living clocks govern growth, sleep, reproduction, physical activity, and even susceptibility to injury and disease.

Obviously, natural rhythms or biological cycles are imprecise and inconvenient in relation to our modern scheduling needs. For most purposes, therefore, we've replaced natural time keepers with more convenient and uniform **clock or calendar time**. Because calendar time is so simple to use, we structure our lives to it

28

rather than to the rhythms of human experience and organic needs. Most maps have been dated according to calendar time.

But, while calendar time rules our lives, we mustn't forget how arbitrary it is. Several different origins (year 0) are used on calendars around the world. (While the origin for the Christian calendar is the birth of Christ, the Jewish calendar is based on the assumed date of creation and the Muslim calendar on the flight of Mohammed from Mecca. Thus, the year 1992 on the Christian calendar is 5753 on the Jewish calendar and 1413 A.H. on the Muslim calendar.)

This use of an arbitrary origin as a starting point from which to measure time means that all dates are a form of interval measurement. As we'll see in *Measurement Level* in Chapter 2, map users should view data based on interval measurement with skepticism, since all such data are based on false zeroes. Thus, a date in itself shouldn't be given a precise numerical interpretation. Only the span of time between two dates is numerically meaningful.

We all learn early in life that calendar time fails to capture the essence of our experience. Calendars and clocks are unvarying, but time is relative, seeming to speed up in some situations and slow down in others. Therefore, we must also be aware of **psychological time**, which compresses or extends our sense of time's passing depending on our state of mind.

All these ways of interpreting time underscore the fact that time is by no means a constant factor. It doesn't stand alone as an independent dimension of our environment, as map makers would have us believe. Time comes alive only through the meaning given it by environmental processes. Since map patterns are reflections of these changing processes, we can't ignore time when we use maps, even though most maps themselves are static. To take advantage of maps, we must keep in mind the way the environment changes through time.

Environmental Temporality

Environmental features change over time in two ways. First, the **state** of features is always changing. The soil erodes, lakes freeze, and living things grow old and die. Second, the spatial **position** of some features changes over time.

Change in Place

Change in the state of features has two components. Let's look first at the rate of change. Then we'll see how different rates of change over time produce various patterns of change.

Rate of Change. Not all environmental features change at the same **rate**. Some change with great speed, while others show no perceptible change over long periods. Our notions of rate of change aren't absolute, of course. Changes will seem faster or slower to us depending on our age (temporal perspective), the physical make-up of our senses, our patience and ability to concentrate.

Things that happen too fast we miss. We may also miss changes that happen too slowly. This is a common problem when observing our environment. Pollution creeps into lakes and streams, fields are eroded, and living things

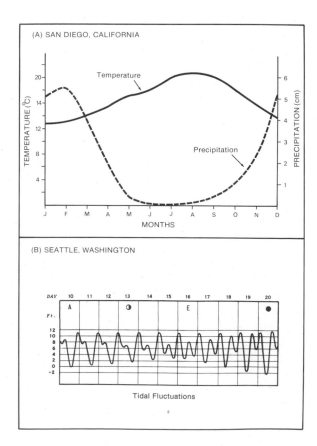

1.11 Many aspects of our surroundings change in cyclical fashion. Examples are annual temperature or precipitation (A) and ocean levels (B).

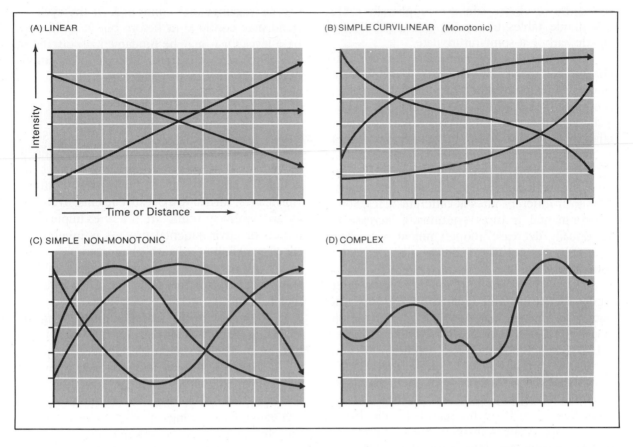

(A) LINEAR

Intensity

Time or Distance

(B) SIMPLE CURVILINEAR (Monotonic)

(C) SIMPLE NON-MONOTONIC

(D) COMPLEX

1.12 Many aspects of the environment change in a non-cyclical way. The pattern of change may be linear (A), simple curvilinear or monotonic (B), non-monotonic (C), or complex (D).

become extinct, all before we realize what's happening. We humans are adept at ignoring the passage of time. That's why high school reunions are so shocking. What a blow to discover that while we haven't aged, all our classmates have!

Old maps are like class reunions—they jog our memories. By letting us contrast past and present, they force us to see that change has occurred. Imperceptible changes may suddenly become obvious. Sometimes just a small change in the rate at which we pass through time creates insight.

Pattern of Change. The features around us vary not only in their rate of change but also in their **pattern** of change. You should be aware of three such patterns: cycles, trends, and catastrophes. Let's look at each in turn.

1. Cycles. Some features vary in a repeatable way, producing cycles. Such features are characterized by returning periodically to previous states or conditions. Once we know the cycle, we can usually make a good guess about the feature's condition at some past or future time. **Figure 1.11A**, for instance, shows the cyclical pattern for temperature and precipitation at San Diego, California. Since seasonal periodicity is well established by a hundred years of weather records, it's safe to predict that average temperature and precipitation for January, 2009, will be near 17°C. (55°F.) and 5.3 centimeters (2.01 inches) respectively.

Cycles aren't always so simple. **Figure 1.11B** portrays a more complex cyclical pattern for tidal fluctuations at Seattle, Washington. If we didn't realize that this pattern had a monthly as well as a daily cycle, the form of the overall pattern would be difficult to decipher. Barring unusual events such as heavy storms or onshore

30

winds, however, we can use empirically established tide tables to predict the depth of the Seattle harbor at some future date.

2. Trends. Environmental features also change in a variety of systematic but non-recurring ways, called trends. The simplest trends are produced by environmental features that change at a constant rate. The result is a **linear** pattern of change which may be increasing (positive), decreasing (negative), or stable (**Figure 1.12A**).

Most trends aren't linear, however. Instead, they fluctuate somewhat, because phenomena change at different rates at different times. Some environmental features continually increase or continually decrease, though not at a constant rate (**Figure 1.12B**). Such trends are called **monotonic**.

Other non-cyclical phenomena show alternately increasing and decreasing patterns. The pattern of change may range from quite simple (**Figure 1.12C**) to extremely complex (**Figure 1.12D**). Sometimes there are cyclical and non-cyclical components to a single trend. Many things change predictably with the seasons, for example, adding a cyclical factor to any trend. It's often helpful to note this seasonal cycle. If you were mapping unemployment rates for June, say, you'd want to take into account the fact that unemployment is always high when people get out of school in June.

3. Catastrophes. Features don't always change in a smooth, gradual way. Some events cause abrupt changes in environmental conditions.* Plants, animals, air, water, and land can be devastated by such catastrophic events as disease, severe weather (tornadoes, hurricanes, frost, drought), earth instability (mudslides, earthquakes, volcanic eruptions), and human activities (grazing, logging, chemical spills). The rate at which these events reoccur is related to an environment's stability and is itself a matter of great interest.

The effects of catastrophes vary but are always characterized by an abrupt "shift" or "step" in the pattern of change (**Figure 1.13**). After a period of adjustment, the original cycle or trend

*It was recognition of the influence of such singular events in biological evolution which led to the concept of **punctuated equilibrium** which is currently in vogue.*

may be regained and continued. Or the cycle or trend may continue as before but at a different base level. Or it may be fundamentally altered in its change rate or pattern. Various combinations of these effects can also be envisioned.

Movement Through Space

As we've seen, all environmental features to some degree change in character through time. Some features also change location with time. Indeed, movement is so integral that many features are defined explicitly in a time-space context. Hurricanes, tornadoes, ocean currents, avalanches, and highway traffic are a few examples. The notion of environmental process is inherent in the very definition of such phenomena.

The nature of movement depends upon a feature's character and geometry. Let's look at a few examples.

Discrete point features move along linear paths. Thus, we can visualize the routes taken by animals, vehicles, and other objects.

Discrete linear features may move at right angles to their linear dimension. Thus, some linear features move over area. Examples include a stream's meanderings, a road's relocation, and the changing ridgeline between adjacent water-

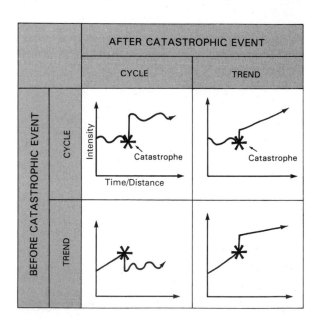

1.13 Catastrophic events may affect trends or cycles in several ways by creating discontinuities, as shown in these graphs. Here, intensity (y-axis) is plotted against time (x-axis).

sheds due to erosion. When such changes occur, we must be sure to adjust political boundaries that follow these linear features. Otherwise, conflicts may result.

Linear features may also move along a linear path. One example is an ice or log jam moving down a river course. Another is the movement of a parade, convoy, or train along its designated route.

Areal features move through space in sheet fashion along a linear front. Outgrowth of a forest edge, soil creep across a slope, surface precipitation runoff, the movement of an oil slick, and the spread of a grass fire fall into this category. When an areal feature is large, we commonly think of its edge as a linear feature. Thus, when the areal feature changes size, we focus on its edge and think of it as the movement of a linear feature. The waxing and waning of the battleline between territories controlled by opposing armies is an example.

Volumetric features move along an areal front. The movement of air masses, ocean currents, and groundwater fit into this category. So do avalanches and landslides. The development and dispersion of plumes of contaminants (such as industrial solvents, pesticides, herbicides, or combustion byproducts) in the soil, groundwater, freestanding water bodies, or the atmosphere also represent this class of feature. Despite the volumetric character of these features, we may be aware only of areal change or the movement of linear edges. We might think of the seasonal rise and fall of a reservoir, for example, as the back-and-forth movement of a linear feature (the shoreline) or the expansion and contraction of an areal feature (the water surface).

To some extent, the movement category into which we place a feature is a conceptual matter. We may think of an animal's movement in terms of a territory or range (areal feature) rather than as a composite of paths (linear features). Conversely, we may think of the sheet movement of an areal feature in terms of several direction lines. In fact, we're adept at viewing the movement of environmental features at different abstraction levels depending on our need at the moment.

Movement of features may take a variety of forms. It may be rhythmic (seasonal) or non-rhythmic. It may be constrained to designated routes, as with road, railroad, pipeline, or river traffic. It may follow multiple but similarly structured interrelated paths (braided streams, lava flows, jet stream paths, migratory bird flyways). It may be purposeful or active in a self-directed sense. Or it may be undirected and tending toward randomness, as in the case of long-term movement of animals within their range. It may even be guided (but not routed) passively by external forces such as gravity, wind, or ocean currents.

These factors are all important, because a feature's location at a particular moment may or may not be an unbiased example of its location through time. Thus, its location at a given instant may be of little value in making generalizations. A series of observations may be required to discern the rate and pattern of movement of even a single feature. Of course, the environment is made up of a multitude of features, each changing at a different rate and in a different pattern. Clearly, capturing this complexity in a map isn't easy.

The movement of environmental features has crucial geographical implications. Thus, if maps are to help us understand the environment, they should isolate and point out movements and movement-related factors. Clashes between moving and fixed features or between two or more moving phenomena are of special interest because they make such an important contribution to environmental dynamics.

CONCLUSION

In this chapter, we reduced the overwhelming detail of our surroundings to a more manageable structure. We did so from a geographical perspective to reveal the essential spatial character of the environment. We found it useful to categorize features according to their geometrical form (point-like, linear, areal, volumetric) and to differentiate further within these categories by feature type (discrete, discontinuous, continuous). We then considered the geometric dimensionality of geographic features. Finally, we explored the truism that the only constant in our environment is change.

Before we go on to the next chapter, it's worth reiterating our earlier caution: The labeling in this chapter is merely a human construct. This construct, as we'll see, not only serves a useful function in human thought and communication but is also basic to understanding the mapping process. In particular, it's vital to remember that human concepts precede mapping; maps don't create concepts. Maps reflect the way we think and are, therefore, superb at helping us visualize concepts.

We're now ready to consider the data available to the cartographer. Maps not only reflect the concepts we hold about our surroundings; they also reflect an adjustment to the data at hand. In the next chapter, we'll look at this relation between the environment to be mapped and the data available to map it.

SELECTED READINGS

Barry, R.G., and Chorley, R.J., *Atmosphere, Weather, and Climate*, 6th ed. (London: Routledge, 1992).

Bloom, A.L., *Geomorphology: A Systematic Analysis of Late Cenozoic Landforms*, 2nd ed. (Englewood Cliffs, NJ: Prentice-Hall, 1991).

Brody, H., *Maps and Dreams* (New York: Pantheon Books, 1981).

Christopherson, R.W., *Geosystems: An Introduction to Physical Geography*, 3rd ed. (Upper Saddle River, NJ: Prentice-Hall, 1997).

deBlij, H.J., and Muller, P.O., *Geography: Realms, Regions, and Concepts*, 8th ed. (New York: John Wiley & Sons, 1997).

deBlij, H.J., and Muller, P.O., *Physical Geography of the Global Environment*, 2nd ed. (New York: John Wiley & Sons, 1996).

Dingman, S.L., *Physical Hydrology* (New York: Macmillan Publishing Co., 1994).

Gerrard, J., *Soil Geomorphology: An Integration of Pedology and Geomorphology* (London: Chapman & Hall, 1992).

Goudie, A., *Nature of the Environment*, 3rd ed. (Oxford: Cambridge University Press, 1993).

Haggett, P., *Geography: A Modern Synthesis*, revised 3rd ed. (New York: Harper & Row, Publishers, 1983).

Hole, F.D., and Campbell, J.B., *Soil Landscape Analysis* (Totowa, NJ: Rowman & Allanheld, Publishers, 1985).

Jordan, T.G., Domosh, M., and Rowntree, L., *The Human Mosaic: A Thematic Introduction to Cultural Geography*, 7th ed. (New York: Addison Wesley Longman, 1997).

Mandelbrot, B.B., *The Fractal Geometry of Nature* (San Francisco: W.H. Freeman, 1982).

Miller, G.T., *Living in the Environment: Principles, Connections, and Solutions*, 8th ed. (Belmont, CA: Wadsworth Publishing Co., 1994).

Ritta, D.F., Kochel, R.C., and Miller, J.R., *Process Geomorphology*, 3rd ed. (Dubuque: Wm. C. Brown Publishers, 1995).

Szego, J., *Human Cartography: Mapping the World of Man* (Stockholm: Swedish Council for Building Research, 1987).

Shelton, J.S., *Geology Illustrated* (San Francisco: W.H. Freeman, 1966).

Short, N.M., and Blair, R.W., eds., *Geomorphology from Space: A Global Overview of Regional Landforms* (Washington DC: NASA, 1986).

Strahler, A., and Strahler, A., *Introducing Physical Geography: Environmental Update* (New York: John Wiley & Sons, 1996).

Thompson, D.W., *On Growth and Form* (Cambridge: Cambridge University Press, 1961).

Vankat, J.L., *The Natural Vegetation of North America: An Introduction* (New York: John Wiley & Sons, 1979).

Vernon, J., *The Garden and the Map* (Urbana: University of Illinois Press, 1973).

Also see references in Chapters 21, 22, and 23.

CHAPTER TWO

GEOGRAPHICAL DATA

INTRODUCTION

ACQUISITION METHOD

Ground Survey
    Horizontal Measurements
    Vertical Measurements
    Modern Survey Measurements
Census
Remote Sensing
Compilation

DATA MODEL

Object-Oriented Model
Location-Oriented Model

MEASUREMENT LEVEL

INVENTORY SCHEME

Population Counts
Spatial Samples

SPATIAL PREDICTION

Point to Point Conversions
Area to Point Conversions
Area to Area Conversions
Point to Area Conversions

DERIVED VALUES

CONCLUSION

SELECTED READINGS

"But somebody must have been through there," Wilson objected. "The map has rivers marked on it in that area."

Da Silva smiled at him condescendingly.

"That doesn't mean a thing. Cartographers are like nature: they abhor a vacuum. With so many rivers around, it's logical to assume a few more up there. Also, what sometimes happens is that a Varig pilot comes into Belém and he says, 'Say . . . coming across from Bogotá I thought I saw some water.' And somebody else says, 'Whereabouts?' And he says, 'Oh, somewhere up here,' and he lays his finger anywhere between Manaus and the Pacific Ocean. And a new line goes on the map."

Wilson grinned at this explanation. "At least nobody can argue with them, if nobody's been there."

Da Silva folded the map and stowed it away. . . .

—Robert L. Fish, *The Shrunken Head*

CHAPTER TWO

GEOGRAPHICAL DATA

It's one thing to think about the environment in conceptual terms as we did in the previous chapter. It's another matter to pin down these concepts into concrete data which can be mapped. This data-gathering step is critical for map users. The way map makers collect information will greatly affect the resulting map.

We sometimes forget how difficult it is to obtain environmental data. Information doesn't fall into our laps; it is elusive. Someone must make an effort to capture it. Data gathering, then, is an active, directed process. We must be willing to pay the cost, which can be high. Those who collect data are prone to take shortcuts, to "make do" at every opportunity. Since maps are only as good as the data used in their creation, map quality can suffer.

Since perfect data are rarely available, you must understand the cartographic effects of imperfect data. Your map reading ability will improve if you understand several aspects of information gathering which influence mapped data. These include: (1) the method used to gather data, (2) the way the data are structured, (3) the nature of the quantification achieved, (4) the data inventory scheme, (5) the spatial prediction models used to flesh out data sets, and (6) the derivation of statistical summary measures from raw data values. Let's consider each of these topics in turn.

ACQUISITION METHOD

Information for mapping is collected in several ways. The oldest method is to rely on **direct environmental perception,** using the unaided human senses. The survival of our species is ample testament to the value of such direct sensory data. We apparently possess a natural capacity to think of objects in terms of their locational, directional, and distance relations.

Direct perception has its limitations as a data-gathering technique, however. Due to the vastness of the environment, we need to store up myriad local images in our heads and then combine them into environmental pictures of broader scope. Unfortunately, our mental bookkeeping procedures for creating, storing, and retrieving these images are informal and poorly controlled. We may not be as observant as we should. We make subjective, imprecise judgments. Our memories may fail. Or we may put images together in faulty fashion. Small wonder, then, that our mental impression of a place usually suffers some inaccuracies.

However adequate direct perception was in human evolution, it's limited in relation to modern living spaces and locational accuracy needs. Fortunately, we can improve the quality of our environmental image by using systematic information-gathering procedures. Thus, we've developed technologically-based ground survey, census, and remote sensing methods to gather data for mapping. These formal procedures are more objective, precise, and controllable than unaided sensory methods. Let's look more closely at these three acquisition methods.

Ground Survey

We can specify the positions of environmental features if we can determine their distance and directional relations with other features. When we gather such data, we call it **ground survey** measurement.

Ground survey measurements fall into two categories: horizontal and vertical. We need both types of measurement to determine position in our three-dimensional surroundings. But since map makers often simplify their work by ignoring the vertical dimension, we'll consider horizontal measurements first.

Horizontal Measurements

Although the earth is a three-dimensional solid, in our local surroundings it's convenient to think of it as a flat, two-dimensional surface. That simplification gives us locational information precise enough for many day-to-day activities. It may even serve cartographic purposes if map coverage is limited to the local scene and the map user is a novice.

But to achieve the map accuracy needed for broad areal coverage and for sophisticated map users, locational information must be related to the earth's curved surface. People commonly say the earth is round or, more precisely, a sphere. That is the shape of our globes, and it suits many of our mapping needs.

But since the late 1600s, astronomers and mapping specialists have known that the basically spherical earth is slightly flattened at the poles and bulges slightly at the equator (**Figure 2.1**). To be precise in locating features, then, we must relate position information to this elliptical earth form. The ellipsoid surveyors use in making two-dimensional location measurements is called a **horizontal reference datum.** Such a datum is the basis for the familiar latitude and longitude spatial referencing system commonly found on maps (see *Flattening Continuum* in Appendix C).

There is a problem, however. Surveyors on different continents and in different countries were initially most concerned with their own region. To locate information in their region as accurately as possible, they adopted a reference ellipsoid that best served local needs. As a result, different ellipsoids were used in different parts of the world. This means that the latitude and longitude grid found on maps in different countries may not be based on the same earth shape and may not be simple to relate. Eventually, as global activity (scientific, military, transport, communication) increased, greater effort was made to define a worldwide datum. To further complicate things, ellipsoids in different parts of the world were "adjusted" periodically to better reflect improved

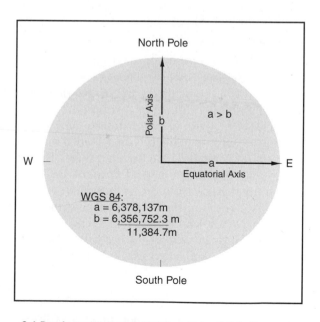

2.1 Due in part to rotation, the earth is slightly flattened at the poles and slightly bulged at the equator, producing an ellipsoid shape.

36

knowledge concerning the shape of the earth. **Table 2.1** lists some of these ellipsoids.

TABLE 2.1
Selected Horizontal Reference Surfaces
Airy Ellipsoid of 1830
Australian Ellipsoid of 1966
Bessel Ellipsoid of 1841
Clarke Ellipsoid of 1866
Clarke Ellipsoid of 1880
European Datum of 1950
European Datum of 1959
Everest Ellipsoid of 1860
International Ellipsoid of 1924
Krasovsky Ellipsoid of 1940
North American Datum of 1983 (NAD83)
(Used on U.S and Canadian maps)
(Based on Clarke 1866)
North American Datum of 1927 (NAD27)
(Used on U.S and Canadian maps)
(Based on Clarke 1866)
Ordinance Survey of Great Britain
Datum of 1936
South American Datum of 1969
World Geodetic System of 1984 (WGS84)
(Entire world for GPS use)

It's the job of highly skilled surveyors, called **geodesists,** to carefully determine positions on the earth with respect to a reference ellipsoid. Because of the high cost (in time, labor, and money) of locating these points, their position on the earth is marked with a special monument so that they can be located later. These markers are called **horizontal control points,** because they guide the work of local surveyors.

Since earth curvature is not pronounced locally, surveyors who stay within a small region can often get by in treating the earth as a flat surface. Thus, they are called **plane surveyors,** to distinguish them from geodesists, who deal with an ellipsoidal earth.

Plane surveyors use many methods, all of which involve making distance or angle (direction) measurements, or both. These ground survey methods had their origin in the invention of simple tools for measuring angles and distances. For example, early surveyors plotted maps by recording the direction and distance of each leg of a course or **transect.** This procedure is a formal version of the navigational technique called **dead reckoning (Figure 2.2A).**

It wasn't till the development of geometry and trigonometry, however, that the immense power of ground survey methods was realized. These mathematical procedures gave surveyors a shortcut. They could compute large amounts of locational, directional, and distance information using only a few observations. Initially, when it was most convenient to measure angles with the tools at hand, surveyors used a procedure called **triangulation (Figure 2.2B).** They used angular measurements to compute the length of a triangle's sides and hence the location of its corners. More recently, as it has become easier to measure distances precisely, a method called trilateration has become popular (**Figure 2.2C**). With trilateration, surveyors use distance measurements to

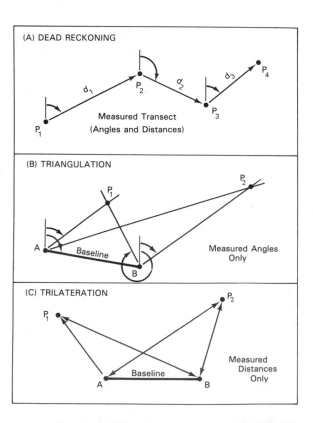

2.2 Ground survey methods may focus on measurement of distances and angles along a transect (A), intersection of sight lines (B), or distances between features (C).

determine angles and locations. In either case, the advantage is that it's unnecessary for the surveyor to physically occupy each site to be mapped.

Vertical Measurements

When we speak of the earth as flat, we don't mean it literally, of course. We're merely saying that the basic form of the surface in our vicinity is flat, but superimposed upon this flat base is an undulating landform surface. There are more ups and downs in the landform in some places than in others, giving the landscape the special character we experience in our daily lives.

For some purposes, then, we want to include the vertical dimension in our positional references. We want a truly three-dimensional way of defining the location of a feature. To do so, we use the term **elevation**. We say that the elevation of the mountain top is 3,200 feet, or that the landform at one place is 500 feet higher than at some other location. But elevation above what? And how are elevation differences determined? There are several options.

What is needed is a **vertical reference datum**. The reference surface widely adopted for this purpose is average sea level, or **mean sea level (MSL)**. Early surveyors chose this datum because of the measurement technology of the day. Surveyors could determine elevation by making gravity measurements at different locations on the landform and relating them to the pull of gravity at sea level. Gravity differences translate into elevation differences.

To make this scheme work, you must imagine that the MSL is extended under the continental land mass. This imaginary average water surface doesn't form a perfect ellipsoid, however, because differences in earth density affect gravity's pull at different locations. Thus, the MSL datum, called the **geoid**, undulates from place to place in irregular fashion (**Figure 2.3**).

The MSL datum is so convenient that it's used to record elevation data around the world. It's the base for the elevation data found on nearly all maps (see Chapter 5: *Landform Portrayal*). But be careful. Better measurements of the geoid have led to updated vertical reference datums. In the United States, for example, the **National Geodetic Vertical Datum of 1929 (NGVD 29)** was adjusted with new data to create the **North American Vertical Datum of 1988 (NAVD 88)**. Be sure you know what vertical datum your map is using.

Times and methods do change. This has led to a second option for measuring elevation. With modern satellite-based survey methods (see *Global Positioning System* in Appendix D), it's more convenient to measure elevation from the center of the earth than from MSL. Therefore, we must convert raw satellite data to the sea level datum before we can use it with existing maps (see Chapter 15: *GPS and Maps*). NAVD 88 was defined to be compatible with these satellite measurements.

Modern Survey Measurements

As you might expect, technological advances over the past several thousand years have improved the efficiency of ground survey methods. Calculations once made laboriously by hand are now handled by computers in a fraction of the time. High-quality magnification optics improve the accuracy and range of sighting devices. Microwaves and laser beams have replaced chains and tapes as a means of measuring distances. Artificial satellites that can send out coded signals reporting their position have reduced the need to take sightings on passive celestial bodies. (See *Global Positioning System* in Appendix D.) Inertial navigational devices (equipment capable of continuously recording changes in direction

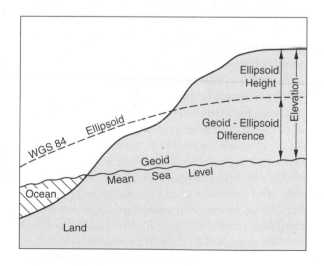

2.3 Elevation measurements for most maps are based on an average sea level datum extended under the continents.

38

and distance) can automatically perform dead reckoning in ships, airplanes, and automobiles. (See *Inertial Positioning Systems* in Appendix D.)

Thus, the speed, accuracy, and convenience of ground survey methods have improved immensely over the years. Ground survey techniques have been used to determine the location of key environmental features in all parts of the world. But ground survey still suffers from the drawback that it's a piecemeal procedure. At best, such surveys give us only a skeletal picture of a region. To do otherwise would require observing and recording the location of every discernible feature in the environment. Obviously, this task would be both overwhelming and impractical.

Census

When our primary concern is the nature of a population distribution rather than the location of individuals in the population, aggregation of data by geographical region may best suit our needs. Such a count of individuals by region is called a **census**.

Federal, state, and local government agencies conduct censuses to learn basic population characteristics. Private research firms focus their census taking on product advertising and marketing. Once data are aggregated, they're published or made available for researchers on computer-compatible tapes or disks. To make it easier to visualize the data, maps may also be produced.

These maps' quality depends largely on how well the target distribution's spatial character was preserved through the census process. There's a limit to the detail such maps can attain, however, since census information doesn't give positions of individual population elements. The map maker knows *how many* things exist within a region but not exactly *where*. Point and line information occurs as a count per region (25 people, say, or 50 miles of road). Areal data show up as absolute units per region (such as 35 acres of industrial land). The distribution of people, roads, or industrial land within the region remains a mystery. Regardless of the information used, therefore, the resulting maps will be highly generalized, or should be treated as though they were.

To assess the quality of census data for mapping, you need to ask yourself several critical questions: Was the census conducted according to high professional standards? Was it executed so that a relatively instantaneous picture was obtained? And what about the geometry of the area partitioning that provided the framework for data aggregation? To what extent did this geometry contribute to an unbiased report of the population? With respect to this last question, keep in mind the spatial data collection units (state, county, census tract, etc.) that were used. Ask yourself: What are the size, shape, and orientation of these data collection units? How might these three factors interact with the distribution under study to give a biased picture? To help answer this question, let's look at these three factors:

1. Size. Because only census unit totals are reported when data are spatially aggregated, areal

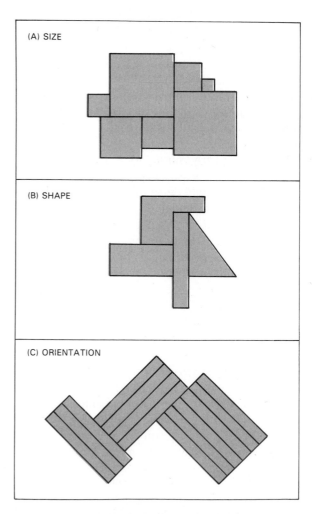

2.4 The size (A), shape (B), and orientation (C) of data collection units all may influence census data quality.

variation within census units is lost in the data. If census units are large relative to the distribution's variation pattern, crucial details may be masked (**Figure 2.4A**). Since distributions vary in detail and structure from one part of their domain to another, a census scheme based on equal-sized areal units will represent the data better in some areas than others. Map detail, for the most part, is limited by the size of the census units, despite what you may be looking for in the map. You may gain an idea of how data are distributed within census units if you know the distributions of related variables. But this attempt to look "into" census tract data is at best a tedious process fraught with guesswork (see *Spatial Prediction* later in this chapter).

2. Shape. The shape of data-gathering units may also influence census data quality. To reduce potential problems, census units should be fairly compact and of similar shape (**Figure 2.4B**). Compactness, however, isn't a simple concept to define. Do we mean compact with respect to space in general, in which case circular shapes are most compact? Or do we mean compact in the sense of keeping areal units as homogeneous as possible with respect to the distribution being studied? On one point there's little disagreement: Shapes that result from politi-

cal **gerrymandering**, in which a region is partitioned according to past voting behavior to ensure re-election of incumbent politicians, are by no means compact (**Figure 2.5**).

3. Orientation. A third aspect of census units that may influence data quality is orientation. The effect of orientation increases as census units' compactness decreases. In the extreme, the orientation of elongated census units may completely mask the distribution's character (see Figure 2.4C). In fact, strong orientation is just as troublesome in a distribution's pattern as in census units themselves.

Clearly, then, it's easy to have a mismatch between census units and the distribution being studied. When a mismatch occurs, census procedures tend to fragment and disperse the data, obscuring the true nature of the environment. Consider the hypothetical example in **Figure 2.6**. Here, four drinking water wells have been contaminated by toxic waste seepage from an abandoned landfill. In situation A, the sites of 400

Democratic senate plan for gerrymandered 27th Congressional District around Austin proposed by state democrats in 1981.

TEXAS

Austin

2.5 Political gerrymandering can lead to census units with very irregular shapes.

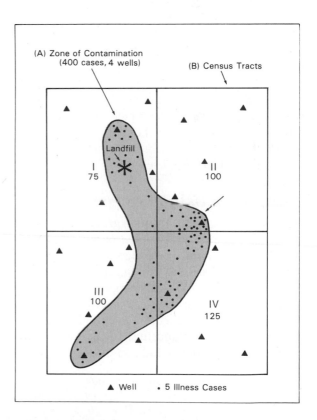

2.6 The effect of environmental toxins on human health (A) may be muted if the data are dispersed among several census units (B).

40

cases of illness traceable to impure water have been recorded, and the boundary of the zone of contamination has been identified. With attention so focused, it's likely that the source of the problem will be determined.

In situation B, however, the 400 cases of illness have been dispersed among four census units. The pattern has been so veiled that analysis of the data is likely to reveal no acute problem. The spatial aspect of the problem has been lost in the data. Under these circumstances, the landfill responsible for contaminating the water may go undetected because attention isn't focused in the vicinity. Unfortunately, we could cite many similar cases.

What we find, then, is a close relation between the geometry of census units and fidelity of census data. Effects of census unit geometry increase as a distribution's spatial character becomes more patterned and distinct. A uniform, smoothly changing distribution is relatively insensitive to the size, shape, or orientation of census units. On the other hand, a distribution with strong patterns and sharp contrasts is highly vulnerable to degradation due to census unit geometry. Recall that many censuses, especially those conducted by government agencies, are of a general-purpose nature. They use existing political partitionings of space for administrative convenience and, therefore, aren't tailored to the spatial character of any individual distribution. Mapping these data will reveal only those problems inherent in the information itself.*

Remote Sensing

Even when controlled through ground survey and census procedures, direct environmental perception gives a limited world view. Indirect experience has always been an important additional source of information for mapping. Reports of distant places have traveled by word of mouth and other forms of communication since the beginning of humankind. In the last century, however, the significance of indirect information gathering, or remote sensing, has grown enormously.

There are two main methods of collecting information through remote sensing:

1. With site-specific devices, we record continuously distributed variables at specific locations. For example, instruments at a weather station give a site-specific measure of temperature, pressure, humidity, and precipitation. Monitors lowered into a scattering of drilled wells give site-specific measures of drinking water quality. Readings at seismic stations provide site-specific indications of bedrock structure that are useful in mineral exploration. Maps of such phenomena are created by compiling information from the scatter of recording stations into a single image.

2. With environmental remote sensing, devices such as the standard camera produce spatial images of the environment directly. Such photography and photo-like electronic sensing from aircraft and spacecraft have given us access to a whole new realm of our environment. Environmental remote sensing lets us observe both continuous and discrete distributions by using materials (films) or recording instruments (electronic sensors) which are sensitive to the energy emitted or reflected from objects (see Appendix B: *Remote Sensing of the Environment*).

The image on film is a directly viewable analog of the environment. Hence it is called an **analog image**. In contrast, electronic sensors yield electrical signals rather than an image. This information must subsequently be transformed into an image. This is done by first representing the signals' strength at regular intervals with numbers, and then converting these digits to tonal levels on film or a computer screen. Since image information from electronic sensors is stored and transmitted as numbers, it is called a **digital image**.

Remote sensing opens up the invisible parts of our environment for mapping. A wide variety of map-like products are produced from these data. Some appear as they came directly from the sensor system. Others represent elaborate computer manipulation of the energy recorded by the sensor (see Chapter 4: *Image Maps*).

It's important to realize that, while remote sensing methods produce images that seem to capture the environment as it is at the moment, they are in fact elaborate technological creations. They contain method-produced artifacts charac-

If there are problems with maps based on census data, then the same problems will exist in statistical analysis based on these data. Although the problems may be harder to visualize in statistical data analysis, they're just as troublesome as in cartographic data analysis.

teristic of the photo-chemical or electronic processes involved. (See *Cartographic Artifacts* in Chapter 25.) Furthermore, many factors can influence the appearance of the resulting image. Such factors include: the sensor vehicle's vantage point, the sensor's spectral sensitivity, the image's spatial resolution, the instruments' technical quality, and atmospheric conditions. Clearly, we must use caution when using maps based on remotely sensed data. This fact is important to keep in mind, for, as we'll see in Chapter 4, remotely sensed images provide the basic information source for many of the maps we use.

Compilation

While ground survey, census, and remote sensing are valuable for generating primary data, such field techniques aren't always practical. Due to constraints on time, labor, or cost, cartographers may have no choice but to gather data for mapping from secondary sources such as tables, graphs, text, or existing maps. This process of data gathering is called **compilation**.

When existing maps provide the data for this compilation procedure, the rule is to proceed from larger-scale (more detailed) to smaller-scale (less detailed) sources (see Appendix A for a discussion of map scale). This strategy ensures that errors and other mapping effects incorporated into the original maps aren't magnified by the compilation procedure (see Chapter 3 for a discussion of the transformational effects of mapping). Commercial mapping firms, for example, commonly derive their small-scale thematic maps and atlases from large-scale maps produced by government agencies.

Violations of the above compilation rule are actually quite common. Someone will enlarge a map on a photocopy machine. A television camera will zoom in on a map designed for wall display. Or a government agency will enlarge small-scale geology maps and lay them over large-scale topographic maps. In each case, the map user can be deceived, because the map isn't being used for its intended purpose. When such situations cannot be avoided, extra map reading care is imperative.

Whenever maps are compiled from existing cartographic products and other secondary sources (text, tables, graphs), it's prudent to ques-

tion their quality. It would be helpful to find the answers to such questions as: Is the map timely? Is it accurate? Is it consistent from region to region? Is the source reliable? What data collection and portrayal methods were used? Are important details masked as a result of these methods? Unfortunately, compiled maps rarely include information of this sort beyond, possibly, the name of the source.

DATA MODEL

To gather, store, and manipulate geographical information using modern electronic equipment, we must adopt a spatial data model. Two such models are widely used. One is based on recognized environmental entities, such as point, linear, and volumetric features. The other is based on the recording of attributes or values found at environmental locations. Which model is chosen has a strong impact on how we gather, store, and manipulate the data. So let's look at both these data models.

Object-Oriented Model

When we view the environment, we see objects. Yet we know our eyes receive light energy reflected from the environment on a cell by cell basis. Apparently, our brain is more interested in objects such as trees, rocks, and rivers than in tiny specks of color data. We quickly process raw sensory data into object-oriented constructs. This is very efficient, since object coding reduces the amount of data we must handle.

It's natural, then, that we would use an **object-oriented model** for digital mapping (**Figure 2.7A**). In this case, the process is called **entity by entity coding**. Point features are coded by coordinate (x,y) location. Lines are coded as a string of points. Areas are coded as lines that close on themselves. Machines called **digitizers** convert graphical information feature by feature into digital form.

Location-Oriented Model

The task of coding environmental information entity by entity is overwhelming. Fortunately, we have another option, which is to code environmental information on a **location by location** basis.

42

It's impractical to record information for every location on earth, of course. In practice, then, information is recorded for a **matrix** or **grid** of cells (**Figure 2.7B**).* The smaller the cells, the more detail in the database, but the more data that must be gathered, stored, and manipulated. Overall, the grid approach is very inefficient because the same amount of data is stored whether the cells are empty or full. This is in stark contrast to the efficiency of object-oriented coding.

The salvation for the grid approach is that modern technology works in grid fashion. This is true of digital computers, electronic scanners, laser printers, and so forth. Thus, inefficiencies in coding are far offset by data processing and display efficiencies. In fact, object-oriented data are commonly converted to cellular form for mapping purposes. A large amount of geographical information is now coded in matrix form, as we'll see in later chapters.

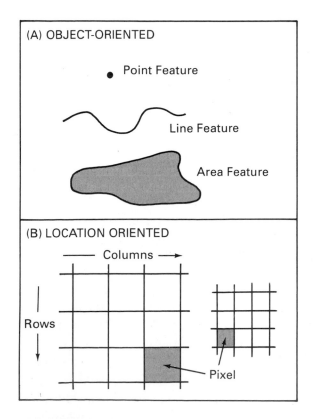

2.7 In gathering environmental data, we may either use an **object-oriented** data model, based on point, line, area, and volume entities (A) or a **location-oriented** data model, based on a grid of cells (B).

MEASUREMENT LEVEL

In addition to knowing how information was gathered and structured, the map user should understand how that information was treated when it was collected and mapped. What is the inherent nature of the mapped data? How does it differ from the nature of all possible phenomena available for mapping? And how has mapping changed its character? To answer these questions, we must be able to divide the information into different measurement levels, with each level telling us something about the nature of the information.

We commonly group data according to two simple measurement levels. The information is either qualitative or quantitative. **Qualitative** information tells only *what* things exist—lakes, rivers, roads, cities, farms, etc. **Quantitative** information measures the *magnitude* of these things, telling how many, large, wide, fast, high, etc., they are.

This simple dichotomy between qualitative and quantitative data pervades our conception of the environment. But to confine measurement of all environmental features to only two categories is needlessly restrictive. It's more useful to measure things in terms of a four-level hierarchy. One level (nominal) is associated with qualitative information, and three levels (ordinal, interval, and ratio) deal with quantitative data (**Table 2.2**). The nature of the information that results from applying these different measurement levels varies greatly. Thus, understanding the properties of the four levels is fundamental to map use.

1. Nominal. At the most primitive level, we can characterize features at a strictly classificatory, or nominal level. Phenomena within a class are assumed to be relatively homogeneous, while elements of different classes are considered dissimilar. Nominal measurement might be used, for instance, to divide the earth's surface into land and water classes.

2. Ordinal. A somewhat less primitive measurement level occurs when environmental features aren't only partitioned into separate groups but are also ranked according to some

*In the case of image data, the cells are called picture elements, or pixels (see Chapter 4: Image Maps).

continuum. This ordinal measurement is characterized by "greater than" and "less than" (> <) relations between classes. How much more or less one class is than another isn't specified, however. Numerical values aren't given. We might use ordinal scaling, for example, to class roads in terms of driving safety: Interstate highways tend to be safer than state highways, which in turn are safer than county roads.

3. Interval. A still higher measurement level is achieved with interval scaling. Here the intervals between groups have meaning, and numbers are used. The numbers themselves don't have absolute value, however, because the zero point in the scale is arbitrary. Temperature scales are a good example. We know exactly how much more 40° is than 32°. Yet the actual numbers are meaningless, as evidenced by the fact that the temperature can be 32°F. and 0°C. at the same time. Calendar dates are also a form of interval measurement, as we saw in *The Nature of Time* in Chapter 1.

4. Ratio. The fourth and most sophisticated level is ratio measurement. With ratio measurement, the numbers do have absolute meaning. This is the case with measurements of length, volume, density, and similar dimensions that use true zero in their scaling.

In general, measurement sophistication increases and the degree of information generalization decreases from nominal to ratio levels. The advantage of higher levels is that they provide information of the greatest accuracy and detail. The map maker can therefore give more information to the map user. But there is a price. These sophisticated measurement levels are the

TABLE 2.2

Measurement Levels

Scale	Defining Relations	Examples
Nominal	(a) Equivalence 　　Class A = Class A 　　Class A ≠ Class B	(a) Land-water classification 　　of earth's surface (b) Land-use classes 　　(urban-rural)
Ordinal	(a) Equivalence (b) Greater-less than 　　A > B 　　B < A	(a) City classification 　　(small-medium-large) (b) Terrain classification 　　(plain-hill-mountain) (c) Population density classification 　　(low-medium-high)
Interval	(a) Equivalence (b) Greater-less than (c) Ratio of any two intervals 　　(assumed arbitrary 0 value)	(a) Temperature 　　(0°C. = 32°F.) (b) Time 　　(1980 Christian calendar = 　　1400 A.H. Muslim calendar)
Ratio	(a) Equivalence (b) Greater-less than (c) Ratio of any two intervals (d) Ratio of any two scale 　　values 　　(assumed true 0 value)	(a) Density of population (b) Volume of stream discharge (c) Area of countries

44

most costly and difficult to attain. This means that higher-level information may not be available for mapping even though it would be desirable.

When high measurement levels have been achieved, the information can be handled with the greatest mapping flexibility. If map makers have information more complex than they need, they can preprocess it into a simpler form before mapping. Higher measurement levels can be generalized to lower ones to fit mapping requirements.

The lower levels of measurement are the simplest and least costly to attain. As a result, information is most commonly available in this relatively low-detail form. Maps made from this information also convey comparatively little information. Furthermore, lower-level information provides the fewest mapping options. If the mapping situation calls for greater detail, there's nothing the map makers can do. It isn't possible to increase the measurement level of the information available; there is no way to "ungeneralize."

INVENTORY SCHEME

Another important aspect of information gathering is the strategy used to collect the information, or the **inventory scheme**. Map makers have two choices. They can observe every element of a distribution; this method is called a **population count**. Or they can observe only a portion of the population; such an inventory is called a **sample.** Suppose, for instance, that they are making a state map showing cities. Should they include every city in the state on their map? Or should they show only a selection of cities? The question may be purely academic, since information is often available only in sample form. It's worthwhile, though, to take a look at the relative merits of population and sample information.

Population Counts

It may seem logical that a map including the whole population would be of higher quality than one showing only a sample. This is probably true in most cases. But not always. For one thing, a number of errors may creep into the observation of population information. These mistakes can be attributed to **instrumental**, **methodological**, and **human** deficiencies during information gath-

ering. Such errors are usually well disguised in maps.

Take the case of the United States Census of Population and Housing, conducted each decade. Since every household in the country is surveyed, maps produced from the statistics will of course be faultless....Or will they? A full head count of over two hundred million people is an immense job. Look at the facts.

Once every 10 years, the Census Bureau pulls together a nation-wide work force from the ranks of the unemployed. These census takers are asked to put their hearts into a low-paying job that lasts only a few weeks. They must brave strange neighborhoods and repeat questions from a long, dull questionnaire on every doorstep. The people to be interviewed often aren't home; when they are, they may be hostile. They're supposed to respond truthfully even though this means telling secrets that could get them in trouble with their landlords, the welfare office, or local authorities. Finally, after all the information has been gathered, it still has to be processed, analyzed, and mapped.

We see here the potential for all three types of errors: instrumental (interviewer), methodological (questionnaire method), and human (at all levels). Yet the Census Bureau has an electronic display which at any time will give you the "actual" number of people in the United States. Be your own judge of how accurate and current this population count is!

Spatial Samples

As we saw in Chapter 1, **discrete** environmental features (such as trees, lakes, or people) are isolated and finite. Consequently, we can count and locate their populations if we have enough time, money, and labor to devote to the task. The problem is that these resources are often not available.

On the other hand, the elements of a **continuous** distribution (such as temperature) are located everywhere. There's no way that the temperature of every spot in the United States can be observed. Even if the needed resources were available, the task would be theoretically impossible.

Clearly, then, we need an alternative to a full population inventory. We must find a method we can use for all continuous distributions and also for discrete distributions when a full population inventory is impractical. The solution is to use a limited amount of **sample** information to estimate what the population is like.

The idea behind sampling is to use a small part of the population to find out what we want to know about the larger population. We can divide the population according to any number of factors—socio-economic groups, age, gender, and so on. When a sample is based on environmental locations, we call it **geographical** or **plane sampling.**

There are several components to plane sampling. The quality of the sample (and therefore of subsequent maps) is determined by how well these sampling components are handled (**Figure 2.8**). First, the people collecting the data have to decide what sampling unit to use—whether to sample information at a point, along a line (transect), or in an area (quadrant). Next, they must determine how many sampling units to use. How large or small is the sample going to be? Finally, they must decide how to spread these sampling units through the environment. Sampling units can be scattered **randomly**, with

no perceptible pattern, **systematically** (say, every two miles in a square pattern), or in a stratified fashion. With **stratified** sampling, the area is divided into groups in proportion to their known characteristics.

Stratified sampling is used in such fields as market research and opinion polling. The Gallup poll, which predicts election results, and the Nielsen rating, which determines how many people watch various TV programs, make good use of stratified sampling. The pollsters divide the population not only in terms of geographical regions but according to a variety of other elements as well. If they know that 35 percent of the total population has only a high school education, say, they assign 35 percent of their sample to that group. If 72 percent of the population is married, then married people will make up 72 percent of the sample.

There's some debate as to the accuracy of the Nielsen rating, but it's hard to argue the reliability of the Gallup poll, since it consistently predicts election outcomes to within a percentage point. Such results make a good case for the effec-

2.8 Plane sampling is based on a random or systematic spatial array of point, line, or areal observation units.

tiveness of stratified sampling. In fact, Gallup and Nielsen pollsters claim that their stratified sampling techniques reflect the truth about a population even more accurately than a total population inventory, such as that carried out by the Census Bureau. When you remember the problems we discussed in association with the Census Bureau inventory, you may agree.

The advantage of stratified sampling is that it takes into consideration what we already know about an area or population. Of course we don't always have such helpful advance knowledge. In such cases—and they are in the majority—we must resort to random or systematic sampling.

Whichever sampling method is used, all samples must strive to be as **representative** as possible of the larger population. If an important aspect of a distribution is missed by the sample, a false impression of reality results. If most of the population is clumped into one corner of a county and that corner isn't inventoried, the sample will be unrepresentative or **biased**. Biased samples lead to poor maps.

For an idea of how samples relate to sampled distributions, look at our attempts to map the world's oil reserves. Life-shaking decisions depend on oil as a source of energy. Yet our knowledge of oil reserves seems to be based on an extremely small and uneven scatter of drill holes. Isn't there a good chance that a slight change in the sample would reveal entirely new oil fields? Wasn't this how the North Slope reserve was found?

The problem with this reasoning is that drilling for oil is based on a far more efficient sample than might be apparent on a map. Exploration has been closely matched to promising geologic structures. In other words, the sample has been stratified, using the best knowledge available. To significantly increase known reserves, then, what we really have to do is find new geologic structures. Since oil well drilling provides a great deal of our geologic knowledge, the high cost (millions of dollars per hole) of expanding the sample has to be balanced by the promise of increasing the world's known resources. Our fondest dream is that major fields have been missed—that our sample has been negatively biased.

Sampling always incorporates an element of chance into data selection and, therefore, map-

ping. The inventory of a relatively small area is being used to predict the variable distribution over a much larger area. Map quality depends on how representative the sample is. Yet sampling bias is seldom ascertained by the map maker and rarely passed on to the map user. In too few cases is a reliability diagram provided along with a map. For the map user, then, it pays to be slightly suspicious of the quality of a map unless some indication of map accuracy is given.

SPATIAL PREDICTION

There are four common situations in which map makers must make a spatial prediction. In the first, they use known spatial sample data to predict what is happening at other (non-sample) locations. In the second, they aggregate data within region boundaries, assign the aggregated value to a centroid within the region, and then predict values at other locations. With the third, they convert data from one set of spatial census units to another with different geometrical characteristics. And with the fourth, they partition a region into subregions by attaching area to the closest known location. Let's consider each situation in some detail.

1. Point to Point Conversions

Spatial sampling may save time and effort, but it gives an incomplete picture of the environment. There's no problem if we're satisfied merely to map what's found at sample sites, as when temperatures at selected weather stations are shown on a U.S. map.

But maps that portray environmental data only at a scattering of sample points often aren't deemed sufficient by such professionals as meteorologists or geologists, who understand that the distributions being mapped are in reality continuous. To satisfy these professionals, it's common to produce maps on which the spaces between sample locations are filled in with map symbols. The U.S. weather map on the TV news, for example, uses bands of color representing temperature zones even though weather information is available only for a scatter of official weather stations (**Figure 2.9**). While such maps give the impression of showing a complete environmental pattern, the in-between data that have been added are nothing more than **spatial predictions**—guesses based on the known sample data. If a representative sample has been taken and if the prediction scheme was valid, a decent map may have been produced. If not, the map may be useless.

Spatial predictions can take several forms. If the prediction is made at a spot that falls between locations with known values, the process is called **interpolation (Figure 2.10)**. If the prediction is made for a spot that falls beyond (to the side of) locations with known values, the process is called **extrapolation**. As a rule, interpolation is the more accurate of the two methods. It should also be clear that large, well-scattered samples support more accurate predictions than small, clustered ones.

How do cartographers manage to convert information from a sparse spatial scattering of

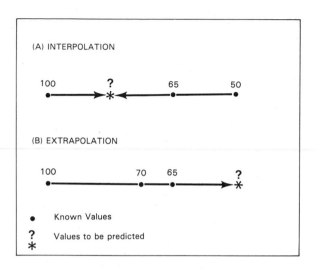

2.10 When spatial prediction is made between known values, it is called interpolation; when it is made beyond known values, it is called extrapolation.

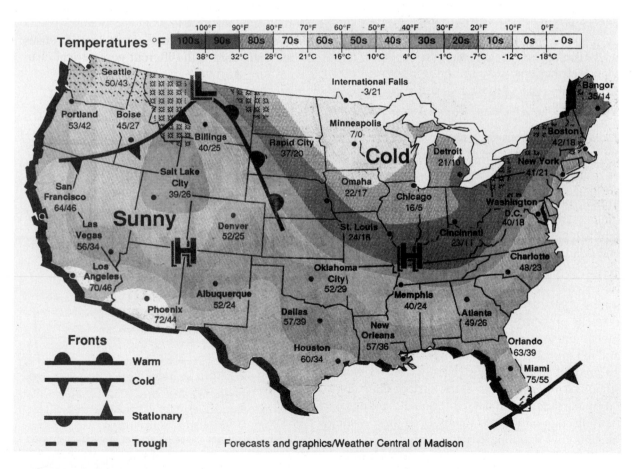

2.9 Although weather conditions are officially measured at relatively few locations, predictive methods are used to show conditions at all locations.

48

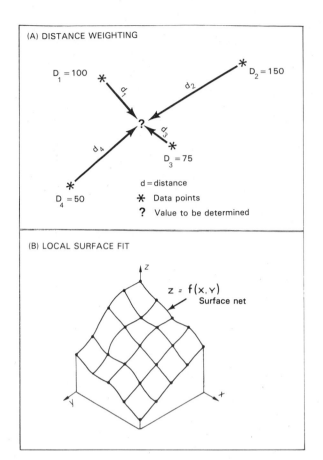

2.11 Point to point spatial prediction models are based either on weighted distance and direction relations (A) or on surface fitting (B).

available, algebraic models are used more often because they can be executed on computers. Some of these models, called **local operator models**, predict the value at a point on the basis of weighted distance and direction relations with known neighborhood values (**Figure 2.11A**). Others, known as **surface fitting models**, involve fitting an equation to all known sample values and then solving the equation for the coordinates of each point of interest (**Figure 2.11B**).

From carefully controlled research, we know what factors affect the accuracy of predicted values. These factors include: the spatial scatter of points, sample size, prediction model, and complexity of the distribution (**Figure 2.12**). Of these, spatial scatter seems to be most critical. Thus, you would expect maps based on predicted values to at least indicate the sample scatter used. Unfortunately, few maps do so, leaving you to guess at the map's fidelity. When you suspect that spatial prediction has been used, then, be careful. Don't assign meaning to what are merely artifacts of the prediction method. (See *Cartographic Artifacts* in Chapter 25.)

sample points to a continuous surface in mapping? There are several approaches, each of which involves making assumptions about reality and building those assumptions into the structural rules of a spatial prediction model. The assumptions generally deal with the expected form of the sampled surface. Specifically, are gradients linear, convex, or concave? Does the surface extend higher and lower than the sample data maximum and minimum? How strongly self (auto) correlated are the surface values (in other words, how smooth is the surface?). Is the surface interrupted by barriers of some sort? Should the surface pass through all sample values, or is there some likelihood of sampling error?

Map makers use the answers to such questions to set structural parameters within spatial prediction models. Although graphic models are

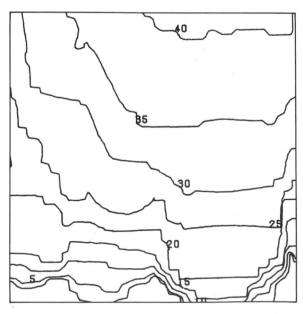

2.12 When maps are based on spatial prediction, method-produced artifacts are sometimes evident. The linear, geometric character of the isolines shown here is an obvious example. (See *Isoline Maps* in Chapter 7 for a discussion of isoline mapping.)

2. Area to Point Conversions

In the previous section, we discussed making spatial predictions based on sample data. We assumed the phenomenon to be mapped had been measured at a scattering of locations. This is appropriate for continuous features such as temperature, but not all phenomena are of this type. If we want to map population density, for example, we can't go to a location and take a measurement. We need another approach to deal with population density and similar derived features.

Census methods yield data counts aggregated by region (see *Census* earlier in this chapter). We can transform these data into a smooth, continuous density surface. We can then map this surface by making several assumptions (**Figure 2.13**). First, we compute population density on a region by region basis so that counts for large regions are standardized with those of small regions. Next, we assign each density figure to a point within its respective region. We'll probably want to choose a central location, but there are other ways to define such a **centroid** (see *Centroid* in Chapter 16). Finally, we predict density values at non-centroid locations, using one of the "point to point" interpolation methods discussed in the previous section.

This is a large number of assumptions! The consequence is that not too much credence should be given to predicted values at specific locations, including centroid points. The overall surface representation can be quite good, however, with the exception that it exhibits less variation (is smoother and less detailed) than the original data. But there's a host of potential problems. The original distribution's character won't be sampled uniformly if data collection regions vary in size, shape, and orientation. Each assumption will also have an impact. In addition, map makers do make design errors, such as assigning raw data counts rather than density figures to centroids. Once again, then, it pays to be cautious when using maps based on spatial prediction.

3. Area to Area Conversions

Like point models, area prediction models should be treated with caution. In this case, cartographers have converted data between different census unit schemes. For instance, they might convert per-capita income information, collected by three-digit zip code zones, so that it is spatially compatible with population data collected by county units.

Cartographers use several approaches to make this conversion between **source zones** (in this case zip code regions) and **target zones** (in this case counties). The most common method is called **spatial overlay** (**Figure 2.14**). With this technique, they determine how much of each source zone's data falls in each target zone. They do so by superimposing target zones on source zones and then determining the extent of overlap as a proportion of each source zone area. Since they assume a homogeneous population density, the proportion of spatial overlap is equivalent to a proportion of the data. Finally, they sum these proportionate data values to arrive at target zone totals.

Obviously, it would be useful if cartographers let map users know when they've used areal models to predict values for mapping. As with point models, however, you'll rarely find this information on maps. Again, caution is in order if you suspect such a procedure has been used, since homogeneity within data collection zones and abrupt breaks at zone boundaries have likely been assumed. If these aren't reasonable assumptions (and they rarely are), then maps based on the predicted data can be quite deceptive.

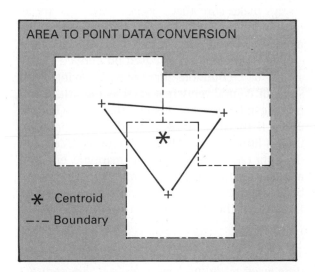

AREA TO POINT DATA CONVERSION

✱ Centroid
--- Boundary

2.13 Area to point conversions involve aggregating data within region boundaries, assigning the aggregated value to a centroid within the region, and then predicting values at other locations.

50

4. Point to Area Conversions

We sometimes use spatial prediction to assign regions to points. For example, we might measure soil type at a scattering of locations. Then we might use these data to exhaustively partition the landscape into soil class subregions. Or, we might try to guess likely service areas around a business such as a bank or store (see Chapter 19: *GIS and Map Analysis Software*).

The assumption we make in these point to area conversions is that of geographical homogeneity. We assume the background environment to be everywhere the same. Under this condition, we partition space by letting each point capture the area closer to it than to any other point. In the soil class case, we assume the landscape near measured locations to be similar. In the service area case, we expect buyers to patronize the nearest (as the crow flies) source of their desire or need. In both cases, we partition space by bisecting the distance between neighboring points, as

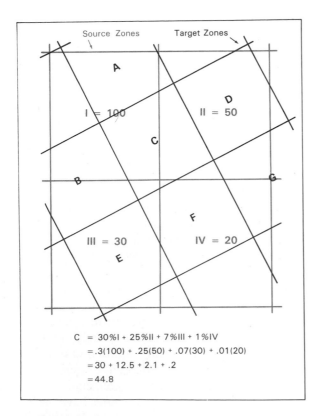

C = 30%I + 25%II + 7%III + 1%IV

= .3(100) + .25(50) + .07(30) + .01(20)

= 30 + 12.5 + 2.1 + .2

= 44.8

2.14 Spatial overlay is an "area to area" method used to convert data from one scheme of spatial data collection units (source zones) to another (target zones).

shown in **Figure 2.15**. Then we choose some attribute within each region created by the partitioning. Finally, we link that attribute somehow to the centroid location.

This strategy for making point to area conversions may yield fairly good predicted values in an all-things-being-equal world. But that isn't our day-to-day reality. In practice, variations in behavior and diversity in the geographical setting make the predicted values, at best, rough estimates.

DERIVED VALUES

In a sense, all data generated with the aid of a spatial prediction model can be thought of as derived data. But, for purposes of this discussion, we'll use the term "derived" in a narrower sense. Cartographers often use simple statistical techniques to manipulate data before mapping. It is these data, generated through statistical processing of raw data values, that we call **derived values**.

In today's computer age, cartographers routinely manipulate raw information in statistical ways to make it more suitable for mapping. The result is a variety of averages, ratios, indexes, potentials, dimensions/factors, deviations/variations, and regressions/residuals.* These measures range widely in conceptual and mathematical sophistication. Unfortunately, cartographers don't always make sure that mapped measures are as meaningful to the map user as they are mathematically elegant.

Meaningless maps based on derived values are in fact common. Mappings involving measures of central tendency, such as the arithmetic mean, can be used to illustrate this point (**Figure 2.16**). If the data show a trendless distribution, there's little problem. But if a trend is present in the data (as might happen in mapping environmental pollution data, for example), the mean will be deceptive because it's constantly changing. Likewise, if the data exhibit a cyclical character,

*It isn't appropriate to go into much detail concerning these measures in this book. Consult a basic statistics text if you need terms clarified. Basic geography texts which deal with statistics also illustrate geographical applications of these measures. (See Selected Readings at the ends of Chapters 16, 17, and 18.)

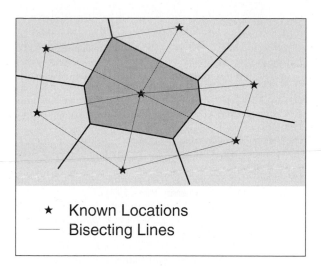

★ Known Locations
— Bisecting Lines

2.15 A region is sometimes partitioned into subregions by attaching area to the closest known location.

the mean isn't very representative of individual population values. Consider, for instance, how meaningful it is to know the average monthly precipitation for a city if this distribution pattern is at all erratic. As a rule, it's better not to map trends and cycles using means. Unfortunately, cartographers rarely reveal the nature of data distributions used in mapping, and you're left to speculate on the nature of the data.

A second example will further illustrate why caution is in order when derived values are mapped. Measures of environmental suitability, trafficability, vulnerability, susceptibility, yield, and potential are frequently mapped for use by planning and regulatory agencies. Indeed, these indexes are thought to represent the ultimate achievement in merging statistical and cartographical methods. The problem is that these measures appear to be objective and meaningful when in fact they are elaborate conceptual creations.

We say these indexes are creations because they represent weighted composites of several variables. An index of soil erosion potential, for example, might take into consideration slope, soil composition, crop cover, local farming practice, storm characteristics, and so forth. To make such an index, cartographers have had to choose which variables to include and how much weight to give each variable. These choices are a matter

of human judgment. Such judgments are always **value laden**.

Imagine, for example, that we want to derive a land suitability index to aid in deciding whether land should be zoned for industrial, agricultural, recreational, commercial, or residential use. Consider the choices that the cartographers will have to make. They will need to assign values to aesthetics, human convenience, and the preservation of air, water, soil, landforms, vegetation, and wildlife.

The problem is that different people hold different values, and a person's values change with time and circumstances. This explains why lists rating the "best" places to live are always so controversial. As for the map user, when cartographers portray numerical indexes of any sort, their maps warrant scrutiny with a skeptical eye.

Faced with a map depicting derived measures, what can the map user do? For one thing, it can't hurt to become well versed in the ways of statistics. Beyond that, it is important to recog-

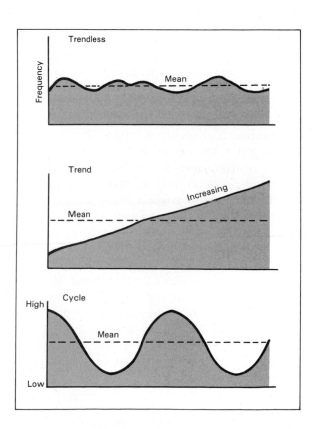

2.16 Measures of central tendency, such as the arithmetic mean, poorly represent data that exhibit trends or cycles.

52

nize that improper statistical manipulations can diminish the quality of good data as easily as they can mask the shortcomings of poor data.

More and more, we will have to appraise the appropriateness of mapped statistical measures. It may help to ask yourself several questions. What was done statistically to the data? Why was it done? What are the potential effects of these statistical manipulations on the appearance of the map and the conclusions you are likely to draw from the map?

CONCLUSION

We saw in the previous chapter that poor maps may result from a deficiency in environmental conception. In the present chapter, we saw that the process of converting environmental conceptions into geographical data further adds to the potential for map failure. The best insurance against both problems is to understand the impact of how we view the environment and how we gather data for mapping.

Cartographers are fond of saying that anything which has a spatial distribution can be mapped. In a sense this is true. But the statement fails to consider the varying nature of environmental phenomena. It also fails to take into account the time, effort, and cost associated with capturing environmental data in a form which can support high-quality mapping. Since we as a society get what we are willing to pay for, the quality of data varies dramatically from topic to topic depending on what is considered important or worthwhile. As a direct consequence, some things are far easier to map well than others, and everything isn't mapped equally well.

Our understanding of environmental concepts (Chapter 1) and the nature of geographical data (Chapter 2) provides the foundation for us, as map users, to evaluate the cartographic process. Thus, we're now ready to move on to the topic of map design. We'll begin by considering basic mapping principles (Chapter 3) and then explore characteristics of common cartographic expressions (Chapters 4 through 7).

SELECTED READINGS

Blalock, H.M., Jr., *Conceptualization and Measurement in the Social Sciences* (Beverly Hills: Sage Publications, 1982).

Burrough, P.A., and Frank, A.U., *Geographic Objects with Indeterminate Boundaries* (London: Taylor & Francis, 1996).

Crosby, A.W., *The Measure of Reality: Quantification and Western Society* (Cambridge: Cambridge University Press, 1997).

Danielson, D., *Wisconsin Geodetic Control, Guide 2* (Madison, WI: Wisconsin State Cartographer's Office, 1992).

Daugherty, R., *Science in Geography: Data Collection* (London: Oxford University Press, 1974).

Gilbertson, D.D., Kent, M., and Pyatt, F.B., *Practical Ecology for Geography and Biology: Survey, Mapping, and Data Analysis* (London: Hutchinson Education, 1985).

Griffiths, J.C., and Ondrick, C.W., *Sampling a Geological Population,* Computer Contribution 30 (Lawrence, KS: State Geological Survey, 1968).

Holmes, J.H., "The Theory of Plane Sampling and Its Applications in Geographic Research," *Economic Geography*, 46, 2 (Supplement) (June 1970), pp. 379-392.

Hurn, J., GPS: *A Guide to the Next Utility* (Sunnyvale, CA: Trimble Navigation Ltd., 1989).

Kent, W., *Data and Reality: Basic Assumptions on Data Processing Reconsidered* (New York: North-Holland Publishing Co., 1978).

Lillesand, T.M., and Kiefer, R.N., *Remote Sensing and Image Interpretation*, 3rd ed. (New York: John Wiley & Sons, 1994).

Lounsbury, J.F., and Aldrich, F.T., *Introduction to Geographic Field Methods and Techniques* (Columbus, OH: Charles E. Merrill Publishing Co., 1979).

Mathews, H., and Foster, I., *Geographical Data: Sources, Presentation and Analysis* (New York: Oxford University Press, 1989).

Montgomery, G.E., and Schuch, H., *GIS Data Conversion Handbook* (Ft. Collins, CO: GIS World, Inc., 1993).

Morain, S., and Baros, S., eds., *Raster Imagery in Geographic Information Systems* (Santa Fe, NM: On Word Press, 1996).

Morrison, J.L., *Method-Produced Error in Isarithmic Mapping,* Technical Monograph No. CA-5 (Washington, DC: American Congress on Surveying and Mapping, 1971).

Muehrcke, P.C., "Concepts of Scaling from the Map Reader's Point of View," *The American Cartographer*, 3 (1976), pp. 123-141.

NRC Mapping Science Committee, *Toward a Coordinated Spatial Data Infrastructure for the Nation* (Washington, DC: National Academy Press, 1993).

Perkins, C.R., and Parry, R.B., eds., *Information Sources in Cartography* (London: Bowker-Saur, 1990).

Peuquet, D.J., "Representation of Geographic Space: Toward a Conceptual Synthesis," *Annals of the Association of American Geographers*, 78, 3 (1988), pp. 375-394.

Quattrochi, D.A., and Goodchild, M.F., *Scale in Remote Sensing and GIS* (Boca Raton, FL: CRC Press, Inc., 1997).

Robinson, A.H., "The Elusive Longitude," *Surveying and Mapping*, 33, 4 (1973), pp. 447-454.

Schmidt, M.O., and Rayner, W.H., *Fundamentals of Surveying*, 2nd ed. (New York: D. Van Nostrand Co., 1978).

Smith, J.R., *Basic Geodesy: An Introduction to the History and Concepts of Modern Geodesy Without Mathematics* (Rancho Cordova, CA: Landmark Enterprises, 1988).

Stoddard, R.H., *Field Techniques and Research Methods in Geography* (Dubuque, IA: Kendall Hunt Publishing Co., 1982).

Summerfield, M.A., "Populations, Samples and Statistical Inferences in Geography," *Professional Geographer*, 35 (1983), pp. 143-149.

Williams, J., *Geographic Information from Space: Processing and Applications of Geocoded Satellite Images* (New York: John Wiley & Sons, 1995).

Wolf, P.R., and Briner, R.C., *Elementary Surveying*, 9th ed. (New York: Harper Collins, 1994).

53

PART I
*Map
Reading*

CHAPTER THREE
MAP ABSTRACTION PROCESS

SELECTION

Selecting a Region and Time Frame
Selecting Variables to be Mapped
Selecting a Scale
Gathering Information
Selecting a Perspective
    A Flat Earth
        Stereographic (True) Perspective
        Central Perspective
        Parallel Perspective
    A Round Earth
    Perspective and Map Use

CLASSIFICATION

Number of Classes
Class Limits
    Constant Intervals
    Variable Intervals
        Systematically Varying Intervals
        Irregularly Varying Intervals

SIMPLIFICATION

Feature Elimination
Smoothing
Shape Abstraction
Aggregation
Change of Dimensionality
Measurement Level Reduction
Compacted Variables

EXAGGERATION

SYMBOLIZATION

Imagery
Graphics
    Pictographic Symbols
    Geometric Symbols
Symbol-Abstraction Gradient
Symbol-Referent Coordination

CONCLUSION

SELECTED READINGS

3

CHAPTER THREE

MAP ABSTRACTION PROCESS

A map allows us to carry the world around in our pocket. It is a Houdini-like trick, setting free the multi-dimensional, ever-changing environment onto a convenient slip of paper. It is reality transformed.

For map makers to perform this almost magical feat, they must carry out several generalizing operations. This process of transforming physical reality to a map is called **cartographic abstraction**.

This process involves far more than simple reduction. A map doesn't merely show the environment in miniature, preserving all features in scaled-down form. Maps are really **caricatures.** Think of how a cartoonist captures a person's essence by emphasizing certain features and de-emphasizing others. In the same way, the map maker attempts to portray the essence of a situation, as defined by the map's purpose. The true detail and variety of geographical reality can never survive this process. In the cartoon that begins this chapter, for example, notice how little of the landscape's distinctive character ends up on the map. Yet the resulting map is, for certain purposes, more useful than reality itself.

The abstraction process that leads to a map is made up of five primary activities: **selection, classification, simplification, exaggeration**, and **symbolization** (although not necessarily in that order). These activities are the fundamental building blocks of the cartographic method. They can be difficult to study, however, because they are interdependent and take on meaning with respect to one another only within the context of the map.

Since a change in one activity can affect all other activities in the map abstraction system, each activity's implications for the map user can be difficult to pin down. Yet, despite their elusiveness, the importance of these mapping activities can't be overestimated. The better you understand them, the richer will be your image of the environment gained through map study. So let's look at each of these mapping activities in turn.

SELECTION

Map makers, obviously, can't include everything; if they did, their map would be a worthless mess. Each time they add one thing, they must leave off something else. The first requirement of map abstraction, then, is to reduce the plethora of environmental phenomena to a more manageable number. Map makers do so in a multitude of ways, depending primarily on their responsibility and the purpose for which the map is intended. The fact that we can't portray everything on one map, or even on several maps, explains why map collections are so vast and diverse.

Map makers' first job, then, is to **select** the information they are going to map. To do so, they ask themselves four things: "Where? When? What? Why?" They may decide, for example, to make a map of Oregon (where?) showing cities of 10,000 or more population (what?) in 1992 (when?) to be used for toxic waste disposal planning (why?). They have thus set **thresholds** (cut-off points) for time, space, and the type of information to be mapped.

These thresholds are arbitrary. There's nothing special about the mapped information except that it happened to meet the threshold requirements. It's not that cities of less than 10,000 people aren't important, or that other states aren't interesting, or that it wouldn't be nice to know what the state looked like in 1960. It's just that these things didn't meet the thresholds set up for this particular map. Other thresholds would lead to different maps.

All these decisions made by the cartographers were determined by the map's purpose. If you use the map for a different purpose, you may have problems. Sometimes a map made for some other reason can be salvaged for your needs. At other times, the only maps available may be totally inadequate. Then you may want to reject maps altogether in favor of other forms of information.

Selecting a Region and Time Frame

When searching for a suitable map, your first concern is with the region and time frame it shows. The answer to your "where-when?" question hinges largely on the purpose for which you need the map but also depends on information availability. The perfect map for your particular need isn't always at hand.

You may, for instance, find a map that covers the region but not the **time frame** of interest to you. Suppose you want a current map of Washington, but all you can find is a 1970 Washington map left over from some past trip. The only solution may be to make do with what you have. This requires making assumptions about what has happened since 1970. If you're good at comparing the landscape with the map, you can probably sketch in changes that have taken place. If your assumptions are wrong, of course, you may find yourself wandering helplessly through a maze of uncharted freeways.

On the other hand, your map may not cover the **region** in which you're interested. Your Washington map is of scant value when you cross into Idaho. This problem of "falling off the edge of a map" is common, because map borders are artificial.* The boundaries of most maps are determined by political units (such as states or countries) or by latitude-longitude grids. These unnatural borderlines have little to do with normal travel plans. If you journey far, you're sure to cross from one map to another.

Here again, you may be able to get by with the map you have. It may hold clues you can use to make assumptions about neighboring regions. Physical and cultural features don't change just because one map ends and another begins. You can usually presume that wooded areas will continue to be wooded, that streams will keep flowing in roughly the same direction, and so on. Of course, specific details of your conjured-up image will be missing. Also, prediction will become more difficult as the region's geography becomes more complex, and as you venture deeper into unmapped territory.

Maps drawn from computer memory are in concept borderless and can be centered at any location. Thus, computerized map navigation systems in automobiles allow drivers to keep themselves centered on the map in the display window at all times. (See Electronic Navigators in Appendix D.)

58

Selecting Variables to be Mapped

Besides deciding "where?" and "when?", map makers must choose "what" to include on their map. This choice depends partly on map size related to ground area extent. It also hinges on the map's **purpose** and the **availability** of information.

Mapping purpose alone is often a misleading guide to information selection for mapping. You would expect that once the map's purpose is known, the phenomena most appropriate for that map would be chosen for inclusion. In practice, however, this isn't always true. Map makers' interests, methods, and instruments have a great influence on which information they include.

Imagine, for example, the creation of a map to be used by canoeists on a remote Canadian river. The map purpose is clear, and the map makers have included such data as location of the river, roads, and campsites. However, they don't know if there are any waterfalls on the river. Since there's no convenient way for them to obtain this information, and time is short, they make the map anyway. If canoeists using this map assume that all relevant information has been included, they could be in deep trouble.

Even when map makers include everything that seems relevant to the map's purpose, they may inadvertently leave off important variables or include irrelevant ones. Suppose that the cartographers' task is to create a hiking map. They have assembled all the information they think the hiker will need. What the map makers don't know, however, is that much of the water in the hiking area is contaminated. Thus, one of the most vital variables for their map—where to find drinkable water—won't be included, simply because they are unaware of it.

Such problems are inevitable, because map makers are all too human. No matter how clearly the map purpose is defined, map makers aren't always aware of user requirements, and the best information may not be available to them. They also make mistakes, especially when maps become detailed and complex.

The biases of map makers carry over into all maps. Just browse through some of the maps that have been published. You'll quickly discover that things of a visible, tangible, static, physical, or historical nature have been mapped far more frequently than invisible, dynamic, human, and futuristic aspects of the world. There's no sound theoretical reason for such a selection process. Rather, the reason is a practical one: There is simply more tangible than intangible information accessible to map makers.

Since intangibles are every bit as important as tangibles, why isn't more intangible information available? The reason has its roots in the way we view our environment. We gain our conception of the world primarily through the senses of sight and touch. Thus, the physical or material aspects of our surroundings dominate our environmental image. Non-material elements of the environment (such as temperature, pressure, humidity, smell, sound, taste, and extrasensory factors) play a secondary role.

Material things are also much easier to measure than non-material ones. Distinct objects, such as houses, can simply be located and counted. Phenomena distributed in a continuous pattern, such as land surface elevation, can be measured at different locations. It is natural, then, that most environmental information available for mapping is of the physical sort.

For millenniums, people have conceptualized their surroundings based on the relatively small awareness gained through their senses. Upper and lower limits to this awareness were set by the individual's sensitivity and tolerance. This situation is changing, however, as we acquire more devices designed to measure the non-material environment. Such instruments extend the unaided human senses or replace subjective impressions with precise quantitative measures. We use spectrometers to measure light, infrared sensors to record temperature, and radar to measure microwaves. (See Appendix B for more information on *remote sensing* capabilities.)

Such extensions of our ability to measure information have been rapid and spectacular. No longer must we view our environment merely through our senses' limited awareness. As we learn to look beyond the realm of our senses, the traditional bias of maps in favor of the physical environment should also change. We should expect more dynamic maps and more maps of relatively short-lived phenomena, for the time and cost of making them with modern computers is decreasing rapidly.

All these new machines for extending our awareness, useful as they are, also create a host of new challenges. Although a whole new part of our environment is opened up for us, it's an unfamiliar part. We no longer have the advantage of generations of practice but must learn new techniques. The type of information being mapped is no longer intuitive and familiar. The map reader may be more confused than enlightened unless special information is added to the map legend.

Selecting a Scale

We've now discussed how map makers go about choosing a region, a time frame, and the information to be mapped. As we've seen, we can look at our world in many ways. But always the problem is the same. Our environment is so vast relative to our size that it is difficult to perceive the overall picture. It's up to map makers to reduce the immensity of our world to more manageable proportions. How to go about making this size reduction is one of their most important decisions. Should they look at many things up close or a few things far away? In other words, they must decide at what **scale** to make their map. (Map scale is considered in detail in Appendix A.)

The term scale can be confusing because of a difference between common and cartographic usage. In everyday use, the word scale has two meanings. When it refers to the extent of coverage, "small-scale" means "limited in scope." When it refers to the detail of coverage, "small-scale" means "fine resolution."

In contrast, the term map scale has a precise meaning related to the size reduction from environment to map. Specifically, **map scale is the ratio of map distance to ground distance**, and is often expressed as a fraction. A large ratio such as 1/500 yields a large-scale map of high (fine) spatial resolution (small details can be seen). Conversely, a small ratio such as 1/5,000,000 produces a small-scale map of low (coarse) resolution (only large features can be seen).

The scale relationship between map and reality depends more on map purpose than anything else. Different map scales have the effect of placing you at different viewing distances from your environment. There is also a direct relationship between viewing distance and scope of

view. Thus, a satellite picture will cover more ground area than will a photo from a conventional low-altitude aircraft.

The question of most appropriate map scale naturally arises. Lewis Carroll suggests an answer in *Sylvie and Bruno Conclude*d (p. 169).

> "What do you consider the largest map that would be really useful?"
>
> "About six inches to the mile."
>
> "Only six inches!" exclaimed Mein Herr. "We very soon got to six yards to the mile. Then we tried a hundred yards to the mile. And then came the grandest idea of all! We actually made a map of the country on the scale of a mile to the mile!"
>
> "Have you used it much?" I enquired.
>
> "It has never been spread out, yet," said Mein Herr: "the farmers objected; they said it would cover the whole country and shut out the sunlight! So we now use the country itself, as its own map, and I assure you it does nearly as well."

As Carroll makes clear, it isn't of much value to copy the environment at its natural size. What, then, is the best scale reduction for mapping?

The answer is that there is no best scale—only a most convenient one (see **Table 3.1** and **Box 3.1**). Small-scale maps cover large areas but with little detail, while large-scale maps show great detail but only cover a small area. Somehow you must find a map that strikes a proper compromise between detail and area coverage. Unfortunately, your needs are often incompatible. If you're traveling from Chicago to Milwaukee, you'll want a small-scale map showing the route between the two cities. Yet for getting out of one city and into the next, you need relatively large-scale city street maps.

You could solve this problem by using three different maps. Or you could use a map with **insets** at different scales. **Figure 3.1** shows how insets allow you to work with drastically different scales on the same map sheet.

Whether you use insets or several individual maps, you'll have to shift your thinking from one scale to another. Usually, though, the advantage of having several scales available outweighs this disadvantage. In most cases, then, a variety of special maps is more useful than a single general-purpose map.

60

No matter how many tricks we perform with scale, however, we return to the same problem. The space constraint on the greatly reduced map surface is always severe. A direct functional relationship exists between this poverty of space and the number and detail of phenomena that can be mapped. Invariably, many more things could be represented on the map to your benefit if competition for the limited map area weren't so fierce. Indeed, it's probably fair to say that map scale more than any other factor controls the degree of map abstraction.

One of the main things to remember about map scale is that it isn't independent of the dimensional character of mapped phenomena. In other words, there's a close relationship between the map's scale and the way it represents environmental features of different sizes. What at large scale seems to be a boundary concern, at small scale becomes a matter of location.

For example, we know that a city extends in area for many square miles, and this fact is shown clearly on a large-scale map of the city and its surrounding environment. Yet the same city becomes a mere point on a map of the entire country. On a city map, concern focuses naturally on the rural-urban boundary, while on a small-scale map, attention is directed to the city's location.

The map makers' choice of scale is a vital part of their selection process. Their choices of scale and variables to be mapped are totally interrelated. The variables they plan to show determine the appropriate scale. At the same time, the

scale influences how many variables they can include; they can't put a great many variables on a small-scale map. The scale will have an especially significant effect on the map makers' next step in the selection process—information gathering.

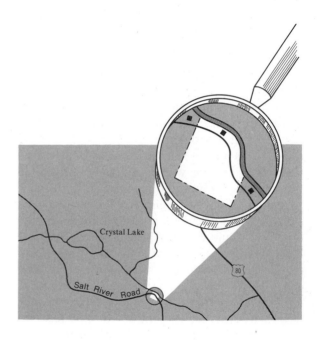

Crystal Lake

Salt River Road

80

3.1 Insets can give a closer view than the map provides, but the resulting spatial discontinuity and change of scale may be confusing.

TABLE 3.1

Convenient Map Scales

Type of Map	Use	Area Covered (Square Miles)
Airline map of U.S.	Trans-continental travel	5,000,000
Page in auto atlas	Interstate travel	250,000
State highway map	Intra-state travel	100,000
National forest map	General recreation	20,000
City street map	Daily travel	200
Low altitude air photo	Special recreation/engineering	5

Gathering Information

After the map makers have decided to include something on a map, they must then gather information about it. This step in map making is critical for the map user, because the procedures followed in collecting information will influence the quality of the resulting map. Your map-reading ability will improve if you keep in mind the aspects of information gathering which go into the making of any map. These factors are considered in detail in Chapter 2.

Selecting a Perspective

Our hypothetical map makers have now selected the variables they are going to map and the scale at which to portray them, and have gathered

BOX 3.1 A QUESTION OF SCALE

Children easily accept scaled-down versions of objects. They have no trouble recognizing a doll or toy car as a smaller rendition of a baby or automobile. This is somewhat surprising, considering how unlike the real thing some toys are. Features which would be invisible or tiny at reduced scales are often given undue emphasis. Other details, which should be clearly perceptible, may be omitted altogether.

The main function of the scaling process is to reduce objects to a manageable size, permitting children to enjoy and understand things that at true scale would remain beyond their grasp. So it is with maps. The earth is so huge compared to us that the size and spatial relationships of its features fall beyond the range of our perception. Maps bring the world within our grasp.

Yet the principle of map scale seems to be one of the hardest transformational concepts for children and unsophisticated map users to accept. The reaction of the mother in Richard Llewellyn's *How Green Was My Valley* (p. 460) is a common one among people unfamiliar with maps:

> With my atlas I tried to show my mother where her children had gone. I drew pencil lines from us to Owen and Gwilym across the Atlantic, and to Angharad down there in Cape Town, and to Davy in New Zealand, and to Ianto in Germany.
> She looked at the page with her head back as though it had a smell....."All that way," my mother said. "Goodness gracious, boy, how far, then, if they can have it all on a little piece of paper?"

Many people share the mother's bewilderment at the idea of reducing the whole world to a single page. And even more confusing are the differences from one scale to the next. A change in map scale gives us a whole new perspective. Consider this description of a woman's feelings when her lover goes on a trip to Lerici, Italy, leaving her in London:

> I had known in advance how long the time would seem—for what else had I to do with my time, what other distractions—but I had not forseen this sensation of physical absence, this terror at the thought of the widening space, the hundreds of miles of land and water between us. It made me feel sick. On the first evening, I got down my atlas, and stared at the size of France and Italy, and then went off to the bathroom and vomited. Then I came downstairs again, and looked through the atlas until I found a page—a map of the whole of Europe, it was—that made Lerici look quite on London's doorstep, and that made me feel much better.
> (Drabble, 1969, p. 144)

This lonely woman is in the opposite situation from the man in an old joke. His problem was that he hated to drive all day and only go an inch on the map. A large-scale map would give this man more of a sense of accomplishment, just as a small-scale map made the woman feel closer to her distant lover.

information about them. The selection process isn't quite complete, however, for there is one more important choice to be made. From what point of view are they going to look at the environment? They can take several perspectives, each from any one of many different vantage or viewing points.

As the map user, then, you must realize that different perspectives and vantage points lead to maps with different spatial characteristics. Remember, too, that features may take on new looks when seen from other points of view. Thus, it's important to learn the geometrical nature of the map that results from each perspective. This task is simplified by the fact that only a few basic observation points are regularly assumed in map making. Once you're familiar with these, you can make accurate statements about spatial relations in the mapped environment whatever the perspective taken in mapping.

Flat Earth

To simplify matters, let's assume that the earth is flat and that an undulating landform surface is superimposed upon it. This is by no means an unreasonable assumption, since most of our daily spatial behavior is conducted as if it true. The portion of the environment in which we spend most of our lives is so small that we can usually ignore the world's roundness. A person walking away from us across a plain becomes invisible long before the earth's curvature interrupts the line of sight.

Since most of us travel only short distances each day, it's natural to use maps showing only the local region. Under these circumstances, it makes more sense to consider the vantage points and perspectives taken in mapping than to worry about the earth's spherical nature.

The **vantage point** is the position that the map maker takes with respect to the earth's surface. There are three components (**Figure 3.2**).

The first aspect of vantage point is the **horizontal viewing angle**, or **viewing azimuth**. A region may appear quite different when viewed from the northeast rather than from the south.

The second aspect of vantage point is the **vertical viewing angle** which the map maker's line of sight makes with the ground surface to be mapped. Vantage points are usually classified according to this second viewing angle as vertical, oblique, or horizontal.

But there's a third, sometimes overlooked aspect to vantage points—the map maker's **viewing distance** from the ground surface. To understand how important viewing distance is on the quality of the resulting map, think of photography. Consider the different effects you get by photographing the same thing with a normal, wide-angle, and telephoto lens. You can compare these dissimilar photos to differences in viewing the environment from various distances.

Whatever their vantage point, map makers can view the world from three main **perspectives**. If they use both eyes, the result is stereographic perspective. By closing one eye, they achieve central perspective. And if they assume a God-like omnipresence, with eyes everywhere, parallel perspective results. Let's see how each one works.

Stereographic (True) Perspective. People with normal vision see their environment in **true** or **stereographic perspective**. The images focused on the retina of each eye are slightly different because our eyes provide two vantage points (**Figure 3.3**). The brain translates the differences between the two images provided by the eyes into an effect we call depth.

This depth-perceptive ability, known as **stereographic** or **binocular vision**, yields a great deal of information about our three-dimensional environment. Thus, map makers have long tried to incorporate depth, or an illusion of depth, into their maps to gain realism and excitement.

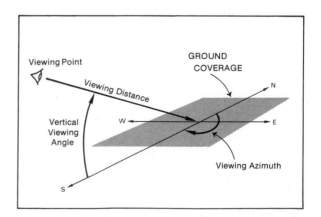

3.2 The viewing azimuth, the vertical viewing angle, and the viewing distance define the map maker's vantage point. Multiple vantage points may be assumed.

There are many such maps, and we'll discuss them in detail in Chapter 5: *Landform Portrayal*.

Central Perspective. The use of one rather than two vantage points removes stereoscopic depth cues and produces a monoscopic or fake perspective. If one of your eyes is much weaker than the other, this is the way you usually view your surroundings. It's also the perspective of a standard photograph. Since light rays radiating from the environment converge on the vantage point, we call this **central perspective (Figure 3.4)**. The essential feature of central perspective is that all objects appear to become smaller as they recede from the observer, creating the effect of distance. Because maps from this perspective are comparatively difficult and tedious to draw, photographs are used whenever possible.

As with all perspectives, the vantage point from which the photographer views the environment has a striking effect on the final photo. There is an infinite number of possible vantage points. These can, however, be broken into three main types—the horizontal, vertical, and oblique.

Horizontal Vantage Point. When we take photographs, we usually hold the camera in horizontal position. The resulting **horizontal photos** aren't usually thought of as maps, although they should be. Their non-map reputation stems from the fact that we generally think of maps as emphasizing the environment's **spatial** aspects—how things are arranged in relation to one another. Instead, horizontal photographs emphasize **vertical** stratification—the ups and downs of the landscape (**Figure 3.4A**). Sometimes this may be all we want from a map, and horizontal photos will serve us well.

An example of a horizontal image that would make a fine map might be a photo of a city such as San Francisco taken from the vantage point of a harbor ferry or a photo of the Rocky Mountain front taken from a vantage point in eastern Colorado. The result in each case is a familiar view which is intuitively easy to understand. Foreground features do tend to block background features, however. Furthermore, the image's scale decreases rapidly away from the vantage point, making background features difficult to identify.

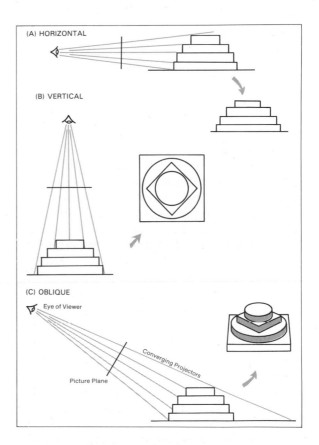

3-D STEREOMODEL

Optic Nerves

Left Eye

Visual Cortex

Right Eye

Visual Field Overlap

3.3 Through eye-brain interpretation, we can merge the slightly different images falling on each retina into a sense of depth.

(A) HORIZONTAL

(B) VERTICAL

(C) OBLIQUE

Eye of Viewer

Converging Projectors

Picture Plane

3.4 Central perspective somewhat distorts the geometry of an image. The vantage point, however, has an even more pronounced effect on an object's appearance, as these three vertical viewing angles suggest.

64

Vertical Vantage Point. At the opposite extreme from horizontal photos are images produced with the camera pointing straight down from an airplane. These **vertical photographs** give us a good idea of the spatial arrangement of features (**Figure 3.4B**). Since we see only the tops of things, however, we receive no impression of **topography**, or vertical relief. Mountains, valleys, and all the interesting ups and downs of our world blend together. But, even though they provide the most unfamiliar representation of the environment and show only a relatively small ground area, vertical photos are widely used in mapping. People like the idea of seeing the earth spread out below them.

On vertical photos, feature size reduction occurs with increasing distance from the center of the picture. But unless the viewing point is far removed from the mapped environment or a wide-angle lens is used, size distortion isn't generally great enough to be a bother.

Oblique Vantage Point. When the camera is held with a sight line falling somewhere between the horizontal and vertical, the result is an **oblique photograph**. The oblique vantage point is the most common angular relation between observer and environment used in photo mapping for non-engineering purposes. Emphasis is placed on both vertical and horizontal components of the environment (**Figure 3.4C**). We can see spatial relationships and still gain a sense of landform relief.

In discussing central perspective maps, we've spoken mainly of photography. While it's a convenient way to produce such maps, photography isn't always possible. The region to be mapped may be inaccessible, or the required photographic equipment and supplies may not be available. In other cases, the information to be mapped is of an intangible or theoretical nature which precludes photography. In these situations, the map maker must either use a computer to compute and plot the central perspective image or laboriously compute and draw the image by hand. Alternatively, a physical model may be constructed and photographed to attain a central perspective image.

Parallel Perspective. Several substitutes for genuine perspective are also used in mapping, some because they're more easily constructed than true perspective, and others because they reduce

scale distortion while still giving a pictorial effect. The most common imitation or pseudo-perspective method is the **parallel** or **orthographic perspective**. The practical effect is that of having a separate vantage point for each line of projection—an infinity of vantage points (**Figure 3.5**). (Some people prefer to think of parallel perspective as the case in which a single vantage point is, in theory, assumed to be located at an infinite distance from the environment.) The result is that the projection lines are parallel to one another rather than converging as in true or central perspective. Parallel perspective usually doesn't give as vivid a pictorial effect as true perspective methods. But several special cases do exhibit extremely useful properties, as we'll see in the following sections.

Horizontal Vantage Point. When the environment is mapped in parallel perspective with an infinity of horizontal sight lines, the perspective effect is lost entirely. The map in essence

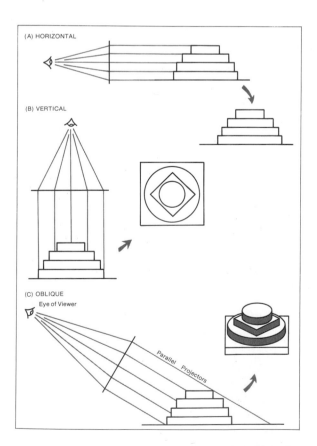

3.5 Scale distortion is minimized with parallel perspective representations. The effect of vantage points is still pronounced, however (compare with Figure 3.4).

becomes a silhouette or profile (**Figure 3.5A**). The advantage is that physical image distortion, so characteristic of central perspective, is eliminated. Panoramic paintings of mountain systems, such as the Rockies from the Colorado plains or the Cascades from the Puget Sound lowland, are examples of horizontal images produced in parallel perspective. The scale is constant from one side of the image to the other.

Vertical Vantage Point. The vertical form of parallel perspective is far more useful than the horizontal one. For centuries, most handmade maps have been vertical images in parallel perspective. This is the form of the standard geographical line map—the model against which all others are compared. (See *Graphics* later in this chapter.)

The mapping technique required to create vertical images in parallel perspective makes good common sense, even though it is foreign to actual human experience. The observer assumes a vantage point directly above each mapped point simultaneously (**Figure 3.5B**). The result is a **plan** view, like the floor plan of a house. The process is called **planimetric mapping**. Accurate spatial dimensions, including size relations, are preserved at all spots on the map. Thus, the spatial form (or **geometry**) of the map is true-to-earth. We say that features are shown in **true planimetry**. This makes it possible to determine the spatial character of all features simply and quickly, permitting all kinds of meaningful analyses involving position, direction, and distance relations. The drawback of planimetric mapping is that clues to the environment's vertical aspect are eliminated. Since it's as if we're looking straight down on our environment, we gain no impression of topography.

Oblique Vantage Point. If we move our vantage point from the vertical to the oblique, we come up with another interesting form of parallel perspective. In this case, lines in each of three map dimensions are drawn in their actual length (**Figure 3.5C**). The result is an **isometric** (meaning "equal measure") map. The term is somewhat misleading, since lines not belonging to the three parallel line systems (one vertical and two horizontal dimensions) aren't shown in true scale. But even uniformity along only three axes is valuable. This trait allows us to compare the height and length of landscape features regardless of their positions on the map.

Unfortunately, isometric maps are visually inferior to central perspective maps in their oblique form. Isometric maps appear contrived. The background seems to tilt forward, and the parallel sides of the map give an illusion of divergence.

A Round Earth

Till now, we've used the idea of a flat earth in discussing perspective. This suffices with maps of regions up to the size of the contiguous United States. But if the mapped portion of the earth's surface is much larger than that, distortion of the map image due to earth curvature becomes increasingly more significant.

To visualize how perspective distortion influences map geometry when regions from near-hemispherical to global extent are represented, it's necessary to make allowance for earth rotundity. Thus, rather than treat the earth's surface as though it were flat, as we did in the previous section, let's now consider perspective in relation to a spherical earth.

If we think of the earth in miniature, as viewed from the moon or represented by a globe, it's clear that we can see less than half (one hemisphere) of its surface at once. This is true no matter which perspective we use. Even if we try some tricks, such as assuming the ability to look out from the earth's center or to see through the earth to the opposite side, the scope of our perspective is still severely limited.

Furthermore, extreme distortion of essential spatial characteristics such as shape, direction, distance, and area occur near the edge of the perspective image. Picture a giant, flat mirror, held up so that it touches (is **tangent** to) the earth. There will be little geometrical difference between the earth's image in the mirror and the earth's surface itself for some distance around the point of contact. With increasing distance from the point of tangency, however, differences between the geometry of the mirrored image and the environment will occur at an ever increasing rate. These distortions may pose an even more serious problem in map use than the spatial scope limitation.

Map makers have learned to overcome problems of scope and distortion at and beyond the hemispherical level by using **global map projection** methods. Conceptually, the secret is

66

to assume a vantage point directly above each position in the mapped environment. If you handle a globe for a moment, however, the impossibility of the task is evident. Only a God's-eye view could capture the spatial aspects of a round earth simultaneously. Since a sphere can't be flattened without distorting the image, every map projection is a compromise. If we retain the correct shape of features, we can't show the correct areas of regions. If correct area is important, then we must forego shape. But we can't have both. To preserve one, we must distort the other. There can be no single perfect map projection solution.

In the absence of a single true solution to the map projection problem, map makers provide you with a wide variety of approximate or partial solutions. By way of example, imagine that an image of the earth's surface has been etched onto the rind of a grapefruit. If you squash the fruit underfoot, the result will be a flattened (albeit stretched and torn) image of the earth's round surface (**Figure 3.6A**). Or, less messily, you could peel the grapefruit and systematically flatten the rind, using a series of carefully placed cuts (**Figure 3.6B**). Clearly, there are many such near solutions to the grapefruit flattening exercise. Indeed, the number of alternatives is infinite.

These map projection examples illustrate two important facts. The "squashed grapefruit" instance produced an **uncontrolled projection**, one which bore no systematic relation to the earth's surface. As might be expected, this type of projection isn't too desirable since it is one of a kind and would be difficult to duplicate. It would also be hard to compare with other projections for the purpose of ascertaining its relative utility.

On the other hand, the case of the "peeled grapefruit" produced a **controlled projection**, bearing a systematic relationship to the earth's surface. This type of projection is most desirable, for it can be easily replicated and compared with other projections. The more control that is exercised in creating projections, the more useful the result becomes and the easier it is to use.

Actually, any system of coordinates that relates points on the earth's surface to points on some other surface can be thought of as a map projection. We'll limit ourselves here, however, to projections onto **plane** (flat) surfaces. Although all points in earth space undergo transformation, the relationship between environmental geometry and map space is easiest to visualize by focusing on the transformational aspects of a rather simple spatial pattern. Makers of global maps usually help you do so by superimposing on the map a coarse network of lines showing latitude (parallels) and longitude (meridians). This system of lines is referred to as the **geographical grid** or **graticule**. (See Figure 11.1 in Chapter 11: *Locational Reference Systems*.)

With such a grid available, it's easy to compare the map's spatial character with the real world or the geometry of one map projection with another. Note that on a spherical earth, meridians converge at the poles; meridians and parallels cross at right angles; and meridians are all of equal length, while the length of parallels varies.

It may be easiest to visualize what a map projection implies if you imagine mapping the earth's surface directly onto a plane or indirectly onto a figure such as a cone or cylinder, which can then be flattened. Although only a few projections are actually made this way, almost all projections can be grouped into one of three families—planar, conic, or cylindric. Since each family has a characteristic distortion pattern, this grouping technique can be extremely helpful

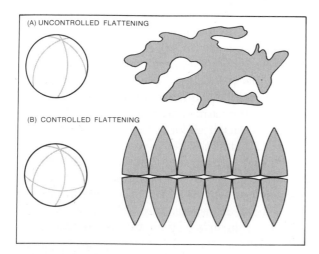

3.6 There is a multitude of ways to flatten the globe so that its entire surface is instantaneously visible. Although all these projections involve geometric distortion, that distortion can be controlled and systematized to advantage.

when using maps. If you aren't familiar with global map projections, please read Appendix C.

Perspective and Map Use

As a map user, then, you need to know what perspective the map maker has chosen and how that decision has affected the map. If only a single map is available, it may be crucial for you to understand its basic geometrical nature. On the other hand, if you have a choice of maps based on different projections, you must select the best one on the basis of the virtues and limitations of each type of projection.

You have two basic concerns as a map user. First, you want to know the perspective of your map so that you can figure out what properties it possesses. This step is simplified if some idea of the image geometry has been incorporated into the map. The geographical grid serves this purpose on small-scale maps. (See *Geographical Grid* in Chapter 11.)

But large-scale maps such as oblique photographs rarely are augmented with an explicit indication of perspective geometry. You're left to piece together this information on the basis of depth and distance cues. You won't have much trouble, though, if the map includes some regular geometric features. Environmental structures that form a parallel pattern (such as roads) are especially helpful.

Your second problem as a map user is to reconcile the projection's distortion properties with your map-use task. What impact might the characteristics of a particular projection have in your map-use situation? Ask yourself two questions:

1. Is the region of interest so large or poorly situated in the projection that image distortion is worth worrying about?
2. Considering the size and location of the region of interest, is there enough projection distortion to have a significant influence on your environmental image?

If image distortion appears to be of no consequence, then you may go on to other matters. But what if you decide that the map projection could be a concern? Since distortion isn't uniform throughout the map image, your first step would be to consider the extent to which the region of interest falls within, straddles, or falls outside the acceptable distortion zone on that particular pro-

jection. Once you know where and how much distortion exists, you can decide what adjustments to make when analyzing and interpreting the map.

Map projections cause the most problems when we want to study environmental features in the context of absolute space. Fortunately, however, the absolute size or position of objects is rarely critical in our daily use of maps. Most of the time we seek only topological information, such as the way to get from one spot to another. These relations between features are handled sufficiently by most projections.

Like many people, you may have been convinced that projection distortion is the most critical problem in map use. This is not so. For standard maps of small regions, in fact, a concern with projections could be more distracting than beneficial. In many situations, a map's projection might best be ignored completely, freeing your attention for more pressing map-use matters. Remember that the choice of a perspective is only one small part of the map maker's selection process. And the selection process itself is just one part of the larger generalizing operation which transforms reality to a map. Let's turn now to the second of these generalizing activities— classification.

CLASSIFICATION

A man who lived on the border between Canada and Alaska couldn't decide which country his property was in. He finally raised enough money to hire a surveyor. When the fellow finished his survey, he informed the landowner that his property was in Canada. "Thank God!" the man cried. "Now I won't have to live through another one of those terrible Alaska winters!"

The story may be apocryphal, but it reflects several important facts. Grouping or **classification** is the basis of communication. We make distinctions between classes of things in our environment and attach labels to the classes. Language then frees us from our surroundings by letting us manipulate these labels rather than real objects.

But no two objects are alike, and our labels don't consider all individual differences. The advantage is that we have far fewer labels to

68

worry about than there are environmental features. Communication is facilitated. The disadvantage is that there is variation within each class, some things fitting better than others. Information is lost by classifying.

Arbitrary as our classes are, we feel more comfortable when we can slip something into its proper niche. Like the man on the Canadian border, we like to know where things fit. But we must keep in mind that classification is an artificial system. We must be especially wary of taking classes at face value when we use maps.

Classification is central to mapping. When information is selected for mapping, it is grouped into a relatively small number of categories. Consequently, map makers start out with information that has already been classed. In a sense, they are only making visual the conceptions people hold of the environment.

In addition, only rarely can features selected for mapping be portrayed as unique entities. Map makers further classify to reduce their maps' complexity. Instead of showing individual trees, for instance, they might divide their map into forested and nonforested regions. In reality, of course, there is no such distinct boundary between groups. The border between "trees" and "no trees" exists only on the map.

Clearly, then, classification reflects the point of view taken by those gathering information and making maps more than it does inherent phenomenal traits. There are no classes in reality; classes are the product of human cognition. Classification reflects a compromise between the belief that everything in our environment is unique and the attitude that individual features only represent specific cases of general groupings. Data classification for mapping reduces reality to manageable proportions and thus is convenient both for map makers and map users.

In a well designed classification scheme, a population element belongs to one, and only one, class. The classes, in other words, are mutually exclusive. A good classification scheme will also deal with all elements of the population without the need for an "Other" category. The classes are thus exhaustive as well as mutually exclusive.

Most important, a good classification scheme serves a useful function. Classes are formed only for convenience and shouldn't be construed to have meaning in themselves. When artificial classes no longer serve a meaningful purpose, they should be abandoned.

Number of Classes

Map makers' first classification chore is to decide how many data classes they will use. It's really a question of how general a viewpoint they should take. Say they're mapping the distribution of discrete entities, such as trees. The crudest classification would lump all tree species into a single group. In such a scheme, an area is either forested or not forested; there are no alternatives. On a map, forested areas might be indicated in green and unforested areas left blank. This one-group classification is simplest in terms of both map making and the appearance of the portrayed distribution. But as far as communication of information about vegetation, it's also the most trivial classification scheme. Such extreme grouping or **aggregation** of details doesn't leave the map user much to work with.

If the map user needs more information about vegetation than the one-class scheme provides, more classes must be used. Even a binary classification of vegetation into deciduous and coniferous species would provide considerably more information.

If this two-way classification were still not sufficient, either vegetation grouping could be further divided. Deciduous trees might be segmented into oak, maple, and hickory classes. These groups could be divided in turn. Oaks might be broken into red and white oak. Even these classes could be further segmented if there were interest in still more detail.

If cartographers are mapping a continuous distribution, they can again take a more or less general attitude. With continuous distributions, progressive subdivision into smaller groups simply involves reducing the intervals between numerical class limits. Take the case of a temperature map at a given synoptic hour (one of four times a day when all stations agree to take weather readings). It would be simplest if only two classes (above 62°F. and below 62°F.) were used. It would be more complex if three classes were used: low (less than 50°F.), medium (50°F. to 75°F.), and high (greater than 75°F.) temperatures. The classification would be most complex if the temperature at each station became its own class, so that there were as many classes as there were recorded temperatures.

Indeed, the extremes in classification range from complete generalization, where just one class represents the entire population, to complete fragmentation (or **disaggregation**), where each population element is treated as unique and given a separate class. Maps made at different levels of classification will vary greatly in appearance, even when the same things are mapped. The number of classes has little to do with the nature of the mapped information; rather, it's the map maker's arbitrary decision.

In view of this arbitrary nature of classification, we may well wonder how meaningful map classes really are. Problems arise particularly when a continuum is divided into a small number of discrete categories. The fewer classes we have, the greater the trouble becomes.

Figure 3.7 illustrates why. Obviously, some locations in the "above -10°F. average minimum temperature" class will in fact have below -10°F. average minimum temperature. The closer a location is to the line between the two zones, the more likely it is to be misclassified on the map. Local conditions of slope, relief, sun exposure, and prevailing winds will all influence average minimum temperature at a particular spot. Indeed, when a phenomenon is diverse in scope and variable within its range, classification into a few categories may be virtually meaningless. Variation of population elements within the groups may actually become greater than differences between groups.

Such difficulties can often be overcome by establishing more classes. But this solution creates its own problems. Each additional class makes the graphic portrayal of the distribution more complex. The limitations of our eyes and brains set severe constraints on the amount of information that can be mapped simultaneously and still be understood. Having many classes also compounds the problem of artificial boundaries. Every time another boundary is added, it's a potential source of confusion for map users.

The truth is that classification problems can't be avoided. When only a few classes are used in mapping, there's likely to be significant within-group variation, but the problems of dealing with arbitrary boundaries are minimized and the resulting map pattern is fairly simple (possibly oversimplified). When many classes are used, there isn't too much within-group variability, but the problem of coping with boundaries is increased and the map pattern is relatively complex (perhaps overwhelmingly so). There seems to be no solution to this dilemma.

Class Limits

However many classes map makers decide on, they must then set class limits. At what point will they end one group and begin another? How, for instance, will they determine the border between vegetation and no vegetation? Here again, the decision isn't clear-cut, for all borders are artificial. Thus, various methods of setting class limits lead to quite different maps, even when the same information is used.

When **discrete** entities are mapped, class limits are usually set according to one or more **qualitative** attributes. Plants might be classed according to such qualities as leaf shape or flower type. On a road map, a distinction might be made between improved and unimproved roads.

Continuously distributed phenomena, on the other hand, are usually classed according to **quantitative** (numerical) measures. Since continuous distributions have a range of value from high to low, the class limits simply segment this range, forming a series of increasing numbers. A map of per capita income might divide the population into people earning less than $5,000, those earning $5,000 to $10,000, and so on. Classification, obviously, will never capture the true continuity

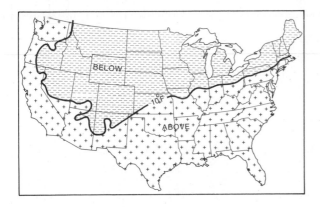

3.7 Most dichotomies are vast generalizations. This simple two-class map showing average minimum temperature zones is no exception. View the boundary between the classes with caution.

70

of continuous distributions. By its very nature, classification breaks things into discrete groups. Thus, according to the above scheme, a person who makes no money at all will be clumped with someone who earns $4,999.97 a year.

Actually, the dichotomy between discrete and continuous phenomena is sometimes confusing. Discrete entities may be viewed as a continuous distribution if the population elements are first related to a spatial neighborhood. Rather than saying that Wisconsin has 4.5 million people, we could say that there are approximately 85 people per square mile in the state. The result is a "count per unit area" or density measure, which constitutes a continuous classification by area. Density itself may subsequently be classed numerically. On a population density map of a state, for instance, the county values may be grouped into high, medium, and low classes.

Constant Intervals

Constant class interval mapping is the simplest way for the map maker to group continuous distributions. The range in population values is merely divided by the desired number of classes. This produces an arithmetic series which determines the class limits. If the percentage of people who took flu shots is mapped by county in Wisconsin, and five classes are used, the range in percent (100) is simply divided by the number of classes (5) to yield class intervals of 20 percent. Therefore, the upper class limits are 20, 40, 60, 80, and 100 percent (**Figure 3.8A**). Such a grouping seems to be intuitively meaningful and easy to understand. Equal class intervals appeal to the same basic human data-handling mechanism that makes percentage figures so attractive to us. Our minds are comfortable with the idea of segmenting the number 100 into equal fractional parts.

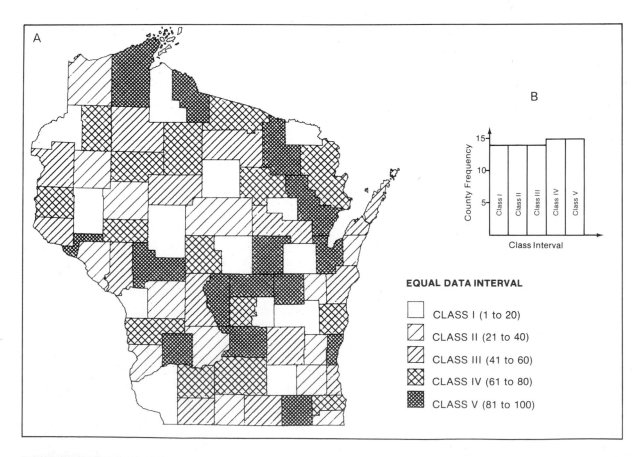

EQUAL DATA INTERVAL

☐ CLASS I (1 to 20)

▨ CLASS II (21 to 40)

▨ CLASS III (41 to 60)

▨ CLASS IV (61 to 80)

▨ CLASS V (81 to 100)

3.8 Constant class intervals have been used to show the percentage of Wisconsin residents by county who took flu shots in 1978. As the data histogram shows, each class is about equally represented.

Constant class intervals make for an attractive and useful map if each class is equally represented. For this to occur, population values must be equally distributed throughout their range. To decide if this condition has been met, we can create a frequency-by-class graph called a **histogram** (**Figure 3.8B**). To do so, we plot frequency of counties on the graph's y-axis and population value on the x-axis. If population values are equally distributed, the result will be a flat frequency distribution. Since the horizontal frequency plot forms a rectangle with the x-axis, the graph is called a **rectangular histogram**.

Sometimes a geographical distribution is rectangular but the size of data-gathering regions, such as counties, varies greatly. If a constant class interval scheme is used in this case, each class won't cover the same map surface. Instead, some classes may extend over large portions of the map, while others are hardly visible.

In addition, most geographical distributions aren't rectangular when segmented with constant class intervals. The histogram of population by county in Wisconsin is unbalanced toward the first (lowest) class (**Figure 3.9**). There are many counties with a low population and few with a high population. In this situation, constant intervals produce a strange map indeed. Most counties fall into one class, while some classes are empty, with no counties at all. Although this map may be useful in showing the vast differences in county populations, it lacks overall detail and is a poor communicator of information.

Variable Intervals

As the previous example shows, constant intervals won't always suit the mapping purpose. In such predicaments, mappers turn to **variable class intervals**. Whatever their mapping advantages, variable intervals lack the symmetry of con-

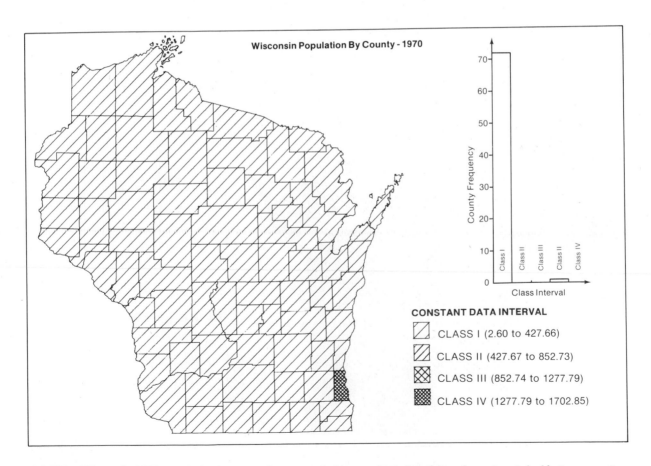

3.9 When Wisconsin 1970 population by county is represented by constant class intervals, a strange-looking map results. Most values fall into the lowest class, and several classes are empty!

72

stant class intervals. You can no longer rely on the intuition that was so helpful when dealing with constant interval maps.

There are two types of variable intervals— those that change systematically and those that vary irregularly. Each suits a different purpose.

Systematically Varying Intervals. Sometimes a distribution displays a concentration of values in a particular part of its range, but otherwise the values are **systematically** distributed. The frequency-by-class plot of such a distribution will produce a graph which looks like a series of steps, with a different frequency in each class. This stair-like graph is called a **stepped histogram**.

Map makers often transform such non-rectangular distributions into rectangular ones for mapping purposes. They do so by using arithmetic, geometric, or other simple mathematical series of class limits. The result is a map with intervals of a **systematically changing** nature. Its

characteristic feature is that class limits become progressively farther apart or closer together from one part of the distribution to another.

Some distributions of population frequencies increase in the lower values and decrease toward the higher value classes. This is the case, as we have seen, with Wisconsin's county population. The effect of mapping such a distribution using progressively larger class intervals is illustrated in **Figure 3.10**. Compare this map with the one in Figure 3.9, which was made using a constant interval. The constant interval map exhibits unbalanced frequencies in map classes, while the variable interval map does not.

Irregularly Varying Intervals. On some maps, the size of class intervals varies in an **irregular** way. Why, you may wonder, have the map makers abandoned systematic intervals?

To answer that question, first ask yourself whether each class covers about the same

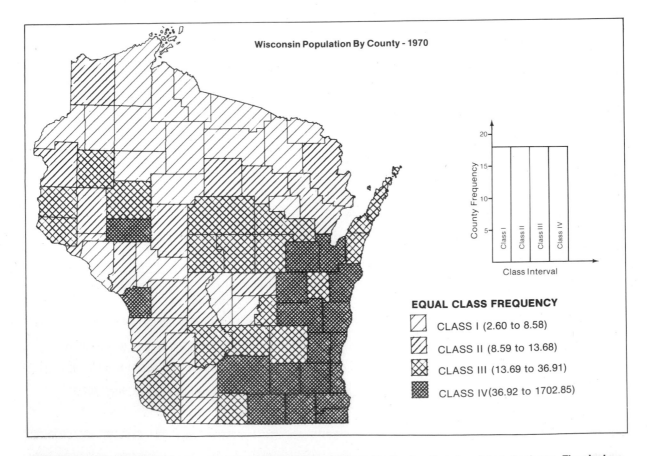

3.10 Wisconsin 1970 population by county is represented by a systematically changing class interval scheme. The aim here was to have about the same number of counties fall into each class.

amount of map area. If so, the explanation for the irregularity may be that the histogram of the distribution was itself irregular. Consequently, the intervals needed to produce an even class frequency couldn't be based on simple mathematical progressions.

A second explanation might be that areal data display units, such as counties, vary greatly in size; thus, area rather than frequency was mapped evenly into the separate classes. Either of these irregular interval maps is difficult to interpret because a simple explanation of the pattern of classes won't suffice.

What if you decide that each class on your irregular interval map does not cover the same amount of area? Now how do you explain the irregularity of class intervals? In this situation, the chances are that the goal of producing even class frequencies was abandoned in favor of a classification scheme which accentuates certain aspects of the mapped distribution. Instead of letting

class limits fall where they might, according to some numerical scheme, the map makers determined class limits with some purpose, some mapping **logic**, in mind.

Their mapping logic in one case may have been to establish class limits at **natural breaks** in the distribution. They decided that these breaks had some geographical significance and were therefore worth preserving on the map. Natural groupings of population elements around certain values are revealed by a **clinographic curve**, which is merely a cumulative plot of population values (Y-axis) against number of observations (X-axis). As **Figure 3.11** shows, changes in the slope of the curve indicate breaks in the data; therefore, the class limits are set at these points.

In another case, the mapping logic might have been to rely on **critical values** to determine class limits. A critical value is one which has special meaning. It may be a significant aspect of the distribution itself, such as the temperature below

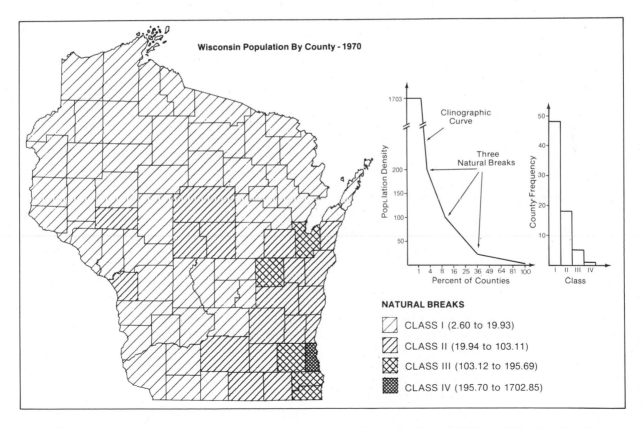

NATURAL BREAKS

⊡ CLASS I (2.60 to 19.93)

⊡ CLASS II (19.94 to 103.11)

⊞ CLASS III (103.12 to 195.69)

⊞ CLASS IV (195.70 to 1702.85)

3.11 Wisconsin 1970 population by county is represented by a class interval scheme which is sensitive to natural breaks in the data distribution. The idea is that these natural breaks may have some functional significance.

which a crop will freeze. Or it may be solely a function of mapping purpose—for example, to show which counties fall below an artificially devised "poverty" line and therefore are eligible for special government assistance.

SIMPLIFICATION

In addition to selecting and classifying information, map makers must **simplify** the variables they have chosen to map. In a way, this is what classification accomplishes. But simplification goes even further. It includes eliminating unwanted features, smoothing the fine details from boundaries, abstracting the shape of features, aggregating features into clusters or regions, changing the dimensionality of features, reducing data measurement levels, and combining variables into ratios or indexes.

The aim of simplification is to produce clear and legible representations at different map scales. Problems in map use arise because the degree of simplification tends to vary from place to place and from one phenomenon to another. To put those problems into focus, let's look further at each of the aspects of simplification mentioned above.

Feature Elimination

Information gathering and mapping activities serve as environmental filters. Some features are ignored while others catch our attention. This is as it should be, because it is impossible to make a map which preserves the full richness of environmental detail.

Features are eliminated from maps both passively and actively. We have no control over **passive** feature elimination. It occurs automatically due to the sensitivity of our data-gathering procedures. We simply can't see individual houses on a conventional photograph taken from the window of an airplane 35,000 feet above the earth. Other information-gathering methods or devices will have different sensitivities, of course. Houses would show clearly on a photo taken from the same altitude if special aerial cameras and films were used.

The sensitivity of our means of gathering information, and therefore our ability to detect environmental features, is also a product of the times. Consider how radically our conception of earthquakes has changed as the sensitivity of monitoring equipment has improved. Previously imperceptible movements of the earth's surface along fault zones are now easily detected using electronic distance measuring and surveying instruments. Many such features of our environment, which were there all the time, were once eliminated from maps simply because our instruments weren't accurate enough to record them.

In contrast, we can design our instruments to exclude certain things even though we know they exist. We can thus eliminate features not in a passive but in an **active** way. Only information which exceeds certain threshold values is collected. For instance, we can manipulate the scanner cell size or film grain size so that it serves as an active spatial filter. A remote sensor can be set to record only those wheat fields which exceed 40 acres, only those trees which are in advanced stages of dying, and so forth.

Additionally, the mapping activity itself can serve as an environmental filter. Features can be actively eliminated from available information during the mapping process. Tributary streams beyond a certain order or cities of less than a given population may simply be left off the map (**Figure 3.12**).

Since information is seldom collected with a particular map in mind, cartographers often end up with more bits of data than they need for their map and must reject some of them. They must be especially ruthless in discarding features when creating a small-scale map from high-resolution, or finely-detailed, information. They will also have to eliminate features when they reduce existing maps to smaller scales or transform them into less complex representations.

If you aren't aware of feature elimination when you use a map, you'll soon become bewildered. When you cross a bridge that isn't on your map, you're likely to think you've erred. Keep an open mind and consider the possibility that it isn't you but the map that is lacking. Always remember that something can exist in reality without being on a map.

You may find yourself puzzling over why one particular lake or road has been left off a map while many other lakes and roads were mapped. You may never know for sure. Feature elimination occurs for a variety of reasons, some related to size of features, others to map scale, some to feature density, and still others to the relative importance of features as established by the map's purpose. Once you've accepted this fact, it will be easier to overcome your sense of disbelief and confusion when you encounter something in the environment that isn't on your map.

Smoothing

Even when environmental features are portrayed on maps, the intricacy of their form is rarely preserved in the cartographic representation. Although the basic form of the features is

retained, it is generally simplified by removing details. This smoothing of mapped features is most evident with linear objects, such as roads or streams. But it also occurs with the edges of areal features and the surfaces of volumetric features (**Figure 3.13**). In all cases, the level of detail is reduced by straightening minor fluctuations.

Although it's not always clear by looking at a map, smoothing is inversely proportional to the map scale. On a large-scale map, therefore, roads are less smoothed than on a small-scale map.

Also, smoothing is directly proportional to the natural detail of features. Thus, winding country roads are more generalized than interstate highways.

In other words, for every feature there's a map scale below which it will be smoothed, and above which it won't. This scale "cusp" or threshold changes from feature to feature, and perhaps from location to location for a single feature as

3.12 One way to simplify a map visually is to eliminate point, linear, areal, and volumetric features. Feature elimination may increase the complexity of the map in conceptual terms, however.

3.13 The form of linear features, areas, boundaries, and surfaces may be smoothed as a way to simplify a map visually.

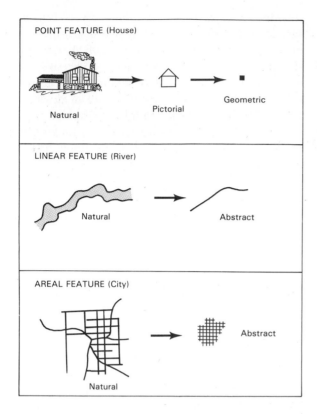

POINT FEATURE (House)

Natural → Pictorial → Geometric

LINEAR FEATURE (River)

Natural → Abstract

AREAL FEATURE (City)

Natural → Abstract

	LARGE SCALE MAP	SMALL SCALE MAP
WOODS		
BRAIDED STREAM		
FACTORY BUILDINGS		

3.14 Shape abstraction simplifies both the map construction task and the map's appearance.

3.15 The appearance of a map can be greatly simplified by using symbols that represent aggregates of features.

well. This threshold scale is smaller with high-quality map production and reproduction methods than with low-quality methods.

When you use maps, be sure to take this smoothing into account. If that road which appears ruler-straight on your map turns out to be a snarl of bends, don't be dismayed. It was merely the victim of cartographic smoothing. Since smoothing reduces the length, sinuosity, and complexity of features, be sure to consider these factors when making mathematical analyses of maps (see Part II: *Map Analysis*).

Shape Abstraction

When cartographers take smoothing to the limit, it becomes **shape abstraction**. The aim of this map simplification method is to replace complex natural shapes with symbols that are visually simpler, more compact, and easier to construct (see *Symbolization* later in this chapter).

Shape abstraction of point features may require more effort in map reading, but it leads to

few other problems. Shape abstraction of linear and areal features, on the other hand, not only adds to map reading effort but also changes spatial relations, which may affect map analysis. Consider the implications, for example, of mapping a river with a symbol of constant width, or mapping a city with a circular symbol (**Figure 3.14**). We'll return to this topic in Part II when discussing map analysis.

Aggregation

A simplification method that takes shape abstraction still further involves using symbols to represent **aggregates** of features. A farmstead might be mapped by a single point symbol, a braided stream by a single line symbol, or a discontinuous clustering of forested patches by a single areal symbol (**Figure 3.15**). The location of symbols representing aggregates is determined by the cartographer's judgment.

To appreciate the map use implications of this cartographic judgment, consider the case of areal aggregates. At least three methods might have been used to create the aggregate symbol (**Figure 3.16**). A **give-and-take** boundary might have been drawn so that the area of the aggregate symbol is the same as that of the discontinuous component features. Alternatively, a maximum areal **extent** or **range criterion** might have been used, leading to an increase of areal coverage over what would be found in the environment. And, finally, the region might initially have been divided into cells and then a **majority area threshold** used to decide how each cell was to be mapped. This last procedure has become routine, for example, when converting remote sensing data into landcover maps.

What aggregation means for you, the map user, is that you can't take the map symbols literally. There can be profound discrepancies between what the map shows at a location and what you might find through a site inspection in the field. Furthermore, the discrepancy tends to increase as map scale decreases. The map symbols are just that—symbols. This symbolic character of maps is one more thing to consider when using maps as aids to environmental thought, communication, and mobility.

Change of Dimensionality

A change of dimension often occurs between an environmental feature and its map representa-tion. Volumetric, areal, linear, and point features may be mapped into symbols having a point, line, area, or volume emphasis. See **Figure 3.17**, for example. Notice that features in the lower left half of this figure are mapped below their natural level of dimensionality, while those in the upper right are mapped above their natural level of dimensionality.

The cartographer may have changed dimensions in this way to make symbols more compact at reduced map scales or as a means of generalizing map features in the interest of map legibility. In either case, a change in dimensionality reflects a change in the way the phenomenon being represented is cartographically defined, which leads to a new level of environmental conceptualization. Once again we see how the cartographer creates a map world rather than merely mapping features passively as they occur in the environment.

The scale "cusps" at which change of feature dimensionality occurs can be critical in using maps. When features are mapped at dimensionalities other than their natural ones, they cross a threshold from physical to conceptual reality. Analytical map uses that are appropriate when no change of dimensionality is involved may no longer be appropriate. For instance, the dispersion of oil wells may be used to define an oil field, but the former won't be found at every location in the latter. Map abuse can occur if this factor isn't taken into account (see *Abuse* in Chapter 25).

Measurement Level Reduction

Another way to simplify a map is to reduce the measurement level. As we discussed in *Measurement Level* in Chapter 2, the four levels of measurement are (from lowest to highest) nominal, ordinal, interval, and ratio. In general, the higher the measurement level used in mapping, the more accurate and complex the map. This is true because each measurement level incorporates all lower levels. Theoretically, then, ratio-level symbols yield the most information. With each lowering of the measurement level, more information is lost.

Both map makers and users can simplify a map by reducing the measurement level. For map makers, this merely involves depicting information at a measurement level below that of the data they

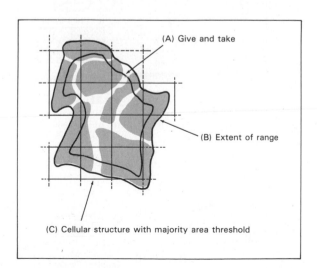

(A) Give and take

(B) Extent of range

(C) Cellular structure with majority area threshold

3.16 At least three methods might be used to aggregate features into simplified symbols. Each method can produce a different visual result.

78

have on hand. Elevation readings at an interval level, say, could be grouped into above and below average classes (ordinal measurement) for mapping. The result would be a simplified map image.

As a map user, you may also work with symbols below their level of measurement. Although this implies a "loss" of information, the reduction of measurement level may fit your needs better. Suppose, for instance, that you have an aerial photograph showing a zone of transition from low to high tree density (ratio measurement). If you wish, you can reduce the measurement level by classifying the photo into only forested and non-forested regions (nominal measurement).

Compacted Variables

Often a map that looks simple turns out upon further inspection to be extremely complex. The reason may be that the map makers indulged in some form of pre-map data processing, thereby turning raw data with relatively low information content into **compact variables** bloated with information (see *Derived Values* in Chapter 2).

Data can be compacted in several ways. Summary measures may be used to reduce a mass of information concerning a single variable; several variables may be combined into a single index; or a large number of variables may be condensed into a few basic factors.

3.17 Mapping often involves change of dimensionality. In these examples, point, linear, areal, and volumetric phenomena are mapped with symbols having a point, line, area, or volume emphasis.

Maps based on compacted data contain far more information than is apparent at first glance. Note, for example, the seismic risk map in **Figure 3.18**. Although the map appears rather simplistic, the data it shows have undergone sophisticated analysis prior to mapping. Areas on the map have been classed according to their susceptibility to, and the degree of potential damage from, earthquake effects such as ground faulting, ground shaking, landsliding, and flooding. The result is a map that exhibits a much higher sensitivity to earthquake severity than might be gained through direct visual observation.

There are several reasons for compacting variables. The motivation could merely be one of **mapping convenience**—the desire of map makers to simplify their job. They may find it easier to show monthly precipitation summaries than daily precipitation records on a single map. Similarly, if they reduce a large number of raw variables to a few "super variables," they may have less trouble clearly symbolizing the information.

On the other hand, variables might be compacted for the **convenience of map users**. The goal may simply be to reduce the clutter that would result if the unprocessed raw data were mapped. This motivation is admirable considering how confusing maps can become as more information is added.

Another aim behind compacting variables may be to provide you with a more sophisticated map than is possible by showing raw data alone. Say that you're interested in how a population has changed over time and space. You could use a map which shows the raw population statistics for 1990 and 1992. But you might well prefer a map giving the percent change in population between the two years. Because the map maker has figured out the rate of population change during this period for you, you can concentrate on other concerns.

Most maps using "super variables" require more effort to read than those showing only raw data. Some of these compacted data maps are easy enough to understand once the underlying concept is familiar. But others are based on such mathematically sophisticated pre-processing methods that they are hard to fathom. Many such maps can be fully appreciated only by expert map readers. The average person is unable to take advantage of compacted maps.

And yet they look the same as any other map. Don't be fooled by their simple appearance. Be sure to consult the map legend, because if compacted variables have been used, the map makers will tell you so there. It's crucial to realize that the mapped phenomena are really composite measures which aren't comparable to raw variables. Proper map reading is likely to be so difficult that it may seem a bit unfair to describe the compacting technique as one of simplification. What is a simplification for the map maker may be a complication for the map user!

EXAGGERATION

We have seen how cartographers select, classify, and simplify the information they map. In addition, it is common for them to enhance or amplify that information. This **exaggeration** of environmental features on maps is one of the most powerful elements of the cartographic abstraction process. If mapped with symbols that were strictly proportionate, certain features would become unidentifiable and eventually disappear as map scale decreased. To counteract this

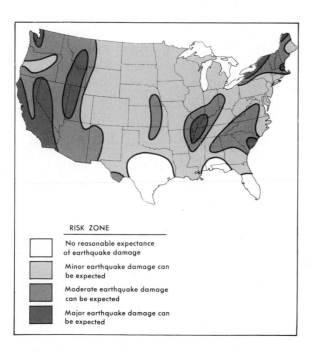

RISK ZONE

☐ No reasonable expectance of earthquake damage

▨ Minor earthquake damage can be expected

▨ Moderate earthquake damage can be expected

▨ Major earthquake damage can be expected

3.18 Environmental data often have undergone extensive manipulation and analysis prior to mapping, as is the case with this seismic risk map of the contiguous United States.

80

problem, it is standard mapping practice to deliberately exaggerate buildings, rivers, roads, elongated islands or lakes, bays, and similar features (**Figure 3.19A**). In extreme cases, the map area covered by symbols may represent hundreds of times the ground area naturally covered by the features depicted. This emphasis of features in terms of their perceived importance with respect to the map purpose reinforces the selectivity of cartographic representation.

Exaggeration may affect the map user in several ways. First, there is only so much space on the map, and disproportionate symbols take more than their share. Thus, exaggeration of some features is only possible at the expense of others.

Second, when the scaled dimensions of a symbolized feature on the map are greater than its actual size in the environment, the relative spatial relations between features become distorted. If the map user misreads this artifact of the mapping process for reality, errors in map analysis may result.

Finally, the locational shifts of feature boundaries resulting from their exaggeration often lead to displacement of other (non-exaggerated) features. This might occur, for example, if a river with cottages along its banks and a parallel access road were all mapped together (**Figure 3.19B**).

SYMBOLIZATION

Features that survive the map makers' selection, classification, simplification, and exaggeration hurdles are incorporated into maps not in a literal but in a **symbolic** way. The relation between symbol and reality varies. Sometimes there is a strong physical resemblance between real and mapped features, while at other times the relationship is based solely on convention. In still other cases, features are mapped with arbitrary symbols which require definition in a legend or key.

The most realistic map symbols are miniature three-dimensional objects such as houses, cars, and trees which are used to make large-scale physical models. Some of these models are actually constructed using materials from the physical environment, such as rocks, vegetation, or sand. But most map symbolism on **physical models** is characterized by a mode change: Buildings are made of styrofoam, grass from sand painted green, and trees from plastic.

Such three-dimensional symbols are used frequently by landscape architects and urban planners to provide decision makers with the most realistic idea possible of how a proposed development would look if implemented. Unfortunately, physical models are extremely expensive to make and awkward to handle. Therefore, most maps are made on a flat medium using less realistic **imagery** and **graphic** methods. In spite of their flatness, these maps can have strong visual appeal. They are also relatively inexpensive to produce and convenient to use.

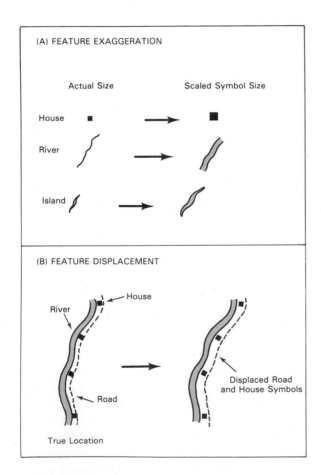

3.19 Exaggeration of the size of environmental features in map symbols is a powerful tool of cartographic abstraction. Disproportionate symbols can lead to apparent feature displacement, however.

Imagery

Next to physical models, **photographic symbols** provide the most "true-to-nature" coordinations with real-life features. We don't usually think of photographs as being made up of symbols, but they are. We're letting splotches of dye on the film emulsion stand for a complex assortment of environmental features.

All photos aren't of the same quality, of course (see Chapter 4: *Image Maps*). Color photos are more natural than standard black-and-white photos. High-resolution photos are more natural than those of low resolution. Least natural are images of the invisible environment, such as infrared and microwave pictures. On these images, environmental detail is depicted with colors or gray tones bearing an arbitrary relationship to mapped phenomena. On false-color infrared photographs, for example, healthy vegetation appears bright red, while diseased vegetation is dull red and many cultural features are blue. Due to modern remote sensing and image processing techniques, such unlikely coordinations of photographic symbols with mapped features have become commonplace. (See Appendix B: *Remote Sensing of the Environment.*)

One drawback of photographs is that most environmental features appear in true relative scale. This means that only those features large enough to be seen from the vantage point of the camera will be mapped. Another disadvantage is that photos are restricted to tangible phenomena. Intangible distributions, such as income or ethnic groups, can only be symbolized by using graphic methods.

Graphics

A typical flat map, made up of a system of graphic symbols, is called a **line map**, or **sketch map**. (This is the type of map most commonly used by the general public and is, therefore, what many people first think of when they hear the word "map.") Its name derives from the fact that all information is depicted in sketchy outline form, using some combination of simple point, line, and area symbols.

These graphic symbols can range widely in appearance. Some symbols look quite natural, while others are totally abstract. Between these

extremes are a variety of semi-natural (or semi-abstract) symbols. The type of symbolism varies with map scale, pattern complexity, and intended audience. The two main types of graphic symbols are pictographic and geometric.

Pictographic Symbols

Pictographic (or **pictorial**) symbols can provide very realistic pictures of environmental features. (See the top panel in Figure 3.14, earlier in this chapter.) Such symbols range from people to trees to railroads. Since they are designed by map makers, pictographic symbols are more flexible than photographic ones. Features of any size can be mapped. But, like photographic symbols, pictographic symbols are limited mainly to tangible phenomena, because the goal is to produce symbols map users will recognize through natural association. In practice, the meaning of many pictographic symbols will be so obscure that you'll need to check the map legend for clarification.

Another problem is that maps with pictographic symbols are relatively expensive and difficult to make. It's especially hard for cartographers to draw easily distinguishable pictographic symbols when mapping many different features at once.

Geometric Symbols

Map makers get around these problems by using **geometric** symbols, such as circles or squares (see Figures 6.6 in Chapter 6 and 7.2 in Chapter 7). These are the most abstract symbols of all. A triangle might represent a tree, a dashed line a road, and a cross-hatched line pattern a city.

The coordination of geometric symbols with reality is sometimes established by mapping convention. A capital city, for example, is often represented by a star inside a circle. More commonly, however, the relation between symbol and environmental feature changes from map to map. In both cases, the coordination will be explained in the map legend or through symbol **annotation** (labeling) directly on the map.

Although pictographic symbols have the most aesthetic appeal and seem to be liked best by children and unsophisticated map users, geometric symbols are most commonly used on maps. The main reason is that geometric symbols provide the greatest mapping flexibility. Features of any size can be shown on maps of any scale.

82

Much more information can be packed into a map using geometric symbols, since they take up less space than natural-appearing ones. In addition, whereas photographic and pictographic symbols are restricted to visible things such as houses or rivers, geometric symbols can be used to portray intangible phenomena such as economic status or incidence of disease.

Geometric symbols do have some disadvantages, however. They look nothing like the features they represent. Also, map makers have trouble designing appropriate symbols for intangible phenomena. As a result, map users must pay close attention to the legend to determine each symbol's meaning.

A quality common to all line maps, whether made up of pictographic or geometric symbols, is that subtle changes in the environment have been transformed into rather simplistic textures, shapes, and linkages. Line maps separate reality, working against subtlety. Thus, the drawback of line maps is that they aren't true to life. It may take a great deal of effort and skill to decode their symbolic abstractions. The advantage, of course, is that using abstract symbols makes it possible to portray anything. But more important still, an extremely small number of simple mapping techniques can be used to represent an unlimited variety of phenomena.

Symbol-Abstraction Gradient

To summarize our discussion of symbols, it may be helpful to think of the different types of symbols arrayed along a gradient of shape abstraction (see *Shape Abstraction* earlier in the chapter). In decreasing order of **visual complexity**, we have photographic (or natural), pictorial, and geometric symbols, respectively (see Figure 3.14). Geometric symbols can be used in greater densities, smaller sizes, and more variations than realistic symbols and still be visually legible.

But visual complexity deals with only half the problem of reading map symbols. Notice that the **conceptual complexity** gradient for these symbol types is just the reverse of the visual complexity gradient. In other words, it takes more thought to read geometric symbols than it does to read realistic symbols. Pictographic symbols fall somewhere between these extremes.

Symbol-Referent Coordination

To appreciate the complexity of map symbolism, it's necessary to understand the problems facing map makers. Somehow they must transform geographical information into symbolized form. Exactly what does this entail?

First, we can think of environmental features as falling into four geometric categories: point, linear, areal, and volumetric. Features falling into these categories can have widely ranging characteristics. Some are discrete, others continuous, and still others discontinuous. In addition, the definition along features' edges can vary from sharply defined to fuzzy. To complicate matters further, you'll recall that each of these categories of information has been gathered at one of four measurement levels: nominal, ordinal, interval, or ratio.

Yet to map this wide array of environmental information, map makers have available only four **categories of symbols**: points, lines, areas, and volumes.* Each of these symbol categories, however, is subject to a number of design variations. The **graphic elements of symbols** include **size, shape, pattern,** and **color**. Pattern can be further divided into **arrangement, orientation,** and **texture**. Color can be segmented into **hue, value** (lightness or darkness), and **intensity** (brightness or dullness).

Obviously, then, matching a symbol to an environmental feature isn't a one-to-one process. Far from it. **Figure 3.20** gives you an idea of some of the decision-making considerations which enter into the process of cartographic symbolization.

Maps are easiest to read if map makers have exploited the intuitive nature of graphic symbols. When they do so, their symbols naturally give the impression of representing attribute (qualitative) differences on one hand or magnitude (quantitative) differences on the other. The graphic elements that have a qualitative connotation (corresponding to the nominal level of measurement) are shape, color hue, pattern orientation, and pattern arrangement (**Figure 3.21**). Symbols which intuitively connote ordered or quantitative

---

Truly volumetric symbols are found only on physical models and, therefore, are rare. More commonly, area symbols are used to denote volumes, in which case the symbols are often labeled with numerical values representing the third dimension.

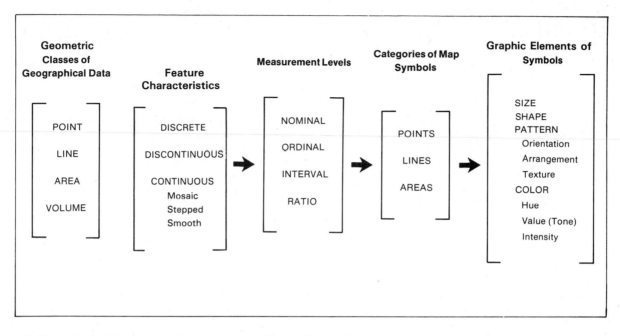

3.20 The matching of map symbol to environmental feature isn't a one-to-one process but, rather, has a transformational character.

differences (the ordinal, interval, and ratio measurement levels) are size, pattern texture, color value, and color intensity (**Figure 3.22**).

Sad to say, map makers don't adhere rigorously to this logical correspondence between graphic elements and the measurement level of geographical phenomena. One reason is that they don't always pay enough attention to user requirements when designing maps. Another is that the symbol system on a given map may become so complex that it seems necessary to rely on non-intuitive coordinations between sym-

bol and environment; otherwise, the symbols would be swallowed up in detail and difficult to recognize.

When non-intuitive matchings of symbol and reality are used, you'll need extra information to read the symbolism. You may find this supplemental information in a legend or as annotations on the map itself. In either case, your first step in using a map should be to decide just what has been represented and how the five cartographic abstraction activities have influenced the way information is portrayed on the map.

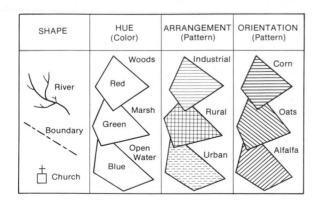

3.21 Graphic elements with a class connotation are best used to symbolize qualitative or attribute data.

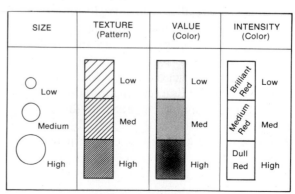

3.22 Graphic elements with a magnitude connotation are best used to symbolize quantitative data.

84

CONCLUSION

In this chapter, we've seen that cartographic abstraction—the process of transforming reality to map form—is a feat of staggering complexity. In discussing the map maker's job, we've broken the abstraction process into the five activities of selection, classification, simplification, exaggeration, and symbolization. These categories are merely for convenience, of course. There's likely to be considerable cycling back and forth between these different activities during the design stage of map making.

The overall effect of cartographic abstraction is to create an image of the environment that's more useful than reality for certain purposes. But by now it should be clear that this image is full of distortions. In its map reflection, reality undergoes a metamorphosis more involved than that created by a multi-dimensional fun-house mirror. Or perhaps it's more accurate to say that a map isn't a mirror so much as a prism. As a drop of water refracts ordinary light into a rainbow of brilliant colors, maps just as dramatically separate and emphasize the many subtle dimensions of reality.

Understandably, then, it takes a vast leap of the imagination to arrive at a lifelike conception of reality by looking at symbols on a highly generalized map. Your job as a map user is to find meanings trapped in abstract graphic symbols and to turn them loose into useful environmental images. The better your understanding of the problems that map makers face and the different ways they deal with these problems, the better those environmental images will be.

We've already given some hint of these problems in showing how cartographers manipulate the abstraction process. In the next four chapters, we'll discuss still further how cartographers' abstraction decisions lead to a wide range of effects through different mapping techniques. We'll begin in the next chapter with image maps, since they constitute the least abstract—and therefore the most intuitive—class of maps.

SELECTED READINGS

Anson, R.W., and Ormeling, F.J., *Basic Cartography: For Students and Technicians*, 3 volumes (Newton, MA: Butterworth-Heinemann, 1995-96).

Benson, B.J. and Mackenzie, M.D., "Effects of Sensor Spatial Resolutions on Landscape Structure Parameters," *Landscape Ecology*, 10 (1995), pp. 113-120.

Buttenfield, B., and McMaster, R.B., eds., *Map Generalization: Making Rules for Knowledge Representation* (New York: John Wiley & Sons, 1991).

Cromley, R.G., "Hierarchical Methods of Line Simplification," *Cartography and Geographical Information Systems*, 18, 2 (April 1991), pp. 125-131.

Dent, B.D., *Cartography: Thematic Map Design*, 4th ed. (Dubuque, IA: Wm. C. Brown Publishers, 1996).

Hearnshaw, H.M., and Unwin, D.J., eds., *Visualization in Geographical Information Systems* (New York: John Wiley & Sons, 1994).

Keates, J.S., *Cartographic Design and Production*, 2nd ed. (New York: John Wiley & Sons, Inc., 1989).

Keates, J.S., *Understanding Maps*, 2nd ed. (Essex: Addison Wesley Longman, Ltd., 1996).

MacEachren, A.M., *Some Truth with Maps: A Primer on Symbolization and Design* (Washington, DC: Association of American Geographers, 1994).

MacEachren, A.M., *How Maps Work: Representation, Visualization and Design* (New York: The Guilford Press, 1995).

McMaster, R.B., and Shea, K.S., *Generalization in Digital Cartography* (Washington, DC: Association of American Geographers, 1992).

Monmonier, M., *Drawing the Line* (New York: Henry Holt & Co., Inc., 1995).

Monmonier, M., *Mapping It Out: Expository Cartography for the Humanities and Social Sciences* (Chicago: The University of Chicago Press, 1993).

Muehrcke, P.C., "Concepts of Scaling from the Map Reader's Point of View," *The American Cartographer*, 3, 2 (1976), pp. 123-141.

Muller, J.C., Lagrange, J.P., and Weibel, R., *GIS and Generalization: Methodology and Practice* (London: Taylor & Francis, 1995).

Robinson, A.H., et al., *Elements of Cartography*, 6th ed. (New York: John Wiley & Sons, 1995).

Tufte, E.R., *Envisioning Information* (Cheshire, CT: Graphics Press, 1990).

Tyner, J., *Introduction to Thematic Cartography* (Englewood Cliffs, NJ: Prentice-Hall, 1992).

Wood, C.H., and Keller, C.P., eds., *Cartographic Design: Theoretical and Practical Perspectives* (New York: John Wiley & Sons, 1996).

CHAPTER FOUR

IMAGE MAPS

Our maps...are drawn by computers from
satellite photos, and that suggests that the
Earth has lost its capacity to keep secrets.

—Peter Steinhart, *Names on a Map*

CHAPTER FOUR

IMAGE MAPS

As we saw in the previous chapter, map makers use cartographic abstraction in many ways. But the end product is one of three map types: image maps, physical models, and line maps. In this chapter we'll discuss image maps. We'll explore physical models and line maps in the next three chapters.

Of the three map types, image maps come closest to depicting the environment the way we see it. This means it is the least abstract type of map. An **image map*** is any photographic or electronic image of the earth's surface. (For a more detailed discussion of these recording devices, see Appendix B, *Remote Sensing of the Environment*.) More of the United States has been mapped at large scales with image maps than with any other type of map. For most regions, coverage has been repeated a half dozen or more times since image mapping began in the 1930s.

IMAGING SYSTEMS

Image maps are usually made with cameras, but images produced by non-photographic electronic-imaging methods are becoming more and more common. Electronic-imaging systems fall into two categories: (1) camera-based systems and (2) scanning-based systems. It's important to distinguish between these different types of image maps because, even though they often look similar, there are major differences between them.

Traditional photographic cameras are the most familiar. These sensors capture the entire ground scene simultaneously on film (**Figure 4.1A**). Newer **electronic cameras**, in which film is replaced by a two-dimensional array of microscopic detectors etched into a computer chip, also capture the ground scene instantaneously (**Figure 4.2**). Images recorded by these **digital cameras** look like conventional photographs and have similar geometry.

*In the past, the term "photomap" was used instead of "image map." But with today's electronic technology, many images that look like photos really aren't. Thus, the more general term "image map" is more appropriate and will be used throughout this book.

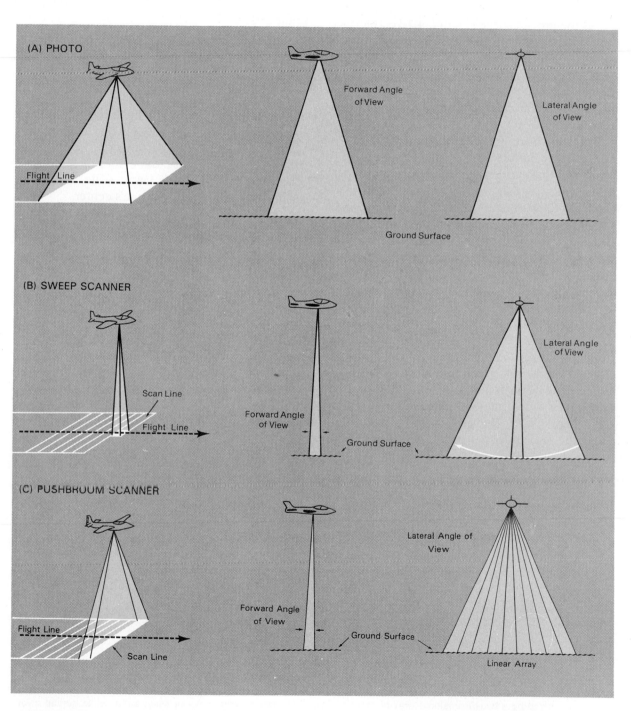

(A) PHOTO

Forward Angle of View

Lateral Angle of View

Flight Line

Ground Surface

(B) SWEEP SCANNER

Scan Line

Flight Line

Forward Angle of View

Ground Surface

Lateral Angle of View

(C) PUSHBROOM SCANNER

Flight Line

Scan Line

Forward Angle of View

Ground Surface

Lateral Angle of View

Linear Array

4.1 A comparison among photography (A), side-sweep scanning (B), and pushbroom scanning (C) shows the differences among these three image mapping techniques.

88

In contrast to camera systems, another class of sensors, called **electronic scanners**, create images in a sequential manner. (See *Electronic Imaging* in Appendix B.) The older **side-sweep scanners** produce an image by recording energy cell by cell in a series of swaths or **scan lines** across the ground scene (**Figure 4.1B**). The cells that make up the image are called **pixels** (an abbreviated form of **picture elements**). Although each scan line is a nearly instantaneous record of the landscape, the sensor vehicle (aircraft or satellite) advances after each ground sweep of the scanner. The effect is like sweeping a spotlight back and forth under the sensor vehicle.

Newer **pushbroom scanners** consist of a linear array of hundreds of signal detectors that record energy for all pixels in a scan line simultaneously (**Figure 4.1C**). As the sensor vehicle moves forward, additional scan lines are added to make up the ground scene. With both types of scanners, time passes between the recording of the first and last scan line. This time lapse allows the ground scene to shift due to earth rotation and short-lived phenomena to change in the meantime.

A second difference between photos and electronic images is their **spatial resolution**. (The higher the spatial resolution of an image, the more detail it shows.) The resolution of a standard photo is determined by the size of the film grain (**Figure 4.3**). The smaller the grain size, the better the resolution of spatial details. The resolu-

tion of electronic imagery, on the other hand, is determined mainly by the size of the pixels (**Figure 4.4**). Smaller pixels yield better spatial resolution. Since these picture elements are generally larger than the grain size of film, electronic images tend to be of lower resolution than photographs.

Third, scanner and camera imagery differ in their scale characteristics. On a camera image, taken with a film or digital camera, scale distortion occurs in all directions outward from the image's center. A scanned image's scale, in contrast, is true along the line of flight but may be distorted outward from the flight line along each scan line. In other words, while the center of the camera image is a point, the center of a scanner image is a line. In both cases, scale distortion occurs outward from the image's center.

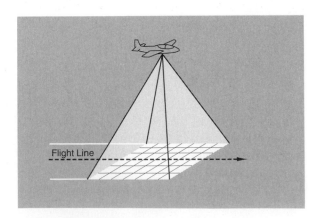

4.2 A digital camera captures the entire ground scene simultaneously using a two-dimensional array of detectors. The resulting pixelized image is similar to a single frame produced by the familiar home camcorder.

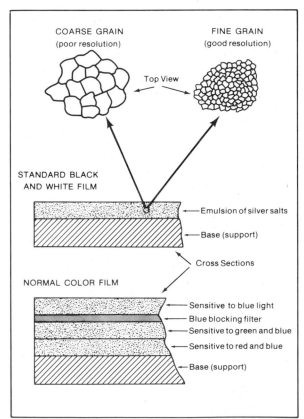

4.3 Standard black-and-white film emulsions contain a single layer of light-sensitive silver salts, while normal color film contains several layers.

Although scanner images are constantly improving, they still vary in quality. If the sensor platform is stable in its flight path, as is true of satellites and high-altitude aircraft, the scan lines will be parallel. The result is a scanner image of high quality. In fact, it is sometimes difficult to tell the difference between a good scanner image and a photograph. If the sensor platform isn't stable in its flight path, however, the scan lines won't be parallel. This is usually what happens when a scanner is carried on a low-altitude aircraft, because light planes tend to be jostled by atmospheric disturbances as they move along their flight lines. The result may be an image of relatively poor quality, on which apparent scan lines dominate the scene. On these low-quality scanner images, linear features such as roads may appear wavy.

Whether they are made with camera or scanner images, image maps vary greatly in scale and resolution. The differences between them depend in large measure on the height above the ground of the sensor device (camera or scanner) when the image was created. An image taken from a conventional airplane looks quite different from one taken from a high-altitude aircraft or a satellite, and each serves a different purpose.

IMAGE VANTAGE POINT

An image represents the landscape the way you'd see it with one eye closed or with both eyes open but at a long distance. Relief cues are provided by shadows cast from raised features and by the outlines of features in profile. The quality of these cues depends primarily on the sensor's vantage point, which may be horizontal, oblique, or vertical (**Figure 4.5**).

Horizontal

Images taken with the sensor held parallel with the land surface provide the most familiar image of environmental features, because this is the way we normally see our surroundings. From this vantage point, vertical aspects of the landscape are seen in profile, making features easy to recognize. But since the breadth of areal coverage increases with distance from the sensor, near features appear larger than distant ones of the same size. This distortion of feature size can be a major handicap.

There's another drawback to seeing the landscape in profile. If there is much foreground relief, background features will be blocked from view. Even when features aren't hidden from sight, we can still see only their near sides, and we can't tell very accurately where features are locat-

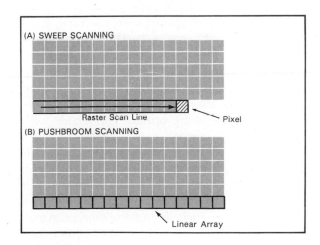

4.4 Electronic scanner images of the sweep (A) and pushbroom (B) types have a cellular structure.

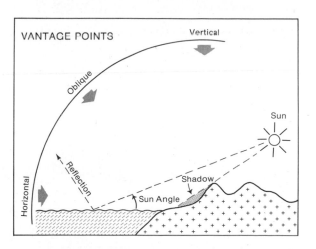

4.5 The relationship among earth, sun, and sensor in aerial image mapping can greatly affect the appearance of the portrayal.

ed in space. For these reasons, horizontal images make relatively poor maps for geographical uses.

Oblique

Images taken with the sensor at an angle between 0° and 90° from the horizontal provide a somewhat less familiar image than horizontal images, because we don't commonly see the landscape from an elevated vantage point. But oblique images have several useful characteristics. For one thing, features seen in semi-profile show the landscape almost as clearly as the true profile of horizontal images. In addition, feature size on oblique images is less distorted with increasing distance from the sensor, and blocking of background

areas due to foreground relief is less severe than on horizontal images.

Even on oblique images, however, size distortion and blocking can occur. These problems are greatest on **high obliques**, which result when the sensor is inclined between 0° and 45° from the horizontal. High oblique photographs are distinguished by the fact that the horizon is visible (**Figure 4.6A**). There is little problem in the foreground of such images, but progressive scale reduction (including the height of features) toward the background of the image severely degrades the quality of representation.

Scale distortion and blocking of features will be balanced more evenly over an oblique image if the sensor is tilted between 45° and 90° from the horizontal. The result is a **low oblique** image, which can be quite effective in portraying the landscape. On these images, the horizon isn't visible, and scale reduction toward the background of the image isn't as pronounced as on high obliques (**Figure 4.6B**). There's a drawback to using a vantage point with such a high vertical angle, however: Features may no longer be in sufficient profile to provide strong relief cues. The closer the vantage point is to the vertical, then, the more you'll have to rely on shadow cues to help you recognize features.

Vertical

The most unfamiliar view of the landscape is provided by **vertical** photos (taken with the sensor perpendicular to the earth's surface), because we're rarely in a position to see the earth from directly above (**Figure 4.7**). The advantage of these aerial views is that blocking is minimized—it's hard for one feature to hide behind another. But at the same time, relief isn't readily apparent unless features vary greatly in height and unless shadow conditions are optimal (preferably with the sun at a low angle).

A great advantage of vertical images is that scale variation is minimized. When it does occur, features are displaced radially from the center of the picture, as we'll see in the next section. The tops of features such as buildings or hills may appear more distant from the image's center than they really are, while the bottoms of buildings or valleys may be displaced toward the image's center. Since this radial distortion is predictable, we

4.6 Different vertical viewing angles produced these high oblique (A) and low oblique (B) aerial photos.

4.7 A portion of a low-altitude, black-and-white aerial photograph taken from a vertical vantage point (Iowa County, Wisconsin, 1937).

can compensate for it with the help of other photos taken from different vantage points.

Clearly, the sensor's vantage point has an important impact on the appearance of the imaged ground scene. It's crucial that you learn to deal with all these vantage point problems, because standard image maps have no legend to clarify things for you. Thus, the main trait of a good image map user is the ability to visualize what environmental features seen daily from the ground would look like from elevated vantage points. Luckily, you can develop this skill through practice. Seize every chance to gaze down on the world. Have lunch in restaurants on top of high buildings, or drive to the crest of a hill and notice how the city looks from above. Best of all, take advantage of the view provided by window seats on airplanes. There's no better way to gain a feel for how image maps relate to the ground than from a plane. With practice, this way of viewing the world will become natural. Even when earthbound, you'll begin to visualize how your environment would look on an image map.

RAW IMAGE MAPS

A **standard** or **conventional** image map is plain and unadorned, just as it comes from the camera or scanner, before it has been modified in any way. Even though these raw images have no labels

to explain things for you, you can still recognize many features on them. Your ability to read these images will improve if you pay attention to the impact of viewing distance, tonal variations, and scale variations. Let's look first at viewing distance.

Viewing Distance

The distance between the sensor device and the landscape is an important factor to consider because it determines the spatial resolution of the image. With a given sensor, a short viewing distance will yield more detailed environmental images than long viewing distances.

Figure 4.7, for example, shows a portion of a standard large-scale aerial photo taken from an airplane flying at an altitude of approximately 300 meters (10,000 feet). Roads, buildings, field patterns, trees, and small streams are all evident.

Compare this standard photo to the scanner image in **Figure 4.8**. This image was taken from a satellite in orbit about 917 kilometers (570 miles) above the earth. Although the fine details apparent in the previous photo are missing, regional patterns can be seen. Forests, bays, large rivers, cities, and water pollution are all visible. An

4.8 This portion of a Landsat multispectral scanner (MSS) image depicts the upper Chesapeake Bay region. Washington, D.C., appears in the lower left corner, and Baltimore, Maryland, can be seen in the upper center.

92

experienced map reader could extract a wealth of additional information from either of these standard image maps.

The differences between these two figures are caused more by the viewing distance than by the equipment used to produce the images. In fact, the similarities of photos and scanner images are greater than their differences.

Tonal Variation

The appearance of a ground scene is also determined by light and shadow conditions. One aspect of this illumination factor is the sun's position with respect to the sensor view. Note how the lakes in Figure 24.4 vary in tone from black to white. Don't be fooled into thinking that there's some basic difference between the lakes themselves. The explanation is that some lakes are reflecting sunlight into the sensor, while other lakes aren't (**Figure 4.9**). As a rule, a ground scene illuminated with the sun behind the sensor will give a much better picture of the landscape than an image taken into the sun's reflected rays.

A second aspect of the illumination factor is the angle at which the sun's rays strike the ground. With higher sun angles, objects cast smaller shadows, thus obscuring less ground area but also providing fewer shadow cues for feature identification. Image mappers try to strike a compromise by taking their images during the midday period in the summer. On images taken

between 10:00 a.m. and 2:00 p.m., shadows are long enough to let you identify features clearly without hiding too much detail. Not all image maps, however, are so carefully crafted.

In addition to daily changes of light and shadow, the environment passes through a seasonal cycle. An image taken in the winter may give a much different impression of the landscape than one taken in the summer (see Figure 8.1). In farm country, the ground scene changes weekly as crops pass through their rapid growth cycle. Likewise, a lake may change appearance over a period of days as algae build up on hot summer days or as storms in the drainage basin create murky runoff.

The fact that images change through time in this way is sometimes a distraction. If you use an image map taken at a different time of year or under different conditions, it may bear scant resemblance to the environment around you. On photos taken during the summer period of heavy foliage, essential landmarks such as roads, streams, and buildings are often obscured. On other photos, atmospheric phenomena such as smog, clouds, or dust may obliterate crucial ground features. Gazing at a photo of the top of a cloud or forest canopy yields few insights for the ground traveler. Such problems tend to reduce the utility of image maps.

Scale Variation

The image map user must also learn to anticipate scale distortions. Conventional photographs are central perspective images (these were discussed under *Selecting a Perspective* in Chapter 3). This means that on vertical photos, which are the most commonly used in image mapping, the scale will most likely be distorted away from the image's center. To provide a simple way to determine the photo center, map makers place special **fiducial marks** at the margins of photos taken with precision aerial cameras (**Figure 4.10**). If you draw lines between opposite pairs of fiducial marks, these lines will intersect at the center of the photo. This is the point that fell directly below the camera when the photo was taken and is called the **plumb** or **principal point**.

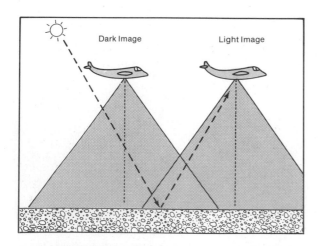

4.9 Features of the same class may appear in a light tone on one part of an aerial photo and dark on another due to the varying light reflectance angle.

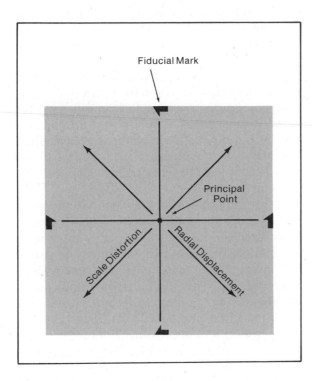

4.10 Format of a standard vertical photograph with the principal point and fiducial marks identified.

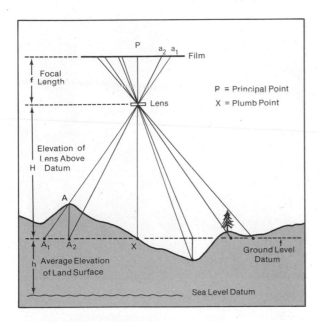

4.11 The radial displacement of features in central perspective maps can be seen in this profile view. Notice how ground point A has been shifted outward on the film.

The main reason that radial scale distortion is characteristic of vertical photos is that objects of different heights are displaced radially about the principal point. If the top of a feature is higher than average ground level, it will be displaced outward. Inward displacement occurs with objects lying below average ground level. The geometric explanation for this pattern of radial displacement is provided in **Figure 4.11**. Notice the relation between the position of features on the ground and on the film. The greater the height or depth of features relative to the ground, and the farther features are from the center of the photo, the greater their radial displacement.

The amount of radial distortion is also influenced by the height of the camera above the ground. The higher the camera, the less the radial distortion. Thus, satellite photos may exhibit so little distortion that they can be overlaid on planimetrically correct maps with only small locational discrepancies. In contrast, displacement is great on low-altitude vertical photos; features such as buildings and trees seem to be leaning out from the center of the photograph.

All these problems with scale variance are minimized when image maps are made using a relatively small field of view. Narrow-view camera lenses and short side-to-side scanner sweeps produce images with little scale distortion. This is assuming, however, that the terrain surface is relatively flat and that the image is truly vertical. If the region is hilly or if the camera is tilted when the photo is taken, scale distortion may be so great that the resulting image map will be difficult or impossible to use. In such cases, standard image maps are often adjusted to compensate for these distortions.

GEOMETRICAL CORRECTIONS

Fortunately, we aren't stuck with the geometry and content of image maps as they come from a camera or scanner. They may be modified in several ways to serve special needs. Some image maps are rectified by having distortions removed; others are made into a mosaic of different images; and still others are enhanced to accentuate specific features.

94

Scale distortions in a vertical image due to camera tilt can be removed from raw image maps by physically altering the geometry of the photo. The process is called photo rectification and is relatively simple to execute.

Rectified image maps still contain radial displacement due to difference in the heights of features, however. To remove this radial distortion, it is necessary to turn the central perspective photo into a parallel perspective one. Rather than looking out from a central point to each feature, we will then be looking directly down on the landscape. Thus, all features will appear in true planimetric position.

The conversion from central to parallel perspective on vertical image maps is a demanding process. Fortunately, it is readily accomplished with computers and is therefore increasingly common. The resulting modified image is called an **orthophoto** or **orthophotomap** (**Figure 4.12**). The prefix *ortho* means "corrected."

Since relations between ground features on orthophotomaps are true in the horizontal dimension, objects don't appear to lean out from the center of the photo. Consequently, orthophotos can be laid directly over other parallel perspective maps, such as standard road maps, with no problems of positional discrepancy between features on the two maps.

Orthophotos represent such an important breakthrough in image mapping technology that federal agencies in the United States are cooperating with state and local governments, as well as the private sector, to create nationwide coverage. The products, called **digital orthophoto quadrangles (DOQ)** are derived from 1/40,000-scale black-and-white photography, yielding 256 gray levels in pixels of approximately one-meter spatial resolution (**Figure 4.13**). These image maps will be available to the public for display and manipulation on desktop computers. Thus, they will serve as a uniform, high-quality base for a vari-

(A) DISTORTED IMAGE

(B) CORRECTED IMAGE

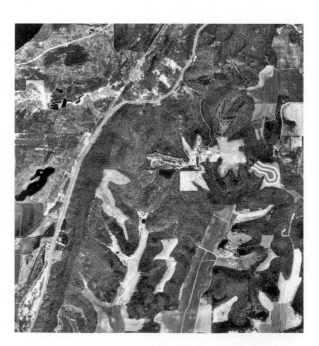

4.12 Relief distortion in the vertical aerial photo (A) gives the cleared powerline right-of-way a wiggly appearance. On the orthophoto, on which relief distortion has been removed (B), you can see that the powerline consists of three straight segments.

4.13 A section of a digital orthophoto quadrangle (DOQ) for the Black Earth area in Dane County, Wisconsin.

ety of mapping, geographical study, and planning activities.

IMAGE MOSAICS

Sometimes several image maps are spliced together to show a broader area than could be covered by one alone. This collage of photos is called a **mosaic**.

Mosaics may be created in several ways. With one method, the image maps are positioned roughly where they belong, stapled together, and then rephotographed (**Figure 4.14A**). These are called **uncontrolled mosaics**, because no adjustments have been made for planimetric distortion of the component photos.

On some uncontrolled mosaics, precise matching of features along the edges of individual images is lacking (**Figure 4.14B**). On others, the photos are stretched and shrunk when making the collage so that edge features do match quite well (**Figure 4.14C**). These uncontrolled mosaics may give a good overall picture of a region. But, due to the geometric distortions associated with

each photo in the mosaic, they aren't suitable for any sort of precision work.

With a second method, each photo is precisely matched to the next, and planimetric distortion is taken into account. This procedure produces a **controlled mosaic**, which meets planimetric accuracy standards. You can easily make your own controlled image map mosaic if you use orthophotos as your component images. Since orthophotos are planimetrically true for small regions, they will fit together perfectly when laid side by side. This is how space image maps, such as the one in Figure 4.8, are created.

Mosaics made by hand from existing images suffer one flaw which may cause confusion for the unwary user. Since each image map is created under different light and shadow conditions, tones and contrast may vary from image to image. The consequence is that even the most carefully made mosaic is inclined to have a mottled appearance (refer again to Figure 4.14). This effect is especially pronounced if the images have been taken at different times of the year or (as is the case with many photos taken from satellites) over several years.

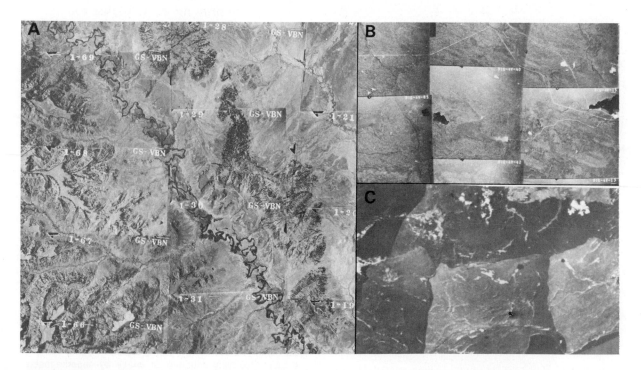

4.14 Uncontrolled mosaics of aerial photographs range in quality from those made by photographing a layout of stapled-together photos (A and B) to those which have been carefully cut and matched along prominent features (C).

96

Image-to-image tonal variation can be smoothed out using digital image-editing software, thus avoiding the mottled appearance of handmade mosaics. As more images have become available in electronic form, so has this practice of image editing. You can now expect that most medium-scale to small-scale mosaics of regional coverage, such as Figure 4.8, will look like a single image rather than a collage.

IMAGE ENHANCEMENTS

Although image maps are excellent at showing some aspects of the landscape, they may fail miserably at depicting others. Intangible features, such as political boundaries, aren't commonly picked up on photographic or scanner images. Such useful aids as geographical names, map scale, direction indicators, and positional reference grids are absent from raw image maps. Features on standard image maps aren't classified and identified in a key or legend. Magnitude infor-

mation rarely comes through well with image mapping. Even those features that do appear on image maps are sometimes so subtle or obscure that they are difficult to identify.

For all these reasons, image maps are often made more "intelligent" by cartographically **enhancing** them with lines, words, numbers, and colors. These features are laid over the image base, producing an **image-based map**. The older **orthophotoquads**, produced by the United States Geological Survey (USGS) to supplement its 1:24,000 series, provide an example. On these maps, a rectified high-altitude aerial photo is printed in shades of gray. Grid lines, place names, and marginal notes are then added (**Figure 4.15**).

Feature Overlays

Modern electronic mapping systems simplify image enhancement through feature overlays. Geographical information system software is particularly well-suited for this task (see Chapter 19: *GIS and Map Analysis Software*). When you're working with an image on a computer screen, this software lets you superimpose symbols for roads, political boundaries, and other features (**Figure 4.16**). You can print the result so that you have a permanent copy.

4.15 Portion of an orthophotoquad published by the U.S. Geological Survey at a scale of 1:24,000.

4.16 When you use an integrated digital mapping system, you can effectively enhance an image by superimposing graphic symbols for roads, boundaries, and other special features.

Perhaps the most dramatic examples of image enhancement through overlay occur not when features are superimposed on the image but when the image is "draped" over a three-dimensional rendering of the terrain surface. With a proper computer system, you can pick a vantage point and then view the result (see Figure 5.30 in the next chapter). You aren't restricted to use of raw images, of course. Thus, you can overlay features such as roads and boundaries on an image, and then drape it over the terrain surface. Since with the best systems you can pick and choose what you see and how it is displayed, we have here the essence of a powerful user-controlled procedure for using maps.

The USGS carries cartographic enhancement still further with the orthophotomaps in its 1:24,000 series (see *Geometrical Corrections* earlier in this chapter for a description of orthophotos). On these orthophotomaps, grids, boundaries, and geographical names have been added; features have been outlined; classes of roads have been indicated with different symbols; and colors have been used to differentiate between classes

of features (**Figure 4.17**). Grasslands are yellow, brush and forest green, lakes blue, and landform contours red.

There is an important difference between orthophotomaps and orthophotoquads. On the "quads," all photographic information remains intact, whereas on the "maps" some of this information has been removed and shown in some other way. For instance, major roads have been resymbolized with lines and colors, while open water has been recolored a flat blue. If this practice of substituting abstract symbols for photographic tones were carried to its logical extreme, the result would no longer resemble the original image map.

Image Classification

Ever since aerial photography was first used, people have classified images manually. Photo interpreters (see Chapter 24: *Image Map Interpretation*) would study an image, and then outline and label features (**Figure 4.18**). Since intricate and fuzzy-edged features need to be generalized in classification, the result is more abstract than the original image. Misclassifications may also occur.

Although a great deal of manual image classification still is done, automated image process-

4.17 Portion of an orthophotomap published by the U.S. Geological Survey at a scale of 1:24,000.

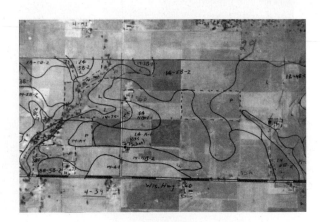

4.18 Photo interpreters traditionally classified features by outlining and naming them on the image.

98

ing is now widely practiced (see *Image Classification* in Chapter 24). Computerized image classification has yet to evolve to such a point that we can distinguish between individual features such as a school and a hospital. We can, however, use electronic procedures to differentiate among land, water, forest, agriculture, urban development, and other forms of ground cover (**Figure 4.19**). The techniques can even be used to determine subclasses within these broad groups. For example, it is possible to distinguish areas in which different tree species are the dominant vegetation.

INDEXES

One of the difficulties in using image maps is to find coverage for a given location. This task is simplified with satellite imagery because the same scene is revisited on subsequent passes of the satellite. Individual scenes form a regular grid in which each cell has a path/row identification code. (See Figure B.19 in Appendix B: *Remote Sensing of the Environment.*)

When images are taken from aircraft, atmosphere turbulence prevents precise sensor positioning and alignment. Furthermore, no standardized spatial imaging format is used with these images. As a result, ground coverage of individual images varies from project to project. To find the

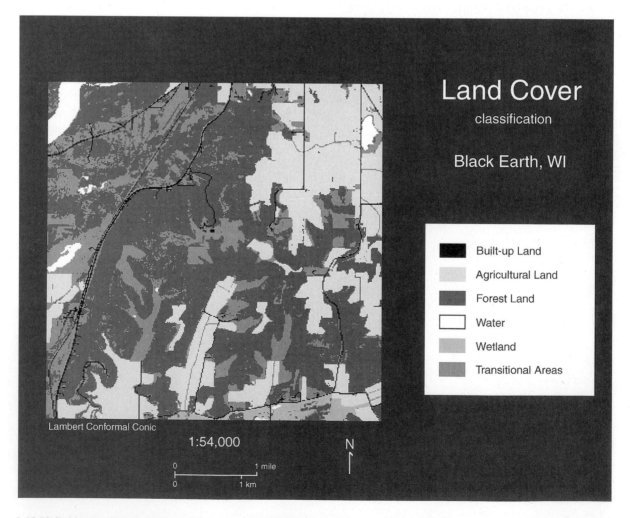

4.19 Digital image classification uses spectral (waveband) information on a pixel by pixel basis to distinguish automatically among general landcover classes. Objects aren't identified as wholes, as is done in visual photo interpretation.

appropriate image for a site, you'll have to refer to some indexing system. Two forms are common. Most widespread are **photo index maps**. These are conventional line maps on which the center of each image is indicated (**Figure 4.20A**). You merely find your location and count image frames along the appropriate flight line.

A second form of index shows a small-scale mosaic of actual images. These **photo mosaic indexes** give you image identification information directly (**Figure 4.20B**). But you may have

trouble finding your target location without the help of a line map of the region.

CONCLUSION

In this chapter, we've stressed that a photo, no matter how realistic and believable it seems, isn't a distortion-free representation of the environment. In its own way, each of the imaging techniques depends on symbolism. Image enhancement moves us along a gradient toward greater abstraction. A completely modified photo or scanner image, such as an orthophotomap, becomes a line map. (As we saw in *Graphics* in Chapter 3, line maps use some combination of graphic point, line, and area symbols to portray reality.) We'll consider line maps in the next three chapters.

SELECTED READINGS

Barrett, E.C., and Curtis, L.F., *Introduction to Environmental Remote Sensing*, 3rd ed. (London: Chapman & Hall, 1992).

Ciciarelli, J.A., *Practical Guide to Aerial Photography: With an Introduction to Surveying* (New York: Van Nostrand Reinhold, 1991).

Cracknell, A.P., and Hayes, L.W., *Introduction to Remote Sensing* (New York: Taylor & Francis, 1991).

Dickinson, G.C., *Maps and Air Photographs*, 2nd ed. (New York: John Wiley & Sons, 1979).

Falkner, E., *Aerial Mapping* (Boca Raton, FL: CRC Press, Inc., 1994).

Lillisand, T.M., and Kiefer, R.W., *Remote Sensing and Image Interpretation*, 3rd ed. (New York: John Wiley & Sons, 1994).

Rees, W.G., *Physical Principles of Remote Sensing* (New York: Cambridge University Press, 1990).

Also see references in Chapter 24 and Appendix B.

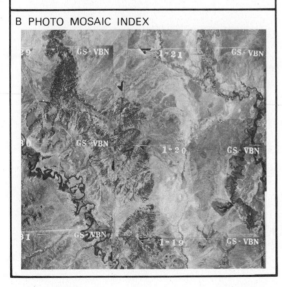

4.20 Photo indexes make it possible to determine the ground coverage and identification code of individual images.

CHAPTER FIVE

LANDFORM PORTRAYAL

INTRODUCTION

RELATIVE RELIEF METHODS

Relief Globes
Relief Models
Image Maps
  Standard Photographs
    Single Photos
    Stereo Photos
  Radar and Sonar Images
Landscape Drawings
Block Diagrams
Smooth Shading
Perspective Profiles
Hachures
Stylized Drawings
Combined Relative Relief Methods

ABSOLUTE RELIEF METHODS

Physical Models
Digital Terrain Data
  Spot Heights
  Digital Elevation Models (DEMs)
Contour Lines
  Special Contours
  Stereo Models
Enhanced Contour Lines
  Shaded Contours
  Shadowed Contours
Combined Absolute Relief Methods

COMPOSITE RELIEF METHODS

Superimposed Representations
Dual Representations
Active Representations

DYNAMIC RELIEF METHODS

Animated Methods
Interactive Methods

CONCLUSION

SELECTED READINGS

Using mountains, for what might be called real-world purposes, is too much trouble; there is always that nagging, debilitating gradient to deal with....The permanent residents of the mountains seldom have the energy left over, after dealing with the gradient, to invent new games.
—John Jerome, *On Mountains: Thinking About Terrain*

When you get down to it, a map is something impossible,... because it transforms something elevated into something flat.
—Sten Nadolny, *The Discovery of Slowness*

5

CHAPTER FIVE

LANDFORM PORTRAYAL

The terrain surface provides the foundation upon which our lives are played out. Nothing in the environment is immune from landform influences. Human orientation, mobility, and environmental understanding are all affected by the terrain surface.

Yet it's easy to forget the significance of the third, or vertical, dimension of our environment, because most of the time we live in a flat world. The floor of our house is flat; most yards and streets are fairly flat; the space between buildings and trees is flat. Thus, we tend to think of geographical position in purely horizontal terms. This is often a perfectly good way to simplify our world. But sometimes such a simplified viewpoint causes conflict. Ships run aground, airplanes crash into mountainsides, and hikers die of exposure at high altitudes—all because the third dimension wasn't properly taken into account.

Maps treat the vertical dimension of our environment in several ways. Some maps ignore it and give only horizontal information, as we will see in the next two chapters. These maps are useful when the mapped area is essentially flat or when facts about an area's relief (variations in the land surface) aren't important to your needs. In such situations, relief information would merely clutter the map with unnecessary detail.

At other times, the ups and downs of the environment are crucial in establishing position and spatial associations. When vertical information about the land is important, planimetric maps aren't of much use. In such cases, you should turn to **landform** or **topographic maps**, which show the configuration of the land surface. There are two basic types of topographic maps—those that show relief in a **relative** way and those that use **absolute** relief methods to give precise elevation information. Which sort to use depends on how accurate a picture of relief you need.

RELATIVE RELIEF METHODS

In our day-to-day life, we're usually concerned with the local range between high and low heights, or the **relative relief**. We think of relief in terms of plains and hills, mountains and valleys. Something is

102

above us or below us, up or down, high or low.

Some topographic maps appeal directly to these relief notions of ours by creating a descriptive terrain picture. On these maps, relative relief methods are used to give a visual three-dimensional effect. The ultimate in realism is achieved when the landform surface is depicted in raised relief, as is done on relief globes.

Relief Globes

Since globes present the truest picture of the earth as a whole (see Appendix C for a discussion of globes), we might conclude that relief globes provide the most realistic and useful portrayal of the vertical dimension. But there is a flaw in this reasoning. The entire extent of the earth's relief, from the top of the highest mountain to the bottom of the deepest ocean, is only about 19 kilometers (12 miles). If we exclude ocean depth, the total is a mere 9.5 kilometers (six miles). This height difference is minuscule when compared with the overall dimensions of the earth—approximately 40,225 kilometers (25,000 miles) in circumference, 12,711 kilometers (7,900 miles) in diameter. What happens, then, when we reduce the world to the size of a globe? Relief fea-

5.1 Apparent elevation variation on a relief globe has to be greatly exaggerated to give a reasonable impression of the landform.

tures, if kept at the same scale as the rest of the globe, shrink to practically nothing.

Even a large globe would show little relief if it were constructed in true proportion to the earth. On a globe with a diameter of 60 centimeters (24 inches), representing a 21,000,000 to 1 reduction, the vertical dimension would be about .9 mm. (.037 inch), and only half that value if ocean depth weren't shown. In fact, if the earth were reduced to the size of a bowling ball (a common globe size), the earth would be "smoother" than the ball!

Clearly, some exaggeration of the globe's vertical dimension is necessary to make landforms visible and somewhat realistic in appearance (**Figure 5.1**). In practice, a vertical exaggeration of about 20 to 1 is typical on relief globes of a 60-centimeter (24-inch) diameter. Therefore, in addition to the highly generalized nature and the handling and storage inconvenience of globes, users of relief globes must also face the problem of vast vertical distortion.

Relief Models

We can minimize the problem of vertical distortion by using physical models rather than globes. Models are in effect chunks of a giant globe. They let us focus on one small portion of the earth at large scale. Thus, relief is shown in much more correct scale than on globes.

Some relief models are crudely built up of **discrete** elevation layers (**Figure 5.2A**). The stepped effect usually results from the mapping technique, not the nature of the landform surface. Although layered landforms do occur in regions of terraced agriculture, open pit mining, and horizontal sedimentary beds of varying resistance to erosion, these landscapes are relatively rare.

More realistic models are constructed with a smooth, **continuous** landform surface (**Figure 5.2B**). These relief models probably provide the clearest picture of the landform that a map can produce. Unfortunately, like all physical models, they suffer from their bulk, weight, and high cost of production.

For these reasons, physical models are usually used only in permanent or semi-permanent displays. They are frequently found in the lobbies of government and private agencies which deal with environmental problems, in city-regional

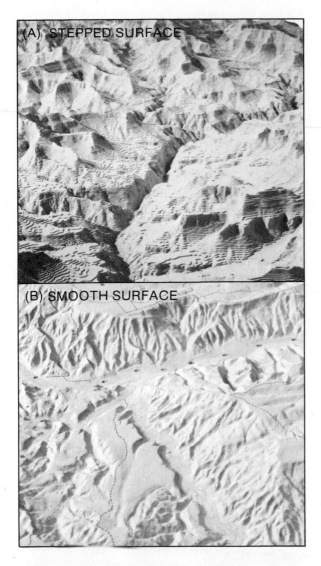

(A) STEPPED SURFACE

(B) SMOOTH SURFACE

5.2 The layer by layer construction of physical models often leaves them with a stepped surface (A), although smoothing out the "cliffs" creates a more realistic portrayal (B).

Maps in the series may be joined together to create a mosaic of an entire region.

5.3 A plastic topographic map molded to form a raised relief surface.

planning exhibits, and in university geology, geography, and landscape architecture departments. People working on high-intensity promotional schemes or research projects are especially fond of using physical models. Parks, urban renewal projects, malls, and dam sites are favorite subjects. For many such purposes, the inconvenience of models is offset by the true-to-life impression of the landscape they provide. The child in each of us responds to the touchable character of physical models.

There is one type of physical model that partially sidesteps the problems of bulkiness and high cost. This is the **raised relief topographic map**. It is made by taking an ordinary flat map printed on a sheet of plastic and using heat to mold it into a three-dimensional model (**Figure 5.3**). The resulting map isn't a chunk of the globe, as is the genuine physical model. It is really just a flat map with an undulating landform surface. Thus, its base will always be flat (unlike models, whose bases often show the curve of the earth).

The raised relief topographic map, which gives a dramatic regional picture of the landform, is widely available from private mapping firms.* It does cost about 10 times more than a conventional map of the same size, and it is relatively fragile and difficult to store. But the realism of its relief often compensates for these drawbacks. A more serious concern is that geographical features aren't portrayed very accurately. This is inevitable because of the displacement caused by stretching a flat map of true planimetry over a three-dimensional model. The inaccuracy problem is compounded by the fact that this type of relief map is usually produced at medium to small scale so as to have wider sales appeal.

A selection of raised relief topographic maps is available from: Hubbard, P.O. Box 104, Northbrook, IL 60062.

104

Image Maps

Most of us aren't concerned enough with realism to put up with costly, awkward physical models. We need maps we can fold up and carry with us. Cartographers have given us a number of convenient flat-map relief portrayals. The most realistic of these is the image map, which we discussed in detail in Chapter 4.

Although image maps are more handy to use than physical models, their depiction of relief isn't quite so straightforward. When you look at a three-dimensional model of the landscape, you can perceive depth directly from any vantage point. That is, you can choose your vantage point by moving around the model. This isn't true of image maps.

In discussing landform portrayal, it's convenient to break image maps into two main types—standard photographs and radar or sonar images. Let's first discuss standard photos.

Standard Photographs

Photos are flat images of the landform as seen in central perspective from the single vantage point of the camera. The quality of photographic relief portrayal depends both on the camera's vantage point and on sun and camera angles related to orientation of landform features. We discussed these critical relations in the previous chapter (see Figure 4.5).

Single Photos. When you look at a single photo, you gain a sense of the landform by using relief cues. Both shadow and profile information provide helpful cues but, due to the background nature of the terrain surface, shadow is the more important of the two. Oblique camera angles and low sun angles give the landform the best visual definition (see Figure 4.6). But you can have too much of a good thing. On oblique images, raised foreground terrain may block your view of background features. Likewise, low sun angles cast long shadows from prominent features, which can obscure less-prominent neighboring landforms.

Another problem with oblique images is that the scale is larger in the foreground than in the background. In other words, near features appear larger on the image than far features. For this reason, a vertical image is usually preferred for more rigorous applications. This doesn't mean such an image is free of scale distortion, however. Features of different heights on the ground will appear at slightly different scales and locations on a vertical image. For general reference use, this may not be a problem, but it is a concern in professional work.

Vertical and low oblique air photos have a curious trait. Our impression of relief depends on the way we hold the photograph. If we orient it so that the shadows fall toward us, we see the terrain in proper relief. But if we view the photo with the shadows falling away from us, **terrain reversal** often occurs. You can see this unexplained phenomenon for yourself by looking at **Figure 5.4** with the book held upside down. *Voilá*—the volcanic cones become craters! Terrain reversal has led to a great deal of map use confusion, especially since we may need to view vertical photos of regions in the Northern Hemisphere with north at the bottom—just the reverse of line map convention—to compensate for this phenomenon. Fortunately, we can easily correct the problem if we understand the reversal effect.

Stereo Photos. When we look at an individual air photo, the relief doesn't always stand out dramatically. To make relief more obvious, a clever method that takes advantage of our normal binocular vision has been devised. Two photos are taken of the same landform from slightly different observation points. The successive pic-

5.4 Shadow orientation is an important relief cue. If this figure is viewed when holding the book upside down, relief reversal occurs.

tures are commonly taken with a single camera pointed straight down from a moving airplane. The result is a number of vertical photos which overlap so that all features appear on at least two images (**Figure 5.5**). These two photos, called a **stereopair**, are then viewed stereoscopically— that is, with each eye simultaneously focused on a different photo.

Some people can achieve stereoscopic vision merely by holding the stereopair of photos side by side at normal viewing distance and consciously focusing one eye on each photo. But most of us find some visual aid helpful—if not essential—in attaining stereovision. For this purpose, special stereo-viewing devices, called **lens stereoscopes**, are available (**Figure 5.6A**). You

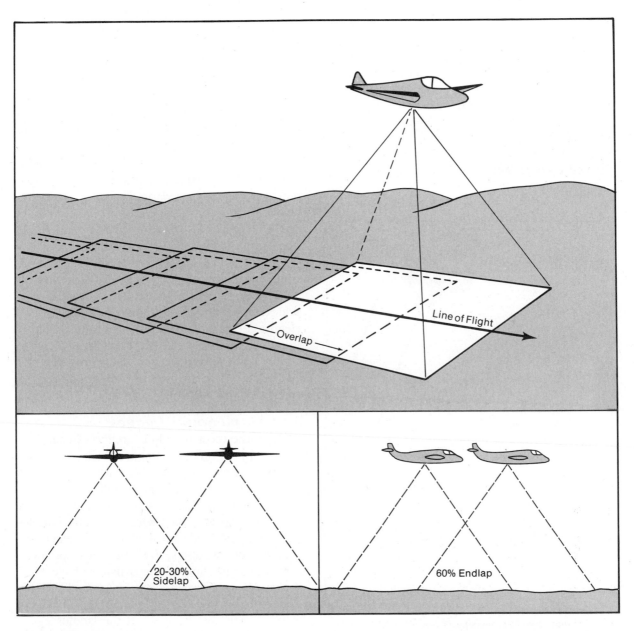

5.5 Aerial photos need to overlap 60 percent along the line of flight (endlap) and 20 to 30 percent between the lines of flight (sidelap) to ensure stereographic ground coverage.

106

simply arrange the two photos side by side and place the stereoscope over them so that each lens is centered over a common point. Since your eyes are spaced about 65 mm. (2.5 inches) apart, that is approximately the distance there should be between common features on the two photos. Looking through the stereoscope, you then move one of the photos slightly until the common points merge into a single mental image and the landscape appears in three dimensions.

Unless one of your eyes is much weaker than the other, you'll soon be able to achieve the stereoscopic effect with ease. Your task will be simplified if both photos in the stereopair have been printed together on one sheet; these side-by-side photos are called **stereograms (Figure 5.7)**. When you're working with stereograms, you can bring up the relief simply by moving the stereoscope slightly.

On other relief maps, the depth illusion is created by superimposing pairs of images taken from different vantage points. Sometimes the two photos are printed (or projected onto a screen) in different colors, one red and one green. You view the picture through special glasses containing one red and one green lens. Each eye is thus limited to seeing only one image. If you've ever been to a 3-D movie, you're familiar with this dramatic technique. You can gain the same effect by projecting the two photos onto a screen using differently polarized lenses. If you then view the screen with special glasses containing lenses of the same two polarities, you'll see the image in three dimensions.

No matter how you achieve stereovision, the effect is the same. The two photos merge into a single landform picture in your mind's eye, just as the two images of the environment provided by your normal binocular visual system combine to create depth perception.

Stereovision is by far the most effective form of relief portrayal. It has its disadvantages, however. Properly overlapping photos and stereoviewing aids aren't commonly at hand. In addition, stereopairs are more expensive than single photos. A further drawback is that simple lens stereoscopes are only convenient to use with relatively small photographs, since the same area on two photos must be brought into proximity to achieve simultaneous eye contact. If you want to view large photos, you could use a special type of stereoscope—one with mirrors that reflect the widely spaced images into your eyes (**Figure 5.6B**). But these **mirror stereoscopes** are so costly that you will rarely have access to them.

Radar and Sonar Images

Some of the most revealing landform images are actually of a non-photographic origin. The landform portrayals made possible with Side Looking Airborne Radar (SLAR), for example, are truly dramatic. (See the volcanic cone in Central America shown in **Figure 5.8A**.) With this high-technology device, the landform is illuminated electronically, casting "shadows" over the landscape away from the flight line of the sensor vehicle. (See *Active Microwave Imaging* in Appendix B for more on this vivid radar technique.) The electronic signals that bounce off the landform and return to the sensor are then used to create the photographic image.

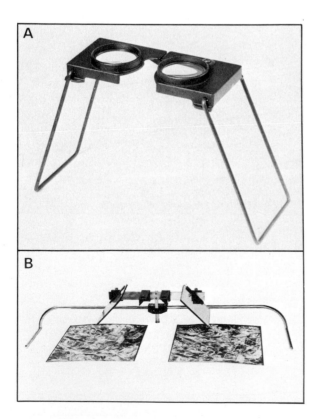

5.6 A simple lens stereoscope (A) is a useful aid when viewing aerial photographs stereoscopically, but a mirror stereoscope (B) is much more versatile.

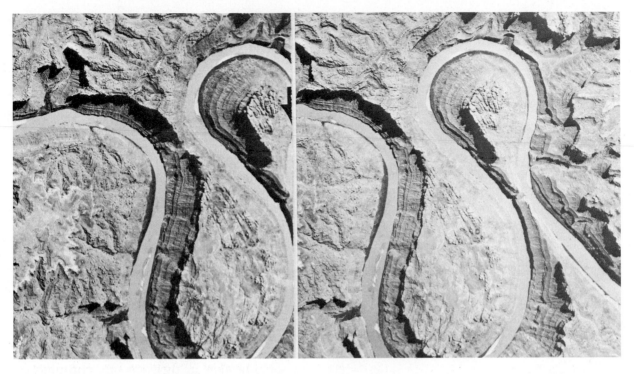

5.7 A specially prepared stereogram greatly simplifies stereoscopic viewing.

Although at first glance SLAR imagery may look like conventional photography, there are crucial differences that affect how you use the images. For one thing, the electronic shadows are black, completely obscuring landscape details. This means that the quality of the SLAR image is directly related to the flying height of the sensor vehicle. There is a basic conflict here, because low flying heights are needed to accentuate the relief effect, but they also lead to longer shadows and a consequent increase in detail obstruction. A compromise needs to be found between these two factors.

Despite these possible drawbacks, SLAR imagery is a boon for map users. It can reveal subtle landscape details such as fault lines. Also, since it contains its own source of illumination, it provides a day-or-night mapping capability in regions in which cloud cover commonly obscures landforms.

Perhaps the ultimate test of cartographers' ability to work under obscured conditions is seafloor mapping. Here cartographers use sonar waves, beamed down in a fanlike pattern. These sonar waves reflect off underwater features and return to the surface, where they are picked up by a sensor. A shipboard computer can then use these data to produce pictures such as the one of seabed volcanoes off the California coast in **Figure 5.8B**. To be most effective visually, these maps must be held with the sonar shadows falling toward the observer, just as with above-water radar portrayals of the landform.

Landscape Drawings

Artistically rendered maps, called **landscape** or **landform drawings**, can provide nearly photo-realistic terrain portrayals (**Figure 5.9**). Due to the immense amount of hand labor involved in their construction, the best-developed examples are found for regions of special interest, such as national parks and popular mountain resorts. Landscape drawings have become popular as ski area posters.

Block Diagrams

Another effective relief impression is provided by oblique drawings that look much like diagrams of the landform. These **block diagrams** are made in both discrete and continuous surface forms. **Discrete surface** block diagrams usually appear

108

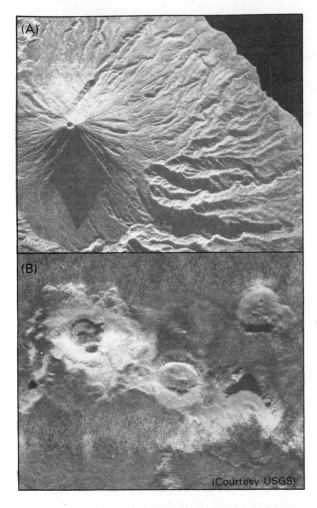

5.8 Microwave mapping can provide dramatic views of the landform, as these SLAR (A) and sonar (B) images attest.

artificial and abstract since surface cues have been held to a minimum, due either to a lack of information or to cut costs. Sometimes the image is created by slicing the landform into vertical zones and then stacking these layers (see Figure 5.2A). The horizontal layers of different heights create a "stepped" image, much like that found with certain erosional surfaces, terrain agriculture, and strip mining landscapes. Generally, however, the relief portrayal only grossly resembles the mapped landform.

Other discrete surface block diagrams are created by making parallel traces across the landform and then "banking" the successive surface profiles in perspective. There appears to be no natural basis for this method of slicing the landform surface vertically. But the relief portrayal can be good, especially if traces in opposite directions are used together to produce a wire-frame or fishnet effect (see Figure 7.7B).

Block diagrams reach their highest degree of sophistication in their smooth, **continuous**

5.9 Landform drawings represent the highest achievement in artistic rendering of the terrain surface.

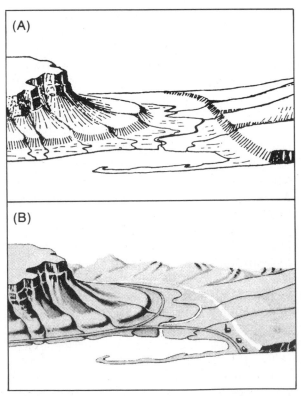

5.10 Oblique drawings (A) and shadings (B) of the landform surface can provide useful terrain representations.

surface form, where an attempt is made to give an artistic picture of the actual land surface. The natural appearance of the landform can be achieved in two ways—by using sketch lines to accentuate those terrain features which give distinct form to the landscape (**Figure 5.10A**) or by shading the surface continuously (**Figure 5.10B**). Either technique makes the landform easily understandable.

Popular magazines and advertisements take advantage of the realistic terrain picture provided by these smooth surface block diagrams. The illustrations in geology, physical geography, and other environmental textbooks are also commonly of this type. Unfortunately, this natural form of relief portrayal is seldom available at large scale and hence is used primarily for laboratory-oriented map study.

With block diagrams, the quality of relief depiction depends on the vantage point taken by the map maker. A horizontal vantage point will produce only a terrain profile, while a vertical vantage point will give no direct relief impression whatsoever (**Figure 5.11**). Therefore, an oblique vantage point is generally the most useful.

Notice in Figure 5.11 that as the quality of relief portrayal increases, so does the problem of terrain blocking. As the vantage point approaches the horizontal, relief is accentuated, but blocking of background features becomes more severe. To circumvent the blocking problem, you can sometimes "look behind the hill" if you use two maps, each with a different viewing direction. Normally, however, only one map is available and you don't have the advantage of this revealing option.

To create a realistic impression of relief, map makers exaggerate the scale of most block diagrams in the vertical dimension (another example of how maps must lie to tell the truth). A 2 or 3 to 1 ratio between vertical and horizontal distance is common with large-scale block diagrams, while a 50 to 1 exaggeration is often used for mapping regions as large as a state. Regions of little relief are exaggerated more than regions of substantial relief. Since different degrees of **vertical exaggeration** can produce quite different relief impressions, you should make it a practice to check the legend of block diagrams to see if a vertical exaggeration factor has been indicated.

The three-dimensional character of block diagrams can be visually enhanced even further if these maps are presented as stereopairs (**Figure 5.12**). The stereopair is made up of two perspective views of the landform taken from slightly different vantage points. Thus, when viewed with a stereoscope as you would a photographic stereopair (see *Stereo Photos* earlier in this chapter), a single three-dimensional model is seen. If the two vantage points are carefully selected to best represent the surface form, the visual effects of such simple line drawings can be quite dramatic. Constructing these stereopairs with computers, using digital terrain data, is a routine matter. Thus,

A [0°]

B [45°]

C [90°]

5.11 Changing vertical viewing angles may drastically alter landform portrayal, as this sequence of 0°, 45°, and 90° angles demonstrates.

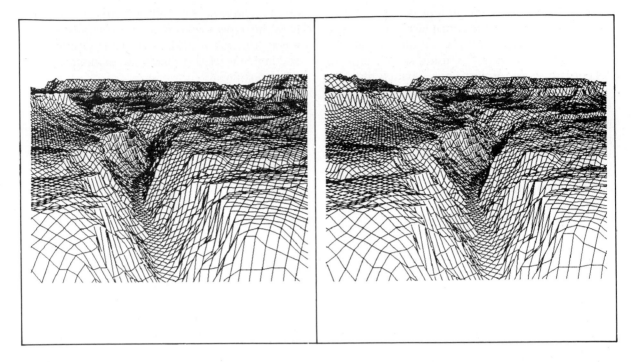

5.12 By using a stereopair of block diagrams with a stereoscope, we can greatly enhance the three-dimensional character of the surface.

we can expect this mapping method to grow in popularity.

Smooth Shading

A still more abstract way to show relative relief on maps is by using shading methods. With **shaded relief** techniques, also called **smooth** or **plastic shading**, cartographers rely on a shadow effect. They know that patterns of light and shade give us the strongest impression of relief in reality. Thus, they try to recreate that pattern on maps to give the same powerful three-dimensional effect.

One method is to shade the relief systematically as though a light were shining down onto the surface from directly above all points. No shadows are cast with this **vertical illumination** technique, but a shading effect is still created because a sloping surface covers more area than a horizontal one. As a result, the light is more widely dispersed (producing darker tones) on slopes than on horizontal ground (**Figure 5.13A**).

With vertical illumination, tone density is directly proportional to slope steepness, and all slopes of the same gradient have the same tone. Therefore, you can receive an impression of rela-tive steepness from one region to another simply by comparing the tonal values. Due to problems of visual differentiation, however, trying to distin-guish one tone from another is impractical in regions of low relative relief.

Another way to achieve plastic shading is to move the imaginary light source to a fixed posi-tion lying off the northwest corner of the map (**Figure 5.13B**). All slopes receive some shading with this simple **oblique illumination** tech-nique. The lightest shading occurs on northwest-facing slopes, which are approximately at right angles to the imaginary light rays. The darkest shadows are cast over southeast-facing slopes, with darker tones assigned to steeper slopes. Tonal value, then, is determined not only by slope steep-ness but also by terrain orientation with respect to the light source. Thus, slopes of the same steep-ness won't necessarily have the same tone. Be sure to keep this in mind, for if you try to pick up gra-dient cues merely by comparing tonal density, as you did with vertically illuminated maps, you may receive a mistaken relief impression.

There's another thing to remember when you use obliquely illuminated maps. Just as was

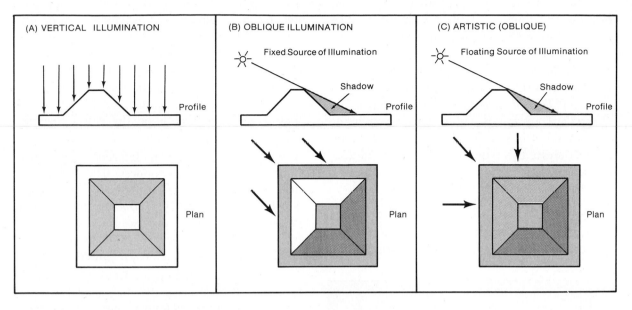

5.13 Continuous shading methods of relief portrayal vary in appearance, depending on the position(s) of the source of illumination. Here, vertical illumination (A), oblique illumination with a fixed light source (B), and oblique illumination with a variable light source (C) are demonstrated.

the case with aerial photos (see Figure 5.4), relief reversal will occur if you turn the map so that the imaginary shadows are cast away from you. An upside-down map will produce exactly the opposite effect from what was intended. Place names, of course, will usually provide an obvious clue to proper map orientation. Still, you should develop the habit of checking the map orientation before interpreting any shaded relief map.

Another drawback to simple oblique illumination from a fixed light source is more serious. Relief features oriented roughly parallel to the imaginary light rays (northwest to southeast) don't pick up enough shadow to give proper relief cues. To circumvent this problem of insufficient shadow, map makers often let the imaginary light source "float" around to the map's west and north sides so that terrain with north-south and east-west orientation also receives effective shading (**Figure 5.13C**). This use of a variable light source, known as **artistic shading**, is probably the best way of all to show relative relief on a single flat map (**Figure 5.14A**). The map may look as real as a picture of a physical relief model of the landform. But artistic shading should be treated with the same caution that was suggested for oblique illumination. In particular, relief reversal

can occur, and the shading density isn't directly proportional to slope steepness.

Until recently, relief shading was a laborious manual chore that required a great deal of artistic skill and a thorough understanding of geomorphology (the study of landforms and terrain forming processes). The expense involved in producing shaded relief maps by hand could rarely be justified. Thus, despite the dramatic visualization relief shading affords, for practical reasons not many such maps have been made. This situation is improving, however, since relief shading by computer is now feasible. As more and more terrain data become available in computer compatible form, we should see increased emphasis on shaded landform portrayal (**Figure 5.14B**). (See *Digital Elevation Models* later in this chapter.)

Perspective Profiles

The effect of a continuous, undulating surface can be produced with lines as well as with smooth shading. Several examples of a **perspective profile** method appeared earlier in the chapter. In Figure 5.11, for example, parallel terrain profiles (see *Profiles* in Chapter 17) are drawn diagonally across the terrain surface. In contrast, the maps in Figure 5.12 exhibit profiles drawn across the land-

112

form at right angles to each other. This second example is sometimes called a **fishnet map**, because it resembles a net draped over the distribution of highs and lows.

More profiles produce a smoother surface. But they also require a finer-mesh grid of terrain data (see *Digital Elevation Models* later in this chapter). They are also more time-consuming to construct. But now that computers are routinely used to create this type of map, they are increasing in popularity.

Hachures

On large-scale maps, the landform is sometimes rendered with tiny, short lines called **hachures**,

arranged so that they face downhill. Each hachure line lies in the direction of the steepest slope, giving a realistic impression of landform shape.

Hachure maps can also show the degree of slope with some accuracy. They do so in two ways:

1. When hachures are all the same width, steepness is shown by the number or density of the lines. The steeper the slope, the closer together the hachures (**Figure 5.15A**).

2. When hachures are of different thicknesses, their width indicates steepness. The greater the degree of slope, the wider the hachures (**Figure 5.15B**). This is called the *Lehmann system*, after its founder. Although precise, the technique is tedious to execute, obscures other map features, and isn't commonly used in the United States.

Whichever method was used, it is up to you to decide how precise the map maker was. At times, the hachure technique has been so rigorously applied that you can derive numerical slope values by comparing a zone of uniform slope with the map legend. (This procedure is explained under the heading *Gradient* in Chapter 16.) More commonly, only an impression of steepness was intended.

Stylized Drawings

The stylized drawing is one of the oldest relief methods. Yet, even today, it is a remarkably effective way to show relief, particularly on medium-scale to small-scale maps. It is commonly found on recreational, advertising, and similar maps designed for the general public, where only a general impression of landform character is needed.

Stylized drawings take several forms. Some are simply *profile* or *oblique* pictures of hills and mountains. These may be highly abstract representations that bear no natural resemblance to the form of the features symbolized (**Figure 5.16A**). Or they may be realistic portrayals that capture the features' natural shape (**Figure 5.16B**). When natural symbolism is used to show rocky crags and cliffs, the term **rock drawing** is often applied (**Figure 5.16C**).

Profile drawings and oblique views have strong intuitive appeal and a high level of readability. This accounts for their popularity on everyday maps. But there is a problem. On these maps, you can't place features at their true loca-

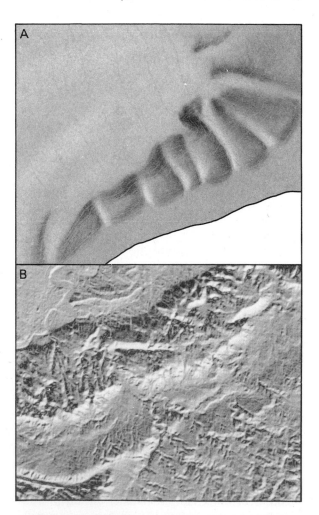

5.14 The use of artistic (or plastic) shading to create the impression of a continuous landform surface (A) can be approximated with elaborate computer-shading methods (B).

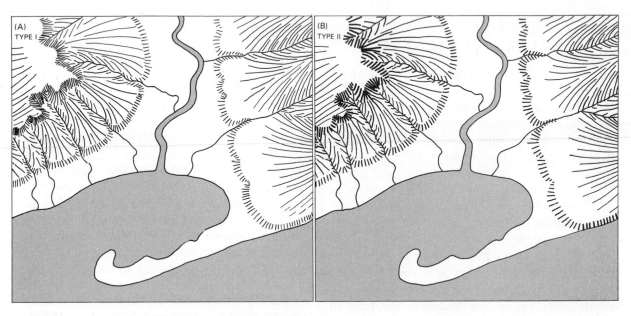

5.15 With the hachure method, relief can be portrayed by varying the density of constant-width lines (A) or by varying the width of the lines themselves (B).

tion. Positional displacement of a relief feature occurs in direct proportion to the height of its symbol. The true map position can be located for

(A) PROFILES

Abstract

(B) OBLIQUE VIEW

Pictorial

(C) ROCK DRAWINGS

(D) PLAN VIEW

"Wooly Worm"
Mountain Range

Cliff

5.16 Stylized drawings of landform features are common on maps designed for general public use. Here we see figures in profile (A), in oblique view (B), as rock drawings (C), and in plan view (D).

the top, bottom, or middle of the feature—but not all three at once.

This problem can be solved by using *planimetric* forms of stylized drawings. Although they aren't as intuitively appealing as profiles, such drawings possess the advantage that relief is symbolized in correct planimetry. The top of a hill or mountain is located on the map at its true horizontal position. The most common example of this type of stylized drawing is the "caterpillar" or "wooly worm." It is most suitably named, as you can see from the illustration in **Figure 5.16D**.

Combined Relative Relief Methods

Mappers often combine different relief methods. They may, for example, supplement hachures with vertical or oblique shading. Or they may add hachures or shading to physical models or block diagrams. Such combinations enhance the map's overall three-dimensional impact.

Yet each of these hybrid representations still gives only an impression of relative relief. If you need to know the actual height of the landform, maps using relative relief methods won't suffice. You'll want another kind of topographic map, one that uses **absolute relief** procedures.

114

ABSOLUTE RELIEF METHODS

Maps showing relative relief become inadequate when it is necessary to deal with terrain detail in analytical terms. Engineers, scientists, surveyors, and other map users who work analytically with the land surface require more than an impression of relative relief. Absolute relief methods provide the metric elevation information they need.

When the relative "up-down" concept of relief isn't sufficient, it is possible to give the vertical position of different points on the earth's surface a precise numerical interpretation. The simplest way to do this is to treat one of the points (usually the lower) as a base (or zero) value. Since by so doing we have arbitrarily created an interval scale (see *Measurement Level* in Chapter 2), we can then simply measure the vertical separation between the two points. In **Figure 5.17A**, for instance, we can see that the highest point is 4,000 feet above the left valley floor and 6,000 feet above the right valley floor. One valley is 2,000 feet higher in elevation than the other.

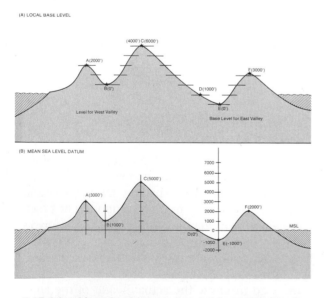

5.17 A local base level (A) can be used to specify the elevation of the landform surface, but a universal datum such as mean sea level (B) is preferred, because it facilitates regional comparisons.

Such an arbitrary system of elevation measurement may serve local needs perfectly well. But it is of limited value in making regional comparisons between different hills and valleys. Nor is it of any value in revealing information about atmospheric pressure and temperature gradients associated with elevation above sea level. To avoid the problems of establishing an arbitrary zero elevation level for each map, people making topographic maps have agreed to use one of several **tidal surfaces of reference**. These 0-elevation base levels from which elevations any place in the world can be measured are called **datums**.

The most useful of the tidal reference datums is **mean sea level** (**MSL**), which is the average of all recorded sea levels over a 19-year period (see *Ground Survey* in Chapter 2). This average ocean surface is theoretically extended under or through the continental land masses around the globe (**Figure 5.17B**). Thus, the elevation of any spot on earth can be given with reference to this world-wide datum.

The advantage of using MSL as a datum is that atmospheric pressure, which is easy to measure, can be used as a substitute for measuring elevation itself. This trait is what makes the **altimeter** of a car or plane so useful. The altimeter actually measures atmospheric pressure and then converts it to elevation by comparing it to the atmospheric pressure at mean sea level. It may not matter much in a car, but in a plane it's vital to remember that the altimeter measures elevation above mean sea level, not ground level. An altimeter may show that a plane is at 5,000 feet, but this doesn't mean that a mountain may not loom in its path.

Mean sea level provides the base for most topographic maps. You shouldn't assume, however, that elevation values on a given map were determined with reference to MSL. You may encounter other datums, especially on maps giving "negative" elevations of depth reading. These datums include the arithmetic average of all the low water levels recorded over a 19-year period, called **mean low water** (**MLW**), and the arithmetic average of the height of all the lower low water levels recorded over a 19-year period, called **mean lower low water** (**MLLW**). MLW is used on hydrographic charts of the Atlantic and Gulf coasts, while MLLW is used on hydrographic charts of the Pacific coast of the United States.

We tolerate the possible confusion of using these different low water datums on nautical charts because we're sympathetic to the special problems of ship captains. They are given the job of moving a three-dimensional craft along a horizontal path through a three-dimensional environment, while their path's elevation changes constantly with tidal fluctuations. This means, for one thing, that ship captains need to decide whether there's enough clearance for their vessels between the changing water surface and a fixed submerged obstacle, such as the harbor bottom or a wreck. To do so, they must determine the minimum depth likely to be encountered at a given position. If overhead clearance is the concern, as when moving under a fixed bridge, the situation is reversed and a maximum high water datum would be most useful. The best map would give both maximum and minimum figures or provide tidal range information as a map annotation.

Since different datums are used as bases from which to measure absolute relief, elevation values are a form of interval measurement (see *Measurement Level*, Chapter 2). In theory, this means that they have no direct magnitude interpretation: The elevation of the same spot can be given varying figures, depending on which datum is used. On a single topographic map of a coastal region, you might find that depth (bathymetric) values are based on a low water datum, the shoreline is based on a high water datum, and the height of the dry land surface is based on MSL.

If the differences among these three datums aren't given on the map (they often aren't), you'll be unable to determine the absolute vertical separation between a position on the harbor bottom and the top of a nearby hill. Fortunately, however, most topographic maps use only MSL. For practical purposes, therefore, the fact that elevation values are a type of interval measurement may never be a matter of concern.

Physical Models

Physical models are the only maps that show the actual height of the landform above some datum for all map locations. Yet models are rarely used to give elevation information, because it is so hard to obtain an elevation figure for a particular point on the surface.

It is theoretically possible to make a physical model that would yield absolute relief information, say by probing through the surface to a base level and then reading the height off the graduated probe. Elevations along a line could likewise be obtained by cutting the model in cross-section. But neither procedure is common because of its impracticality. There are better ways to provide the map user with precise topographic detail, as we'll see in the following sections.

Digital Terrain Data

The terrain representations we've discussed so far all hide actual elevation values behind a mask of graphic rendering. Now we'll look at two methods that keep the numbers visible—spot heights and digital elevation models.

Spot Heights

On some maps, the elevation of the surface is given numerically at a scatter of points. These selected elevation values are called **spot heights**. At some locations, the elevation has been determined by precise surveying methods, and a permanently fixed brass plate, called a **bench mark**,

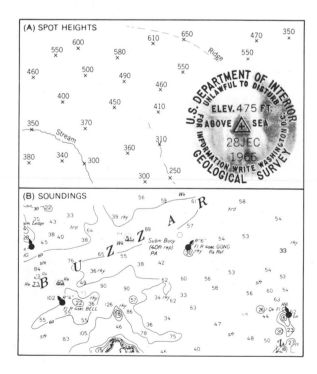

5.18 Elevation may be shown at specific locations on a map using spot heights (A) or soundings (B).

has been installed on the ground. Bench marks are symbolized on USGS topographic quadrangles by a small cross next to the elevation figure (**Figure 5.18A**). On some maps, the identifier "BM" (for "bench mark) precedes the number. Spot heights may also be used on hydrographic charts. Here they refer to depth readings and are called **soundings** (**Figure 5.18B**).

Spot heights of either form are, as their name forewarns, a spotty way of giving topographic information. You're faced with a point sample of elevation readings from which you must conjure up an impression of continuous topographic detail. Your ability to do so depends on how well the scatter of sample elevation values captures the land surface's essential features. You can usually reconstruct a relatively simple terrain surface from almost any small sample. But a more complex surface will generally require a large, well placed sample. Ask yourself this: Does the sample let you detect significant changes in relief, or might it conceal important landform fea-

tures? You must weigh the consequences of making errors in predicting elevation values from spot heights and proceed accordingly.

Digital Elevation Models (DEMs)

When the elevation sampling is taken on a regular grid, the result is called a **DEM** (**digital elevation model**). Although DEMs, such as the one in **Figure 5.19**, may not look very impressive, they are tremendously important in modern mapping and map use. The reason is that it is convenient for computers to work with a matrix of digital terrain data, just as it is convenient for computers to work with a regular grid of image pixels (see *Image Enhancements* in Chapter 4).

A number of government and private organizations are involved in creating matrices of numerical elevation values. The most ambitious project is a spinoff of the digital orthophoto quadrangle program (see *Geometrical Corrections* in Chapter 4). In this project, the USGS and cooperators are rapidly completing DEM coverage of the country at a spatial resolution of roughly one meter in latitude and longitude. The USGS is also well along in sampling the terrain surface portrayed on its 1:24,000 topographic quadrangles at an interval of 30 meters in latitude and longitude. DEMS for the entire United States with a spatial resolution of three arc seconds (latitude and longitude) and taken from 1/250,000-scale topographic quadrangles have been available for some time. Much of the rest of the "developed" world has also been completed, although the base maps used tend to be of even smaller scales.

A DEM isn't a geographical map in the sense we are using the term in this book. Indeed, military personnel fondly call DEMs "digital dirt." Strictly speaking, a DEM is a digital database of ele-

```
                ⟶ Columns ⟶

   10760 10460 10180 10040 10580 10560

   10560 10480 10160 10230 10640 10650

   10480 10310 10280 10540 10800 10680

   10540 10350 10270 10560 10990 11310

 R 11080 11000 10990 10670 10730 11020
 o
 w 11680 12320 11360 12100 11280 11700
 s
   12350 12650 12430 12570 12280 11900

   12080 12250 11800 11560 11080 11520

   12060 12140 11640 11590 11150 10980

   11040 11880 11680 11280 11360 10920
                    ⬉
                    Elevation Value
```

5.19 Digital elevation models (DEMs) provide the foundation for electronic mapping and map analysis.

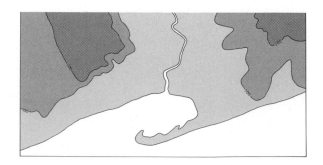

5.20 A contour map based on a 20-foot contour interval.

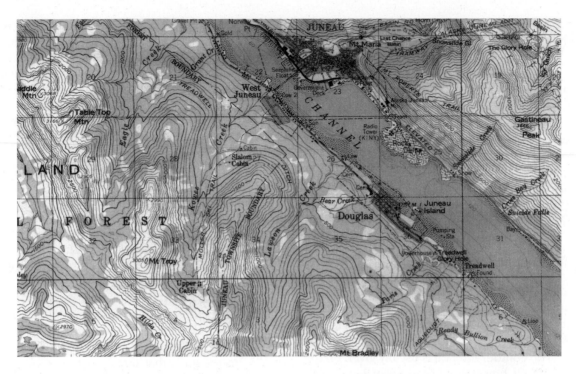

5.21 A USGS 1:24,000 topographic quadrangle shows a variety of physical and cultural features in addition to contour information, making it an excellent general reference map.

vation values. Thus, it's better to think of a DEM as a **cartographic product**, rather than as a map. From this perspective, DEMs serve the same role as other forms of digital cartographic data, such as those generated by electronic scanners and digitizers. The computer-executed landform maps in this book used these digital elevation databases.

Contour Lines

To make digital information truly useful, we need to portray it in graphic form. This is the logic behind the **contour map**. It is a pattern of lines, with each line drawn through points of equal elevation (**Figure 5.20**). If these lines were actually drawn on the earth, they would follow the contour of the landform. Thus, they are called **contour lines** if they are drawn above sea level. If drawn below sea level, they are known as **bathymetric contours**, or **isobaths**. Many countries have a special series of topographic maps that show the landform with contours. The portion of a USGS topographic quadrangle in **Figure 5.21** is representative of this type of map.* Isobaths, on the other hand, are most likely to be found on special nautical charts.

To gain an idea of the logic behind contour lines, imagine that you are on a small sandy island in the ocean. If you walked around the island at the shoreline when the tide was at mean sea level, you would trace out the 0-level or datum contour. By using the water's edge as a guide, you would neither gain nor lose altitude; thus, you would return precisely to your starting point. This is important to remember, since all contour paths eventually rejoin themselves, although the closed curve won't always be fully depicted on a single map sheet.

Now suppose that you climb the side of the island until you reach an elevation of 100 feet above mean sea level (assume this is the current ocean surface). If you again follow the contour around the island, all points on your path will be

Government topographic map series usually show the same region at a number of scales. The U.S. Geological Survey, for example, publishes topographic quadrangles at scales of 1:24,000, 1:62,500 (now inactive), 1:00,000, and 1:250,000. They also publish topographic maps at other scales, such as state maps at 1:500,000.

of the same elevation, and again you will return to your starting point. The effect is the same as if you had walked along the shoreline after the ocean surface was raised 100 feet. If you did the same thing for elevations of 200 feet, 300 feet, and so forth, and the paths you walked were projected vertically onto a flat map, the result would be something like **Figure 5.22**. If the island were viewed in profile, it would look as though it had been sliced into layers by imaginary horizontal planes. (The procedure used to create a profile from a contour map is explained under *Profiles* in Chapter 17.)

In our island example, the vertical distance between contours, called the **contour interval**, was 100 feet. The map maker, of course, may select a contour interval of 20 feet, 50 feet, or whatever seems appropriate. The smaller the interval used, the more detailed the landform portrayal will be.

The contour interval is usually given on the map; if it isn't, however, you can easily figure it out for yourself by comparing the numbers on the contour lines. Once you know the interval, it's a simple matter to "read between the lines." If the spot in which you're interested lies halfway between the 1,000-foot and 1,200-foot contours, you can conclude that it's around 1,100 feet high.

Also note that the interval in our island example was constant; each contour line was the same vertical distance from the next. Map makers usually use a constant interval, but not always. They could use any of the methods for choosing intervals which we discussed in *Classification* in Chapter 3. They might, for instance, use an irregular interval to accentuate natural breaks in the terrain.

The configuration of contours on a map depends mainly on the nature of the terrain. When contour lines are close together, they show a steep slope; when they are far apart, the slope is gentle. Notice in Figure 5.22, for example, how much closer the contour lines are on the left (sharply sloped) than on the right (moderately sloped) side of the island.

It's not quite that simple, however. Whether a particular relief feature is outlined by the contour lines depends on three additional factors: the position of the datum, the method used to select the interval between contours, and the size of the interval. Various interactions between these variables can produce contour configurations with much different detail. All the examples in **Figure 5.23** show the same island as Figure 5.22, but by altering the three crucial variables we've greatly changed the look of the contour pattern.

The land itself hasn't changed, of course; only the impression you'll receive of it has. The bump on the side of the ridge in Figure 5.23 is obvious from the third and fourth contour pictures but unseen on the first two because it fell "between the contours." The only difference is that on the third map the contours were begun at a different datum and on the fourth map a variable contour interval was used. The same thing can occur if we change the size of the contour interval slightly; small hills or valleys may appear as if out of nowhere. Such small irregularities may seem insignificant, but if you are using contour maps in the field, it's the little things that count. If a 10-foot cliff, invisible on your map, suddenly rises ahead, you may wish you had checked a map with a different contour interval.

All of which returns us to our same caution: Just because something isn't on the map

5.22 The logic of the contour method of landform portrayal is illustrated here by converting the contour intersections with a straight transect (top) into a profile (bottom).

MSL Datum

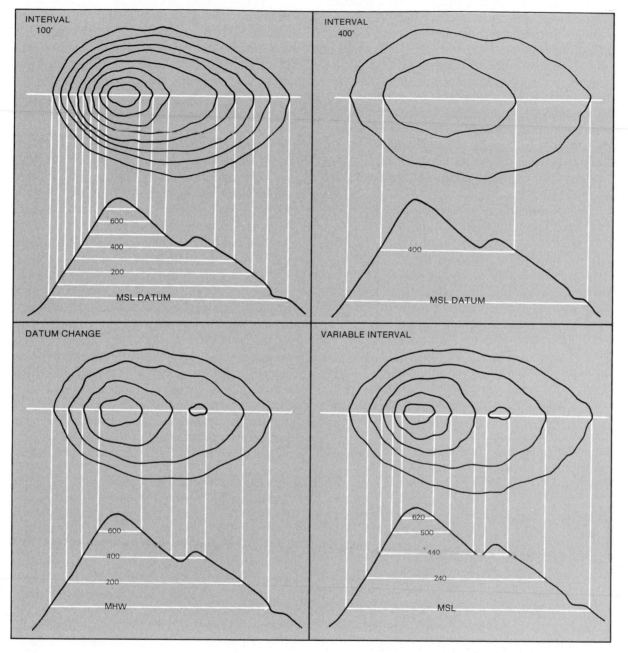

5.23 The appearance of a contour map is readily altered by changing contour parameters, such as the interval and the datum.

doesn't mean it's not on the ground. The reverse is equally true. Just because something shows up in the contour lines doesn't mean that there is anything especially meaningful about it. There's nothing sacred about a particular contour configuration; it merely reflects what a certain sample of the terrain surface looks like.

On most contour maps, an MSL datum and a constant interval are used, regardless of the nature of the terrain. You are usually safe in treating these factors as constants. This leaves only the size of the interval as a variable factor. In general, you will find that the greater the relative relief on a map, the larger the contour interval. Map mak-

120

ers have had to establish this functional relationship between relief and contour interval to keep contour lines from becoming too dense in areas of high relief and too sparse in areas of low relief.

Variable contour line density is desirable, of course, because it provides important information about changing terrain slope. But there can be too much of a good thing. Closely spaced contour lines clutter the map and become difficult to differentiate. In contrast, widely spaced contour lines make it hard to determine the trend of the landform and to predict elevation at points falling between contours.

Vast differences in elevation and steepness of the terrain on the same map call for clever use of a variable contour interval to control the density of contour lines. Sad to say, many map makers, especially those relying on automated computer methods, don't take this extra care in executing their craft. Consequently, their maps exhibit contour line densities ranging from good to poor.

There are other problems with the use of contour maps. Contours are **line samples** of the landform and, like all samples, should be unbiased. Here again, however, map makers don't always treat contours as samples. Instead, they may merely decide on a contour interval and map the result. As a consequence, contour lines often aren't selected carefully enough to provide an unbiased terrain picture.

Furthermore, because of the vast scale reduction in mapping, all contour lines are simplified, their form smoothed. How much smoothing is done depends on the degree of generalization used to produce the map. The discrepancy between the real-world contour and the map contour line will become greater as the complexity of the landform increases and as map scale decreases.

A special problem arises when the landform configuration changes markedly from one part of the map to another. When this occurs, it is quite possible that several different but constant intervals may have been used on the same map. This might happen, for example, with map sheets spanning high to low relief, as is the case along the Rocky Mountain front in the Denver area.

Of all the things you can learn about contour lines, one of the most useful is the simple fact that they point upstream when they cross a valley or river (**Figure 5.24**). Keeping this fact in mind, you can quickly get a feel for the lay of the drainage pattern and background landform. When it comes to landform details, the angle at which contours cross streams or valley bottoms is also revealing. A sharp, acute angle means a narrow valley with cut-in watercourse, while a crossing near 90 degrees indicates a stream close to the surrounding ground level in a relatively broad valley.

Special Contours

Several modifications of standard contours are used to portray special aspects of the land surface and to simplify map reading. To aid in identifying closed depressions or basin-like features, for instance, hachures may be added to the downslope (or inside) of contour lines (**Figure 5.25A**). These **depression** or **hachured contours** help to focus the map user's attention when the depression is small relative to the size of the map sheet. Hachured contours are especially useful in distinguishing between small hills and depressions, since there is seldom enough space for the map maker to label the contours of these features with their elevation values.

When depression contours are used, they are sometimes labeled, sometimes not. In either case, note that the first (outside) depression contour is always of the same elevation as the adjacent standard contour. Moreover, depression contours merely represent special cases of the

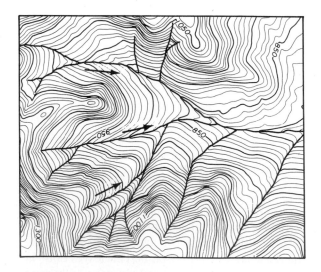

5.24 Knowing that contour lines bend upstream is very helpful when trying to visualize the character of the landform.

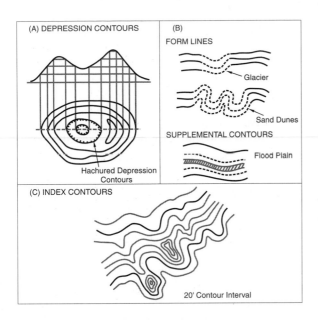

5.25 Depression contours (A), form lines (B), and index contours (C) are used to portray special landform features and to make the map easier to analyze.

standard contour lines on the map and thus share the same interval and elevation values.

Sometimes you will come across dashed segments of standard contours or will find dashed lines falling between the standard contour lines. These line segments are called **form lines**. They are used to indicate the approximate location of contours where the information isn't reliable, as might be the case in extending standard contour lines across a glacial or sand dune surface (**Figure 5.25B**).

Form lines may also provide important topographic detail that otherwise wouldn't be shown by the standard contour lines. These **supplemental contour lines** are often used in floodplain areas where a slight change in relief might have a major impact on the stream channel and flooding pattern. Although form lines can contribute valuable information, they should be viewed with caution. They are arranged to give a general impression of topology, not precise elevation figures.

On most maps, you'll find that not every contour line is marked with its elevation value; instead, every fourth, fifth, or tenth line is labeled. The labeled or **index contours** are usually bolder than the others (**Figure 5.25C**). While these eye-catching contour lines facilitate rapid map reading, they may also cause problems. Many map readers skip over the less conspicuous contour lines and look only at the index contours. Their impression of the terrain may suffer greatly—and needlessly, for they are ignoring much good information which is right in front of them. The resulting detail loss is the same as if the size of the contour interval were increased by a large factor.

5.26 When contour map stereopairs are viewed stereoscopically, dramatic relief effects can be achieved.

122

Stereo Models

We can visualize the landform even more clearly by using **contour map stereopairs** (**Figure 5.26**). The stereovision mechanism is the same as that used to view photographic stereopairs (see *Stereo Photos* earlier in this chapter). In this case, we use central perspective contour maps of the terrain surface from two vantage points. When we view these two graphics with a stereoscope, the eye-brain system merges them into a single three-dimensional model of the landform.

A special form of stereo model may be produced by printing a stereopair of contour maps in different colors and then superimposing one upon the other. The resulting contour map, with patterns of overlapping blue-green and red contour lines, is favored by geologists. It is called an **anaglyph**. By viewing the anaglyph with special glasses equipped with red and blue-green lenses, we see the landform in stereovision.*

Although contour map stereopairs and anaglyphs are effective, they are also somewhat impractical. They cost more to produce and require more viewing effort than standard contour maps. And because the relief impression is created in the brain, not on a sheet of paper, the image is ephemeral and not subject to analytical map use procedures. Despite these drawbacks, however, anaglyphs are used extensively in certain earth sciences, such as geology. They are also destined to become more common in the future, since they are easily constructed by computer.

Enhanced Contour Lines

Reading naked contour lines challenges even the most skilled map users. The reason is that it can be difficult to visualize the terrain when relative relief cues are lacking. To remedy this problem, yet maintain the metric character of the landform portrayal, some form of contour line enhancement is common. Two techniques are discussed here—shaded contours and shadowed contours.

Anaglyphs are sometimes created using photo stereopairs overprinted in green and red ink. They are used in the same way as contour anaglyphs but have the advantage that they provide a more realistic (continuous) tonal surface representation in the minds of their users.

Shaded Contours

Shaded contour maps have a tiered effect, much like a layer cake. On these maps, the landform has been broken up by contour lines into different elevation zones (such as low, medium, and high), and each zone has been given a distinct gray tone or color, called a **hypsometric** or **layer tint**.

When gray tones are used, the usual rule is: The darker the tone, the higher the elevation (**Figure 5.27**). If the non-linearity of human vision was taken into consideration when designing the map, you will receive a "stepped" relief impression equivalent to the value of the class intervals. But layer tints aren't always properly chosen by the map maker, nor do darker tones always signify higher elevations. Thus, it's especially important to check the legend before using these maps.

If color is used, layer tints of a single hue but of different intensities may have been assigned to the elevation zones. The effect is the same as that achieved with gray tones. Higher intensities usually signify higher elevations, but there are exceptions. Again, you should routinely consult the map legend.

Sometimes layer tints of different hues are assigned to different elevation zones. This technique is called a **spectral scheme**. It is frequently used in making wall maps for schools. The highest elevation zone is usually shown in dark brown or red, the intermediate zones in buff and light brown, and the lowest zone in dark green. Water is blue.

The spectral scheme introduces special problems, since it is based on the psychological

5.27 The hypsometric (or layer tint) method of portraying relief creates the impression of a stepped surface.

notion that some colors such as blue are "cold" and visually fall away from you, while others such as red are "warm" and visually rise toward you. Although this "warm-cold" scheme is widely used, its effectiveness hasn't been satisfactorily proven. When you come across spectral layer tints, then, you should proceed with caution.

You should also be wary of black-and-white copies of maps, since the original may have possessed spectral schemes of layer tinting. A xerographic copy, for example, will probably bear no tonal relation to the original map. If you assume that tone increases with elevation, such a copy will give you a warped idea of relief.

When map makers use layer tints, they are really just using selected contour lines to divide the landscape into elevation classes. As we saw under *Classification* in Chapter 3, all borders between classes are artificial to some degree. The same is true for elevation zone boundaries created by contour lines. While layer tints show a sharp change from one elevation to another, no such abrupt difference exists in reality. You will rarely come across a hill like the one in Figure 5.2A—except on a map. Yet layer tints are likely to leave you with just such an impression of the environment.

The boundary problem can be minimized by gradually merging one tint into the next along the contour lines, rather than making distinct divisions between colors or tones. The technique, called **feathering** or **vignetting** is readily achieved using computer methods, and the result is more realistic. Boundary problems, of course, can never be completely eliminated. As always, you should view every border line with some skepticism.

Because of their unrealistic contour-line boundaries, stepped shading maps give only a simplistic picture of relief. Consequently, this method is reserved primarily for small-scale maps and maps created for special purposes. Large-scale maps, in contrast, are usually shaded continuously, giving a more true-to-life impression of the terrain (see *Smooth Shading* earlier in this chapter).

Shadowed Contours

Between-contour shading isn't the only way map makers give contour-map users a sense of relative relief. Another method, involving **shadowed contours**, is also effective, especially on smaller-

scale maps (**Figure 5.28**). This technique takes advantage of the same shadow phenomenon we mentioned when discussing relief reversal (see Figure 5.4) and smooth shading (see Figure 5.13). There, we learned that a relief effect occurs if shadows fall toward the viewer's lower right from terrain features.

By making contour lines on the lower-right side of terrain features (as you view the map) heavier than those on the upper-left side of these features, map makers create a shadow effect. This results in the impression that the contour lines are stacked, layer upon layer. The effect is similar to the discrete terrain model you saw in Figure 5.2A. Since shadowed contour lines are easy to produce with the aid of computers and digital terrain data, maps employing them are becoming more common.

Combined Absolute Relief Methods

There is only a remote chance that the summit of a hill will coincide exactly with a contour line. Therefore, when you play the guessing game of "reading between the contours," you can seldom give precise elevation values to hilltops and valley

5.28 By making contour lines on the lower-right side of terrain features heavier than those on the upper-left side, an impression of shadowing occurs, creating a relief effect.

124

bottoms. To help you out, map makers frequently combine spot height and contour methods of showing elevation. Spot heights, giving the exact elevation of the tops of hills and bottoms of depressions, are interspersed between contour lines. The result is a truly useful picture of absolute relief.

COMPOSITE RELIEF METHODS

But the best overall image of essential landform features isn't gained by either relative or absolute methods alone. It is achieved when highly informative (but comparatively hard to read) absolute relief methods are combined with the strong visual effect of relative relief symbolism. We then have the "real" look of the land surface and the precision of elevation information as well. The same end can be achieved with the help of computers and computer-driven graphics devices which permit user interaction with an electronically displayed map. Three landform mapping procedures fall into the category of composite relief methods: superimposed representations, dual representations, and active representations.

Superimposed Representations

By far the most common type of composite relief map is made merely by superimposing one type of map symbolism onto another. Some of the many possible combinations are block diagrams with contour lines, hachures with contour lines, colored layer tints with shading, and contour lines with shading (**Figure 5.29**).

You will note that many of the landform portrayals in this chapter show a naked, bald terrain, denuded of land cover features. With the aid of computers, this problem has recently been overcome. It is now common to use aerial photography or satellite imagery draped over a digital elevation model (**Figure 5.30**). This electronic enhancement of the landform with land cover information can be very effective. Furthermore, since all data are in digital form, we can view the terrain from any number of different vantage points (see *Dynamic Relief Methods* later in this chapter).

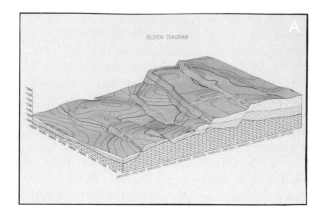

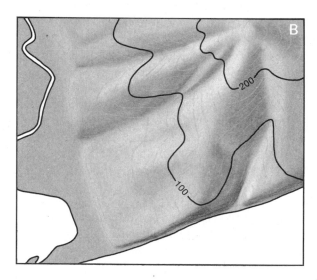

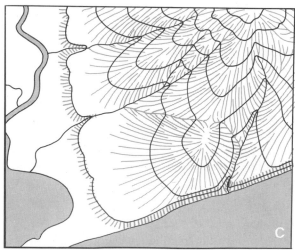

5.29 Composite relative-absolute relief portrayal methods provide the best view of the landform, because visualization is combined with metric information.

5.30 A realistic three-dimensional view of the landform is created by draping an image showing land cover over a digital elevation model.

There can be problems when trying to use maps consisting of superimposed representations. For instance, one graphic method may visually obscure the other. This explains why the rather open contour method is usually used as one of the two techniques which are superimposed. Furthermore, the combined effect of the two graphic methods may so clutter the map that very little additional information can be portrayed. Finally, in the case of oblique (pseudo) three-dimensional portrayals, parts of the surface may be blocked from view.

Dual Representations

One way to get around the problems associated with superimposed representations is to portray the landscape in dual form, using two different mapping techniques. Commonly, a contour map is "floated" in spatial registry over or under a pseudo three-dimensional surface portrayal, and both are viewed obliquely (**Figure 5.31**). By looking back and forth from one representation to the other, we have the best of both worlds (absolute and relative relief information). However, since both representations are necessarily oblique, scale-related questions can be difficult to answer precisely. A separate planimetrically true map may be needed for this purpose.

Active Representations

If you are fortunate enough to have access to appropriate computer mapping systems, compos-

126

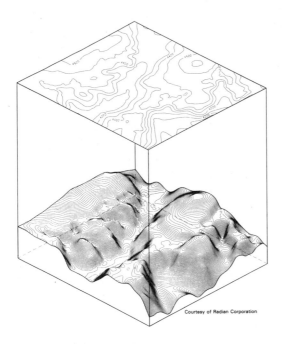

Courtesy of Radian Corporation

5.31 This vertical layering of fishnet and isoline depiction provides more information than either alone.

5.32 When a map displayed on an electronic screen is asked about elevation at a point, the computer can query the database used to make the map to receive the answer.

ite relief methods can assume an active character (**Figure 5.32**). The action takes place in a series of steps. First, terrain data are displayed on an electronic screen using a relative relief technique, such as continuous shading. Second, you "point" at the location whose elevation you are seeking. The pointing may be done by touching a touch-sensitive screen or by aiming some electronic device designed for that purpose.

Next, you "ask the map" what the elevation is at the indicated point or what a terrain profile is like along a given path. You may do so through a keyboard, by verbal query, or by pointing to an electronic menu of questions displayed on the side of the screen. Finally, the computer will note the location or path you indicated, search through the elevation data records used to make the map, perform the necessary computations, and provide you with the requested elevation data or profile.

With these "point and ask" portrayals, the map merely provides a graphic version of the landform, and you direct analytical questions to the underlying digital terrain data. In other words, the map serves as a window on the data. By not burdening the map with the need to portray absolute relief information, the quality of visual-

ization can be improved. At the same time, elevation values can be determined with greater precision than would be possible with a graphic portrayal alone. (Also see Chapter 19: *GIS and Map Analysis Software.*)

DYNAMIC RELIEF METHODS

Electronic technology has made it possible to put landform representation into motion. If landform portrayals from a sequence of vantage points are animated, we get the impression that we are flying and the terrain is passing by under and around us. The visualization of space and movement can be so realistic that we may actually feel pangs of airsickness! This **fly-over** effect occurs because our minds find it easier to accept our bodies moving than the terrain moving.

Animated Methods

The age of cinema introduced us to the potential of animated mapping. By viewing a motion picture taken by flying a camera over and around a region, we can gain a dramatic, dynamic impression of the landform. The effect is similar to that achieved by viewing a physical model. In both cases, we have the advantage of being able to change vantage points and, therefore, change perspectives (although in the cinema version the sequence of movement is preprogrammed). In fact, animated landform maps are commonly made by rotating a movie camera over and around a physical model of the terrain rather than the landform itself. Simulators to train pilots and astronauts, for example, have used this dynamic mapping method. (See *Simulation* in Chapter 8.)

Inexpensive video (television) cameras have brought new life to animated mapping in recent years. (See *Animation* in Chapter 8.) But the most important advance came with the advent of high-speed, digital computers and their associated video display terminals. With the aid of computers and sufficient numerical data representing the terrain, there is no longer a need to photograph or videotape a physical model or the terrain surface itself. Instead, the images can be created from the digital database through a series of calculations which take into consideration the vantage point of the observer, the orientation of the surface, and the nature of some source of illumination. The images are then displayed on a video screen and may be recorded electronically in video mode for subsequent playback.

Interactive Methods

Interactive maps take animated methods one step further. While animation takes you over the terrain on the path chosen by the animator, interactive relief maps put you in control. You can call up any image onto the screen, in any sequence. If you operate the controls, you can simulate movement realistically from one vantage point to any other. You control the fly-over path. You might start up high to get the overall view, then fly in closer to get a better look at features of special interest. You can view the terrain from as many heights and directions as needed to get a feel for the nature of the landform. You get the sensation of flying over a static terrain, but of course it's the changing view of the terrain that is creating that effect.

CONCLUSION

Clearly, a wide variety of cartographic methods may be used to portray the landform. Since each

has weaknesses as well as strengths, none is best suited to serve all map user needs. As always, the "best" map will depend on your purpose.

Although the tangible terrain surface was the subject of mapping in this chapter, the methods used in landform portrayal are general ones which can be used to map all sorts of other tangible and intangible phenomena. Our discussion of the nature of cartographic techniques in this chapter is equally applicable to these other mappings. In the chapters to come, we'll be working with these mapping techniques in a variety of map analysis and interpretation contexts.

SELECTED READINGS

Baldock, E.D., "Cartographic Relief Portrayal," *International Yearbook of Cartography*, 11 (1971), pp. 75-78.

Barry, M., *Wisconsin Topographic Mapping*, Guide 1 (Madison, WI: Wisconsin State Cartographer's Office, 1992).

Castner, H.W., and Wheate, R., "Reassessing the Role Played by Shaded Relief Methods in Topographic Scale Maps," *The Cartographic Journal*, 16 (1979), pp. 77-85.

Crawford, P.V., and Marks, R.A., "The Visual Effects of Geometric Relationships on Three-Dimensional Maps," *The Professional Geographer*, 25, 3 (August 1973), pp. 223-238.

Curran, J.P., "Cartographic Relief Portrayal," *The Cartographer*, 4, 1 (June 1967), pp. 28-38.

Grotch, S.L., "Three-Dimensional and Stereoscopic Graphics for Scientific Data Display and Analysis," *IEEE Computer Graphics and Applications*, 3, 11 (1983), pp. 31-43.

Imhof, E., *Cartographic Relief Representation*. Translated and edited by H.J. Steward (New York: Walter de Gruyter, 1982).

Irwin, D., "The Historical Development of Terrain Representation in American Cartography," *International Yearbook of Cartography*, 16 (1976), pp. 70-83.

Jeffery, T., "Mimicking Mountains," *Byte* (December 1987), pp. 337-344.

Jenks, G.F., et al., "Illustrating the Concepts of the Contour Symbol, Interval, and Spacing Via 3-D Maps," *Journal of Geography*, 70, 5 (May 1971), pp. 280-288.

Kumler, M.P., *An Intensive Comparison of Triangulated Irregular Networks (TINs) and Digital Elevation Models (DEMs)* (Toronto: University of Toronto Press, Inc., 1995).

Lobeck, A.K., *Block Diagrams and Other Graphic Methods Used in Geology and Geography*, 2nd ed. (Amherst, MA: Emerson-Trussel Book Co., 1958).

Miller, V.C., and Westerback, M.E., *Interpretation of Topographic Maps* (Columbus, OH: Merrill Publishing Co., 1989).

Mitchell, C.W., *Terrain Evaluation*, 2nd ed. (New York: Longman, 1991).

Petrie, G., and Kennie, T.J.M., eds., *Terrain Modelling in Surveying and Civil Engineering* (New York: McGraw-Hill, Inc., 1991).

Robinson, A.H., et al., "Portraying the Land-Surface Form" in *Elements of Cartography*, 6th ed. (New York: John Wiley &

128

Sons, 1995), pp. 527-548.

Ryerson, C.C., "Relief Model Symbolization," *The American Cartographer*, 11, 2 (1984), pp. 160-164.

Schou, *The Construction and Drawing of Block Diagrams* (London: Thomas Nelson & Sons, Ltd., 1962).

Thompson, M.M., *Maps for America*, 3rd ed. (Washington, DC: U.S. Geological Survey, 1988).

Toth, G., "Terrain Representation—Past and Present—At the National Geographical Society," *Proceedings* of the Fall ACSM Convention, Lake Buena Vista, Fla., October 2-5, 1973.

United States Geological Survey, *Topographic Maps*, Pamphlet (1992).

Watson, D.F., *Contouring* (New York: Pergamon Press, 1992).

Yoeli, P., "Digital Terrain Models and their Cartographic and Cartometric Utilization," *The Cartographic Journal*, 20, 1 (1983), pp. 17-23.

CHAPTER SIX

ATTRIBUTE AND DISTRIBUTION MAPS

INTRODUCTION

SINGLE-VARIABLE SYMBOLS

Point Emphasis
Line Emphasis
Area Emphasis

MULTIVARIATE SYMBOLS

Point Emphasis
Line Emphasis
Area Emphasis

LINEAR CARTOGRAMS

Routed
Unrouted

SELECTED READINGS

Miss Dove had seen paintings done in the art class—great, free, brilliant blobs of color running into the margins, and had shuddered to imagine maps executed with such techniques!

—Frances Gray Patton, *Good Morning, Miss Dove*

6

CHAPTER SIX

ATTRIBUTE AND DISTRIBUTION MAPS

In the previous chapter, we saw how line maps show landforms. Since everyone has experience with the land surface, this was a good way to explore map abstraction. In this chapter, we take another step along this abstraction gradient by stripping the landform surface from maps. When we remove the terrain, surface features drop to positions on a **plane**. When we do this with a map viewed in parallel perspective from a vertical vantage point, the result is a **planimetric map**. (See *Vertical Vantage Point* in Chapter 3.)

One type of planimetric map is the **attribute** map. It focuses on locations of specific environment features or attributes. One such map is the state road map (**Figure 6.1A**), which shows such features as highways, towns, parks, and rivers. The map is intended to serve as a reference for travelers.

When a map focuses on the spatial variation of one environmental feature or theme, it is called a **distribution** map. A geology map falls in this category (**Figure 6.1B**). It gives you a view of bedrock types underlying soil and other material. The emphasis is on variation of rock type through space.

On both attribute and distribution maps, cartographers use **qualitative symbols**—symbols which simply show the location of some feature. (In Chapter 7, we'll see how cartographers use quantitative symbols to show how much of something exists at a location.)

In this chapter, we explore the possibilities of attribute and distribution maps. First, we divide qualitative map symbols into two categories, according to whether they stand for a single variable or a number of variables. Second, we class each symbol on the basis of whether it emphasizes information at a point, a line, or an area. Finally, we introduce an alternative to conventional line maps.

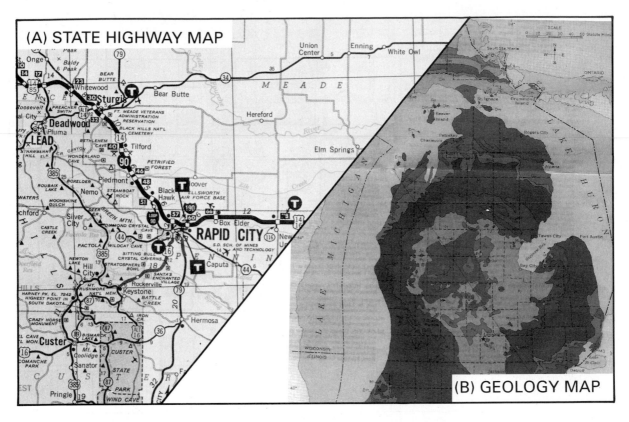

6.1 On a highway map (A), the focus is on environmental attributes of special interest to motorists. In contrast, a geology map (B) emphasizes spatial variation of a single attribute—bedrock type. Both maps originally were printed in color, greatly facilitating distinctions between different symbols.

SINGLE-VARIABLE SYMBOLS

The simplest and most common qualitative map symbols are those that represent one kind of feature and nothing else. Most symbols on road maps and other general purpose maps are of this type. To read these single-variable qualitative symbols, we must first determine what phenomenon has been shown.

As we saw under *Symbolization* in Chapter 3, symbols are easiest to interpret if the map maker has taken advantage of their intuitive nature. The graphic elements which evoke the proper image of **qualitative** symbols are **shape, pattern arrangement, pattern orientation,** and **color hue (Figure 6.2)**. Each of these elements gives the impression that objects are separate in type or kind but not more or less in magnitude.

Keep in mind, however, that map makers don't always design maps as well as they might. Thus, they may use some other graphic element (size, texture, color value, or color intensity) which really should be reserved for showing quantitative differences. (See Chapter 7 for a discussion of quantitative symbols.) When maps are badly made in this way, your first reaction will be that quantitative rather than qualitative information is being shown.

Say, for instance, that the map makers have made lakes blue, land brown, and parks green. They have quite properly used hue to differentiate one region from another. But what if they've also varied the parks' color intensity, making some parks deeper green than others to distinguish between public and private parks? In this case, you could easily get the impression that the parks differed in some quantitative way, such as in entrance fees charged. The only way to keep from being misled by such poorly designed maps is to

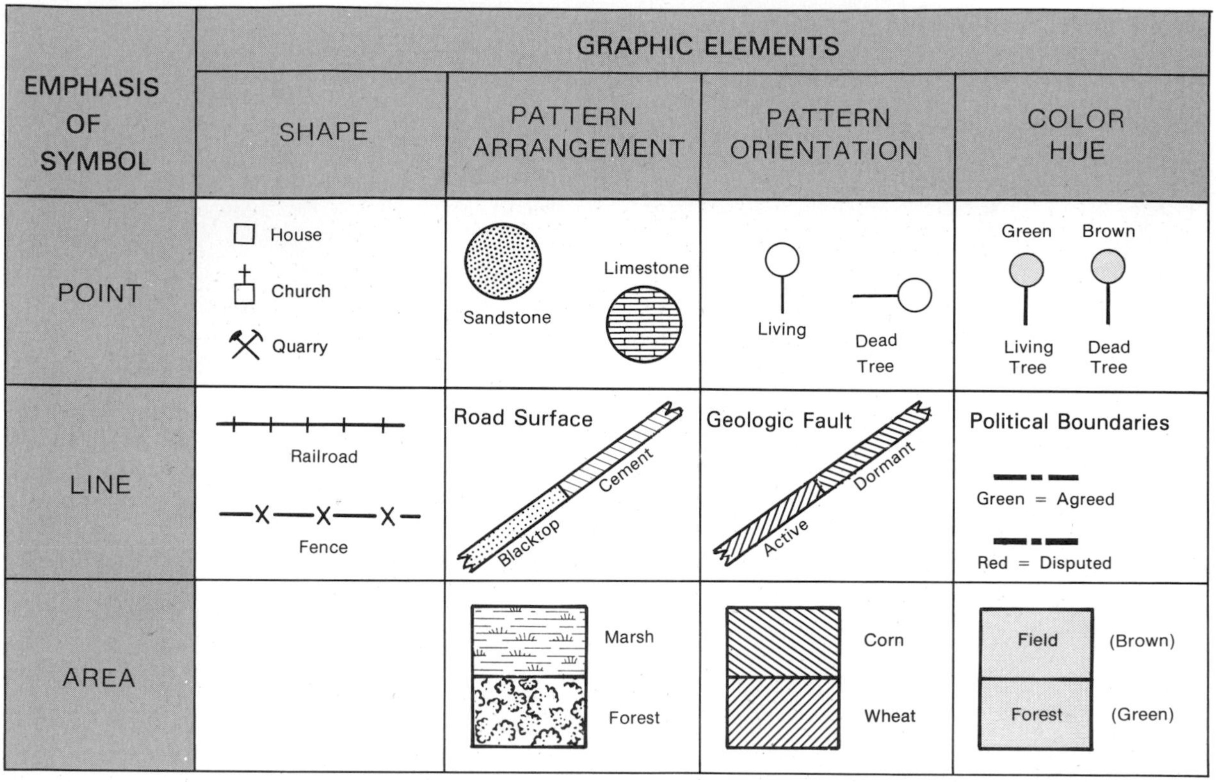

EMPHASIS OF SYMBOL	GRAPHIC ELEMENTS			
	SHAPE	PATTERN ARRANGEMENT	PATTERN ORIENTATION	COLOR HUE
POINT	☐ House ⌂ Church ⚒ Quarry	Sandstone Limestone	Living Dead Tree	Green Brown Living Dead Tree Tree
LINE	┼┼┼┼┼┼ Railroad —X—X—X— Fence	Road Surface Cement Blacktop	Geologic Fault Dormant Active	Political Boundaries ▬ ▪ ▬ ▪ Green = Agreed ▬ ▪ ▪ ▬ Red = Disputed
AREA		Marsh Forest	Corn Wheat	Field (Brown) Forest (Green)

6.2 The graphic elements which naturally evoke a qualitative impression are shape, pattern arrangement, pattern orientation, and color hue.

be sure to consult the legend to see what the symbols actually represent.

Point Emphasis

A map symbol which emphasizes existence of something at a specific location is called a **point symbol**. The word "point" has a rather loose interpretation here. It isn't being used in the strict mathematical sense of a non-dimensional figure; if it were, then a point symbol would be unable to show anything except pure location. In practice, then, a point symbol may actually be a circle, a cube, or some other figure.

Qualitative point features are usually represented with pictographic or geometric point symbols. **Pictographic** symbols are designed to "look like" miniature versions of the features represented. They give the map a light, childlike appearance (**Figure 6.3A**) and are commonly used on maps for children and tourists.

A special type of pictographic symbol is the **standard** symbol (**Figure 6.3B**). Standard symbols have a more professional, less childlike look than most pictographic symbols. But they still suffer problems associated with pictographic symbols in general. They have to be relatively large for details to be apparent, which means the map must be rather simple. In addition, only a limited number of environmental features can be successfully symbolized pictographically. What, for example, is an obvious icon for a museum? Although these symbols are intended to be intuitive at a glance, in practice you will often have to go to the map legend to determine what is symbolized.

The drawbacks of pictographic symbols are overcome by using **geometric** symbols such as circles, squares, triangles, and so forth. Although these symbols may look sterile, they can be distinguished even when very small. This lets map makers pack more information into the map than

(A) 3-D PICTOGRAPHIC SYMBOLS

(B) STANDARD SIGNS/SYMBOLS

6.3 Pictographic symbols on maps range from the childlike (A) to more sedate standard signs (B).

they can with larger pictographic symbols. Furthermore, since the correspondence between real-world feature and geometric symbol is strictly arbitrary, any feature can be represented in this way. The greater level of abstraction embodied in geometric symbols increases their flexibility as representational tools. It also requires close study of the legend to determine what is being symbolized.

Line Emphasis

Map makers usually use line symbols to show linear features, such as roads, streams, or boundaries. As with point symbols, the word "line" isn't used here in the strict mathematical sense of a one-dimensional figure. Line symbols usually have

obvious width as well as length. If the lines are wide enough, map makers may use graphic elements such as color, arrangement, or orientation to signify different classes of information.

Shape (form) is the graphic element usually used to distinguish line symbols (**Figure 6.4**). The symbols may be either pictographic or geometric. As always, pictographic symbols are easier to read than geometric ones. Linear features, however, seem to be more difficult to miniaturize than point features. Therefore, with the exception of the pictographic symbols used to depict tangible features such as railroads, fences, and powerlines, most line symbols are geometric abstractions. Intangible features such as political boundaries are almost always symbolized geometrically.

134

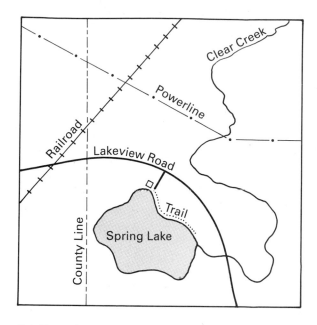

6.4 Maps show a variety of linear features with line symbols of different forms and colors.

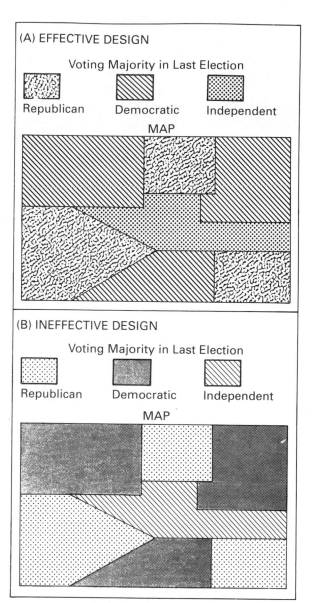

6.5 Area symbols can be used to distinguish regions from each other on the basis of attributes (A). But improper choice of symbols causes confusion (B).

Area Emphasis

Qualitative area symbols emphasize features that extend uniformly over regions. As with point and line symbols, the word "area" isn't restricted to a mathematically defined two-dimensional figure. In practice, point and line symbols are sometimes used to show areal phenomena. Point symbols of different geometric shapes might be used to show the existence of various features in a region. Or a cross-hatched pattern of lines might indicate a zone of groundwater contamination. Moreover, point and linear features are commonly represented with area symbols. A collection of oil wells might be represented on the map by an area symbol for an oil field. Similarly, instead of showing the grid of roads in a town, the map maker may simply color in the built-up area.

In general, however, when we think of qualitative area symbols, we're referring to an areal mosaic (see *Mosaic Surfaces* in Chapter 1). For example, a map might use area symbols to show the pattern of states that voted for one political party or another (**Figure 6.5A**). On such maps, environmental attributes are best symbolized using visual elements that give the impression of differences in kind. To create the most readable map, then, map makers should use the visual ele-

ments of hue, arrangement, and orientation. If map makers instead use visual elements that give a magnitude impression, such as value, intensity, texture, or size, you're likely to find the map confusing (**Figure 6.5B**). You'll tend to think one symbol depicts more of something than another symbol, even though this wasn't the map makers' intent.

MULTIVARIATE SYMBOLS

Most attribute and distribution maps use a separate symbol to represent each variable. But sometimes map makers show several variables with the same symbol. They accomplish this feat in two ways.

One method is to use a different symbol dimension to show each variable. Theoretically, then, by varying symbol shape, hue, texture, and arrangement, map makers could show four different variables at once. In practice, symbols showing more than two or three variables are rarely made, because there is so much possibility of error in using them. You will usually have no trouble telling when this method has been used, because the symbols will appear more complex than those showing only a single variable. It is important to refer to the legend, however, since at least one (and likely all) of the variables will be symbolized in geometric rather than pictographic fashion.

With the second method of symbolizing multivariate information, map makers show composite data rather than raw variables. Thus, they may combine a number of variables and show them with a single symbol. It is here that map reading becomes especially tricky, for these multivariate symbols look exactly like single-variable ones. Only the nature of the information symbolized, not the form of the symbols, has been changed. More than ever, therefore, it is essential to check the legend as your initial step in map reading.

Point Emphasis

Map makers like to use point symbols to show multivariate qualitative information because they can pack information into several dimensions at once (**Figure 6.6**). Some multivariate point symbols are pictographic, but most are geometric. For example, a symbol's shape may represent one feature, while its hue represents another. Cartographers also may use multiples of the same graphic element. For instance, they may use two shapes, such as a square within a circle. Although they should use graphic elements with qualitative connotations to construct these symbols, they don't always do so. One reason is that they may not be aware of the proper cartographic language. Another is that they often try to code so many variables into their point symbols that they can't adhere to intuitive graphic elements in their designs.

Line Emphasis

Map makers don't often use line symbols to portray multivariate qualitative data. One reason is that such line symbols aren't as easily extended

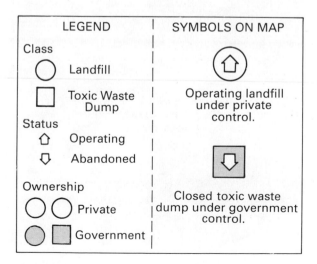

6.6 A great deal of attribute information can be designed into a map through use of multivariate point symbols.

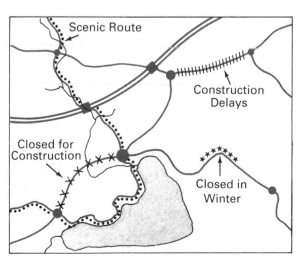

6.7 To a limited extent, multiple line symbols can be used to depict multivariate linear information on a map.

136

into different dimensions as are point symbols. Multiple lines, each with a different shape or color, are sometimes used, as on highway maps enhanced with driving status or "scenic" route symbols (**Figure 6.7**). This technique only works with a few variables, however, because of the limits of using overlapping or repetitive symbols.

An alternative to repetitive line symbols is to use lines wide enough to accommodate color, arrangement, or orientation marks within their edges. These **fat line** symbols tend to cover an inordinate amount of map space, however. Map makers normally would rather make separate maps of the individual variables than clutter a single map with fat lines that distract from the rest of the map information.

Area Emphasis

Sometimes map makers make multivariate symbols with area emphasis by overlapping two area symbols to form a third (**Figure 6.8**). This technique is quite effective if one of the symbols is relatively transparent. This is the case, for example, when blue water and a grass symbol pattern are merged to form a marsh symbol. But in other cases, as when yellow and blue symbols overlap to form a green symbol, the coding may go unrecognized, because green is normally seen as a separate color, not a mixture of the other two. In such cases, it's necessary to refer to the map legend.

At first glance, many maps seem to show a single variable when they actually show a variable composite. This is the case with climate and soils maps, for example (**Figure 6.9**). Climate zone borders are defined by temperature and precipitation conditions (pattern and magnitude) as well as typical vegetation. We may think of climate as a single variable, but each component of the composite plays a crucial part. Similarly, a soil class is defined by a set of soil conditions, including fertility, slope, depth, drainage, color, and texture. You can probably think of other examples of environmental phenomena that are determined by a composite of variables.

LINEAR CARTOGRAMS

Conventional line maps are limited to depicting features in their correct locations. There are times, however, when physical location is less important than functional relationships between features. We may, for example, care more about the time it takes to get to work than about the distance in miles or kilometers. To serve this desire,

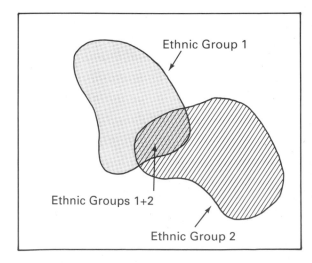

6.8 The overlap of separate area symbols can create a hybrid symbol with a multivariate character.

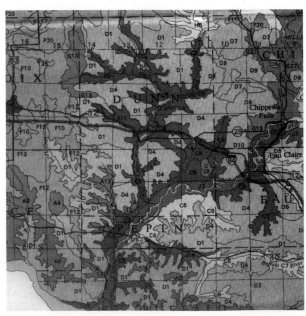

6.9 Symbols representing soil classes on a map signify zones in which certain combinations of environmental conditions exist.

map makers sometimes distort the map's geography to show relations that are more meaningful to our lives. The resulting "super-distorted" maps are called **linear cartograms**. They will probably strike you as rather strange-looking, because familiar physical space is scaled in some less tangible measure (such as time, effort, cost, or fear) which is strongly felt but not easily visualized.

Linear cartograms may be either routed or unrouted. Let's look at both types.

Routed Cartograms

On **routed** cartograms, map makers consider functional distance only as it's measured along some route, such as a road or path. If you're restricted to travel along these routes, it makes sense to use this type of cartogram.

Routed cartograms are of two types. The first type is called a **route-segment cartogram**, since mapped routes are broken into segments, with the functional length of each segment shown. You're undoubtedly familiar with route-segment cartograms that appear as insets on highway and airline maps to show estimated travel time between cities. Better roads and faster planes "shrink" effective (or functional) distance, while poor roads and slow commuter flights "stretch" effective distance. Since time is usually more important to us than miles, these cartograms can be very helpful in travel planning.

A simple route-segment cartogram is shown in **Figure 6.10**. Distances between prominent landmarks along a hiking path have been measured in terms of walking time rather than physical units. If we were planning a hike, this map might be more useful than one showing physical distance. What we really want to know about a path isn't its exact length in kilometers or miles but how long it will take to walk it.

Despite its unusual appearance, a route-segment cartogram is simple to read. If it takes a long time to travel a certain stretch of path, that segment will be long on the map, regardless of its physical length. Likewise, a path which can be traversed quickly will be short. The result is a map whose very make-up is based on time, not physical distance. Instead of the usual map scale of centimeters to the kilometer or inches to the

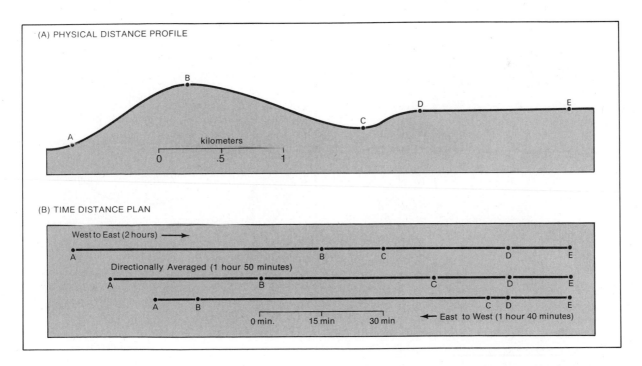

6.10 A landform profile (A) has been transformed into a route-segment cartogram based on walking time (B). Small-scale, route-segment cartograms showing between-city "distances" work well because the "effort" in opposite directions is about equal.

138

mile, the scale is centimeters or inches to units of time elapsed.

If walking time were the same on all paths in the region, there would be no difference between the cartogram and a conventional map. But this is rarely the case. Travel is nearly always faster or slower on some routes than others. In Figure 6.10, note how downhill route segments are compacted on the cartogram, while uphill segments are expanded. In extreme situations of alternate route stretching and shrinking, the cartogram may bear little resemblance to a conventional map, except that the connections between places will be preserved. Position, direction, shape, and area will all be grossly distorted.

The most serious drawback of route-segment linear cartograms is the problem of **directionality**. Directionality isn't a critical factor when planning between-city trips because travel times are roughly equal in each direction. But for local trips, directionality can be a problem. For instance, it takes more time to walk uphill than to walk the same route downhill. Likewise, a one-way street shortens the route in one direction but lengthens it in the other. On a route-segment cartogram, the time required to walk a stretch of path must be averaged in the two directions, often making the result meaningless if not deceptive.

Map makers overcome this problem of directionality on the second type of routed linear

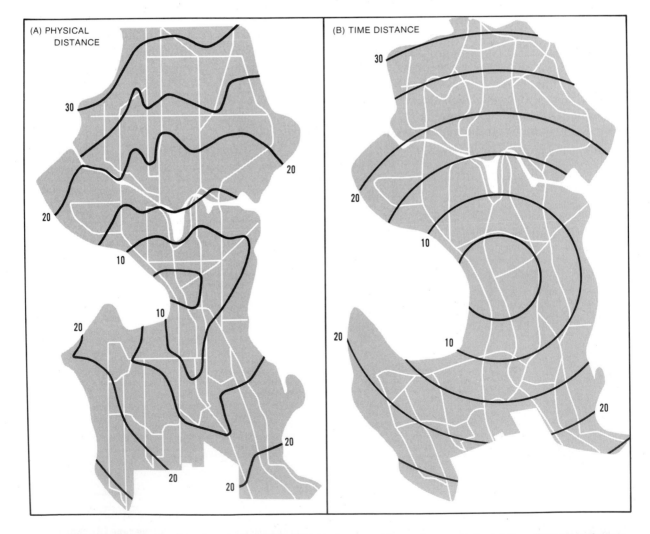

6.11 Driving times in minutes from downtown Seattle (A) have been used to create a central-point time-distance cartogram of the city (B). Since this is an old (pre-expressway) map of the city, it shouldn't be used to plan a Starbucks rendezvous in present-day Seattle.

cartogram. They do so by giving distances in some meaningful measure from a central point. To demonstrate the idea behind these **central-point cartograms**, let's again use time as our measure. Now suppose we figure out how far we can drive in various directions from a central point, assuming that we travel for the same amount of time in each direction. Next, imagine that we draw these equal-time lines on an ordinary map (**Figure 6.11A**). If a road has a low speed limit, a great many stop signs, or congested traffic, the line for that route will be long on the map. Major thoroughfares or streets with light traffic, on the other hand, will result in a short line, since it will take much less time to travel the same distance.

To create a central-point cartogram, map makers merely transform the equal-time lines from the map in Figure 6.11A into equally spaced concentric circles (**Figure 6.11B**). In doing so, they distort the geography of the map: Features are pulled apart in congested areas and squeezed together along high-speed paths.

The scale of this time-distance cartogram is one cm. (.3937 inch) on the map to five minutes of travel time on the ground. The scale is correct, however, only along established routes from the central point. Off-route distances and distances to the central point aren't correct.

Unrouted Cartograms

Instead of showing distance along a path, map makers can create linear cartograms without considering routes. These unrouted cartograms assume that travel or communication can take place over space without restriction. If some symmetry exists about a point, map makers can show some measure of distance in every direction from that location. They might, for instance, show the effort required to reach the top of a mountain from all directions. Such a map would be useful if you were planning to hike up the mountain. With a conventional map, you would have to use indirect means to determine climbing effort (**Figure 6.12A**). An effort-distance cartogram of the same mountain would be more direct and simple to use (**Figure 6.12B**). Such a map, on which slope steepness and altitude have been converted into a measure of climbing difficulty, would help you determine how many days it would take to reach the summit and, therefore, the amount of food

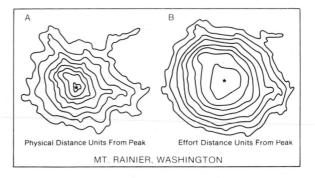

A — Physical Distance Units From Peak

B — Effort Distance Units From Peak

MT. RAINIER, WASHINGTON

6.12 A map of the landform of Mt. Ranier, Washington (A), has been transformed into an unrouted effort-distance cartogram (B).

and supplies needed for the climb. The cartogram's constant effort-distance scale would thus facilitate direct route planning.

Sometimes unrouted cartograms are made to aid environmental studies. Take, for example, our geographical awareness of distant places. Studies have shown that we care most about what we know best and that our knowledge of the country dwindles with distance from home (see *Mental Maps* in the introductory chapter). To put our relations with different parts of the country in perspective, then, it might be useful to work with a cognitive-distance transformation rather than a conventional map.

SELECTED READINGS

Bertin, J., *Graphics and Graphic Information-Processing* (New York: Walter de Gruyter, 1981).

Carnachan, R., *Wisconsin Soil Mapping*, Guide 4 (Madison, WI: Wisconsin State Cartographer's Office, 1993).

Chaston, P.R., *Weather Maps: How to Read and Interpret All Basic Weather Charts* (Kearney, MO: Chaston Scientific, Inc., 1995).

Dent, B.D., *Cartography: Thematic Map Design*, 4th ed. (Englewood Cliffs, NJ: Prentice-Hall, Inc., 1996).

Hole, F.D., and Campbell, J.B., *Soil Landscape Analysis* (Totowa, NJ: Rowman & Allanheld, Publishers, 1985).

Holmes, N., *Pictorial Maps* (New York: Watson-Guptill Publications, 1991).

Jordan, J., and Carnachan, R., *Wisconsin Geologic Mapping, Guide 6* (Madison, WI: Wisconsin State Cartographer's Office, 1994).

Kuchler, A.W., and Zonneveld, I.S., eds., *Vegetation Mapping* (Boston, MA: Kluwer Academic, 1988).

Lisle, R.J., *Geological Structures & Maps* (New York: Pergamon Press, 1988).

Maltman, A., *Geological Maps: An Introduction* (New York: Van Nostrand Reinhold, 1990).

Monmonier, M., *Cartographies of Danger* (Chicago: The

140

University of Chicago Press, 1997).

Monmonier, M., and Schnell, G.A., *Map Appreciation* (Englewood Cliffs, NJ: Prentice Hall, 1988).

Robinson, et al., *Elements of Cartography*, 6th ed. (New York: John Wiley & Sons, 1995).

Saint-Martin, F., *Semiotics of Visual Language* (Bloomington, IN: University Press, 1990).

Spencer, E.W., *Geologic Maps* (Englewood Cliffs: Prentice-Hall, Inc., 1993).

Tufte, E.R., *Visual Explanations: Images and Quantities, Evidence and Narrative* (Cheshire, CT: Graphics Press, 1997).

Wrigley, N., *Categorical Data Analysis for Geographers and Environmental Scientists* (New York: Longman, Inc., 1985).

Also see references in Chapter 3.

CHAPTER SEVEN

STATISTICAL MAPS

INTRODUCTION

SINGLE-VARIABLE SYMBOLS

Point Emphasis
Line Emphasis
Area Emphasis
    Three-Dimensional Area Maps
    Two-Dimensional Area Maps
        Isoline Maps
        Shaded Isoline Maps
        Choropleth Maps
        Dasymetric Maps
        Dot Maps
        Area-Emphasizing Point Symbols

MULTIVARIATE SYMBOLS

Point Emphasis
Line Emphasis
Area Emphasis

AREA CARTOGRAMS

Disjoint
Pseudo-Continuous
Continuous

CONCLUSION

SELECTED READINGS

7

CHAPTER SEVEN

STATISTICAL MAPS

In the previous chapter, we discussed maps that emphasize the location of different kinds of environmental features. Sometimes we want to know not only *what* and *where* but also *how much* of something exists at some location. In such cases, we need to turn to **statistical maps**.

On statistical maps, cartographers use **quantitative symbols** to depict magnitude information (**Figure 7.1**). (See *Symbol-Referent Coordination* in Chapter 3 for a discussion of qualitative vs. quantitative symbols. Also see Chapter 6 for a detailed look at qualitative symbols.) The graphic elements which evoke the proper image of quantitative symbols are **size, pattern texture, color value,** and **color intensity**. These dimensions give an impression of magnitude rather than simply the location of a feature.

If map makers were careful to use the correct graphic elements, we can usually tell quantitative from qualitative symbols. That, however, is only the first step in reading statistical map symbols. We must next determine what type of quantitative information is portrayed. Do the data reflect a single theme or variable, such as a ranking of cities by average family income? Or do the data reflect a composite of several variables, as in a ranking of cities by desirability for raising a family? Although these two maps may look identical, the conceptual basis and meaning of symbols on the two maps are very different.

SINGLE-VARIABLE SYMBOLS

The simplest quantitative map symbols are those that represent a single variable. Once we grasp the nature of the mapped data, we need to determine whether the symbols emphasize information at a point, a line, or an area.

Point Emphasis

To show quantitative information at specific points, map makers simply vary some graphic element of the symbol in proportion to different magnitudes. Symbols which are varied in this way are called **variable** or **proportional** point symbols. Proportional symbols may be either pictographic—miniature ver-

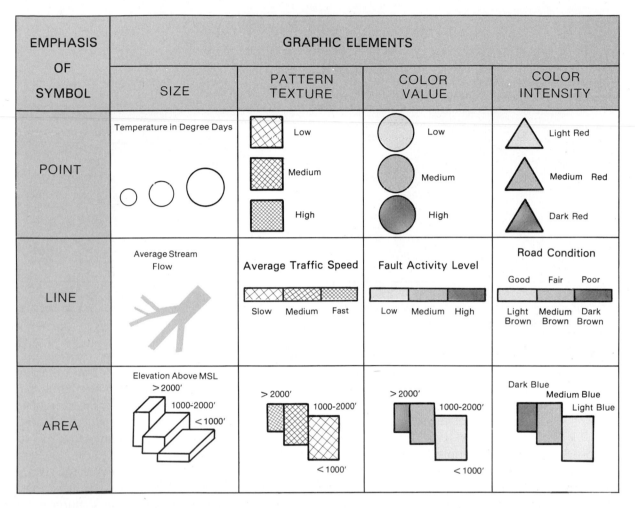

EMPHASIS OF SYMBOL	GRAPHIC ELEMENTS			
	SIZE	PATTERN TEXTURE	COLOR VALUE	COLOR INTENSITY
POINT	Temperature in Degree Days	Low / Medium / High	Low / Medium / High	Light Red / Medium Red / Dark Red
LINE	Average Stream Flow	Average Traffic Speed — Slow Medium Fast	Fault Activity Level — Low Medium High	Road Condition — Good Fair Poor — Light Brown Medium Brown Dark Brown
AREA	Elevation Above MSL >2000' / 1000-2000' / <1000'	>2000' / 1000-2000' / <1000'	>2000' / 1000-2000' / <1000'	Dark Blue / Medium Blue / Light Blue

7.1 The graphic elements which naturally evoke a quantitative impression are size, pattern texture, color value, and color intensity.

sions of the features shown—or geometric—forms such as circles, squares, or triangles (**Figure 7.2**). (See Chapters 3 and 6 for more discussion of pictographic and geometric symbols.)

If the symbols are pictographic, they will usually be varied only in terms of size (**Figure 7.2A**). For example, a human figure of one size may indicate a town of 100 people, while a symbol 10 times as large would show a town of 1,000 residents.

If proportional symbols are geometric, their texture, color value, and color intensity, as well as size, may be varied to show changes in magnitude (**Figure 7.2B**). Deeper shades of red, for instance, might indicate larger populations.

Even with geometric symbols, however, the most common way of showing changes in magnitude is to vary the size dimensions (length, area, or volume) of the symbols. Reading these symbols isn't as straightforward as it might seem. The difficulty arises because of the way the human eye and brain work. The eye doesn't receive information in a linear way; instead, the size of geometric symbols is progressively underperceived as the length, area, or volume of the symbols increases. This discrepancy between the **apparent magnitude** and **absolute magnitude** of map symbols is minimal with respect to length, is worse with respect to area, and becomes a major problem with three-dimensional symbols (**Figure**

144

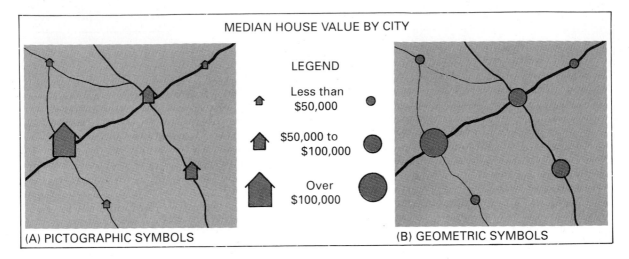

7.2 Point symbols are commonly used to show quantitative information. Pictographic symbols (A) may look interesting, but simple geometric symbols (B) are usually easier to use in map analysis.

7.3A) Apparently, readers respond to three-dimensional symbols' *extent* rather than to their volume. Thus, the area which a cube covers on the map, not its volume, is what we're likely to see.

The human eye also has problems perceiving changes in texture, color value, and color intensity of area shading tints on maps. We see low texture, value, or color intensity levels as greater than they actually are. At the same time, we underperceive the magnitude of higher levels of texture, value, or color intensity. The human response to map symbols of different gray tones has been determined experimentally and is shown in **Figure 7.3B**.

The problems of using proportional point symbols are greatest when a continuous gradation of symbols has been used. The human eye simply doesn't function precisely enough to differentiate between such slight variations between symbols. The inevitable result is that much of the effort that went into making the map isn't appreciated by the map user. In fact, continuous magnitude gradation of symbols may actually contribute to map reading error because of the increased confusion it may cause.

Such difficulties are largely avoided when symbols are limited to a small number of discrete classes. With this classification approach (some-

times called **range grading**), the symbols are usually different enough so that the eye can easily tell them apart (**Figure 7.4**). Although some information may have been lost in the classification process, these maps are generally the easiest to read of the single-variable quantitative point symbol type.

Most map makers are aware of the tricks played by the human eye and have devised various methods to counteract them. One solution is to over-emphasize the things that are usually underperceived by the map user. For instance, the map user normally sees larger symbols as smaller than they really are. So the map maker may increase the size of larger symbols (**Figure 7.5A**). Absolute and apparent magnitudes should then coincide. In the same way, map makers may use the curve of the gray spectrum to determine appropriate symbol texture, value, or intensity (**Figure 7.5B**). Since the symbols show apparent rather than absolute magnitude, this method is known as **apparent magnitude symbol scaling**.

With apparent magnitude scaling, map makers are trying to bring absolute and apparent magnitudes together. In doing so, they are compensating for the "average" effects of nonlinear vision. The trouble is that you aren't necessarily the "typical" map user. Consequently, your impres-

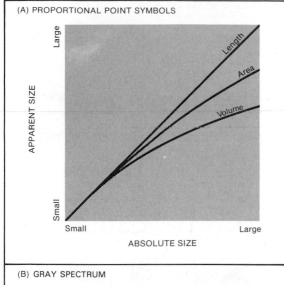

(A) PROPORTIONAL POINT SYMBOLS

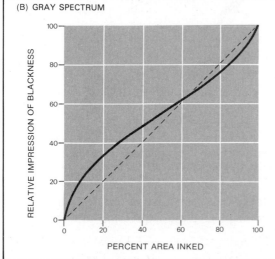

(B) GRAY SPECTRUM

7.3 The apparent magnitude of a proportional point symbol (A) or a gray tone (B) may deviate substantially from its absolute magnitude.

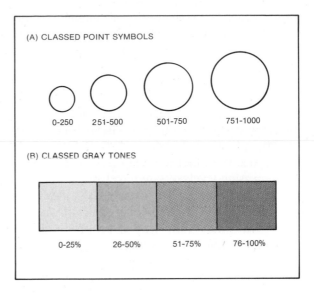

7.4 If proportional point symbols (A) and area shading tints (B) are classified prior to mapping, their values are more easily determined visually.

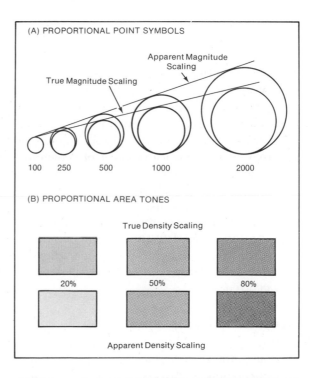

7.5 The use of apparent magnitude scaling of proportional point symbols (A) and gray tones (B) is one way to compensate for the nonlinearity of human vision.

sion of magnitude may or may not coincide with the absolute magnitude of the symbolized information. The main thing to remember is to check the map legend. If apparent magnitude symbol scaling has been used, the map maker will probably say so there.

Line Emphasis

Map makers use a variety of **proportional**, or **ordered**, **line symbols** to show quantitative information associated with linear features. With

146

proportional line symbols, cartographers first decide where they want the lines to go and then show how some phenomenon changes along or between those lines.

Two types of proportional line symbols are used to show changes. With the first type, lines representing different features that vary in magnitude are designed to form a **visual hierarchy**. An example would be the road symbols found on the typical state highway map (see Figure 6.1A). In decreasing levels of safe travel speed and visual symbol rank, you find expressways, U.S. highways, state highways, and county roads.

With the second type of proportional line symbol, the line representing a single feature is varied in visual weight from one place to another. Map makers usually accomplish this by making the width of the line continuously proportionate to some magnitude (such as traffic deaths, speed of travel, toxicity, danger, construction cost, etc.) (**Figure 7.6A**). Although in this example data aren't classed, map makers sometimes class data into line segments with proportional width symbols.

Alternatively, visual weight may be created by using the graphic elements of texture, value, or intensity as a "fill" within **fat lines**. The level of earthquake risk along California's San Andreas Fault has been mapped this way (**Figure 7.6B**). As with other proportional line symbols, data are usually classed and ranked to simplify mapping.

A problem with proportional line symbols from your perspective as a map user is that the symbols are disproportionately large. This means that they may cover a great deal of geography. Thus, only a limited number of such symbols can be used, and lines which are close together may be displaced. For the map to make sense, the geographical base data themselves may be displaced to accommodate the proportional lines. Whenever you see proportional line symbols, then, you should suspect that such displacement has occurred.

Area Emphasis

With quantitative area symbols, map makers want to show both the area extent and the magnitude of a phenomenon. To show changes in magnitude, they may vary size, pattern texture, color value, or color intensity. The most dramatic maps

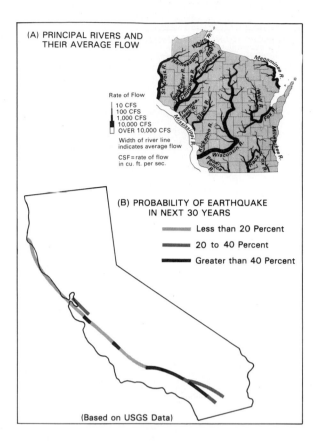

7.6 Proportional line symbols may be of the variable-width flow-line type (A) or the fixed-width fat-line type (B).

are made by varying size in the third dimension. These maps give the impression of a volumetric surface.

Three-Dimensional Area Maps

One type of three-dimensional map is the **region-bounded** map. It is made by dividing the mapped area into regions and showing how much of something exists in each region.

Since the information to be mapped is usually collected according to such zones as states, counties, or census tracts, it is easiest for cartographers to divide their maps into these same regions. They will then be able to use the information just as it comes from the data collectors. Such a map, showing average population density by state, is shown in **Figure 7.7A**. Each state boundary has been raised obliquely above the base level to a height proportionate to its average density. The result looks like a three-dimensional, stepped surface.

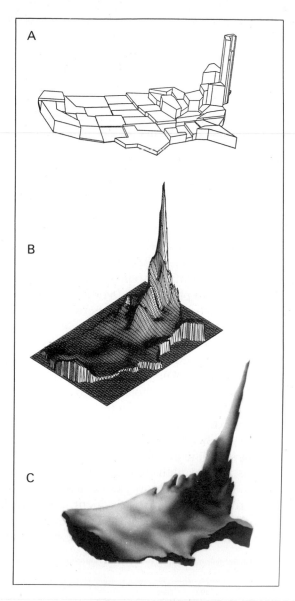

7.7 Three-dimensional area mapping methods which can be used to represent thematic information include symbols of the stepped (A), fishnet (B), and shading (C) types.

regions. Population density doesn't change abruptly at state boundaries, although the uncritical map user might get just such an idea from the region-bounded map.

We can solve this problem by using smooth, continuous symbols rather than discrete, step-like ones. If the map maker constructs closely spaced line profiles in two directions and in oblique view, we gain an impression not of individual lines but of a whole area (**Figure 7.7B**). This is called a **perspective profile** map (see *Perspective Profiles* in Chapter 5). Here is a case in which lines are effectively used as area symbols. Notice how our attention is focused not on any one line but on the general form of the surface. Note, too, how much more realistically this map shows the variability in population density across the United States than does the region-bounded map.

A still more visually realistic portrayal of the same United States population density information is provided on maps which use **continuous surface shading** in oblique view. On these maps, changes in magnitude are shown by altering the graphic elements of color value or intensity. Again, a three-dimensional effect is created (**Figure 7.7C**).

All three types of three-dimensional maps are visually impressive, but there are several problems with them. For one thing, although highs and lows are apparent, the exact height of the surface at a given location is difficult to determine. In addition, if the information which was mapped ranged greatly in value, map makers may have transformed it to a more convenient mathematical form. For example, if the population density of the United States by state were mapped as raw data, the few high-density states would be so much greater in magnitude than the bulk of the low-density states that the map would show little magnitude variation between most states. But by mapping the square root of the state population density averages, the effect is to exaggerate the differences among the low-population-density states. Considering the impact of such data transformation on the appearance of a map, your first map-reading step should be to ascertain whether the map data have been manipulated by the map maker and, if so, how.

A final problem with these three-dimensional area maps is that they are all drawn in

The problem with a region-bounded map is that it uses discrete area symbols to show what in reality is a continuously changing distribution. In other words, it gives the impression that the mapped variable (in this case, population density) is uniformly distributed within the regions and that sharp breaks in the distribution occur at region boundaries. We know that this rarely, if ever, happens. The density pattern is a reflection of landscape factors, not of data-gathering

148

oblique view. This means that the vantage point taken in map making is crucial to their appearance. A poor choice of viewing direction or vertical angle may lead to blocking of locations or features essential to effective map use. If you suspect this problem, it may be best to search for a different map or, at least, to use supplemental map information.

Two-Dimensional Area Maps

Map makers can circumvent these problems associated with three-dimensional area maps by taking a vertical, parallel perspective view. The result is a two-dimensional area map. Being planimetric views, these statistical maps exhibit better metric qualities than three-dimensional representations. But this trait is achieved at a price. The map maker has to rely on either the visual elements of tone, texture, or intensity, or on some form of symbol annotation (labeling with numbers). None of these methods is as intuitive as is symbol size on three-dimensional displays. This means it will require more effort on your part to visualize the magnitude surface represented. You will find this task more difficult with some two-dimensional methods than with others.

Isoline Maps. The most common method used in two-dimensional areal maps is to connect points of equal value with uniform line symbols called **isolines** (the prefix *iso* means equal).* In Chapter 5 we saw how these lines may be used to signify the tangible land surface, in which case the isolines are called **contour lines**. These versatile lines may also be used to point out variation in such intangible distributions as temperature or precipitation.

To construct an isoline, map makers begin by selecting a certain value. Let's say they want to show where it would be practical to plant a certain type of nursery stock. Let's also assume that the species can't tolerate average minimum temperatures below -10°F. Using a base map of the United States, the map maker simply puts a pen on a spot at which the average minimum temper-

ature is -10°F., draws a line to the nearest spot with the same value, and so on. The result is an irregular horizontal trace across the United States, connecting locations with the chosen -10°F. value (see Figure 3.7). Spots on one side of the isoline (in this case north) receive minimum temperatures below -10°F. and would therefore be unsuitable for the nursery stock. Places on the other side of the line experience higher minimum temperatures, and we could expect the nursery stock to survive.

Rarely are isolines used in isolation, however. More commonly, a family of isolines, each tracing out the path of a different value, is used to give a general impression of variations in a spatial distribution (**Figure 7.8**).

To create an isoline map, cartographers must decide how many isolines to draw and how close together to place them. In other words, they must decide what the **interval** between successive isolines will be. This is really a problem of classification. As we saw in our discussion of classification procedures (see *Classification* in Chapter 3), map makers can choose a constant or variable interval. That choice will have a major effect on the map's appearance.

Consider Figure 7.8 again. Here, isoline mapping has been used to show average annual hours of sunshine across the United States. Each isoline is labeled with its value so that regional variation in sunshine hours can be determined. A strong regional pattern is evident. Sunniness clearly decreases as we move from the Southwest to the Northwest and Northeast. The high near

---

*Isolines are also known as **isarithms**. In addition, they have been given many different names according to what type of information they show—**isotherms** showing points of equal temperature, **isobars** showing equal atmospheric pressure, **isohyets** showing equal precipitation, etc.*

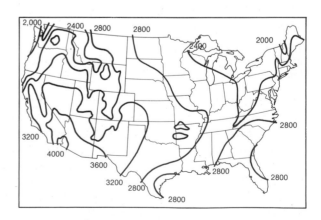

7.8 This isoline map shows average hours of sunshine received annually at various locations.

the Arizona-California border is about double the lows in parts of the Pacific Northwest and the New England states. In creating this map, the cartographers had to make a series of choices. They decided that 2,000 annual hours of sunshine would be the lowest value they showed; they chose a constant class interval of 400 hours; and they decided to draw six isolines. Changing any one of these factors might well alter the appearance of the map. If more isolines were shown, for instance, we would see more detail, although the look of the general regional pattern would remain the same.

An isoline is, of course, a completely artificial device of the map maker. But these symbolic lines on the map are extremely useful for drawing attention to important geographical relations in our world. They make clear what is too abstract or covers too large an area for us to see with our unaided natural senses.

Here again we see, as we did with perspective profiles (see Figure 7.7B) how line symbols can be used to show areas. When a series of isolines are shown together, no single line stands out as a special symbol. Instead, our attention is shifted to the spatial form of the distribution.

The ideal way to read an isoline map is to ignore individual isolines and use the overall isoline pattern to visualize the distribution. Some people find this hard to do, however. To assist map users who have trouble focusing on the pattern rather than on separate isolines, some quantitative area maps are made using a shaded isoline procedure.

Shaded Isoline Maps. The **shaded isoline** technique differs from standard isoline mapping only in that discrete area shadings of texture, value, or intensity are added between the isolines, creating a strong proportional symbol effect (see Figure 7.15). With this procedure, the main function of the isolines is to outline different magnitude zones. The isolines usually aren't labeled with numbers—a fact which further encourages us to see the general pattern of highs and lows rather than to concentrate on individual isolines.

One drawback of shaded isoline maps is that only a relatively small number of visually distinct area shadings can be used at one time. Thus, shaded isoline maps tend to be highly generalized. Furthermore, even though a continuous distribution is assumed when using isolines, the

discrete between-isoline shadings may leave us with the false impression that the mapped phenomenon has a step-like pattern.

Choropleth Maps. In contrast to shaded isoline maps, some quantitative area maps are made using a **choropleth** procedure. With this technique, the distribution isn't segmented according to different magnitude zones, as is done with shaded isolines. Instead, appropriate area shadings (value, texture, or intensity) are assigned to the regions used for collecting information prior to mapping.

The effect of mapping Wisconsin population density by county in this way is illustrated in Figures 3.8 through 3.11. The impression of a stepped distribution is created by the discrete county shadings.

Actually, this technique is the same as the one used for three-dimensional region-bounded maps except that shading rather than size is varied to show magnitude. And the choropleth map may cause the same map reading confusion as we saw with the three-dimensional region-bounded map; it gives the idea that sharp changes in the population density pattern occur at county boundaries.

Dasymetric Maps. An area mapping technique which represents a compromise between the choropleth and shaded isoline methods is called dasymetric mapping. On **dasymetric** maps, zone boundaries are created where abrupt changes take place in the distribution. As a result,

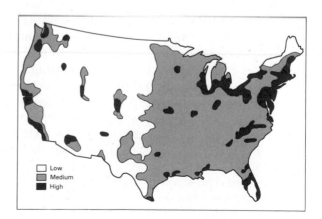

7.9 Population density in the United States (1970) is portrayed using a dasymetric technique with low, medium, and high classes.

150

the zones themselves are relatively homogeneous in nature (**Figure 7.9**). Since smooth gradients don't always exist in reality, as shaded isolines would have us believe, a zone of medium magnitude doesn't have to fall between areas of high and low magnitudes. Nor are dasymetric zones rigidly constrained by artificial data collection units, as is the case with choropleth maps.

Despite its many advantages, the dasymetric technique is still limited to the use of discrete area symbols. Thus, a step-like appearance is created—although with dasymetric maps the "steps" are designed to conform as closely as possible to variations in the actual distribution.

All three types of maps—choropleth, shaded isoline, and dasymetric—share the problems associated with using discrete rather than continuous shading. All three have a step-like appearance, with the steps supposedly indicating increases and decreases in the distribution. To show increasing magnitude, cartographers make the color darker or brighter or the texture finer. If they don't choose their shadings properly, however, we won't see the steps in the distribution correctly. Unless they make careful use of apparent magnitude scaling, we probably won't gain a true picture of reality. Furthermore, due to poor map design and reproduction, it's common to find map zones which blend together so that we can't differentiate between them. These problems are worst with complex maps which show too many classes without sufficient visual difference between area shadings.

Dot Maps. We have seen how line symbols can be used to show areas. In much the same way, point symbols can also show area information. In fact, point symbols are the basis for one of the most effective ways of showing spatial magnitudes. The procedure is called **dot mapping**.

With this technique, the map maker repeats the same point symbol as many times as necessary to give a picture of the distribution's form (**Figure 7.10A**). Although the dot is the most common symbol used in dot mapping, any geometric figure, such as a square, circle, or triangle, may be used. The shape is irrelevant, since the symbol's meaning lies solely in its repetition.

An understanding of the difference between a point symbol map and a dot map is crucial to map reading. On point symbol maps, each symbol represents only one population ele-

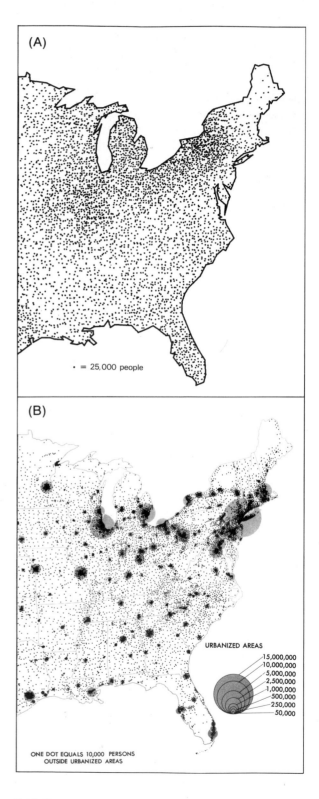

7.10 Simple dot map (A) and composite dot and proportional point symbol map (B) of the United States population.

ment, such as a city. Spatial variation from one location to another is shown by changing the form of the symbol—making it larger or darker, for instance, to show a larger city. With dot mapping, on the other hand, each symbol stands for several population elements, and spatial variation is shown by using more or fewer symbols, not by changing the symbol's form.

To create a dot map, cartographers first choose a value for each symbol. For example, they may decide, as they did for the map in Figure 7.10A, that each dot represents 25,000 people. They then divide the population by this **unit value**. The resulting number tells them how many dots to put on their map. Dot maps usually include only a single legend item defining the unit symbol value. (In this case, the legend indicates that one dot equals 25,000 people.)

While point symbol maps show where things are located, symbols on a dot map can't exist at the same locations as the population elements do in reality, because each symbol represents more than one population element. The aim of dot maps isn't to give precise locational information but to present an image of changing density from one region to the next. Thus, if the dot map is well made, your eye won't be attracted to individual dots but to a general impression of changing spatial density. Not all dot maps meet this criterion, however. The symbols may be too large or too small in size, too few or too many in number. When this happens, there's danger that you'll receive a mistaken impression of the distribution.

Dot maps look simple, but that is a deception. They can be some of the most difficult maps to read. For one thing, as we have already seen, the human eye tends to underperceive magnitudes. This perceptual nonlinearity may cause a problem when viewing dot maps. Psychological experiments have shown that as the density of dots increases, our estimates of the density tend to fall below the absolute values at an increasing rate. The result is that people viewing dot maps typically receive the impression that the range in dot density—and therefore the contrast in density from one region to another—is less than it actually is. For this reason, you may find it necessary to compensate mentally for perceptual nonlinearity in your own density judgments to gain a true picture of the mapped distribution.

A second problem with dot maps is that the data collection method and dot placement scheme can distort the map's accuracy. Take the case in which information is gathered by region prior to mapping and dots are then placed uniformly within each map region. This might happen, for example, if a dot map of the United States were made using only state population totals. In this situation, the dot map's accuracy depends on several factors. First, how representative were the data collection units (states) in gathering information? Also, how well did the uniform dot-placing scheme match the population distribution in reality?

There's little cause for concern when a geographical distribution varies rather smoothly from region to region. In such cases, the regions' size, shape, and orientation will combine with the uniform dot location scheme to make the dot map a fairly accurate reflection of reality.

Serious problems may arise, however, if abrupt changes occur in a geographical distribution. These sharp gradients may not be picked up by the data collection net for several reasons: The regions may be too large, not well oriented with the population distribution, or variable in size and shape. Whatever the reason, the characteristics of the original distribution won't be reflected on the dot map.

As a rule, whenever dots are distributed rather uniformly within map region boundaries, you have a right to be skeptical, because you are given the impression of a stepped distribution. Geographical distributions rarely conform so neatly to such boundaries.

The alternative to placing dots uniformly within data collection regions is to create a smooth density gradient across the data collection unit boundaries. To do so, map makers first assign the region population total to a centroid. Then they place dots as though there were a smooth surface gradient to neighboring region centroids. This was done to produce Figure 7.10A.

Clearly, dot maps can be confusing, if not downright misleading. And the more clustered the distribution, the more pronounced the discrepancy between reality and the dot map. Thus, a dot map of California might give the impression that population is scattered rather evenly over the state, while in reality most of California's population can be attributed to Los Angeles and other

152

urban areas. Likewise, note how the highly-concentrated urban population in New York, Michigan, and Illinois has been spread over the countryside in Figure 7.10A.

Map makers can solve many of the problems of dot maps if they combine dot mapping with some other method. The false impression of population we gained from Figure 7.10A can be corrected if we use point and area symbols on the same map. Notice how we improve the map's clarity when we separate cities of over 200,000 people from the rest of the population and map them with proportional point symbols (**Figure 7.10B**). In this case a unit value of 10,000 has been used to represent the rural population.

Area-Emphasizing Point Symbols. Possibly the most confusing quantitative area maps are those which use proportional point symbols to represent data aggregated by regions (**Figure 7.11**). The problem is that you are led to think you're looking at data concentrated at a point when that isn't the case at all. The cartographer has placed the symbol at some centroid location within the region used to gather the data (see *Census* and *Spatial Samples* in Chapter 2). Most commonly, the data are unevenly distributed throughout the region. These maps also suffer

problems common to all maps that use proportional point symbols, such as symbols overlapping the boundaries of data collection units (see *Point Emphasis* earlier in this chapter).

MULTIVARIATE SYMBOLS

Sometimes map makers show several variables with the same symbol. As we saw in Chapter 6, they may do so in two ways.

First, they may use a different symbol dimension to show each variable. The symbol's size might represent per capita income, for example, while color intensity within the symbol outline might represent years of education.

Second, they may show composite data rather than raw variables. For instance, they may use a single symbol to represent an index or ratio.

With quantitative multivariate symbols, as with single-variable ones, the best map designs use combinations of symbol size, texture, value, and intensity. These are the magnitude-suggesting elements of visual design. Just as with multivariate qualitative symbols, however (see previous chapter), unskilled map makers don't always adhere to these intuitive symbol dimensions. Instead, they may try merely to accommodate multivariate information coding in the easiest possible way. An intuitive graphic element may be used for one variable but not for others. Still worse, you may encounter multivariate quantitative maps in which no symbol dimension is intuitively matched to magnitude-suggesting visual elements. This is why it's important that you learn to deal with bad as well as good examples of map design.

Again, point, line, and area symbols are different enough to warrant looking at each in turn. Let's begin by considering point symbols.

Point Emphasis

When quantitative, multivariate point information is displayed in **raw** form, it is the size dimension which is most frequently manipulated. The results are divided bars (bar graphs), circles (pie graphs and circular graphs), triangles, and cubes (**Figure 7.12**). In each instance, the symbol is segmented to represent proportions of some total

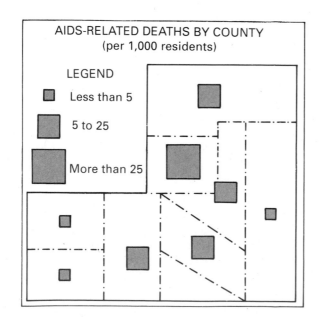

7.11 When data have been aggregated by region, proportional point symbols located at region centroids are often used to show the information.

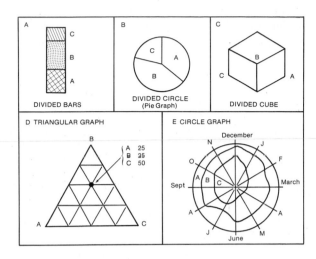

7.12 A variety of quantitative point symbols are used to represent multivariate data.

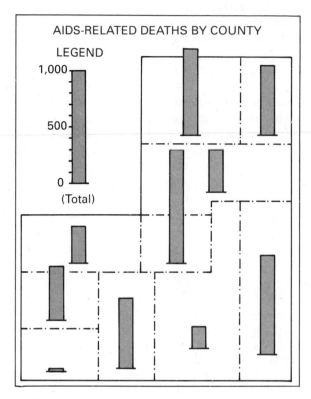

7.13 When bar symbols are used with data exhibiting a large magnitude range, it is difficult to show data variation between regions without having high-value symbols extend beyond region boundaries.

magnitude. The use of any of these symbols requires judging the relative amount of length, area, or volume falling within each segment.

Divided bars are somewhat easier than divided circles for most people to read and analyze with precision, because they require only the estimation of relative length. The problem with divided bars is that they often project out of the data region, because only length can be varied. When bars extend beyond map space, as they do in **Figure 7.13**, a propaganda effect is achieved (see Chapter 25: *Maps and Reality*).

On other maps, quantitative, multivariate point information is depicted in composite form using a single graphic element. For example, the simple ratio between crop yield and land value may be mapped as proportional circles for a selection of farms. Or the multivariate index may be more complex. For instance, the seismic risk map shown in Figure 3.18 takes into consideration a number of factors which combine to cause overall earthquake damage. All these factors could be shown in index form by varying the size of proportional symbols for a selection of cities. At first glance, such symbols would look no different from symbols showing a simple ratio—or even from single-variable symbols showing merely the size of cities! Yet the three types of information mapped by the same technique would require quite different reading effort.

Line Emphasis

Quantitative multivariate line symbols are relatively uncommon for the same reason as are qualitative ones: If they are made large enough to be effective, they take up too much room on the map. But you may occasionally encounter route lines or profiles which show multivariate information. These look exactly like the single-variable route lines and profiles which we discussed earlier (see Figure 7.6). The only difference is that extra information has been added by varying the size, texture, or color of the line symbols. Since this category of line symbols is relatively neglected by cartographers, we won't pursue it further here.

Area Emphasis

Area symbols representing multivariate data in quantitative form commonly show ratios or

154

indexes rather than raw data. The map maker often derives or makes up geographical distributions by relating some feature to the environment (such as people per square kilometer or miles per hour) or by relating one feature to another (such as incidence of disease per 10,000 people). In concept, values for these concocted distributions exist everywhere, even though they can't be seen directly. They are contrived things—purely the artificial configurations of the map maker's mind. Nonetheless, they can be very helpful in understanding the environment.

A common way to create a multivariate surface is to collect data by census region and then assign these data to a region centroid (area, population, minimum aggregate travel). The centroid data are then related to the region area, creating a density. These density figures are then mapped using the isoline method.

An isoline drawn across any of these contrived distributions is called an **isopleth**. Isopleths look identical to standard isolines, but they differ in that they show values which in practice cannot exist at points (**Figure 7.14**). There's no way, for instance, that 20 people per square kilometer can exist at one spot. Therefore, you can't be satisfied with knowing simply the

value of the isopleth line—you also have to keep in mind the relation between this value and some other aspect of the environment. In the case of densities, try to think of the **spatial neighborhood** that has been incorporated into the figures. In other words, how far out from the isopleth must you go to find the number of people the isopleth depicts? If the isopleth shows the number of people per square kilometer, then a square kilometer is the spatial neighborhood. It may help to draw a square kilometer box or circle in the legend. This will give you a concrete base for reading the map.

A further problem with isopleths is that the values indicated by the map at a location may not even exist within the surrounding neighborhood. Recall that the map is made by assigning census region totals to region centroids and then creating a smooth density surface using the centroids as sample points. This means the map is at best an abstract, generalized representation of the data. Suppose, for example, that an isopleth shows the population density as 100 individuals per square mile. At a given position along that isopleth, you may find no people, or you may find 5,000! The map is only intended to give a general impression of varying density over space. It is not to be analyzed location by location. Such is the nature of abstraction.

Isopleths which show the incidence of something, such as rate of divorce per 20,000 people, can be treated in much the same way as density isopleths. In this case, you want to know how far out from the isopleth you must go to find 20,000 people. The answer can become a bit complicated, since if population densities aren't uniform (and they rarely are), the spatial neighborhood may vary from large in sparsely populated regions to small in densely populated areas. If no indication of density has been given, your ability to make sense of this type of map may be severely limited.

With isopleth maps, your eye is drawn to the lines themselves. But these multivariate area symbols are actually depicting areal ratios, such as population density, which are defined within census tracts or other data aggregation units. A better impression results if your attention is drawn to the area between the lines. This effect is achieved when map makers add tone, intensity, or texture to the map. In the **shaded isopleth** case, for

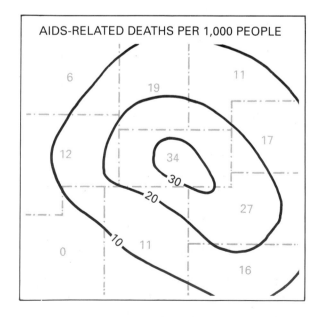

AIDS-RELATED DEATHS PER 1,000 PEOPLE

6   11   19   17   12   34   30   20   27   10   11   0   16

7.14 When isolines are drawn through a field of derived or aggregated data, such as population density values by county, the result is called an isopleth map.

example, map makers add area shadings between a series of isopleths, just as they do with shaded isoline maps. (See *Shaded Isoline Maps* earlier in this chapter.) The result is to draw your attention away from individual line symbols and focus it on the area nature of the distribution (**Figure 7.15**). In fact, this map design procedure has the visual effect of creating a stepped surface or distribution. On these shaded isopleth maps, the isopleths are often unlabeled. Numerical information associated with each shading class is provided solely in the legend.

Another type of statistical map uses point symbols to portray multivariate data aggregated by area. Most use geometric symbols such as the familiar pie graph. But some, such as the example in **Figure 7.16**, show multivariate quantitative data with the aid of pictographic symbols. In this case, different facial expressions are used to depict four social status factors. The shape of the face shows levels of affluence; the mouth indicates unemployment rate; the eyes represent urban stress; and the tone of the symbol represents the proportion of the population that is white. The combined effect is so striking that you can almost sense how people in different sections of the city might feel.

AREA CARTOGRAMS

After our discussion of quantitative symbolization on conventional line maps, we can hardly help but respect cartographers for their ingenuity in portraying magnitude information. Some of their intricate quantitative symbols are true masterpieces. Considering how well thought out they are, it is too bad that these cleverly contrived symbols often fail to convey the magnitude message.

The problem is that conventional line maps are limited to depicting features in their correct locational positions. There are times, however, when it is more important to give an impression of the magnitudes of features than their exact spatial locations. Thus, map makers sometimes distort the geographical size of regions to show

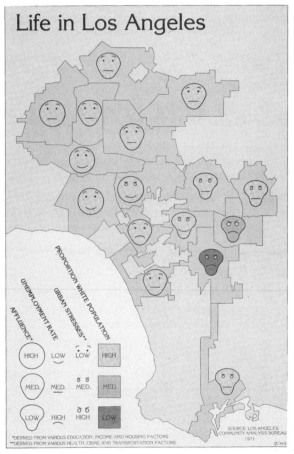

7.16 This multivariate map of Los Angeles shows four social status factors, each divided into three classes (low, medium, high) (courtesy of Eugene Turner).

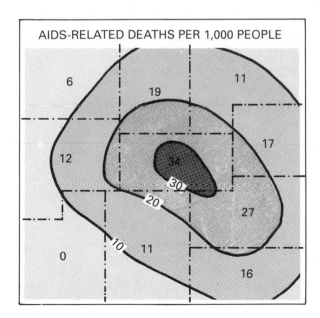

7.15 To overcome the difficulty of visualizing data depicted by naked isopleths, the inter-isopleth zones are often shaded, producing the visual effect of a stepped surface.

156

magnitudes. The resulting maps are called **area cartograms.**

Rather than focusing attention on non-physical distances, as do linear cartograms (see previous chapter), area cartograms draw attention to magnitudes within regions. The size of each state, for example, might be made proportional to its population rather than its geographical area.

To use an area cartogram effectively, you must compare sizes of regions in the cartogram with those same regions on conventional maps, which show the area in square miles or kilometers. If the size relationships of area units (states, countries, etc.) in a region aren't familiar to you, an area cartogram can be difficult to use, because you'll need to compare two unfamiliar-looking maps. For this reason, area cartograms are most successful when the subject region is familiar. This explains why the "world by country" or "country by state" representations are most common.

Ideally, in converting physical space to magnitudes, map makers retain as many spatial attributes of conventional maps as possible. Preserving shape, proximity, and continuity relations will make it easier to compare a cartogram with a standard map. But each of these factors can be preserved only by distorting one or more of the others.

Disjoint Cartograms

Disjoint or **non-continuous cartograms** are the crudest area cartograms (**Figure 7.17**).

They're also the most common, because they're the easiest to make. To create such a cartogram, map makers enlarge or reduce each region in proportion to the magnitude being shown. (This magnitude might be anything from population to amount of gasoline, decongestants, or painkillers consumed.) They then replace these transformed regions in their correct geographical positions—or as nearly as that can be managed. As Figure 7.17 indicates, preserving the shapes of regions makes it easy to recognize and compare them with their counterparts on a conventional map. But as the figure also shows, proximity relations are only roughly maintained, and continuity is sacrificed completely.

On some disjoint area cartograms, map makers represent shapes with simple geometrical figures, such as squares, rectangles, or circles. With these geometric area cartograms, relative position is the sole clue in recognizing regions and making comparisons. Thus, these cartograms may be more difficult to use than those which preserve shape.

Pseudo-Continuous Cartograms

Some cartograms appear continuous at first glance but upon closer inspection turn out only to give the illusion of continuity. These cartograms, unlike disjoint ones, are all one piece, but their regions don't really fit together properly.

These **pseudo-continuous cartograms** are made by transforming each region into some

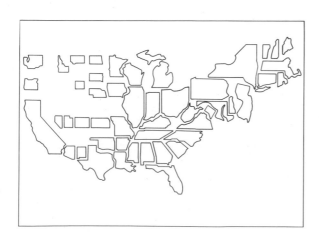

7.17 A disjoint population-by-area cartogram of the United States (1970 data).

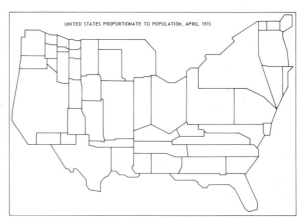

7.18 Pseudo-continuous rectangular area cartogram of the 1970 U.S. population by state.

geometrical shape of correct proportion to the magnitude being shown. Rectangles are the shapes most commonly used. The new shapes are then arranged in what resembles their correct geographical position. When rectangles are used, the result is called a **rectangular area cartogram**. By sacrificing shape and proximity, these cartograms can maintain a considerable degree of continuity.

The rectangular area cartogram idea is commonly modified by using simple straight-line approximations to the shape of regions, as in **Figure 7.18**. But if we study this figure, we see that states don't fit together as they do in reality.

Such pseudo-continuous cartograms are actually no better than disjoint ones—perhaps worse, because some map readers may believe them to be truly continuous when in fact they aren't. The popularity of pseudo-continuous cartograms is probably better explained by the fact that they are easy to construct (only graph paper is needed) than by any theoretical advantage they might possess.

Continuous Cartograms

Truly **continuous** cartograms are by far the most realistic and useful type. On these cartograms, absolute proximity and continuity relations are maintained, although this is accomplished at the expense of shape. The shapes of regions are usually distorted in a rather artistic, **uncontrolled** way. Therefore, the results of several map makers would likely look quite different.

This lack of rigid mapping control is evident in the oil and coal cartograms from a 1970s-era Exxon ad (**Figure 7.19A**). Notice that while the shapes of some countries are fairly well preserved, other countries don't look like themselves at all. Yet, despite this distortion, Exxon's cartograms are extremely effective; with only a glance, we can see precisely which countries control the oil and coal resources of the world. This would seem to indicate that the variable quality of shape preservation from one region to the next isn't always a major distraction. We appear able to accept a fair degree of shape distortion before figures become unrecognizable.

A bigger problem with continuous cartograms is that they are difficult and time-consuming to make. To draw even a simple

cartogram well requires a vast amount of labor, not to mention artistic talent. As a result, this intriguing map type has, in the past, been regarded more as a novelty than as a working document in environmental applications.

But both problems—uncontrolled distortion and difficulty of construction—can be solved if computers are used. It takes little effort or artistic talent to create cartograms by computer. In addition, computers produce **controlled** cartograms. **Figure 7.19B** shows such a computer-produced, controlled cartogram of U.S. population by state. Note how much like itself each state looks. Although shape has been distorted, it has been done in a recognizable way.

With increasing use of computers, cartograms of all types will become more available each year. In deciding whether to use a cartogram or a conventional map, you must decide if

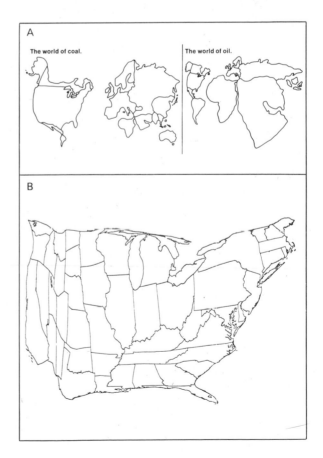

7.19 Continuous area cartograms range from those drawn manually (A) to those produced by computer (B).

you prefer emphasis on a distribution's magnitude or on a region's geography. With standard line maps, you face the problem of decoding magnitude information from complex symbols. Cartograms make these magnitudes obvious, but in distorting physical space, they force you to rely on your own familiarity with geography. The optimal solution, of course, is to use a mix of both types of maps.

CONCLUSION

In the previous four chapters, we have seen that our environment can be mapped in a wealth of ways. Even the same data can be depicted in very different-looking representations. We have discussed some of the many techniques map makers use to pack reality into symbols. Your goal, as we have said, shouldn't be to memorize a list of mapping techniques but, rather, to discover how reality has been transformed in each case. Once you

understand the logic of that transformation, you will be better able to imagine the reality which has been captured by each map symbol.

SELECTED READINGS

Bertin, J., *Semiology of Graphics* (Madison: University of Wisconsin Press, 1983).

Dent, B.D., *Cartography: Thematic Map Design*, 4th ed. (Dubuque, IA: Wm. C. Brown Publishers, 1996).

Robinson, A.H., et al., *Elements of Cartography*, 6th ed. (New York: John Wiley & Sons, 1995).

Slocum, T.A., and Egbert, S.L., "Cartographic Data Display," Chapter 9 in D.R.F. Taylor, *Geographical Information Systems: The Microcomputer in Modern Cartography* (New York: Pergamon Press, 1991).

Tyner, J., *Introduction to Thematic Cartography* (Englewood Cliffs, NJ: Prentice-Hall, 1992).

Tufte, E.R., *The Visual Display of Quantitative Information* (Cheshire, CT: Graphics Press, 1983).

Tufte, E.R., *Envisioning Information* (Cheshire, CT: Graphics Press, 1990).

Wright, J.K., "The Terminology of Certain Map Symbols," *The Geographic Review*, 34, 4 (1944), pp. 654-655.

Also see references in Chapter 3.

CHAPTER EIGHT

TIME AND MAPS

INTRODUCTION

STATIC MAPS

Temporal Aspects
Completion Date
Datedness
Mapping Period
Elapsed Time
Temporal Sensitivity of Features
Historical Perspective
Symbolizing Dynamic Features
Environmental Change Maps
Time Composite Maps
Change in Position
Change in Character
Travel Time Maps
Time Cartograms
Time Bias of Maps
Mapping Cyclical Phenomena
Mapping Trend Phenomena

DYNAMIC MAPS

Animation
Fixed-Sequence Mapping
Interactive Mapping
Stored Images
Computed Images
Simulation

CONCLUSION

SELECTED READINGS

What did Einstein do? Very little. He refused to accept the established
judgment of others, that time is an irrelevant constant.

—Jacob Bronowski, *Science and Human Values*

8

CHAPTER EIGHT

TIME AND MAPS

In Chapter 1, we discussed the dynamic nature of the environment (see *Environmental Change*). We learned that time, like space, is a vital part of human experience. All features in our three-dimensional world are continually aging. Some objects also change their spatial position over time. Thus, to locate something—a place, an object, or an event—we must view it in a four-dimensional space-time continuum.

We'll now consider how cartographers try to preserve this spatial flux in their map symbols. What we find is that time is commonly overlooked by map maker and map user alike.

Environmental change has long frustrated map makers, for the task of mapping a changing world is never complete. By the time a new map is finished, the more dynamic features may already have moved or changed. As fast as new maps can be created, existing maps become out of date.

Being overworked but basically clever, map makers have maintained their sanity by concentrating on phenomena that change relatively slowly. This practice gives their maps greater longevity if not greater utility. It also shifts the burden of dealing with environmental temporality to you, the map user.

You should view time, like space, as a relative rather than absolute attribute of the environment. But there's a big difference between space and time. You can move through space without restriction; there's no beginning or end, no inherent direction. Unlike space, time is a directed quality—it is irreversible. We can speak of evolution into the future but can regain the past only in memory. To explore the profound implications of directed time on map use, we'll first consider how static maps treat time. Then we'll discuss cartographers' attempts to map the changing environment with dynamic media.

STATIC MAPS

Not only have cartographers focused their attention primarily on relatively static phenomena, but they have also for the most part portrayed these features as if time were absent. Mute, static maps have been with us from the beginning of cartography. Maps scratched in the sand, printed on paper, painted on

BOX 8.1 A MATTER OF TIME

The relation of time to maps is a difficult concept for many map users to grasp. Unsophisticated map users tend to cling to the belief that maps are timeless, never-changing geographical devices, and this viewpoint is frequently reflected in literature. Antoine de Saint-Exupéry pinpoints this bias in *The Little Prince* (1943, p. 54):

> "Geographies," said the geographer, "are the books which, of all books, are most concerned with matters of consequence. They never become old-fashioned. It is very rarely that a mountain changes its position. It is very rarely that an ocean empties itself of its waters. We write of eternal things."
> "But extinct volcanoes may come to life again," the little prince interrupted....
> "Whether volcanoes are extinct or alive, it comes to the same thing for us," said the geographer.

This view of maps as frozen adjuncts to geography is echoed by C.P. Snow (1960, p. 58):

> "I'm only just beginning to realize," said George, "what a wonderful invention a map is. Geography would be incomprehensible without maps. They've reduced a tremendous muddle of facts into something you can read at a glance. Now I suspect economics is fundamentally no more difficult than geography. Except that it's about things in motion. If only somebody could invent a dynamic map—"

Although the truly dynamic map may be in the future, maps are produced frequently enough so that they do keep up with the changing environment fairly well. Whether volcanoes are extinct or alive *is* of importance to map makers, who are always striving to keep abreast of the times. The fact that maps must reflect a constantly changing world is pointed out by an advertisement for a Rand McNally atlas:

> **Whatever happened to Alice?**
> Alice, Colorado, went the way of 200 other small communities in the past ten years—gone from the face of Rand McNally maps. A turnpike gobbled up Bill's Place, Pennsylvania while DeSoto Beach, Florida is now part of the missile base at Cape Kennedy....
> At Rand McNally we're used to changes. In fact, there were over 40,000 made in our city and state maps last year. Businessmen and travelers demand up-to-date, accurate information on their maps, and we supply it.

A recognition of this changing nature of maps has led to a second viewpoint in literature. As John Steinbeck put it in *Travels With Charley* (1963, p. 70):

> ...roads change, increase, are widened or abandoned so often in our country that one must buy road maps like daily newspapers.

Perhaps the final literary word on the relation of maps and geography to a mutable world should go to Miss Dove, a character who is herself a geography teacher:

> "Is that the same map?" Jincey asked. She pointed to the large map of the world that hung, rolled up for the summer, above the blackboard behind Miss Dove. "Is China still orange?"
> "It is a new map," Miss Dove said. "China is purple."
> "I liked the old map," Jincey said. "I liked the old world."
> "Cartography is a fluid art," said Miss Dove.
>
> (Frances Gray Patton, *Good Morning, Miss Dove*, 1956, p. 56)

162

walls, or designed into floor tile mosaics all fall into this category.

These static maps do have some advantages. They're relatively inexpensive and, in paper form, convenient to handle and store. They lend themselves to detailed study, especially when visual information retrieval and processing are desired. Furthermore, a variety of simple, fairly inexpensive, and easy-to-use tools are available for analytical purposes, as we'll see in Part II: *Map Analysis*.

You can think of static maps as representing a slice in time, analogous to a "freeze-frame" on your videotape or optical disk player. As such, static maps give the impression of a stable, immobile environment. By making static maps of relatively static features, cartographers may simplify their job, but they largely ignore the fact that time is a vital part of the map user's world. Even with modern technology, it isn't possible to define the geography of the earth's surface at a given moment with absolute precision, as maps pretend to do. The map maker's ability to "freeze motion" is nothing but an illusion (see **Box 8.1**). Making maps static doesn't necessarily make them easier to use. Quite the contrary. Static maps give a false impression of the changing environment which only skilled and imaginative map interpretation

can overcome. You can lessen these problems, however, by understanding the relation between time and the map display.

Temporal Aspects of Maps

Maps that show what conditions were like at one specific time are, at least in part, out of date before map users even see them. All static maps aren't equally time specific, however.

Conventional line maps, because of their abstract symbolism and long production time, are the least tied to a specific time. Consequently, if we compare line maps created at different times, we see changes in spatial position—roads that have been moved, towns that have grown or dwindled, or dams that have been built.

If we compare image maps made at different times, on the other hand, we see changes in the *state* as well as the placement of features. For instance, trees shed their leaves and lakes are covered with ice in the winter, thus changing their appearance even though they haven't moved in space (**Figure 8.1**). Image maps, because of their less abstract symbolism and their shorter production time, show these changing states better than line maps, which usually depict average or typical states—a blue lake or green forest, for instance,

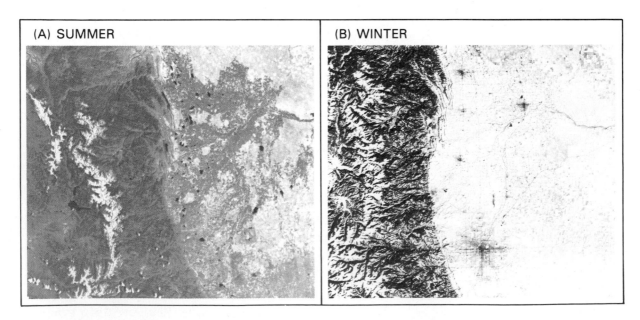

(A) SUMMER

(B) WINTER

8.1 There can be considerable seasonal specificity in the appearance of an image map, as demonstrated by these winter and summer scenes of the Denver region, seen from space.

regardless of season. (See Chapters 4 and 24 for more on image maps.)

Many people dislike image maps for this very reason—they are *too* time-specific. Different light conditions, seasonal change, and aging all transform the look of stationary features. Other features, such as cars or trains, may appear on one image map but not on another taken a few minutes later. Frustrating though this may sometimes be, that's the way our world is. Image maps remind us of the temporal nature of the environment and thus keep us in touch with reality.

And in using maps it's vital to keep time in mind. With the continual changes in our environment, even a year-old map may be significantly outdated. Before you use any map, you ought to know when it was completed and how long it took to make. These facts will help you judge how to use the map most effectively at the pre-

sent time. Let's take a closer look at these two important temporal aspects of map use.

Completion Date

One of the first things you should do when you pick up any map is to look at the date it was completed. Here you may immediately run into trouble, for many maps aren't dated. At times the date is left off inadvertently. At other times, map makers deliberately avoid adding dates so that maps won't appear outdated through long revision cycles. Even if there is a date, it may be hidden in a corner of the map, written in a cryptic code. Tracking down the approximate date of these maps may take some detective work (such as looking on the map for a spot you know has been altered recently). But if it saves you frustration later, the effort is worth it.

On many maps, of course, a completion date is clearly shown. The date on standard image maps tends to be the most specific. Most dates on standard low-altitude photographs, for instance, are given to the nearest day (**Figure 8.2A**).

Dates on line maps are usually less specific—as we would suspect, since line maps aren't as closely tied to temporal changes as image maps. Therefore, as **Figure 8.2B** shows, the completion date may be just one of several dates connected with producing a line map.

Datedness

It would be ideal if we had only up-to-date maps available. But no map is completely free of datedness. Even maps which are changed at short intervals, such as space photos and special navigational charts, are never truly up to date. Most ephemeral features, such as icebergs or severe storms, are inaccurately shown or remain unmapped and must be dealt with directly in the field or through supplementary sources of information. The only way to keep your maps updated is to annotate them with information from other sources, including other maps.

An outdated map can lead to serious, even deadly, driving confusion. If new interchanges have been constructed since information was collected for your map, you may miss the correct exit and become disoriented. Cartographers sometimes try to extend a map's practical life by mapping interchanges which have been planned but not yet built. The problem is that if the proposed

8.2 It's good practice to pay attention to the dates printed on maps. The date on the air photo (A) is specific enough, but the primary date (1959) on the topographic quad (B) is only one of several dates critical to the mapping process.

164

roads are never constructed or aren't completed on schedule, as often happens, the map will be more misleading than ever.

The question, then, is how "dated" a map can be and still serve a useful function. As usual, there is no one answer. We can tolerate different degrees of datedness with respect to different phenomena and in different circumstances. Map datedness depends on both the rate and pattern of change of environmental features and on our ability to imagine how the environment might look five, 10, or 25 years after the map was made. Most of all, our tolerance of map datedness depends on the consequences of arriving at a wrong conclusion about our environment through map use. Sometimes an outdated map may merely be inconvenient; at other times, it may be fatal.

Three factors can make a map outdated. First, the time it took to complete the map, or the mapping period, might have been excessive. Second, a long time may have elapsed since the map was made. Finally, the varying temporal sensitivity of environmental features must be considered. Let's examine each of these factors in turn.

Mapping Period. The first factor in map datedness, mapping period, is often overlooked, but it can have a major effect on map use. If the time between initial data collection and final map printing is lengthy and if phenomena change rapidly, the map can be badly out of date before it is even completed.

Clearly, then, a map's completion date tells only part of the story. It is equally important to know the mapping period. But if the completion date isn't always given directly on a map, the length of the mapping period almost never is. Some maps do include the dates of source information, though, and these dates will give you a clue to mapping period. USGS topographic quadrangles, for example, tell when photographs were taken and when the field check of map compilation was made. (Refer again to Figure 8.2B.) Maps that use census information usually give the date of data collection. Most maps, however, won't give you even that much help. The solution then is the same one you use when faced with a missing completion date: Think of several features you know have changed at certain dates and check their condition on your map.

Look again at the map in Figure 8.2B. Note that the completion date of the last photorevised edition is 1974 but that some compilation was done in 1957. In some respects, then, the map was effectively 17 years old when first published! It's important to realize that even a new map may, in a sense, be old if the mapping period was long.

Confusion over mapping period sometimes arises where least expected. Image maps are a good example. Many people assume that photos, for instance, give a simultaneous view of environmental features, and this is usually true of large-scale image maps. But image maps covering large ground areas at smaller scales are often created by taking a number of photos and then putting them together into a regional mosaic. (Figure 4.14 in Chapter 4 shows such a mosaic.) These photos may have been gathered over a period of hours, days, months, or—in the case of space image maps made up of several satellite images—years.

Usually, however, image maps have a shorter mapping period than conventional line maps. This means that image maps are generally better than line maps at representing rapidly changing features such as plant diseases or water pollution.

If line maps are produced by computer, however, their mapping period may be shortened remarkably. These computer maps can be completed only minutes after information is collected, especially if automated recording stations send information directly to the computer. Computer maps of a short-lived or rapidly changing feature can be in the user's hands while the feature still exists—not after it is of only historical interest, as with most handmade maps (see Chapter 9: *Software for Map Retrieval*).

Elapsed Time. The second factor in map datedness is the time that has elapsed since the map was completed. A map which provided an accurate picture of conditions when it was printed may be of little use today because too much has changed. The faster environmental features change, the shorter the acceptable elapsed time since mapping.

Sometimes an elapsed time problem is caused by the fact that maps of a certain region haven't been revised for a long time. Map makers tend to give higher priority to mapping new regions than to updating old maps. Their logic is that it's easier for the user to cope with an outdated map than no map at all.

At other times, the trouble is that, although updated maps have been made, you don't happen to have one. Who hasn't known the frustration of trying to use a 10-year-old road map unearthed from the depths of the glove compartment? These outdated maps can cause no end of confusion. If you are such a skilled and confident map user that you instantly spot changes in the environment and know what decisive action to take, you may be able to manage with an old map. But most people caught in this situation could better spend their effort locating a new map.

The elapsed time problem can be circumvented by producing maps on display screens from current information stored in computer memory (**Figure 8.3**). Since you view the screen directly, there is no lapse in time. There are difficulties with these electronic maps, however, primarily because not enough information has yet been stored in computers and because display units are still bulky and expensive. It shouldn't be long, though, before you'll be able to create up-to-date maps at will on your home television screen or on a display console in your car (see Chapter 9: *Software for Map Retrieval*).

Temporal Sensitivity of Features. Map use problems stemming from mapping period and elapsed time are complicated further by the varying temporal sensitivity of environmental features. Different features on the same map change at different rates. As a result, some features will hardly have changed since the map was begun, while others will be vastly different or will have disappeared altogether.

Some environmental features are also more sensitive than others to short-term, intermittent datedness. Roads are temporarily closed, for example, due to routine roadbed and bridge maintenance. Storms may cause temporary highway blockages. Rivers swollen by spring runoff or storm-induced flooding may be unnavigable for short periods. Certain soils may become impassable to farm equipment or recreational vehicles during spring break-up and periods of rainfall. To read maps effectively, we must grasp the effects of these and similar conditions. We'll return to this topic under the heading *Functional Distance* in Chapter 13.

Historical Perspective

Sometimes outdated maps are exactly what you want. By collecting and analyzing a series of maps of the environment over a sequence of times, you often gain valuable historical insight. You may compare the maps in several ways—by viewing them one after the next in proper sequence, by laying them side by side and viewing them simultaneously, or by using map overlays, one on top of another.

Such a time-sequence view of maps is particularly useful in monitoring dynamic phenomena such as storms. The series of maps in **Figure 8.4**, for example, plot the changing character and position of a hurricane as it moves across the Gulf of Mexico toward the Texas coast. We can learn a great deal by studying such map sequences.

In practice, the task of comparing a time series of maps is fraught with complications, however. The maps to be compared seem invariably to be of different scales, sizes, and symbolism. It is difficult to avoid this problem when using static maps. Fortunately, we can often gain a temporal perspective by using maps which deal with time

8.3 Electronic display screens make it possible to keep maps up to date. This photo shows an electronic map display unit mounted in a police car.

| SATURDAY, 1 P.M. | SUNDAY, 1 A.M. | SUNDAY, 6 P.M. |

8.4 This series of weather satellite images of a hurricane in the Gulf of Mexico could serve as individual frames for an animated map sequence.

directly. In the next section, we'll explore some ways cartographers symbolize dynamic features.

Symbolizing Dynamic Features

Environmental change has long frustrated map makers. Till recently, it took so much time, effort, and money to make maps that dynamic features weren't attractive candidates for cartographic representation. There are signs, however, that cartographers, encouraged by high-speed computer mapping procedures, are no longer ignoring dynamic features. With growing frequency, they are creating **time-related maps**—maps which deal with time explicitly, either in the mapped information or in the symbols themselves. In other words, time is actually built into these maps, not simply added on as a date in the map's margin.

Time-related maps are conceptually and cartographically more complex than static ones and thus require more effort to decipher. But the temporal insight we gain makes the extra effort worthwhile. The simplest of these time-related maps is the environmental change map.

Environmental Change Maps

Environmental change maps show change which has taken place over a particular time span. There are two main types—qualitative and quantitative.

Qualitative change maps show only the features which have been added to or removed from the environment during the period in question. In effect, these maps show the features that would remain if an older map were subtracted from a recent one. **Figure 8.5**, for instance, demonstrates the result of subtracting the pattern of forest cover on a 1937 aerial photo from the forest cover on a 1968 photo of the same area. From this figure, it's obvious that forest in the region expanded far more than it decreased during the 30-year period. Likewise, subtracting features on a 1965 quadrangle from those on a 1975 quadrangle would make it possible to see at a glance how many roads, subdivisions, landfills, and so on, were constructed during those 10 years.

Qualitative environmental change maps are simple to make and can show changes for many environmental phenomena simultaneously, especially if each type of feature is given a separate symbol. Such maps are of limited use, however, because only the changed features are shown. Thus, it's hard to place these changes in the broader geographical context.

Quantitative environmental change maps go a bit further than qualitative ones and show the changes in magnitude which have taken place—the increased or decreased size of a state's

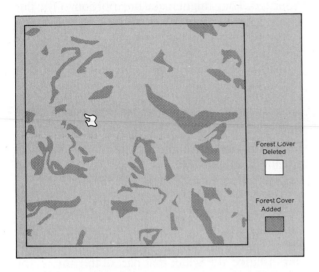

8.5 This qualitative change map depicts change in forest cover between 1937 and 1968 in a four-square-mile portion of Iowa County, Wisconsin.

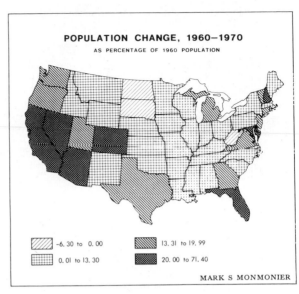

8.6 This quantitative change map shows the percent change in U.S. population by state between 1960 and 1970. Note that the base populations upon which these percentage changes are figured vary greatly.

population density, say, or amount of pollution in a lake. These maps may show only the direction of change (whether the magnitudes have gotten larger or smaller), or they may give the absolute values of magnitude change. Maps showing absolute changes are somewhat difficult to interpret, because the base magnitude isn't provided. We don't know whether a change of 100 people is based on a city of 500 or 500,000, although that information clearly makes quite a difference.

Quantitative change maps can also show the proportionate increase or decrease in a population over a specified time period, as in **Figure 8.6**. This map was made by forming a ratio between the state population figures for 1970 and those for 1960. If a state had 10 million people in 1960 and 11 million 10 years later, the ratio would be 11/10 million, representing a 10 percent increase. We have to be careful when using this type of map, because the same percentage of change doesn't necessarily mean that the same number of people have been added. If a populous state such as California increases its population by 10 percent, it is gaining far more people than if a sparsely populated state such as Wyoming adds 10 percent to its population. This is a good place for propagandists to misuse statistics for their own ends (see *Propaganda* in Chapter 25).

Time Composite Maps

We can circumvent the shortcomings of a single environmental change map by superimposing a map of one date on that of another. We can then see exactly what changes have taken place since the earlier map was made. Such a map, showing change through a succession of time intervals, can be thought of as a **time composite**. Such maps can show two kinds of change—change in position and change in character. Let's look at both these types of change.

Change in Position. Time composite maps are often used to trace the path along which something moves. Since point, linear, areal, and volumetric features vary in the way they change location through time, we'll consider them separately.

Point Features. Movements associated with discrete point features are often mapped as simple route lines. For instance, **Figure 8.7A** shows the route Lewis and Clark took on their historic journey to the west coast. A temporal context is created by showing the times at which they passed various points along their route.

When point features' movements aren't routed, multiple tracks are often plotted to create

168

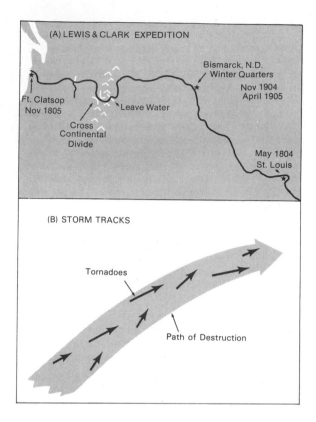

8.7 Simple route maps (A) show the changing location of a feature through time, whereas multiple track route maps (B) show different paths taken by a repetitive feature or event over time.

the impression of a temporal composite (**Figure 8.7B**). These temporal composites are commonly generalized to a higher level conception and mapped as paths or corridors. Thus you might find a map of "Tornado Alley" or the "Mississippi Flyway" on which an areal zone rather than a series of individual paths is depicted. Be sure you recognize the conceptually sophisticated nature of such a zone map.

The most common symbols showing point features' movement in quantitative terms are **flow lines**. These route lines show the varying amounts of flow of something—traffic, goods, services, and so on—between two points. Flow lines may be of constant or changing width.

On flow lines of **constant** width, changes in amount of flow are shown by varying texture, color value, or color intensity of the lines. Say that map makers want to show how many artichokes are being freighted along a line from California to

Chicago. They might make one portion of the line three times darker than another to show that three times more artichokes are being shipped along it. The trouble is that the lines have to be quite wide to make these differences clear (see Figure 7.1). This "fat line" problem could be solved by repeating thin lines of constant width. Thus, if one line stands for 1,000 artichokes, three thin lines indicate that 3,000 artichokes are being moved along that route. This solution is only marginally successful, though, since three thin lines take up about as much space as one fat one.

More common than constant-width flow lines are those of **changing** width. Here the thickness of the lines indicates magnitude. The more water that flows down a segment of a river, for instance, the wider that part of the line on the map will be (see Figure 7.6). The problem with these flow lines is that the human eye is not sharp enough to discriminate between slight changes in size. One solution is to divide the information into a small number of separate classes. The thinnest line might indicate 0-1,000 cubic feet of water per minute, the next thinnest line 1,000-2,000 cubic feet of water, and so on. The widths of the lines will therefore be different enough to be clearly identifiable.

When you read any type of flow line, focus your attention on the magnitude information, not on the line's precise location. Map makers often distort true geography to accommodate flow lines. A flow line showing the volume of ship traffic through the Straits of Gibraltar, for example, might be too wide to fit into the small space. Thus, the straits must be widened on the map; otherwise, it will look as if things are being shipped over land.

Linear Features. Maps rarely portray movement connected with linear features. When they do, they generally depict two different types of linear change.

On one type of map, changes in the location of a line feature such as a road may be shown by superimposing the paths followed at different times. In **Figure 8.8A**, road curvature likely was progressively smoothed and straightened as travel speeds and volume increased through the years.

A second type of linear change that you may find mapped is movement along routes. Thus, a map might show the movement of a train carrying nuclear waste along a track or the move-

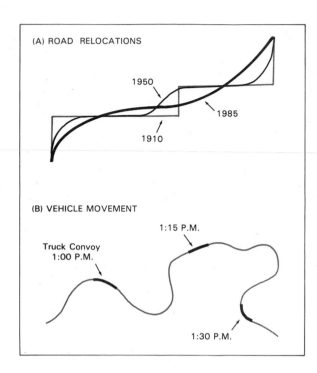

8.8 Time composite maps of linear features can show the changing location of a route through time (A) or the changing position of a vehicle along a route (B).

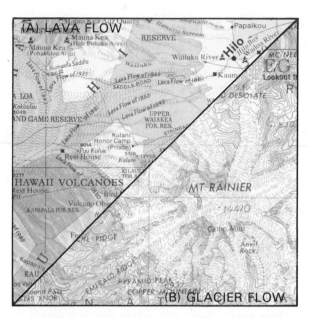

8.9 Repetition of simple map marks can be used to create symbols which suggest spatial flow processes, as these areal time composite maps of lava flows and glaciers illustrate.

ment of a toxic chemical spill down a river (**Figure 8.8B**).

Clearly, the scarcity of maps showing linear change doesn't reflect their lack of importance. Rather, the data needed to make such maps haven't been readily available. Fortunately, this condition is changing now that remote sensing is becoming commonplace (see Appendix B: *Remote Sensing of the Environment*).

Areal Features. Since movement of areal features occurs at their edge, they move along a linear front. This movement is shown on maps as a zone or area of change. The tidal zone is an example. As we saw in Chapter 1, what we think of as areal features may be more a matter of conception than of physical reality. Thus, a forest is composed of individual trees, and an urban area is made up of a composite of buildings and utilities. Change in the location of these areal conceptions is mapped in the same way as change in physically occurring areal features.

Cartographers sometimes try to suggest spatial process in the design of areal feature symbols. The symbols for lava flows or glaciers are

examples (**Figure 8.9**). Although such a symbol depicts the current extent of the feature, it also gives the impression that the feature is closely linked with a flow process.

Even more sophisticated areal conceptions are mapped in the form of spatial diffusions of discrete point phenomena. **Figure 8.10**, for example, shows the systematic areal expansion of gypsy moths in the eastern United States. The acres of forest land defoliated by this imported insect pest appear to be expanding at an accelerating rate. Since the mapping method is perfectly general, the inland movement of European settlers from the eastern seaboard in the 18th and 19th centuries could be similarly shown. So could the retreating snowcover in the upper Midwest during a typical spring thaw.

When working with this type of map, remember that you're dealing as much with conception as fact. The map pattern isn't in any strict sense verifiable in the field (see *Thematic Maps* in the introductory chapter).

Volumetric Features. Volumetric features move along an areal front which, for the most part, is difficult to show on a two-dimensional map. Thus, true volumetric change mapping is

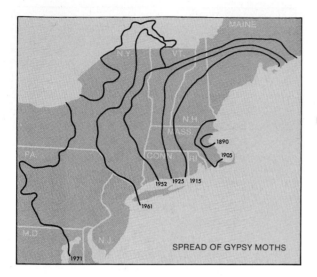

8.10 The progressive expansion or contraction of an areal feature can be shown with isolines. This map depicts the spread of gypsy moths.

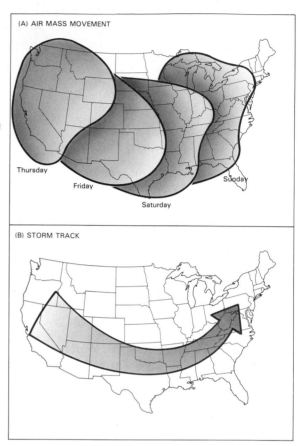

8.11 Volumetric features are commonly depicted on maps by areal flow symbols (A) or linear flow symbols (B).

rare. Instead, volumes are commonly collapsed into an areal form by projecting them down or up onto the ground level surface, and then these data are mapped as areal flow symbols. This is the standard method of mapping air mass movement (**Figure 8.11A**). Sometimes even greater abstraction is used, and the movement of volumetric features is collapsed into linear flow symbols. You're probably familiar with this conceptual leap through maps of the jet stream on TV weather reports (**Figure 8.11B**).

Change in Character. In addition to showing change in features' position, time composite maps also portray change in the character of the environment. The USGS, for example, uses this time compositing method to make interim photorevisions of their topographic quadrangles. Qualitative changes which have taken place since the earlier edition of the quadrangle are indicated by a magenta overprint. On some USGS quads, several photorevisions have been made, and variously colored overprints representing a succession of different time periods may have been added.

Composite point symbols (point symbols which indicate change through time) are often used to show cyclical phenomena. An annual graph might be used to portray the yearly cycle of temperature or rainfall at a specific point (see Figure 7.12E). Maps using these or similar time-sequence graphs allow us to compare seasonal variations at selected weather stations or to study the variation through time at a single station.

Travel Time Maps

We often turn to maps to decide how much time it will take to travel from one place to another. To do so with conventional maps, we must first find the travel distance in miles or similar ground units and then use our expected travel speed to convert these figures to a travel-time estimate. Cartographers sometimes try to simplify this process by annotating conventional maps with travel time estimates. These are at best average figures, of course (see *Behavioral Distance Annotations* in Chapter 13).

Rate of travel information can also be incorporated into the map symbols themselves. Thus, roads on which we can travel at more than 40 kilometers (25 miles) an hour might be symbolized by lines 2.5 millimeters wide, 40-kilometer-an-hour roads by lines 1.25 millimeters wide, and slower roads (such as school zones) by .5-millimeter-wide lines. Thus, the wider the line symbol, the faster the rate of travel. Such road symbols are often more useful than the usual sort showing number of lanes or type of surface. Most of the time, after all, what we really want to know about roads is the time it takes to drive them.

Time Cartograms

We have discussed a variety of ways in which cartographers build time into their map symbols. Some of these procedures are indeed quite ingenious. But perhaps the most novel approach to capturing time in maps is to incorporate the temporal dimension not into the map symbols but directly into the map geometry. The result is a linear cartogram on which time has been substituted for physical distance. These **time cartograms** have the same properties as all linear cartograms (which we discussed in Chapter 6).

There are two types of time cartograms. On one type, individual route segments have been made proportional to travel time. The scale in time units is supposed to be correct in both directions along a route. Such a **non-directional** map is shown in Figure 6.10. Problems arise with this type of map, since travel time is rarely equal in opposite directions along a route. Environmental factors such as sun angle, wind, ground slope, and one-way streets may exert a greater influence on travel time in one direction than the other. More often than not, therefore, these non-directional linear cartograms represent the average of travel times in opposite directions, something which is rarely experienced in reality.

On the other type of time cartogram, distance is given in travel time only from a central point. Figure 6.11 shows such a **directional** cartogram of Seattle based on evening rush hour driving times at five-minute intervals from the downtown. The map scale is one inch to five minutes' driving time, but the scale is correct only in one direction—*from* the central point. Travel times *to* the central point or between outlying points are incorrect. (For a more detailed discus-sion of route-segment and central-point linear cartograms, see *Linear Cartograms* in Chapter 6.)

Time Bias of Maps

No matter how maps deal with the changing environment, temporal bias is a fact of cartographic life. We owe it to ourselves, therefore, to assess each map to see how well it represents the environment in which we live. What we find will to some degree depend on whether the environmental features of interest are changing in a cyclical or in a trend-like manner.

Mapping Cyclical Phenomena

The mapping of phenomena that change in cyclical fashion poses special problems for the map user (see *Pattern of Change* in Chapter 1). In particular, it's important to know when in the cycle information was collected for mapping and how long it took to gather the information. If, for example, you looked at a map of average July temperatures for U.S. cities, what could you say about temperatures across the United States in general? Obviously, your answer would be greatly limited by the representativeness of the July data.

A map based on a single observation point is unreliable because it may represent the top of the cycle, the bottom, or some point in between (**Figure 8.12A**). To generalize from such a map can easily lead to a false impression of the environment. Consider the cyclical pattern of people going to work, to lunch, back to work, and home again. A population sample of a city taken at noon would show a much different distribution of people than a sample taken at midnight.

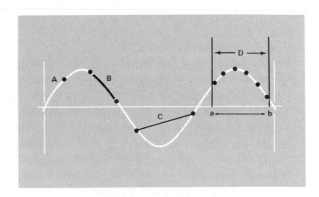

8.12 A few observations can easily give a biased view of phenomena which exhibit cycles or trends.

172

Even if maps are available for two observation points, you still have no guarantee of an unbiased view (Figure **8.12B**). A phenomenon may appear to be decreasing, increasing, or remaining the same, depending solely on where the sample points are located in the cycle. And even if you view a collection of maps representing a large sample of observation points, you can still have problems. Unless the phenomenon has been sampled repeatedly at a frequency that's half or less that of its basic cycle, the resulting information will be distorted. Peaks and valleys of the cycle will be lost or attenuated, as **Figure 8.12C** shows. The periodic nature of many environmental features is undoubtedly lost because their basic period is small relative to the mapping frequency.

The cyclical nature of phenomena can also be masked when averages are used. It is common to average information gathered over a month or a year and to provide only the average figure on the map. If just a single time span has been mapped, you will always gain the impression that the phenomenon is static. In addition, the state you observe will vary according to whether the map represents the top or bottom of the cycle or some span between these extremes (**Figure 8.12D**).

When a phenomenon is mapped over a succession of time spans, the result is quite different. A completely unsuspected cyclical pattern may emerge. Take monthly temperature and precipitation averages. There may not seem to be a day-to-day or month-to-month pattern, but when information is pooled over many years a strong cycle emerges. Just as cyclical patterns can escape detection because we observe them over intervals that are too long, they can also evade notice if our observation intervals are too short.

Mapping Trend Phenomena

When environmental change takes place in a non-cyclical way, we say there is a **trend**. Meaningful maps of trend phenomena are even more difficult to come by than those of cyclical phenomena. The problem with trends of all types is that you can't be certain that the duration of the observation period has given an unbiased picture of the way a feature changes over time. Maps based on three different observation periods might give you three different impressions of an environmental change. Your ability to make predictions

using trends is always influenced by the possibility that the pattern of change in the past or future can't be determined with the information you have in hand.

Sometimes cyclical phenomena may appear as a trend, as Figure 8.12D suggests. The time span shown (*ab*) wouldn't provide the information you need to detect periodicity. In practice, many cyclical phenomena that change slowly in relation to our life span and duration of record keeping have been treated (and are doubtless still being treated) as noncyclical.

DYNAMIC MAPS

A changing environment begs for a changing map. Despite all the clever map making devices we've discussed so far, the result is still a passive, static representation of a dynamic environment.

Dissatisfied with these static images, people use several methods to put the map into motion. One is to manipulate symbols on a map base such as a physical model. As we saw in Chapter 5: *Landform Portrayal*, physical models often provide the next best thing to "being there" in the environment. Thus, planners and military strategists often play out real-life scenarios by moving symbolic pieces on a base map as if playing chess. Such dynamic maps allow them to physically move around on the map display and thereby gain the advantage of tactual learning. They can practice actions over and over until procedures are finetuned and problems are worked out.

Unfortunately, such physical models are expensive and unwieldy. For these reasons, their use is restricted to situations in which cost isn't a primary concern and bulkiness is offset by the grave consequences of making wrong decisions.

A more general solution to dynamism in mapping is to put the entire map, rather than just a few symbols, into motion. How do cartographers accomplish this feat? We'll answer that question in the rest of this chapter.

Animation

Map makers can bring maps alive through several animation techniques. The least flexible of these involves playing through a fixed sequence of images from beginning to end. More sophisticated animation lets the viewer interact with the system, choosing the starting point and the sequence of images to follow. Let's look at both these animation methods.

Fixed-Sequence Mapping

The simplest way to build a time sequence into maps is to make a motion picture from a series of static maps. On such **fixed-sequence** animated maps, each frame is a separate map from a different time period. Time-lapse film and video methods transform the changes from one image to the next into a sense of motion. Dramatic animated maps have been made, for example, using hourly weather satellite images of the earth (see Figure 8.4). We watch the cloud patterns build up, swirl across the land surface, and dissipate from day to day as though we were sitting in a rocking chair 20,000 miles out in space. The differences in cloud patterns from one image to the next are slight enough so that we gain the impression of continual motion. Similarly striking animated maps are available on such diverse topics as landscape change, urban population growth, traffic crashes, and transportation network expansion.

One of the advantages of fixed-sequence animation over conventional static maps is that changes of geographical pattern can be viewed sequentially with all mapping variables held constant. Changes that have taken place in a region over a period of several generations can be viewed at a single sitting. Thus, fixed-sequence animated maps can point out changes which otherwise might escape us. Although the animated map images are ephemeral, any frame or sequence of frames may be stopped, slowed down, speeded up, or played backward. Each technique gives a different perspective.

Fixed-sequence animated maps often give us important insights into the nature of slowly changing phenomena. The first time we watch a time-lapse movie of a flower blooming, we are awestruck. The same effect could be achieved by viewing a city's air pollution over a single day; once we were made so graphically aware of how pollution is correlated with traffic, we might do more about decreasing auto exhaust pollutants.

Fixed-sequence animated mapping needn't be confined to temporal sequences. It is also possible to produce motion pictures of existing static maps (or ground scenes), using animation to **pan** over the landscape or to **zoom** up or down map scales. Thus, if a realistic physical model of, say, a national park is used as the basis of the motion picture, the animation can be quite life-like and informative (see *Simulation* later in this chapter).

The problem with many past attempts at fixed-sequence animated mapping was that the individual static maps were first produced by hand, à la Walt Disney. Due to the immense effort required, mappers usually didn't use enough maps to create the illusion of smooth motion; instead, the simulated motion on these maps tended to be jumpy. Furthermore, to keep costs within reason, the line maps used were generally rather simple. The increasing use of video and computer methods is rapidly overcoming this problem, although costs are still so high that the full potential of fixed-sequence animated mapping is far from being realized.

Interactive Mapping

Although fixed-sequence animated mapping can provide dynamic environmental portrayals through space and time, their pre-programmed, linear character prevents the map user from directly interacting with the map beyond stopping, reversing, or changing the speed of the sequence. As new technologies are developed, cartographers are creating more **interactive** map forms—maps which provide feedback to map users' queries or respond to users' commands. Modern map forms which fall into this interactive category provide some idea of what future map use will be like. We'll take a look at two interactive map forms, one based on stored images and the other based on computed images.

Stored Images. The most sophisticated interactive mapping procedures are still in an experimental, non-commercial phase. But they illustrate the exciting potential of interactive mapping. These systems use an **optical disk** player controlled by a microprocessor. Initially, ground scenes are videotaped, and individual frames are transferred to the disk. Map users then simulate movement through the video-mapped environment by giving commands with a "joystick," "mouse," or other system interface device. These commands call up the appropriate image sequence for display on a computer graphics terminal (**Figure 8.13**).

174

If existing maps are videotaped at different scales, we can use the microprocessor-controlled system to look up the appropriate map image of the region. This scheme has been built into the laser-disk car display navigational system with which Chrysler is currently experimenting (**Figure 8.14**).

Somewhat less ambitious stored-image mapping systems are based on Compact Disk— Read Only Memory (CD-ROM) technology. Although these systems are slower than optical disk systems, they work quite well with personal computers. A number of vendors now market mapping products (see Chapter 9: *Software for Map Retrieval*).

Stored-image animation can be jerky and slow and may not let you see what you want. The reason is that system builders had to anticipate which scenes users might want to see, and then create and store these images. Searching a large image database takes time, and you can't see what isn't there. Smooth motion, because it demands an immense number of images, is commonly slighted.

Computed Images. Problems associated with stored-image systems can be overcome by storing the original database, along with software capable of creating images on demand (see *Dynamic Relief Methods* in Chapter 5). Vehicle navigation systems sometimes use this method to recompute and update the street grid display as the vehicle moves along its path. Road networks are relatively simple, which means the database and computing requirements are modest. Computing full-motion video images on demand is another matter. At present, only the most powerful and expensive computers can handle a chore of that magnitude. This limits full-motion video capability to a few specialists.

Despite these implementation problems, this form of interactive map is, in theory, the map of our dreams. It will thrust map analysis and interpretation fully into the electronic age. It will do so by permitting a free question and answer exchange between you and the map. Through a series of prompts and queries, you can ask the computer to determine such factors as the area of a lake, elevation at a point, distance along a route, direction between two points, least-effort path, and so forth (**Figure 8.15**). The map serves as a convenient visual interface to the numerical data records stored in great detail in computer memory. The map display need only show enough information to help you direct questions to the data records. You use the maps for visualization and the map data for analysis. The computer provides the link between the two modes of storing geographical data. In such an environment, map

8.13 A single frame from a microcomputer-driven video disk map of Aspen, Colorado, called *Movie Map*, is shown.

8.14 Chrysler Corporation is experimenting with a video disk map navigation system which is guided by satellite positioning signals.

analysis can actually be fun! This is especially true if you can interact with the computer through verbal commands or by pointing.

Simulation

Maps aren't restricted to showing existing phenomena. One of the great strengths of mapping is that it lets us play out "What if?" scenarios. As we noted earlier, planners and military strategists have long simulated future events through mapping. Their concern is that poor decisions can lead to avoidable expense, environmental degradation, and loss of life. When this "cost" of taking wrong actions is high, it's a good idea to play out the consequences of different options through practice. When it isn't possible to manipulate the environment itself, the next best thing is often to manipulate a map representation. This was done, for example, by military commanders planning for ground operations in Desert Storm (see **Box 8.2**).

The imaginative power of simulation reaches its ultimate form with modern electronic technology. Special machines called **simulators** can respond to a number of human commands. When animated maps are used in these machines, the effect is one of actually moving within or through a three-dimensional environment. (See *Animated Methods* in Chapter 5.) The term **virtual reality** is now commonly used for the modern "goggles and glove" approach to simulation. In this implementation, a person wears a glove equipped with motion detectors and goggles containing a miniature TV screen for each eye. Hand motions cause changes in the screen images, producing the sensation of body movement through a three-dimensional setting.

Simulators are used to familiarize pilots with landing and take-off procedures before they climb into the cockpit of a real aircraft. In the same way, NASA astronauts were trained to land their spacecrafts on the moon by using stored video images. (These images were constructed using photos taken during previous orbital flights.) Likewise, driving-test simulators can, in several minutes of "action," gauge your response to several lifetimes of traffic crises.

In most modern simulators, computer-controlled video frames (stored-image systems) are giving way to fully electronic computer graphics display systems. In this case, the image is created on command from digital (numerical) data files which reside in the computer's memory and which represent the ground scene. The three-dimensional modeling procedures used in these simulators incorporate knowledge of hidden surfaces, shading, shadow, and texture to create dramatically realistic maps (**Figure 8.16**).

8.15 With growing frequency, map users can use electronic display screens to analyze and interact with environmental data.

8.16 Three-dimensional solid modeling by computer has become highly sophisticated, as this illustration shows.

BOX 8.2 COUNTDOWN TO WAR

Far north in the desert of western Saudi Arabia, Major General Barry McCaffrey gathered the battalion and brigade commanders of the U.S. Army's 24th Infantry Division (Mechanized) and their staffs for a fifth and final review of the war plan. This was known as "Map-Ex," for map exercise....

Inside the tents, headquarters personnel had constructed a large plywood-topped table that zigged and zagged for some thirty feet on both sides; only the top and bottom ends of the table were cut straight. On both sides of the long table, they had pieced together dozens of map sheets....

With McCaffrey's aides watching closely, junior officers from the Division Operations staff drew black greasepaint lines in the yellow of the map's desert. The more prominent were labeled Main Supply Routes Yankee and X-ray. The greasepaint lines snaked north into the heart of Iraq. There were also phase lines labeled Opus, Colt, Charger, Ram, Smash, Jet, and Viking. These divided the desert along east-west lines. Next were the objectives of McCaffrey's division. These were marked Brown, Red, Gray, and Orange. They were described with little circles. These were the targets toward which McCaffrey's mobile forces would aim. There were areas of operation marked Hammer, Stewart, Vanguard, Saber, Liberty, Cougar, Wolf, and Fox. There were battle positions marked 101, 102, and 103.

Finally, flags were placed on the map table—one for every unit in McCaffrey's division....During the course of the map exercise, the flags would be moved over and over again.

Gathered around the map table with McCaffrey were his staff chiefs for operations, intelligence, and communications....Altogether, there were sixty men and women crowded around the map table. There was not a single chair anywhere. Everyone had to stand.

Sipping from a cup of coffee, McCaffrey ordered the attack to begin. As he watched silently, his commanders began taking turns maneuvering their forces on the map table by moving the tiny flags on their wooden bases. What the movement of the flags described was a high-speed attack by the heaviest armored division ever fielded by the U.S. Army....

The map exercise dragged on for thirty-six hours over two days before it was concluded. "Well," McCaffrey said, "I guess that's it. Anyone have any questions or comments?"

Bill Chamberlain, a lieutenant colonel..., raised his hand. "Sir," Chamberlain said, "I just want to say that I would rather be shot in combat than go through another Map-Ex."

Out of the crowd of sweating soldiers around the map table came the voice of another battalion commander: "Sir, I agree. I, too, would rather see Bill shot than go through another Map-Ex."

(*Triumph Without Victory: The Unreported History of the Persian Gulf War*, by the staff of *U.S. News & World Report*, New York: Times Books, 1992)

CONCLUSION

When using maps of any type, we're inclined to use our relatively short life cycle as a temporal yardstick. We think of time flow in terms of lifetimes or generations, not always realizing how vague such concepts are from a quantitative standpoint.

The earth's origin dates back roughly five billion years. Multicellular life on earth stretches back about 600 million years. The human species has been around nearly a million years. The agricultural revolution began approximately 8,000 years ago. These numbers stagger the imagination. They represent such huge multiples of our temporal scope that we can't comprehend them.

The short duration of the human life span in relation to the scope of environmental processes contributes to an abusive attitude toward our surroundings. We find it difficult to deal effectively with long-range environmental management plans. It is hard for us to believe that the little pollution or population increment added to our environment each day could, over a period of several hundred years, destroy us.

To overcome the shortcomings of our relatively short temporal perspective, we may need to take the point of view of philosophers who consider environmental features to be events rather than objects. People are more permanent than sand dunes, trees more durable than people, lakes more long-lasting than trees, and geologic formations more enduring than lakes. But all these things are mere events on a time scale of billions of years. If we would treat all environmental features, including ourselves, as events rather than objects, we would minimize our tendency to simplify reality on the basis of longevity. Once we understood that all things change (though not with the same pattern and rate), we might be encouraged to treat the whole environment with greater respect. Long-range plans would be just as important as short-range ones.

Considering the significance of time, it seems incredible that it is rarely treated as an essential component in mapping. Map makers have treated time casually (if at all) simply for the sake of convenience, not because time is an inconsequential concern for the map user. In fact, time is probably the most important facet of our environment—even more crucial than space. We can learn to cope with spatial problems, but there's nothing we can do to stop time. Like it or not, we and everything around us are changing, second by second. If map makers disregard the temporal dimension, that is all the more reason that we, the map users, must bring to maps an awareness of its vital importance.

SELECTED READINGS

Boorstin, D.J., "Book I: Time," *The Discoverers* (New York: Vintage Books, A Division of Random House, 1985).

Brookfield, H., and Doube, L., eds., *Global Change: The Human Dimensions* (Canberra, Australia: Academy of the Social Sciences in Australia, 1990).

Campbell, D.S. and E.L. Egbert, "Animated Cartography: 30 Years of Scratching the Surface," *Cartographica*, 26, 2 (1990), pp. 24-46.

Carlstein, T., Parkes, D., and Thrift, N., eds., *Timing Space and Spacing Time*, 3 volumes (New York: Halsted Press, John Wiley & Sons, 1978).

DiBiase, D., "Visualization in the Earth Sciences," *Earth and Mineral Sciences*, 59, 2 (1990), pp. 13-18.

Earnshaw, R.A. and D. Watson, *Animation and Scientific Visualization: Tools and Applications* (San Diego: Academic Press, Inc., 1994).

Egbert, S.L., and Slocum, T.A., "Explore Map: An Exploration System for Choropleth Maps," *Annals of the Association of American Geographers*, 82, 2 (1992), pp. 275-288.

Eyton, J.R., "Rate-of-Change Maps," *Cartography and Geographical Information Systems*, 18, 2 (April 1991), pp. 87-103.

Gersmehl, P.J., "Choosing Tools: Nine Metaphors of Four-Dimensional Cartography," *Cartographic Perspectives*, 5 (1990), pp. 3-17.

Langran, G., *Time in Geographic Information Systems* (New York: Taylor & Frances, 1992).

Lynch, K., *What Time Is This Place?* (Cambridge: MIT Press, 1972).

MacEachren, A.M., and DiBiase, D., "Animated Maps of Aggregate Data: Conceptual and Practical Problems," *Cartography and Geographical Information Systems*, 18, 4 (October 1991), pp. 221-229.

MacEachren, A.M., and Taylor, D.R.F., eds., *Visualization in Modern Cartography: Setting the Agenda* (New York: Pergamon, 1994).

Monmonier, M.S., "Authoring Graphic Scripts: Experiences and Principles," *Cartography and Geographical Information Systems*, 1, 4 (1992), pp. 247-260.

Monmonier, M.S., "Strategies for the Visualization of Geographic Time-Series Data," *Cartographica*, 27, 1 (1990), pp. 30-45.

Morrill, R.L., Gaile, G.L., and Thrall, G.I., *Spatial Diffusion* (Newbury Park, CA: Sage Publications, Inc., 1988).

Parks, D., and Thrift, N., *Times, Spaces, and Places* (Chichester: John Wiley & Sons, 1980).

Peterson, M.P., "Interactive Cartographic Animation," *Cartography and Geographical Information Systems*, 20, 1 (1993), pp. 40-44.

177

PART I
Map Reading

178

Peterson, M.P., *Interactive and Animated Cartography* (Englewood Cliffs: Prentice Hall, 1995).

Roberts, N., ed., *The Changing Global Environment* (Oxford: Basil Blackwell, Ltd., 1994).

Robinson, V., ed., *Geography and Migration* (Brookfield, VT: Edward Elgar Publishing Co., 1996).

Singh, R.B., ed., *Global Environmental Change: Perspectives of Remote Sensing and Geographic Information Systems* (Rotterdam: A.A. Balkema, 1995).

Weber, C.R. and B.P. Buttenfield, "A Cartographic Animation of Average Yearly Surface Temperatures for the 48 Continuous United States: 1897-1986," *Cartography and Geographic Information Systems*, 20,3 (1993), pp. 141-150.

Zachmann, W.F., "Simulation: The Ultimate Virtual Reality," *PC Magazine*, (March 31, 1992), p. 107.

CHAPTER NINE
SOFTWARE FOR MAP RETRIEVAL

INTRODUCTION

DIGITAL CARTOGRAPHIC DATABASES

Location-Oriented Data
　　Scanned Landscapes
　　Scanned Maps
　　Extracted Map Data
Feature-Oriented Data
Database Trends

DISPLAYING RETRIEVED MAPS

CREATING MAPS FROM DATA

Reference Mapping
Statistical Mapping
Thematic Mapping
Image Mapping
　　Paint and Image Editing
　　Image Processing

DYNAMIC AND INTERACTIVE MAPPING

Interactive Multimedia
Animation and Simulation
Fly-Overs
　　Predetermined Sequence
　　User-Specified Sequence

YOU-ARE-HERE MAPS

HERE-IT-IS MAPS

CONCLUSION

SELECTED READINGS

9

CHAPTER NINE

SOFTWARE FOR MAP RETRIEVAL

Traditional printed maps are inexpensive, convenient to handle, and require no special equipment to view. These traits are so desirable that sheet maps have survived centuries of technological changes and will likely survive the information age as well. While printed maps won't become extinct in the foreseeable future, electronic technology is bringing us alternatives too useful to ignore.

Electronic mapping requires special equipment, programs of instructions, and large digital databases, all of which are costly and demanding of resources. Fortunately, these resources are fast becoming available on the Internet (see next chapter). Electronic mapping also requires some level of computer literacy on the part of map users. But the result is often worth the extra cost and effort required to develop and use computer-assisted mapping systems.

A variety of electronic map products are now on the market. They range from low to high conceptual sophistication and demand an equal range of user skill. New, more attractive products rapidly replace earlier, more primitive efforts. The products discussed in this chapter all serve the function of map retrieval and reference. All programs permit maps or geocoded data stored in a database to be displayed on a screen. With some products, data can also be linked to displayed maps. But the map retrieval and reference software we'll discuss in this chapter has no provision for analyzing map data. Software for map analysis is discussed in Chapter 19.

DIGITAL CARTOGRAPHIC DATABASES

Digital data are the foundation of electronic mapping systems. Each year, more geographical information is gathered in digital form directly in the field. But, for the most part, numerical information suitable for electronic mapping is the result of converting existing printed maps into digital files (see Chapter 2: *Geographical Data*). Unfortunately, different formats and structures are used in developing these digital cartographic databases. Mapping software must be matched to these different ways of organizing the data.

There are two fundamentally different data formats. Our computing, scanning, and printing technology all work in a matrix or grid format. In this **raster format**, data are recorded, stored, and processed on a cell-by-cell basis. In the case of image data, the cells are called **pixels**.

The alternative to the location-oriented (cell) focus is to think of the environment as being a collection of features of varying geometrical character. These features may be represented in a database as points, lines, areas, and volumes. We use the term **vector format** in referring to software and data having this focus on environmental **objects**.

Location-Oriented Data

The simplest way map makers convert existing maps to digital form is to scan the map as a whole. Many location-oriented databases are available. Some were made using a camcorder or electronic still camera set up to download individual image frames to a digital computer. Others were made by scanning maps with desktop electronic scanners capable of recording the full range of colors found on a printed map or image. Because this process is so straightforward, location-oriented cartographic databases are common.

The spatial resolution of both scanners and computer screens is limited, however. If the entire map is covered on one image, therefore, most of the original detail will be lost when the image is later displayed on a screen for viewing. To obtain an image that better matches the detail on printed maps, cartographers have to image the map in approximately 3–5 inch sections.

The advantage of whole-image databases is that they can be created relatively quickly and inexpensively from existing maps. A disadvantage is that only the information on the original map is included in the database. The original map design dominates subsequent displays of the information. Furthermore, the image is represented in the database in one layer as a whole. This means that

individual features in the image can't be manipulated separately from others. Thus, mapping flexibility is limited.

Let's look at several widely used location-oriented databases. These represent examples of databases created in three ways: scanning the environment directly, scanning maps, and extracting map data. As far as software is concerned, it doesn't matter how the databases were created, of course.

Scanned Landscapes

Electronic scanner imagery from satellites has been available for civilian applications since the early 1970s. (See Appendix B for more information on remote sensing.) Massive volumes of data now exist in these image databases. The *Landsat Multispectral Scanner (MSS)*, begun in 1972, generates gridded data at a pixel resolution of 80 meters and is suitable for mapping at 1:250,000 scale. The *Landsat Thematic Mapper (TM)*, operational since 1983, generates pixels of 30-meter resolution, which is suitable for mapping at a scale of 1:100,000.

The French *SPOT Image* satellites (in orbit since 1986) generate pixel grids of 20-meter (color) and 10-meter (black-and-white) resolution. The color imagery makes good 1:60,000-scale maps, while the panchromatic imagery is suitable for mapping at 1:40,000.

The Indian Space Research Organization has launched five remote sensing satellites since 1988 in their IRS series (-1A, -1B, -P2, -1C, -P3). These satellites have generated large image databases with multispectral resolutions of 180, 72, 36, and 20 meters. Their pancromatic images with five-meter pixels, available since 1995 (IRS-1C satellite), represent the highest spatial resolution satellite coverage available commercially. It is well-suited to 1:25,000-scale mapping. Plans call for a satellite with 2.5-meter panchromatic imagery in 1998.

Due to commercialization, however, major changes are taking place in remote sensing from space. A number of private vendors worldwide are gearing up to launch their own satellite systems. Some of these are designed to record data in hundreds of narrow wavebands, producing what is called **hyperspectral imagery**. Most of these satellites are also designed to achieve extremely high spatial resolution. Plans call for these **high-**

182

resolution satellites to record environmental phenomena with pixels ranging in size from one meter (panchromatic) to five meters (color). At least some of these data may be available commercially in 1998.

Scanned Maps

The USGS decided in the mid-1990s to scan its topographic coverage of the United States. The product is called a **digital raster graphic (DRG)**. The USGS began producing DRGs of its 1:24,000 maps in the mid-1990s, with plans to eventually do all its topographic maps. The DRG project at 1:24,000 scale is now complete for some states, and the rest of the states will be done within a year or so (**Figure 9.1**)

Paper maps are scanned at 250-dpi spatial resolution, converted to an 8-bit color image, and referenced to a UTM projection (see Chapter 11

and Appendix C for more on the UTM projection). These data are then compressed into a Tagged Image File Format (TIFF). Compressed files for a 7½-minute quadrangle range from 5 to 15 megabytes of data, so you need a robust computer to display the images. DRGs are available on CD-ROM for 1 x 1 degree quadrangles, which include about 64 files of 1:24,000-scale maps.

The USGS also decided to provide complete **digital orthophoto quadrangle (DOQ)** coverage of the United States by the end of the century (see Figure 4.13). The program uses 1:40,000-scale aerial photos that are centered in each 3.75' x 3.75' quarter of a 7½-minute topographic quadrangle. These photos are scanned, and the resulting matrix of one-meter pixels is processed to correct for scale distortions due to height variation of landscape features. The topographically corrected data are georeferenced to a

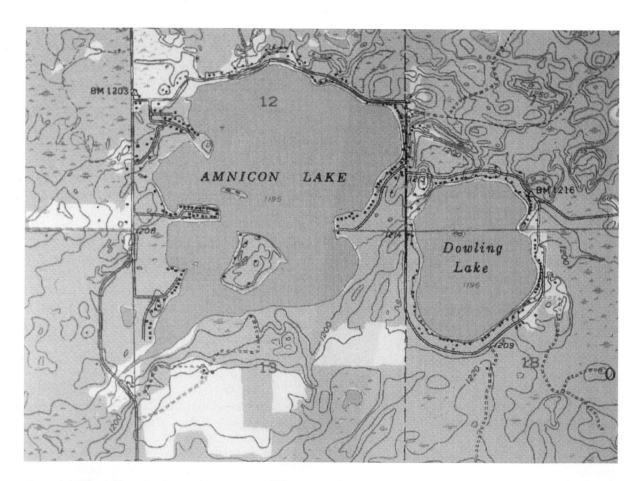

Figure 9.1 This portion of a digital raster graphic (DRG) of a 1:24,000-scale quadrangle illustrates the level of detail available in this electronic version of the USGS topographic quadrangle series.

UTM projection and the NAD83 datum (see Chapter 2 for more on datums). Since the DOQs provide the same ground coverage as each quarter of a 1:24,000 topographic map, they are sometimes referred to as **digital orthophoto quarter-quadrangles (DOQQ)**.

Each color band is stored in 256 (eight-bit) gray levels. Files are distributed in a compressed-image format of about five mb per DOQ. Data meet National Map Accuracy Standards (see Chapter 20: *Map Accuracy*) for 1:12,000-scale mapping (+/-33 feet on the ground). For more information on orthophotos, see Chapter 4.

Extracted Map Data

Regular grids of topographic data, called *digital elevation models (DEMs)*, are produced by many government agencies and private firms. In the United States, DEMs are available at two scales in the USGS's US Geodata program. Contour lines for the entire country were digitized from 1:250,000 quads by the Defense Mapping Agency. This information was then interpolated to a grid with a ground spacing of approximately 200 feet. These data are also available at a 3" (latitude-longitude) sampling interval. The digital files are split into two paths, one for the east and one for the west half of the quad.

The USGS is also producing DEMs from its 1:24,000 quads, using a ground distance sampling interval of 30 meters. The data are derived from digitized contours or from a scanned stereo-model of high-altitude photographs. The USGS divides its DEMs into two vertical accuracy classes, one falling between 0-7 meters and the other between 8-15 meters. Plans are to have 1:24,000 DEM coverage of the United States completed by the year 2000. (For more information on DEMs, see *Digital Elevation Models* in Chapter 5.)

Finally, the USGS is producing DEMs as a by-product of its digital orthophoto quadrangle program. Pixel size is one meter, so these DEMs also have a one-meter sampling interval on the ground. These high-resolution digital elevation data provide one of the key Digital Cartographic Databases in the U.S. National Spatial Data Infrastructure (NSDI) effort. Geodetic control and landcover are other key databases. The federal government's aim is to keep these databases updated so that they will serve the needs of both public and private institutions in the coming decades.

Feature-Oriented Data

Cartographers also create databases by converting existing maps to digital form on a feature-by-feature basis. They scan or digitize roads, rivers, political boundaries, and other features as layers into separate data files. The graphic aspects of the original map design don't persist in these vector databases to the extent they do in the whole-image approach. The resulting database is complex in structure but more flexible in use.

The problem with feature-oriented databases is that data gathering is time-consuming and expensive. The extra cost is often justified, however, because individual features as well as feature layers in the database can be manipulated and tailored to a wide variety of user needs. Let's look at some of the better-known databases of this feature-oriented type.

DIME/TIGER. The U.S. Census Bureau began creating *Dual Independent Map Encoding (DIME)* files of urban streets for the 1970 decennial census. These files were updated and coverage was expanded for the 1980 census. For the 1990 census, the system was modified, further expanded, and renamed the *Topologically Integrated Geographic Encoding and Referencing (TIGER)* database. TIGER is based on planimetric data from USGS 1:100,000 quadrangles and was developed with USGS assistance. (For information on USGS topographic quads, see *Land Navigation* in Chapter 14.) Features include roads, addresses, hydrography, railroads, miscellaneous transportation, and census unit boundaries. TIGER data, usually in upgraded form, are widely used by private vendors in their digital mapping products.

US Geodata. The USGS uses the term US Geodata* in reference to digital cartographic databases. Its digitizing activity began in the 1960s. The first database effort was to digitize 1:250,000 and 1:100,000 *Land Use* and *Land Cover* maps. Planimetric coverage of the entire United States was completed from *National Atlas* reference maps at 1:2,000,000 in 1982.

*Information on US Geodata can be obtained from the National Cartographic Information Center, U.S. Geological Survey, 507 National Center, Reston, VA 22092, 703-860-6045.

184

The USGS began digitizing planimetric data from its 1:100,000 quad maps in the early 1980s. These files were called **Digital Line Graphs (DLGs)**, in reference to their topological structure. This meant that each line segment in the database had a beginning and ending point, and a right and left neighbor. The program was restructured in the early 1990s. The new files were feature-based, characterized by objects, attributes, and relationships. The new database is called **Digital Line Graph–Enhanced (DLG-E)**.

Modified and supplemented versions of TIGER files, taken from 1:1,000,000 quads, are being completed with partners in the business community. Currently, the USGS and its private-sector partners are modifying and supplementing the 1:100,000 TIGER files and completing 1:24,000 coverage. Both these databases use latitude-longitude and UTM coordinates. (See Chapter 11: *Locational Reference Systems* for information on UTM.) When the program is complete, all features on the 1:100,000 and 1:24,000 quads will be coded in digital form.

WDBII. The *World Data Bank II (WDBII)* was completed by the Central Intelligence Agency (CIA) in the early 1980s by digitizing map sheets at scales from 1:1,000,000 to 1:4,000,000. It includes over six million latitude-longitude coordinates and covers international boundaries, hydrography, coastlines, and U.S. state boundaries. The database has undergone continual revision and update through the years. WDBII is the basis for many digital mapping products sold by private vendors.

DCW. The *Digital Chart of the World (DCW)* was developed by the U.S. Defense Mapping Agency in conjunction with private contractors. It represents the most detailed worldwide cartographic database and was originally released in 1992.

To create the database, a series of 1:1,000,000 maps that cover the world, called *Operational Navigation Charts (ONC)*, were scanned at 1,000 dots per inch. These raster files were then converted to ESRI's PC ARC/INFO* vec-

tor format. The data were sorted by feature type into 17 information layers, divided into 5 x 5 degree tiles, and stored on a set of four CD-ROMs in a non-proprietary format. There are 1.7 gigabytes of DCW data on these CD-ROMs! You can preview DCW tiles on ESRI's Web site (see Chapter 10). The DCW data (coastlines, international boundaries, cities, airports, contours, roads, railroads, water features, cultural landmarks, and other base-map information), and special desktop software for using the data, are available from ESRI.

Commercial. Several private firms now distribute proprietary vector cartographic databases. Some of these commercial databases have been developed from scratch. Others are modifications and updates of public-domain databases such as those discussed previously. The four examples we discuss here are chosen because they're used by so many developers and providers of digital mapping products.

1. *EtakMap** databases focus on roads and streets. They meet USGS standards for 1:24,000 mapping in urban areas and 1:100,000 in rural areas. Roads are named and classified by type, and address ranges, zip codes, and geographic coordinates (latitude-longitude) are provided. These top-quality databases cover over 75 percent of major population centers in the United States, and coverage is being expanded to other parts of the world.

2. DeLorme Mapping's *Street Atlas USA*** is a comprehensive road and street atlas of the United States. It is bundled with easy-to-use software that makes the extensive cartographic data held on CD-ROM come to life (**Figure 9.2**). You can search on phone number, ZIP-code, place, and street to retrieve a map to the screen. You can view the same location at a wide range of map scales, depending on the amount of geographic detail and extent of geo-

---

Arc/Info is a geographical information system (GIS) developed and marketed by Environmental System Research Institute (ESRI), 380 New York Street, Redlands, CA 92373, 714-793-2853. See Chapter 19: GIS and Map Analysis Software.

Information on EtakMap databases can be obtained from Etak, Inc., 1430 O'Brien Drive, Menlo Park, CA 94025, 415-328-3825.

**Information on DeLorme's databases are available from DeLorme Mapping, P.O. Box 298, Lower Main Street, Freeport, ME 04032, 207-865-1234.*

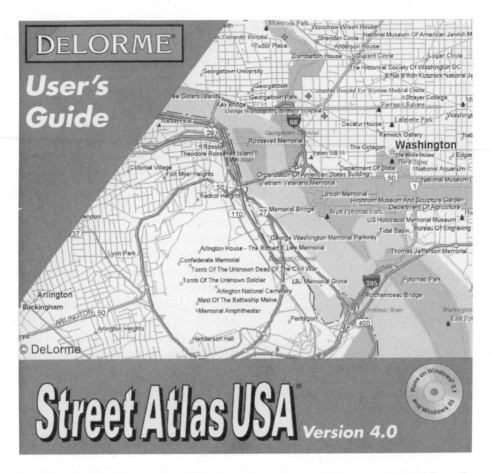

Figure 9.2 Street Atlas USA is representative of the tremendous volume of highway and street information now available on CD-ROM. This database is used with many electronic navigation map display systems. (Courtesy DeLorme Mapping.)

graphic coverage you desire. You can customize maps to suit your needs and print out maps for handy reference in the field.

3. One of the oldest commercial suppliers of cartographic databases is Geographic Data Technology (GDT).* Its highly regarded *Dynamap* products include a street network database (streets, addresses), postal (ZIP-code) boundaries, political boundaries, census district boundaries, landmark layers (airports, railroads, parks, recreation areas, transportation terminals, institutions, major retail centers, large urban landmarks), insurance rate territories, hydrography, coastal windstorm areas,

GDT, 11 Lafayette Street, Lebanon, NH 03766-1445, http://www.geographic.com.

postal carrier routes, and other features. GDT has had a long and intimate relation with the U.S. Census Bureau's DIME and TIGER file development.

4. Environmental System Research Institute (ESRI) markets a 1.2-gigabyte database on a CD-ROM titled *Maps & Data, Volume I*. These ready-to-use data provide access to worldwide mapping files and let software developers put maps into their applications easily. This company is expanding rapidly into the cartographic database arena.

Database Trends

The databases discussed in the previous sections represent only a portion of the digital data now

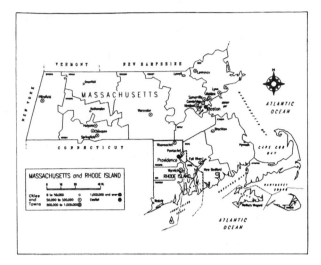

9.3 Clip-art maps can be displayed, altered, and printed for reference purposes, but they aren't suited for data manipulation or analysis.

available for use with mapping software. Additional data are being gathered at a growing pace. While a decade ago government agencies dominated database development, the momentum is shifting rapidly to the private sector.

Databases are being commercialized by vendors who see a profit to be made in selling digital cartographic products. These databases are used in a wide variety of applications that are affecting the way we use maps. Clearly, competition between private vendors is stimulating development of an array of exciting new mapping products. We'll discuss some of the mapping possibilities in the remainder of this chapter.

DISPLAYING RETRIEVED MAPS

People commonly use a map as a geographical dictionary. They look to a map when they want to know where a place is located in relation to other environmental features. Since people vary greatly in their backgrounds and needs, such maps must show a variety of features for spatial reference purposes. On these **general-purpose maps**, then, you'll find features such as coastlines, rivers,

roads, political boundaries, and cities. Because these features define the basic geographic structure of a region, such reference maps are called **base maps**.

The most primitive collections of electronic maps are skeletal base maps that can be displayed and printed or plotted (**Figure 9.3**). They are called **clip-art maps**, in reference to their cut-and-paste nature. Most of these maps are "dumb" in the sense that they stand alone, simply to be looked at. You can't interact with data used to make the map or information associated with the mapped region (in contrast to *Creating Maps from Data*, discussed later in this chapter).

Simple base maps are widely available as clip-art in word processing and desktop mapping software. More extensive collections are marketed in conjunction with **presentation graphics*** and **illustration**** software. Specialized clip-art vendors sell vast collections of electronic maps. Although these maps are commonly spliced "as is" into a document, the maps can also be tailored on screen to meet individual needs. Features can be added or deleted, color and other symbols changed, and the size or style of type modified.

As a rule, you can interact with these clip-art map collections only in a very limited way. Base map collections usually come with a reference manual, which shows pictures of the maps along with their titles (disk file names). To call up a map on your computer screen, you select its file name from a list. Within limits, you can see the displayed map in more detail by zooming in on a portion of it. The maximum level of detail is determined by the scale of the original map that was digitized or scanned to create the electronic data. Remember that digitizers approximate curves with straight-line segments, and scanner resolution is determined by its pixel size. Thus, if

*See, for example, Freelance Maps (Lotus Development Corp., 55 Cambridge Parkway, Cambridge, MA 02142, 800-345-1043.

**Illustration software includes such programs as Illustrator (Adobe Systems, Inc., 345 Park Ave., San Jose, CA 95110), CorelDRAW (Corel Systems Corp., 1600 Carling Ave., Ottawa, Ontario K1Z 8R7), Designer (Micrografx, 1303 Arapaho Rd., Richardson, TX 75081), and Freehand (Aldus Corp., 411 First Ave. S., Seattle, WA 98104).

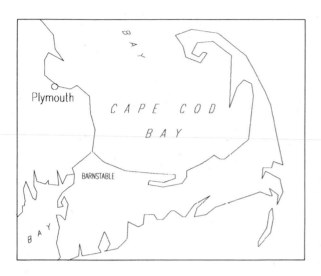

9.4 If clip-art maps are enlarged much beyond the scale of the source maps, the spatial resolution of scanning or dig-itizing will become apparent in the form of straight or jagged line artifacts.

Figure 9.5 Map clip art is available in a full array of map-ping styles and types for use by advertisers and publishers to add eye-catching appeal to their documents.

you enlarge a clip-art map too much, you will see these straight or jagged line artifacts (**Figure 9.4**).

More elaborate clip-art map collections contain maps of graphic quality comparable to that found in atlases (**Figure 9.5**). These collec-tions serve the same function as an atlas. Recently, collections of novel maps, terrain views, and 3-D globes have emerged to serve the market for "eye-catching" special-effects maps in publishing and advertising.* But people want more. They often want to know things about the pictured area that aren't part of the map design. This need is addressed by tailoring maps from databases.

An excellent example of high-end map clip-art collec-tions is MapArt (Cartesia Software, 80 Lambert Lane, P.O. Box 757, Lambertville, NJ 08530, 609-397-1611). CD-ROMs of raster and vector data include U.S.Terrain, Geopolitical Deluxe World, and USA Bundle. At least 32 mb of computer memory, as well as image editing and illustration software, are required. For other examples of clip art, see Globe Shots and Cool Maps and Mountain High Maps (Digital Wisdom, P.O. Box 2070, Tappahannock, VA 22560, 800-800-8560).

CREATING MAPS FROM DATA

One of the great benefits of the computer age is increased access to information. We have had text, statistics, and maps for centuries. But we had to deal with them as separate sources of informa-tion. Shifting back and forth between these three forms of information was rarely convenient and often impractical. Much of the frustration of working with these different data forms can be avoided if they are recorded in computer-com-patible (digital) form. This has already been done for a great deal of information, and the process is progressing rapidly.

Mapping software that will let you link a map with a database is now available in a variety of commercial products. The functionality of this software ranges widely. Some programs are designed to work on desktop computers, while others provide assistance for drivers (see *You-Are-Here Maps* later in this chapter). The source of data may be a prerecorded disk, or it may be telecommunicated on demand from an external source. Hardware demands also vary widely.

188

Reference Mapping

Atlas-style maps and limited quantities of linked data are widely available in CD-ROM format. Because of the enormous data capacity of CD-ROMs, software in this category can offer vast libraries of maps and related environmental data in easily transportable form. Products distributed on CD-ROM include such titles as *World Atlas* (The Software Toolworks), *Encarta 97 World Atlas* (Microsoft), *Compton's Interactive World Atlas* (1997 Edition), *Mindscape's U.S. Atlas and Almanac, ArcAtlas: Our Earth* (ESRI), and the National Geographic Society's *Picture Atlas of the World*. A selection of these programs is available in most computer software stores.

These digital atlases all function in much the same way. Your session begins with a base map of the world on the screen and a main menu bar running along the map's top-left edge (**Figure 9.6**). Both map and menu bar are active; thus, you can work from map to text or from text to map. For example, select any country name on the world base map (point-and-click with mouse or use cursor arrows and enter on keyboard), and a base map of that country appears on your screen. Select a city, and a pop-up "Text" keyword submenu appears. Submenu commands include geography, people, education, health, government,

crime, economy, agriculture, communication, and travel. Select one of these topics, and you bring up a list of related data. Your mapping options include dozens of map styles for world and country or region coverage. Aerial views, 3-D maps, detailed street maps for major cities, satellite images, video clips, ground photos, and other items let you discover and explore every part of the world.

If you prefer, you can start with the menu bar rather than the map. Selecting any of the main menu keywords produces a drop-down submenu of commands. Choosing one of these commands produces either a map or a list of data associated with a mapped region (country) or location (city). Picking the keyword "Index" in the main menu, for example, may give you a secondary menu of letters in the alphabet. Selecting any of these letters will give you an alphabetized list of geographical names. Highlighting one of these names will give you the country map on which the name is found.

These atlas products now have links to Internet sites about cities and places (see next chapter). This gives you online access to unlimited volumes of information not contained on the CD-ROM. It also provides you with the most current information available worldwide. You can even customize a map and print it for personal use.

Statistical Mapping

Large volumes of census information and other statistical data are now stored in computer-compatible digital form. A variety of mapping programs can be used to display these data in their geographical context. Some statistical mapping programs contain a statistical database along with the software. These programs usually ask you to select a mapping technique and a data subject from lists of options. You may also be asked to specify design parameters, such as a vantage point (with 3-D methods), the number of class intervals, and class limits. When you've selected these items, a map appears on the screen.

The problem with self-contained mapping packages is that it may be difficult or impossible to map data other than what is provided with the software. At the worst, data upgrades must be purchased from the software vendor. As an alternative, some statistical mapping programs let you

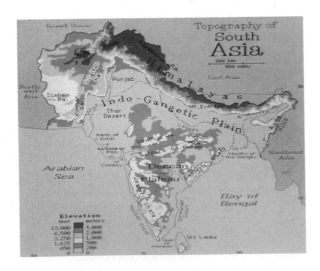

9.6 This map is taken from *World Atlas,* **which is representative of map retrieval packages that take advantage of the enormous data storage capacity of CD-ROM technology. (Courtesy The Software Toolworks.)**

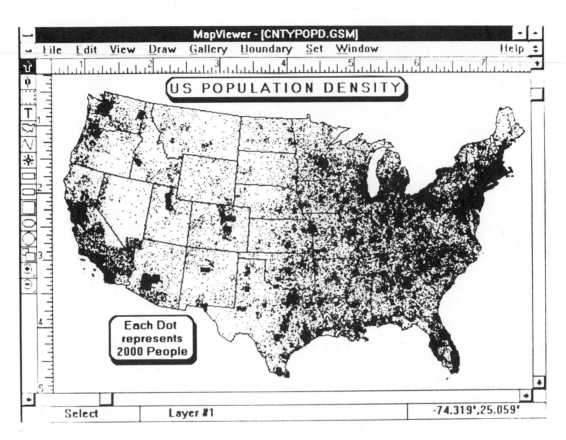

9.7 High-end statistical mapping packages provide a variety of options for displaying user-supplied statistical data. This map was produced using *MapViewer*.

use external databases. Programs such as *MapInfo, Atlas*GIS, MapLinx, MapViewer*, and *Surfer** are representative of these high-end pro-

grams (**Figure 9.7**). You can use this type of software to map your own data. Since these programs must be able to handle a variety of data exchange formats, they tend to be more expensive than self-contained packages.

Most computer spreadsheets now include a statistical mapping capability. Once you have centered data on the spreadsheet and manipulated it to your desire, you have a variety of options for cartographic display. As an alternative, you may decide to export your spreadsheet data to a stand-alone statistical mapping package. Most such mapping software accepts data in a range of spreadsheet formats.

*MapInfo *is marketed by MapInfo Corp., 200 Broadway, Troy, NY 12180, 518-274-8673. Atlas*GIS *is marketed by Strategic Locations Planning Inc., 4030 Moorpark Avenue, San Jose, CA 95117, 408-985-7400. ArcView GIS *is sold by ESRI, 380 New York Street, Redlands, CA 92373, 714-793-2853. MapLinx *is marketed by MapLinx Corporation, 5068 W. Plano Pkwy., Plano, Texas 75093, 214-231-1400. MapViewer *and* Surfer *are marketed by Golden Software, Inc., 809 14th Street, Golden, CO 80402-0281, 303-279-1021.*

190

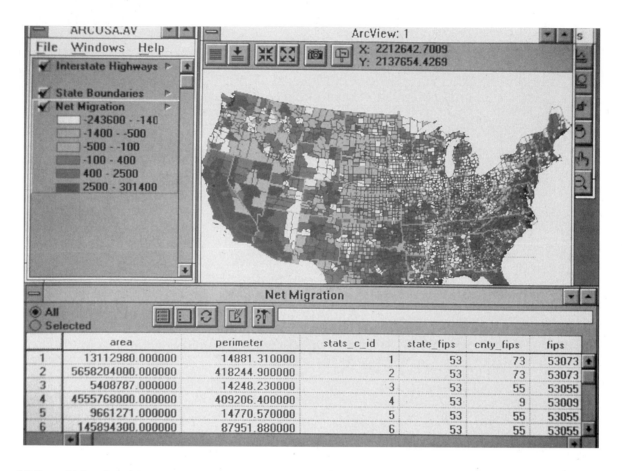

9.8 Some high-end mapping packages provide options for displaying user-supplied attribute data, such as the location of geographic features (roads, rivers, etc.) and landcover classes. This map was produced using *ArcView*.

Thematic Mapping

A variety of programs permit mapping of attribute data, such as land-use or landcover classes. *ArcView* is one of the best, because it lets you display digital information available in Arc/Info and many other popular data formats (**Figure 9.8**).* *ArcView* represents the high end of digital

map retrieval software and exhibits some analytical features as well (see Chapter 19: *GIS and Map Analysis Software*).

Image Mapping

Earlier in this chapter (see *Location-Oriented Data*), we discussed how raster photo databases are created directly by scanning the landscape or indirectly by scanning photos of the landscape. Image mapping software that takes advantage of these digital photo databases is of two types. Let's look at each one.

*ArcView is marketed by ESRI, 380 New York Street, Redlands, CA 92373, 714-793-2853. Arc/Info is a geographical information system (GIS) also marketed by ESRI (see earlier footnote).

BOX 9.1 REALITY CHECK

I have almost two decades of family pictures in a shopping bag—undated, unsorted, prints and negatives spilling out of their envelopes, the old and the new hopelessly jumbled. All but the latest dozen or so. These are taking up virtual space instead, on the hard disk of my computer. They are cleverly labeled: Harry at Ballpark, Harry with Astro, Harry on Stoop.

They are a little on the fuzzy side, and to make them I spent $900 on a digital camera roughly equivalent in quality to a traditional camera costing $50. But let's face it. The chemical technologies that produced most of the images in this magazine, not to mention just about all the 70 billion amateur pictures developed worldwide last year—technologies that require the support of a multi-billion-dollar worldwide photo-processing infrastructure—have reached the end of their useful lives. Those technologies were a temporary accident, the best we humans could do for a while, like illumination by whale oil. Now it's farewell to silver halide, goodbye Kodachrome, forget about Polaroid. R.I.P.

In a digital camera, light passes through the lens and strikes an electronic detector instead of the multilayered film, saturated with tiny crystals of silver salts, that unrolls and slides behind a mechanical shutter. The digital images are stored in the camera's memory or in a match-book-size add-in with 150 times the memory of the original I.B.M. personal computer. You see each picture immediately on a tiny screen, and if you don't like it, you can erase it to make room for more.

Then you've got . . . bits. Bits are lightweight. You can plug the camera into a computer and transfer the bits. You can display them on a monitor. You can send them by E-mail. You can show them on your Web page. When it occurs to your local photo shop to install a suitable printer next to all that darkroom equipment, you should be able to walk in and get instant color prints. Or for about $500, you can buy a new photographic printer that lets you make your own snapshots or 8-by-10's, matte or glossy, not to mention greeting cards, postcards and calendars.

Bits are fast, and news photographers have been among the first professionals to take advantage of digital photography. The pattern of photons bouncing off the President's face can make its way by satellite or land line back to a newspaper office at light speed, more or less. Art photography will not succumb so readily. Artists adopting digital photography have tended so far to a science-fictiony, special-effects style. For the infinitely delicate gradations of shading in fine art photography, film, for now, remains superior. Bits are just a sampling of reality. Still, the gradations of film are not really infinite—film has grains, digital in their way, just as electronic detectors have pixels. Eventually, film will be to photography what vinyl is to recorded music: an antique medium with a special, nostalgic feel.

Bits are also changeable. With any decent photographic software, you can transform an image with two-dimensional and three-dimensional effects: pixelation, edge detection, wet paint, pinch-punch, whirlpool, zigzag. You can paint in new textures and backgrounds. You can enhance, adjust or substitute colors with infinite freedom. You can add artistic effects: alchemy, canvas, glass block, impressionist, smoked glass, terrazzo, vignette. You can sharpen images or soften them. You can add motion blur, or throw in some random noise, or, if you are in a perverse mood, simulate a mathematically perfect lens flare—a spot of light designed to mimic an optical reflection that you would be desperate to remove if your lens had caused it. If you happen to miss the graininess of film, you can add that, too.

Other software lets you make subtle changes to the size of any element in a picture, without obviously distorting anything else (shrink those ears; stretch that nose). You can push, slide,

continued on next page

Reality Check continued from previous page

brush and nudge the pixels of a photograph as though they were a liquid. Of course you can move that moon to a more artistically suitable spot in the sky, or excise nonpersons from group portraits. . . .

So much for reality. Some photographers have always tried to give people skin tone that was realer than real or to increase the grandeur of nature. "To say that 'the camera cannot lie,'" Marshall McLuhan wrote a generation ago, "is merely to underline the multiple deceits that are now practiced in its name." We have long had distorting lenses and air brushes. Still, we trust photographs, or we did. We admit them into evidence. Some of the truthfulness we ascribe to photography has to do with the sheer inconvenience of chemicals and papers and darkrooms, as the particular sound of a violin has to do with old wood and yellowed resin. Now photography is becoming as slippery as water. . . .

(James Gleick, *New York Times Magazine*, 1997)

Paint and Image Editing

At the low end of image display software are common paint programs.* These come bundled with computer operating systems and some office suite software. They are also offered as stand-alone programs, and a variety can be downloaded on the Internet free or as shareware.

Most paint software will let you import and export images in a variety of graphic file formats. They also provide tools and menus that allow you to manipulate the image in a number of ways. In all cases you create special effects by adjusting tone or color information on a pixel-by-pixel basis.

More sophisticated programs called **image editors** expand the functionality of inexpensive paint programs.** These programs let you import and export images in a wide variety of graphic file formats. This software also lets you do everything found in paint programs and more. For example, you can pre-define and then manipulate blocks of pixels that represent image features or objects.

Image editors have largely replaced manual photo processing in a darkroom. You now can perform dramatic image enhancements at your computer. For example, you can delete or add entire features, change the background, and perform other creative tricks, with no visible evidence of the tampering. Indeed, the certainty of photographic evidence in now subverted by digital technology for manipulating images. "Seeing is believing" no longer holds true for photos and other images (see **Box 9.1**).

Image Processing Software

The high end of image display software is represented by **image processing** software (see Chapter 24: *Image Map Interpretation*).* These programs are designed for professional use and take some effort to master. But their capability goes well beyond that of image editors. You can import and export images in a long list of graphic file formats. Most important, you can set rules for processing the entire image automatically. The processing is based on a **local operator** procedure, whereby each pixel in the image is manipulated in accordance with information found in neighboring pixels.

Examples of paint programs include Publisher's Paintbrush, CA-Criket Paint, Painter, *and* Halo Desktop Imager. *Check your local computer software store for current versions.*

**Examples of image editors include* Photoshop, PhotoFinish, PhotoStyler, Photo-Paint, Picture It, PhotoSuite, PhotoImpact, *and* Picture Publisher. *Check your local software store for current versions.*

Examples of image processing programs include ERDAS Imagine *(ERDAS, Inc., 2801 Buford Highway, Atlanta, GA 30329),* ER Mapper *(Earth Resources Mapping, 4370 La Jolla Village Drive, Suite 900, San Diego, CA 92122),* ENVI *(PCI Remote Sensing Corp., 1925 N. Lynn Street, Arlington, VA 22209), and* Image Analyst for ArcView GIS *(ESRI, 380 New York Street, Redlands, CA 92373). This software is designed for use by professionals in the mapping sciences and is not available in software stores serving the general public.*

Image processing software lets you super-impose layers of geocoded data on the image base. Thus, buildings, roads, floodplains, and other geographic features can be used to enhance the photographic data. Perhaps the most dramatic function of image processing software is to let you drape the image over digital elevation models, creating an oblique three-dimensional view of the landscape. If these landscape scenes are animated, you can create a fly-over, which we'll discuss in the next section.

DYNAMIC AND INTERACTIVE MAPPING

Static paper maps have served human needs for centuries. But they have a "take-it-or-leave-it" character that isn't sensitive to your special needs. As a result, you often find yourself trying to make do with a map that isn't designed for your particular use. Electronic media offer a welcome alternative to traditional static maps. Digital displays let you interact with and manipulate your map in many ways that were once impossible.

Furthermore, electronic maps need not be static representations. You can now have dynamic, moving maps. These may simply be animations of traditional static maps, or they may be simulations of environmental conditions or processes. You can follow your moving position on these maps with the help of positioning technology. You can also simulate flight over the landscape. Let's look more closely at these examples of dynamic and interactive maps.

Interactive Multimedia

The potential of modern information technology is best achieved by **interactive multimedia** software. The term **multimedia** is used in reference to a system capable of handling sound (music, speech, special effects), text, numbers, still images, and video graphics.

Current multimedia mapping systems are probably best represented by electronic encyclopedias. Examples of multimedia encyclopedias include *Encarta* (Microsoft), *World Book* (IBM), and *Grolier* (Grolier Interactive, Inc.). They are available in most computer software stores. These programs contain hundreds of static maps and dozens of animated map sequences. More important, the maps are fully integrated with text, statistics, music, video clips, photos, and other items that let you explore subjects, events, people, places, and times.

The great benefit of this multimedia software is that it encourages us to move freely between maps and other forms of knowledge representation (sound, video, still photos, drawings, text, numbers). Of course, we could interact with all these media before the advent of multimedia technology. But we were usually discouraged from exploring their full potential because of the effort and frustration involved.

Current multimedia software based on CD-ROM technology is not without limitations, however. Problems such as slow screen redraws and slow-motion video are related to the limited power and speed of hardware in common use today. Since new generations of hardware and software appear every six to 18 months in the computer industry, these limitations should become less of a concern.

No matter how sophisticated the new technology, however, we seem to push it quickly to its limits and desire more. In multimedia terms, this implies we won't be satisfied until all knowledge is readily accessible, starting with any piece of information. This is a big challenge for the technocrats!

Animation and Simulation

Many problems in creating map animation and simulation with CD-ROMs can be overcome with **optical videodisk** technology. Optical disks the size of vinyl LP records are used as the storage medium. Each disk can hold up to 54,000 still images or one hour of full-motion video, depending on the design of the system used to play the disk. Although this technology is not as popular as CD-ROM systems, it is widely used in training, education, marketing, and entertainment applications. Due to the high quality of imagery, some people use videodisk systems to show feature movies at home.

In addition to providing excellent image quality, videodisk technology lends itself to interactivity. Low-level systems permit the same level

9.9 Optical videodisk technology is ideal for storing and providing access to a large photo database. Here we see one frame from the Wisconsin DOT's *Photolog* project.

of interaction as videotape and VCR systems. But the most powerful and flexible videodisk systems, those linked with a personal computer, give you complete control of the system. With the help of special software and properly coded images, you can go directly to any image on the disk and view any sequence of images at any speed you desire. You can also enhance a video image by overlaying computer graphics.

Mapping applications of videodisk technology are still limited. Indeed, the technology forces us to rethink what we mean by the term "map." For example, one of the most interesting applications is the *Photolog* project developed by the Wisconsin Department of Transportation (DOT). The DOT has taken images in each direction at 52-foot intervals along Wisconsin's highways and put this information on videodisks. Using a videodisk player controlled by a personal computer, you can go to any point in the highway system and look down the road in either direction (**Figure 9.9**). You can also step through a sequence of images at simulated highway speeds. A mass of auxiliary highway data is also linked to each frame so that you can view this information as well.

Whereas *Photolog* is an operational system, many videodisk mapping projects are still experimental. *Movie Map*, for example, was created in Aspen, Colorado, by the Architecture Machine

Group at Massachusetts Institute of Technology. For this project, eye-level video frames were taken at 10-foot intervals along roads, streets, and building access paths and halls. Maps and plan views were also put on videodisk. You can thus simulate driving through town along any chosen route, and walking into buildings, by interacting with menu commands on a touch-sensitive screen (see Figure 8.13 in Chapter 8). You can turn at any corner, speed up, slow down, reverse direction, and stop at will. You can even switch from summer to winter images.

So why don't we all have access to videodisk mapping so that we can get to know a place before we actually go there? Part of the reason is cost. It takes great effort and expense to produce the original master disk, which can then be copied relatively inexpensively. It takes a large potential market to justify the cost of producing the master disk. In addition, videodisk players are still more expensive than VCRs and aren't nearly as popular. Videodisk use has thus been limited primarily to business and institutional settings.

The interactive capacity of videodisk technology, but not its full-motion video, is available in compact disk format in a technology called **CD-I (Compact Disk—Interactive).*** CD-I is audio CD compatible so that you can use it to play your collection of CD music disks. But CD-I differs from audio CD because the disks also can carry still photos and graphics, either of which can be animated.

A CD-I system plugs directly into a TV and stereo speakers. It can also be plugged into a personal computer equipped with a special video card that can handle a VCR or TV input signal. A "thumbstick remote" (the CD-I version of the video-game "joystick") controls all disk action.

A CD-I title of special interest to map users is Rand McNally's *America: United States Atlas.*** The disk holds maps for the United States on topics such as economy, people, and environment. At

For information on CD-I systems, contact Philips Consumer Electronics Company, 440 N. Medinah Road, Roselle, IL 60172, 708-307-3000.

**For information on CD-I titles, contact Philips Interactive Media of America, 11111 Santa Monica Blvd., Los Angeles, CA 90025.*

the state level, it shows simple base maps with major features and a few thematic maps. You can access state maps by selecting a state from an alphabetized list or a U.S. outline map. By saving two maps to a clipboard, you can fade from one to the other for comparison. To take a tour, you choose the states you want to visit from a U.S. outline map. Tours consist of a narration of each states's primary characteristics and attractions, accompanied by still images of landscape scenes. There is a hint of greatness here but, overall, the impression is that this is a rather crude first attempt at harnessing powerful CD-I technology. The addition of full-motion video would help, as would larger-scale maps with "hot" links to other information.

As this example shows, current CD-I technology does have limitations. There is no full-motion video because present systems can't move the required volume of data quickly enough to provide the 30-image-per-second TV standard. The advanced video compression technology needed to surmount this problem is coming. In the meantime, you only have access to slow-motion, animated sequences of still images. More serious, perhaps, is that CD-I is a self-contained system that plugs into standard TV and stereo jacks with no special cables or connectors. This means it isn't compatible with computers unless the computer is first equipped with an expensive video board.

Probably the most serious problem with CD-I technology is that it has not been widely accepted by consumers. One of the newer formats, such as some form of digital compact disk, seems to hold more promise (see **Box 9.2**).

Despite current problems, CD-I and the other multimedia systems discussed here hint at the tremendous promise technology holds for the map user. Fully developed systems will have an active map interface. This will let you begin your retrieval of information by pointing to a location on a map. Such systems will also have a full linkage network among all knowledge in the database so that you can easily move from any topic to any other related information.

BOX 9.2
DVD: PURE MAGIC ON A PLASTIC PLATER

Watch out in the coming months for DVD. It promises to burn holes in every database, game, and multimedia archive that you've ever carried around on CD-ROM.

Actually, like Windows CE, nobody's entirely sure just what the initials mean (whatever it was, it has morphed into the logical Digital Video Disk), but that's the information age for you. . . .

In this case, DVD may just live up to the inevitable hype. It mimics the size and shape of a CD, but can carry between 1.36 and 15.9 gigabytes of data. At the high end, that's the equivalent of 24 CD-ROMs. Put another way, a DVD can easily hold two hours of video and sound, or three million pages of text. . . .

Three kinds of DVD exist. DVD-Video plays movies, etc., on your TV via a special player, similar to your VCR system. DVD-Audio, as the name suggests, plays on a properly equipped stereo system. DVD-ROM . . . runs on a computer and will eventually replace CD-ROM as the permanent and portable storage medium of choice. . . .

DVD-ROM drives can play CD-ROM disks and Audio-CD (although not laserdiscs), but CD-ROM drives can't return the favor. . . . DVD-ROM drives can also play DVD-Video and DVD-Audio. . . .

DVD-ROM brings a hefty advantage to multimedia storage and quality. It offers the average user the opportunity to own gigabyte-level portable libraries, encyclopedias and databases; provides software developers with a delivery medium for the (inevitable) next generation of megaprograms; and brings us one step closer to realizing true PC Theater.

(David Bragi, *Portable Computing Direct Shopper*, August 1997)

9.10 This three-dimensional perspective image was created using a powerful roadway design system called *RoadCalc*, which is marketed by Engineering Design Systems (Dubuque, Iowa).

Fly-Overs

Programs that simulate flight over the landscape are creating a great deal of excitement. Multimedia atlases boast of dozens of fly-over clips. Scientists use fly-overs to study the landscape from all angles to better grasp the nature of their subject.

For such fly-overs to be realistic, full-motion video is required. Thus, a powerful computer is needed to produce the 30 or so frames a second required for smooth motion. A digital terrain database (see Chapter 5: *Landform Portrayal*) is also needed to create these fly-over electronic maps. If surface rendering with natural textures or landcover is desired, databases holding this information must be available. Supporting software must be able to produce an image of the landscape from any chosen vantage point.

Once the appropriate system components are assembled, the developers of fly-over products have several choices. Which approach they take depends primarily on the sophistication of available hardware, database, and software. Basically, it's a question of how much they are able to expend in human and monetary terms. Less ambitious systems will show a rather skeletal terrain from only a few vantage points. More advanced systems will provide a realistic terrain view in full motion.

Predetermined Sequence

The least flexible and most inexpensive fly-over systems display images from vantage points in a pre-selected flight path. The most primitive products generate only still pictures, as shown in **Figure 9.10**. Although a number of such images can be created by repeating the commands with new vantage points, rarely would more than a few images be called for by a map user.

The exception is when someone puts together a sequence of images to simulate slow-motion animation or a full-motion fly-over. This was done, for example, with the Los Angeles

9.11 Here we see one of over 3,000 frames used to make the Los Angeles Basin fly-over called *LA—The Movie.*

Figure 9.12 A laptop computer linked to a satellite positioning receiver and loaded with the proper navigation software and cartographic database can display your map position as you move through the environment.

Basin* fly-over that has been widely broadcast in commercials and Cable News Network (CNN) "Science & Technology" segments. To produce this fly-over, thousands of scenes depicting the terrain surface were overlaid with a Landsat satellite image showing landcover. These scenes were computed from vantage points along a pre-chosen flight path (**Figure 9.11**). Since this fly-over is produced in video format, the sequence of images was set by its creator. With an appropriate VCR, you can achieve such special effects as freeze-frame, slow-motion, fast-forward, and reverse. But that is the extent of your control.

User-Specified Sequence

The inflexibility and lack of user control that characterizes predetermined sequences is overcome in more sophisticated interactive systems. One such approach involves computing views from a multitude of vantage points and storing them for subsequent retrieval by a system user.

With such a system, you are provided with an interface that lets you choose a three-dimensional path. Once you specify this path, the appropriate selection of images is displayed.

*LA—The Movie *was created from a single Landsat TM scene (July 3, 1985) and a digital elevation model. It was produced by the Science Data Systems Group, Jet Propulsion Lab, 4800 Oak Grove Drive, Pasadena, California 91109, 818-354-4016.*

The computational demands on such a system are enormous. Numerous scenes must be pre-computed. An immense amount of information must be retrieved in random-access fashion. This information must be displayed at the full-motion rate of 30 frames a second. The only way to perform all these computations is to use the most powerful computers made (called supercomputers). Even then, you are limited by the availability of stored images.

This stored-image problem is overcome with systems that provide the software and database needed to compute a sequence of views as you specify new vantage points. You may perform such a **real-time fly-over** by moving a joystick or entering a series of vantage point coordinates from a keyboard. The advantage of this approach is that you have complete flexibility in choosing a flight path. The drawback is that a supercomputer is needed to support the computations and data-transfer rates. Cost restricts this approach to flight-simulation applications, special graphic effects in film-making, and other users who demand the best and have the resources to pay for it. Even then, in an attempt to save computational time, image quality usually falls somewhat short of photo-realism.

198

BOX 9.3 BOOSTING YOUR CAR'S IQ

You may never stop and ask directions again with Oldsmobile's GUIDESTAR system, a sophisticated mapping and routing device that literally tells you where you are and how to get where you're going.

Olds's system uses a combination of global-positioning satellite (GPS) readings, an inertial guidance system for dead reckoning, and sophisticated computer map-matching techniques to establish the car's precise location and plot a route to your chosen destination. A 4-inch color monitor mounted on the dashboard asks literally, "Where do you want to go?" The menu-driven software lets you answer by entering a street address, an intersection, a freeway entrance or exit, a "point of interest" (including tourist attractions, major businesses, hospitals, schools, and service stations), or a previous trip's destination stored in the computer's memory. The system then offers you a choice of routes—the most direct or the one using mostly expressways, for example.

As you drive, the system traces your progress. The monitor displays the number of miles to your next turn, and a synthesized male voice tells you well in advance when to make it. If you take a wrong turn and get lost despite all this computerized prompting, the system establishes your current position and recalculates a route, all at the touch of a button....

GPS locating and mapping systems for automobiles aren't exactly new. About 6,000 motorists in Japan currently have them on their cars. American consumers, on the other hand, have historically been more cautious about high-tech advances, and such caution partly explains their high cost and limited availability here....

Ultimately, any device that boosts a car's IQ must win the confidence of the car's true guiding intelligence—the driver.

(Joseph D. Younger, *AAA World*, November-December 1994)

YOU-ARE-HERE MAPS

One of the most exciting developments in electronic mapping is the use of map displays in vehicle navigation systems. In this application, a base map on a computer screen indicates your location (**Figure 9.12**).* This is the digital map equivalent of the familiar "you-are-here" maps that you find hanging on walls at critical locations.

But the electronic maps go a step further. As you drive along, your position on the map display is updated as well (see **Box 9.3**). What makes these maps do their magic is modern spatial positioning technology. These navigation systems are discussed in more detail in Chapter 15: *GPS and Maps.*

In the more sophisticated systems, the map display is linked by cellular phone or radio signals to local databases so that you can receive traffic updates and other useful information as you travel. Vast databases of lodging, restaurant, and other travel information, as well as trip planning software, are also available to assist in your travels.

HERE-IT-IS MAPS

Always knowing your map position can be comforting and useful, as we saw in the previous section. But sometimes you want to know the location of something distant from your present position. Fortunately, the same software that uses GPS technology to pinpoint your position can also find those distant locations.

Software such as Road Scholar *(Road Scholar Software, Houston, TX),* TripMate *(DeLorme Mapping, P.O. Box 298, Freeport, ME 04032),* SkyMap *(Etak, Inc., 1430 O'Brien Drive, Menlo Park, CA 94025),* GeoLink PowerMap *(GeoResearch), and* Compass-3800 *(Chicago Map Corp., 15419 127th Street, Lemont, IL 60439) provide this function.*

Many mapping programs serve this "here-it-is" market.* Features vary between vendors, but most software will let you call up a map with the target location marked with a symbol. You can make your request by entering a telephone area code, postal ZIP-code, street name, street intersection, building address, or geographic place name (city, national park, and so on). Often these programs are linked with electronic Yellow Pages so that you can find the location of anything in the phone book. Alternatively, you can find locations of target businesses or attractions near an address. The software will also give you the nearest address if you click on a specific map location.

Simple "here-it-is" mapping software commonly includes **trip planning** enhancements or links to software that has those additions. You might think of these programs as ROAD ATLAS + TRAVEL AGENT + TOUR GUIDE on a CD-ROM with Internet links. This software truly makes planning half the fun of travel. While still at home or in your car (if you have a laptop computer), you can check out restaurants, lodging, campgrounds, and other things to see and do near a given address or along a specified route.** Interactive maps let you explore such places as national parks.

You can customize software settings with a profile of your travel preferences so that only your personal favorites are displayed. Internet links to vendors' Web pages and other sites provide access to volumes of additional travel-related information, including road conditions and weather.

Examples include Street Atlas USA *(DeLorme Mapping, Lower Main St., Freeport, ME 04032),* SelectStreet Atlas *(www.procd.com),* Precision Street Map USA *and* Precision Mapping Streets *(Chicago Map Corp.),* Streetfinder 1997 *(Rand McNally, 8255 N. Central Park Ave., Skokie, IL 60076),* Streets Plus *(Microsoft Automap, www.microsoft.com/automap/), and* Streets on a Disk *(Klynas Engineering, P.O. Box 499, Simi Valley, CA 93062).*

**Popular trip planning programs include:* Tripmaker 1997 *(Rand McNally, 8255 N. Central Park Ave., Skokie, IL 60076),* AAA Map'n'Go—Trip Planner *and* Global Explorer *(DeLorme Mapping, Lower Main Street, Freeport, ME 04032), and* Trip Planner *(Microsoft Automap, www.microsoft.com/automap/).*

CONCLUSION

Two incompatible technologies are currently associated with electronic maps. One is the **personal computer**, with its associated peripheral devices, such as display screens, digitizers, scanners, printers, CD-ROMs, modems, faxes, and the like. Personal computers brought word processing, spreadsheets, databases, statistical processing, mapping, desktop publishing, and graphic design to the desktop. Recently the personal computer has provided the basis for multimedia.

The other technology is **consumer electronics**. This category includes VCRs, TVs, camcorders, stereos, cassette players, laser disk players, compact disk players, and so on. Whereas personal computers changed the workplace, consumer electronics changed recreation.

At present, electronic map products are designed for one or the other of these two incompatible technologies. Even worse, they are designed for incompatible equipment within each category. IBM-style personal computers are not compatible with Apple's machines, and so on. Fortunately, the trend is toward increasing compatibility between the two technologies and between products within each category. Focus is shifting from building proprietary systems that lock out other applications to producing creative products. Not only will this reduce frustration levels immensely, it will also mean that resources aren't spread so thinly across a myriad of incompatible products. The map user is bound to gain. This is especially true when it comes to using the Internet for mapping purposes, as you will see in the next chapter.

SELECTED READINGS

Arlinghaus, S.L., ed., *Practical Handbook of Digital Mapping: Terms and Concepts* (Boca Raton, FL: CRC Press, 1994).

Benzon, W., ed., *Desktop Mapping the MapInfo Way: A Primer on the New Technology for Data Visualization and Analysis* (Troy, NY: MapInfo Press, 1991).

Canning, S.H., "Never Be Lost Again," *Portable Computing Direct Shopper* (August 1997), pp. 108-110.

Carter, J.R., *Computer Mapping: Progress in the '80's* (Washington, DC: Association of American Geographers, 1984).

Clarke, K.C., *Analytical and Computer Cartography*, 2nd ed. (Englewood Cliffs, NJ: Prentice-Hall, 1995).

Cromley, E., *Digital Cartography* (Englewood Cliffs, NJ: Prentice-Hall, 1993).

DeLacey, M.A., *Inside ArcCAD* (Santa Fe, NM: OnWord Press, 1995).

ESRI, *Understanding GIS: The ARC/INFO Method—PC or Unix Version* (Redlands, CA: Environmental Systems Research Institution, 1995).

Hutchinson, S. and Daniel, L., *Inside ArcView GIS*, 2nd ed. (Santa Fe, NM: OnWord Press, 1997).

Maguire, J.G., "Interactive Magazines," *Computer Graphics World* (August 1991), pp. 33-40.

Monmonier, M.S., *Technological Transition in Cartography* (Madison: University of Wisconsin Press, 1985).

Muller, J.C., ed., *Advances in Cartography* (London: Elsevier Applied Science, 1991).

Pazner, M., *Simple Computer Imaging and Mapping* (Fort Collins, CO: GIS World and the World Bank, 1993).

Rogers, M., "Is This the Next VCR?," *Newsweek* (July 8, 1991), p. 50.

Smith, T., and Frank, A., *Report on Workshop on Very Large Spatial Databases*, Technical Paper 90-4 (Santa Barbara, CA: National Center for Geographic Information and Analysis, 1990).

Stettner, W.R., Lanfear, K.J., and Aitken, D.S., *User's Manual for a Method of Map Scanning and Digital Editing for Thematic Map Production and Data-Base Construction*, USGS Circular 1054 (Reston, VA: U.S. Geological Survey, 1990).

Taylor, D.R.F., *Geographic Information Systems: The Microcomputer and Modern Cartography* (New York: Pergamon Press, 1991).

Thalmann, D., ed., *Scientific Visualization and Graphic Simulation*, New York: John Wiley & Sons, 1990.

Werner, R., and Young, J., "A Checklist to Evaluate Mapping Software," *Journal of Geography*, 90, 3 (1991) pp. 118-120.

Wyatt, P., *TIGER: The Coast-to-Coast Map Data Base* (Washington, DC: Data User Services Division, Bureau of the Census, 1990).

Wilke, T., "Computer Software for Displaying Map Projections and Comparing Distortions," *Journal of Geography*, 90, 6 (1991), pp. 264-266.

CHAPTER TEN

MAPS ON THE INTERNET

WARNING

INTRODUCTION

INTERNET JARGON

WEB SITE CATEGORIES

Links to Mapping Sites
Static Map Collections
Historical Maps
Maps and Data
Remote Sensing Information
Image Map Collections
Image Map Vendors
Remote Sensing Data Processors
Geographic Names
Address Matching
Business Address Search
Land Parcel Search
Digital Cartographic Databases
Route Selection
Statistical Mapping
Global Positioning System (GPS)
GPS and Maps
Geographic Information Systems (GIS)
Spatial Analysis
Animated Maps
Professional Information Sites
Trade Publications
State Government Agencies

USEFUL KEYWORDS

INTERNET SEARCH HELPERS

Search Engines
Search Services
Searchable Directories

CONCLUSION

SELECTED READINGS

To me, this is the real digital revolution—not computers,
not networks, but brains connecting to brains.

—Louis Rossetto

CHAPTER TEN

MAPS ON THE INTERNET

Warning: Much of the following information could be obsolete by the time you read this chapter. This is the nature of the fast-evolving Internet. Rapid change should be expected by anyone using this global information network, commonly called the **information highway**. Some sites will have disappeared, some will have stagnated, and others will have expanded. Many new sites will have come on line. The information provided here should be sufficient, however, to launch you into the exciting future of online mapping.

The desktop mapping we discussed in the previous chapter (also see Chapter 19: *GIS and Map Analysis Software*) can be frustratingly slow. The reason is that enormous amounts of geographical data must be processed to create a readable image on the screen. The software and computer equipment needed to store and process these large amounts of data are also expensive. This means that desktop mapping isn't practical for many would-be users.

Fortunately, there's an alternative to desktop mapping. The solution is to let someone else make the maps or process the data and send the results to you over the information highway we call the **Internet**. With access to digital maps and cartographic data at locations (called sites) around the world, your computer only needs to download an existing product. With this greatly reduced workload, you can often get your map more quickly and inexpensively than by making it yourself. Even if you have to pay a communications hookup charge or product user royalty, you may still be ahead financially.

Indeed, the Internet now beckons the map user to locations around the world where maps and map-related information can be found. Thousands of sites have some cartographic content. Furthermore, this content is rapidly growing more sophisticated. More and more, you can expect full-color images and animation in addition to traditional static maps.

Now one of your biggest problems is to sort out sites that are of personal interest. To this end we have selected a few sites representing a variety of information categories. These are chosen to illustrate the scope and depth of information available. Despite this list's limited size, these sites should serve as handy access points to the wealth of information available in electronic form.

Before moving on to our electronic sources of map information, we need to comment on the graphic quality of maps found on the Internet. To be blunt, it is generally poor. There are several reasons for the low design quality of Internet maps.

Existing maps must be digitized or scanned to be computer readable. When they're scanned, it usually is done at relatively low spatial resolution. The reason is that the size of data files grows exponentially as spatial resolution increases. Large files are more costly (in time and money) to store, transmit, and process. Since computer screens also have poor spatial resolution (about equivalent to what is found in a newspaper), we can't appreciate a high-resolution image when viewing a screen display. So maps on the Internet are characteristically lacking in fine detail. This may be a problem if you intend to print out the map and use it for detailed work.

The second quality issue concerns maps created from vector cartographic databases. Although the original data may have been digitized at high resolution, desktop mapping software and screens or printers are often unable to take advantage of high-resolution data. Thus, maps will lack fine detail regardless of the quality of the database used to create them. It takes the work of a professional using more powerful graphics software and computers to take full advantage of high-resolution databases.

As computers grow more powerful and graphics software becomes easier to use, at least some of these quality issues will be alleviated. In the meantime, however, you'll have to live with rather crude Internet maps. If you insist on high graphic quality, maps printed using traditional graphic arts equipment may be the better choice.

TABLE 10.1

Internet Terms

Browser: A program that serves as a graphical interface between you and the Web.

Document: A stand-alone item at a Web address, such as a block of text, a table, or a picture.

Home Page: The opening screen of a Web site.

Hot Link: A highlighted word, picture, or icon in a Web document that serves as a link (also see hypertext).

Hypertext: Words, pictures, and icons that serve as links to jump you from one document to another.

Internet: An invention of the U.S. Department of Defense to let researchers communicate worldwide over a loose, dynamic, disorganized network of computers.

Link: Cross-references and pointers to other sites with related information.

Net: Abbreviation of Internet.

News: Abbreviation of newsgroup.

Newsgroup: Organized site on the Internet with a subject focus where users post messages and share information and opinions.

On-line Services: Began as commercial vendor's user-friendly alternative to the Internet but now redesigned to offer full Web access.

Page: A screen of content at a Web site.

Query: A search for one or more keywords likely to be found on a Web page.

Searchable Directory: Lists of Web sites sorted into categories that are good for browsing rather than looking for a specific item.

Search Engine: A program that generates a list of sites using your keywords.

Site: An address or location on the Web.

Surf (Surfing): Popular term for browsing through resources on the Internet to see what you find rather than with a specific goal in mind.

Telnet: Lets you log on (connect to) a distant computer to execute programs and look for files.

Usenet: Text-only portion of the Internet. It all began here (before the Web).

Web: Abbreviation of World Wide Web (www), the graphical portion of the Internet which organizes information as hypertext.

204

INTERNET JARGON

The Internet is the creation of youthful computer "techies." Thirty years old is ancient in this crowd. For them to discuss each new idea or invention, they had to call it something. So they gave it a techie name. To talk about or work with the Internet, you are forced to deal with this high-tech jargon.

These cryptic terms account for much of the mystery of the Internet. Once you master the terminology, things will be far less confusing and frustrating. You will also make fewer mistakes entering long address codes if you understand what the terms mean and in what sequence they must occur. If you are already familiar with the Internet you may want to skip ahead to the next section.

If the Internet is new to you, read on. To pick up the needed jargon we advise you to consult at least one of the references under *Selected Readings* at the end of this chapter. We have summarized some of the material found in those thick volumes in a few tables for quick reference.

In **Table 10.1** we have listed terms associated with Internet use. Although the meaning of many of these terms is not too hard to figure out, the meaning of others is not apparent. Browsing through this table should answer many of your questions.

The Internet began as a U.S. Department of Defense attempt to let their researchers around the world communicate and share information electronically. They linked the scientists' computers into a loosely organized network. The idea was to create a system with no central control and enough redundancy (multiple linkages) to be operational even if parts of the system failed.

The early Internet was character based. Scientists were quite happy communicating in text and numbers. It took a major effort to learn how to get computers of all makes and models around the world to work with each other. But dedicated professionals were willing to make this effort.

As casual and recreational users discovered the power of the Internet, pressure mounted to make the system easier to use. Most of what you encounter today in using the Internet is a result of the rapid commercialization of the system that followed. The biggest addition was the graphical interface that let people see what they were doing.

All sorts of helpful programs and products now make the Internet user-friendly to even the

---

TABLE 10.2
Internet Acronyms

ftp — **File Transfer Protocol.** Software and standards used to send and receive files between computers. Accesses anonymous ftp sites and Web pages at older sites.

html — **Hypertext Makeup Language.** Code that tells the browser what typeface to use and how to format the text and how digitized pictures are integrated with the text on a page.

http:// — **Hypertext Transfer Protocol.** The language (protocol) that a Web page uses. Accesses Web pages.

ppp — **Point-to-Point Protocol.** Code that integrates your computer, modem, and phoneline into the Internet so that the pieces work together as a unit.

SLIP — **Serial Line Internet Protocol.** Code that integrates your computer, modem, and phoneline into the Internet so that the pieces work together as a unit.

TCP/IP — **Transmission Control Protocol/Internet Protocol.** A common language that holds the Internet together.

URL — **Uniform Resource Locator.** Technical name for a Web address (http://www. . . .) that is used to access a site.

WWW — **World Wide Web.** Graphical portion of the Internet that lets you integrate text, sound, and graphics.

computer novice. The point and click interface gives you almost instant access to information stored in computers worldwide. But there is a price to pay in learning how to use the system effectively and efficiently. This learning curve is extended by terminology that is far less obvious than that listed in Table 10.1.

In **Table 10.2** we have listed common acronyms associated with the Internet. These are serious jargon. They look like mysterious nonsense words. But you can make some sense of them if you know the words behind the acronyms. If you are new to the Internet, we suggest you browse through this table so you can begin speaking the language of the information highway.

WEB SITE CATEGORIES

The large number and obscure addresses of Internet sites can be confusing. One solution is to sort them into a few categories based on common traits. But there is no agreement on how many categories should be used or what they should be called. Our aim in creating the following list is to draw your attention to a wide variety of functions.

We also want to warn you that the browser capability needed to run the mapping applications mentioned vary from site to site. The site's home page usually will tell you what the needed browser capability is. If your browser doesn't meet the requirements stated, you won't be able to take full advantage of the services at that site.

Links to Mapping Sites

http://kartoserver.frw.ruu.nl/HTML/staff/ oddens/oddens.html. No person even remotely interested in maps should miss the Oddens's Book Marks site. It contains a list of links to about 1,500 other sites of cartographic interest. Many of the sites pointed to here contain viewable images of scanned maps.

http://wings.buffalo.edu/geoweb/services. html. This is a "must visit" site for anyone who wants a hint of what the future hold for maps on the Internet. It contains links to a list of geographic information retrieval services. These sites offer a wide variety of GIS and online mapping capabilities.

http://www.ciesin.org/. This is the site of the Consortium for International Earth Science Information Network (CIESIN). It provides links to other sites offering various interactive mapping applications.

Static Map Collections

http://www.loc.gov/. Access to the U.S. Library of Congress collection of maps in the Geography and Map Division. Over 200,000 cartographic items are expected to be on-line soon.

http://www.lib.berkeley.edu. Access to the Map Library collection at the University of California—Berkeley.

http://www.lib.utexas.edu. Access to the Perry-Castaneda Library map collection at the University of Texas. This is one of the best sites for viewing, printing, or downloading scanned copies of non-copyrighted, public-domain maps. Coverage is world-wide.

http://www.nais.ccm.emr.ca/schoolnet/. Versions in English and French. Here you can view maps from the *National Atlas of Canada* as well as a variety of other maps focusing on the Canadian environment.

http:/fermi.jhaupl.edu/states/states.html. This site is at the Applied Physics Laboratory at Johns Hopkins University. You can view topographic and county maps of every U.S. state. There are also links to map lists at other Web sites.

http://www.dartmouth.edu/-atlas. Sample maps from the *Atlas of Health Care in the United States* are available for on-line viewing. "Hot-issue" maps are also posted at this site.

http://www.appgeo.com. View the coastal atlas of Massachusetts, including public access sites.

Historical Maps

http://elvis.necp.wisc.edu/~cdean/index. html. This is the site of the monumental History of Cartography Project. Here you can explore the history of mapping in relation to other cultural developments around the world.

206

http:/scarlett.libs.uga.edu/darchive/hargrett/maps/maps.html. This is the Hargrett Library site at the University of Georgia Library. Hundreds of rare maps dating as far back as the 1500s can be viewed and downloaded. Beware of large file sizes!

Maps and Data

http://www.epa.gov/enviro/. At this site you can use Maps on Demand (MOD) to interactively create maps that display environmental information for any ZIP code, county, watershed, or other specified site in the contiguous United States. Data relate to various Environmental Protection Agency (EPA) management and health concerns.

http://www.maconusa.com. Source of digital maps and spatial datasets for desktop mapping (ArcInfo, ArcView, Atlas, IDRISI, MapInfo). Currently has U.S. and European editions, with expansion into other regions planned.

http://www.magellangeo.com. Offers a worldwide collection of 2D and 3D digital maps for viewing and downloading. Helps users find, license, and purchase digital images.

http:/://www.unh-ecs.sr.unh.edu. At this University of New Hampshire site you can interactively map various environmental and base data in the Amazon region of Brazil.

Remote Sensing Information

http://www/ersc.sisc.edu/ersc. This is the home page of the University of Wisconsin's Environmental Remote Sensing Center. It is a source of extensive remote sensing information and news.

Image Map Collections

http://edcwww.cr.usgs.gov/glis/hyper/guide/disp. Access to a user's guide to declassified satellite photos collected during the 1960s and early 1970s by the United States intelligence community. You can browse scanned images of the photos. The service is provided by the Global Land Information System (GLIS).

http://www.digitalglobe.com. At this site you can view EarthWatch's Digital Globe orthophoto datasets for a number of large cities in the United States and Canada. Pixel resolution is .5 meter for these black-and-white photos.

http://shark1.esrin.esa.it/home.html. At this site the European Space Agency provides an easy-to-use interface to call up a satellite image for any place in the world. The images come from the AVHRR Global Land Data Set (1 x 4 km. pixel resolution). Four features (water, bare soil, vegetation, clouds) are color-coded.

Image Map Vendors

http://www.spot.com. SPOT Image Corporation's site lets you browse a worldwide catalog of over four million scenes.

http://www/digitalglobe.com, http://www.orbimage.com, http://www.spaceimage.com. Sites of commercial vendors of upcoming high-resolution satellite imagery. Spatial resolution as fine as .5 meters and revisit times as short as one day are planned.

Remote Sensing Data Processors

http://www.erim.org. Access to the Environmental Research Institute of Michigan (ERIM), one of the world's largest non-government satellite image processing facilities.

http://www.earthsat.com. Access to the Earth Satellite Corporation, a project-oriented company that specializes in processing high-quality digital imagery and photographic products.

Geographic Names

http://www-nmd.usgs.gov/pub/gnis/. Access to the USGS collection of two million official domestic geographic names. You can search the database by area or feature type. Also available on CD-ROM. This list is widely used in government and private mapping activities.

Address Matching

http://www.usps.gov. This U.S. Postal Service Web site provides a ZIP code lookup service (you enter the street address, city and state). State abbreviations and other information are also available.

http://maps.yahoo.com/yahoo/. One of the leading search engines on the Web allows you to see a street-level map of any location in the United States by entering the address, city, state, and ZIP code. Accesses Etak map database.

http://www.mapblast.com. Street level address matching and mapping for the United States are available at this site. Map will be sent to your site (or someone else's) upon command. Plans to add European countries.

Business Address Search

http://visa.infonow.net/powersearch/html. Given an address, the locations of the three nearest ATM machines will be shown on a street map. Works for the United States, Canada, and Australia.

http://www.innsandouts.com. Access to a comprehensive guide with maps to United States bed-and-breakfast information.

http://www.bigbook.com. This is an electronic Yellow Pages service with a mapping capability. This site will produce site maps (from Etak database) and other information for over 11 million businesses in the United States.

http://www.mapquest.com. GeoWeb's "Mapquest" lets you interactively map businesses and points of interest from various geocoded databases. Lets you view home pages of businesses if available. Uses Etak digital maps.

http://www.citysearch.com. This site has maps for many business sites in a selection of U.S. cities.

Land Parcel Search

http://199.35.5.101/indes1.htm. In "The Map Room," developed by Oakland, California, you can zoom in on the outline of a land parcel superimposed on an orthophotograph base. Various parcel data are also retrievable.

Digital Cartographic Databases

http://ilm425.nlh.no/gis/dcw/dcw.html. Access to the Digital Chart of the World, a 1.7 gigabyte global cartographic database taken from 1:1,000,000 scale maps. Originally published on four CD-ROMS.

http://maps.esri.com/ESRI/ArcView/demos. htm. This site provides mapping demonstrations that use the Digital Chart of the Word database for the Middle East and permit access to country-specific data from the *CIA World Factbook.*

http://pubweb.parc.xerox.com/map/. The Xerox Palo Alto Research Center (PARC) provides the PARC Web Map Viewer as an experiment in dynamic information retrieval. You can create a small-scale base map of any part of the world (from the CIA World Data Base II), and a similar scale but more detailed base map of any area of the United States (from the USGS 1:2,000,000 DLG database).

http://www.etak.com. Etak Incorporated is one of the largest suppliers of digital cartographic data in the commercial sector. Many vendors and Web sites use their databases. You can see product demonstrations at this site. (Also see the DeLorme site at http://www.delorme.com/.)

http://nsdi.usgs.gov/nsdi/. This is the USGS node at the National Geospatial Data Clearinghouse. It provides access to data associated with the National Spatial Data Infrastructure and is a rich source of digital information.

http://www.ngs.noaa.gov. This National Geodetic Survey (NGS) site is the source for geodetic datum information concerning horizontal and vertical control points for the United States.

http://www.ngdc.noaa.gov/mgg/. This is a rich source of information for worldwide marine geological and geophysical data held by the U.S. National Geophysical Data Center.

Route Selection

http://www.travroute.com. "Road Trips Door to Door" comes with a complete street atlas of the United States. You can determine routes from one address to another over seven million miles of roads and between 100,000,000 home and business street addresses.

http://www.randmcnally.com. "Tripmaker" multimedia files contain detailed maps, business listings in 37 categories, video, scenic tours, and a walking guide feature.

208

http://www.mapsOnUs.com. Gives driving directions between addresses entered by user, but provides no maps.

Statistical Mapping

http://maps.esri.com/ESRI/Mapobjects/demos.htm. In addition to viewing a series of demos showcasing software capabilities, at this site you can use 1990 Census Bureau demographic data to make a statistical map of any state in the U.S.

http://sedac.ciesin.org/plue/ddi/ewer/. "Demographic Data Viewer" provides for manipulation and statistical mapping (choropleth and 3-D) of over 100 variables from the U.S. census. Statistical analysis is also possible.

http://tiger.census.gov/egi-bin/. Tiger Mapping Service provides base maps for cities or sites within cities. Also permits construction of statistical (choropleth) maps from census data down to the block group level.

Global Positioning System (GPS)

http://www.utexas.edu/depts/grg/gcraft/notes/gps/gps.html. This site is a good source of up-to-date GPS information.

http://www.navnet.com. Good source of GPS, tracking, and navigation market and product information. Over 1,000 products are profiled.

http://nmaa.org/navtech.com/navtech.html. Site of Navtech Seminars and GPS Supply in Arlington, Virginia. The Navtech bookstore offers an extensive list of software and book titles related to GPS.

GPS and Maps

http://delorme.com. "Map'n'Go" lets you hook up to a GPS receiver to retrieve a map of your surroundings and shows the route you are taking.

Geographical Information Systems (GIS)

http://www.esri.com. This colorful and extensive site is a net-surfing bonanza for anyone interested in GIS information.

http://www.intergraph.com. At this site you can use "GeoMedia Web Map" to browse and query vector databases formatted for use with Intergraph's mapping and GIS software.

http://www.idrisi.clarku.edu. At this site you can review information related to the raster-based GIS software called Idrisi, which is widely used in educational institutions.

Spatial Analysis

http://gs213.sp.cs.emu.edu/prog/dist. Gives distance between any two U.S. cities, ZIP code centroids, or latitude-longitude positions. Also creates maps centered on locations using the PARC Map Viewer (see http://www.xerox.com/map/).

Animated Maps

http://hum.amu.edu.pl/~zbzw/glob/glob1.htm. The "Great Globe Gallery" provides a collection of rotating globes portraying a variety of earth science data.

Professional Information Sites

http://www.ncgia.ucsb.edu/. This is the Web site of the National Science Foundation's National Center for Geographical Information and Analysis at the University of California at Santa Barbara. Information can be found on publications, research initiatives, conferences, curriculum materials, and a wide range of other items related to GIS.

http://www.ucgis.org. This is the site for the University Consortium for Geographic Information Science (UCGIS), which is a consortium of 34 universities and other research institutions in the United States. Information is available here on activities and priorities of the organization.

http://alexandria.sdc.ucsb.edu. Here you can find information about the Alexandria Digital Library (ADL) Project, which is exploring ways to provide seamless access to line and image maps as well as large spatial databases. Available at this site are tutorials, information about spatial data sources, and provision for browsing and retrieving digital data and maps.

http://www./andsurveyor.com/acsm/. The American Congress on Surveying and Mapping

(ACSM) Web site has no maps or spatial data, but is a good source of information on professions that deal with maps and spatial data.

http://dgl.ssc.mass.edu. Provides access to information concerning educational programs (degrees, seminars, institutes, consulting services, and on-site training) at the Center for Geographic Technologies, Analysis, and Information at Salem State College.

http://feature.geography.wisc.edu/sco/sco. html. The extensive home page of the Wisconsin State Cartographer's office has information on a wide range of mapping topics, news items, and activities. It also has links to related Web sites. Viewing a copy of the Wisconsin Mapping Bulletin is well worth the visit.

http://www.maptrade.org/maptrade. Home page of the International Map Trade Association. Provides information about acquiring maps, data on map and related product publishers and manufacturers, an index of map specialty retailers, and a newsletter called *The Map Report*.

http://www.nationalgeographic.com. This site provides access to the colorful and exotic world of the National Geographic magazine and related projects and products.

Trade Publications

http://www.gisworld.com. Information related to free trade publications such as *Business Geographics* and *GIS World*.

http://www.geoinfosystems.com. Information related to the free trade publication titled *Geo Info Systems*, including article index, calendar of events, GIS products and services, and GIS resource links.

http:/www.gpsworld.com. Information related to the free trade publication titled *GPS World*.

State Government Agencies

http://www.dnr.state.wi.us/geo. The home page of the Geoservices Division of the Wisconsin Department of Natural Resources is a rich source of GIS and mapping information. An interesting newsletter called *WALWRIS Notes* features current projects and news items.

http://nris.mt.gov/gis/gis.html. The home page of the Montana Natural Resources Information System is a good source of digital maps, databases, and news. Check out the *Montana GIS News*, an informative source of mapping and GIS information. It also contains summaries of current state projects.

USEFUL KEYWORDS

The sites we have listed will give you a glimpse of what the information highway can provide. You could use these sites as links to track down other sites of interest. But a better approach might be to make a direct search using keywords. Search engines could then do the work of finding sites of interest (see *Search Engines* in the next section). You might, for example, use any of the following keywords to start your search: maps, mapping, cartography, aerial photographs, satellite images, geographical information systems (GIS), global positioning system (GPS), surveying, remote sensing, environmental monitoring, photogrammetry, geodesy, map design, positioning, path-finding, orienteering, compass, lost, spatial data, geography, earth science, weather, climate, meteorology, space science, geology, oceanography, and travel.

The problem with using such general keywords is that you may get hundreds or even thousands of hits, most of which are not of interest. To narrow your search, use modifiers, such as thematic, statistical, animated, interactive, historical, climatic, soils, and so forth. You might also focus your search by time or place. The command "soils maps of Michigan" will yield a much more manageable list than the command "maps."

INTERNET SEARCH HELPERS

Your task of searching the Internet is greatly eased by various software aids. These can be instructed to do much of your work automatically. We will discuss three categories of these helpful assistants.

210

Search Engines

Software aids called **search engines** help you find information on a topic of interest. Try different search engines, because each has strengths and weaknesses (**Table 10.3**).

To use a search engine, you enter a subject or keyword combination, and the software will generate a list of sites where that topic is found. You can then go to these targeted sites to see if the information is what you want. Often you get a false hit, but this still is more efficient than random browsing.

Search Services

Search engines are specific vendor products designed to search the Internet on a given topic. As Table 10.3 shows, however, there are many search engines available; and each is a little different. To perform a thorough Internet search, you would have to try a number of these engines.

This task is simplified by **search services**. This software loads your query simultaneously into more than one search engine (**Table 10.4**).

In other words, by going through one of these metasearch engines, you can launch multiple searches with the same effort that it would take to run a single search engine.

Searchable Directories

A third category of software that eases your search task is called a **searchable directory**. This software reads through Web home pages and groups the sites by category into lists (**Table 10.5**). They are excellent for browsing but not convenient when looking for a specific item.

CONCLUSION

The Internet is in its infancy. There is no way to predict what is to come. But what you can conclude from your surfing of the sites mentioned in this chapter, and sites linked to those sites, is that

---

TABLE 10.3

Popular Search Engines

Alta Vista
http://www.altavista.digital.com

Deja News
http://www.dejanews.com

Excite
http://www.excite.com

Hotbot
http://www.hotbot.com

Infoseek Guide
http://www2.infoseek.com

Lycos
http://www.lycos.com

OpenText
http://index.opentext.net

Webcrawler
http://www.webcrawler.com

TABLE 10.4

Search Services

(Metasearch Engines)

All-in-One
http://www.albany.net/allinone

C/net
http:/www.cnet.com

Search.com
http://www.search.com

TABLE 10.5

Popular Searchable Directories

Magellan	http://www.mckinley.com
Point.com	http://www.pontcom.com
Yahoo	http://www.yahoo.com

Also available from the home page of popular browsers (Netscape Navigator, Microsoft Internet Explorer).

something of great importance to the mapping community is fast becoming reality.

Computer specialists refer to the electronic world we are entering as **distributed computing**. By this they mean you no longer need a self-contained computer equipped with software and data sufficient to accomplish your goals. You now have access to networked resources. This means your computer configuration can be quite modest yet you can perform major chores.

You do this by having data held in a Seattle archive and software held at a vendor site in Toronto sent to a world-class computer in Paris. You may then instruct the Paris computer to process the data using the software and to send the results to a business partner in Moscow. You may have to pay each participant in this scenario a royalty to use their resources, but the cost is insignificant compared to what you would pay to own a computer system of the same capability. Besides, the different data, hardware, and software suppliers would all be responsible for keeping their resources up to date and operating smoothly. You would thus avoid the frustration and cost of rapid obsolescence of your own resources.

Clearly, electronic technology is rapidly changing things in the mapping community. In our next chapter, we begin discussing map analysis, which benefits from electronic technology more than any other aspect of map use.

Selected Readings

Cady, G.H., and McGregor, P., *Mastering the Internet*, 2nd ed. (San Francisco, CA: SYBEX, Inc., 1996).

Eager, B., et al., *Using the World Wide Web*, 2nd ed. (Indianapolis, IN: QUE Corporation, 1996).

English, K., ed., *Most Popular Web Sites* (Emeryville, CA: LYCOS Press, An Imprint of Macmillan Computer Publishing USA, 1996).

Hahn, H., *The Internet Complete Reference*, 2nd ed. (Berkeley, CA: Osborne McGraw-Hill, 1996).

Honeycutte, J., et al., *Using the Internet*, 3rd ed. (Indianapolis, IN: QUE Corporation, 1996).

Hudson, David, *Rewired* (Indianapolis, IN: Macmillan Technical Publishing, 1997).

Pfaffenberger, B., *Discover the Internet* (Foster City, CA: IDG Books Worldwide, Inc., 1997).

Also check your bookstore's computer section for books on browsers, search engines, on-line services, and other topics discussed in this chapter. Internet Yellow Pages are republished frequently and are a good source of Internet addresses.

PART TWO

MAP ANALYSIS

In our study of map reading in Part I, we've learned what we might expect to find on a map and gained an appreciation for the conceptual nature of the mapping process. This information provides the necessary background for the second phase of map use—analysis. Here our goal is to analyze and describe spatial structure and relations.

Theoretically, we could carry out spatial analysis directly in the environment. This is rarely done, however—and rightly so, since the same results can be obtained much more easily and inexpensively by analyzing features on maps. A map cuts through the confusion of the environment and makes spatial relationships easier to see. Even a map, however, doesn't make everything apparent at a glance. The purpose of map analysis, therefore, is to reduce the muddle of information on a map to some sort of order so that we can understand it and describe it to other people.

It is possible to do this visually—to view mapped information and describe it by saying, for example, "This area looks hilly" or "That pattern is complex" or "There seems to be a strong correlation between those variables." Traditionally, map analysis has been performed in just such a way. There are problems, however, with a visual approach to map analysis. First of all, such terms as "hilly," "complex," or "correlated" are subjective and vague. They are merely estimates based on personal experience. Two or more people looking at the same map would probably use different terms to describe it. We would also have a hard time conjuring up an image of the landscape on the basis of their nebulous descriptions. What picture comes to mind, for instance, if someone says that a hillside is "steep"? Your mental image of steepness may be quite different from that of the person sitting next to you. Besides, how do you know that you can trust the person who described the hill as steep in the first place? Perhaps his judgment was biased by his poor physical condition and the hill isn't steep at all. Furthermore, all these problems with visual analysis are compounded as patterns grow more complex, as details in mapped configurations become more subtle, and as the number of variables increases.

Obviously, then, if we're to extract information from a map so that someone else will understand what we have in mind, we need an objective way to describe mapped phenomena. By "objective," we mean repeatable: Two people looking at the same map pattern would describe it in the same way, and we could be sure that their descriptions were trustworthy. Such objectivity is provided by quantitative analysis, in which we use numbers rather than words and replace visual estimation with counting, measurement, and mathematical pattern comparison. These activities let us convert mapped information to numerical data in a rigorous way. We may be satisfied simply with raw numbers—the area and depth of a lake, say, or the measurement of its shoreline, or the number of houses along it. But it's often more interesting to combine raw numbers to obtain more sophisticated information. We might, for instance, want to add up the incomes of people in a state to acquire a state average. This average could then be compared with average incomes from other states. There are hundreds of similar ways to combine, compare, and manipulate quantitative spatial information.

In theory, quantitative analysis is strictly repeatable. Using the same map and analytical procedures, each map user should arrive at the same conclusions. But there's no limit to the number of mathematical methods from which to choose. Moreover, the choice of best or most appropriate method is by no means obvious, even for someone knowledgeable about quantitative analysis. This means that even with rigorous analysis, there's no guarantee that two or more people will come to identical conclusions when working from the same map.

In general, however, variations in conclusions are far less with quantitative than with visual analysis. We must decide whether the added objectivity and precision gained by using quantitative methods will be great enough to warrant the extra effort required. In many situations, estimates based on simple observation are all we need. The advantages of quantitative procedures will be more fully exploited, of course, as computers are increasingly used to do the mathematical work for us.

In theory, too, quantitative methods are absolute and precise. In practice, however, there are several potential sources of error. As we saw in our discussion of map reading in Part I, the map itself is not error-free. The tools, materials, and techniques of the data collector and the map maker lead to many distortions of mapped information. Even if the map is perfect, map analysts add their own errors. Some of these errors are random and can be minimized only by exercising great care while figuring. Other potential errors are systematic. Some of these are caused by inaccuracies built into our tools of analysis. Others can be attributed to human bias, such as the fact that perception is non-linear (we tend to increasingly underperceive magnitudes as they become larger). We can compensate for both types of systematic error once we know they exist.

Two other cautionary notes are warranted. First, map analysis is based on the assumption that we're working with physical space. In other words, the greater the discrepancy between behavioral and physical space, the less valid the results of map analysis. This problem has plagued nearly everyone who has tried to conduct analytical studies based on map information. The second caution is that map analysis gives us descriptions, not explanations or interpretations. Analyzing a map's geometry is designed to facilitate map interpretation, not to substitute for it. Map analysis merely converts the complex pattern of symbols to usable form.

A fascinating thing about map analysis is that we can, in a sense, get more out of a map than was put into it. When map makers show a few features in proper spatial relationship, they allow us to determine all sorts of things—directions, distances, densities, and so on—that they may not have had specifically in mind. Peppermint Patty's confusing story problem (see cartoon) would be greatly simplified, for example, if she would only measure the distance between the cities on a map. This is one of the beauties of map analysis. It can make complex geographic relations more readily understandable.

The following discussion of map analysis is divided into nine chapters. The first three chapters explore the spatial elements of location (Chapter 11), direction (Chapter 12), and distance (Chapter 13). Next, we discuss how to use these spatial elements when working with a map and compass (Chapter 14) and a GPS receiver (Chapter 15) to locate our position and to find our way. In Chapter 16, we see how to use these same spatial elements to perform cartometric analysis. In Chapter 17, we search for spatial order in the environment, and in Chapter 18 we move our focus to spatial associations among patterns. Chapter 19 covers software to assist in GIS and map analysis. And in Chapter 20, we stress the importance of understanding map accuracy before making decisions about spatial issues.

As we move from map reading to analysis, we're shifting our attention from the theory behind maps to their practical use. It is here that the real fun of maps begins. However beautiful a map may be in theory and in design, it is at its most beautiful when it is being used.

CHAPTER ELEVEN
LOCATIONAL REFERENCE SYSTEMS

Latitude and longitude were to the measurement
of space what the mechanical clock was to the
measurement of time.
—Daniel J. Boorstin, *The Discoverers*

"...but then I wonder what Latitude or Longitude
I've got to?" (Alice had not the slightest idea
what Latitude was, or Longitude either, but she
thought they were nice grand words to say).
—Lewis Carroll, *Alice in Wonderland*

11
CHAPTER ELEVEN

LOCATIONAL REFERENCE SYSTEMS

Most of the time, we feel comfortable thinking of our environment in only two dimensions. In other words, we relate to the earth's surface as though it were unchanging and flat. This vast oversimplification causes little conflict with much of our spatial behavior. Many environmental features change so slowly that we see them as functionally static. Our access to automobiles and airplanes also means that landform undulations have a minimal impact on our daily behavior.

Maps encourage this "flat earth" concept because they're eminently suited to providing static pictures of the environment on flat media. Indeed, most maps are created by projecting geographic features onto a flat surface, such as a sheet of paper. The advantage of the flat earth concept is that we can locate something by using a simple two-axis reference system. Length and width suffice.

Of all the jobs maps do for us, one stands out. They tell us where things are and let us communicate that information efficiently to someone else. This more than any other factor accounts for maps' popularity. It's convenient to make locational decisions by studying maps, knowing that our purposes will be served as well as if we'd gone into the environment directly—sometimes better, for maps can reveal relations between features that we would have trouble seeing on the ground. They give us a superb **spatial reference system**—a way of pinpointing the position of something in space. Thus, maps appeal to a deep need in all of us—to know where things are. The more things we can locate, the more secure we feel.

There are many ways to pinpoint location, as we'll see in this chapter. All these locational methods are relative: The position of one feature is defined in relation to the position of something else. The "something else" may be a concrete object, or it may be an arbitrary grid of some sort. In either case, it is called a **frame of reference**.

CONCRETE FRAMES OF REFERENCE

As babies, one of the first things we seek is information about the position of objects in our environment. We begin by locating things with reference to the known position of some local reference object. This local reference object may be personal or environmental.

At the most primitive level, the location of an object may be designated merely by pointing. This simple way of locating something, of course, requires that we be close enough to see it.

Since we soon learn that pointing isn't only primitive but impolite, we move on to more sophisticated methods of showing position. We can eliminate pointing with no loss of communication power if we refer to the orientation of a person's body. ("Look at the waterfall!" "Where?" "Off to the right.") To communicate position in this way, both people must be close enough to see the waterfall; both must agree on what is meant by the egocentrically-based indicators of "left" and "right"; and both must be facing the same direction.

Position can be further abstracted so that we specify location in terms of direction and distance relationships. Someone may tell you to "drive north along Route 5 till you get to the Hi Ho Tavern; then turn west on the county road and drive five miles." The success of such a location-finding scheme depends on your initial position and your ability to maintain a course along a network of pathways. In addition, you must know the cardinal directions (north, south, east, west) and be able to determine distance in miles. The directions given on many roadside signs provide a good test of your skills with this locational system.

In each of the above instances, position was egocentrically derived. Everything was related to where *you* were. At a still more abstract level, it is possible to remove the individual from the scene and communicate positional information indirectly. You may hear, for instance, that there is an interesting archaeological site halfway up Vertigo Mountain, directly east of Dead Man's Rapids. No matter where you are, you can get to the site—as long as you know the location of Vertigo Mountain and Dead Man's Rapids. This system, then, depends on a knowledge of **place names**—the identifying labels given to unique

sites and features in our environment (see **Box 11.1**). For this reason, such a locational scheme may suffice for people who are familiar with local place naming but be of little value to someone who isn't acquainted with the area. There is no offhand way to find the corner of Crestview and Maple Streets in a strange city. This is where maps become indispensable; without them, the place name system could never work. Maps free us from relying on hearsay or our own limited experience in locating unfamiliar named places.

Yet even with the aid of maps, the place name method isn't very efficient. For one thing, many spots have been given the same names. *The Atlas of Wisconsin* lists 115 lakes called, graphically if unimaginatively, Mud Lake. If you aren't sure which one you're searching for, even a map can't help you.

To add to the confusion, place names don't always stay the same. A street or park or city may be retitled to honor someone or something. Truth or Consequences, New Mexico (formerly called Hot Springs) probably holds the distinction of being the only town to change its name in honor of a TV show. More commonly, places are rechristened in memory of great leaders, as happened when Cape Canaveral became Cape Kennedy after President Kennedy's death in 1963. Many people had just begun to adjust to the new name when it was changed back to Cape Canaveral in 1973.

The motives behind name changing may be even more capricious. Those in authority may simply decide that a name is in bad taste and take it upon themselves to "clean up the map." Until the early 1970s, for instance, there was a place in Oregon known as Whorehouse Meadows (named after some enterprising women who used to entertain sheepherders there). The Bureau of Land Management, in the process of sanitizing their maps, changed this admirably frank name to the more discrete Naughty Girl Meadows. An r was slipped into the name of another Oregon town so that it became Bullshirt Springs. In Washington state, S.O.B. Creek is now Sob Creek, while in Oregon, Shit House Mountain and Bull Shit Canyon have become S.H. Mountain and B.S. Canyon.

Although we may protest the loss of colorful bits of history, such changes are inevitable. And they occur so rapidly that sometimes only

BOX 11.1 WHAT'S IN A NAME?

The study of American place names can yield many fascinating historical insights. The physical features the settlers saw (or thought they saw) are often evident in the names of places throughout the United States. In some areas, the names paint a fairly clear picture of the physical environment in settlement days and thus provide a standard against which to compare the contemporary landscape.

Place names also suggest who settled where, providing insight into ethno-cultural factors of influence in the settlement period. The settlers' beliefs, hopes, fears, prejudices, expectations, and the quality of their lives may be revealed. Hungry Hill, Suicide, Desperation Point, Goshelpme Creek, and Terror Ridge hint at grim realities. The implication is that people who settled in Gnaw Bone and Lickskillet were so destitute that they had to chew on bones and lick every morsel from their dishes, while Aristocracy Hill and Quality Row poke fun at those settlers who struck it rich and started putting on airs. The large number of frontier communities called Hell, Helltown, Hell Hole, Hell Hollow, Hell-for-Sure, or some such variation makes it clear that a great many places were the very devil to get through (although some of these appellations, it must be noted, may commemorate a place where the settlers had a "hell of a good time").

The true derivation of place names is, in fact, often a matter of controversy, although there are some general categories of names which are fairly typical. Many place names (Madison, Washington, Jefferson City) originate with an important person, while other spots are named after local personages. Some places receive their names from a distant locality (because Napoleon defeated the Austrians at Lodi, Italy, we now have towns called Lodi in Ohio, Wisconsin, and California). Some place names (Rushingwater Creek, Blue Ridge, or Stinking Spring) are graphic physical descriptions. The cultural setting has also left some colorful descriptive labels (Whiskey Creek, Poverty Hollow, Society Corners). Other place names, such as Pleasant View or Paradise, are subjectively descriptive. Towns such as Liberty, Progress, Hope, and Pride reflect inspirational and symbolic place naming. A wealth of other named places, from Idaho to Tennessee, represent phonetic spellings—or outright perversions—of Native American names.

Obviously, there are dangers in trying to read too much into a place name. For one thing, the people who named a new settlement weren't always as perceptive as they might have been. Also, many early place names (Prosperity, Richland, Zenith, Eden, etc.) were dreamed up in hopes of attracting settlers and hence reflected aspirations rather than realities. In addition, most place names have several possible origins. The name Lodi mentioned earlier, for example, may have come directly from a racehorse by that name and only indirectly from the town in Italy.

To be sure, research on place names, particularly the most off-color or suggestive ones, rarely supports what our imaginations would have us believe. Whatever Bitch Creek, Idaho, might conjure up, for instance, it is actually derived from the French biche, meaning "cow elk," while Intercourse, Pennsylvania, is probably one of those frontier names meant to attract settlers, for the common meaning of "intercourse" at the time was "commerce."

While place names may be interesting and descriptive, very few give any indication of location. We can find some locational information in such names as Northport, West Fork, or East Branch, but the usefulness of most such information is limited by its relative nature. Since the thrust of the renaming effort being conducted by government agencies is toward locational place names, we can expect to see more of this class of names in the future.

Locational place names may sometimes be helpful in finding our way, but at other times they may be misleading. We must be wary of trying to extract information about location from a place's name, as the following excerpt from a newspaper article illustrates:

> East is east and West is west, but evidently nobody told the colonial settlers of Massachusetts. The automobile legal association reported this week that South Chatham is west of Chatham. West Dennis is south of Dennis, West Yarmouth is south of Yarmouth. South Wareham is west of Wareham and West Wareham is to the north. North West Duxbury is east of West Duxbury and East Bridgewater is north of Bridgewater. West of Falmouth is nothing but ocean so West Falmouth is—what else?—north of Falmouth.

> (*The San Francisco Chronicle*, August 24, 1967)

Despite all these problems, the practice of giving names to places is a firmly rooted tradition. People often become deeply attached to place names: Witness the nationwide storm of protest which resulted when Atlantic City, New Jersey, proposed changing the names of Baltic and Mediterranean Avenues—names known to every Monopoly player. As one of the executives in the company which manufactures the game argued at the time:

> Baltic and Mediterranean are not just local street names. They must be included in the category containing such thoroughfares as Broadway, Trafalgar Square and the Champs-Elysés. Who would ever suggest changing their names? Baltic and Mediterranean Avenue belong to America.

> (*Newsweek*, January 22, 1973)

the most up-to-date map is of any use in finding a place by its name. (On the other hand, since local people usually call places by their original names, a new map may often be more bewildering than an ancient one!)

Moreover, even familiar names may escape us in moments of stress. Police officers, fire fighters, ambulance drivers, and others who answer crisis calls are sadly aware of the trouble people have, under tension, of recalling place names. The star of the ambulance squad is the person who knows all the old as well as modern names, for in emergencies people revert to calling places what they did in the past.

Some of these problems are avoided if the names of places give an indication of relative position. Streets running parallel in an east-west direction could be named after U.S. Presidents in the order they took office. North-south streets might be named after states in the order they joined the union. To take advantage of such a system, however, you must know the "code"; thus, most such attempts at spatial referencing are of little practical value.

Places can also be named with numbers. The U.S. and interstate highway systems are good examples of rather crude numerical place naming. In the U.S. system, east-west highways are given ascending even numbers from north to south, while north-south highways have ascending odd numbers from east to west. The interstate system maintains this odd-even pattern but reverses the order of the numbers.

Numbered highways may seem to provide a better locational method than the names of Presidents or states. But the fragmented and irregular nature of the numbering system creates many problems for its users. A highway whose number suggests that it should be running east-west often runs north-south for short stretches. Furthermore, the network of highways is far from regular; it fluctuates from very dense in some places to sparse in others.

A much better numbered place naming scheme is found in rectangularly gridded cities with a pair of right-angled base lines, such as Main Street and Main Avenue. All streets are numbered sequentially away from these north-south and east-west base lines. With such a system, we can easily locate a place when only the address is given. It is a simple matter to find the corner of 4th Street and 22nd Avenue, on the ground as well as on the map. In a sense, the city becomes its own map.

The most abstract position-finding system of all uses arbitrary grids which are independent of the observer and bear no natural relation to the environment. In other words, the frame of reference is an abstract concept. A variety of such locational systems are used on maps, as we'll see in the following section.

ABSTRACT FRAMES OF REFERENCE

Abstract spatial reference systems fall into two categories. Point locating systems use mathematical coordinates to define the position of grid intersections. In contrast, zone locating systems use letter and number coordinate notation to define the position of grid cells. Each type of referencing system has a special use, as we'll see in the remainder of this chapter.

Point Locating Systems

In choosing a **point locating system**, we must find a balance between accuracy and convenience. The least convenient but most accurate system is tied directly to the earth's spherical form. It is known as the **geographical grid**, or **graticule**. Less accurate but more convenient systems involve superimposing a square grid on a flat map. Since these grids treat the earth as a flat surface, they are called **plane grids**. Let's look more closely at these two types of point locating systems.

Geographical Grid

The geographical grid is made up of longitude lines (called meridians) which run in a north-south direction between the north and south poles, and latitude lines (called parallels) which run in an east-west direction around the earth parallel to the equator (**Figure 11.1**). Coordinates for the geographical grid, called **geographical coordinates**, are measured in common angular units. Since a circle contains 360 degrees (°) of arc, there are 360° of longitude around the equator and 180° of latitude from pole to pole. Each degree can be divided into 60 minutes (60'), and each minute can be further divided into 60 seconds (60").

Geographical coordinates are given on maps with respect to an arbitrarily chosen origin (0° latitude, 0° longitude). The east-west base line (0° latitude) follows the equator and thus lies halfway between the true north and south poles. The north-south base line (0° longitude) is called the **prime meridian**. Coordinates for a position are given in degrees of arc up to 180° east or west of the prime meridian and in degrees of arc up to 90° north or south of the equator. A typical reading might be 89°23'03"W longitude, 43°04'29"N latitude (the position of the capitol dome in Madison, Wisconsin. By carrying the readings to the nearest second (1") of latitude and longitude in this way, we can in theory specify a position to within 100 feet of its true location on the earth.

That is quite an accurate system. Yet it's not as universally eloquent as you might think. Since the prime meridian is an arbitrary line, it can be placed wherever a country pleases. For English-speaking countries, it has been placed so that it follows the meridian on which the Royal Observatory is located (near London, England, in the suburb of Greenwich). But over the years a variety of other prime meridians have appeared on foreign maps. The whimsical way in which prime meridians are established is evident when

Table 11.1 Prime Meridians Used on Foreign Maps with Longitudinal Distances from Greenwich

Amsterdam, Netherlands	4°53'01"E
Antwerp, Belgium	4°22'50"E
Athens, Greece	23°42'59"E
Batavia (Djakarta), Java, Indonesia	106°48'28"E
Berlin, Germany	13°23'55"E
Bern, Switzerland	7°26'22"E
Brussels, Belgium	4°22'06"E
Copenhagen, Denmark	12°34'40"E
Ferro, Canary Islands (French)	17°39'46"W
Ferro, Canary Islands (German)	17°40'00"W
Helsinki, Finland	24°57'17"E
Istanbul, Turkey	28°58'50"E
Leningrad, Russia	30°18'59"E
Lisbon, Portugal	09°07'55"W
London, England	0°05'43"W
Madrid, Spain	3°41'15"W
Moscow, Russia	37°34'15"E
Munich, Germany	11°36'31"E
Oslo, Norway	10°43'23"E
Padang, Sumatra, Indonesia	100°22'01"E
Paris, France	2°20'14"E
Peking, China	116°28'10"E
Pulkovo, Russia	30°19'89"E
Rio de Janeiro, Brazil	43°10'21"W
Rome (Monte Mario), Italy	12°27'08"E
Rotterdam, Netherlands	4°29'46"E
Singkawang, Borneo, Indonesia	108°59'41"E
Stockholm, Sweden	18°03'30"E
Tirane, Albania	19°46'45"E
Tokyo, Japan	139°44'41"E

you consider that more than two dozen different ones can be found on these maps (**Table 11.1**).

Because the origin of the geographical grid is located in such an arbitrary way, longitude values are a form of interval measurement. As we discussed in *Measurement Level* in Chapter 2, interval scaling is based on a false zero; thus, none of the numbers has any direct meaning. Spatial reference systems provide a good example of the need for caution with interval measurement. The longitude of a particular location is a meaningless number; on a map using a different origin, the longitude value would be completely different. When reading foreign maps, then, be sure to check which prime meridian was used.

Fortunately, you can convert longitude readings from one prime meridian to another as easily as you change temperature from Fahrenheit to Centigrade. If you should note in an old Turkish atlas that the longitude of Seattle, Washington, is

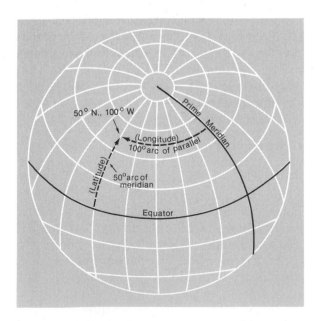

11.1 The latitude and longitude lines that make up the geographical grid have their origin at the intersection of the equator and prime meridian.

151°16'W (based on the Istanbul meridian) and you know that the Greenwich longitude of Seattle is 122°17'W, you can determine the Greenwich longitude of Istanbul through subtraction: 151°16' – 122°17' = 28°59'E.

This example gives you an idea of how awkward it is to make computations with spherical latitude-longitude coordinates. You're dealing in 60s, not 10s, when changing one unit (degree, minute, second) to another. Most people find this troublesome, especially if a great many calculations must be made.

A related problem when using spherical coordinates is that arc units aren't everywhere constant. A degree of latitude varies slightly in length between the equator and the poles, but averages about 69 miles (111 kilometers) at every point on the earth's surface (see Table E.6). In contrast, a degree of longitude varies in length from about 69 miles at the equator to 0 miles at the poles (see **Figure 11.2** and Table E.7).

In general, the length of a degree of longitude is equal to the cosine of the latitude times the average length of a degree of latitude. At 45 degrees north or south of the equator, for example, the cosine (of 45 degrees) is .7071 (see Table E.5). Therefore, the length of a degree of longitude is approximately 69 x .7071, or close to 50 statute miles. This is roughly 19 miles shorter than the length at the equator.

As a rule, then, a degree of longitude is rarely equivalent to a degree of latitude, and the relation between the two changes with different locations on the earth's surface. This undesirable trait of geographical coordinates results from fitting a grid to a spherical surface and is unavoidable.

Another disadvantage of geographical coordinates is that you can't observe them in the field without special instruments. In the Northern Hemisphere, you obtain latitude by measuring the angle between the horizon and North Star. To obtain longitude, you measure the difference between local and Greenwich (prime meridian) time. And you can't make such measurements without technical devices.

But that's no reason to give up on geographical coordinates. To the rescue come modern satellite positioning systems that give latitude and longitude readings quickly and accurately (see Appendix D: *Navigation Instruments*). All you need is an inexpensive hand-held receiver to decode satellite signals. These devices are widely used for precision ground survey work (see Chapter 2: *Geographical Data*) and are becoming common navigational aids in airplanes, boats, and ground vehicles (see Chapter 15: *GPS and Maps*).

While geographical coordinates were once restricted to indoor map study or to surveyors, navigators, and other well trained and equipped professionals, the situation has changed due to GPS technology. GPS-equipped hikers, boaters, hunters, and others now find geographical coordinates a welcome navigation aid.

Even if you haven't yet joined the growing GPS crowd, you shouldn't ignore the geographical grid. Indeed, it's often the only coordinate reference system found on small-scale maps and is also used on many government-produced series of large-scale maps. In particular, USGS topographic quadrangles receive their name from the fact that they're bounded by parallels on the north and south and by meridians on the east and west (see Chapter 5: *Landform Portrayal*). U.S. aeronautical charts, too, are produced within a geographical grid framework. Depending on the map series and scale, the geographical grid network may be printed in full over the map image, or it may be indicated only by marginal ticks (lines not extended across the map image) and projected crossed lines within the map boundaries (**Figure 11.3**). In either case, you'll have to interpolate the actual geographical coordinates for most positions.

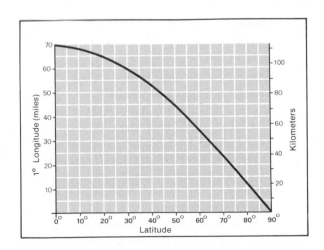

11.2 This plot shows the shrinking nature of longitude as latitude increases.

222

Plane Coordinates

As we've seen, we face many problems when we use the geographical grid to locate point features. We can trace most of these difficulties to the fact that the latitude-longitude system is based on the structure of **spherical coordinates**. In other words, it uses coordinates that show position on a rounded surface. Obviously, it would be much simpler if we could designate location on a flat surface using **plane coordinates**. We could then simply read coordinates from a square grid of intersecting straight lines.

To devise such a system, we would have to deal somehow with earth curvature. We know that transferring something round to something flat always causes distortion. But we also know that map projection distortion due to earth rotundity is minimal for fairly small regions. If we superimpose a square grid onto flat maps of small areas, therefore, we can achieve spatial reference accuracy for many purposes. We can also avoid the frustration of using inconvenient latitude-longitude notation.

A major issue with plane coordinate systems is the choice of origin for the grid. On large-scale maps intended for local use, the origin is often chosen arbitrarily to suit the available map format. For maps in a series, and for maps intended to be used with other maps, it's common to tie the origin to the ground, creating a terrestrial reference system. Let's look first at arbitrary local grids, and then we'll discuss some examples of terrestrial systems.

Arbitrary Local Grids. When an arbitrary square grid of reference lines is superimposed on mapped features, it's called a **local grid**. A flat map has only two dimensions—width (left to right) and length (top to bottom). If we superimpose a plane grid on the map, with division left to right labeled as x-coordinates and division top to bottom labeled as y-coordinates, we have established the familiar **cartesian coordinate system** (**Figure 11.4**). We can now pinpoint any location on the map precisely and objectively by giving its two numbered coordinates (x, y).

Such a simple way of showing position has a great convenience advantage over the geographical grid. Local grids are especially handy in the laboratory for such analytical procedures as

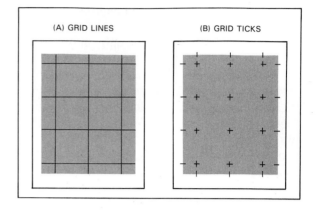

11.3 The geographical grid is shown on maps published by the U.S. Geological Survey either by grid lines (A) or grid ticks (B).

locating environmental features and finding the distance or direction between them.

When we use local grid coordinates, however, we face some special challenges. One problem arises because there's no single logical origin—or zero point—for such a system. Since the earth's surface doesn't provide any natural origin, the map maker's choice is arbitrary. Thus, almost as many different origins are used as there are coordinate schemes. One consequence of using more than one origin is that the precise numerical values of coordinates may vary from one map to the next.

Another problem with using local grids is that field use is limited unless you have a GPS receiver that allows entry of a user-defined grid (see Chapter 15: *GPS and Maps*). If you have such a receiver and take the time to customize it to your local map grid, you can put the local coordinate information to practical use.

State Plane Coordinates (SPC). The SPC system overcomes many problems associated with arbitrary local grids. It does so because it is a terrestrial reference system—an official standardized system that is tied systematically to the ground.

The SPC system was created in the 1930s to serve several purposes. First, it would completely cover the United States with a flat grid network at a constant scale. Second, maximum scale distortion error wouldn't exceed one in 10,000 (100 parts per million). Thus, distance measured over a

10,000-foot course would be accurate within a foot of the true measure. This level of accuracy couldn't be achieved if only one grid enveloped the whole country; the area is too large. The solution was to divide the United States into a minimum number of smaller zones and make a separate grid for each zone.

The country was eventually broken into 125 zones, each having its own projection surface (see Appendix C for a discussion of map projections). Most states have several zones, as **Figure 11.5** shows. A section from a Lambert conformal projection was used for states of predominantly east-west extent, and a transverse Mercator projection was used for states of mainly north-south extent. This explains the orientation of the individual zones.

The logic of SPC is quite simple. Zone boundaries follow state and county boundaries. Each zone has its own centrally located **origin**, through which passes its own **central meridian**. A false origin is established to the west and south of the zone, usually 2,000,000 feet west of the central meridian. In the case of Wisconsin in **Figure 11.6**, the Lambert conic projection provides the base for each of the three zones (north, central, and south). You read coordinates first to the east of the false origin and then to the north of the false origin, giving rise to the terms **false eastings** and **false northings**. Since north is conventionally at the top of the map, it may be helpful to remember that you read coordinates **right-up**. Specifically, the correct form of SPC notation is to give the false easting in feet, the false northing in feet, the state, and the zone. For example, you would give the location of the state capitol dome in Madison, Wisconsin, in abbreviated form as:

2,164,606 feet E; 392,285 feet N; Wisconsin, S.

State Plane Coordinates have been widely used for public works and land surveys. Although a full SPC grid isn't superimposed on many maps, 10,000-foot grid lines are indicated by black ticks along the margin of recent USGS quadrangles of the topographic, orthophotoquad, and orthophotomap series.

While the SPC system served the needs of the states when it was created and is still a convenience for the casual map user, it is now largely obsolete as far as surveyors and other professional map users are concerned. One reason is that accuracy of 100 parts per million (one in 10,000) in locating points is now easily achieved using modern surveying methods. Also, each SPC zone is a separate entity with its own defining characteristics—a fact that frustrates and discourages joint operations across zone boundaries.

You may find the SPC grid useful for analyzing maps in the laboratory. For field use, you can enter key SPC map parameters into your GPS receiver as a user-defined grid (see Chapter 15: *GPS and Maps*).

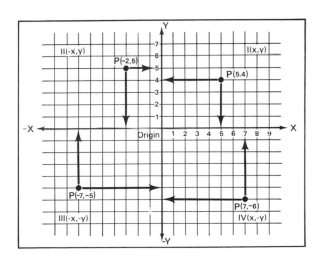

11.4 The structure of the cartesian coordinate system, including basic notation. Notice the different signs of the x and y coordinates in the four quadrants.

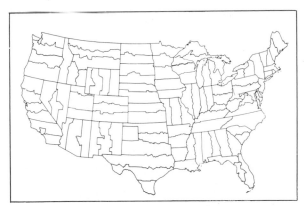

11.5 Zones of the State Plane Coordinate System for the contiguous United States. Notice that the zones are oriented either north-south or east-west, depending on the shape of the state.

224

Universal Transverse Mercator (UTM) Grid.
The convenience of a flat grid can also be enjoyed at the global level if enough zones are used to ensure reasonable accuracy. Probably the best known plane coordinate system of international scope is the **Universal Transverse Mercator (UTM)** grid. All vendors program its specifications into their GPS receivers.

The UTM grid extends around the world from 84° North to 80° South. Sixty north-south zones are used. Each one covers six degrees of longitude, with an overlap of 30 minutes with the zones on either side (**Figure 11.7**). A section from a transverse Mercator projection is used to develop a separate grid for each of the 60 zones. This method makes it possible (assuming a constant scale) to achieve an accuracy level of one part in 2,500 maximum error within the zone.

The logic of the UTM grid is similar to that of SPC. Each zone is individually numbered from west to east, beginning at the 180° meridian. Each zone has its own origin, located at the intersection of the equator, and its own central meridian (**Figure 11.8**). A false origin for the north half of the zone lies on the equator 500,000 meters west of the origin, and a false origin for the south half of the zone lies 500,000 meters west and 10,000,000 meters south of the origin (or 10,000,000 meters directly south of the false origin for the north half of the zone). You read coordinates as for SPC—first to the east and then to the north of the appropriate false origin. You give the false easting in meters, the false northing in meters, the zone number, and the zone hemisphere (north or south). Thus, you would designate the location of the capitol dome in Madison, Wisconsin, in abbreviated form as:

305,904 meters E; 4,771,651 meters N; 16, N.

Because UTM zones are formatted according to the geographical grid and not state boundaries, it usually takes more than one UTM zone to cover a state completely. Wisconsin falls into two zones: 15 and 16 (see Figure 11.7).

It's also of special interest that the equator has two false northings:

$0^{m\ (meters)}$N in the northern half
and
$10,000,000^{m}$N in the southern half.

11.6 State Plane Coordinate zones and notation for Wisconsin.

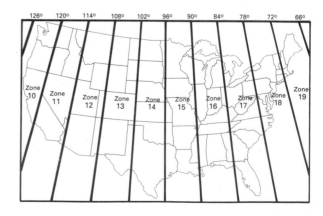

11.7 Zones of the Universal Transverse Mercator grid in the contiguous United States.

This means that every location on the equator has two sets of grid coordinates. For example, the coordinates for the zone origin are:

500,000ᵐE, 0ᵐN in the northern half
and
500,000ᵐE, 10,000,000ᵐN in the southern half.

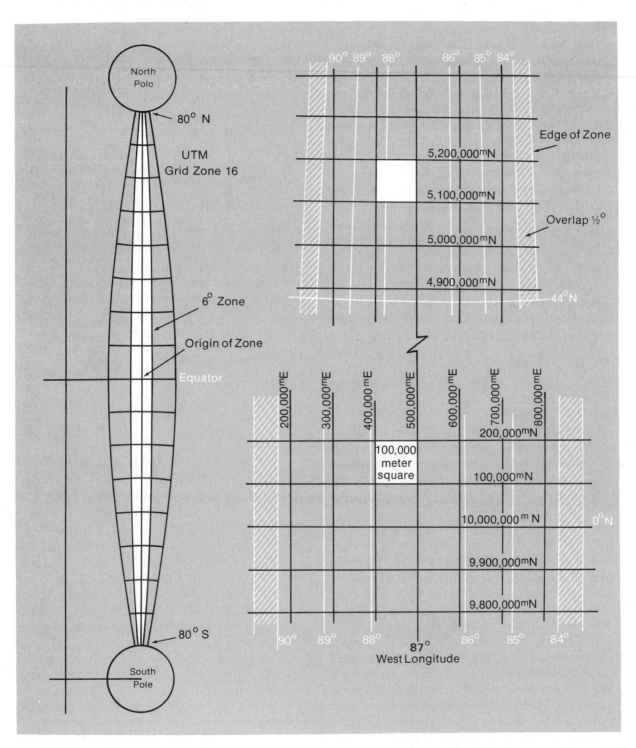

11.8 The Universal Transverse Mercator grid is shown here for selected portions of zone 16.

226

The near universal scope of the UTM grid makes it a valuable point referencing system. The UTM grid is indicated on many foreign maps and on all recent USGS quadrangles in the topographic, orthophotoquad, and orthophotomap series. The position of selected grid lines is shown either by a superimposed full grid or by marginal grid ticks. These lines or ticks are spaced at 1,000 or 10,000 meter intervals, depending on the map scale. On USGS quadrangles of the topographic series, 1,000-meter grid ticks are printed in blue. These ticks are labeled (in black) with their false easting or false northing values along each margin of the map. The principal digits—those which represent the 1,000-meter grid tick values—are printed in larger type with the trailing digits (000) dropped from all but one label along each edge of the map.

Universal Polar Stereographic (UPS) Grid. As mentioned above, the UTM grid extends only from 84°N to 80°S latitude. To complete global coverage, a complementary rectangular coordinate system called the **Universal Polar Stereographic (UPS)** grid was created. The UPS grid consists of a North Zone and a South Zone. Each zone is superimposed upon a polar stereographic projection and covers a circular region. To provide overlap with the UTM grid, an additional half degree of latitude is provided.

Modified Grids. The growing popularity of digital methods in all phases of mapping has kindled the desire for coordinate grids tailored to specific needs. States that fall into several UTM zones, for example, often create a special state coordinate grid by shifting the central meridian of a UTM zone to the center of the state. Thus, Wisconsin routinely records and reports data formatted in the **Wisconsin Transverse Mercator (WTM)** coordinate system. UTM and WTM have the same accuracy potential, but WTM avoids the problem of having two UTM zones. Thus, it's more convenient to use within the state.

Even counties have gotten into the spirit of grid adjustments. Each of Wisconsin's 72 counties has a grid optimized for its own region. County data are recorded and reported on these plane coordinate grids. Since counties are such small regions relative to the earth's size, a county-based plane grid can provide extremely accurate spatial referencing.

Coordinate Determination and Plotting

Although the structure of map coordinate systems is relatively easy to understand, it may take practice to gain skill in solving spatial problems using map coordinates. Sometimes you'll want to determine an environmental feature's coordinates or location. At other times you'll need to know the ground position of a feature whose coordinates are given. You should approach both problems systematically.

Say, for instance, that you want to determine the rectangular coordinates of a building. If a full reference grid isn't printed over the map, use the marginal grid ticks and a straightedge to construct the grid lines lying immediately to the south and north, and east and west, of the building (**Figure 11.9A**). Note the coordinate values of the grid lines lying to the west and south of the building. Next, measure the inter-grid northing and easting of the building, and form ratios between these values and the grid interval distance in map units (centimeters or inches). Multiply these proportions by the grid interval distance in coordinate units, and add the results to the west and south grid line values. Thus, in Figure 11.9A, the map reference of the building is:

$$easting = 305,000^m + 903.6^m = 305,903.6^m$$
and
$$northing = 4,771,000^m + 650.6^m = 4,771,650.6^m.$$

Now imagine that you want to plot the location of a feature for which you know the rectangular coordinates. This problem is essentially the reverse of reading map references. First, determine the grid line values that fall immediately above and below the coordinate values (**Figure 11.9B**). If these grid lines aren't plotted on the map, use the grid ticks and a straightedge to do so. Next, subtract the grid line value immediately west of the easting from the easting, and subtract the grid line value immediately south of the northing from the northing. Form ratios between these inter-grid differences and the grid interval distance. Now multiply these proportions by the inter-grid interval in map units to obtain the inter-grid easting and northing in map units. Finally, plot these inter-grid distances from the western and southern grid lines. The two plotted lines will intersect at the desired coordinate location.

If you'll be working with a single coordinate system on maps of a certain scale over and over, it may pay to construct a simple computational aid called a **roamer**.* You can make this

---

Many map-scale and grid-using aids are available commercially. These clear plastic devices have calibrated rulers etched into their surface. The rulers match standard topographic map formats. Check your local map specialty store to get one of these handy ready-made products.

graphic device using the right-angle corner of an ordinary sheet of paper, although you may wish to use more durable material. To construct a roamer, merely mark off the grid interval distance along each edge of the paper, starting at the corner. Then divide these distances into units fine enough to suit your map reference needs. Millimeters or tenths of inches should suffice.

By aligning the roamer with the north-south and east-west grid lines, you can determine map references and plot coordinate locations

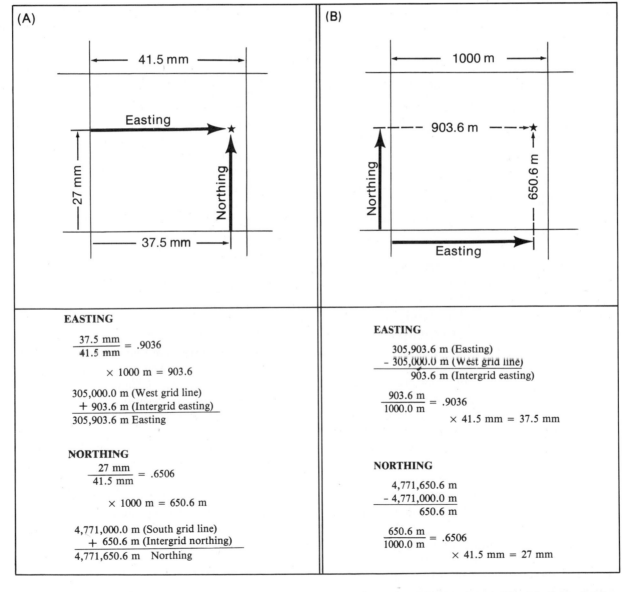

(A)

EASTING

$$\frac{37.5 \text{ mm}}{41.5 \text{ mm}} = .9036$$

$$\times 1000 \text{ m} = 903.6$$

305,000.0 m (West grid line)
+ 903.6 m (Intergrid easting)
305,903.6 m Easting

NORTHING

$$\frac{27 \text{ mm}}{41.5 \text{ mm}} = .6506$$

$$\times 1000 \text{ m} = 650.6 \text{ m}$$

4,771,000.0 m (South grid line)
+ 650.6 m (Intergrid northing)
4,771,650.6 m Northing

(B)

EASTING

305,903.6 m (Easting)
− 305,000.0 m (West grid line)
903.6 m (Intergrid easting)

$$\frac{903.6 \text{ m}}{1000.0 \text{ m}} = .9036$$

$$\times 41.5 \text{ mm} = 37.5 \text{ mm}$$

NORTHING

4,771,650.6 m
− 4,771,000.0 m
650.6 m

$$\frac{650.6 \text{ m}}{1000.0 \text{ m}} = .6506$$

$$\times 41.5 \text{ mm} = 27 \text{ mm}$$

11.9 To determine the UTM coordinates of the Wisconsin state capitol dome, follow the steps outlined in A. To plot the dome's location from UTM coordinates, follow the procedure in B.

228

quickly and accurately (**Figure 11.10**). You'll need a separate roamer for each map scale and grid system, of course. Therefore, you may want to put UTM and SPC roamers for standard USGS quadrangles on opposite corners of the same sheet of paper.

Zone Locating Systems

The abstract coordinate reference systems that we've discussed all use point coordinates. Several reference grids found on maps provide for zone rather than point descriptions. These **zone coordinates** consist of an alphanumeric code which locates cells. In this section, we'll explore several such systems.

Arbitrary Local Zones

The most primitive zone coordinate system is the arbitrary grid of reference lines that make up **local grid zones**. This grid is superimposed over geographic features on many city, state highway, recreational, and atlas maps. The grid is usually keyed to a place name index. If you're seeking Obscure Street, you simply look it up in the index, where you'll find its local coordinates (say, M-2). Then, by referring to the place where Row M crosses Column 2, you will roughly determine the position of Obscure Street.

"Roughly" is the appropriate word, because rows and columns intersect at an area (or cell), not a point. Thus, you'll still have to locate the feature within the grid cell. This can become especially maddening if the density of names is great or the cell is large relative to the extent of Obscure Street. The problem of searching "within the square" for a difficult-to-spot street name is even greater when grid lines are indicated only by marginal ticks. Most of us know the resulting frustration well and may thus be somewhat skeptical of map indexing. The only remedy is patience. Persistent searching will usually turn up the place name in the end.

Remember, too, that each local grid is specific to the map for which it was drawn. If your friends ask you where Obscure Street is and you tell them, "M-2," the information won't be of any help unless they have the same map you do. Keep this in mind when you use maps that include insets. Since each inset may have its own local grid, the same place may be represented by various pairs of coordinates. You are effectively working with different maps.

Proprietary Grids

In recent years, mapping has become more and more commercialized. Commercial vendors have developed and marketed several zone reference systems for use with their products. These proprietary grids may be map related, or they may be related to the use of maps in conjunction with specialized instruments. Let's look at a few examples.

Map Publishers. Atlases have their own version of local grid zone referencing. To complete the spatial reference, you need the name of the atlas and the page number of the gridded map. The index might indicate, for example, that you'll find London at M-5 on page 12 of the atlas.

This scheme is the basis for proprietary grid systems packaged with GPS equipment from some vendors (see Chapter 15: *GPS and Maps*). For example, the well-known map publisher Thomas Brothers Maps®** has created the *Page and Grid*™ system for use with their three scales of maps covering the continental United States. Through special arrangement with the GPS vendor Trimble Navigation,** Thomas Brothers Maps® supplies a grid-related product called *Thomas Guides*™. Trimble, in turn, markets a coordinate extension called *Trimble Atlas*™ (supplied by Thomas Brothers Maps®) which is designed to increase the locational precision of Page and Grid™ references.

The more specific the zone reference, the larger the scale of the map that is referenced. The result is a tailored package. Your GPS receiver locates you on your map, letting you zoom in or out in scale to see the desired level of detail. As more vendors market electronic navigation systems that display maps on a portable computer screen, such linking of zone coordinates to map features will become more common.

Amateur Radio Operators. Another proprietary grid is that developed and used by ama-

*Thomas Brothers Maps (R), 17731 Cowan, Irvine, CA 92714, 800-899-MAPS, www.thomas.com.

**Trimble Navigation, 645 N. Mary Avenue, Sunnyvale, CA 94086, 800-487-4662.

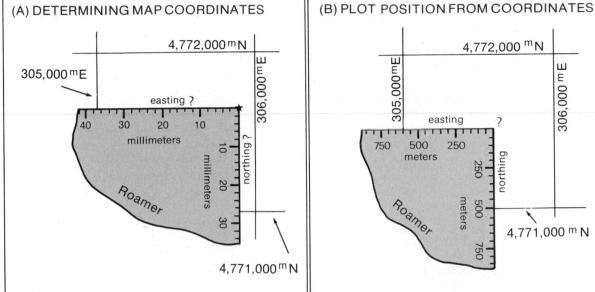

(A) DETERMINING MAP COORDINATES

(B) PLOT POSITION FROM COORDINATES

PROBLEM: Determine UTM coordinates of building.
Step 1: Align roamer so that its edges are parallel with the grid lines and its corner is positioned at the center of the building.
Step 2: Read the intergrid easting and intergrid northing from the edges of the roamer.
Step 3: Add the intergrid easting and intergrid northing to the west and east grid line values, respectively.
RESULT: [305,903ᵐE, 4,771,650ᵐN]

PROBLEM: Plot the location of the building with UTM coordinates (305,600ᵐE, 4,771,500ᵐN).
Step 1: Determine the intergrid easting and northing by subtracting the value of the west and south grid lines from the easting and northing, respectively.
Step 2: Slide the roamer across the map to the point where its edge scales provide the proper intergrid easting and northing.
Step 3: Mark the map at the corner of the roamer. This is the plotted position.

11.10 You can use a roamer to determine rectangular coordinates for a feature (A) or to plot a feature's position from known coordinates (B).

tcur (HAM) radio operators.* This terrestrial reference scheme is based on the **Maidenhead** global system, which partitions the earth into progressively smaller quadrilaterals of latitude and longitude. The first two letters in the reference divide the earth into 20° by 10° fields. Pairs of numbers designate 2° by 1° squares within these fields. Two more letters are used to define 5' by 2.5' sub-squares within each square. Thus a six-character code can locate any place on earth within a rectangular zone of up to 5½ by 3 miles.

As with the Page and Grid™ scheme, Trimble has extended the Maidenhead grid so that it provides more precise spatial referencing. This extension makes the grid more suitable for use with their GPS receivers. The extension, called the *Trimble Grid Locator*™, adds a pair of numbers and a pair of letters to the six-character Maidenhead code.

Military Grid

Another terrestrial reference scheme is the **U.S. Military Grid Reference System**. It is used with UTM and UPS grids. In devising this system, the military aimed to minimize confusion when using long numerical coordinates (up to 15 digits may be required) and numerical zone specifica-

Grid locator maps are available from the Headquarters of the American Radio Relay League, 225 Main Street, Newington, CT 06111.

230

tions. This modification was achieved by substituting single letters for several numerals.

In the Military Grid, each 6° zone (there are 60 in all) is divided into 19 quadrangles of 8° of latitude and one (the northmost) of 12° of latitude, forming a grid of cells.* The rows of quadrangles are assigned letters C through X consecutively, beginning at 80°S latitude (**Figure 11.11A**). Letters I and O are omitted to avoid pos-

---

Only the UTM version of the Military Grid will be discussed in detail, since most map users have little call for making coordinate references in polar regions.

sible confusion with similar-appearing numerals. Each grid cell is designated by the appropriate alphanumeric code, referring first to the zone number (column) and next to the row letter. Wisconsin's capitol building, for example, is located in the 6° x 8° quadrangle designated 16T.

Each quadrangle is next divided into 100,000-meter squares, and each square is identified by two letters which are unique within the grid zone designation. The first letter is the column designation; the second letter is the row designation (**Figure 11.11B**). Letters I and O are

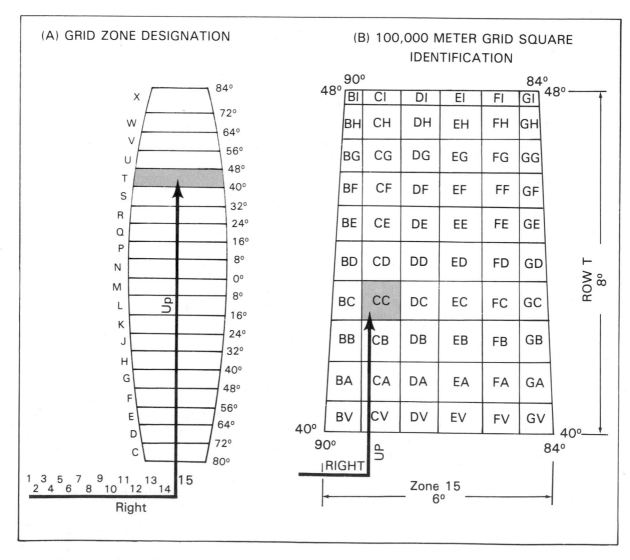

11.11 With the **Military Grid**, the 6° UTM zones are first divided into 8° latitude bands and lettered from south to north **(A)**. Next, each of these 6° by 8° zones is divided into 100,000-meter squares and given a unique letter code within its zone **(B)**.

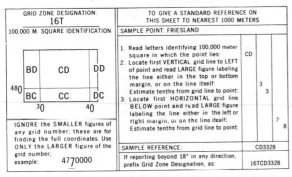

GRID ZONE DESIGNATION:
16T

100,000 M. SQUARE IDENTIFICATION

BD	CD	DD
BC	CC	DC

480

30   40

IGNORE the SMALLER figures of any grid number; these are for finding the full coordinates. Use ONLY the LARGER figure of the grid number; example: 4770000

TO GIVE A STANDARD REFERENCE ON THIS SHEET TO NEAREST 1000 METERS

SAMPLE POINT: FRIESLAND

1. Read letters identifying 100,000 meter square in which the point lies: CD
2. Locate first VERTICAL grid line to LEFT of point and read LARGE figure labeling the line either in the top or bottom margin, or on the line itself: 3
   Estimate tenths from grid line to point: 3
3. Locate first HORIZONTAL grid line BELOW point and read LARGE figure labeling the line either in the left or right margin, or on the line itself: 2
   Estimate tenths from grid line to point: 8

SAMPLE REFERENCE: CD3328

If reporting beyond 18° in any direction, prefix Grid Zone Designation, as: 16TCD3328

MADISON, WISCONSIN

11.12 A map sheet miniature showing the 100,000-meter square identification letters can be found in the marginal grid reference box on maps which use the Military Grid.

again omitted to avoid possible confusion with numerals. The 100,000-meter square containing Madison, Wisconsin, is designated 16TCC. To assist the user, the 100,000-meter square identification letters for each map sheet are generally shown in the sheet miniature, which is a part of the grid reference box found in the lower margin of the map (**Figure 11.12**).

For more precise designation of locational coordinates, the Military Grid uses the standard UTM numerals. Thus, the regularly spaced lines that make up the UTM grid on any large-scale map are divisions of the 100,000-meter square. These lines are used to locate a point with the desired precision within the 100,000-meter square. Dividing the square by 10 adds a pair of single-digit numerals which designate a cell of 10,000

11.13 Military Grid coordinate designations within 100,000-meter squares involve progressive subdivision by 10 and use standard UTM numerals.

232

meters on a side (**Figure 11.13**). Wisconsin's capitol dome is located in the 10,000-meter cell designated 16TCC07. Further division by 10 requires a pair of two-digit numbers, yielding the designation 16TCC0571 for the 1,000-meter cell containing the capitol. The process can be continued until the desired level of precision is achieved. In each instance, the coordinate pair designates the southwest corner of the grid cell at the specified level of precision.

LAND PARTITIONING SYSTEMS

People have long had a need for a spatial reference system that was convenient for land partitioning. Land ownership, zoning, taxation, and resource management are just a few of the purposes to be served by such a system. The system that was needed had to be simple enough conceptually so that it could be generally understood and simple enough technically so that it could be readily implemented in the field at the time of settlement.

"Time of settlement" is the key phrase here. The point and zone coordinate grids discussed previously may be appropriate for land partitioning today, but they would have been impractical at the time most regions were settled.

When European settlers first arrived in the United States, they brought a host of land partitioning methods. Two distinct systems were soon in vogue in the colonies. An unsystematic scheme prevailed in the South and Southwest, while a systematic plan was more common in New England.

Unsystematic Methods

Much land in the United States colonized before 1800 was characterized by scattered settlements. This was particularly true in the South, where climate was moderate and agriculture was practiced on a large scale. These conditions encouraged people to settle far apart rather than to cluster together as they did in the North. A family usually acquired a grant of a certain size, say 400 acres, through a gift or purchase. The family was then permitted to select a 400-acre parcel to their liking on any part of the unappropriated area. Consequently, the shape of parcels was decided mainly by the geography of the local setting; people naturally snatched up the best land they could, regardless of its shape. Convenience of land parcel description was only an afterthought. An irregular parcel would be harder to describe than a simple geometrical figure such as a square, but the extra effort might be worth it if the enclosed land was substantially better. So some of the lots had strange shapes indeed.

The problem, then, was to define these asymmetrical parcels well enough to make clear whose land began where. The solution was to follow a connected path around a parcel's boundaries, noting landmarks along the way. A parcel might be described, using only natural features, as:

> That parcel of land enclosed by a boundary beginning at the falls on Green River, thence downstream to the confluence of the North Fork, thence up the North Fork to the first falls, thence along Black Rock Escarpment to the point of beginning.

This self-contained form of land description is referred to as the **metes and bounds** system. With this method, little skill was required to delineate a boundary. The legal description was down to earth and remained useful as long as neighbors agreed with the place names and accepted the boundaries.

Parcels didn't have to be described using only natural features, of course. The parcel shown in Figure **11.14A**, for instance, could be given the following metes and bounds description, based on artificial as well as natural features:

> Parcel beginning at the point where Pine Road crosses Beaver Creek, thence due east to the big rock pile, thence northeasterly to the confluence of Beaver Creek and Pine Creek, thence northwesterly to the N.E. corner of Tom Smith's fence, thence back to the point of beginning.

After survey methods arrived, it became less common to use environmental features in land parcel descriptions. Descriptions became more abstract, based on distance and direction from an established point. The abstract form of the previous crude description is shown in Figure **11.14B**; it would read as follows:

> Parcel beginning at the N.E. corner of the Pine Road bridge over Beaver Creek, thence along a compass sighting of 90° for 500 yards, thence along a compass sighting of 10° for

PART II
*Map
Analysis*

500 yards, thence along a compass sighting of 300° for 950 yards, and thence along a compass sighting of 170° for 1,000 yards back to the point of beginning.

If survey methods were available, the description would likely include the parcel's size in common areal units, such as acres, as well.

Metes and bounds land parcel descriptions were most common in the southern colonies but were used to some extent throughout all regions settled before 1800. English settlements in the relatively humid East and South were located mainly with respect to soil and timber resources **(Figure 11.15A)**, while in the Southwest the Spanish settlers were more concerned with water (riparian) resources **(Figure 11.15B)**. The spatial arrangement of the English and Spanish schemes was similar.

French settlements, on the other hand, had quite a different land parcel arrangement. Settlement usually took place along rivers or lakes, which provided the chief source of transportation and communication for the French. Boundaries ran back from the waterfront as parallel lines, creating ribbon farms or **long lots (Figure 11.15C)**. Through subsequent subdivision, the parcels often became so narrow that they were no longer practical to farm.

With all these unsystematic settlement schemes, the land was settled before surveys were made. This free-for-all system encouraged inefficient partitioning of area—at least from the government's taxing point of view. The first people into a region had a virtual monopoly over the choicest lands. Later settlers found only swamps, steep slopes, or poor soils available. In many areas, fragments of poor land remained unowned and unwanted long after a region was "fully" settled.

Furthermore, land claims often overlapped, and boundary errors were common. In homogeneous environments, it was hard to establish accurate borders in the first place. In

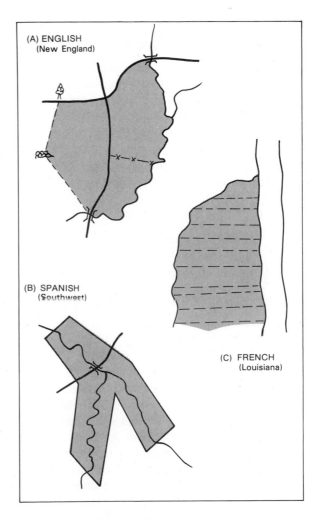

11.14 Metes and bounds descriptions may consist of landmarks and approximate directions (A) or precise distance and direction readings (B).

11.15 The English (A), Spanish (B), and French (C) systems of land settlement vary in their basic geometry and relation to environmental features.

234

any setting, boundary mistakes naturally occurred as the land passed through various owners and environmental changes. Good fences, as Robert Frost pointed out, did make good neighbors, because they clarified irregular boundaries. It used to be the custom for neighboring landowners to walk together around their lots each spring. The excursion was far more than a social outing; it made sure that all owners agreed on the borders between their land. Problems arose, however, when later generations ignored the boundary-walking tradition. Many markers were shifted or destroyed through time: Fences fell away; trees died or were chopped down; lakes dried up; rock piles were moved. The result has been a host of legal battles over property boundaries of unsystematically settled land.

Systematic Methods

The alternative to the scattered settlement of irregular parcels was to survey and divide the land systematically before settlers arrived. This practice was followed in many of the colonies, occasionally in the South but mostly in the North. Areas were laid out and surveyed, and maps of the parcels (called **plats**) prepared and recorded, all prior to settlement. Let's take a look at the New England system, which was typical of these systematic land-partitioning systems.

New England Towns

In New England, the environment was less hospitable than in the South, and settlers needed a land partitioning system that would provide mutual help during severe winters and accommodate the small-scale agriculture practiced in the area. The idea the colonists hit upon was to divide the land into squares, called **towns** or **townships**, and to break up these large parcels further into **lots** or **sections**. New townships were laid out with reference to neighboring ones, creating a compact and systematic settlement pattern. With this plan, it wasn't easy for one person to gain control of the best land, as was the case with unsystematic settlement. Settlers had to take the poor land along with the good. This system simplified the task of providing services to the settlers, while at the same time generating the maximum amount in land taxes.

United States Public Land Survey (USPLS)

In 1776, the United States Congress of the brand-new Confederation of 13 states was faced with an urgent need for a national land policy. They had to devise some way to manage the western lands which had been ceded to the Confederation. Quick action was important for several reasons. Land had been promised to Revolutionary soldiers; a source of income was necessary to run the new country; and future states had to be carved out of the wilderness. Most important, the country needed a land policy that the people on the frontier could understand.

By the time the lands west and north of the Ohio River (the Northwest Territories) were opened to settlement in the late 1700s, the newly formed United States government had come up with what seemed to be an orderly way to transfer land to settlers. The solution was called the Land Ordinance of 1785, otherwise known as the Township and Range System or, more commonly, the **United States Public Land Survey (USPLS)**. This plan called for regular, systematic partitioning of land into easily discernible parcels prior to settlement and required that all grants be carefully recorded. Settlers were able, however, to select previously surveyed parcels to their liking. Thus, the USPLS approach combined features of the systematic New England and unsystematic southern systems.

The USPLS was implemented in the Northwest Territories and subsequently in the remaining central and western states. The first step was arbitrarily to select an **initial point (Figure 11.16A)**. The parallel and meridian which intersected at that point were determined by field survey. The parallel was called the **base line** or **geographer's line** (surveyors were called geographers in those days). The intersecting meridian was called the **principal meridian**. **Range lines** were then surveyed along meridians at six-mile intervals north and south of the base line. **Township lines** were surveyed along parallels at six-mile intervals east and west of the principal meridian **(Figure 11.16B)**. The 6 x 6 mile squares bounded by these intersecting township and range lines were called **survey or congressional townships**.

The surveyors encountered a problem, however. Because the earth is round, meridians converge toward the north pole, and the effect of this meridional convergence is additive. Thus, the square township grid couldn't be extended indef-initely outward from the initial survey point with-out becoming distorted, and the trouble became worse with increasing distance east and west of the principal meridian. To reduce the problem of unequal township dimensions to a practical level,

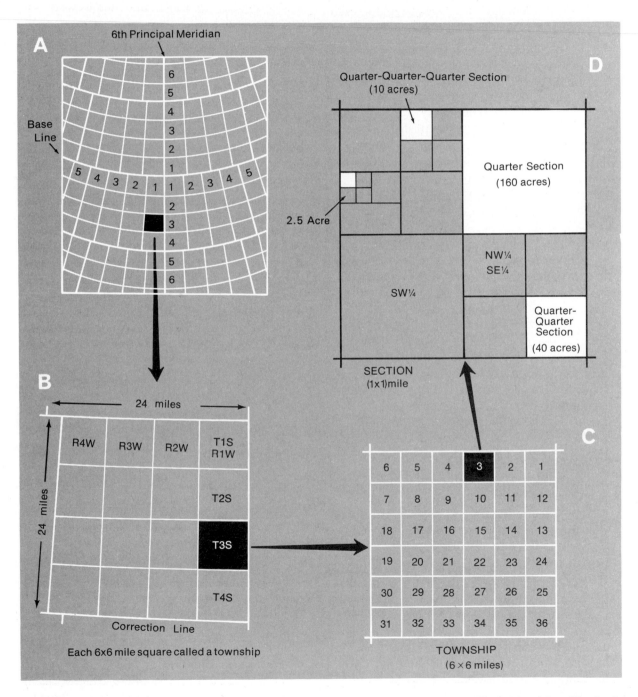

11.16 The structure and notation of the United States Public Land Survey provides a systematic means of describing land parcels as small as 10 acres.

236

standard parallels were established at every fourth township line, and guide meridians were placed at every fourth range line. These standard parallels and guide meridians formed grid cells approximately 24 miles square. Within each cell, there were 16 idealized townships. Note the words "approximately" and "idealized," for each zone couldn't be an exact 24 x 24 mile square, nor could each township be truly six miles on a side.

But at least distortion could be limited by modifying each zone. The solution was to readjust guide meridians along standard parallels so that each zone's southern boundary was 24 miles long. This correction was accomplished by offsetting guide meridians along standard parallels; for this reason, the term correction line is often used as a synonym for standard parallel.

To further reduce the effect of converging meridians, new base lines were established at con-venient intervals as the USPLS expanded west-ward. As Figure 11.17 demonstrates, each base line was intersected by a principal meridian. Each principal meridian was given a name, which was used to identify surveyed parcels within the region. For example, as Figure 11.17 shows, parts of Wisconsin, Minnesota, and Illinois were sur-veyed using the 4th Principal Meridian.

In addition, each township was partitioned into 36 square-mile parcels of 640 acres, called sections. Every section was then given a number from 1 to 36, depending on its position in the township (Figure 11.16C). A section could be further divided into halves, quarters, and similar fractional parts. With this system, each land par-cel's legal description is unique and unambigu-ous. If full details of the partitioning are given, you can locate a parcel with impressive accuracy. The 10-acre piece of land in Figure 11.16D, for exam-ple, would be described in abbreviated form as:

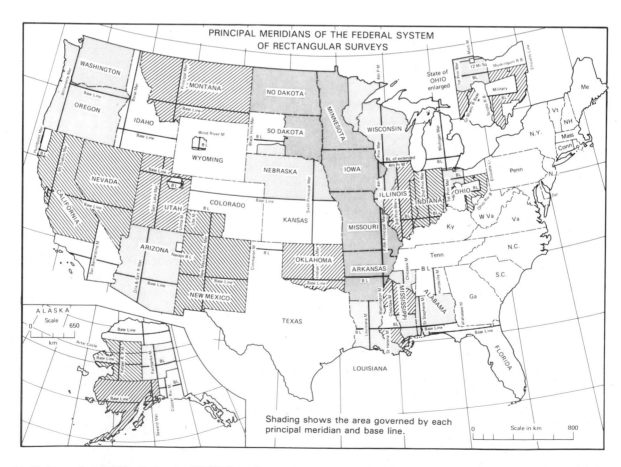

11.17 Areas governed by their own USPLS base lines and principal meridians are shown here for the contiguous United States.

NW¼, NE¼, NW¼, Sec. 3, T.3S, R.1W, 1st Principal Meridian.

In expanded form, the description reads:

> The Northwest quarter of the Northeast quarter of the Northwest quarter of Section 3 of Township 3 South, Range 1 West, first Principal Meridian.

To locate a parcel from its legal description, the trick is to read backwards, beginning with the principal meridian and working back through the township and range, the section, and the fractional section. To give the parcel's legal description, you simply reverse the above procedure and work up from the smallest division to the principal meridian. Peruse the examples in **Figure 11.18** until you feel comfortable with the system,

because the USPLS is the basis for abstracts, deeds, and most other land ownership documents in the United States. Note in particular that separate (disjoint) parcels or parcels overlapping certain survey lines can't be given a single description. This explains why there may be several deeds to your family property even though it is a single unit of land.

There are some exceptions to the use of the USPLS, even in areas generally covered by the system. One exception occurs when most of a small parcel falls under a water body. Such a parcel, called a **government lot**, is usually described solely by a number **(Figure 11.19A)**. Parcels in a platted subdivision of building sites are also specified by lot numbers **(Figure 11.19B)**. Other

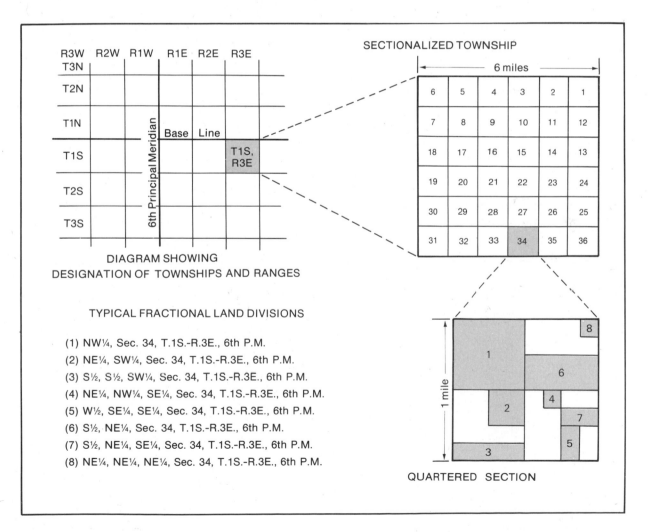

DIAGRAM SHOWING
DESIGNATION OF TOWNSHIPS AND RANGES

SECTIONALIZED TOWNSHIP

QUARTERED SECTION

TYPICAL FRACTIONAL LAND DIVISIONS

(1) NW¼, Sec. 34, T.1S.-R.3E., 6th P.M.
(2) NE¼, SW¼, Sec. 34, T.1S.-R.3E., 6th P.M.
(3) S½, S½, SW¼, Sec. 34, T.1S.-R.3E., 6th P.M.
(4) NE¼, NW¼, SE¼, Sec. 34, T.1S.-R.3E., 6th P.M.
(5) W½, SE¼, SE¼, Sec. 34, T.1S.-R.3E., 6th P.M.
(6) S½, NE¼, Sec. 34, T.1S.-R.3E., 6th P.M.
(7) S½, NE¼, SE¼, Sec. 34, T.1S.-R.3E., 6th P.M.
(8) NE¼, NE¼, NE¼, Sec. 34, T.1S.-R.3E., 6th P.M.

11.18 Fractional land divisions in the USPLS and their legal descriptions.

238

exceptions are small (less than 10 acre) and irregular land parcels, which were often given metes and bounds, rather than USPLS, descriptions.

In practice, the idealized structure of the USPLS frequently broke down. Errors in the original survey occurred due to poor instrumentation, rugged terrain, or just plain sloppy work by surveyors, who were paid on the basis of total miles surveyed (**Figure 11.20**). These survey errors have persisted, largely because historical boundaries hold legal precedence over new survey evidence.

Parcel excesses and flaws resulting from survey errors weren't the only obstacles to regular land partitioning. Again, the pinching effect of converging meridians on a round earth complicated the surveyors' job of laying out a square grid of townships. To systematize the distribution of shape and area distortions, surveyors put off all errors to the western and northern tiers of sections within each township. The result was to create **fractional lots**, which may depart radically from the ideal 640-acre sections (**Figure 11.21**).

Distortions due to earth curvature led to still other problems. Errors became worse as surveyors traveled farther from their initial point. Thus, they eventually gave up, established a new initial point, and started extending grid lines all over again from this new spot. The result is a great many different grid systems which, where they come together, rarely mesh (**Figure 11.22A**). In the zones of contact between these clashing systems, some confusing USPLS descriptions can occur. This is especially true for parcels straddling the contact zone, since for them two deeds—and reference to two principal meridians—are required.

A similar problem may occur when the USPLS grid comes into contact with other reference systems; this can happen in regions settled before 1785 or any area that was still unsurveyed at the time of settlement (**Figure 11.22B**). Some land has never been surveyed under the USPLS system, mainly because it was reserved for national forests, Indian reservations, or other government use. Setting aside these regions eliminated the need to partition them for subsequent land give-away purposes.

The USPLS grid has been incorporated into the symbolism of many maps. On planimetric maps made by government agencies, for example, the USPLS grid is often included because it is so closely associated with the boundaries of townships, counties, and other political units. The USPLS grid probably finds its fullest expression on USGS quadrangle maps in the topographic series. On these maps, section lines, section numbers, and marginal township-range notations are all printed in red. Unlike boundaries on maps oriented to political regions, however, quadrangle boundaries rarely follow USPLS lines.

As we've seen, the USPLS grid shown on these topographic and planimetric maps lets us

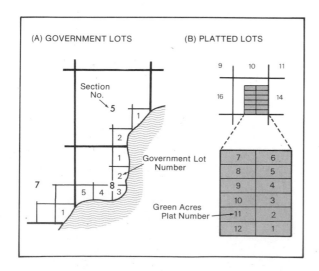

11.19 Small parcels, such as government lots (A) and platted lots (B), are numbered separately in the USPLS.

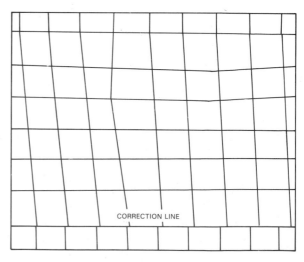

11.20 Converging meridians and survey errors are evident in the USPLS section line grid.

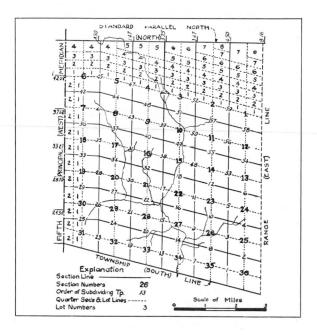

11.21 Survey error is, by USPLS design, distributed to the northern and western sections in each township.

partition a region into easily defined areal parcels. By slightly modifying the USPLS, however, we can also use it as a crude point referencing system. To do so, we state the location of environmental features with reference to the corner or center of a standard USPLS parcel. We can pinpoint many features this way, since the cultural landscape has been aligned to the USPLS grid in many parts of the country. For instance, Wisconsin's capitol dome is centered on the northeast corner of Section 23 in T.7N, R.9E. As a rule, of course, one of the special point referencing systems is the preferred method of indicating point locations.

LAND RECORDS

For centuries, people have felt a need to keep land information records. Physical characteristics, resource reserves, market value, ownership, improvements, accessibility, and restrictions on land use are but a few of the items entered in these records. Traditionally, the basic spatial unit for this record keeping is the **land parcel**. A land parcel is the smallest unit of ownership or, as in the case of a farm field, a unit of uniform use.

Types of Land Records

We call the records kept on land parcels the **cadastre**. Although we can use the term cadastre in an all-encompassing sense, it is usually classified into several types. **Fiscal cadastres** are among the oldest (not surprisingly, since govern-

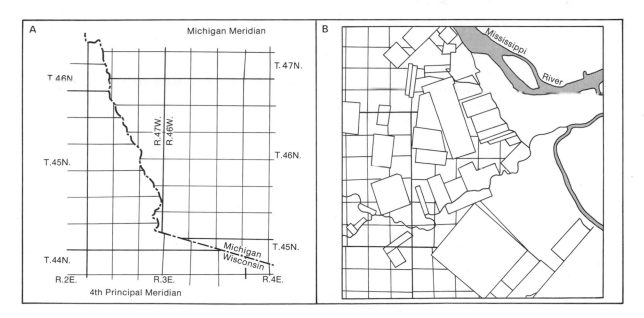

11.22 Irregularities in the USPLS system can often be attributed to base line and principal meridian origins (A) and prior claims (B).

240

NAME & ADDRESS OF OWNER	DESCRIPTION OF PROPERTY	ASSESSED VALUES	
30-20-401 30-11139 Ditsch, Roman S. RFD 1 Blue Mounds, WI 53517 20.0 acres	School 3794 Fire MH Sec 20-7-6 E1/2 NW1/4 SW1/4 643/377	Land Improvements Total	6,450 6,450
30-20-402 30-11162 Anderson, A. Duane 2665 Marshall Pkwy Madison, WI 53713 20.0 acres	School 3794 Fire MH Sec 20-7-6 W1/2 NW1/4 SW1/4 794/11	Land Improvements Total	3,600 3,600
30-20-403 30-11185 Blumer, Harold RFD 1 Blue Mounds, WI 53517 40.0 acres	School 3794 Fire MH Sec 20-7-6 SW1/4 SW1/4 830/354	Land Improvements Total	8,400 8,400
30-20-404 30-11208 Blumer, Harold RFD 1 Blue Mounds, WI 53517 40.0 acres	School 3794 Fire MH Sec 20-7-6 SE1/4 SW1/4 830/354	Land Improvements Total	10,300 10,300

11.23 This portion of a page from the Dane County, Wisconsin, tax rolls held in the county treasurer's office shows the types of land records that make up the fiscal cadastre.

ments have taxed property since the beginning of recorded history). Fiscal cadastres include the owner's name and address, parcel description and size, the parcel's assessed value and any improvements, and the current tax levy (**Figure 11.23**). In the United States, the fiscal cadastre for rural areas is the responsibility of county government and is housed in the county treasurer's office in the county seat (often the courthouse). The fiscal cadastre for city property is the responsibility of municipal government.

11.24 The legal cadastre contains records concerning proprietary interests in land parcels, deeds, titles, easements, legal encumbrances, and so forth.

Another type of cadastre is the **legal cadastre (Figure 11.24)**. It includes records concerning proprietary interests in land parcels.* These records contain the current owner's name and address, legal description of the property, deed, title, abstract, and legal encumbrances (such as easements, mineral rights, and transfer restrictions). In the United States, some of this information is held by the property taxing authority, but the rest may be scattered among several agencies. Abstract and title companies do a booming business helping people track down these elusive records.

Fiscal and legal cadastres are of limited value for administrators, managers, and planners who make decisions involving natural resources, land use, or infrastructure considerations (fire, police, ambulance, disaster relief services) in the course of their work. These land information specialists need extensive, reliable attribute (or feature) information about land parcels, including land slope and aspect, soil characteristics, drainage, vegetation cover, number of residents, building construction, access road width and surface material, utility service, and zoning restrictions. The body of land records containing this information is called the **multipurpose cadastre**. It is this third type of cadastre that is currently attracting the most attention. Environmental administrators, managers, and planners realize that they could do their jobs better if this information was reliably recorded and accessible.

Structure of Land Records

Cadastres are generally made up of two complementary parts. One part contains the written record, or **register**, which provides information concerning land ownership. It may include all manner of documents, forms, official seals, and stamps of approval that characterize bureaucratic activities. Figures 11.23 and 11.24 illustrate typical register entries. These written records have traditionally been widely scattered among government offices, each with a different mission and authority. Assembling the register material can therefore be frustrating, time consuming, and costly.

In practice, there is a great deal of overlap and duplication between fiscal and legal cadastres.

The second part of most cadastres—which is, ideally, thoroughly cross-referenced with the first part—contains detailed locational descriptions of each parcel. These descriptions may be in the form of the original **cadastral survey data (Figure 11.25A)** or in the form of **cadastral**, or **land ownership, maps** plotted from these data **(Figure 11.25B)**. In either case, you can determine the location and areal extent of each parcel from these records. Cadastral survey data are generally tied to the ground through a system of field markers at the time of survey. Thus, at least in theory, you can use cadastral survey data to trace a parcel's boundaries in the field.

In fact, a key function of cadastral surveys is to provide the foundation for a system of land

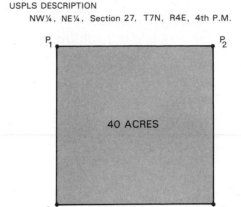

USPLS DESCRIPTION

NW¼, NE¼, Section 27, T7N, R4E, 4th P.M.

COORDINATE DESCRIPTION (IN UTM COORDINATES)

$P_1 = (742,970^{m}E, 4,771,670^{m}N)$
$P_2 = (743,500^{m}E, 4,771,700^{m}N)$
$P_3 = (743,530^{m}E, 4,771,170^{m}N)$
$P_4 = (743,000^{m}E, 4,771,140^{m}N)$

11.26 In the future, land parcels will probably have several descriptions. For example, parcels designated as "forties" (40 acres) in the USPLS system will also be described by pairs of coordinates.

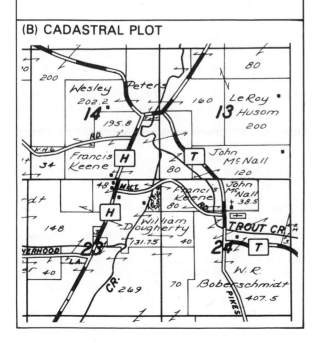

(A) LEGAL DESCRIPTION

SE¼, NW¼, NE¼, SW¼, Section 26, T.10N., R.15E., 4th Principal Meridian

(B) CADASTRAL PLOT

11.25 A detailed boundary description, in the form of cadastral survey data (A) or cadastral maps (B), lets you determine each parcel's location and extent in the field.

rights transfer. It's necessary to know a parcel's boundaries before it can be conveyed without ambiguity from one owner to the next. Land conveyance involves more than a geographic description of a parcel, of course, because such a description says nothing about possible restrictions or encumbrances on the property. It is for this reason that the cadastral survey is cross-referenced with the register, and it is important to consult both land records when transferring property rights.

Land Information Systems

Automated **land information systems** represent a recent attempt to integrate the various cadastres into a useful whole. Such systems stress data compatibility, sharing, and cooperation. They also incorporate powerful statistical and graphic tools to help users analyze data, generate land information, and make decisions (see *Geographical Information Systems* in Chapter 19).

The cadastre represents an important part of the database of a modern land information system. As such, it must meet two requirements:

1. All entries should be **spatially referenced**, using some form of coordinate referencing system. In other words, there must be some

241

PART II
*Map
Analysis*

242

provision for moving from the data records to the appropriate ground positions.

2. There must be **compatibility** among the spatial referencing entries. It is preferred that all spatial reference data be identified with some terrestrial system. Latitude-longitude coordinates are ideal because they are universal, but State Plane Coordinates and Universal Transverse Mercator coordinates are also acceptable if we're willing to accept the zone boundary problems they introduce. If several spatial reference systems are used in recording data, they should at least be transformable from one to the other.

Here we have a major problem. Land partitioning systems that accommodated the early settlers aren't best suited today when **land records management** is the primary concern. The USPLS is a case in point. It was an excellent system when the government's main concern was selling or giving away land parcels as quickly and efficiently as possible. It also served land transfer needs fairly well in subsequent years.

But for purposes of land management, the current USPLS is an administrative nightmare. The problem is that locations of corners and boundaries aren't tied to a terrestrial coordinate system such as latitude and longitude. Rather, these locations are known only in reference to other points and boundaries in the system. This means that there is no convenient way to determine which parcel contains a particular location or what resources are found in a specific parcel. Learning whose land has been damaged by a flood, for example, usually involves laboriously rescaling and overlaying several maps, as well as searching through a diversity of textual and tabular records.

This procedure is very inefficient in a computer age which uses digits as the language of high-speed information processing. We can perform overlay and correlation operations much more quickly and accurately with computers than we can manually. For this reason, efforts are being made to identify locations of land parcel corners and boundaries with abstract terrestrial coordinates such as those provided by latitude-longitude, UTM, and SPC grids. Although the old system will undoubtedly persist for years to come, we can expect land parcels in the future to be described for analytical purposes by strings of abstract coordinates (**Figure 11.26**). We'll return to this topic in Chapter 19, where we discuss automated geographical information systems.

SELECTED READINGS

Atwill, L., "What's Up (and Down) at the USGS," *Field & Stream* (May 1997), pp. 54-55.

Crossfield, J.K., "Evolution of the United States Public Land Survey System," *Surveying and Mapping*, 44, 3 (1984), pp. 259-265.

Department of the Army, *Universal Transverse Mercator Grid*, TMS 241-8, Washington, DC, 1958; Departments of the Army and Air Force, TM 5-241, Washington, DC, 1951.

Department of Commerce, Coast and Geodetic Survey, *Plane Coordinate Intersection Tables (2 Minute): Wisconsin*, Special Publication No. 308, Washington, DC, 1953 (series to cover each state).

Estopinal, S.V., *Guide to Understanding Land Surveys* (Eau Claire, WI: Professional Education Systems, 1989).

Fuson, R.H., *Fundamental Place-Name Geography*, 6th ed. (Dubuque, IA: Wm. C. Brown, 1989).

Hart, J.F., "Land Division in America" in *The Look of the Land* (Englewood Cliffs, NJ: Prentice-Hall, 1975), pp. 45-66.

Johnson, H.B., *Order Upon the Land: The U.S. Rectangular Land Survey and the Upper Mississippi Country* (London: Oxford University Press, 1976).

Maling, D.H., *Coordinate Systems and Map Projections*, 2nd ed. (New York: Pergamon Press, 1992).

Mitchel, H.C., and Simmons, L.G., *The State Coordinate Systems: A Manual for Surveyors*, U.S. Department of Commerce, Coast and Geodetic Survey, Special Publication No. 235, 1945.

National Research Council, *Modernization of the Public Land Survey System* (Washington, DC: National Academy Press, 1982).

National Research Council, *Need for a Multipurpose Cadastre* (Washington, DC: National Academy Press, 1980).

National Research Council, *Procedures and Standards for a Multipurpose Cadastre* (Washington, DC: National Academy Press, 1982).

Quimby, M.J., *Scratch Ankle, U.S.A.: American Place Names and Their Derivation* (New York: A.S. Barnes & Co., 1969).

Robinson, A.H., et al., "Scale, Reference, and Coordinate Systems," Chapter 6 in *Elements of Cartography*, 6th ed. (New York: John Wiley & Sons, 1995), pp. 92-111.

Stewart, G.R., *Names on the Globe* (New York: Oxford University Press, 1975).

Stewart, G.R., *Names on the Land: A Historical Account of Place-Naming in the United States* (New York: Random House, 1945).

Thrower, N.J.W., "Cadastral Survey and County Atlases of the United States," *The Cartographic Journal*, 9, 1 (June 1972), pp. 43-51.

Trewartha, G.T., "Types of Rural Settlement in Colonial America," *Geographical Review*, 36, 4 (1946), pp. 568-596.

Ventura, S.J., *Implementation of Land Information Systems in Local Government—Steps Toward Land Records Modernization in Wisconsin* (Madison: Wisconsin State Cartographer's Office, 1991).

Vonderohe, Alan P., et al., *Introduction to Local Land Information Systems for Wisconsin's Future* (Madison: Wisconsin State Cartographer's Office, 1991).

Also see references listed in Appendix C and Chapter 15.

CHAPTER 12

DIRECTION

INTRODUCTION

FLAT EARTH

Geographical Reference Lines
    True North
    Grid North
    Magnetic North
        Declination
        Declination Diagram
        Deviation

ROUND EARTH

    True Direction
    Constant Direction
    The Navigator's Dilemma

CONCLUSION

SELECTED READINGS

12

CHAPTER TWELVE

DIRECTION

Some people like to think that animals have an inborn **sense of direction** which the true outdoors-
people among us have somehow retained. If this is true, however, how do we account for the many animals as well as famed backwoods guides who become lost? A better explanation for the
direction-knowing powers of animals, "primitive" people, and guides is that they have learned to be more
observant than the rest of us. This is good news, for it means that anyone can learn to tell direction and,
with practice, can share the distinction of having a "sense of direction."

That expression, as a matter of fact, is nonsensical. If we say that certain people have a "sense of
direction," what do we mean? That they always know where the North Star is? Or the North Pole? Or that,
like Lassie, they can always find their way home? Direction, by definition, can only be determined with
reference to something. The reference point may be near at hand or far away, concrete or abstract. This
reference point, whether it is some object or some known position, establishes a **reference line**, or **base
line**, between you and it. Direction is measured along or to either side of this reference line.

The more different reference lines you learn, then, the better you will be at telling direction. The
aim of this chapter is to acquaint you with some useful base lines and the referencing systems built on
them. Let's begin by discussing direction in terms of a flat earth, since that is our usual way of perceiving the world.

FLAT EARTH

In its simplest form, direction is determined **egocentrically**. Your reference line is established by the
way you are facing. You go left or right, "this way" or "that way," straight ahead or back, up or down the
road—all in relation to an imaginary line pointing out from the front of your body.

Egocentric direction is often modified to include reference to landmarks. You are told to turn left
at Hardee's or right at Taco Bell. In familiar areas, this form of *landmark direction* may work well, except
for two problems. Landmarks change frequently—Hardee's or Taco Bell may have gone out of business.

PART II
Map Analysis

And far-off landmarks, such as mountain peaks, may be obscured by fog or snowstorms.

In an interesting refinement of egocentric direction, a symbolic clock face is used. You are assumed to be located at its center, facing 12:00. Your base line is the line projected from your position to 12:00. Now say that you want to find the direction to a distant object. Another imaginary line from you to that object is called the **direction line** (sometimes referred to as a **lubbers line** or **point line**). Direction is given in angular units as the difference between the base line and the direction line. Something directly to your right would be located at 3:00, something behind you at 6:00, and something to your left at 9:00 (**Figure 12.1A**).

The usefulness of all these egocentric direction indicators is limited. Our direction-finding ability will be more far-ranging if we learn to think **geocentrically** in terms of the cardinal directions. With this system, as with the clock face, direction is measured in angular units of a circle (**Figure 12.1B**). Direction to a distant object is given as the angle between our direction line and a **north-south base line**.

For everyday purposes, we give this angle verbally as east, northwest, southeast, and so forth. When we need greater accuracy, we use numerical systems of angular measurement. We break the circle of the earth into 360 degrees, each degree into 60 minutes, each minute into 60 seconds. This **sexagesimal** measurement scheme is the most common one used in the English-speaking world. If it sounds familiar, it is because our hour/minutes/seconds time notation uses the same units.

Early in life most of us discovered that time computations are awkward and frustrating. We overcame the inconvenient temporal units to some extent by converting to fractions. Thus, we say 1½ hours or 1.5 hours rather than 1 hour and 30 minutes. In the same way, people often convert angle measures to fractional or decimal units. For instance, the angle 50°30'15" becomes the equivalent but more convenient 50°30.24' or 50.50417° in decimal degrees. (The key to these conversions is to remember that there are 3,600" (60' x 60") in one degree.)

You may find other angle notations used on some maps. These systems are based on such

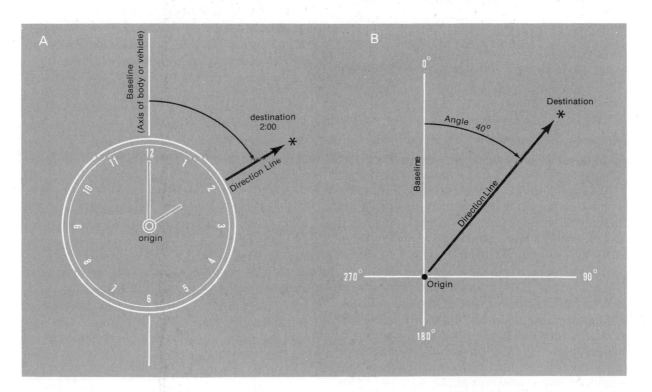

12.1 Direction is defined as the angular deviation from a base line. Sometimes a clock face is used as a directional reference system (A), but more commonly direction is measured in degrees from north or south (B).

246

units as **radians** (2π radians = 360°), **mils** (1 mil = 1/6400 of 360°), or **grads** (1 grad = 1/400 of 360°).

No matter which of these angular units we use, we must have some zero point on the circle from which to begin measuring. The starting point which has been chosen is north. In other words, north is equivalent to 12:00 on our symbolic clock face. This is probably why we tend to think of north as "up" and why north is customarily placed at the top of standard line maps. Oddly enough, the convention of topping a map with north is also found in the Southern Hemisphere—most likely because early European settlers carried the custom there.

The reason that the cardinal directions are so useful is that our reference line is no longer oriented to our own body, as it was with egocentric directional methods. No matter which way we turn, north remains the same. To make this system universally functional, all we need do is find some reference line on the earth's surface which will tie the cardinal directions to the ground.

Geographical Reference Lines

Before we can find such a universal reference line, however, we must face up to a startling fact. There can be no single north base line, because there isn't just one north. There are actually *three norths*. Each has its advantages and disadvantages as a reference point, and each is best suited for certain purposes. The north used on most maps is called true north.

True North

True (or **geographical**) **north** is the direction to a real place—the north pole of the axis of earth rotation. A line from any point on earth to the North Pole—that is, a line of longitude—is known as a **true north base line**. Thus, any meridian can serve as our reference line in finding true north.

The advantage of true north is that it can often be found in the field without the use of any special instruments. We can determine direction simply by making reference to natural features, much as animals do. Bees, for instance, use the sun to establish direction from hive to flowers, while geese are guided by the stars on their long nighttime migrations. People, too, have used both sun and stars as directional markers since they first began observing nature. As a matter of fact,

north was probably chosen as the zero point on maps because there are such good celestial signs to help us find it.

One of the oldest and most reliable indicators of true north is the North Star (Polaris). It is positioned in the Northern Hemisphere sky almost directly above the North Pole. The discrepancy between North Star and North Pole is only about one degree. To find true north, then, we merely find Polaris—quite a simple matter, since it is one of the brightest stars in the sky and is conveniently located at the tip of the handle of the Little Dipper (**Figure 12.2**). If you patiently observe the night sky, the North Star will be further pinpointed for you. Because the earth is rotating on its axis, all the stars seem to move in concentric paths around Polaris (**Figure 12.3**). We could hardly ask for a more dramatic reference mark.

We can use the sun as well as the stars to tell direction. For centuries, people have found the direction of true north by using the sun, a shadow cast by an object, and a bit of patience. Their method still works. The first step is to find an object which casts a well-defined shadow (**Figure 12.4A**). Next, mark the spot at which the top of the shadow touches the ground. After waiting 30 minutes, again mark the tip of the shadow. A line drawn between your two marks will be an east-

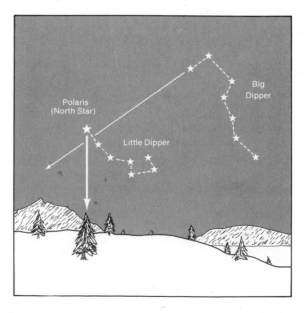

12.2 True north can easily be determined by observing the stars in the Northern Hemisphere sky at night.

12.3 A time-lapse photo of the night sky in the Northern Hemisphere captures the apparent movement of stars around a stationary North Star. In fact, the earth, not the stars, is turning.

west line. Since the sun rises in the east and sets in the west (actually, the earth travels from west to east), the shadow travels in the opposite direction. Therefore, your first mark will be on the west end of the line and your second mark on the east end. If you know the relationship between the cardinal directions, you will have no trouble filling in north, northeast, and all the other points on your ground sketch. When you divide a circle into directional segments in this way, you are **boxing the compass**. (The word "compass" derives from the Old French *compasser,* meaning "to go round.")

Sun determination of true north can be refined considerably if a watch is handy. Simply hold a thin stick or similar object upright in the center of the dial and then turn the watch until the shadow cast by the stick lies over the hour hand (**Figure 12.4B**). Now picture a spot halfway between the hour hand and 12:00, reading counterclockwise from 12:00 in the a.m. hours and clockwise in the p.m. hours. An imaginary line

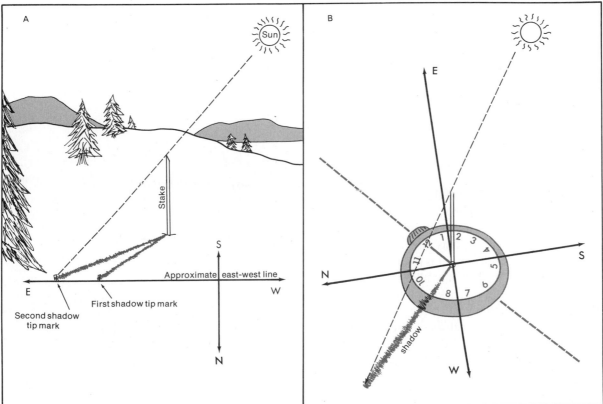

12.4 True north can be determined in the daytime by using shadows cast by the sun in conjunction with stakes placed in the ground (A) or with a clock face (B).

248

extended from the center of the dial through that spot will point to true north.

An alternative procedure for using a watch and the sun to determine direction is to point the hour hand directly toward the sun. As before, read counterclockwise from 12:00 in the a.m. and clockwise in the p.m. hours. South lies halfway between the hour hand and 12:00.

The problem with relying on the sun or other heavenly body as a reference mark is that it can be hidden by clouds or storms. To overcome this difficulty, people have created their own "artificial stars" in the form of navigation satellites. The constellation of satellites developed and operated by the U.S. military is called the **global positioning system (GPS)** (see Appendix D: *Navigation Instruments*).

Since these satellites communicate with the earth electronically on a 24-hour basis, we now have an all-weather, day-or-night ability to determine the direction of the true north baseline. It couldn't be easier. You merely turn on your GPS receiver, press some buttons, and in seconds you can determine the direction to a distant position with respect to true north (see Chapter 15: *GPS and Maps*).

But what do you do when you don't have a GPS receiver and the natural heavenly bodies (sun, planets, stars) are obscured? When this happens, people sometimes revert to an ancient body of folklore to find true north. It has been observed, for example, that growth rings are wider and branches heavier on a tree's sunny side (in the Northern Hemisphere, this is the tree's south side). Moss grows thickest on the shaded side of trees. In some regions, winds prevail from a certain direction. The tips of some trees, especially hemlock, point to the sun. In dry areas, such as the mountains of the American West, heavy timber is found on the shady north slope of mountains, while grass grows on the sunny south slope. Flocks of birds move south in the fall and north in the spring.

Such natural indicators of direction may be helpful in some instances. But what really matters is whether they are correct at the time you need them. It becomes a question of probability. A single indicator is less likely to be reliable than several indicators which are in basic agreement. As a rule, it isn't a good idea to depend too heavily on these natural guides to true north.

Grid North

Geographical north may be the true north, but it isn't always the most useful north. On maps which have a rectangular grid, you will find a second north—**grid north**. Unlike true north, it doesn't refer to any geographical place. It is purely artificial, established for the convenience of those who work with maps in the laboratory. Rectangular grids are often superimposed on maps to make it easier to use a protractor when computing distance and direction. The vertical lines on these grids point to grid north.

Grids may be added by the map user when working with maps in the lab. Or they may be included by the map publisher, as is common with large-scale maps such as those in the topographic map series (see Chapter 11: *Locational Reference Systems*). The UTM and SPC grids are standardized systems, in which the grid lines running from top to bottom are oriented to true north by convention.

But grid north isn't necessarily the same as true north. Grid north lines run parallel, straight up and down on a map, while true north lines (meridians) converge toward the north and south poles of earth rotation. If a map is centered on a

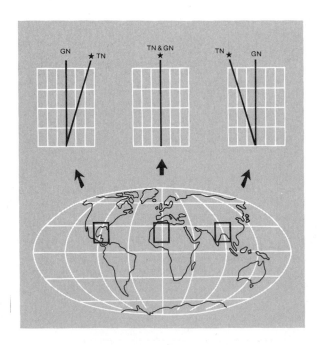

12.5 There can be considerable discrepancy between true north and grid north from one margin to the other of a small-scale map.

meridian, therefore, only the grid line in the center of the map will point to true north (**Figure 12.5**). The farther the grid lines are from the center of the map, the more deviation there will be between the two norths. There's little problem if only a small area is mapped. If the mapped region is large, however, the grid lines toward the edges of the map may point far from true north.

Another problem is that a particular grid can only be oriented to a single meridian. Thus, when two or more grid systems occur on a single map, grid north will seldom be the same for each grid. On USGS quads, for example, north on the SPC grid probably won't coincide with north on the UTM grid. The discrepancy between these two grid norths on the Madison West, Wisconsin, quadrangle is illustrated in **Figure 12.6**.

Magnetic North

True north is most valuable to map makers, and grid north is a helpful aid to map study in the laboratory. The third north—**magnetic north**—is most convenient for the map user in the field. To find magnetic north, we needn't look for celestial or natural clues to direction. We don't even need a map. All we need is a simple, easy-to-carry little

device called a **magnetic compass**. (See Appendix D: *Navigation Instruments* for a discussion of the magnetic compass.) This invaluable instrument (in theory at least) homes in on the magnetic north pole.

The logic of using magnetic north as a directional base line is quite simple. In effect, the earth is a giant magnet, with its magnetic field (or the **geomagnetic field**, since *geo* means "earth") running roughly north and south (**Figure 12.7**). A small magnet, too, has a magnetic field running between its north and south poles. The magnetic property which makes a compass work is that when two magnets are put together, their like poles repel and unlike poles attract. Thus, a free-floating magnetized needle will align itself with the earth's magnetic field. The needle's south pole will point to the north and its north pole to the south. If the end of the needle which points toward the earth's north magnetic pole is marked distinctly, say with red paint or with the letter *N*, it will point out the magnetic base line for us.

The latest version of a magnetic compass is the modern GPS receiver (see Appendix D: *Navigation Instruments*). Most such devices

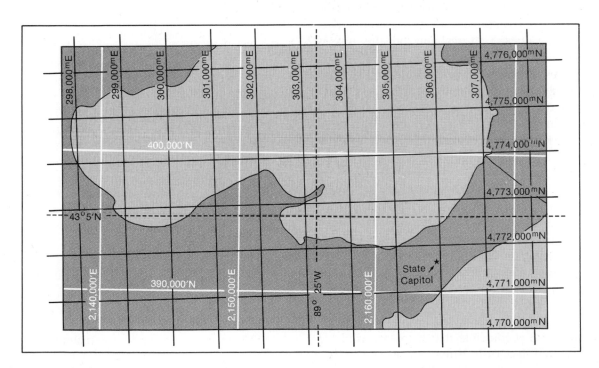

12.6 Grid north differs substantially from true north (indicated by a longitude line) for the UTM and SPC systems on this Madison West, Wisconsin, USGS 1:24,000 quadrangle.

250

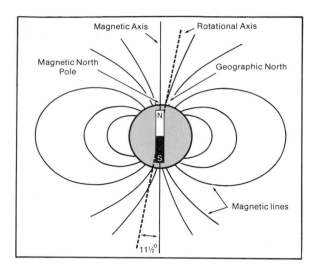

12.7 The earth's magnetic field resembles that of a simple bar magnet. There is a discrepancy of approximately 11 degrees between the magnetic and geographic poles.

have a magnetic north mode and thus serve as a **GPS compass**. You merely enter the coordinates for any two locations and press a few buttons. The receiver will display the magnetic direction from one location to the other.

Theoretically, the needle of a magnetic compass will point to the magnetic north pole from any place on the earth's surface. In practice, however, it doesn't always work out this way, as we'll see.

Declination. We've already seen that grid north may differ significantly from true north. The angular difference between these two norths is called **grid declination**. A similar problem occurs with magnetic north. The north pole of the earth's magnetic field is located in the Northwest Territories of Canada (north of Bathurst Island), approximately 1,300 kilometers (800 miles) south of the true North Pole (**Figure 12.8**). This discrepancy between the positions of the two poles means that the true north and magnetic north base lines only rarely coincide. The magnetic compass seldom points to true north!

The angular difference between true and magnetic north (called **magnetic declination** on maps and **compass variation** on nautical charts) is so predictable that maps are available which show **isogonic lines**, or lines of constant angular difference between the two norths. Such an isogonic map is shown in **Figure 12.9**.

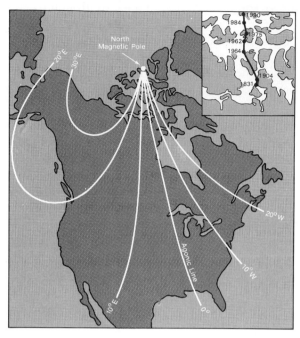

12.8 Magnetic north and true north rarely coincide at a location, as this 1990 map makes clear. It shows the north magnetic pole located about 1,300 kilometers south of the true North Pole.

Since GPS receivers have electronic memory capability, they can store declination data for the entire world. With these data in memory, the receiver can make the proper declination adjustments for direction readings taken any place on earth.

As Figure 12.9 shows, a line of "no declination" runs through the east-central part of the United States. At any position along this **agonic line**, the true and magnetic north poles are aligned. In contrast, magnetic declination exceeds 22 degrees in the northwestern and northeastern corners of the country.

In Washington State's Puget Sound, the compass will point far east of true north, while in Maine the compass will point far west of true north. Compass users in Chicago may be blithely unaware of magnetic declination, but if they go for a backpacking vacation in the Cascades they could be in for a shock.

To make matters worse, the magnetic declination for a given location is always changing. The magnetic poles are *wandering*, albeit in a predictable manner (see Figure 12.8). For this reason, the date shown on an isogonic map such as the one in Figure 12.9 is a critical piece of information for the map user. If the map were used a decade or so later, the declination might have changed significantly. Most nautical charts, which strive to be scrupulously up to date, tell exactly how much the variation is changing each year and in what direction.

The fact that the magnetic poles are wandering, while it leads to many problems, also provides strong evidence in support of one of the most important theories of all time. Some years ago, an interesting phenomenon was noticed. Iron crystals, during the process of changing from a molten state to rock, orient themselves with the local geomagnetic field, just as a compass needle does. This process of crystal alignment was given the term **chemical magnetism.**

Their curiosity aroused, scientists began to study the crystal orientation in rocks of different ages around the world. They discovered that each continent has a unique polar-wandering curve. When they plotted crystal alignment over the years on different continents, they found that the pole had moved in a different pattern with respect to each continent. Since there is just one magnetic north pole, the only explanation is that the continents themselves have moved, as predicted by the theory of **continental drift**. (See the section *Continental Drift* in Chapter 21.) Such confirmation of continental drift is momentous, for this theory helps explain the location of earthquakes and volcanoes and is thus crucial to our lives.

Declination Diagram. Declination is important to keep in mind, especially when you're in the field. It will, of course, be more critical to take note of declination at some times than others, depending on how much accuracy is needed. Surveyors and other professionals who work with precise directional information must always be conscious of declination. Someone building a solar house would also want a precise

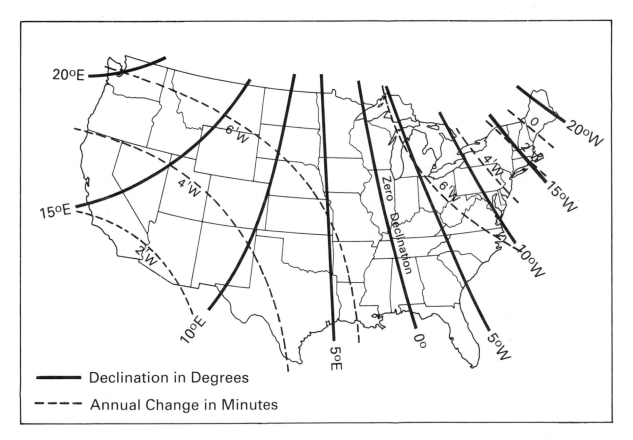

12.9 Isogonic (or declination) chart of the contiguous United States (1990). The 0-declination line is slowly shifting to the west.

252

determination of true north so that the structure could be aligned as effectively as possible. The rest of us may sometimes disregard declination, sometimes not.

If you live in the east-central United States, you'll have little problem with magnetic declination for everyday purposes. But when you use a compass in the northwest or northeast parts of the country, you can't ignore the discrepancy between true and magnetic north.

Declination problems are also compounded with distance. You might be able to tolerate 10 degrees of declination over a distance of 1 kilometer (.62 mile), since the ground distance discrepancy is only 174 meters (571 feet). But over a range of 9 kilometers (5.6 miles), the same ground distance discrepancy will occur with a declination of only 1 degree. Table E.11 in Appendix E gives an idea of the relation between declination angle and ground distance discrepancy.

Large-scale maps are designed purposefully to be used with a compass in the field. Nautical and aeronautical charts clearly fall into this cate-gory. A **compass variation diagram** is provided as standard information somewhere on the face of these charts (**Figure 12.10**). The outer ring in this diagram is oriented to true north, while the inner ring is oriented to magnetic north. The discrepancy between the 0-degree points on the two rings indicates the compass variation at the time the chart was made. Notice that the annual change in compass variation is also shown near the center of the diagram so that the navigator may update the chart if necessary.

The standard topographic quadrangle series for the United States published by the USGS is another good example of a large-scale map designed for use with a compass in the field. On these maps a **declination diagram** is provided as standard marginal information. Relations among the three north base lines, taken from the Madison West, Wisconsin, USGS 1:24,000 quad, are illustrated in **Figure 12.11**. Notice that UTM grid declination and magnetic north declination are given for the *center* of the sheet. Declination in areas toward the sides of the map could be slightly different. The larger the area covered by the map, the greater the change in declination from one part of the map to another.

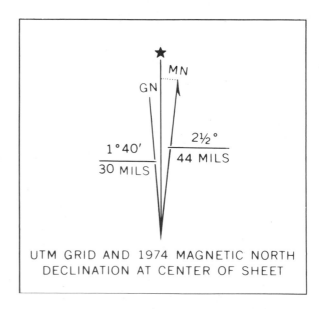

12.10 A typical compass variation diagram from a modern nautical chart. The diagram is positioned on the chart so that 0 degrees on the outer circle shows true north, while 0 degrees on the inner circle shows magnetic north. Compass variation and its annual change are also indicated near the center of the diagram.

12.11 Declination diagram showing relations among true, grid, and magnetic north base lines on the Madison West, Wisconsin, USGS 1:24,000 quadrangle. A mil is an angular division equal to 1:6,400 of the circumference of a circle.

The declination diagram which is found in the lower left margin of 1:24,000 USGS quadrangles is too small to be used conveniently with either a protractor in the laboratory or a compass in the field. To make the declination information easier to use at different map locations, you can extend the lines of the diagram across the map sheet. You might want to extend all three north base lines, or you may wish to extend one base line and then supplement it with additional parallel lines. Before you do either of these things, however, check to see whether the declination diagram has been drawn in true proportion. Are measured angles between base lines the same as the declination measurements given? If they aren't—and this is usually the case when declination angles are small—you'll have to use a protractor to compute the base lines.

By comparing the three base lines in the declination diagram, you can tell where the region covered by the map is located relative to the central meridian of the UTM grid and the isogonic chart of the country. If the north-south UTM grid lines tilt to the east, you know that the mapped region lies to the east of the central meridian. If the magnetic north lines slant to the east, you know that your mapped region is west of the agonic line. The reverse is true, of course, if the lines slant to the west. In the declination diagram shown in Figure 12.11, for example, grid lines tilt west and magnetic lines east. Consequently, you can tell that the Madison West quadrangle is located west of both the agonic line and the central meridian of the UTM zone.

The declination diagram also provides the information you need to change direction measures from one base line to another. This is a common task when figuring direction on maps. You can make conversions simply by adding or subtracting appropriate values. The logic of whether to add or subtract may be somewhat confusing, however. The best strategy is to work conversions out graphically. To do so, first remember that declination is measured from the true north base line. Next, decide whether the direction line lies to the west, to the east, or between the base lines involved in the conversion.

Now suppose that you want to convert a direction line from an eastern to a western base line when the direction line lies east of both base lines. In **Figure 12.12**, for instance, you might want to convert direction line D from the magnetic value of 12°E to a true direction value. You would merely add the magnetic declination to the magnetic angle. Thus, 12°E + 15°E = 27°E (true).

Conversely, you can convert a direction line from a *western* to an *eastern* base line when the direction line lies east of both base lines. To convert direction line D from grid to magnetic direction, subtract the sum of the grid and magnetic declinations from the grid angle. Thus, 37° (grid azimuth) – 15°E (magnetic declination) + 10°E (grid declination) = 12°E (magnetic).

Sometimes the direction line lies between the two base lines involved in a conversion. This is the case when you convert the magnetic value of 7°W (direction line C) to a true direction value. To make the conversion, subtract the magnetic declination from the magnetic angle, and drop the minus sign if the declination is larger than the original angle. Therefore, 7°W (magnetic angle) – 15°E (magnetic declination) = –8°E = 8°E (true).

And, finally, you will sometimes want to make conversions when both base lines lie east of the direction line. Say, for example, that you want to convert the magnetic value of 40°W (direction line A) to a true value. Simply subtract the magnetic declination from the magnetic angle. Thus, 40°W – 15°E = 25°W (true).

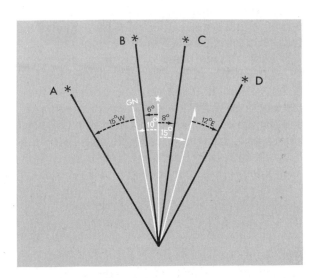

12.12 It is sometimes necessary to make conversions from one base line to another. Conversions to lines A, B, C, and D are described in the text.

These are just a few of the conversions illustrated in Figure 12.12. If you review the conversions discussed here and try some additional ones on your own, the concept of converting from one base line to another will become clear. It will also be evident that a direction line can be specified by any of three numerical values, depending on the base line chosen as your zero reference. This means that direction values, like temperature and elevation values, are an interval form of measurement (see *Measurement Level* in Chapter 2: *Geographical Data*).

Thus, direction values should be treated with the same caution given to all information based on a false zero reference. To ignore the fact that a direction line can have different numerical values is to risk making directional errors.

Deviation. Important as the declination diagram is, it doesn't tell the whole story. Not only does the compass needle rarely point to *true* north—it often doesn't even point to *magnetic* north! This discrepancy is called **deviation.**

Some of this deviation from magnetic north is caused by extramagnetic forces, such as regional variation in earth density, or by stray magnetism, such as that produced by magnetic ore bodies. Fortunately, these regional disturbances in the otherwise systematic pattern of isogonic lines are fairly well documented and predictable and thus will cause you few problems. All you need is an isogonic map, such as the one in Figure 12.9. Notice on this map how the isogonic lines wander here and there rather than heading straight for the magnetic pole. These irregularities show locations of major magnetic disturbances.

Compass deviation isn't always so predictable, though. It may also be caused by local disturbances, such as power lines, thunderstorms, and iron objects. Since this second source of deviation won't show up on isogonic maps, you must be constantly watchful for it. Try to keep away from known disturbances and be on the lookout for unknown ones, which may make your compass needle pull "off" north or act erratically.

ROUND EARTH

"Sail west to the east" goes an old mariner's saying—and that, of course, was what Columbus did. "Fly north to get east" was Lindbergh's philoso-phy when he reached Japan by flying over the North Pole. Determining direction on a round earth, as every ship and plane pilot knows, is a far different matter from flat-world direction finding.

Till now, we've defined direction as the angle between a direction line and base line. But when we're dealing with distances of over a hundred miles or need a high degree of precision, we must alter this flat-earth definition to account for earth rotundity. On the spherical earth, we can interpret direction in two ways—as the shortest-distance route between two points, called the **true azimuth**, or as the path determined by constant compass readings, called the **constant azimuth**. Let's look at both these types of direction.

True Direction

If we extend a direction line from its origin far enough, it will eventually return to its point of beginning. A direction line which forms a full circle in this way is called a **true azimuth.*** A true azimuth circling the earth at any angle other than east-west or in any direction from a point on the equator will be a **great circle**.

A great circle has a number of significant properties. It is the largest possible circle on the globe. Its center is the center of the earth. Every great circle is the circumference of the earth and divides the earth's surface into halves. But the trait which makes the great circle most valuable to navigators is that it is the shortest possible route between two locations on the spherical earth. To save time, then, navigators traveling long-distance routes will want to move along a great-circle path. They will also want to use a projection which correctly shows all true azimuths, regardless of their origin and destination points on the map.

The only projection which has this important property is the gnomonic projection, on which all great circles project as straight lines (**Figure 12.13A**). Gnomonic projections aren't always useful, however, because they are limited to showing less than a hemisphere (see Appendix

*Some writers, especially those in the GPS field (see Chapter 15) use the term bearing *in place of* azimuth. *This can be confusing if you're familiar with the bearing compass (see Appendix D). It's the concept of different direction lines, not the terminology, that's important to grasp in this section.*

C: *Map Projections*). In some cases, navigators turn to other azimuthal projections.* Since these projections are all symmetrical about their central points, all great circles passing through their centers are shown as straight lines on the map. And since great circles are the shortest-distance routes on the earth's surface, it follows that true direction to and from the center of an azimuthal projection is preserved (**Figure 12.13B**). Because all other azimuths are incorrectly represented, however, azimuthal projections aren't always useful, either. There is really no way to show true azimuths for the whole world on a single map.

There is another problem with navigating a true azimuth route. When navigators travel along a great circle (with the exception of the equator or a meridian), compass direction varies constantly. When using a compass to navigate, then, they may soon grow weary of continually making directional computations and steering their craft to keep on a great-circle course. They can alleviate these problems by following a constant-azimuth path.

Constant Direction

A direction line which is extended so that it crosses each meridian at the same angle is called a **constant azimuth** (or a **rhumb** or **loxodrome**). Rhumbs are routes of constant compass readings and are therefore extremely useful to navigators. If they follow one of these lines, navigators can maintain a course without constantly figuring out new headings and making turns. They merely check the compass to be sure that they are crossing each meridian at the angle of their rhumb line. Their *path* may bend, but their compass direction won't.

Rhumb lines running east-west along the equator or north-south along a meridian return eventually to their points of origin and are actually great circles. Those running east-west along parallels other than the equator also close on themselves but are small circles, not shortest-distance routes.

Rarely, however, are rhumb lines either great or small circles. More commonly they cross meridians at an oblique angle, tracing out an odd-

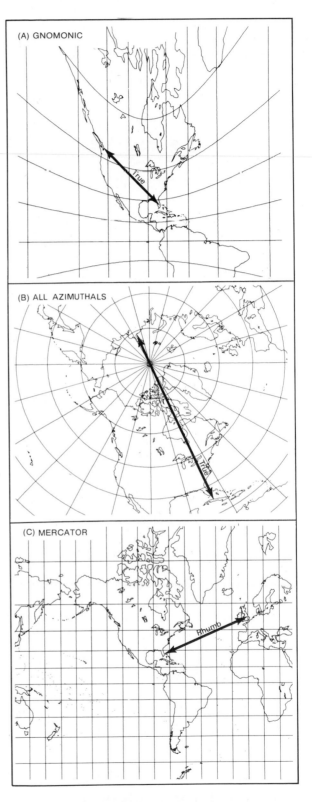

12.13 Direction-preserving projections have such properties as straight great circles (A), straight azimuths through the center (B), and straight compass lines (C).

The gnomonic projection is a member of the azimuthal class. As such, it has all the properties of azimuthal projections, and more.

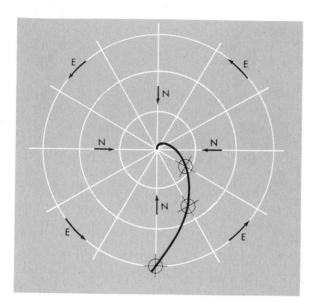

12.14 A constant heading of 45 degrees will trace out an equiangular spiral (or loxodromic curve).

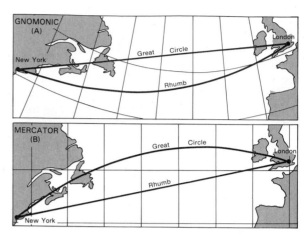

12.15 Long-distance navigators find it convenient to plot courses back and forth between gnomonic projections (A) and Mercator projections (B).

looking path. To cross each meridian at the same angle, the oblique rhumb line has to keep curving. Its path, therefore, will form a spiral, known as a **loxodromic curve**. **Figure 12.14** shows the loxodromic curve that results when a constant northeasterly direction line (one which intersects every meridian at an angle of 45 degrees) converges on the North Pole.

To preserve constant bearings on maps, a special projection is required. The problem is to show compass directions between any two points as a straight line—a considerable feat on a round earth. Mercator solved this problem, as Figure **12.13C** shows, by pulling the meridians and parallels apart at higher latitudes. On a Mercator projection, then, rhumb lines have been straightened. This valuable trait makes navigation by compass and straightedge quite straightforward. There are no complicated computations to make, as there are with great-circle routes. The compass course, however, is almost never the shortest-distance path. By replacing true azimuths with constant ones, navigators make their job easier but lengthen their route.

The Navigator's Dilemma

We see, then, that even when projections "preserve" direction relations, some maps give us

truth of direction for shortest-distance routes, while others maintain truth of direction with respect to constant azimuths. Long-distance navigators are thus presented with a dilemma. Should they use true azimuths and save time, while doing a great deal of work? Or should they turn to constant azimuths, simplifying navigation but going the longer way around?

There is a solution to the navigator's dilemma. Both types of azimuths may be used together. First, the desired course is plotted as a straight line between origin and destination on a gnomonic projection (**Figure 12.15A**). Next, this shortest-distance path is transferred to a Mercator projection as a curve (**Figure 12.15B**). This curve, which is always concave toward the equator, is then approximated with a series of straight-line segments. A compass may now be used to sail or fly in a straight line along each leg of the route, making only a few turns. When you fly in a commercial plane, you can often sense when the pilot is making these "corrections."*

---

*In practice, commercial airline flights are constrained to established air **corridors**, which represent a balance between the desire for direct routing on one hand and concern for minimizing air traffic congestion and maximizing safety on the other. Thus, the corrections in flight direction which you experience represent a shift from one straight-line corridor segment to the next.*

CONCLUSION

As our discussion of true versus constant azimuths has demonstrated, different directional methods lead to routes of different distances. Direction and distance are intertwined. Direction, however, doesn't usually influence our spatial behavior as much as distance does. It is that important attribute, **distance**, to which we turn in the next chapter.

SELECTED READINGS

Dixon, C., *Using GPS* (Dobbs Ferry, NY: Sheridan House, 1994).

Letham, L., *GPS Made Easy: Using Global Positioning Systems in the Outdoors* (Seattle: The Mountaineers, 1995).

Selwyn, V., *Plan Your Route: The New Approach to Map Reading* (London: David & Charles, 1987).

United States Army, Chapter 5 ("Directions") in *Map Reading*, Field Manual, FM 21-26 (Washington, DC: Superintendent of Documents, 1969), pp. 5-1 to 5-27.

United States Army, *Map Reading*, Programmed Text 2169 (Fort Benjamin Harrison, Indiana: Adjutant General School, 1972), pp. 89-141.

Also see references in Chapters 14 and 15 and Appendix D.

CHAPTER THIRTEEN

DISTANCE

INTRODUCTION

PHYSICAL DISTANCE

FUNCTIONAL DISTANCE

SELECTED READINGS

How far is a mile?
Well, you learn that right off.
It's peculiarly different from ten tenths on the odometer.
It's one thousand seven hundred and sixty steps on the dead level . . .
It's at least ten and maybe a million times that on the hills
And no river bed ever does run straight.

—Jerry & Renny Russell, *On the Loose*

Certainly my own memorable hikes can be classified as Shortcuts that Backfired.

—Edward Abbey, *The Journey Home*

13
CHAPTER THIRTEEN

DISTANCE

In our fast-moving, energy-devouring society, we sometimes overlook the importance of distance. With scarcely a thought, we commute an hour to work each day, travel from state to state on the weekend, and fly across the country several times a year. Because energy is inexpensive, we can ignore some effects of distance. We can do so, however, only till our supplies of fuel are used up or become so expensive that we can no longer afford them. Unless some energy miracle occurs, we'll one day come face to face with the formidable barrier of distance.

As we discuss this important aspect of our environment, keep in mind that you can interpret "distance" in two ways. When working with maps, we usually think of the **physical distance** between places. Since we assume that the map shows locations correctly, we expect a close relation between map and ground distance. We measure map distance with a ruler and ground distance in kilometers or miles—usually along the shortest or "as-the-crow-flies" route.

In our everyday lives, however, it's more natural to think not of physical but of **functional distance**. Most of us have little notion of how long a kilometer or mile is. Instead, we view distance in terms of the time, cost, or energy we must expend to get from here to there. We ask not "How many miles?" but "How long does it take?" or "How hard is it to get there?" Even when we do measure functional distance in miles or kilometers, we do so along the routes we must follow rather than cross-country, because we aren't crows.

Although a few maps do provide information on functional distance, most are based on physical distance units. Our first concern, therefore, is to learn to determine physical distance from maps. Then we'll see how we can use maps to determine functional distance.

260

PHYSICAL DISTANCE

We measure physical distance in equal units in any direction from a point. For us to communicate and make comparisons, these units of distance must be standardized. But since there is no natural and agreed-upon distance unit, a variety of standards have come into use. Some of these units have a basis in our natural surroundings, while others are artificial.

Units in our familiar English system of measurement, for example, are artificial. The unit known as the **yard** (representing three feet or 36 inches) was decreed by King Henry I to be the distance from the tip of his nose to the end of his thumb with arm outstretched—clearly an egocentric way of determining distance!

When people talk about a mile, they usually mean a **statute mile** (1,760 yards or 5,280 feet). And when we use the term "mile" in this book, unless otherwise noted, we'll be referring to this familiar statute mile. But as you use maps, you'll discover other miles. Unlike the statute mile, these are geocentrically derived and represent a specific part of a degree on the earth. One such measure is the **geographical mile** (6,087.1 feet), which is one minute of the equatorial great circle. The **admiralty mile** has been rounded off to 6,080 feet. The **international nautical mile** (6,076.1 feet or 1,852 meters) represents one minute of a great circle of a perfect sphere whose area is equal to the area of the earth.*

In contrast to the English system, units in the metric system are geocentrically derived. The meter, which is roughly equivalent to the yard (39.37 inches), represents a definite distance on the earth's surface. A meter is one ten-millionth of the distance from equator to pole (as that distance was thought to be when the meter was defined. The distance is known to be somewhat different today.)

When you use the metric system to work with maps, you'll usually measure ground distance in kilometers (km.) and map distance in centimeters (cm.) Conveniently, each kilometer equals 1,000 meters, and each centimeter is one-hundredth of a meter. Indeed, convenience is the metric system's great advantage. It's much easier to use than the English system because all units are in multiples of 10—a real boon when multiplying or dividing numbers.

The overwhelming convenience of the metric system is hard to ignore. Thus, be prepared: Metric maps are coming. Even such large English-speaking countries as the United States are drifting toward the metric standard for their official government maps. GPS receivers sold around the world have a metric option for reporting distances.

You should be familiar with both the metric and English systems, because there are situations in which one is more convenient than the other. This means you'll often have to convert from one system to the other. Tables E.3 and E.4 in Appendix E will help you make these conversions. A GPS receiver holds the conversion parameters in its memory and thus can perform the same chore.

All these distance units have little real meaning in themselves, of course. They take on significance only when we use them to specify the separation between geographical locations. Let's look now at this important function—determining distance.

Determining Distance

When you need distance information, it's usually impractical to measure distance between places directly. Nor is it often practical to look up distance information in logs or tables. The solution is to turn to maps. Map and earth space are so closely related that measurements made on the proper maps can be nearly as precise as ground measurements themselves.

Using maps to measure distances isn't straightforward, however. A map is always smaller than the environment it depicts. Map distances of centimeters or inches represent ground distances of kilometers or miles. To convert map to ground distance, you need to know the map's reduction factor, or scale. (To learn more about map scale, see Appendix A.) An understanding of scale is vital in using maps to measure distances.

---

*Although not too familiar to most of us, the nautical mile is important because it serves as the standard unit of distance in water and air navigation. It also provides the basis for the mariner's **knot**, which is the velocity of one nautical mile per hour. Knots are used in computing the speed of ships, planes, and wind.*

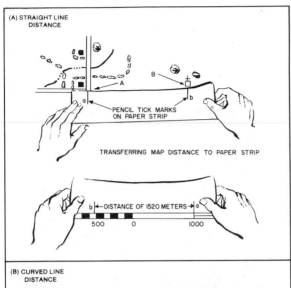

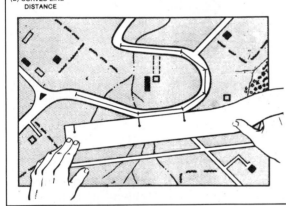

13.1 You can use the graphic scale to compute the ground distance between two map features along a straight line (A) or a curved line (B).

13.2 Mechanical distance measuring devices, such as this "road runner," are helpful if the route isn't intricately detailed.

There are two ways to use a map to find distances between places. You may use the map's scale, or you may use simple algebra along with coordinate references. Let's look at each of these methods.

Determining Distance by Scale

The easiest way to figure distance is to use the **graphic scale,*** the ruler-like markings found on most maps. To do so, mark the distance between two map locations on a piece of paper or string. Then compare this measured distance with the graphic scale (**Figure 13.1A**). No ruler or mathematical computation is necessary. The distance value you obtain won't be too precise, however, especially if you try to determine the length of a winding route (**Figure 13.1B**).

You can also compute distance using the **representative fraction**, or **RF**,* which is also found on most maps. Simply measure the distance between two points with a ruler and then multiply that figure by the denominator of the RF. For instance, if the RF is 1:24,000 and the between-feature distance is 3.3 inches, then:

$$24{,}000 \times 3.3'' = 79{,}200''.$$

You'll want to convert this distance to practical ground units such as miles or kilometers. Thus:

$$79{,}200'' \div 63{,}360'' = 1.25, \text{ or } 1^{1}/_{4} \text{ miles.}$$

Again, the accuracy of this figure depends on how much the measured route twists and turns.

With either an RF or a graphic scale, you can speed your task with a "**road runner**" or **distance measurer**. This device consists of a wheel and one or more counters. Simply set the counter to 0, then roll the wheel along the desired path. The counter will give you the map distance in inches or centimeters. To convert this value to

*See Appendix A for more details on graphic scales and representative fractions.

262

ground distance, multiply it by the denominator of the RF. Or roll the wheel backward on the graphic scale to return the counter to 0.

On the distance measurer in **Figure 13.2**, the inner dial points to one foot and the outer dial to five inches, giving a reading of 1'5". Since the map scale is 1:24,000, the ground distance is 1'5" x 24,000 = 17" x 24,000 = 408,000". This figure is best understood by converting it to miles: 408,000" ÷ 63,360" = 6.44 miles.

Mechanical distance measurers work best when the path between the two points is relatively smooth. Keeping the small wheel on a winding road or stream is a real exercise in finger control. If the wheel slips or binds on tight curves, errors result.

Determining Distance by Coordinates

Map scale computations can become boring if you must do many of them. If you wanted to know the distance from each of 10 cities to each of the other nine, you would have to make 45 calculations—quite a chore. But there is an alternative. If you use **coordinates*** to determine distance, you need only figure out the coordinates of the cities once and then use them over and over in your distance computations. You can save yourself even more time with this method because you can use digitizers to extract coordinates from the map and computers to process these coordinates and give you the distance values you want.

You can also use your GPS receiver as a convenient distance calculator. To do so, you merely enter the coordinates of the two points in question, press a few buttons, and the receiver will display the distance between them (see Chapter 15: *GPS and Maps*).

Such modern procedures eliminate the need to know a great deal about either mathematics or computers. You'll feel more comfortable with the technique, however, if you understand the basic mathematical process behind it. Thus, we'll work through some coordinate distance computations so that you'll know how to do them, although you may never have to perform them by hand.

For a discussion of map coordinates, see Chapter 11: Locational Reference Systems.

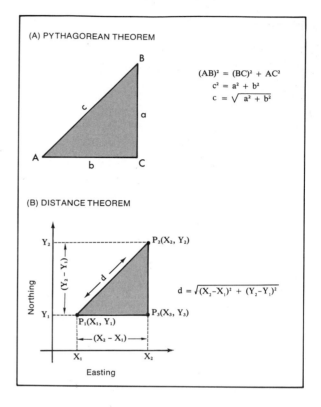

13.3 You can compute the distance between two points from their coordinates using the Pythagorean theorem.

Plane Coordinates. You can determine distances within a small region—up to the size of a state—by using a plane coordinate system, such as the UTM or SPC grid. (These grids are discussed in Chapter 11.) Assume that the distance you want to measure is the hypotenuse of a right triangle. The **Pythagorean theorem** tells us that if a, b, and c represent the sides of a right triangle, and c is the hypotenuse, then $c^2 = a^2 + b^2$ (**Figure 13.3A**). To find the distance between two points, we restate the Pythagorean theorem, changing c to d, which will represent distance. So:

$$d = \sqrt{a^2 + b^2}$$

or

$$d = \sqrt{(x_2 - x_1)^2 + (y_2 - y_1)^2} \, ,$$

where (x_1, y_1) and (x_2, y_2) are the coordinates of the locations between which the distance is to be determined. This formula is called the **distance**

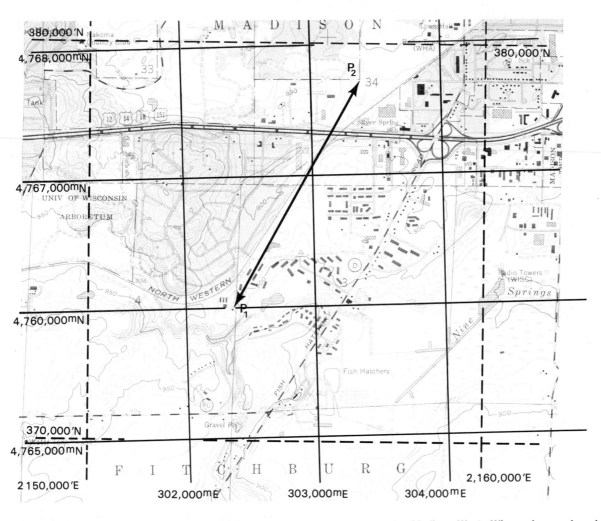

13.4 Using coordinates to compute the distance between two points on the Madison West, Wisconsin, quadrangle (see text).

theorem. It states that you can determine the distance between any two points on your map by taking the square root of the sum of the squares of the differences in the x and y coordinates of the two points (**Figure 13.3B**).

The usefulness of the distance theorem is demonstrated in **Figure 13.4**, using data derived from UTM and SPC systems found on the Madison West, Wisconsin, 7' topographic quadrangle. Let's say we want to find the distance between a corner of the University of Wisconsin Arboretum (P₂) and a building to the southwest (P₁).

Step 1: Extend the marginal ticks on the map to form boundaries around the UTM and SPC grid cells in which the two places are located.

Step 2: Determine the UTM and SPC eastings (x) and northings (y) for each point (as was explained in Chapter 11). These are:

P_1
$$\begin{cases} \text{SPC} & \begin{cases} x = 2,153,600' \\ y = 373,320' \end{cases} \\ \\ \text{UTM} & \begin{cases} x = 302,348 \text{ meters} \\ y = 4,766,000 \text{ meters} \end{cases} \end{cases}$$

P_2
$$\begin{cases} \text{SPC} & \begin{cases} x = 2,156,800' \\ y = 379,100' \end{cases} \\ \\ \text{UTM} & \begin{cases} x = 303,384 \text{ meters} \\ y = 4,767,726 \text{ meters} \end{cases} \end{cases}$$

264

Step 3: Now transfer the numerical values determined in Step 2 to the distance formula:

d_{SPC}

$$= \sqrt{(2{,}156{,}800 - 2{,}153{,}600)^2 + (379{,}100 - 373{,}320)^2}$$

$$= \sqrt{3{,}200^2 + 5{,}780^2}$$

$$= \sqrt{10{,}240{,}000 + 33{,}408{,}400}$$

$$= \sqrt{43{,}648{,}400}$$

$$= \quad 6607' \text{ or } 2013.7 \text{ meters}$$

d_{UTM}

$$= \sqrt{(303{,}384 - 302{,}348)^2 + (4{,}767{,}726 - 4{,}766{,}000)^2}$$

$$= \sqrt{1{,}036^2 + 1{,}726^2}$$

$$= \sqrt{1{,}073{,}296 + 2{,}979{,}076}$$

$$= \sqrt{4{,}052{,}372}$$

$$= \quad 2013 \text{ meters or } 6604'$$

Thus, the computed distance from the UTM coordinates is 2,013 meters or 6,604 feet. SPCs yielded a distance of 2,013.7 meters or 6,607 feet—a discrepancy of only three feet between the two computations. These computed distances also compare favorably with the distance we obtain by using the map scale. The measured map distance is 3.3", which, at a map scale of 1:24,000, yields a ground distance of 3.3" x 24,000" = 79,200" ÷ 12" = 6,600'. The close agreement between the distances computed from coordinates and from the map scale is remarkable considering the difficulties of making fine measurements on maps.

There's no doubt that using plane coordinates to find distances is a simple, accurate method. Its disadvantage is that you can use it only for relatively small regions: Both places must lie within a single grid zone. Your use of SPCs is thus limited to areas the size of a small state, while UTM coordinates are restricted to zones of 6° longitude.

Nor can you solve this problem by extending plane coordinates over larger regions. Larger grids incorporate greater distortion, since the earth curves progressively away from a plane surface. Grids of greater extent decrease accuracy in distance computations.

Spherical Coordinates. Fortunately, there is a solution. You can find the distance between any two places on earth by using spherical coordinates. The geographical grid serves this purpose. To find the distance between two locations, you need only know the latitude and longitude of each place and use trigonometric tables. GPS receivers perform this task automatically, but it's good to understand the procedure used.

Suppose you want to know how far it is from Seattle to Miami along a great circle route. Follow these steps:

Step 1: Look up the latitude and longitude of the two cities, using Table E.8 in Appendix E. This table shows that Seattle is located at 47°36'N, 122°20'W, and Miami is located at 25°45'N, 80°11'W.

Step 2: Form a triangle, the sides of which are arcs of great circles. Construct this spherical triangle by connecting Seattle and Miami with the arc of a great circle. Extend arcs of great circles along meridians from each city to the North Pole (**Figure 13.5A**).

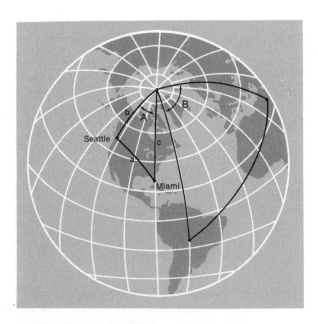

13.5 You can find the distance between widely separated points by using spherical coordinates.

Step 3: Consider what you know about this spherical triangle. You know that the distance from equator to pole is 90°. Thus, you can calculate side c by subtracting the latitude of city B (Miami) from 90°. Or, c = 90° - 25°45' = 64°15'. Similarly, side b = 90° - 47°36' = 42°24'. Angle A, which is the distance of arc along a parallel between the two cities, can be found by subtracting their respective longitudes. Thus, 122°20' (Seattle) - 80°11' (Miami) = 42°9'.

Step 4: Convert the angles determined in Step 3 to trigonometric functions using Table E.5 in Appendix E:

cos A = cos 42°9' = .74139
cos c = cos 64°15' = .43445
sin c = sin 64°15' = .90070
cos b = cos 42°24' = .73846
sin b = sin 42°24' = .67430

Step 5: Transfer the numerical values from Step 4 to the following adaptation of the Pythagorean theorem:

cos a
= (cos b)(cos c) + (sin b)(sin c)(cos A)
=
(.73846)(.43445) + (.67430)(.90070)(.74137)
= .32082 + .45028
= .77110

$$\left[\begin{array}{l} \text{From Table E.5: The angle whose cos is} \\ .77110 \text{ is } 39°32'50'' \end{array} \right.$$

Step 6: What proportion of 360° is an angular measurement of 39°32'50"? The question is best answered in stages to overcome the complications of using sexagesimal units. First, convert the arc units (39°32'50") to a decimal value in degrees. Do so by converting the minutes and seconds portion of the arc to a decimal fraction of 1° (60'). In other words, what proportion of a degree is 32'50"? Answer: 32'50" = 32 5/6' = 32.84 ÷ 60 = .53889.

Next, add this decimal value to the arc degrees (39° + .53889 = 39.53889°). Divide this sum by 360° to find the arc's proportion of a great circle:

39.53889 ÷ 360 = .10983, or 11 percent.

Step 7: Multiply this percentage by 25,000 miles, which is the approximate length of a great circle:

.11 x 25,000 = 2,750 miles.

Thus, you have discovered that the great circle route from Seattle to Miami is 2,750 miles.

You'll have to adjust this approach if the two cities fall in different hemispherical quadrants. This situation occurs when the great circle distance to be computed crosses the 180° meridian, the prime meridian (0°), or the equator (**Figure 13.5B**). If one city is north and the other south of the equator, for example, you'll have to add the latitude of the southern hemisphere city to 90°, rather than subtract it, to obtain its meridional arc (side b or c of the spherical triangle). When both cities lie south of the equator, you can either add both latitudes to 90° or use the South rather than the North Pole as a meridional reference point. If one city is east and the other west of the prime meridian, you add rather than subtract their respective longitudes to obtain angle A. Except for these slight changes, you compute spherical distance just as you did when both cities fell in the same hemispherical quadrant.

Coordinate Distance Along Complex Lines. You've now seen how to use coordinates to compute distances along straight lines. You can also use coordinates to find the length of a complex line. All you need to do is break the line into short, straight segments. Then use the coordinate method for each segment. Finally, add the segment lengths to obtain the total distance (**Figure 13.6A**). This approach is used by GPS receivers to determine distance traveled or the length of a route involving several legs.

Digitizing machines make it easier to record the strings of coordinates you need for these computations. Once you've traced the line with the digitizer, just "click" on the length function, and the software will compute the distance.

You can use the same method to determine the length of a curved line. All you do is approximate the curve with a series of straight lines (**Figure 13.6B**). You must decide how long to make the lines, of course, and this decision will affect the accuracy of your results. Although

266

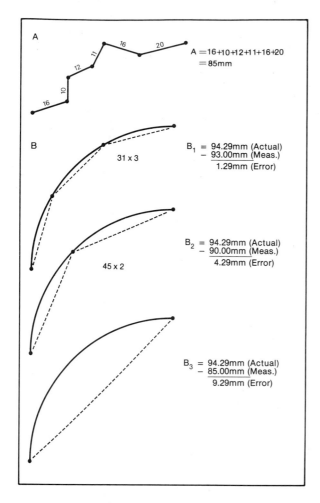

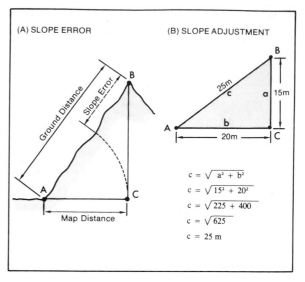

13.7 When computing distance between two points (A), it may be necessary to adjust for ground slope (B).

13.6 You can figure out the length of a complex line if you break it into short, straight segments (A). You can also approximate curved lines with straight line segments (B).

shorter lines lead to less error, they also require more computations. You must reach a balance between accuracy and effort.

Error Factors

No matter how you determine distance from maps, some error is bound to slip into your results. The methods you use, the judgments you make, or the figuring you do may be faulty. These might be called **external error factors**, since you impose them on the map from the outside. To minimize them, use only proven techniques and instruments, and take care to avoid mistakes in computation.

But even if you make no external errors, your final distance figure is still likely to be inaccurate. The reason is found in the nature of the map itself. A variety of distance distortions are built into the process of transforming reality to a map. Fortunately, you can compensate for these **internal error factors** if you're aware of their existence. Let's look at some of these internal errors and see how you can overcome them.

Slope Error. Your first problem is that map distance is given as if the surface were flat. Thus, it is always shorter than true ground distance—except in the rare case of perfectly flat terrain. As **Figure 13.7A** shows, the steeper the slope and the longer the ground distance over which slopes occur, the greater the error between true and computed distance.

To compensate for this **slope error**, recall the Pythagorean theorem discussed earlier in this chapter. Consider **Figure 13.7B**. To compute ground-distance c between points A and B, use the horizontal (map) distance b and the vertical (elevation) distance a, both of which you can determine from a topographic map. In this case, the discrepancy between map and ground distance is five meters. (Note that, although it may make a big difference to you whether the slope is "up" or "down" in relation to your position, the distance will be increased by the same amount in either case.)

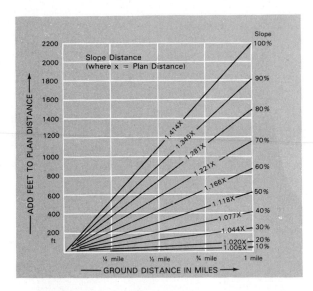

13.8 Use the slope error figures on this graph's vertical axis to adjust map distance (horizontal axis) for the effects of ground slope.

In theory, then, it's not much trouble to compensate for slope. If the terrain undulates quite a bit, however, there can be a great many slope adjustments to make. If you aren't concerned with absolute accuracy, you can avoid all these computations by making one overall (but highly approximate) correction. Just determine the region's approximate degree of slope, and then compensate for this slope by using the information in **Figure 13.8**. From this table, for instance, you can see that if you walk 10 miles along a 40 percent slope, you'll travel a ground distance of 10 x 1.077 = 10.77 miles, or about three-fourths mile farther than the map scale suggests.

Smoothing Error. A second type of distance error can be traced to map makers' smoothing of line symbols. When they show linear features such as roads and rivers, map makers straighten curves and smooth irregularities. As a result, the measured route along a highway, railroad, or hiking trail may deviate from the ground distance. Likewise, map distance along a shore or down a stream may mislead a canoeist.

This **smoothing error** has something in common with slope error: Both add to the measured map distance. A ground distance route may be the same length or longer than the map distance estimate, but it can never be shorter. Unless

the ground is completely flat and the route perfectly straight, your computed figure will always fall short of true ground distance.

Although elevation figures are available to help you overcome slope error, you have no way of knowing how much map makers have smoothed linear features. There are, however, a few useful guidelines. One good rule to remember is that the smaller the map scale and the more irregular the ground route, the more smoothing map makers use. Thus, the discrepancy between map and ground distance increases as map scale decreases. In other words, you can minimize this whole problem if you *use large-scale maps.*

It's not quite that simple, however. Even on large-scale maps, some roads, rivers, and boundaries will be more generalized than others. The more detailed and intricate the feature, the more it will be simplified. County roads, for instance, will always be more smoothed than freeways, because they are more convoluted to start with. The map legend is rarely of much help in sorting out the effects of this **variable smoothing** of line symbols. Intuition is your best guide. You would naturally expect highways to be more irregular (and therefore more smoothed by the map maker) than railroads, streams to be less regular than roads, and state highways to be less regular than freeways. Additionally, linear features in rugged, rocky regions will be more irregular (and thus more smoothed on the map) than the same features in flat, sandy regions. As you use your common sense and anticipate these differences within the same map, you'll be able to figure distance more and more accurately.

Scale Error. Another problem in determining distance occurs because a single map scale rarely tells the whole truth. This fact is illustrated in **Figure 13.9** using large-scale maps depicting the same grid of lines on the ground. Clearly, scale accuracy depends on the point of view taken by map makers. If they take a parallel perspective view from a vertical vantage point, scale will be true in all directions from every point. Central perspective maps from a vertical vantage point will have fairly true scale near the center but will show scale variation toward the edges if relief or earth curvature is significant. The oblique images show greater scale distortion than the vertical images. Oblique maps in parallel

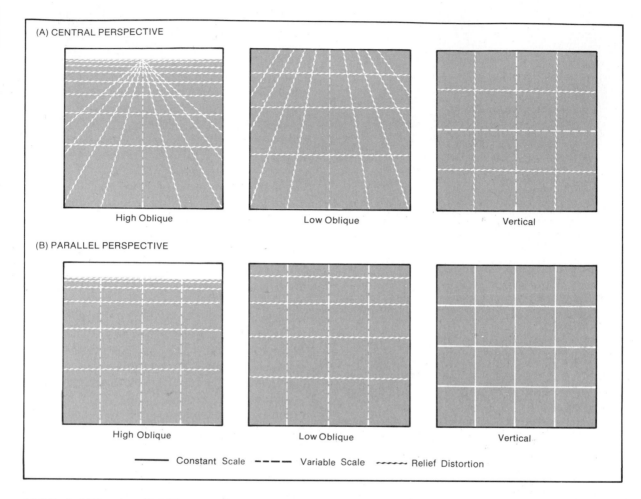

(A) CENTRAL PERSPECTIVE

High Oblique   Low Oblique   Vertical

(B) PARALLEL PERSPECTIVE

High Oblique   Low Oblique   Vertical

——— Constant Scale - - - - Variable Scale ⌒⌒⌒ Relief Distortion

13.9 Central (A) and parallel (B) perspectives influence distance relations between points on large-scale maps in different ways.

perspective show scale distortion in one less dimension than those in central perspective.

In addition, the larger the mapped region, the greater the potential scale error. When you use small-scale maps of continents or hemispheres, it is good advice to trust the scale only near the center of the map or along the major map projection axes, such as standard meridians or parallels.

Since distance relations are such an important aspect of our environment, aren't there any maps designed to keep distances in true scale? The answer is yes and no. For a small-scale map projection to preserve distance relations perfectly, it would have to show the shortest spherical distance between any two points as a straight line—and do so at true scale. That's a mathematical impossibility. We can, however, keep true distance along certain lines. Several map projections do exactly that.

Recall that with projections of the azimuthal group, great circles passing through the projection center become straight lines on the map. Therefore, we can easily adjust the radial scale on azimuthal projections so that distance is true along these great circles (**Figure 13.10A**). The result is the **azimuthal equidistant** projection. Distance from all points to this projection's center, or to points on a great circle passing through the projection's center, are true to scale. Distances between all other points are incorrect, however, and scale distortion increases with radial distance from the map center. This creates a problem for the map user: To take best advantage

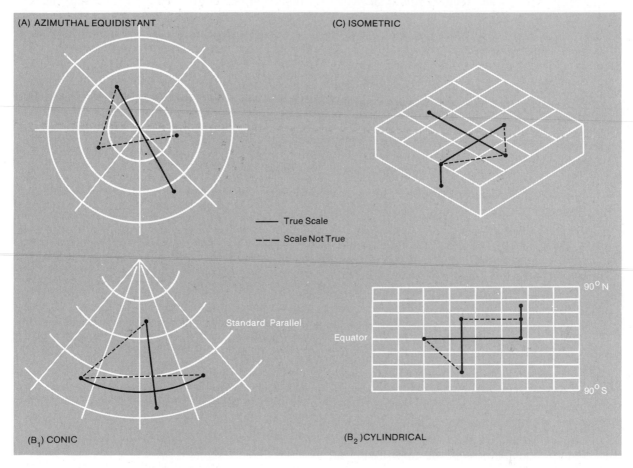

13.10 The property of true distance is, at best, only partially preserved on small-scale maps. The solid lines indicate true scale, and the dashed lines aren't true.

of the azimuthal equidistant projection, you need a separate map for each point of interest.

A second form of partially equidistant map is based on modified conic or cylindric projection models. Equal distance is achieved along the line of contact between cone or cylinder (**Figure 13.10B**). These line-oriented equidistant projections are of little use except for mapping narrow regions, since scale deteriorates with distance from the center line. Thus, with these projections, as with azimuthal equidistant ones, equal distance isn't a general property, since it's limited to directions from certain points.

Distance is also preserved somewhat on large-scale maps in isometric perspective. But again, even though **isometric** means "equal measure," true scale isn't an overall property. Only

three systems of parallel lines are laid off in true length. Distance measurement along all other "non-isometric" lines is distorted (**Figure 13.10C**). Yet the uniformity of scale which is preserved and the ease with which isometric maps can be created by computer make this form of perspective the most common basis for block diagrams.

Thus, we find that no flat map can exhibit true distance from all points in all directions simultaneously. True scale relations can only be maintained in a few directions from a few points—and, even then, only at a price. We must be willing to accept greater than usual scale distortion from other points.

When this scale distortion forms a systematic pattern over the map, you'll sometimes find a variable graphic scale (see *Graphic Scale* in Appendix A) on the map. If such a scale isn't given, consider constructing your own variable scale. Figure A.1 shows a variable graphic scale found on Mercator projections. This scale lets you figure distances in two directions (latitude and longitude) from any point, despite the great scale distortion on Mercator projections. It will, of course, be harder to figure distance between widely spaced points or in directions other than those of latitude-longitude lines.

Disproportionate Symbol Error. A fourth source of error in figuring distance arises because most map features aren't symbolized in correct scale. If they were, the symbols wouldn't be large enough to see. Take, for instance, a road which is 30 feet wide. It might be shown by a thin line (.01 inch wide) on a map with a scale of 1:125,000. This would give it an effective width of 104 feet!

This problem becomes more extreme when a feature such as a political boundary, which has no width, is shown by a symbol which is effectively several miles wide. And the trouble becomes worse as map scale decreases. There's simply not enough space to include everything. As a result, cartographers overemphasize features selected for the map, while de-emphasizing all other features. By the very nature of symbolism, depicting one feature leads to excluding, distorting, or displacing its neighbor.

Consider the case of a house on a 105-foot lot between a road and a river (**Figure 13.11A**). If the river and road were both symbolized by lines .01 inch wide at a map scale of 1:63,360, they alone would use up 52.8 feet, or half the space available. There wouldn't be enough room for the building symbol (which at .1" x .1" would itself take up 528 feet) or for the space necessary *between* the symbols.

If map makers want to preserve all three features, they'll need to "pull them apart" in violation of planimetric truth. Such distortion is essential to retain the relative spatial relations between features: We can't have the road and river running through the house. But the result is that distance accuracy is compromised.

Be wary, then, of any distance measurements involving symbols. If, in **Figure 13.11B**, you computed the distance between the centers of the river and road from the map, you would come up with a ground figure of 686 feet, while the two are really 105 feet apart. If you didn't know about disproportionate symbols, you might even try to figure the distance across the river and deduce that the river is 52.8 feet wide when it is actually only 10 feet across.

Map users who recognize the problems of disproportionate symbolism on conventional maps sometimes overlook the fact that the same thing occurs on photographic and scanner images. Contrary to what many people believe, a photograph does not show all environmental features in correct proportion. Since photography is based on reflected light, a shiny, highly reflective object looks disproportionately large on a photograph. Mapping teams have made use of this fact for years. Before taking photos, they place highly reflective targets on the ground. These targets stand out on the photos, helping the mappers locate known positions and correct distortions when using the photos to plot topographic maps.

The same thing happens with images from non-visible parts of the electromagnetic spectrum. An extremely hot object will appear overly large on a thermal image. Buildings made of certain materials and oriented in certain ways appear on radar images as large bright spots.

If these occurrences seem to defy logic, even more baffling is the fact that linear features

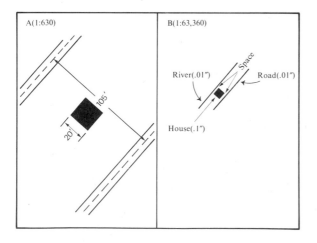

13.11 Disproportionate map symbols can have a major distorting effect on distance determinations between closely spaced features, as these 1:630 and 1:63,360 ways of depicting the same setting demonstrate.

appear on photos at far larger than their natural size. Powerlines are often visible on a photo even though the high transmission towers holding them up are not. Railroad tracks can be seen when a car can't. On satellite images with a scanner cell size of 200 by 200 feet, there is no logical way that a 60-foot-wide road would show up—yet it does! These examples should remind us to keep disproportionate symbol error in mind when we make measurements on image maps as well as conventional line maps.

Dimensional Instability Error. Unless maps are printed on a dimensionally stable material such as plastic, glass, or metal, they will stretch and shrink with changes of temperature and humidity. A map the size of the USGS 1:24,000 series, if printed on paper, can change as much as one centimeter (.39 inch) from one day to the next. This stretching and shrinking may cause errors in your distance measurements. Be especially careful if you're measuring a long distance.

Like slope, smoothing, scale, and symbol error, paper instability error plays havoc with distance calculations. No matter how precisely you compute distance from maps, no matter how carefully you wheel your mechanical distance finder along wiggles in the road, your final figure will be only approximate.

Ground Distance Figures
All these errors occur because map distance isn't the same as ground distance. Such problems could be eliminated, then, if someone physically measured the distance on the *ground* and put it on the map for us. That's just what has been done on some maps—road maps in particular. Supplementary ground distance figures are an invaluable aid in determining route length and choosing between routes. Let's look at some of the ways these figures have been added to maps.

Segment Numbers. On some maps, ground distance figures are added between such nodes as towns, intersections, or special features (**Figure 13.12A**). Routes are thus divided into segments, with the length of each segment given. To find the distance between two points, you merely add up all the numbers along the route.

If your route is very long, of course, you'll soon tire of adding numbers. To help you out, map

makers may provide a second level of distance figures. Second-level route segments are longer than the first and have as their end points major cities and intersections. These special points are shown by such symbols as stars or tick marks (**Figure 13.12B**). The symbols and segment numbers are usually printed in a different color to reduce confusion with the first-level figures.

The segment number method is the simplest and most common way to give ground distance information on road maps. The figures let you compute your route's length without having to measure winding lines on the map. The only problem is that some map makers become carried away with a good thing and cover the map with blue, black, and red numbers in such profusion that it becomes difficult to tell which distance figure refers to which road segment.

Distance Insets. To show the distance between widely separated points, map makers often include **distance insets.** Insets are usually double-ended arrows with names of features, such as cities, and distances between them (**Figure 13.12C**). Insets can be useful, though they may be hard to locate and are far from complete. All too often you'll find that the map maker ignored the route length of interest to you.

Distance Diagrams. The deficiencies of segment numbers and distance insets are somewhat overcome when a **distance diagram** is

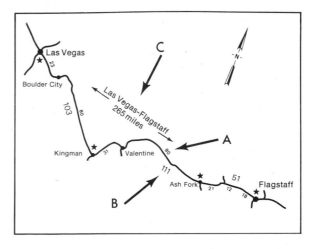

13.12 Distance information is often incorporated into the design of road maps to help in determining route length.

CHAPTER 13 - DISTANCE

added to the map (**Figure 13.13**). On such a diagram, routes between major features are abstracted to straight lines, with the length of each route given. These lines aren't meant to duplicate real roads but only to show that one point is connected to another. The result is much easier to read than the original map.

The main disadvantage of distance diagrams is their size. They are usually relegated to a corner of the map and are so small that most cities must be left off. Furthermore, you have the same problem you did with segment numbers: You must add a lot of numbers together. To find the distance from Cumberland to Washington in Figure 13.13, for instance, you must add at least six numbers.

Distance Charts. The problem of having to add a great many numbers is avoided if distance figures are arranged in charts. There are two types of distance charts. On a **rectangular table**, key features are listed alphabetically along the top and side. You find the distance between two cities by looking up one name along the top and the other along the side. Then follow down the column and across the row to where they intersect. To find the distance from Chicago to Fairbanks in **Figure 13.14A**, locate Chicago in the left margin and Fairbanks on the top, and read the row-column intersection as 3,804 miles. Or look up Fairbanks on the left and Chicago on the top—the result will be the same.

Distance charts aren't all-inclusive. You may find one of the cities you're looking for but not the other, or both places may be missing from the chart. On such occasions, you can sometimes arrive at an approximate figure by looking up the distance between nearby features.

As we saw in the last example, a rectangular distance chart is 50 percent redundant. To let you look up either name in either margin, the chart's upper right half is the same as the lower left half. To avoid this duplication and to save space, map makers often use a **triangular distance chart**. On these charts, feature names need occur only once. In **Figure 13.14B**, you can find the distance between Charlotte and Atlanta by following down the column from Atlanta until it intersects the row opposite Charlotte. The distance is 241 miles.

Distance Databases. The modern way to determine the distance between cities and other "official" geographical places such as national parks, is to access a computer database holding these data. These databases come bundled with route-finding software for your personal computer (see Chapter 19: *GIS and Map Analysis Software*). You can also consult these data at sites on the Internet (see Chapter 10: *Maps on the Internet*). Both sources may have the option for straight-line or routed distances.

FUNCTIONAL DISTANCE

But all these physical distance figures tell only a small part of the story. Consider the following examples:

> Distances as measured in miles had no meaning for him, so I computed the number of moons of hard walking which would be required to cover the length of the river as I had seen it stretched out on the map. He shook his head.
>
> I understand now, although I did not at the time, that my airy and easy sweep of map-traced, staggering distances belittled the journeys he had measured on tired feet. With my big map-talk, I had effaced the magnitude of his cargo-laden, heat-weighted treks.
>
> (Prince Modupe, *I Was A Savage*, pp. 146-147)

> Eventually I had to come out of the tree-hidden roads and do my best to bypass the cities....It takes far longer to go through cities than to drive several hundred miles.
>
> (Steinbeck, *Travels With Charley*, p. 25)

> The drift of the pack since the Endurance was beset had carried them to within about 60 miles of Vahsel Bay—a tantalizingly short distance, it would seem. But 60 miles over hummocky ice with God knows how many impassable tracks of open water in between, carrying at least a year's supply of rations and equipment, plus the lumber for a hut—and all this behind sledges drawn by ill-conditioned and untrained dogs. No, 60 miles could be a very long way, indeed.
>
> (Lansing, *Endurance*, pp. 41-42)

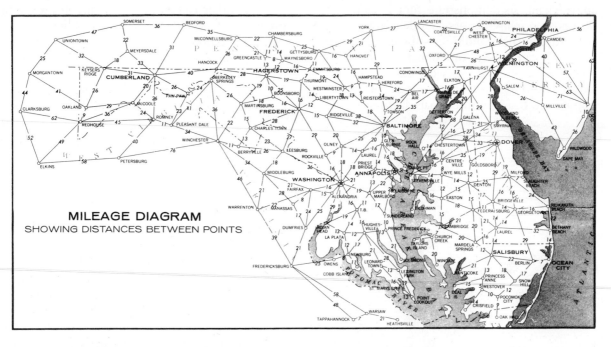

MILEAGE DIAGRAM
SHOWING DISTANCES BETWEEN POINTS

13.13 A distance diagram, such as this one from the Maryland state road map (1973), makes it possible to compute the road distance between any two cities in the state.

This seemed, from the map, the best way. Probably there were better ways. There are usually better ways than the map reader knows of. In almost any area there are better ways, known to those who traverse them daily—ways around traffic, ways that avoid lights; ways, for that matter, which avoid toll booths. But these are hidden to the man who has only a map to go by, whatever his need to hurry.

(Lockridge, *The Devious Ones*, p. 157)

In Los Angeles, with everybody traveling by car on freeways, nobody talks about "miles" anymore, they just say "that's four minutes from here," "that's twenty minutes from here," and so on. The actual straight-line distance doesn't matter. It may be faster to go by a curved route. All anybody cares about is the time.

(Wolfe, *McLuhan: Hot & Cool*, p. 38)

These assorted experiences underline an important point: There's more to distance than physical miles on the ground or measured miles on the map. Physical distance isn't nearly so germane to our lives as functional distance. As the

A

	Alaska Boundary	Anchorage	Chicago, Ill.	Circle	Dawson Creek, B. C.	Delta Junction	Eagle	Edmonton, Alta.	Fairbanks	Glennallen
Alaska Boundary		421	3506	463	1221	201	242	1591	298	232
Anchorage	421		3927	523	1642	340	503	2012	358	189
Chicago, Ill.	3506	3927		3969	2285	3707	3748	1915	3804	3738
Circle	463	523	3969		1684	262	545	2054	165	413
Dawson Creek, B. C.	1221	1642	2285	1684		1422	1463	370	1519	1453
Delta Junction	201	340	3707	262	1422		283	1792	97	151
Eagle	242	503	3748	545	1463	283		1833	380	314
Edmonton, Alta.	1591	2012	1915	2054	370	1792	1833		1889	1823
Fairbanks	298	358	3804	165	1519	97	380	1889		248
Glennallen	232	189	3738	413	1453	151	314	1823	248	

B

ATHENS
ATLANTA / 66
AUGUSTA / 101 / 147
BAMBERG / 161 / 207 / 60
BARNWELL / 143 / 189 / 42 / 21
BATESBURG / 120 / 186 / 44 / 61 / 56
BEAUFORT / 219 / 266 / 119 / 75 / 77 / 130
BENNETTSVILLE / 247 / 310 / 171 / 136 / 153 / 131 / 190
BISHOPVILLE / 202 / 265 / 126 / 91 / 108 / 86 / 145 / 45
CAMDEN / 180 / 243 / 104 / 82 / 91 / 64 / 150 / 67 / 22
CHARLESTON / 244 / 286 / 139 / 79 / 99 / 129 / 69 / 148 / 117 / 124
CHARLOTTE / 192 / 241 / 157 / 150 / 153 / 123 / 220 / 90 / 88 / 76 / 200
CHERAW / 234 / 297 / 158 / 134 / 145 / 118 / 188 / 16 / 43 / 54 / 149 / 74

13.14 Distance charts from Alaska (A) and North Carolina (B) state road maps (1973).

274

above examples demonstrate, functional distance depends on many factors—mode of travel, frame of mind, external conditions—the list is endless.

We can look at functional distance in two ways. The first of these we'll call practical distance. This refers to your route's actual length, as opposed to the computed map distance.

"Bridge River Campground?... Go North about three-fourths of a gallon and then East about a half-gallon."

Practical Distance

You'll often find that your distance calculations have little to do with the distance you end up traveling. One problem may be unexpected detours. A ship or airplane may have to deviate from a direct route to miss a violent storm. Your path through an alpine meadow may be blocked by a grizzly bear, requiring a long detour to gain your course. Road construction, highway accidents, train derailments, floods, and other route obstructions can add to a trip's length.

Unforeseen restrictions on travel can also take you off your planned course. You may be stymied by one-way streets, low overpasses, or load limits on bridges. Such restraints are seldom indicated on maps. Or you may get lost or miss a freeway exit—practical considerations that don't show up in your distance computations.

Another factor that can make nonsense of pre-trip distance figures is a breakdown in your planned method of travel. Planes may be detoured to neighboring airports, requiring a switch to car or bus travel. If your canoe is wrecked, you may find that the distance to your destination on foot is quite different from that by water.

Behavioral Distance

Even practical distance doesn't give the whole distance picture, however. When we consider how far away something is, we usually don't think in terms of kilometers or miles at all. Instead, we measure distance in some more meaningful unit, such as cost, energy, or fear.

We often behave in ways that would seem ridiculous if physical distance were our only guide. But we're not acting irrationally. We don't always *want* to take the shortest physical route. We may decide that we can reach the top of a steep hill more easily if we zigzag than if we climb straight up. In a sailboat, we may cross a lake more quickly by tacking into the wind than by heading directly across. In both cases, we happily lengthen the physical distance in order to shorten the subjective distance, as measured in time or energy. How many times do we deliberately take the "long way around" because we know that we'll avoid a dangerous part of town or a rutted, one-lane road—or just because the scenery is prettier, thus making the time seem to pass more quickly? Scenic beauty, while not a common unit of distance, is nonetheless a valid one.

The most valid of all measurement units, in fact, are those which are intuitively meaningful, for they have the greatest impact on our lives. Most of our spatial behavior is based not on physical distance but on the expenditures of time, money, and effort required to move goods, information, and people from place to place. In a behavioral sense, our modern world has shrunk and distance has collapsed so much that we can often disregard physical distance entirely. It takes about the same time to make a cross-country phone call as to call your next-door neighbor. Due to highway traffic, baggage handling, and takeoff-and-landing delays, a long-distance airplane flight often takes little more time than a flight of much shorter length.

There is similar evidence of a cost-space convergence. It costs the same to send a letter from Maine to California as from one block to the next. By taking advantage of special fares, you can fly from New York City to San Francisco for the same price as a flight from Chicago to Salt Lake City. A cross-town drive during rush hour will cost as much in gas and wear-and-tear on your car as a trip of three times the length on the highway.

Even the geographical pattern of fear is changing. It used to be the most distant place which was the greatest mystery, and the object of our fear was the unknown. We now find that our next-door neighbor might be the real stranger. We frequently feel more comfortable with our friends across town or in another part of the country than with the people down the street. A section of our own city may be more feared than some far-off place.

These are just a few examples of the importance of distance as measured in behavioral and therefore intuitively meaningful terms. Sad to say, map makers have found it difficult to respond effectively to our concern with behavioral distance. In large part it is their own shortsightedness which is at fault. They have concentrated on making maps ever more geographically accurate, thereby satisfying the demands of engineers, land surveyors, and military strategists. In the process, they often overlook the day-to-day needs of the rest of us.

But partly the fault rests with the nature of behavioral distance itself. While physical distance is always the same, distance measured in time or energy depends on many factors. Maps based on physical distance, therefore, aren't only simpler and less costly to make but are also more neutral. They can be used by anyone at any time. Maps which use behavioral distance may be more meaningful for specific purposes, but to be effective they must be tailor-made for each situation.

Faced with this problem, what have map makers done? When they have dealt with functional distance at all, they have done so in several ways. One approach is to add behavioral distance figures as supplementary information on conventional maps.

Behavioral Distance Annotations

The most common behavioral distance unit added to maps is travel time, because it is the easiest to measure. Map makers can determine average travel times simply by studying speed limits

along a route. They may add this information to maps in two ways.

Route Segments. One method, as shown in **Figure 13.15A**, is to give the travel time for each route segment. (The same thing may be done in a distance diagram, rather than on the map itself, as in **Figure 13.15B**.) This procedure is used in road atlases, maps produced by the American Automobile Association, and maps in hiking guidebooks. You find your total travel time by summing the numbers of the segments, just as you do to determine physical distance.

Central Point. The second method is to give travel time information continuously in all directions from a central point. Travel times are usually shown by lines of equal time-distance, called **isochrones** (see Figure 6.11A). Isochrones are arranged concentrically around the central point, with the spacing between them directly proportional to travel speed. They'll be close together in congested traffic areas, far apart along open stretches of road.

This second way of showing travel times is more restrictive than the first, since only time to

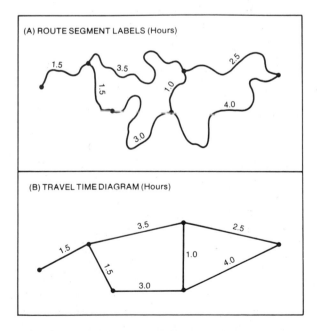

13.15 Behavioral distance annotations may appear directly on maps as route segment labels (A) or off the map as a time diagram (B).

BOX 13.1
MAPPING NON-GEOGRAPHICAL REALITIES

A map maker is both an artist and a surgeon. In his book *Maps*, Gershon Weltman claims that maps "are not the environments themselves but are, instead, displays designed to present an environment in absence; displays designed to 're-present' in such a way as to allow the map reader systematically to derive attributes of the mapped environment." And despite a proliferation of mediocre or misleading maps, there is an active community of exemplary designers who have mastered the techniques of mapping.

Joel Katz, a partner in the Katz Wheeler graphic design firm in Philadelphia, is...a map maker in the most expansive sense of the word. In the following paragraphs, he outlines the considerations of conscientious map makers.

In the area of maps, particularly, there is no developed aesthetic by the public. People have no concept of what makes a good map, because the concept of a map that they're raised on is so banal. It's the atlas the teacher pulls down in third grade. When people come to us for maps, it's because we make maps that work....

What are the simplest questions you would ask yourself if you were doing a map? How would you start? There's one question: what's the purpose of the map? Some maps are to get people from here to there, and other maps have nothing to do with that whatsoever. The purpose of a map or the vocabulary of the map relates to the experience that's appropriate for the person using it to have. There are even cases for nongeographic, straight-line maps that depart from reality.

The clearest, most logical example for the justification of a straight-line, totally nongeographic map is the airplane experience. You have absolutely no control whatsoever. You gain control as you move through the succeeding modes of transportation from trains, subways, buses, and cars to the pedestrian experience, which is at the other end. The kind of map you need is one that relates to what you can see, what you can feel, and the extent to which you can act on information....

[T]he most important thing in mapping—in non-geographic, diagrammatic mapping, modified-view mapping—is consistency. What you have to do is tie the nongeographic diagram with a picture of the nonspecific geography of both. All those things have to connect.

In airline schedules, it doesn't matter what the plane does once it gets up in the air; you want to know where it takes off and where it lands. Headwinds are beyond your control. You can choose a flight that arrives at a particular time, but you can't determine the particular route or the altitude of the plane. Those matters are beyond your repertoire of choice.

But there are aspects that you might want to know about that are hard to find in most airline schedules, such as where does the plane stop? Where are the two stops on my flight to India? What will the plane fly over?

Many flight maps have straight lines between places, many have curved lines because that's supposed to resemble the way an airplane flies. We go up and we come down. But all these lines are of no use. The visual messages don't inform. It would be better to look at a map and understand that there is a plane change, a time change, and a stopover in Mozambique.

(Richard Saul Wurman, *Information Anxiety*)

and from the central point is meaningful. But both methods are useful because they combine physical and behavioral distance measures on the same map. You are given the best of both worlds: You can use physical distance units to compute gas mileage and travel time figures to estimate arrival times, travel fatigue, and other such factors.

All travel time figures are approximate, of course. They will vary with weather, time of day, route, and vehicle. Maps provide average figures, and averages seldom correspond to individual cases.

If maps showing travel times are few, those giving other types of behavioral distance information are nearly nonexistent. Such details as travel comfort, energy consumption, and route safety would all be of interest to map users. The core of the problem is that such information is difficult to gather. And here again, average figures aren't always helpful in individual cases. As widespread automated mapping becomes practical, however, we can envision maps being tailor-made for a particular person and trip. You'll give a computer all the information related to your journey and be presented with your own special and truly functional map.

Distance Cartograms

The most original response to the challenge of showing functional distance on maps is the linear cartogram. (Recall the discussions of linear cartograms in Chapters 6 and 8.) Although cartograms are often dismissed as novelties, they can serve a serious purpose. By carrying abstraction to the extreme, they extend the range of functionality. As **Box 13.1** makes clear, the geography of reality is constrained. Distance cartograms can fill that gap.

As with behavioral annotations, there are two types of linear cartograms. Some are based on route segments (see Figure 6.10). Others are arranged around a central point (see Figures 6.11 and 6.12). These central-point cartograms have many of the same properties as azimuthal equidistant projections. But unlike equidistant map projections, on which the scale is true to or from the central point, the cartogram scale is true only *from* the central point. As on equidistant projections, distance and angles between other points aren't correct.

The best way to appreciate the route-segment or central-point linear cartogram is to compare it with a conventional map. The differences between the two will highlight spatial behavior and use of space which you might otherwise overlook.

The advantages of distance cartograms are largely offset by their lack of general application. As with behavioral annotations, however, automated mapping will eventually change all this. Some day it will be routine to create a special map for any situation.

That day, however, is in the future. What do we do in the meantime?

Behavioral Distance by Inference

In the meantime, the burden lies with you, the map user, to translate physical into functional distance. You could do this by searching out the information elsewhere and adding it to your maps, but such a process is usually too involved to be worth the effort. Your alternative is to supply behavioral distance through a process of inference. You can conjure up a great deal of information from past experience stored in your mental maps.

You probably use the inference process frequently without realizing it. When figuring the length of a trip, for instance, you take traffic conditions into account. You know that a drive across town will take longer during rush hour than at other times. Holiday and weekend traffic is equally predictable, so you leave earlier or stay longer and thus shorten your travel time.

You can probably think of many other functional distance measures. The map scale is merely the starting point for a person with imagination. By drawing on your experience and intuition, in combination with careful map study, you can make many inferences which will bring map and functional distance closer together. Your common sense can add more to maps than cartographers can show.

SELECTED READINGS

Abler, R., "Distance, Intercommunications and Geography," *Proceedings, Association of American Geographers,* 3 (1971), pp. 1-4.

Atwill, L., "What's Up (and Down) at the USGS," *Field & Stream* (May 1997), pp. 54-55.

Bovy, P.H.L., and Stern, E., *Route Choice: Wayfinding in Transport Networks* (Boston: Kluwer Academic Publishers, 1990).

278

Buttenfield, B.P., and McMaster, R.B., *Map Generalization: Making Rules for Knowledge Representation* (Essex: Longman Scientific & Technical, 1991).

Maling, D.H., "The Methods of Measuring Distance," Chapter 3 in *Measurement from Maps* (New York: Pergamon Press, 1989), pp. 30-52.

McMaster, R.B., and Shea, K.S., *Generalization in Digital Cartography* (Washington, DC: Association of American Geographers, 1992).

Muehrcke, P.C., "Functional Map Use," *Journal of Geography,* 77, 7 (December, 1978), pp. 254-262.

Muller, J.C., Lagrange, J.P., and Weibel, R., eds., *GIS and Generalization* (London: Taylor & Francis, 1995).

Monmonier, M.S., *Maps, Distortion and Meaning* (Washington, DC: Association of American Geographers, 1977).

Olsson, G. *Distance and Human Interaction,* Bibliography Series No. 2 (Philadelphia: Regional Science Research Institute, 1965).

Peters, A.B., "Distance-Related Maps," *The American Cartographer,* 11, 2 (1984), pp. 119-131.

Watson, J.W., "Geography: A Discipline in Distance," *Scottish Geographical Magazine,* 71 (1955), pp. 1-13.

Witthuhn, B.O., "Distance: An Extraordinary Spatial Concept," *Journal of Geography,* 78, 5 (1979), pp. 177-181.

Also see references provided in Chapters 14 and 15 and Appendix A.

CHAPTER FOURTEEN

COMPASS AND MAPS

INTRODUCTION

ORIENTING THE MAP

Inspection Method
    Celestial Features
    Terrestrial Features
Compass Method

ESTABLISHING YOUR POSITION

Inspection Method
    Distance Estimation
    Resection
Instrumental Methods
    Celestial Observation
    Electronic Positioning
        Self-Contained Systems
        Signal-Dependent Systems
    Compass Method
        Distance Estimation
        Resection
    Altimeter Method
        Linear Feature
        Sight Line
Local Reference Method

LOCATING A DISTANT POINT

Inspection Method
Compass Method
Radiobeacon Method

ROUTE-FINDING MAPS

Land Navigation
Water Navigation
Air Navigation

ROUTE-FINDING TECHNIQUES

Piloting
    Planning for Piloting
    Piloting a Course
Dead Reckoning
    Planning for Dead Reckoning
    Executing a Dead-Reckoned Course

PRACTICAL NAVIGATION

SELECTED READINGS

14

CHAPTER FOURTEEN

COMPASS AND MAPS

There's no feeling as chilling as realizing you don't know where you are or how to get where you want to go. The most basic aspect of being oriented, then, is to know your position and where distant features are located in relation to you. Knowing this information also lets you move (navigate) from place to place with confidence.

The need to know your position can be so overwhelming that you hesitate to leave your known environment. But you needn't give in to fears of disorientation. If you know how to compare your surroundings with a map, you can brave new horizons without worrying about getting lost.

People have survived a long time relying solely on their powers of observation. But we have enhanced our natural spatial abilities over the centuries by inventing a variety of technical aids. Clocks, compasses, optical sighting devices, electronic direction and distance finders, inertial navigation systems, and global positioning satellites all fall in this category (see Appendix D: *Navigation Instruments*).

No matter how technically sophisticated our position and path-finding aids, however, they share much in common with longstanding "eyeball" methods. They all use distance or direction information. And they all rely on a few geometrical concepts. When our modern technical gadgets fail or aren't at hand, we must fall back on this information and these concepts.

So let's start this chapter by discussing traditional observation and compass techniques that have proven useful for centuries and underlie even the most modern satellite-based methods of position and path finding. For convenience, we'll begin with orienting the map, then consider locating a point, and conclude with navigation issues. We'll bring these methods up to date with GPS applications in the next chapter (*GPS and Maps*).

ORIENTING THE MAP

To **orient** a map means to turn it so that directions on the ground are lined up with those on the map. This is sometimes called **setting** the map.

It's not always essential that you orient your map. Indeed, many people keep the map topside up, no matter which way they're facing. This procedure has the advantage that place names, symbols, and features are easy to read. But it has the disadvantage that map directions aren't usually aligned with ground directions. When you're heading south, right on the map is left in reality. Such reverse thinking can make the mind reel. Imagine trying to make a split-second decision in heavy traffic about which way to turn! Since this may not be much of a problem in familiar settings, it's easy to forget that there is an alternative.

If you are in an unfamiliar, confusing setting, it is usually easier to find your way around if you first orient the map. Turning the map until ground and map features are aligned has the advantage that you can always determine directions directly. Although you may have to read place names and symbols upside down or sideways, this is easier than trying to unscramble backward directions. For most people, therefore, it is simpler to use a map oriented with the ground than to orient the map mentally. This is especially true under conditions of stress.

Inspection Method

For ordinary purposes, the most practical way to orient a map in the field is by the **method of inspection**. With this technique, you don't need to know which way north is. Nor do you need any special tools. Two conditions must be met, however. First, you must be able to see one or more features. (Sometimes—say in the case of a sawmill or feedlot—it may suffice to hear or smell the feature, even if you can't see it). Second, you must be able to identify these same features on the map, or at least to relate their position to the map. Various celestial and terrestrial features satisfy both conditions.

Celestial Features

The position of the sun and stars—particularly the North Star (see Figure 12.2), which is almost directly above the North Pole—can be related to most maps. Combined, they provide convenient directional reference marks for both day and night map orientation. Our use of the sun's position is so basic, in fact, that it is often unconscious. For most people, however, the sun and stars give only a rough idea of direction. Also, celestial marks sometimes become obscured by atmospheric conditions and cannot be used.

Terrestrial Features

On the other hand, many landmarks are shown directly on maps. Thus, they provide a means of orienting the map by inspection which can be used in lieu of (or as a supplement to) celestial reference marks. Often a single linear feature is all you need.

One Linear Feature. There are three forms of alignment with a single linear feature (**Figure 14.1A**). If you can move onto a linear feature such as a road, then you need only turn the map until the mapped road lines up with the real one. Although this is the most accurate form of alignment, a slight variation of this approach is almost as accurate. With this second method, you assume a position which lies on a straight-line extension of the ground feature. Your third option is to take up a position to either side of the linear ground feature and then to align the map feature so that it is parallel with the ground feature. This last form of map orientation is the least accurate of the three methods, but it often must suffice due to the accessibility problems so characteristic of actual field situations.

The first and third of these methods share one serious problem. When you line up the map road with the ground road, you don't know which direction is which, and you could end up going in the opposite direction from what you intend. Because of this potential **reversal of orientation**, you shouldn't rely on a single linear feature if you can avoid it.

Two Linear Features. A better practice is to rely on two or more linear features when orienting the map by inspection. As with a single feature, you have three options. You can move to a position on either of the two linear features, move to a point which lies on a straight-line extension of either feature, or assume a position

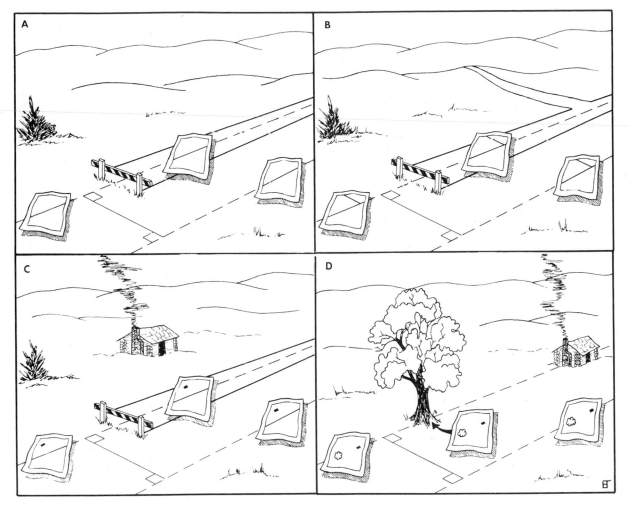

14.1 You may use a number of methods to orient your map by inspection.

off to one side of both features (**Figure 14.1B**). Then you simply turn the map until the two features on the map are aligned with the same features on the ground. Again, the first method is the most accurate, the third approach the least accurate.

Prominent Objects. Reversal in map orientation can also be avoided by using other combinations of two or more features on the ground and map. For example, a linear feature and a prominent object, such as a house, hill, or pond, will do as well as two linear features (**Figure 14.1C**).

Likewise, two prominent objects (one of which could be your position) would also suffice.

In this case, you can move to one of the features or to a position on a line extended through the two features (**Figure 14.1D**). Next, place a ruler or other straightedge between the features on the map. (If a straightedge isn't available, mentally sighting between the two features will do). Then turn the map until you can sight along the straightedge or sight line to the other visible point (when you have moved to one feature) or to both features (when you have moved to an extension-line position). If you are located off to the side of the features, you will have to position your map so that the straightedge sighting is in parallel alignment to the ground features.

The success of map orientation by the inspection method depends primarily on the ability to identify environmental features which are also depicted on the map. When prominent environmental features are unfamiliar or obscured (by vegetation, fog, or terrain) or when they are locally nonexistent (as on a plain or ocean surface), the method of inspection is of little, if any, value. In these special situations, a practical method of map orientation is by means of a magnetic compass.

Compass Method

The compass method of map orientation has several limitations. You must have a compass, and you must know the direction of the magnetic north pole. (See *Magnetic North* in Chapter 12). Once you fulfill these two conditions, though, the compass procedure is straightforward.

First, find the magnetic north indicator on the map. This is usually an arrow in the margin of large-scale maps. Next, holding the map under the compass, turn the map until the compass arrow lines up with magnetic north on the map. Since this procedure accounts for magnetic declination, your map will now be properly oriented with true north as well.

Figure 14.2 illustrates why it is so essential to take magnetic declination into account when orienting a map with the compass method. In this example, the magnetic declination is 20° East. Thus, when the compass card is oriented with the magnetic north base line (A), true north correctly falls 20° west of the magnetic north indicator (the arrow on the compass). Conversely, when the north position on the compass card is oriented with the true north base line (B), the map is incorrectly oriented 20° east of true north.

Unfortunately, magnetic north isn't always indicated on maps, especially not on small-scale and non-topographic maps. Often a topographic map sheet will have been cut into sections or have its margins trimmed off to make its size more manageable, with the result that the magnetic north indicator is lost. For these reasons, it

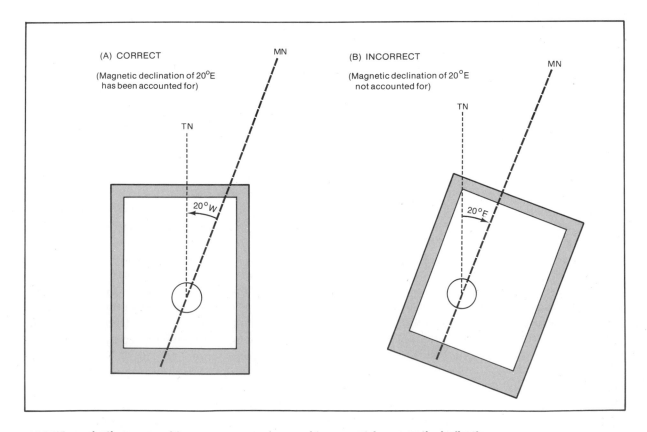

14.2 When orienting a map with a compass, you may need to account for magnetic declination.

makes sense to commit the basic declination pattern to memory. For the contiguous United States, declination varies from approximately 25° West (in the Northeast) to 25° East (in the Pacific Northwest) (see Figure 12.9 in Chapter 12: *Direction*).

If you keep in mind the magnetic declination for the general area in which you are traveling, you need never be too far off in estimating the map direction of magnetic north. For large portions of the Midwest, the declination is close enough to 0 degrees that true north (indicated by longitude lines) provides a reasonable substitute for magnetic north.

ESTABLISHING YOUR POSITION

At times you will orient your map on the basis of a known ground position, or your position will be established in the process of map orientation. At other times, your actual ground location will remain unknown even after you have oriented your map. But once your map is oriented, regardless of whether you have done so mentally or physically, you can then establish your map position. There are three potentially useful methods: by inspection, by instruments, and by local reference.

Inspection Method

When you use the inspection method to locate your map position, the idea is the same as when you used inspection to orient your map. You are simply looking at (or "inspecting") ground features without any special aids. There are two main inspection techniques. With the first, you inspect things on the map and then estimate their distance from you. With the second, you plot lines which intersect at your position.

Distance Estimation Method

The most common inspection technique is distance (or **range**) estimation. To use this method, first orient your map and select a feature on the ground which can also be identified on the map. Next, estimate the range from your ground position to the distant feature, and convert this figure to map distance units by using the map scale.

Now mark out the computed map distance along the proper direction line and you have established your position (**Figure 14.3A**). You can double-check your work by repeating the procedure with several features, but don't be too discouraged if your results don't agree. Distances are hard to judge accurately, although it is possible to improve with practice.

One trick is to use multiples of familiar distance units, such as a football field (100 yards), the side of a 40-acre field (440 yards), or miles. But most people have trouble visualizing these units. A further complication is that as your vision approaches the vanishing point, it becomes more difficult to judge the surface of the ground. The nearest segment of a range is proportionately easier to estimate than more distant segments.

Another trick is to memorize what familiar objects look like at different ranges. Then you can simply compare the size and general appearance of an object, such as a tree, with the "template" that you hold in your mind's eye, and you will have a good idea of the range. There are problems with this procedure, however. The reference object may not be of standard size. Even when it is of typical proportions, troubles may arise. Weather, atmospheric conditions, the relationship of the sun's rays to the object, and the intervening terrain may all compound the difficulties of judging distance on the basis of the size of objects. A feature will appear to be a different distance when seen from a low position over a flat surface than when viewed from one hillside to another. If the object is seen from above or below, it will appear smaller and farther away than it actually is. A back-lighted object will seem farther away than a front-lighted one. A brightly marked feature will appear closer than a dull feature, while both objects will look closer on a bright, dry day than a humid or foggy one.

Given these problems, it isn't surprising that many gadgets to help estimate range are on the market. The simplest device is a card containing the **silhouettes** of objects at different ranges. To estimate the range to a distant feature, hold the card at arm's length. Then determine the best match between the silhouettes on the card and the object in the field, and read off the distance. This technique's accuracy, obviously, depends on how "standard" the object's size and your arm's length are, and how well you can

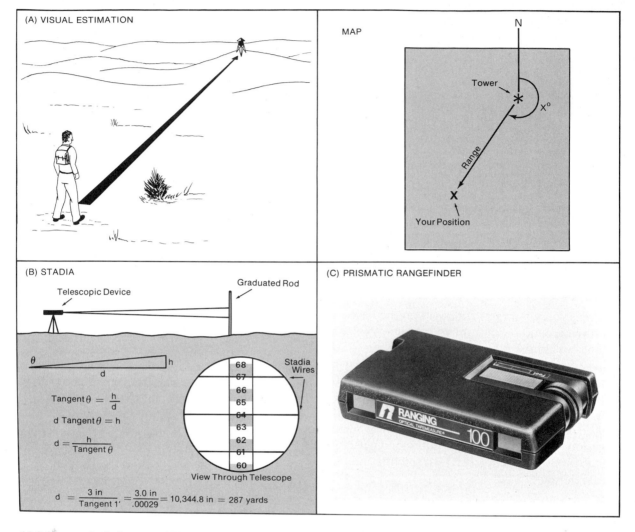

(A) VISUAL ESTIMATION

MAP

(B) STADIA

Telescopic Device

Graduated Rod

$\text{Tangent}\,\theta = \dfrac{h}{d}$

$d\,\text{Tangent}\,\theta = h$

$d = \dfrac{h}{\text{Tangent}\,\theta}$

68
67
66
65
64
63
62
61
60

Stadia Wires

View Through Telescope

$d = \dfrac{3\text{ in}}{\text{Tangent }1'} = \dfrac{3.0\text{ in}}{.00029} = 10{,}344.8\text{ in} = 287\text{ yards}$

(C) PRISMATIC RANGEFINDER

RANGING
OPTICAL TAPEMEASURE
100

14.3 One way to find your position is to use range and direction information gained by inspecting your surroundings.

match the object with a relatively few silhouette sizes.

This "card trick" is crude at best. A more sophisticated and accurate device for measuring distance is the **stadia principle**. It has long been used in optical surveying instruments and hunting scopes. This device has a built-in pair of horizontal wires, or **stadia**, which are spaced to bracket a distance measured in the angle of arc of a circle. The angle subtended is usually on the order of minutes of angle (MOA). One minute of angle (1/60th of a degree) will subtend approximately 1 inch (actually 1.023 inches) at 100 yards, 2 inches at 200 yards, and so forth. Surveyors use

the stadia-equipped instruments to sight at a graduated rod and then compute the intervening distance by using simple trigonometry (**Figure 14.3B**). The technique may be far less accurate if an object must be assumed to be of standard size, as is the case in most non-surveying applications.

Prismatic rangefinders can also be accurate. The ground-glass and split-image rangefinders on many modern single-lens reflex (SLR) cameras are representative of this class of instrument. They generally have such a small distance (usually a few inches) separating their prisms that their effective range is too short for most distance estimates in the field. They are accurate up to their "infinity" of, say, 100 feet. Beyond that distance, they are of no value because all distances appear the same. Under good conditions, however, specially designed optical rangefinders with prisms spaced farther apart can be effective in estimating distances up to several hundred yards with an accuracy of a few yards (**Figure 14.3C**).

The latest technology for distance estimation is the **laser rangefinder**. Although rather expensive, these "point and read" instruments are the most accurate and handy yet invented. Infrared beams built into binoculars or a monocular (1/2 of a binocular) measure distance up to 1,000 yards with an accuracy of one yard at a touch of a button. These laser rangefinders have become indispensable around construction sites and realtor's offices, where they are known as **electronic rulers**.

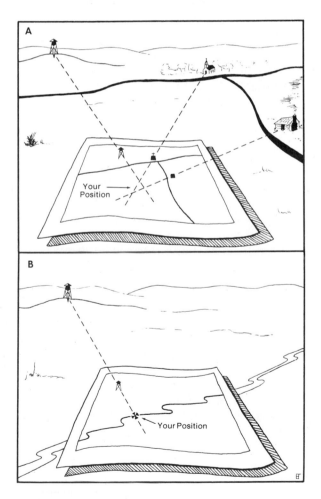

14.4 Position finding can be carried out by inspection using the resection method.

Both prismatic and laser rangefinders can be a lot of fun to use, especially in checking the results of your mental distance estimates. Their cost and weight are directly related to their range and accuracy. But varying from nine ounces to three pounds, they all are portable enough to be carried for many business and recreational uses.

Resection Method

Unless you are one of the few people who has mastered visual range estimation or has the proper equipment available to compute distance, you probably should avoid the distance estimation method if accurate position determination is crucial. For most people, a better technique for locating position by inspection is the resection method. With this technique, you plot lines which cross, or "resect" at your position. You can make this plot with three lines or with two lines.

If possible, it is most accurate to use three lines. First, you must be able to find three outstanding point features on both the ground and the map. Then, with the map properly oriented, place a straightedge on a line between one of the prominent ground features and the same feature on the map, and draw a line along the straightedge. Or, if you have no straightedge, simply draw in your mental **sight line**. (This sight line is really a **backsight** or **back bearing**, since it is drawn from the known position of a distant feature back to your position). Next, draw lines in the same way for the other two features. You know that you are located where the three lines cross on the map (**Figure 14.4A**).

You will get the most reliable position fix when at least two of your sight lines cross at angles close to 90 degrees.* Due to execution inaccuracies, however, even then the three lines will rarely cross at a point but instead will form a **triangle of error** within which you are probably located. If this triangle is small, you can feel confident in your results. If the error triangle is large, however, it is advisable to repeat the previous method, taking greater care. It may be that you were sloppy in your sighting. But there is also the chance that you didn't sight to the correct feature

---

If possible, you should avoid using sight lines which cross at angles smaller than 45 degrees. With small angles, even a slight error in construction may considerably mislocate the point at which the line should intersect.

or that the map maker misplaced the feature on the map in the first place.

If only two outstanding point features are identifiable on both ground and map, you can still use the resection method, proceeding as you did when three features were available. Because only two lines are constructed, they will cross at a point regardless of execution errors on your part. With three lines, the triangle of error makes it obvious if you are far off in your sightings. But having only two lines intersect at a point gives the illusion of accuracy. Any error you made in either of your sightings won't be evident. Whenever two rather than three lines are used, therefore, you must watch out for this potential **hidden error**. If precision position finding is critical, it is good practice to repeat the procedure as an accuracy check.

You can also use resection to find your position by taking advantage of a point and a line feature. First, move to a line feature on the ground. Next, move along the linear ground feature until a distant point feature which is depicted on the map is also visible from your ground position. With your map properly oriented, place a straightedge on a line between the ground feature and its plotted map position and draw a line (**Figure 14.4B**). Your position is thus established where the line intersects the linear feature on the map.

Instrumental Methods

The main problem with the inspection method of position finding is that it is often difficult to locate distinct landmarks on the ground that also show up on your map. Terrain features may be muted; the weather may be stormy; and so on. In these situations, position-finding instruments are invaluable. Let's take a look at some instrumental methods of position finding.

Celestial Observation

The oldest way to determine your position with instruments is by observing the positions, magnitudes, and motions of celestial bodies in conjunction with certain principles of astronomy. The essence of the technique is to establish celestial lines of position (east-west, north-south) by comparing the predicted positions of celestial bodies

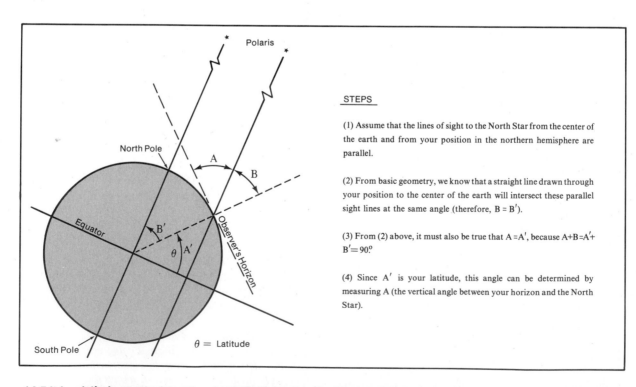

STEPS

(1) Assume that the lines of sight to the North Star from the center of the earth and from your position in the northern hemisphere are parallel.

(2) From basic geometry, we know that a straight line drawn through your position to the center of the earth will intersect these parallel sight lines at the same angle (therefore, B = B').

(3) From (2) above, it must also be true that A = A', because A + B = A' + B' = 90°.

(4) Since A' is your latitude, this angle can be determined by measuring A (the vertical angle between your horizon and the North Star).

14.5 It is relatively easy to determine your latitude by observing the height of the North Star above your apparent location.

with their observed positions. A hand-held instrument, called a **sextant**, is the tool of choice for measuring the angle (or altitude) of a celestial body above the earth's horizon.

One thing soon becomes clear—the universe is in motion. The earth and other planets rotate on their axes and revolve around the sun. The moons of these planets rotate and revolve, the sun rotates, the solar system is moving through space toward the star Vega, and so forth. Astronomers study and tabulate information on the actual motion of celestial bodies, but in fixing your position you need concern yourself only with apparent motion. You stop the earth, so to speak, and watch the celestial bodies rise in the east.

These celestial observations can help you pinpoint your latitude and longitude. Latitude, quite simply, is equivalent to the angle between your horizon and the North Star (or the Southern Cross in the Southern Hemisphere) (**Figure 14.5**). It is more complicated to compute your longitude. You can do so by using elaborate tables in conjunction with the relationships of various celestial bodies. If you have a clock or watch, however, longitude can be figured much more easily. You merely compare your local time with Greenwich mean time. Recall that the prime meridian—or 0 degrees longitude—passes through Greenwich, England. Therefore, each hour difference between your time and that of Greenwich is equivalent to 15 degrees of longitude from Greenwich.

Celestial methods of fixing a position are still used extensively by surveyors and by navigators of ocean-going ships and long-range aircraft. But the skills and special equipment required to make precise fixes place the technique beyond the practical realm of most people. It is far more common to use celestial bodies as a means of establishing a basic reference system. Thus, the position of the sun tells something about direction as well as the time of day and year; the shape of the moon reveals something about the time of the month; and the position of the North Star is useful in establishing the true-north direction line.

Electronic Positioning

Modern position-finding instruments take advantage of electronic technology. Since electronic methods involve data processing as well as hardware components, the term "system" best describes these tools. Two approaches are being taken today. In one case the system is self-contained, while in the other it is dependent on external signals.

Self-Contained Systems. A navigation system that requires no external information source must have some means of keeping track of where it has been. This ancient **dead-reckoning** procedure is in fact the basis for modern **inertial navigation systems (INS)** (see *Route-Finding Techniques* later in this chapter and *Inertial Positioning Systems* in Appendix D). Since inertial systems work by keeping track of positions, they can also serve as position-finding devices.

Inertial navigation systems are complex, bulky, and expensive, which limits their practical use to ships, airplanes, and ground vehicles. But those fortunate enough to have such a device can, at any time, obtain their estimated positional coordinates. Technically advanced systems can even display your current position superimposed on a map background.

Since inertial systems work by keeping track of the distance and direction moved since the last position fix, you do have to get the device started. This means at some prior time you had to know your position. In addition, computational errors accumulate as the system is used (see *Dead Reckoning* later in this chapter). This influences the accuracy of your current position determination.

Signal-Dependent Systems. Problems associated with inertial navigation can in part be overcome by using a device that receives positioning signals from an external source. For several decades, ground-based **radionavigation aids** have served this function (see *Radio Transmitters and Receivers* in Appendix D).

The advantages of electronic position determination over traditional visual methods are that radio signals travel to great distances, function equally well in daylight or darkness, and can penetrate vegetative cover or fog as well as clear sky. Otherwise, electronic and conventional position fixing differ only in the methods of data collection and in the senses used.

There are several ways to fix position by radio waves. One method is to passively receive

290

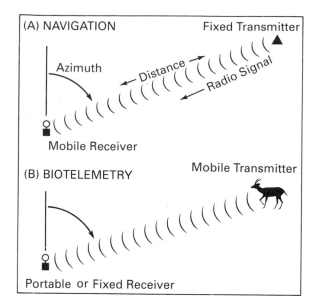

(A) NAVIGATION — Fixed Transmitter

Azimuth — Distance — Radio Signal

Mobile Receiver

(B) BIOTELEMETRY — Mobile Transmitter

Portable or Fixed Receiver

14.6 You can use a radio direction finder (RDF) to determine the direction and, sometimes, the distance from your position to a radiobeacon.

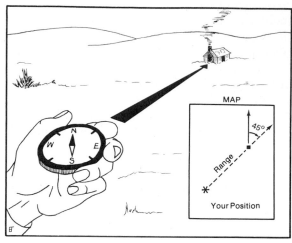

MAP

45°

Range

Your Position

14.7 You can use a magnetic compass to carry out the range and direction method of position finding.

signals transmitted from one or more distant **radiobeacons (Rbns)**. To serve this purpose, a network of RBns has been established around the world. To make use of a radiobeacon's signal, you need a receiving unit, or **radio direction finder (RDF)**. An RDF is sometimes referred to as a **radio compass** because it is an azimuthal instrument which can determine the direction of the sending station (**Figure 14.6**). With some systems, the bearings given by the instrument need to be plotted on a special chart to determine your position.

More sophisticated receiving units are capable of converting signals from one or several transmitting stations to both range (distance) and bearing (direction) readings. Simply turn on the instrument, and distance and bearing information to the radiobeacon (Rbn) is automatically displayed.

Systems that involve passive reception of radio signals suffer the drawback that appropriate sending units must be nearby and transmitting. An alternative is to send out a radio wave which, when it strikes an object, is reflected back to a receiving unit. Examples are **radar (radio detection and ranging)** and **sonar (sound navigation ranging)** systems. In both cases the range of an object is determined from the time lag between signal transmission and receipt of the

reflected wave, while the bearing of the object depends on the direction of the transmitting antenna at the time that the signal was sent out. When a radar scope is used to combine the range and bearing information, your position with respect to surrounding objects can be seen directly.

The latest and most promising signal-dependent positioning technology is based on a constellation of satellite transmitters rather than a network of ground stations. This **Global Positioning System**, or **GPS**, is maintained by the U.S. Department of Defense. The use of GPS with maps is discussed in Chapter 15, and technical details concerning GPS are found in Appendix D.

Compass Method

The compass method for finding your map position is similar to the method of inspection, discussed earlier. The only difference is that you use a compass to determine direction. An advantage of this compass technique is that you don't need to orient your map before finding your position. As with the inspection method, you can use a compass to establish your position in one of two ways—by estimating distance or by plotting lines of resection.

Distance Estimation Method. To perform the range estimation technique, use your compass to sight on a distant feature and note the

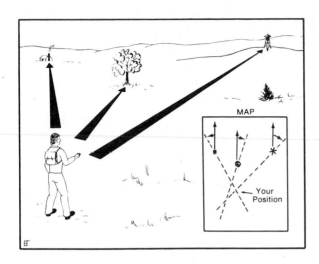

14.8 You can use a magnetic compass to determine your position by resection.

reading. Then determine the ground distance from your position to that feature (using one of the range estimation techniques discussed earlier under *Establishing Your Position*). Now, using the map scale, convert this figure to map distance units. Finally, plot the sighting through the target feature on the map, and mark off the estimated distance, as shown in **Figure 14.7**.

Resection Method. Like the inspection technique, the compass method of resection makes use of backsights as resection lines. You merely use a compass, rather than a straightedge or visual sighting, to determine the resection lines. Again, you can make your resection plot with two or three lines. To use the three-point resection technique, select three outstanding features on the ground which you can also identify on the map. Next, simply sight the three distant points with a compass from your ground position and note the readings obtained. Plot the three sightings through their respective map points by using a protractor (**Figure 14.8**). The three lines will come together to form a triangle of error, just as your lines did when made with a straightedge. Again, you know that your position lies somewhere within that triangle.

The two-point resection technique and the point and line feature resection technique are similar to the inspection method except that you use a compass to make your sightings. We've already discussed the hidden error that may result from using only two sight lines. Therefore, if the consequences of being wrong are critical, be sure to repeat the procedure at least once as an accuracy check.

Altimeter Method

In mountainous regions, particularly those which are heavily forested or cloud-shrouded much of the time, you may be unable to locate enough features on both the ground and map to use the inspection and compass methods of position finding accurately. In this case, you might think the GPS receiver would be your savior. But you would be wrong. Hand-held GPS receivers in common use have such limited altitude capability that they're generally not helpful in such situations (see Chapter 15: *GPS and Maps*).

Instead, a pocket **altimeter** is probably the best position-finding aid in such circumstances. With a contour map and an altimeter, you can fix your position with the help of only a single feature common to your map and your surroundings. An altimeter position fix is easiest if you are located on (or by) a linear feature such as a trail, stream, or ridge line. But it is also possible to determine your position with an altimeter if you are able to make a sighting on a distant feature such as a building, mountain peak, or lake.

Before you rush into the wilderness with an altimeter in your pack, there is something you should know. An altimeter's primary drawback in position finding is that an instrument of portable size and weight is difficult to keep calibrated. These calibrating problems can be traced to the fact that an altimeter is a form of **barometer**. Therefore, it determines elevation by measuring air pressure. Unfortunately, the relation between elevation and air pressure isn't a simple one. Since under ideal conditions air pressure decreases systematically with altitude, the altimeter's scale can in theory be calibrated in meters or feet to reflect changes in elevation. In practice, though, air temperature and humidity also influence atmospheric pressure, and these factors often change rapidly and unpredictably. All things considered, it is best to view pocket altimeter readings as approximate.

You can do several things to increase the accuracy of your altimeter readings, however. One is to pay a little more and obtain a temperature-compensated altimeter. Also, always set your altimeter before you start your trip, using your contour map to obtain accurate elevation data. And, finally, reset your altimeter as often as possible during your travels. You can do so whenever you come to a place where you can clearly discern the elevation. A mountain top, a saddle between two peaks, and the point at which a trail branches or crosses a stream are likely spots to make this instrument calibration. The shorter the time between your altimeter settings, the less chance that changing conditions will distort your elevation readings.

Linear-Feature Altimeter Procedure. To establish your position with an altimeter when you're located on a path or other prominent linear feature, there are two steps. First, read the elevation value from your altimeter, taking care to tap the device several times to be certain that the pointer hasn't stuck in a wrong position. Next, follow along the appropriate linear feature on your map until you come to the elevation value indicated by the altimeter. This will be your approximate current position.

An actual case of position fixing with an altimeter and a linear feature is provided in **Figure 14.9**. Let's assume that you have parked your car at point A, with the intent of hiking up the trail to the north. You note that the parking lot is bisected by the 2,600-foot contour line. Before starting out from your car, therefore, you set your altimeter to this reading. Later, after hiking several hours through dense fog, you stop and

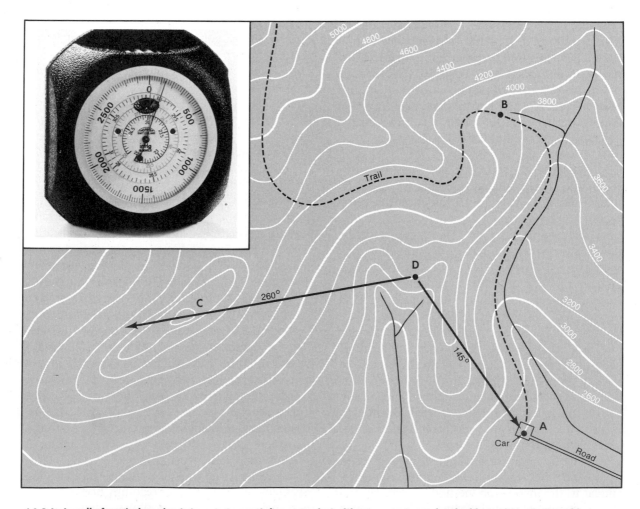

14.9 In heavily forested or cloud-shrouded mountains, a pocket altimeter can be an invaluable position-finding aid.

read your altimeter again. The device indicates that you have climbed to an elevation of 3,900 feet. By tracing your route up the trail, you decide that you must be located near point B, about halfway between the 3,800-foot and 4,000-foot contours.

Sight-Line Altimeter Procedure. If you aren't located on a linear feature, you can still use your altimeter to fix your position if you can make a sighting on a distant object. Three steps are required. First, establish where the sight line from your position to the visible feature falls when plotted on your map. (To do so, you can use either the inspection or the compass methods discussed previously.) Next, read the current elevation value from your altimeter. Finally, follow along the sight line until you come to this elevation value. This should be your approximate position.

An example of this sight-line method of position finding is given in Figure 14.9. In this case, suppose that you lost the trail in a snowslide area shortly after making the position fix described in the previous section. After you have searched for an hour or so, the clouds clear enough so that you can see a mountain peak (C) across a valley off to the southeast of your position. With the help of your compass, you determine that the azimuth to the mountain peak is 260°. At the same point, your altimeter indicates an elevation of 3,600 feet. By plotting the sight line on your map, and then following along the line until you get to the point at which it crosses the 3,600-foot contour line, you establish your current position (D). From this point, you decide that you can cut across country to your car by following an azimuth of 145 degrees.

Local Reference Method

What if you don't have a map or positioning instrument with you when you want to establish your position? Or, what if you want to remember how to get to a certain unmarked position, such as a sunken shipwreck? The **fisher's solution** to either type of problem is simple and reasonably effective, particularly when precise locational information isn't required.

Imagine that you find a terrific fishing spot in the middle of a small lake. How will you find the spot next time you go fishing? This is a com-

mon problem, often solved by fishers in cartoons by marking an "X" on the side of their boat. There is a much better procedure, however. Simply locate two pairs of features which fall on opposite sides of the lake on imaginary lines extending through your position (**Figure 14.10A**). In theory, the wider the angle of separation between sighting lines, the more accurately you will be able to return to the spot. A separation of about 45 degrees is probably a good compromise between theoretical accuracy and the practical problem of trying to make continuous sightings as you approach the desired position.

Obviously, this technique won't work if you are on a large body of water, since you won't be able to see both shores at once. Another method, which is probably more accurate than the previous one even for small bodies of water, is to line up two pairs of features along one shoreline. In

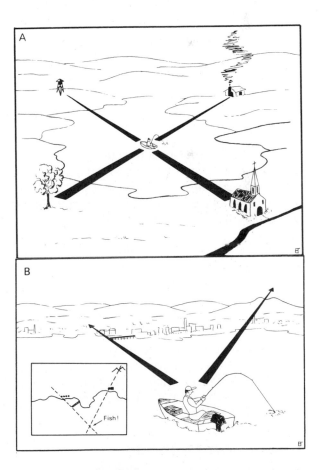

14.10 As any good fisher knows, position finding doesn't require the use of a cartographic map.

294

effect, this procedure establishes your position by crossed backsights and is thus a form of resection. By using this technique to locate a small reef which lies about six miles off the Lake Superior shoreline from Marquette, Michigan (**Figure 14.10B**), some people are able to catch lake trout consistently, while others, without this technique, enjoy only hit-or-miss luck.

LOCATING A DISTANT POINT

It isn't always enough to know how to locate yourself on the map. What if you want to know the position of something else? That pond or house or tree, for instance, may be clearly visible but not shown on your map. How do you figure out its correct map location?

The technique to use here is really just a take-off on the method of resection. You use resection to establish your own position and the method of **intersection** to find the map position of something else. As we have seen, resection lines are formed by backsights or back bearings—lines from a distant feature back to your position. Intersection lines, on the other hand, are made by **foresights** or **cross bearings**—lines from your position to a distant feature.

Using the intersection technique, you sight on the unknown spot from two ground positions whose map locations are known or can be computed. The point at which these foresights intersect establishes the feature's location.

As with resection, the accuracy of the method of intersection is improved by using three rather than two known sighting points. Again, the triangle of error created by using three sight lines will give you a measure of confidence in how accurately you have executed the intersection method.

To locate a distant point, you can use techniques similar to those you used to establish your position. The three main techniques are the inspection method, the compass method, and the radiobeacon method.

Inspection Method

To locate a feature by inspection, first orient your map and determine your position. Next, lay a straightedge (or visually sight) from your map position toward the unknown ground position. Plot this sight line on your map (**Figure 14.11A**). Now move to a second known position, resight the distant feature, and plot this second sight line. The unknown point will be established by the intersecting foresight lines.

If only a single known point is available, you can still use the intersection method if a second point can be computed. Simply follow the above procedure in making a sighting from the known point, and then repeat the procedure from a second point which is a measured distance and direction from the first (**Figure 14.11B**). Just as before, the sight lines will intersect on the map at the desired ground position.

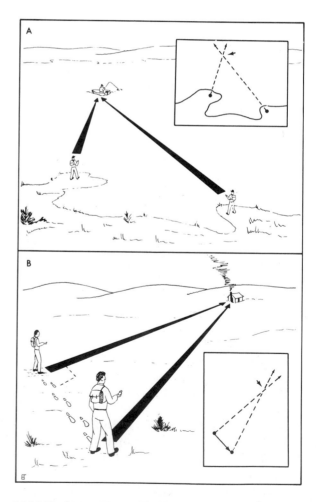

14.11 The intersection method is commonly used to determine the location of a distant point.

Two fixed positions can also be used to determine location of a distant point. Fire towers often serve this purpose. The effect is the same as in the previous examples, except that in the fixed-position case one station must communicate its direction-line information (as measured from the map with a protractor) to the other station to complete the fix.

Compass Method

If a map and compass are both available, you may determine the location of a distant feature by locating your map position, sighting on the unknown location, and recording the direction-line reading (angle). Next, move to a second known position, resight the unknown feature, and record the reading of this second foresight. Now plot the two foresights through their respective map features. The point at which they intersect is the map location of the distant feature. The compass method of intersection can also be used when you're working from two fixed positions or from a fixed position and a computed position. The procedure is similar to the intersection method discussed above.

Radiobeacon Method

Traditional inspection and compass methods for locating distant points have taken an exciting turn in recent years with the help of mobile radio transmitters. Transmitting units as small as a person's fingernail are available. They have been attached to animals (biotelemetry study of bears, sea turtles, salmon, etc.), children, and paroled criminals. Crash-activated units have also been placed in airplanes, greatly assisting search and rescue missions. Whatever the transmitter placement, the location of the tagged feature in reference to the position of the radio direction finder can be determined at any time. More sophisticated units can give both direction and distance readouts.

Satellite positioning technology may provide the ultimate means of locating distant points. As a test of this potential, their use in future crash-avoidance systems for ships and airplanes is under study. If all vehicles carried a GPS receiver as well as a transmitter that sent out positioning signals, the position of all nearby vehicles could be known at all times. By automating the system, a warning could be given as vehicles got within a certain critical distance of each other. Corrective steering instructions for collision avoidance could also be given, either to the human or instrumental operator of the craft.

ROUTE-FINDING MAPS

Once you've learned to determine your position and that of distant features, you're ready to determine how best to get from one known location to another. But before we discuss these methods, it is important to consider the types of special maps and charts* available to assist us in navigation. How we get through our environment will vary depending on what type of map we have at hand and what information it gives us.

With a wide selection of maps available for navigation, your task is to choose the one(s) best suited to your needs. Map aids to route finding can be grouped into those designed for land, open water, and air travel.

Land Navigation

Land travel is often restricted to definite routes such as trails, roads, or railroads. In such cases, travelers are concerned primarily with their route network; they don't much care about the environment as a whole, or about absolute directional relationships. Maps for such travelers can be greatly simplified, therefore, especially if an obvious origin, route, and destination exist.

Making a simple, schematic map which focuses on a particular route isn't a new idea. The Romans schematized their route maps, called **Peutinger tables**, by ignoring directional relationships and concentrating instead on showing the route network and route-side facilities for the traveler.

The distortion of spatial relations in schematic mapping which began with the

---

*By convention, maps used for a special navigational purpose, especially by ship and airplane pilots, are called **charts**.*

296

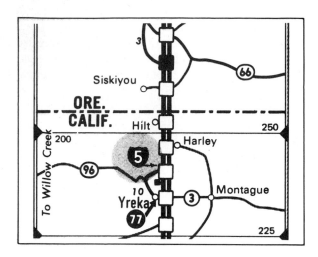

14.12 Modern route maps published by bus lines, railroads, and airlines are often more schematic than planimetrically accurate.

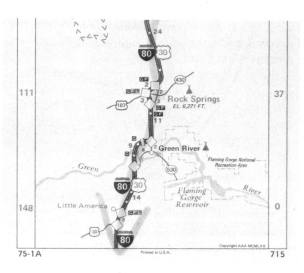

14.13 The American Automobile Association has popularized a type of route map called a Triptik.

Romans has been carried a step further in recent times. Often there is a concerted attempt to mislead the map user. For example, the scale and direction relationships on 19th-century railroad maps were often carefully arranged to create a favorable impression of the company's service in a region. The following commentary from the *Inland Printer* shows how far this practice of planned distortion went:

"This won't do," said the General Passenger Agent, in annoyed tones, to the mapmaker. "I want Chicago moved down here half an inch, so as to come on our direct route to New York. Then take Buffalo and put it a little farther from the lake.

"You've got Detroit and New York on different latitudes, and the impression that that is correct won't help our road.

"And, man, take those two lines that compete with us and make 'em twice as crooked as that. Why, you've got one of 'em almost straight.

"Yank Boston over a little to the west and put New York a little to the west, so as to show passengers that our Buffalo division is the shortest route to Boston.

"When you've done all these things I've said, you may print 10,000 copies—but say, how long have you been in the railroad business, anyway?"

(New York Herald)

The practice of deliberate map distortion continues today, especially in the form of rapid transit, bus, and airline maps. See **Figure 14.12**.

A similar type of simplified route map is the modern "wilderness" hiking or canoeing guide. Again, in an effort to make the maps as simple and uncluttered as possible, only the route network and prominent surrounding landmarks are depicted. On these maps, however, an attempt is made to retain correct directional relations. Such maps are well designed for the amateur outdoorsperson but are generally inadequate for sophisticated map users. Furthermore, there is a danger that some unplanned event such as a damaged canoe will force the user to engage in another mode of transportation for which the map is totally unsuited. The main problem with these simplified route maps, then, is that they aren't flexible. They keep you tied to your route.

You will have more flexibility if you use general-purpose maps on which a route has been marked. One such map, put out by the American Automobile Association, is called a **Triptik** (**Figure 14.13**). The Triptik contains a planned route which you can follow, but in the event of an emergency it also includes a complete base map of the region neighboring the route. A major deviation from your planned route is required to thrust you into "unmapped territory."

The standard road map provides a still more general picture for route finding, since its

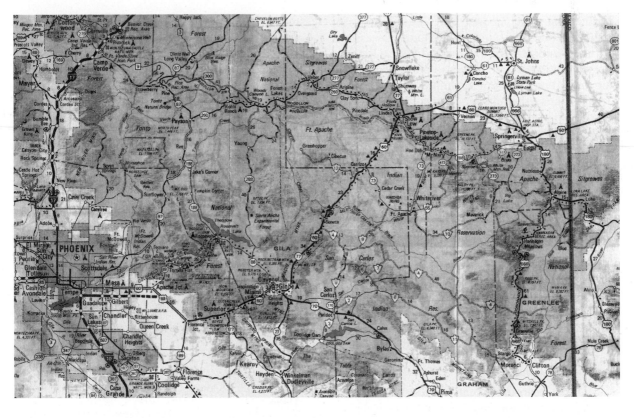

14.14 Road maps usually show a variety of information in addition to highways, making them useful for general reference purposes as well as for navigational assistance.

coverage is defined by state, region, or country (**Figure 14.14**). A variety of information is available to the traveler, including possible alternate routes such as railroads and river systems. Map information selected for the purposes of highway travel doesn't paint a complete picture of the country, of course. The traveler concerned with environmental details falling much beyond the shoulder of the road will likely find road maps inadequate.

Travelers who want more detail on their maps will probably find general-reference maps the most helpful. Several series of maps which provide widespread coverage of the United States are published by the U.S. Geological Survey (USGS) in quadrangle format. These maps make an excellent guide for all but the most sophisticated route finder. They show topography, vegetation, railroads, streams, and many other features which aid local travel (see Figure 5.21). Since maps are available at scales of 1:24,000, 1:62,500, 1:100,000, 1:250,000, 1:500,000 (state oriented),

and 1:1,000,000 (state maps), most travel requirements can be satisfied. Those who want to see even more detail along their route may wish to turn to orthophotomaps and orthophotoquads (refer to Figures 4.15 and 4.17). If these maps still don't show enough detail, the navigator can consult large-scale aerial photographs (see Figures 4.6 and 4.7).

Water Navigation

Nautical charts are published primarily for the mariner, although they serve the public interest in many other ways. They are designed to give all available information necessary for safe marine navigation, including soundings (bathymetric contours), obstructions and hazards, prominent landmarks near shore, and navigational aids such as buoys and lighthouses (**Figure 14.15**).

The scales of nautical charts published for the coastal waters of the United States by the National Ocean Survey range from 1:2,500 to about 1:500,000. Coverage includes the Atlantic,

298

Pacific, and Gulf coasts, and coastal areas of Alaska, Hawaii, and the United States possessions (Virgin Islands, Guam, Samoa, and Puerto Rico).

Hydrographic charts are also published for certain inland waters. For example, charts for the Great Lakes, the upper Hudson River, Lake Champlain, the New York Barge Canals, and part of the Minnesota-Ontario border lakes are issued at various scales and are designed primarily for navigational use. Most of these charts show the hydrography of water areas, together with the topography of limited areas of adjacent shores and islands, including docks, structures, and landmarks visible from the lakes and channels.

Charts designed for flood control, navigation, and recreation on the Mississippi River and connected waters are also published at several scales. The U.S. Army Corps of Engineers is the primary source of these useful charts. In addition, state agencies such as the Department of Natural Resources usually produce hydrographic maps for inland lakes and rivers of significant size or recreational potential.

If you plan to navigate on the water, a good rule is to obtain the largest-scale chart available. This will help ensure that the most comprehen-

sive graphic summary of information pertinent to making navigational decisions is always at hand. Before you use the chart, you should carefully study the notes, symbols, and abbreviations placed near the title or next to map symbols, for they are essential for effective use of the chart. Coast and Geodetic Survey Chart No. 1 shows the symbols and abbreviations used on nautical charts and is recommended to the mariner for study (**Table 14.1**).

TABLE 14.1

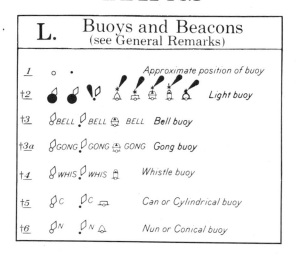

The date of the chart is of such vital importance to the marine navigator that it warrants special attention. When charted information becomes obsolete, further use of the chart for navigation may be extremely dangerous. Natural and artificial changes, many of them critical, are occurring constantly. It is essential, therefore, that navigators obtain up-to-date charts at regular intervals or hand correct their copies for changes advertised in a weekly publication entitled *Notice to Mariners*.

Air Navigation

The aeronautical charts published in the United States are specially designed for use in air navigation, and emphasis is given to features of greatest aeronautical importance (**Figure 14.16**). Every effort is made, therefore, to include the outstanding landmarks in each locality. Environmental features depicted on these charts include population centers, distinctive natural and cultural landmarks,

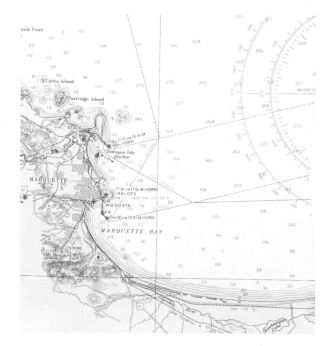

14.15 Nautical charts are designed specifically for the marine navigator.

14.16 Maps designed especially for air navigation are called aeronautical charts.

TABLE 14.2

AERONAUTICAL SYMBOLS
AERODROMES

railroads, and principal roads. Topographic information is shown by spot elevations, contours, and layer tints. Aeronautical information is overprinted in magenta-colored symbols and includes pertinent data such as aerodromes, visual and radio aids to navigation, controlled airspace, restricted areas, and obstructions (**Table 14.2**). The charts are available without the magenta-colored aeronautical data overprint so that they may be used for purposes other than air navigation.

As with nautical charts, once information on an aeronautical chart has become obsolete its further use for navigational purposes becomes a definite hazard. One of the most important things on any chart is its date. On aeronautical charts, the date is usually given in large red type in the lower right margin.

ROUTE-FINDING TECHNIQUES

Path-finding activity is really an extension of simple position finding. But, instead of determining isolated positions, the path finder is concerned with the sequence of positions that define a route. Moving effectively through the environ-

ment is aided by special maps and charts, as we saw in the previous section. But it also requires mastery of some special navigational skills. Actually, there are several methods of route finding, or navigation.

The first is **piloting**. With this method, you find your way by making direct reference to your surroundings. With the second technique, called **dead reckoning**, you use distance and direction logs, paying no direct attention to environmental features. In practice, however, it is often difficult to tell which of these two techniques is being used. For one thing, there are many variations on each procedure, some involving sophisticated instruments and aids to route finding. Also, piloting and dead-reckoning methods are freely mixed in the "anything goes" route-finding experience.

Whatever combination of techniques you use, route finding entails two basic activities. First you need to plan the route. This usually involves map reading, analysis, and interpretation. The importance of this step is made clear by John Steinbeck in *Travels With Charlie* (pp. 128-9):

> In the early morning I had studied maps, drawn a careful line along the way I wished to go. I still have that arrogant plan—into St. Paul on Highway 10, then gently across the Mississippi....That seems simple enough, and perhaps it can be done, but not by me.
>
> First the traffic struck me like a tidal wave and carried me along, a bit of shiny flotsam....As usual I panicked and got lost.

300

Good pre-trip planning allows for contingencies such as heavy traffic or possible detours. Ideally, it will include alternate routes that could be taken if necessary.

After you have planned your trip, you must maintain your route in the field. This second stage involves the navigational problems of ascertaining your present position, determining the direction which will carry you to your destination, and estimating the time of arrival. We will see how both the planning and execution steps can be carried out for piloting and then for dead reckoning.

Piloting

Piloting is the simplest, most common form of route finding. With this method, you use environmental cues to determine your current position. On the basis of this environmental information, you determine the direction and distance that you must travel to reach your destination. The piloting technique is essentially similar whether you are on land, on water, or in the air. Piloting is somewhat more involved if you are on the water or in the air, however, since depth of water and altitude above the land, respectively, then become important considerations.

Planning for Piloting

When you use the method of piloting, you plan your route so that you can follow prominent **navigational marks** (landmarks, skymarks, or seamarks). The variety of suitable reference features is limited on one hand by your powers of observation and knowledge of the surrounding environment, and on the other hand by your map. Your map may possess so little detail that it isn't of much value in piloting. In addition, your surroundings may be so homogeneous that it is hard to find satisfactory landmarks. Yet even in homogeneous areas, there are usually more useful environmental cues than we realize.

To be successful at piloting, you must be observant—and you needn't restrict yourself to what you can see. Tactual, acoustic, and olfactory cues may serve as important aids to piloting under special circumstances. Radio signals have long been the cue of choice in piloting ships and airplanes, and are fast becoming practical in ground vehicles. The recent appearance of inexpensive hand-held receiving units suggests the

foot traveler may soon be using electronic signals for piloting as well.

Computer Aids to Piloting Planning. Those with access to a personal computer can prepare for piloting with the help of special route-finding software. We discussed the map look-up capability of these programs in Chapter 9: *Software for Map Retrieval.* At that time, we mentioned the routing aspect of the software. It is now appropriate to look at this useful function more closely.

Route-finding software gives you a number of options. If you provide an origin and destination city, for example, it can tell you the shortest distance, least time, or most scenic route. If you specify stop-over points en route, the software will direct you through these points as well. You have the choice of seeing your route marked on a map, or seeing an itinerary giving all pertinent route identification and distance data for each route segment (see Figures 19.2 and 19.3). Both map and itinerary can be printed.

Traditional Piloting Planning. Not everyone has access to a route-planning computer, of course. Furthermore, current software is restricted to established routes, such as city streets and primary rural roads. If you're in a non-computer mode or planning a cross-country trek, you'll have to do your route planning by hand, the old-fashioned way. This can be more fun than staring at a map on a coarse-resolution computer screen, however. It is also effective, particularly if you take reasonable care.

You must be especially alert when piloting in wilderness areas or regions of sparse human settlement. Here, most of your route-finding cues will be provided by natural landmarks such as mountain peaks, rivers, lakes, and prominent vegetation features. Familiar skymarks such as the sun and the North Star may also prove useful.

Not all your piloting cues will be natural, though, even in wilderness regions; few parts of this country are so remote that the impact of human occupance is nonexistent. The sound of logging equipment, a train whistle, or the smell of woodsmoke have provided many people with desperately needed piloting aids.

Rural and urban areas provide different piloting marks than wilderness regions. In settled rural areas, the primary aids to piloting will be human features of the landscape, such as water towers, railroad tracks, smokestacks, or buildings, while natural features will play a secondary role. Marked or labeled features, such as roads, rivers, mountains, and towns, are also important in rural piloting. In urban areas, piloting is dominated by labeled features. Streets are named, buildings are numbered, and signs direct you to significant natural and cultural features.

Some people rely on special aids to piloting. Such aids as buoys and beacons are used by amateur plane and boat pilots as well as by hikers, fishers, etc. Other aids, such as radio transmitters and satellites, require training and sophisticated equipment and therefore are used more exclusively by trained professionals. Radio signals are invaluable for ship pilots close to shore, especially in fog, and plane pilots find radio beams a useful supplement to contact flying.

Electronic navigation differs from usual piloting procedures only in the methods of obtaining the position information. No matter what special equipment is used, the idea behind piloting remains the same—to use clues from the environment around you to keep on your planned course.

When planning a trip through a familiar environment, you may only need to think over the route and reflect on the landmarks that will provide piloting cues. If some part of your desired course seems obscure, clarify it before you leave, either by looking at maps or talking to someone who knows the area.

Your planning will be greatly simplified, of course, if you decide to follow a well-defined path, such as a road, since then you will merely have to work out the topology of your course and augment this information with sufficient navigational marks so that you will be prepared to make turns without confusion. Useful navigational marks will depend largely on the time (day or night) and method of travel, and on the aids to your normal senses that you have available (optical, celestial instruments, radio transmitter-receivers, and so forth).

When landmarks are scarce, you may have to stop to ask someone for distance and direction information. You may be told, for instance, to "go south about five miles and take a northeasterly heading across the ridge, and then keep going till you come to a stream." You might think of this as the "buried treasure" method of piloting, since it

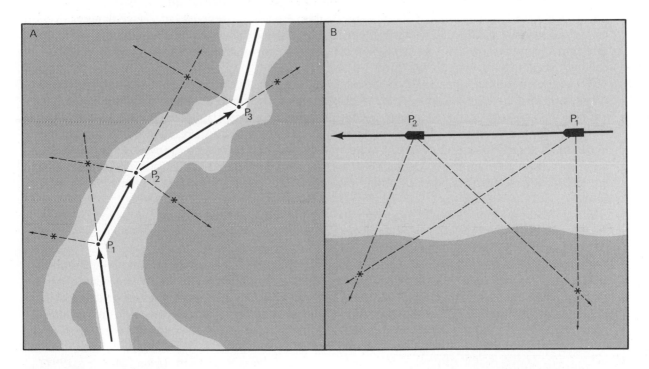

14.17 Piloting a ship through a narrow channel may require a number of precise direction or distance measurements.

302

provides the basis for locating the chest of priceless coins in many stories. If you suspect that it may be necessary to make simple direction and distance measurements from known and observable features, you should make proper preparations, such as to carry a compass, pedometer, and rangefinder.

Sometimes in the course of piloting you may find it useful to compute your position with respect to navigational marks. Suppose, for instance, that on a boating trip it is crucial that you maintain a specified distance from shore to avoid an underwater obstruction. In this case, as part of your pre-trip planning, you should make the computations required to fix a safe course (**Figure 14.17**) and then take this heading information into the field in a convenient form. This procedure can save you a lot of time and hassle when occupied with the pressure of navigating.

Indeed, regardless of your travel situation, it is advisable to make up a course log prior to departure. You may simply do this mentally, but it is often a good idea to write out a series of directions, sketch a map of your route, or mark your course on an existing map. Marking a course on an existing map is the best method, because you will have the information needed to reorient yourself if you happen to stray from your planned course. This may happen inadvertently, or it may be forced upon you by a detour of some sort.

Piloting a Course

Most human spatial behavior takes place in familiar settings. Much of the time, therefore, you will be traveling through regions for which your cognitive map is well developed. In such situations, piloting may be so effortless that it becomes unconscious. Your daily travel routine is likely to be of this nature. Features in your surroundings are so familiar that you can move freely with merely your mental map and natural senses. You probably don't even realize that you are execut-

BOX 14.1 LOST IN THE FOG

Despite justifiable worries about close calls in the sky, the collision of two Northwest airliners at Detroit's Metro Airport last week suggests that airplane passengers face grave dangers even on the ground. The accident, in which eight people were killed and 24 injured, raised a life-and-death question: If runways are so foggy that a pilot can miss two turns and wind up in the path of a plane rolling toward takeoff, why is the airport still open?

Landings had been banned at Metro because of the fog, but takeoffs were allowed to continue because visibility on the runways was declared to be above the required quarter-mile minimum. Captain William Lovelace, making only his 13th flight after a five year absence (he had left to get treatment for a kidney-stone ailment and later opened a gift shop) apparently became disoriented in the murk shortly after pulling his DC-9 away from the gate. According to investigators, he made a left turn onto a wrong taxiway, then failed to turn right onto a second taxiway that would have led him back to his assigned takeoff point. His delayed right turn placed him on the active takeoff runway....

Northwest Flight 299, a 727 carrying 153 people, had just been cleared for takeoff, and was already roaring toward the DC-9. Unable to get above the lost aircraft, pilot Robert Ouellette felt his right wing rip into the DC-9's cabin and tear off one of its tail engines....

Compared with collision-avoidance safeguards in the air, those on the ground are primitive. Only 12 U.S. airports have ground radar (Detroit does not), but it is unreliable, 1960s-vintage equipment. A more modern radar is being tested in Pittsburgh, but technical bugs have delayed its deployment at other airports. A network of stop-and-go-signal lights at taxiway and runway intersections has been tried at New York City's Kennedy Airport, but it was discontinued when its slowness contributed to delays....

(Ed Magnuson, *Time*, January 7, 1991)

ing piloting procedures. Yet you are constantly referring to a host of environmental cues.

Sometimes a familiar setting can become functionally unfamiliar. Normal vision may be obscured by fog, snow, or darkness (see **Box 14.1**). When you are unable to see landmarks, non-visual sense information becomes especially important in piloting. Occasionally, all sensual cues are lost (although this will happen less often in the future as more people rely on electronic positioning methods). When it does happen—in blizzards, for instance, or in "socked-in" mountains or high-altitude "white-outs"—piloting is impossible. Any movement under these conditions is hazardous. Many people who die by falling off cliffs or freezing to death in winter storms do so because they lost their familiar piloting cues and panicked.

Not all your piloting takes place in familiar settings, of course. You often want to establish a route through an unfamiliar region. You can do so in several ways.

Vehicle Piloting Systems. For several decades, navigators of ships and airplanes have relied on electronic piloting devices to maintain a course. The same technology discussed earlier in *Electronic Positioning* is used in navigating between points. Revolutionary recent developments link maps to the radio signals. Thus, you can navigate a ground vehicle by observing your progress along a path on a map and then making route decisions on the ground. Although several approaches are being used, in each case your changing ground position is plotted with a cursor on a map display, much as was done years ago in the prophetic James Bond movie *Goldfinger.*

With one type of system, called inertial navigation, the device monitors vehicle movements and uses this information to update the position of a "you-are-here" cursor on a map display.* You must initialize the system by properly positioning the cursor on the map at the start of your route (see *Self-Contained Systems* earlier in this chap-

....
This is actually a hybrid system, since dead-reckoning technology is used to generate positional information, which is then used to update the cursor location on the map display. (See Dead Reckoning *later in this chapter.)*

ter). Each distance and direction computation also involves some error. Since each subsequent computation is based on the previous one, errors accumulate, and the estimated position tends to "drift."

With primitive systems, the map backdrop may be a simple screen overlay. But more advanced technology uses digital cartographic data held in some form of disk storage (see *Inertial Positioning Systems* in Appendix D). An inertial navigation add-on option may someday be as popular for automobiles as air conditioning and automatic transmissions.

A second type of navigation aid, and one that seems to hold the most promise, is based on radionavigation technology (see *Signal-Dependent Systems* earlier in this chapter). Radionavigation has several advantages over inertial navigation. For one thing, radionavigation can provide an initial position fix, as well as subsequent fixes. More important, each new position determination along a route is computed independently of previous ones. Thus, errors don't accumulate as they do with inertial navigation.

Although ground-based radiobeacons are in widespread use at present, GPS-linked navigators are attracting the most attention (see Chapter 15: *GPS and Maps*). One reason is that they provide spatial coordinates which can be used to retrieve the appropriate map from disk storage. When the vehicle moves off the edge of one map, the next one in the direction of travel is automatically brought up on the display screen.

Potential applications of GPS technology in route finding stagger the imagination. Navigational procedures will soon be transformed into something hardly recognizable today. All the major automobile companies are experimenting with GPS-based dashboard navigator units for their automobiles. (For an idea of the type of experimenting that's taking place, see **Box 14.2**). Many trucking, busing, delivery, and taxi companies are already using the technology. Hand-held GPS receivers weighing as little as nine ounces are available from several vendors for less than $200. Actual manufacturing cost is probably less than half that figure. It seems certain that sometime within the decade, we will have wristwatch-sized consumer products capable of giving route-finding information upon request.

304

Traditional Piloting Procedures. We can't navigate on tomorrow's promises, however. Since vehicle navigation devices are in the development phase, it is difficult to predict which technology will ultimately succeed, and which experiments will be abandoned. Current systems are expensive and limited to places for which electronic maps have been produced in the appropriate format. Furthermore, there is still no electronic system available for the non-vehicular, cross-country traveler. For these reasons, there is still a need to pilot a course by traditional methods.

One thing you'll realize is that an off-the-shelf map isn't complete until you've personalized it. By doing so, you bring it into line with your mental map and make it more pertinent to your needs. Use magic markers to emphasize roads or other features which are meaningful to you, and if you know of any landmarks that aren't on the map, draw them in. Since most maps are made by government agencies, they can't include landmarks such as McDonald's or the First Federal Bank building, because that would be advertising. Yet those landmarks are precisely what people use when they give directions. Therefore, any extra information you can add to your map will make piloting easier.

Once you have an appropriate map, use it to keep yourself oriented at all times. Don't make the mistake of thinking that with a map in the glove compartment of your car or the pocket of your backpack you can't get lost. John Steinbeck (p. 82) has summed up the problem:

> I pulled to the side of the street and got out my book of road maps. But to find where you are going, you must know where you are, and I didn't.

If you wait till you're lost, your map isn't of much use. Stop often, therefore, and orient yourself with your map. Frequent orientation stops

---

BOX 14.2 HOW TO GET THERE? LET CAR COMPUTER DECIDE

Orlando, Fla. (AP) — "Smart cars" designed by General Motors Corp. can steer drivers away from clogged roads, but a GM executive discovered to his chagrin on Tuesday that they can't avoid every obstacle.

GM Vice President Robert Frosch climbed into one of 100 Oldsmobile Toronados fitted with computers, video screens and other equipment that monitor highway conditions and plot the most efficient course to a given destination.

Moments later, Frosch ran over an orange traffic cone inadvertently left in front of the car.

"I believe it has been crushed," Frosch said.

But Frosch eventually made it to downtown Orlando in fine time, following directions dictated by a Swedish-sounding computer voice nicknamed "Sven" by GM engineers.

The cone-crushing was the only gaffe in the day's formal unveiling of GM's travel technology, or "TravTek." The plan is to put all 100 cars on central Florida roads for one year....

Avis Rent-a-Car System Inc. will lease 75 of the vehicles. The rest will be rented to local drivers.

The road test involves 1,200 square miles, 75,000 intersections, and 10,000 miles of roads in central Florida. Drivers punch in a street address or the name of a local destination. The computer then displays the best route on a six-inch video screen, using information from NASA's Global Positioning Satellites, electronic road sensors and video cameras along Interstate 4.

If traffic jams or a road blockage appears, the computer maps a new route. Throughout the journey, the computer's synthesized voice gently reminds the driver where the car is and ought to be.

Tourism officials are happy about another feature: When the car is in park, drivers can browse through a computerized list of local hotels, attractions and city landmarks.

Frosch predicted it would be six to eight years before smart cars will be in widespread use.

(Associated Press, March 25, 1992)

will guarantee that you are never too far from a known position, and this is the most comforting information to have when traversing unknown country.

The trouble is that suitable maps aren't always available. To be sure, most maps are too small in scale (and thus lacking in detail) to be of much use when piloting locally. When you don't have any appropriate maps, it is natural to ask directions from someone whose mental map is more complete than yours. Doing so, of course, places you at the mercy of the other person's environmental image, which may or may not be better than your own. You rarely know how much confidence you should place in these directions. If you get turned around again, therefore, you should obtain a second or third opinion without delay. Don't wander blindly in hope that you will get lucky and find your way.

Sometimes the person to whom you go for information will be helpful enough to draw you a map. The problem with such crude sketch maps is that the obvious is generally assumed and therefore not indicated. In addition, it is natural for people to perceive their environment in functional rather than absolute terms. Consequently, directions obtained from people who live in the area may bear little resemblance to objective reality. Steinbeck again pinpoints the problem (p. 49):

> I had been given written directions on how to go, detailed directions, but have you ever noticed that instructions from one who knows the country gets you more lost than you are, even when they are accurate?

It makes sense, then, to be wary of directions given by a stranger. That doesn't mean that you should hesitate to ask for directions, however. Good navigators realize that it's often the only way to get the information they need.

The piloting technique can be successful only if you are able to see (or otherwise sense) features which are familiar or are identified on the map. But what if you lack electronic navigation gear, and no prominent environmental features are available? For instance, what if you are on a flat, featureless plain or water body or in a heavily forested region where no landmarks stand out? In these and similar situations, you need an alternative to piloting.

Dead Reckoning

If you have no useful piloting cues, it is best to abandon piloting techniques and rely instead on dead reckoning. This second form of navigation is self-contained in the sense that direct contact with the environment isn't needed. Rather than make reference to environmental cues as you progress along your route, you keep track of distance and direction traveled from your starting point. To determine your position, you must know either the direction and distance you've traveled or the direction, speed, and time that has elapsed since you started out.

Unfortunately, you can't determine the direction and distance traveled along a route segment without some error. These errors accumulate as you traverse subsequent route segments. Thus, dead reckoning usually isn't as accurate as piloting. When piloting is unreliable or impossible to use, however, you may need to resort to dead reckoning.

Planning for Dead Reckoning

When you use the method of dead reckoning, you plan your trip by constructing a plot of the desired course. Although you can do this mentally, it's better to do it directly on a map or map overlay. The plotting task consists simply of laying out the proper course line. This is rarely a single line but rather a series of segments or "legs" separated by change-of-direction points (**Figure 14.18**). The first point in the course line is the point of beginning (POB) or origin of the planned route, while the last point in the course line is the point of destination.

Once you've constructed the course line, the next step is to determine the length and direction of each leg.* It's important to remember that your duties as navigator will be so important and exacting that you shouldn't be burdened by work which could be handled during course planning. For instance, if nautical miles will be used during navigation, you create extra work for yourself if you plot the lengths of course legs in statute miles. Likewise, although it may be most conve-

---

Inertial navigation systems simplify this step by making it possible to enter only the beginning and ending coordinates of route segments. Segment distances and directions can then be computed automatically.

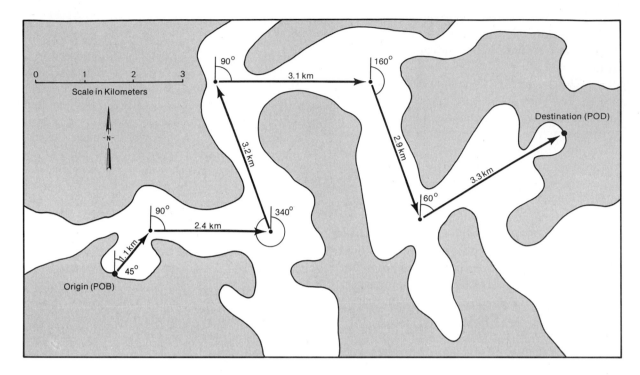

14.18 A dead-reckoned course is made up of a series of straight legs and is defined by the collective length and direction of these legs.

nient to determine angular relations of course segments in terms of relative direction, when you're in the field you'll probably find it simplest to make absolute direction readings. Your planning for dead reckoning should take such considerations into account.

In planning a course, your knowledge of standard distance-direction relations may not be enough. To provide a functional measure of distance and direction, you must also consider forces such as tides, currents, winds, and magnetic deviation. You should incorporate known and constant forces as modifications directly into your planned dead-reckoning course (**Figure 14.19**). You will have to cope with other forces when you execute the planned course.

Time is an important aspect of dead reckoning. You can use your travel-speed and course-length information to compute your estimated passage (or transit) time. Data from the legs in the dead-reckoned course shown in Figure 14.18 are provided in **Table 14.3**. When working from a

fixed departure time, you can use this information to compute your estimated time of arrival (ETA). Or, working from a fixed destination time, you can use the same information to compute your required departure time.

TABLE 14.3

Transit Time for Dead Reckoned Course

Leg	Length	Speed	Time
A	1.1 km.	12 km./hr.	5.5 min.
B	2.4 km.	20 km./hr.	7.2 min.
C	3.2 km.	18 km./hr.	10.7 min.
D	3.1 km.	20 km./hr.	9.3 min.
E	2.9 km.	16 km./hr.	10.9 min.
F	3.3 km.	10 km./hr.	19.8 min.
Total	16.0 km.		63.4 min.

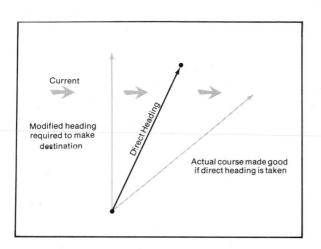

14.19 You should incorporate known and constant environmental forces into your course planning.

Executing a Dead-Reckoned Course

Dead reckoning in the field consists of taking and recording distance and direction data and then

constructing a dead-reckoned plot which you can compare with your planned course. The procedure is similar regardless of whether you use automatic dead-reckoning equipment or strictly manual methods.

Inertial Navigation. For years, ships and airplanes have navigated the earth using dead reckoning assisted by electronic technology (see *Inertial Positioning Systems* in Appendix D). Electronic methods have proven reliable, as transoceanic airline traffic attests. But, as you can see in **Box 14.3**, they are by no means foolproof.

The future of "pure" inertial navigation for ground vehicles isn't promising. It is difficult to imagine someone in a vehicle willingly driving without paying any attention to the outside landscape. Devices that use inertial technology to update your position on a map display, so that you can make route corrections, seem to have far more promise (see *Vehicle Piloting Systems* earlier in this chapter). A portable device for cross-country foot travelers also seems unlikely.

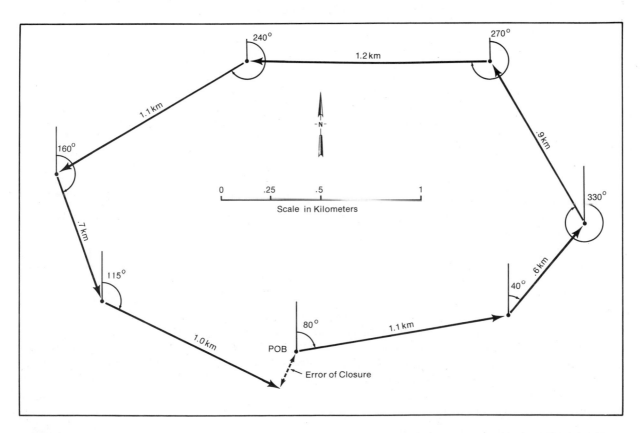

14.20 Executing and plotting a closed traverse is a good way to test your dead-reckoning skills. The error of closure provides a measure of the quality of your work.

308

Manual Dead-Reckoning Procedures. If you aren't able to use an inertial navigation system, you are left to do your path-finding the old fashioned way. Don't despair: People have survived the hazards of dead reckoning for centuries.

The first step is to establish your origin position. From this fix, you draw a course line, usually as a series of straight-line segments, using the compass rose to determine direction and the chart scale to figure distance. You then separate the successive legs of the course line by dead-reckoned, or predicted, positions. In the field, you will determine these dead-reckoned (DR) positions solely on the basis of the distance (speed x

elapsed time) and direction you have traveled from your previously determined position. Thus, you must keep a careful log of this information up to date at all times.

A major problem with dead reckoning is that a number of forces can cause a discrepancy between predicted (DR) and actual position. In addition to the forces mentioned previously (tides, currents, winds), course deviations can be caused by a host of other factors, such as steering error, variations in engine speed, or unexpected obstructions. To maintain your desired course line, you must make heading corrections as you go along. This may entail correcting your next

BOX 14.3 EXPLAINING THE INEXPLICABLE

How could KAL Flight 007 stray so far off its proper course? The Boeing 747 was equipped with three Inertial Navigation Systems (INS), designed to keep the jet on its scheduled flight path and to back one another up in case of malfunctions. Their performance record is excellent: a new study shows that only about one flight in 10,000 strays 50 or more miles off course. In 90% of the cases the deviation is attributed to pilot error. The INS computers are programmed by the crew at the start of the flight. The computers are fed the plane's latitude and longitude at takeoff and the coordinates of way points along the plane's scheduled route. On Flight 007, for example, the computers, made by Litton Industries at $100,000 apiece, were told that the plane should be at its fifth way point, Neeva, above the Aleutian Islands at 172°11 min. east and 54°40 min. north, after the first 900 miles of the trip. Using gyroscopes and acceleration meters, the INS keeps track of the plane's location and guides it along the preprogrammed course.

The initial information fed into the Korean airliner's INS computers at Anchorage, where the flight had refueled, was correct. Flight 007 hit its first five way points as planned. But after Neeva, Flight 007 apparently began to stray.

One possible explanation is that the crew fed the INS computers some erroneous information while aloft. The INS can store only nine sets of coordinates; there were twelve way points along Flight 007's route to Seoul, which means that new sets of latitudes and longitudes had to be plugged in sometime during the trip. The co-pilot, who on Korean Air Lines flights is usually responsible for entering navigational data, might have done so after Neeva. Although each INS is supposed to be programmed separately, in practice the numbers are often put in simultaneously. The co-pilot (or other crew member) on Flight 007 could have simply misread the coordinates from his chart when he punched them into the computer. It is standard procedure for the other crew members to double-check these navigational entries. But airmen have been known to skip this precautionary step.

Another possible explanation for straying off course: a crew member might have used the INS to find out the distance and time remaining to 007's final destination; if he had left the coordinates for Seoul on the screen, and pressed the "insert" button rather than the "clear" button on the electronic console, the plane would have made a beeline for the South Korean capital instead of looping south away from Soviet territory and out of harm's way. In fact, the plane appeared to head straight for Seoul after passing Neeva.

(*Time*, September 19, 1983)

heading to take into consideration forces operating during the previous leg. Or it may involve modifying your next heading to account for forces that will be operating at that time. (See Figure 14.19.)

When the operating forces aren't relatively constant and known, there may be no way to decide what corrections must be made. Thus, the resulting dead-reckoned plot may be of little value. This problem occurs, for example, when people try to maintain a straight course without the benefit of external aids. Over and over, it has been proven that people have an unerring tendency to walk in circles. If we knew what was making us circle, we could compensate for that factor. But since no one has ever been able to explain why we walk in a curved path, there's no way (except with a compass or other external aid) for us to maintain a straight-line course and no way to prepare an accurate dead-reckoned plot.

If you're interested in checking your ability to maintain a course by dead reckoning, you might try to set up and execute what is known as a **closed traverse**. The idea is to follow a course which will take you back to your point of beginning (**Figure 14.20**). Rarely will your start and finish coincide! The gap between them, known as **closing error** or **error of closure,** can never be completely eliminated.

Dead reckoning is generally a graphic means of navigation. In other words, you can see your whole route at once, plotted neatly on a map. The dead-reckoned plot is usually labeled with course-leg direction and distance (or time and speed when they are used to compute distance), the time of departure from the original fix, and the time at which subsequent DR positions are obtained.

You should update the plot as often as necessary to provide for safe navigation. This will depend upon the circumstances and proximity of danger. The plot itself will help you to revise your time-of-arrival estimate.

Ideally, you should check your progress after each course leg. To do so, you must look for navigational marks in your surroundings, which means that you are no longer practicing true dead reckoning but are bringing in piloting techniques. Such mixing of techniques is usually the best strategy and is the essence of practical navigation.

PRACTICAL NAVIGATION

In practice, the navigator's basic rule is that "anything goes." The experienced route finder brings into play simultaneously whatever procedures a situation warrants. Piloting is usually the preferred technique, especially when radio and celestial techniques are brought to bear on the problem.

When dead reckoning is the primary technique you are using, you may still correct headings with piloting information, particularly with radio and celestial procedures. You should always be prepared to switch modes of navigation if problems occur with the method you are using. It is also helpful to check your progress using an entirely different approach to the navigational problem at hand. The more navigational tricks you learn, the easier it will be to improvise in field situations. The key to route finding is the ability to cope with the unfamiliar and the unforeseen.

SELECTED READINGS

Baker, R.R., *Human Navigation and the Sixth Sense* (New York: Simon & Schuster, 1981).

Blandford, P.W., *Maps & Compasses*, 2nd ed. (Blue Ridge Summit, PA: TAB Books, A Division of McGraw-Hill, 1992).

Geary, D., *Using a Map & Compass* (Mechanicsburg, PA: Stackpole Books, 1995).

Hodgson, M.., *Compass & Map Navigator* (Riverton, WY: The Brunton Company, 1997).

Jacobson, C., *The Basic Essentials of Map & Compass*, 2nd ed. (Merrillville, IN: ICS Books, Inc., 1997).

Kjellstrom, B., *Be Expert With Map & Compass: The Complete Orienteering Handbook*, revised ed. (New York: Macmillan General Reference, a Simon & Schuster Macmillan Company, 1994).

Langley, R.B., "The Federal Radionavigation Plan," *GPS World*, 3, 2 (March 1992), pp. 50-53.

Larkin, F.J., *Basic Coastal Navigation: An Introduction to Piloting* (Dobbs Ferry, NY: Sheridan House, 1993).

Randall, G., *The Outward Bound Map & Compass Handbook* (NY: Lyons & Burford, Publishers, 1989).

Seidman, D., *The Essential Wilderness Navigator* (Camden, ME: Ragged Mountain Press, 1995).

Time-Life Books, *Navigation* (Chicago: Time-Life Books, 1975).

United States Army, *Map Reading, Field Manual*, FM 21-26 (Washington, DC: Department of the Army, Headquarters, current ed.).

United States Army, *Map Reading*, Programmed Text 2169 (Fort Benjamin Harrison, Indiana: Adjutant General School, 1972).

Wilkes, K. (revised by P. Langley-Price and P. Ouvry), *Ocean Navigation* (London: Adlard Coles Nautical, 1994).

CHAPTER FIFTEEN

GPS AND MAPS

INTRODUCTION

GPS = COMPUTER

Interface

Tables and Equations

Datums

Grids

Declination

Celestial Extras

Databases

FIELD APPLICATIONS

Use GPS to Orient Map

Use GPS to Find Your Position

Use GPS to Find Distant Position

Use GPS to Plan Route

Use GPS to Follow Route

Where Am I Going?

Where Have I Been?

How Am I Doing?

How Do I Get Back?

GPS LIMITATIONS

Linking GPS to Maps

Paper Maps

Digital Maps

Keep a Notebook

Keep Your Compass

Warning to GPS Novices

PREPPING MAPS FOR GPS USE

Flesh Out Map Grid

Add Grid to Gridless Map

Create Range Grid

Grid-Reading Aids

Digital Database

Portable Grid

Make Your Own

Ready-Made

LOCATION-AWARE DEVICES

CONCLUSION

SELECTED READINGS

GPS will inevitably contribute to our awareness that we all share the same planet. . . .

—Noel J. Hotchkiss

The prudent mariner will not rely solely on any single aid to navigation. . . .

—Nautical Chart, *National Ocean Service*

15

CHAPTER FIFTEEN

GPS AND MAPS

This chapter focuses on how you can use a global positioning system (GPS) with maps. Technical details on how GPS works are found in Appendix D. The aim here is to address the needs of the general (non-professional) user who has a hand-held GPS receiver. Since we must be brief, we advise you to consult at least one of the guides under *Selected Readings* for this chapter. You'll also find the user's manual that comes with your GPS unit to be an essential reference. Although GPS receivers share many traits, vendors use slightly different designs and terminology. Thus, the manual will explain how to use labeled hard keys on the face of the GPS unit, how to use different key combinations and sequences to activate soft keys (items) in the display menus, and what the menu jargon and cryptic acronyms mean.

GPS = COMPUTER

Your GPS receiver has a computer as its heart. The more you pay, the more capable this computer. This means the receiver works with numbers. It makes calculations using equations and tables of data stored in memory. It takes in data from satellites through its antenna. When connected with a cable, it can communicate with other computers. It can access digital databases that hold volumes of useful information.

To take advantage of electronic technology of any sort, we must learn its specialized terminology. GPS technology is no exception. But in this case, you'll have to learn the jargon of navigation as well as technical terms needed to operate your GPS receiver. Since this combined vocabulary is a barrier to first-time GPS users, we've deciphered the cryptic code of GPS abbreviations and acronyms in **Table 15.1** and defined common GPS terms in **Table 15.2**. If you're new to GPS, take time to browse through these tables so the terms will be familiar when you encounter them later.

Interface

The interface of a hand-held GPS receiver is usually rather stark (**Figure 15.1**). You find a small (approximately 2 x 3 inch) black-and-white display screen. This screen has rather poor spatial resolution, which

312

TABLE 15.1

Guide to GPS Abbreviations & Acronyms

ALT:	Altitude (also EL)		**ODOM:**	Odometer
BRG:	Bearing (also azimuth)		**P Code:**	Protected (Precision) Code
C/A:	Coarse (Course) Acquisition Code			(military use)
	(unprotected civilian use)		**PPS:**	Precise Positioning Service
CDI:	Course Deviation Indicator		**S:**	South
CMG:	Course Made Good		**SA:**	Selective Availability
COG:	Course Over the Ground		**SOA:**	Speed of Advance or Speed of
CTS:	Course to Steer			Approach
DMG:	Distance Made Good		**SOG:**	Speed Over Ground
DOP:	Dilution of Precision		**SQ:**	Signal Quality (strength)
DST:	Distance		**SPD:**	Speed
DTG:	Distance to Go		**SPS:**	Standard Positioning Service
DTK:	Desired Track			(civilian use)
E:	East		**STM:**	Statute Miles
EL:	Elevation (also ELEV and ALT)		**STR:**	HDG - BRG
EPE:	Estimated Position Error			(Heading minus Bearing)
ETA:	Estimated Time of Arrival		**2D Fix:**	Two-Dimensional Fix
ETE:	Estimated Time En Route			(latitude-longitude)
FT:	Feet		**2D NAV:**	Two-Dimensional Navigation
GMT:	Greenwich Mean Time		**3D Fix:**	Three-Dimensional Fix
GQ:	Geometric Quality			(latitude-longitude-elevation)
GRI:	Grid		**3D NAV:**	Three-Dimensional Navigation
HDG:	Heading		**TFF:**	Time to First Fix
K:	Kilometers or Knots		**TRK:**	Track
LFX:	Last Fix		**TTG:**	Time to Go
LMK:	Landmark		**TTFF:**	Time to First Fix
M:	Meters or Magnetic		**UTC:**	Universal Time Coordinated
MAG:	Magnetic (north)		**VMG:**	Velocity Made Good
MGRS:	Military Grid Reference System		**VOG:**	Velocity Over the Ground
MOB:	Man Over Board		**W:**	West
MPH:	Miles per Hour		**WGS84:**	World Geodetic System—84
N:	North		**WPT:**	Waypoint
NAV:	Navigation		**XTE:**	Cross Track Error (also **XTK**)

explains why a typical screen display consists of only a few characters or a simple graphic. The frequent use of abbreviations and acronyms is a way to increase the amount of information displayed in a screen image.

On the receiver's face, you also find a few hard (dedicated function) buttons, including a POWER switch and four CURSOR (directional) keys. Several additional hard keys have special functions, such as ENTER, QUIT, PAGE, MARK, AND GOTO.

The **page key** lets you browse through a half dozen or so screen pages or menus. These provide access to most of the functionality of the receiver. On each screen page (**Figure 15.2**), you can cursor to a menu item, or soft key, and then activate that function by pressing ENTER. To enter an alphanumeric character, you must cursor

TABLE 15.2

Guide to GPS Terms

Acquisition: The satellite receiver's process of locating the source of the satellite signal and starting to collect data from the satellites.

Almanac Data: Satellite position information stored by the satellite receiver so that it can determine its own position.

Anywhere Fix: A fix made by a GPS receiver when you don't first initialize it (or tell it approximately where you are in terms of latitude and longitude).

Auto Mag: Adjustment that can be made to a GPS receiver so that it automatically gives magnetic courses and bearings.

Azimuth: See bearing.

Base Station: GPS receiver that's fixed over a known control point.

Bearing (BRG): The direction measured clockwise in degrees from north. This is technically the "azimuth," but most GPS receivers use the term "bearing" instead of azimuth. GPS receivers use either true north or magnetic north, whichever you select in your setup menu.

Channel: The part of the satellite receiver that tunes in on a satellite's signal and sends the information to the receiver's processor to calculate your position.

Checkpoint: Same as waypoint and landmark.

Coarse (or Course) Acquisition Code (C/A): One of two types of signals sent out by GPS satellites. The other is the Precision (P) code. The C/A code is the one sent to civilians and is not as precise as the P code used by the military.

Course: Same as courseline or track.

Course Deviation Indicator (CDI): A graphic way of showing the amount and direction of Cross Track Error (XTE or XTK) in your course.

Course Made Good (CMG): The course you have actually achieved so far.

Course Over the Ground (COG): The direction of travel achieved from your starting point to your present location.

Course to Steer (CTS): The recommended course to maximize your ability to get back on track.

Cross Track Error (XTE or XTK): The distance from your current location to your desired track (DTK).

Courseline: Your planned line of travel from departure point to destination.

Default: The setting automatically chosen by the GPS unit.

Desired Track (DTK): The course you want to travel.

Differential GPS (DGPS): A method in which a base station sends GPS signals to a rover station, thus improving the accuracy of Coarse Acquisition Codes for civilian use.

Dilution of Precision (DOP): Measurement of the accuracy of a fix on a scale of 1 to 10, with 1 the most accurate and 10 the least accurate.

Distance Made Good (DMG): Distance from your last position to your present position.

Distance to Go (DTG): The distance you have yet to travel to reach your destination.

Estimated Position Error (EPE): Estimate of the error of a fix, given in feet.

Estimated Time of Arrival (ETA): The time you should reach your destination, based on your current speed.

Estimated Time En Route (ETE): The amount of time remaining to arrive at your destination, based on your current speed.

continued...

TABLE 15.2 *continued*

Fix: A position given in latitude and longitude (for a two-dimensional fix). A three-dimensional fix gives latitude, longitude, and elevation.

Geometric Quality (GQ): Same as Dilution of Precision.

Global Positioning System (GPS): A system of 24 satellites that can be used with receivers to fix a position.

Goto Function: A function that lets you use a display screen to point the direction you want to travel while your GPS receiver guides you to your destination.

Ground Speed: The speed you're traveling over the ground (as opposed to speed through the water).

Heading (HDG): The direction in which you're moving with respect to either true or magnetic north.

Initialization: The initial act of telling your GPS receiver approximately where you are in terms of latitude and longitude.

Lock-on Time: The time between turning on your GPS receiver and receiving a good signal.

Man Over Board (MOB): A simple keystroke combination you can use to mark a spot quickly so that you can return to it.

Precise Positioning Service (PPS): The accuracy provided by Protected (P) Codes for military use.

Protected (or Precision) Code (P Code): One of two types of signals sent out by GPS satellites. The other is the Coarse Acquisition (C/A) code. The P code, which gives far more accurate fixes than the C/A code, may be used only by the military.

Rover: GPS receiver that can be moved about, in contrast to a fixed base station.

Selective Availability: Method the U.S. Department of Defense uses to deliberately make civilian GPS receivers less accurate by causing an apparent clock error.

Signal Quality (SQ): The strength of the signals from a satellite.

Speed (SPD): The speed at which you're moving with respect to the earth.

Speed of Advance (SOA): Your speed in the direction of your destination. If you're heading directly toward your destination, your SOA is the same as your ground speed. If you're not on course, your SOA is less than your ground speed. The GPS receiver shows a negative SOA as a blank line.

Speed of Approach (SOA): Same as Speed of Advance.

Speed Over Ground (SOG): Same as Ground Speed.

Standard Positioning Service: The accuracy provided by Coarse Acquisition Codes for civilian use.

Status: Estimate of the combined impact of Dilution of Precision (DOP) and Signal Quality (SQ).

Time to First Fix (TTFF or TFF): The time it takes a GPS receiver to make its first position fix after you turn it on. This is the time it takes the receiver to collect position information from every satellite.

Time to Go (TTG): Estimate of the time from your current location to your next waypoint, based on your current speed.

Track: Same as courseline.

Universal Time Coordinated (UTC or UT): The time obtained from GPS satellites, adjusted to Greenwich Mean Time.

Velocity Made Good (VMG): Same as Speed of Advance.

Velocity Over the Ground (VOG): Same as Ground Speed.

Waypoint: The coordinates of a place you want to reach.

World Geodetic System—84 (WGS84): A satellite-based global datum for making horizontal measurements on the earth's surface (see Table 2.1).

through the alphabet (A to Z) or digits (0 to 9) until you reach the desired character, and then press ENTER. You must repeat this process for each letter in a word and each digit in a number.

The GPS receiver interface also includes an antenna. Internal antennas make for a more compact but less flexible unit. External antennas may be fixed to the unit's side and must be rotated into vertical orientation for use. External antennas may also be attached to the unit with a cable so that they can be remotely mounted, say on a vehicle's roof or the top of a backpack. In either case, the antenna must be held upright with a clear

line-of-sight to at least three satellites for a two-dimensional fix or four satellites for three-dimensional positioning.

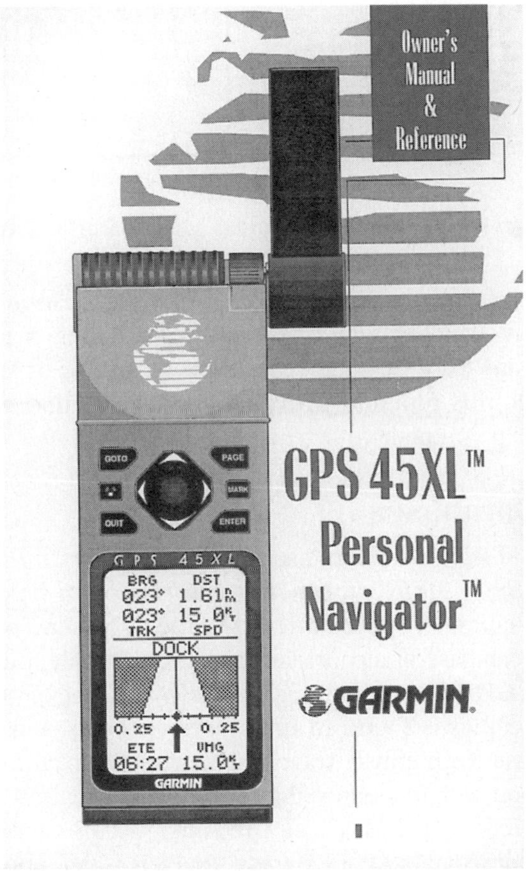

Tables and Equations

The permanent memory of your GPS receiver holds useful equations and tables of data. You can use these equations and tables to process satellite signals. You can also use them to make spatial computations when determining direction (true or magnetic), distance in English or metric units, speed, and position with respect to different grids. These tables and equations also let you process data you enter through the keypad or through a cable link to a stand-alone computer. Let's look more closely at some of these uses.

Datums

The receiver memory holds the data and equations needed to make both horizontal and vertical datum calculations. Parameters for over 100 datums used around the world are held in many hand-held receivers. The computer can make conversions between these datums.

GPS receivers default to the WGS84 horizontal datum. Unfortunately, this datum underlies few existing maps. If you're not using a map based on WGS84, the positional discrepancy between your map datum and WGS84 will create positioning errors beyond those associated with the stated accuracy (EPE) on your receiver. This additional locational error can be as much as 100 meters in the United States and 600 meters worldwide.

To minimize datum errors, you have two choices. You can relate computed positions to your map manually, which is a laborious task. Or you can enter the datum used to make your map and let the receiver make the datum conversion before displaying position coordinates. This second choice best uses the power of the receiver and is preferred.

Grids

The geographical grid (latitude-longitude) is usually the default. But most receivers can convert to several grids. The UTM grid is found on all units. In addition, you might find the military version of UTM, called MUTM, and a variety of regional and proprietary grids. A menu lets you select the grid of your choice. Some units even let you define your own grid.

Figure 15.1 This is an example of the type of interface you are likely to find on a hand-held GPS receiver.

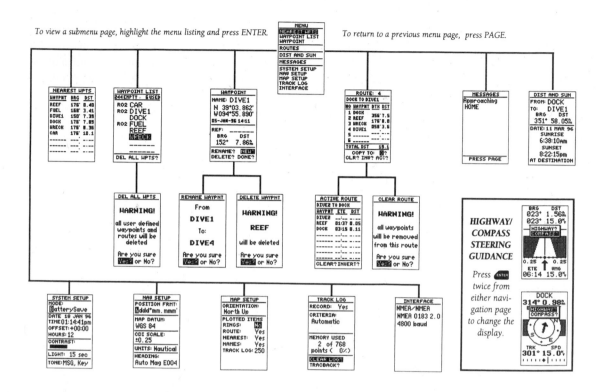

Figure 15.2 This example shows the type of menus you'll encounter when searching through the screen pages of a hand-held GPS receiver.

The choice of grid usually determines units of measurement as well. The UTM grid, for example, uses metric units. The geographical grid uses English units. There is provision in the menus to change to units of your choice.

Declination
GPS receivers report direction with respect to both true and magnetic north. The choice is yours. To make these conversions, the receiver must hold in its permanent memory declination data for the entire earth. Computations done with these data let the receiver serve as a form of electronic compass. But a GPS receiver is no substitute for a conventional magnetic compass, as we'll discuss later in this chapter.

Celestial Extras
GPS receivers commonly hold celestial data in permanent memory. This function lets you request information on sun and moon activity for a given date. You can do so for your location or any place for which you have coordinates. If you want to be at your destination at sunrise or sunset, this function provides information that will help you plan your trip.

Databases
Mid-sized receivers used in vehicles (see *Linking GPS to Maps* later in this chapter) often hold a database of special interest to the GPS user. Thus, a database of airport facilities is commonly found in GPS units used in planes, and a database of port facilities is found in units used by boats. A database for highway travel might contain local fuel, food, lodging, entertainment, and information on interesting sites. These GPS units will also accept a map database, since their screen is large enough in size and fine enough in spatial resolution for useful map display.

Receivers hooked up to a laptop or portable computer have access to even more extensive spatial databases. This volume of data can't be handled by small, hand-held receivers, however. Their screen and internal computer are simply too limited.

FIELD APPLICATIONS

You can best judge the potential of GPS technology by reviewing what it can do. We've said GPS is a revolutionary advance in positioning and navigation technology. So how does it compare with traditional methods of position and route finding? In this section, as we describe what GPS units can do, we invite you to make a direct comparison with the map-and-compass methods discussed in the previous chapter.

Use GPS to Orient Map

1. Turn on your receiver, and it will display coordinates for your present position (**Figure 15.3**). Enter this point as a landmark.

2. Plot present coordinate location on your map.

3. Options:

   A. If you can find a distant landmark on both the map and ground, switch to the observation method (see Chapter 14).

   B. If none of the landmarks you can identify on your map can be seen on the ground (due to darkness, fog, dense vegetation, etc.), enter the coordinates of a map landmark and press the GOTO key. The receiver will display the direction to the distant map landmark.

   C. If none of the landmarks you can see on the ground can be identified on your map, switch to the steering or navigation screen. Then point your receiver in any direction and move (briskly if walking) along a straight path in that direction, keeping your starting point in view. The receiver will display your direction of travel.

   D. As an alternative when faced with the conditions in C, you can move in any direction to a location from which you can see your starting position. Determine the coordinates at your new position. Next, you have

two options: (1) Press GOTO and select your starting point from the landmark list. This will give you a backtrack (or backsight) reading. Reverse the direction of this backtrack angle by adding or subtracting 180 degrees. (2) Or you can use the displayed coordinates to plot your map position. Then press GOTO and select your starting point from the landmark list. The receiver will display the direction back to your starting point.

4. Use the direction information displayed on your receiver screen as a direction line to orient your map as you did in Chapter 14.

Use GPS to Find Your Position

Position determination is the wonder of GPS. It couldn't be simpler. Merely turn the power on, and in a few seconds the receiver displays your three-dimensional position (see Figure 15.3). The horizontal coordinates on a civilian receiver will be accurate within 100 meters (328 feet) 95 percent of the time.* If you take continuous readings at one location and average them over several hours, you may achieve 15-meter (49-foot) accuracy. If you are moving, your accuracy is poorest. Conveniently, the receiver will tell you the estimated position error (EPE) when it displays your coordinates.

The stated positional accuracy of GPS receivers varies dramatically from source to source. Part of the problem is that accuracy is defined in three ways: horizontal (a 2-D circle of a given radius), vertical (height above a datum), and spherical (a 3-D sphere of a given radius). So you first want to ask, "What type of accuracy?" Things get even more confusing because there are several ways to define each type of accuracy. It may be stated with respect to the military design specifications for the system. Since GPS has surpassed design specifications, these figures are conservative. Accuracy may also be stated with respect to the best achieved or the probability of being within a given distance 50, 68, 95, or 100 percent of the time. Accuracy is sometimes stated with respect to a single position fix and sometimes with respect to averaging fixes over a period of time ranging up to six hours. Unfortunately, the proper clarification is often missing when you see a statement of GPS accuracy.

318

You can attain positional accuracy of 10 meters (33 feet) 95 percent of the time with a hand-held receiver if you have access to signal correction data from a second receiver. This is called **differential GPS (DGPS)**, and is explained in the *Global Positioning* section in Appendix D. The second receiver must be positioned over a point for which accurate coordinates are known. You can either get the signal correction data in real time, say by cellular phone, or post-process your GPS readings when you get in from the field, using correction data that you download into your computer. If you're willing to average signals over several hours, you can use your hand-held receiver to achieve DGPS horizontal accuracy as good as three meters (10 feet).

Even better accuracy is possible with the proper equipment and procedures. Accuracy in the meter range is now quite routine with surveyors, and accuracy in the centimeter range is possible under the best of conditions. Such accuracy requires sophisticated equipment and data post-processing using signal correction technology after returning to the laboratory. This is costly in terms of time, equipment, and skilled professionals.

DGPS holds great promise. But its added expense and inconvenience may not be justified if you can live with up to 100-meter positioning accuracy. Surveyors and other mapping professionals need DGPS accuracy in the sub-meter range, however, and are willing to put up with the added labor and cost. In the future it's likely that all receivers will be equipped for DGPS and that the needed correction data will be communicated from permanent ground stations via satellite to your receiver. You could then enjoy 3-meter to 10-meter accuracy worldwide with an inexpensive, hand-held receiver.

Your vertical position is another matter. Civilian receivers, using averaged signals, have a vertical accuracy potential of 46 meters (151 feet), with 95 percent of readings falling within 159 meters (522 feet) for a given fix. This error is greater than the local relief in much of the world!

Such vertical errors may be acceptable in regions of major relief and when using rapid modes of travel. But for travelers in much of the world, elevation information provided by hand-held GPS receivers isn't useful and is best ignored.

You can improve the accuracy of elevation readings to some degree by periodically entering corrected data obtained from your map at known positions. But the advantages are limited. If you

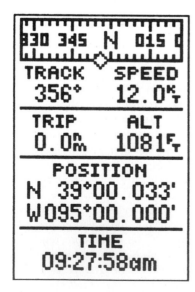

Figure 15.3 The position screen on a GPS receiver displays locational coordinates for your current position.

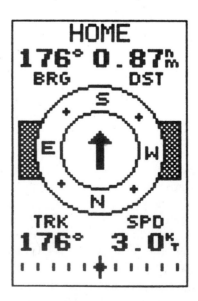

Figure 15.4 The compass or navigation page on your GPS receiver will tell you the direction and distance from your present position to your next landmark (or to your destination if this is the only or final leg of your route).

need precise elevation data, carry an altimeter (see *Altimeter Method* in Chapter 14).

Use GPS to Find Distant Position

A GPS receiver can't be used to find a distant position. It only can determine coordinates for its own location. If you know the coordinates for a distant point, you can enter them. Once you do so, your receiver will be helpful in getting you to that destination.

Use GPS to Plan Route

A GPS receiver is also unsuited to route planning. Your receiver depends on you to enter critical data. If landmarks are stored in your receiver's temporary memory from past data entry or on-site position determinations, you can organize these points into a route sequence. This scavenging of existing coordinate data can save you tedious repeat data entry.

The problem with using coordinates from past trips is that hand-held receivers have limited temporary storage capacity. Most units let you store only a few hundred points organized into 20 or so routes. Once you exceed this capacity, you must clear some coordinates before you can enter new ones. These purged coordinates are lost unless you download them into some other storage device. Some GPS units let you do this to a memory card, disk, or tape. Or you may be able to make the transfer by connecting your receiver to a computer by cable.

Despite these memory problems, it's essential to plan ahead and enter needed data into your receiver. You can obtain the necessary coordinates from maps, gazetteers, Web sites, or other geographical sources. It's wise to save coordinate information for routes you might want to repeat by writing them in a notebook or entering them into your computer. Remember that coordinates held in a GPS receiver can be lost if the unit is damaged.

Use GPS to Follow Route

The awesome power of GPS is revealed when following routes. Your GPS unit tells you which way to go, where you've been, how you're doing, and

how to get back on track if you're off course. Let's look at each of these functions.

Where Am I Going?

As we discussed earlier, it's essential to plan your route by entering your destination's coordinates into your receiver. Once you've done so, you merely press the GOTO button and select your destination from the landmark list. Your receiver will display the direction and distance to your destination on the **compass** or **navigation page** (**Figure 15.4**).

If your route has several legs, your receiver will automatically shift to the next leg when you approach an upcoming landmark. The new direction and distance data will be displayed. This process will be repeated until you reach your destination.

Where Have I Been?

The **map page** displays your progress along a route (**Figure 15.5**). It shows your starting point and each landmark you've visited. It also shows the path you took between landmarks to get to your present position. The plot is crude but sufficient to give you the information you need in the field.

You may want to save information about your route. This might be the case, for example, if you're following a trail or road not found on your map. Later, when you get back to your computer, you can download the route coordinates and plot an overlay. Then you can use the overlay to update your printed map.

How Am I Doing?

Your GPS receiver also provides graphic steering guidance and navigation information en route. This information is often displayed on a graphic page that resembles a highway. Indeed, it is called the **highway page** on some units (**Figure 15.6**)

Compass and highway pages commonly include a course deviation indicator (CDI)—a graphic display showing how far you've strayed left or right of your desired path. This information is called your cross track error (XTE or XTR). Such a portrayal of navigation error can be very useful in guiding you back on course (see Figure 15.6).

Compass and highway pages also display a variety of speed and time information (see Figures 15.4 and 15.6). Speed (SPD), Speed Over Ground (SOG), Velocity Made Good (VMG), Estimated

320

Time En Route (ETE), and Estimated Time of Arrival (ETA) are some of these functions (see Table 15.2 for definitions). They may be useful if you're traveling in a vehicle along a fairly straight course at a constant rate of speed. But at slow speed over an irregular course, such as walking, the data are unreliable. Also remember that the GPS uses straight "crow-flying" distances in making these calculations.

All these GPS navigation functions can be welcome if you get off course. But be careful in using your receiver as a steering device. Constant use will rapidly drain battery power. Ten hours of operation is about what you get from a set of fresh batteries under the most careful power-saving procedures. The best way to conserve batteries is to rely primarily on map and compass. Use your GPS receiver only intermittently to check your progress and make navigation adjustments.

When you near your destination, your receiver may beep or display a message saying "Arrived." At this point, you should be within viewing distance of your ground destination. It's time to look up and study your surroundings. GPS has done its job. Remember, even experienced navigators complete the final few feet of their journey by eye, not by instrument or map!

How Do I Get Back?

Most GPS receivers have a backtrack function that helps you retrace a route back to its starting point (**Figure 15.7**). A press of a few menu keys reverses your route and displays it as a graphic plot. As you follow the route back toward its starting point, the navigation display works the same as when you were out-bound on the route.

An interesting variation on backtracking is the **man over board (MOB)** function. You might use MOB, for example, if you accidentally drop your fishing rod in the water while trolling across a lake. A couple of quick keystrokes activate the function on most receivers, marking the spot with MOB coordinates. Later you can navigate back to this position as you would to any destination. If you've ever tried to recover something dropped in a lake while the boat was moving or you were far from shore, you will appreciate the potential of MOB.

GPS LIMITATIONS

GPS technology is revolutionary, but it is not magical. It knows coordinates, not geography. It uses these coordinates to compute geometric rela-

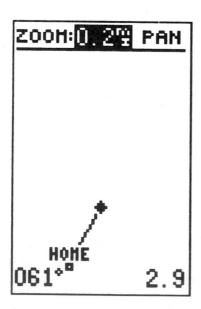

Figure 15.5 The map page displays progress along a route and lets you zoom or pan to vary the detail of the plot.

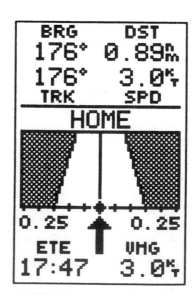

Figure 15.6 Your receiver's graphic steering page (sometimes called the highway page) tells you how far and in what direction you've strayed from your planned route and how to correct for these navigation errors.

tions. From these computations, it is able to report useful data related to location, distance, direction, and speed. It assumes a straight-line path between landmarks when computing distance.

But a GPS receiver lacks the sense of place that makes us feel special about locations. Since it can't read your mind, its computations aren't tempered by such human factors as wants, desires, needs, or dreams. It can tell you the shortest distance as measured in miles, but it can't tell you which route is the quickest, most interesting, least effort, most aesthetic, or least comfortable (in terms of fear, bug bites, sun in your eyes, and so on). You glean such functional information from maps, either those in your head (mental) or those in your hand (cartographic). Maps help you to see spatial relations at a glance, to put the environmental pieces together to form a bigger picture. The map suggests alternate places to visit and routes to take. You can then program these data into your GPS receiver.

Linking GPS to Maps

But how do you make this connection between GPS and maps? The small, coarse-resolution screen on your GPS receiver can display only a

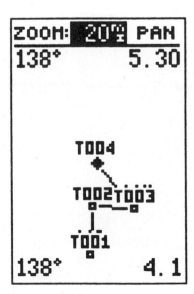

Figure 15.7 GPS receivers have a backtrack function that displays your current route reversed, helping you navigate back to your starting point or the oldest point in the receiver's memory, whichever comes first.

few landmarks and a simple path or two. It can't display a map of any useful detail. This leaves you with two options.

Paper Maps

One option is to carry a conventional paper map along with your GPS receiver. Whenever you check your position with the receiver, you also visually note that location on your map. Some people prefer to plot positions and make annotations on the map as they move across the landscape. Others carry a small notebook in which they keep an annotated log of their route. This record of the geography behind the coordinates can prove invaluable on your return trip or, later, when you want to recall your route.

A big advantage of this option is that it is inexpensive. Paper maps cost relatively little, and you can use the least costly receiver. Another advantage is that the combination is conveniently portable. Inexpensive receivers weigh only a few ounces, and a map weighs next to nothing.

The disadvantage of using traditional paper maps with your GPS receiver is that they demand the most from you. You must continually keep them oriented. You also must be able to work with the scale and reference grids to make sense of the position, distance, direction, and other spatial information supplied by the receiver. Since the map is static and mute, it can't provide assistance in these matters. You must rely on eye and hand methods.

Digital Maps

This brings us to the second option, which is to link a map to the GPS receiver automatically. A screen of readable size and resolution is required, as is a digital map database. The system also must contain the electronics needed to retrieve and display the appropriate map with your present position. Automation of the map link is achieved in several ways.

The most convenient method of linking map to GPS is to build an integrated unit. A typical example is a 10-inch-square box, weighing several pounds, with a 5-by-7-inch black-and-white screen (**Figure 15.8**). These devices are typically used in planes, boats, and highway vehicles where there is ready access to a plug-in source of electrical power. In these vehicles, the added bulk of integrated units is also not a significant factor. But

321

PART II
*Map
Analysis*

322

reduced portability is a major obstacle for the person on foot. Indeed, since these dedicated units can perform only the functions they were designed to do, they are usually permanently mounted.

The map may have been integrated into the machine in several ways. It may have been read into the unit's memory from a digital map database before taking the device into the field. More commonly, a disk holding the desired map is plugged into the unit. After traveling some distance, you may have to insert a new map disk. These disks are often sold by the builders of integrated units and are much more expensive than paper maps.

The added expense is acceptable if automated positioning is your aim, however. An integrated unit will continually update your position and route on the map display screen. You can see the progress you're making toward your destination and get a readout of a wide variety of navigational data in the process. Some integrated units used on boats will show you a sonar depth map as well as a position map (**Figure 15.9**). They may do so by splitting a single screen or by alternating between position and depth displays.

The second method of linking map to GPS automatically is to connect a stand-alone receiver to a general-purpose laptop or desktop computer (**Figure 15.10**). The computer offers major computational power. Since computer memory is vast and the unit can be networked to databases worldwide, all manner of data can be fed into the system. You can also take advantage of the computer display screen, which is bigger, multicolored, and higher in spatial resolution than the screen on most integrated units. This all adds up to a high-quality map display backed up by powerful analytical capabilities. Furthermore, when you're not using the computer for GPS, you can use it for other things.

The laptop-computer approach has the advantage of portability if you're using it from a vehicle or can move a vehicle near your desired location. Since the unit isn't permanently mounted, it can be removed from the vehicle when not needed. This may be the most cost-effective way to bring automated positioning technology into your vehicle travels. Furthermore, when you sell your car you don't lose your navigation device as you do when you have an integrated auto navigation system.

The desktop computer lacks portability but has the most processing and graphic display power. Screens as big as 21 inches in full color can be used to display maps. Desktop computers

Figure 15.8 Integrated GPS receivers include a display screen of sufficient size and resolution to display your position on a readable map called up from its memory.

Figure 15.9 Electronic "fish finders" show your map position and a sonar chart of underwater features.

are commonly used by surveyors and other mapping professionals to process field data in the lab. By making elaborate corrections to field data using information from other sources, experts can make far more precise position determinations than is otherwise possible. This post-processing of DGPS data is essential in geodetic applications and for making the highest-quality maps.

Desktop computers linked to multiple GPS receiver/transmitter units are now commonly used by fleet vehicle companies. Businesses use this method to monitor the position and movement (speed and velocity) of each taxi, truck, ship, train, or plane in their fleet. The military is developing an "electronic battlefield" scenario in which the positions of all friendly troops and vehicles are continuously monitored on a electronic map at a central command center. Field commanders will also have access to these maps on laptop display devices.

Keep a Notebook

We've already discussed how the small size and poor resolution of display screens on hand-held GPS receivers create problems. One difficulty is that displayed terms, graphics, and messages must be abbreviated. Most GPS units will by default code landmarks sequentially by number (001, 002, 003, and so on). Having hundreds of numerical identifiers in your receiver's memory is a nightmare when you want to select a destination or create a route.

Fortunately, receivers have provision for manually entering a short landmark label in place of the default numerical identifier. A label such as "CAR," "CAMP," or "PARK" is easier to use than number identifiers, but you soon run out of meaningful short words and recognizable abbreviations. There is no space to say anything significant about a landmark that you want to recall later.

Figure 15.10 Plugging a GPS receiver into a laptop computer creates a powerful unit for analysis and display of positioning data yet is portable enough to use in moving vehicles.

324

Finally, keying in multiple character identifiers is laborious.

You might get around the landmark entry and recall problems by annotating your map with the proper numerical identifier each time you enter one into your receiver's memory. But that is quite a chore, especially in the field, and it makes a mess of your map if you use it for many trips. Furthermore, you have to add still more annotations to your map to capture the character of the landscape along each leg of your trip. This information is particularly valuable if you decide to backtrack or return at a later time.

A better way to augment landmark identifiers is to keep a notebook (log or diary). In a notebook, you can expand on each short landmark identifier to your heart's content. Later, you can remind yourself of the character of the landscape along routes. You will also know what terrain features to watch for as you approach obscure landmarks. If nothing else, your notebook makes good reading later when you want to daydream about past trips.

Keep Your Compass

We have stressed how maps can help overcome the limitations of GPS technology. The same can be said of the magnetic compass. Your GPS receiver cannot replace your compass. You need both.

True, a GPS receiver can do some of the things compasses and protractors do. For instance, your receiver can give you the true and magnetic directions between any two points for which it has coordinates. This function mimics protractor and map use. In the field, your GPS receiver can give you the direction to a distant point for which it has coordinates. This function mimics compass use. If you're moving along at a brisk walk or faster, it can give you your direction of travel. Again, this mirrors compass use.

But if you aren't moving, your GPS receiver's likeness to a compass breaks down. Under this condition, it doesn't know which way is north or which way you are facing (or if the device is oriented). That is a concern because it makes it difficult to keep your map oriented if you're traveling slowly. It can also be a problem with faster movement over a path that keeps changing direction.

An even more significant difference between GPS and compass technology is that GPS uses rather weak satellite signals that are easily blocked. Terrain, buildings, vegetation, human body parts, and even a canvas boat sail may block line-of-sight satellite signals that are crucial in making a position fix. Signals can also reflect off nearby objects, confusing the GPS receiver and leading to degraded position calculations.

Other things can happen to the satellite signals as well. Problems can occur with signal transmission at the satellite, resulting in a weak signal or none at all. Satellites must be a certain distance above the horizon or their signals will be weak or blocked. And the geometrical configuration of the satellites has an impact on the reliability of position computations. You don't want the satellites to be bunched together in the sky but to be rather evenly dispersed overhead. For an explanation of this phenomenon, see *Operating Conditions* in Appendix D.

GPS receivers need a power supply to run their internal computer. In hand-held units, this power supply is usually a battery. We all know that batteries lose power with time, use, and cold temperatures. Since a loss of power will cause the receiver to fail, batteries must be replaced or recharged after about 10 hours of use.

In contrast, a magnetic compass uses the earth's magnetic field as its energy source and signal. This ubiquitous and reliable force is everywhere powerful enough for the compass to work properly. No electrical power is needed. Magnetic energy is not blocked or reflected by landscape features. (There can be problems with stray magnetism, however, as we discussed in Chapter 14.)

Clearly, GPS and magnetic compass technologies are complementary. One enhances the other. When your GPS receiver fails, and it eventually will, your compass could be life-saving. Carrying both devices is a form of insurance or risk management.

If you choose to ignore this advice, then we can only echo Edward Abbey's suggestion in *The Journey Home*: "Carry water. Avoid the noonday sun. Try to ignore the vultures. Pray frequently."

Warning to GPS Novices

You may know exactly where you are and where you want to go but still be lost. Your GPS receiver will tell you your location and the direction and distance to your desired destination. It will do this every few seconds for hours—until the batteries drain down. But that information is of little use if you can't move (because of a broken leg, bad storm, etc.) and have no way to communicate your location to a would-be rescuer. Before you leave home, then, it's a good idea to arm yourself with a backup device that can let someone know where to find you.

In many parts of the world, a battery-powered radiotelephone (commonly referred to as a cellular phone or cell phone) may get your message out (**see Box 15.1**). This ground-based system depends on line-of-sight signals, which means you must be located within a region (cell) that is served by a transmitter/receiver. The system has the advantage that you can call an existing telephone number, and someone can call you back if you leave a message. The disadvantage of cellular technology is that transmitters are found only in densely populated areas.

Battery-operated two-way and citizen's band (CB) radios have a more limited range (only five miles under optimal conditions) than cellular phones. Also, the signals of these unlicensed units can be blocked by landscape obstructions. Furthermore, your message is broadcast on open air waves. Thus, someone needs to be listening on your waveband when you transmit a message. Despite their drawbacks, these radios can get you help in some circumstances.

Vehicle-mounted CB radios have a greater range than hand-held units and, therefore, can increase your chances of making a contact. But they lack crucial portability for use beyond the range of powerboats and power-driven land vehicles.

Better-quality amateur (ham) radios that operate on batteries have a range up to 10 miles. In the United States, they require a Federal Communications Commission (FCC) license to operate on the restricted two-meter (VHF) ham waveband. These units can link you directly

BOX 15.1
CELL PHONES: A CALL FROM THE WILD

High atop the Grand Teton Mountains, the climbers were caught in a vicious hailstorm. Terrified and desperate, they did what any self-respecting backpackers of the '90s do—whip out the cell phone and yelp for help. Rescuers found a group of tenderfoots astonishingly unprepared, clad in shorts and T-shirts, without extra supplies. Ranger Tom Kimbrough asked them to explain. "I looked at a big pile of gear and I looked at the phone," a climber said. "And the phone was a helluva lot lighter."

So much for survival of the fittest. In an age of cordless communications, the help-on-demand syndrome may be leading to a dangerous mind shift in the wilderness. And the lore of the foolish cell-phone caller is growing among the ranks of search-and-rescue squads. In New Hampshire, a group of hikers pleaded for flashlights because they had only brought along one battery-powered device—the phone. ("Press 1 if you're a bozo. Press 2 if you're merely inconsiderate.") Great Smokies ranger Bob Wightman says he has "real concerns about people beginning to take risks they wouldn't otherwise take, feeling that help is just a phone call away." It often isn't, since phones don't always work in remote locations.

The problem isn't just safety. Once upon a time, the Great Outdoors meant getting away from it all. These days, with so many hikers toting cell phones, the culture clash with purists is dramatic. Sure, the technology has saved lives, but at an esthetic cost. Bob Penney is a millionaire Alaska businessman and avid fisherman. Last summer he took three brokers out on the Russian River at 3 in the morning. Before they even caught anything, Penney recalls, the brokers were on the cell working the markets in New York and Singapore. Penney should've thrown his friends in as bait.

(Daniel Glick and bureau reports, *Newsweek*, July 28, 1997)

326

(called **simplex operation**) or indirectly (through **repeater units**) into the worldwide ham radio network. Thus, there's a good chance someone will hear your message if you're near a populated area. An attractive feature of repeater operation is **autopatch**, which interconnects to the public telephone network so that you can call any phone number.

If you have access to an auxiliary power supply such as those available in planes, boats, cars, or trucks, you have the option of a more powerful CB radio. These FCC-licensed units have a range of tens of miles under good conditions. Someone is likely to hear your message if there are highways or population centers within range.

Coming soon are several constellations of hundreds of communications satellites in low earth orbit. Several commercial vendors are planning to spend billions of dollars in the coming decade to establish these competing satellite-based communication systems. There are so many of these satellites and their orbit is so low that every place on earth will have a satellite nearby. Thus, a signal can be sent or received using little electrical power.

Within the next decade, then, an inexpensive, small, battery-operated, personal communication device will instantaneously connect you to the information highway. GPS technology will surely be built into this device. Ground-based cellular phone technology with its blocked line-of-sight signals and hand-offs between neighboring cells may soon be history.

PREPPING MAPS FOR GPS USE

Few maps are designed for convenient GPS use. The problem is that GPS works with spatial coordinates. A dense spatial reference grid must be overprinted on a map if you are to find your map position accurately from coordinates. A dense grid is also needed to determine the coordinates of a feature or location from a map.

But design specifications for today's maps were set years ago when there was little demand for using coordinates to define location. Thus, most map makers don't clutter their maps with coordinate reference grids.*

Flesh Out Map Grid

Until maps come with a dense grid overprint, you will have to tailor maps for GPS yourself. You should make it a habit to do so before taking your map and GPS receiver into the field. Some maps have a sparse grid of reference lines, some have a denser spacing of ticks along the map margin, and some have both (see Figure 11.3). Whatever form the grid information, it provides the basis for your grid densification task.

If you have a full but sparse grid, you need to subdivide each edge of a grid cell. Then connect matched subdivision marks on opposite sides of the cell to create your dense grid (**Figure 15.11**). Your task is simplest if you use subdivisions based on halves. Thus, you divide the full cell edge into half, divide each half into half to produce quarters, divide each quarter into half to

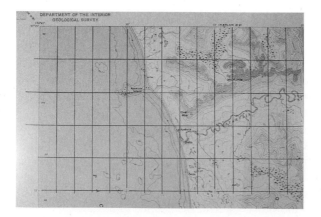

Figure 15.11 By densifying the sparse grid found on a map, you can make it more suitable for use with a GPS receiver.

In the late 1970s, the USGS overprinted a full UTM grid on their experimental metric series 7½ x 15 minute 1:25,000 topographic quadrangles of the Adirondacks (New York state). But the idea was dropped because customers complained. It may have been the metric units for scale and contours, rather than the grid, that was the problem. In any case, it now looks as if the USGS was ahead of the time with this project. In the future, we're sure to return to full grid overprints to make maps easier for GPS use.

produce eights, and so on. This is easy to do, but fractional units of 1/8, 1/16, 1/32, 1/64, and 1/128 are awkward to use later.

We suggest subdivision into tenths, which is easier to use. First, subdivide each cell edge into 10 segments. Then divide each segment into 10 subsegments. Rarely is there need to go beyond subdivision into hundredths. Admittedly, division into tenths is more difficult than repeated halving. If you have forgotten how to subdivide a line of odd length into a given number of subunits, consult Figure A.5 in Appendix A to refresh your memory.

With a little practice, you will breeze through the grid subdivision chore. As an incentive, remember that you are creating a "value-added" product. Densifying the grid is tedious but need not be boring. It speeds things along if you spend this time daydreaming about the trip you will take when the gridding work is done.

If you only find marginal tick marks on your map, it may suffice merely to connect matching tick pairs with lines. Refer to Figure 13.4 to see the result of connecting UTM ticks to create a full UTM grid on a USGS 1:24,000 scale topographic quadrangle. Since the UTM grid ticks were spaced 1,000 meters (1 km.) apart, the grid cells are too large for accurate GPS use, especially if you aren't traveling in a high-speed vehicle.

A civilian GPS receiver gives horizontal position within 100 meters 95 percent of the time. Therefore, we advise that you subdivide the

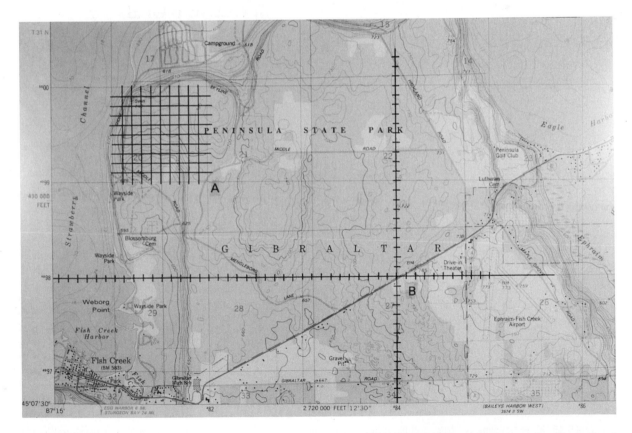

Figure 15.12 To take full advantage of the positional accuracy potential of civilian GPS receivers, you should construct either (A) a full 100-meter grid or (B) 100-meter tick marks along key north-south lines on your map.

328

UTM grid cells in Figure 13.4 by 10. This will yield 100-meter grid cells, a good match for your GPS readings (**Figure 15.12A**). If you find that a full 100-meter grid overprint clutters your map too much, you might simply put 100-meter tick marks along key 1,000-meter grid lines in both the north-south and east-west directions (**Figure 15.12B**). An alternative to constructing these fine-ly-spaced grid lines or ticks is to use a grid-reading aid (see *Grid-Reading Aids* later in this chapter).

Add Grid to Gridless Map

As you saw in the previous section, it helps to have at least some map grid information as a guide when constructing a full grid over a map. But what if your map has no indication of a grid?

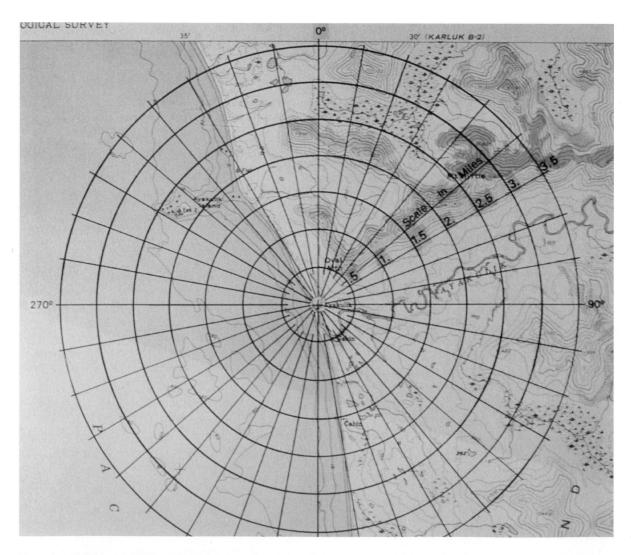

Figure 15.13 When traveling out from and back to one location over a period of time, it's handy to have a range grid superimposed on the home base. Then, from any location, you can quickly determine your current map position, as well as the direction and distance to home base, by pressing the GOTO button and selecting the home base landmark on your receiver.

This is usually the case with image maps, for example.

There are two ways to deal with this challenge. You can obtain coordinates for key features from a map that does have a grid, or you can go into the field with a GPS receiver and determine coordinates for key features. In either case, you then annotate features on your gridless map with these coordinates. Finally, you can use these key locations to anchor a standard grid (such as UTM) to your gridless map. Since the grid construction requires many calculations, it is a chore if done manually but a snap with the proper computer software.

Create Range Grid

You might think of the gridding work you did in the previous section as producing a locationally-neutral spatial reference grid. In other words, you can use the grid from any map position with equal results. There is no positional bias that makes grid readings from one location any easier or more accurate than from any other location. This grid neutrality is ideal if there is no positional focus in your spatial behavior.

But there are situations in which your behavior has a strong positional focus. Say, for example, you intend to use one location for several days as a home base from which you travel out each morning and to which you return each evening. In this case, the ideal grid would be focused on your home base, as shown in **Figure 15.13**.

We call such a grid a **range grid**, because it consists of equally-spaced concentric circles (or range lines) centered on the home base. Radiating out from the home base are equally-spaced azimuth (direction) lines. You may recognize this as a **polar coordinate system**, where coordinates are defined by the distance and direction from the center point. It is a handy mathematical alternative to the more common rectangular (or Cartesian) coordinate system we have mentioned earlier in this book.

When constructing a range grid, you have a choice of orienting it to true, magnetic, or grid north. You can set your GPS receiver to report directions as either true or magnetic. If you will be using a magnetic compass along with your GPS receiver, we recommend constructing your range grid with magnetic north orientation. This will eliminate the need to make conversions from compass readings to true north readings.

To use a range grid, you first enter the home base coordinates. In the case of Figure 15.13, your home base is a cabin near the Ayakulik River on the southwest shore of Kodiak Island, Alaska. The USGS 1:63,360-scale topographic quadrangle was printed in 1952. Latitude-longitude ticks are shown every five minutes, but no other grid is overprinted.

With the coordinates of your home base in your GPS receiver's memory, you merely press the GOTO button on your receiver and select your base from the landmark list. The display will tell you the direction and distance to the base. By looking at your map, you can easily find your current location using the distance (range) and direction data.

Alternatively, you might want to know the distance and direction to a distant point. Suppose, for instance, that yesterday you discovered a particularly good spot to catch halibut. Immediately you marked the position with your GPS receiver. Then you pressed GOTO and recalled the base camp landmark from memory. Your GPS receiver displayed the direction and distance back to camp. This allowed you to plot your good fishing spot on the map (see Figure 15.13). Now, when setting out from camp to go fishing, you press GOTO and recall the landmark. Your GPS receiver directs you to your fishing spot even though it is five miles out in the ocean.

In this part of Alaska, fog and low clouds obscure landmarks for days on end during some parts of the year. These weather conditions make map-and-compass navigation nearly impossible. Under these conditions, a GPS receiver and a range-gridded map can save your life.

The spacing of range and latitude lines is a matter of personal preference. In Figure 15.13, range lines are spaced .5 miles apart, and azimuth lines are 10 degrees apart. This rather open grid is a good compromise between map clutter and position-reading precision. You can visually divide the half-mile azimuth line segments into tenths. This division yields distance units of 2600 feet ÷ 10 = 260 feet. This result is a little better than the lower accuracy of civilian GPS receivers.

330

Direction is another matter. At about the 2½ to 3 mile range, the range line segments are also spaced about .5 miles apart. At this distance, then, you can achieve the same directional accuracy in ground units that you can with range accuracy. Closer in, it's harder to make tenth divisions, but each division represents a shorter distance. Farther out, it gets easier to make divisions, but each division represents a longer distance. So converting direction to position will vary some by location. We must remember, of course, that people navigated successfully for centuries using hand-held magnetic compasses, which in the field can be read with a precision of only +/- 3 degrees.

Grid-Reading Aids

A drawback of the gridding work discussed in the two previous sections is that it has to be repeated for each new map sheet you want to use. It would be nice if you could have a grid for each map without having to repeat all the work. This is indeed possible. Let's look at the options.

Digital Database

The ultimate grid-reading tool is an electronic map. To display a map on a computer screen, you must have a digital database containing coordinate information for every location. With proper software, therefore, you merely "point and click" at a position or feature on the electronic map. The database will give you a coordinate readout. We cover this and other digital methods of map analysis in Chapter 19: *GIS and Map Analysis Software*.

Portable Grid

If you don't have access to a digital database to determine coordinates for you, the next best thing is a portable grid. When it is properly super-

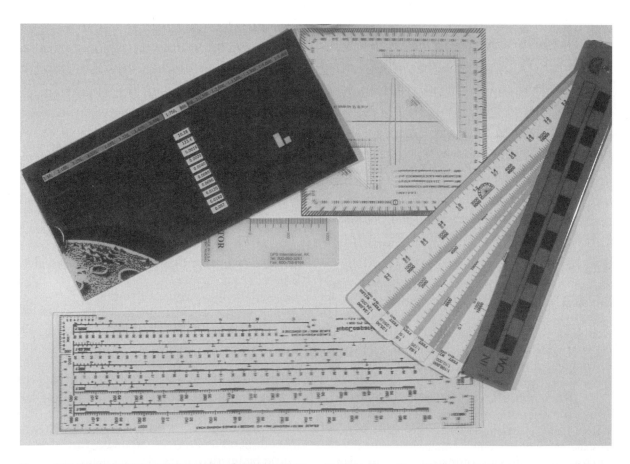

Figure 15.14 Commercial vendors supply an assortment of scale and grid-reading devices etched on a clear plastic base. By properly positioning these aids on your map, you can greatly speed up distance, direction, and grid analysis chores.

imposed on a map, you can use it as you would a permanent grid.

You can make your own portable grid, or you can buy one already made. You'll need several portable grids to accommodate different map scales, projections, and reference systems. Still, the savings in gridding time are immense if you use many different maps.

Make Your Own. If you make your own grid, you have a choice of doing it the old-fashioned way with pencil and paper, or doing it with a drawing program on a computer. If you draw on paper or print your computer image on paper, you can photocopy the grid onto a clear sheet of plastic to make reading map symbols through the grid easier. You can also send your computer file to a graphic arts service bureau where it can be written out to clear film electronically on a film recorder.

But first you have to construct your grid. A square grid is easy to make. Simply start with a piece of conventional graph paper with ruled grid squares as a guide. Then construct right-angle grid lines at a spacing that matches those on a given map. Label the grid in the appropriate units, starting with the origin (x=0, y=0) in the lower-left corner, and proceeding along each axis until you reach some multiple of 10 (10, 100, 1,000).

A range grid is a little more complicated to construct. If you start with a blank sheet of paper, you will need a protractor to lay out the azimuth lines and a drawing compass to construct the range circles. If you use polar-coordinate graph paper as a guide, you will still need a compass to draw the range lines. But you can trace the azimuth lines from the graph paper with a straightedge, thereby eliminating the need for a protractor. Whatever approach you take, you must decide what spacing to use for the azimuth and range lines. It is best to space the range circles in convenient distance units, such as a tenth or a half mile. Closer line spacing is more work and clutters the map, but is more accurate to use if you can see the mapped features through the grid.

Ready-Made. If you have more money than time, you can buy ready-made grids at a local map store or through a map supply catalog. A variety of scale and grid reading aids are sold by different vendors (**Figure 15.14**). Instructions for using these map analysis aids are usually etched onto

the surface of the device, or are available in a separate user guide.

Although specialized grids may be hard to find on the market, some general aids are available. For reading angles, for example, a 360-degree protractor is invaluable (**Figure 15.15**). If you will be traveling out from a home base repeatedly, it pays to construct a north-south or east-west baseline through the home base location. Doing so will speed your azimuth readings and make them more accurate as well. A fairly dense grid drawn over your map will do almost as well, since it will let you orient your protractor at any position with good accuracy.

LOCATION-AWARE DEVICES

A variety of common devices are being enhanced by GPS technology. Especially promising are devices that can transmit their position on demand. The possibilities are limitless. Likely candidates to be GPS-enabled include pet collars, children's necklaces, electronic parole bracelets, cellular phones, wristwatches, cars, trucks, farm tractors, bikes, airplanes, boats, trains, and buses (see **Box 15.2** and **Box 15.3**).

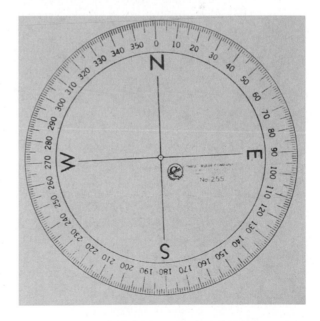

Figure 15.15 A 360-degree protractor is a handy and inexpensive device for determining angles on your map.

332

BOX 15.2 IN MINNESOTA, "SMART" BUSES GETTING A WHIRL

MINNEAPOLIS—Satellites used to direct missiles during the gulf war may keep some commuters from freezing at bus stops this winter as the city embarks on a high-tech program that eventually could make commuting easier for millions nationwide.

Officials say the pilot project set to start in mid-December will be the first of its kind to give commuters direct information about public transportation through home computers and videotex machines, touchscreen kiosks, electronic outdoor signs and indoor monitors. That information will help commuters avoid long waits for buses that break down or fall behind schedules.

"We don't think this will turn everybody into a bus rider," says Melanie Braun of Minnesota Guidestar, the office developing "smart" travel systems. "But it will give commuters information they can use to provide them with more options."

Dispatchers using signals from the Defense Department's Global Positioning System will be able to track 80 of the city's 1,000-bus fleet to within 50 feet of their location.

Breakdowns or other problems will be updated every 30 seconds at a downtown control center and simultaneously sent out to commuters in homes, office buildings and park-and-ride sites.

Commuters also will be able to use the kiosks and home computers to plan trips and access information like car pooling, downtown parking costs and traffic problems.

The one-year, $6.5 million project isn't the first—Denver, Milwaukee and Baltimore use the same technology—but it's the first to include commuter involvement, transit officials say.

"It removes uncertainty, which is a barrier to public transportation," says Bob Gibbons of Metropolitan Council Transit Operations. "And in mid-January in Minnesota, with a wind chill at 30-below, waiting for a bus is not a pleasant experience."

While buses here are relatively safe, the new technology also increases security: If a driver sends a silent alarm on a keyboard used to communicate with the dispatch center, "we can track that bus and send help," Gibbons says.

Officials are looking for about 600 commuters to participate in the program using either videotex machines or computer software programs.

David Smith, 52, of Corcoran, Minn., who commutes over 30 minutes one way each day to his bank job in the city, picked up an application for the program this week at the commuter service center where he buys his bus tickets.

Smith drives 10 miles just to get to the park-and-ride where he catches his bus.

He often drives all the way into the city when he's running late because "if I don't get there at 8, I don't know when the next bus is."

Outdoor messages will give Smith the latest bus schedules as he drives into the parking lot so he can make a better decision about which way to travel.

If the program is successful here, officials hope to expand it to other suburbs and other cities nationwide.

"We're hoping all of this has an impact on the freeway system," Braun says.

(Caroline Pesce,
USA Today, November 28, 1994)

This positioning technology will soon be altering your life in unimaginable ways. As a consequence, your spatial behavior will be safer and more efficient.

CONCLUSION

GPS differs radically from traditional spatial technologies. In the past, people relied on direction-distance relations to locate features and routes. In contrast, GPS technology is based on locational coordinates, from which direction and distance relations are computed. This change takes some getting used to, but the shift is needed to take advantage of a GPS receiver's internal computer.

GPS provides a variety of navigational information that isn't available when you work only with map and compass. GPS can tell you how well

BOX 15.3 NEW FREEDOM IN THE SKY

In a dimly lit room inside the FAA's air-traffic control center on New York's Long Island, dozens of controllers hunch over primitive black and green radar panels. Each controller tracks up to 25 airplanes simultaneously; together they shepherd a total of 6,500 flights a day across the country's most congested airspace. To keep planes separated and on course, controllers guide them down narrow corridors in the sky. Terry Bolerjack, the facility's air-traffic manager, explains by unfolding an aerial map crisscrossed with hundreds of spindly blue lines. "Just like Manhattan," he says. "These are one-way streets."

If a concept called "free flight" takes off, those one-way streets could become three-dimensional superhighways early in the next millennium. The current system may seem orderly, but it's not efficient. Since planes can't pass each other and aren't allowed to stray from the often circuitous airways, the system wastes time, fuel, and, ultimately, money—an estimated $3.5 billion a year. In free flight, navigational satellites would help pilots themselves choose the most efficient route, altitude and speed for their planes. The airlines and the FAA are both on board, and a congressional task force that studied the idea in 1995 proposed its implementation by 2010. "The sky isn't crowded at all; it is air-traffic control that's crowded," says United Airlines systems manager Bill Cotton, considered the "father" of free flight. "This is nothing more than reducing the unnecessary restrictions to flight."

The foundation of free flight is already in place: the Global Positioning System (GPS), a network of 24 satellites launched by the Defense Department starting in the late '70s. The orbiting satellites would give pilots precise information about their position and the positions of other aircraft, while digital transmitters would automatically swap this data between aircraft and the ground. Air-traffic controllers would become managers, intervening only around airports and in case of emergency. To avoid crashes, two imaginary, electronically defined zones would be projected around each plane. A breach in the outer layer, called the "alert zone," would trigger a traffic warning inside the cockpit, prompting the pilot to prevent a further intrusion into the plane's milewide inner layer, called the "protected zone."

. . .[T]he potential benefits of free flight to passengers are enticing: shorter flights and lower fares. An FAA trial called the National Route Program, which allows planes above 29,000 feet and 200 miles from an airport to chart their own courses, has already saved $40 million for the industry this year alone. "It's been the most successful program the FAA has put forward," says Monte Belger, the associate administrator for air-traffic services at the FAA. That sounds promising. Now if they could only do something about legroom.

(Kimberly Martineau and Brad Stone, *Newsweek*, August 25, 1997)

334

you're doing and how to correct for your navigation errors. A GPS receiver derives this useful information by manipulating coordinate data with its internal computer.

In this chapter, we discussed how map analysis, or analysis of cartographic databases, can lead to a variety of useful spatial information. The GPS receiver, having a computer at its core, can quickly make calculations by using stored equations and tables in conjunction with incoming positional data. In the next several chapters, we'll pursue this analytical theme in greater depth.

SELECTED READINGS

Ackroyd, N., and Lorimer, R., *Global Navigation: A GPS User's Guide*, 2nd ed. (London: Lloyd's of London Press, Ltd., 1994).

Clarke, B., *Aviators' Guide to GPS*, 2nd ed. (New York: TAB/McGraw-Hill, 1996).

Dixon, C., *Using GPS* (Dobbs Ferry, NY: Sheridan, 1995).

Hotchkiss, N.J., *A Comprehensive Guide to Land Navigation with GPS*, 2nd ed. (Herndon, VA: Alexis Publishing, 1995).

Hurn, J., *Differential GPS Explained* (Sunnyvale, CA: Trimble Navigation, Ltd., 1993).

Hurn, J., GPS: *A Guide to the Next Utility* (Sunnyvale, CA: Trimble Navigation, Ltd., 1989).

Kennedy, M., *The Global Positioning System and GPS* (Ann Arbor, MI: Ann Arbor Press, Inc., 1996).

Leick, A., *GPS Satellite Surveying*, 2nd ed. (New York: John Wiley & Sons, 1995).

Letham, L., *GPS Made Easy: Using Global Positioning Systems in the Outdoors* (Seattle, WA: The Mountaineers, 1995).

Sonnentag, B., *Precision GPS Navigation the E-Zutm Way* (Gabbs, NV: GPS International Press, 1997).

Van Sickle, J., *GPS for Land Surveyors* (Ann Arbor, MI: Ann Arbor Press, Inc., 1996).

CHAPTER 16
CARTOMETRICS

PRIMARY SPATIAL ELEMENTS

Location
Direction and Distance
Height
    Height of Discrete Features
        Image Displacement Method
        Shadow Length Method
        Parallax Method
    Height of Continuous Surfaces

SECONDARY SPATIAL CONCEPTS

Region
Centroid
Circumference
Area
    Graphic Counting Methods
    Instrumental Methods
    Mathematical Methods
    Area Distortion
Volume
Density
Spatial Change
    Slope
    Gradient

CONCLUSION

SELECTED READINGS

I've heard—who knows the truth—that if you rolled
West Virginia out like a flapjack, it would be as large as Texas.

—William Least Heat-Moon, *Blue Highways*

16
CHAPTER SIXTEEN
CARTOMETRICS

The world around us is rich in variety and interrelated in complex ways. Map analysis implies a search for order in this feature collage. We can begin this search by thinking about the environment in a disciplined manner.

It's in this spirit that, throughout this book, we've treated the environment as a collection of point, linear, areal, and volumetric features. What we need now is an equivalent vocabulary for describing these features' spatial character and geographic relations with each other. This vocabulary need not be new; it can be drawn from ideas you've used—perhaps unconsciously—for a long time.

In fact, we've already made a good start toward this vocabulary building. In previous chapters, we've explored the spatial elements of location, direction, and distance. Now we'll see how we can use these spatial elements to define features and environmental structures and describe relations between them.

We often make judgments about spatial structure and association simply by looking at mapped patterns and describing what we see. However, as we discussed in the introduction to Part II, such judgments are subjective and therefore difficult to communicate to others. Thus, their scientific value is lessened. Furthermore, such judgments vary with the patterns' complexity and the degree of correlation between them. Finally, there's no way to judge the accuracy of visual judgments except to believe those in authority. For all these reasons, it's often better to replace visual judgments of spatial association with objective, repeatable mathematical measures.

Mathematical procedures are more involved than visual analysis. But on the plus side, they have the advantages of precision and repeatability which are so important in scientific work. In addition, mathematical measures of spatial structure and correspondence can in some cases be accompanied by a statement of the statistical confidence you can have in the results' validity.

In view of the advantages of mathematical over visual analysis, in this chapter we'll not only introduce terms to clarify spatial descriptions, but we'll also define these terms mathematically as much as possible.

Map analysis is most basic when we look at the spatial geometry of environmental features. Included at this level of analysis are counting, measuring, and estimating operations, which we refer to as **cartometric analyses**, or **cartometrics**.

It is convenient to group cartometric analyses into primary and secondary classes of operations. Let's begin by exploring primary spatial elements.

PRIMARY SPATIAL ELEMENTS

The first step in sorting out the confusion of our environment is to ask, "What are its basic properties?" What we are seeking are the most essential, most primitive elements we can use to describe the world in all its geographical complexity.*

Fortunately, we can describe all environmental phenomena with only a few basic elements—location, distance, direction, and height. Let's look at each of these primary spatial elements.

Location

The most basic spatial element is that of a dimensionless location, or point. It is without size or shape. It may signify mere existence of something, such as an oil well. Or it may represent the coming together of several linear features, as at a crossroads, in which case we call it a **node**. Location may also represent a numerical designation in a coordinate reference system.

We detailed these aspects of location in Chapter 11. In that chapter, we saw that answering the question "Where?" is central to understanding our environment. We also saw that the question can be asked and answered in either an absolute or a relative way.

Direction and Distance

We can fully describe relations between two points on a horizontal plane by using two rela-

tional spatial elements. First we specify the angular relation, or **direction**, between the points. To define direction, we need a base line, a location (or origin), and a line of sight. As we saw in Chapter 12, direction, like location, can be specified in both absolute and relative terms.

Second, we provide a measure of the separation between the two locations, which we refer to as **distance**. Distance is merely the length of the direction line.

In Chapter 13, we saw that the property of distance, too, has both a relative and absolute definition. Although most maps are made using physical distance units, we tend to define distance in a functional way. To use a map effectively, then, it's usually necessary to convert map distance to some more conceptually meaningful measure.

Height

The earth isn't a flat plane, of course. We live in a three-dimensional environment. In this context, direction has a vertical as well as two horizontal components, and distance is measured along the direction vector. When the direction vector is oriented vertically, we refer to its length or distance as **height**.

Several cartometric procedures let you determine height precisely. Since these procedures differ depending on whether you want height information for discrete features or a continuous surface, we'll discuss each separately.

Height of Discrete Features

Sometimes you may want to know the exact height of environmental features, such as trees or buildings. On line maps, this information may be given directly. On image maps, however, you usually have to figure out the heights of features yourself. You can do so in three ways:

1. Image Displacement Method. Under special conditions, you can determine the height of environmental features quite accurately using a large-scale, vertical photograph. One such method is based on the radial displacement of tall objects which occurs outward from the photo center.

Using this technique, you may determine object heights by the following relationship:

$$\text{Height of object } (h_o) = \frac{d}{r}(H)$$

We are dealing here with the three-dimensional spatial world. Time has been abstracted from consideration at this point.

where   d = the length of the displaced image on the photo.

   r = the radial distance from the principal point to the top of the displaced image. (This must be expressed in the same units as d.)

   H = the aircraft flying height above the base of the displaced object. (This must be expressed in the units desired for the object's height.)

For example, if you assume that the photo in **Figure 16.1** was taken from an altitude of 300 meters, you can compute the tree height as follows:

$$h_o = \frac{5 \text{ mm.}}{50 \text{ mm.}} (300 \text{ m.}) = 30 \text{ m.}$$

The accuracy of this height determination depends on several factors. The photo must be truly vertical (non-tilted) so that the principal point can be accepted as the nadir position (the point directly below the camera, also called the plumb point). You must know the precise flight altitude above the base of the object. Both the base and top of the displaced object must be clearly visible. And, finally, the degree of image displacement must be great enough to be measured with available equipment (such as an engineer's scale). If any of these conditions is open to question, you should regard resulting height determinations as approximate only.

2. Shadow Length Method. You may also compute objects' heights by measuring shadow lengths on a vertical photo. Before you can do so, however, several conditions must be met:

- The object must be vertical (perpendicular to the earth's surface).
- The object's shadow must be cast from its true tip rather than its side.
- The shadow must fall on open ground at the level of the object's base, where it is undistorted and easily measured.
- You must know the angle of the sun above the horizon at the time the photo was taken.

If these conditions are satisfied, you can determine the object's height by using the fact that the length of an object's shadow is directly proportional to its height. As you can see in **Figure 16.2**, height computations involve basic trigonometric principles. The key to the geometric relationship used in determining object heights from shadow measurements is the **sun angle**, or angular elevation of the sun (symbolized as θ in the figure). The tangent of this sun angle (θ) multiplied by the shadow length(s) provides a measure of object height (h_o). Written symbolically,

object height (h_o) = shadow length(s) x tangent θ.

Thus, the basic problem is to determine the sun angle at a given location for a specific time. You can do so in two ways:

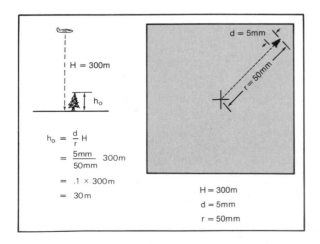

16.1 You can determine the height of a feature from its radial displacement on a vertical aerial photograph.

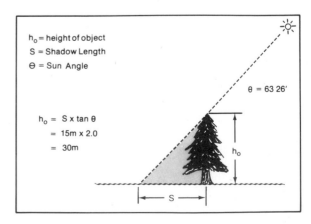

16.2 Under special conditions, you can determine the height of an object on a vertical aerial photograph from its shadow length.

Sun Angle Determination Method 1. If you can find a sharply defined object of known height, such as a building or radio antenna, on the photograph, you can use the shadow it casts to determine the local sun angle at the time the photo was taken. Just transpose the previous equation so that it reads:

$$\text{tangent } \theta = \frac{\text{height of object}}{\text{shadow length (in ground units)}}.$$

Therefore, if you know a building is 50 meters high and it casts a shadow two millimeters long on a photo with a scale of 1:12,500, you can compute the sun angle as

$$\text{tangent } \theta = \frac{50 \text{ m.}}{2 \text{ mm. x } 12,500 \text{ mm.}}$$

$$= \frac{50 \text{ m.}}{25,000 \text{ mm.}} = \frac{50 \text{ m.}}{25 \text{ m.}} = 2.0.$$

Because the sun's rays are parallel, this value remains constant for the entire photo. Thus, you can multiply the shadow lengths of other features on the photo by 2.0 to determine their corresponding object heights. For example, if a tree on the same photo has a shadow length of 15 meters in ground units (1.25 mm. x 12,500 = 1,500 mm.), you can compute the height of the tree as

$$h_o = 15 \text{ m. x } 2.0 = 30 \text{ m.}$$

Sun Angle Determination Method 2. If you can't find an object of known height on the photo, you can determine the local sun angle by using a **solar ephemeris**, which is a collection of special astronomical tables. This second procedure is more complex than the first and requires as basic information, in addition to the astronomical tables, the time (month, day, and hour) of photography, the photo's latitude and longitude, and the photo's scale. Once you have determined the sun angle, the object height computations proceed as before.

To obtain accurate results, you should measure shadow length to the nearest 0.1 millimeter or less. In the previous illustration, for example, an error of only 0.1 millimeter in measuring the tree's shadow length on the photo would lead to a *3.75-meter* difference in the estimated object height (see **Box 16.1**).

Special micrometer devices and magnifying monoculars simplify this measurement task. In general, the precision of shadow length computations improves with larger photo scales, because they permit more accurate shadow measurements.

Box 16.1 Effect of Small Errors in Measuring Shadow Length

Shadow length in ground units = 1.35 mm
(shadow length in map units) × 12,500 (photo scale) = 16,875 mm = 16.875 m

$$h_o = 16.875 \text{ m} \times 2.0 = 33.750 \text{ m}$$

$$\begin{array}{r} 33.750 \text{ m (New Height)} \\ - 30.000 \text{ m (Old Height)} \\ \hline 3.750 \text{ m} \end{array}$$

Thus, there would be a 3.750 m difference in object height given only 0.1 mm difference in measured shadow length.

3. Parallax Method. Although the image displacement and shadow methods of object height determination are useful when only a single photo is available, they depend on so many hard-to-control factors that they don't always provide reliable height measurements. A valuable alternative to use when stereopairs of photographs are available (see *Stereo Photos* in Chapter 5) is the parallax method of height determination. "Parallax" is the term given to the apparent displacement of objects when viewed from the perspective of different vantage points. Parallax is a normal aspect of overlapping vertical photographs called stereopairs.

To determine an object's height using the parallax method, you must first obtain two parallax measurements. Before making these measurements, first align the stereopair along the line of flight, as illustrated in **Figure 16.3**.

Once the photos are properly aligned, the first step is to compute the **absolute stereographic parallax** (P). You can do so by summing the distance (measured parallel to the flight line) from the object base to the nadir of each photo.

The second step is to compute the **differential parallax** (dP). This is simply the difference in absolute stereographic parallax at the top and base of the object being measured.

With these two parallax measurements completed, you can determine the object's height by applying the following equation:

$$\text{Height of object (h}_o\text{)} = (H) \; \frac{dP}{P + dP}$$

where H is the aircraft's height above the object's base (expressed in the units desired for the object height, usually feet or meters), and dP (differential parallax) and P (absolute parallax) are expressed in the same units (usually hundredths of inches or centimeters).

In Figure 16.3, the flying height of the aircraft is given as 500 meters. The absolute parallax is computed to be 45 mm. + 50 mm. = 95 mm., while the differential parallax is computed to be (47 − 45) + (53 − 50) = 5 mm. Thus, by substitution:

$$h_o = 500 \text{ m.} \; \frac{5 \text{ mm.}}{95 \text{ mm.} + 5 \text{ mm.}}$$

$$= 500 \text{ m.} \; \frac{5}{100} = 25 \text{ m.}$$

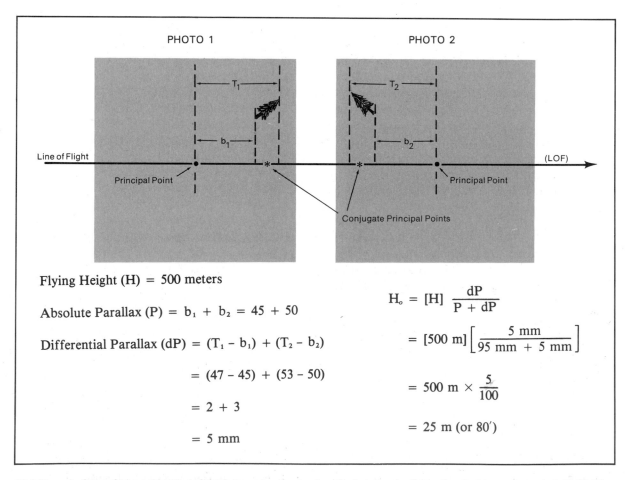

PHOTO 1 PHOTO 2

Line of Flight ——————— (LOF)

Principal Point

Principal Point

Conjugate Principal Points

Flying Height (H) = 500 meters

Absolute Parallax (P) = $b_1 + b_2$ = 45 + 50

Differential Parallax (dP) = $(T_1 - b_1) + (T_2 - b_2)$

$\qquad = (47 - 45) + (53 - 50)$

$\qquad = 2 + 3$

$\qquad = 5 \text{ mm}$

$$H_o = [H] \; \frac{dP}{P + dP}$$

$$= [500 \text{ m}] \left[\frac{5 \text{ mm}}{95 \text{ mm} + 5 \text{ mm}} \right]$$

$$= 500 \text{ m} \times \frac{5}{100}$$

$$= 25 \text{ m (or 80')}$$

16.3 You can determine an object's height from a stereopair of vertical photos by lining the photos up along their flight line and then measuring parallax separation.

The accuracy of this object height estimate depends on how precise the two parallax measurements are and how close the true flying height is to 500 meters. To improve measurement precision, it helps to measure the differential parallax stereoscopically with a special aid such as a **parallax wedge** or **parallax bar** (stereometer). These specialized devices are described in books on photo interpretation (see *Selected Readings* at the end of this chapter).

The precision of stereoscopically determined measurement also depends on your ability to perceive the three-dimensional parallax effect. It helps immensely to have an object clearly imaged on high-resolution photos of known scale and flight altitude.

Height of Continuous Surfaces

We have been treating the land surface as an irregular base from which we can measure the height of discrete environmental features, such as trees or buildings. But we can also measure the height of the terrain surface itself.

As we saw in Chapter 5, *Landform Portrayal*, we can view the landform as a continuous geographic distribution. By "continuous," we mean that for every location we can measure the land surface's height above a base level (or datum). We call this height value "elevation." Some maps show elevation data directly. With other maps, you will have to determine this elevation information on your own.

The same cartometric procedures we use to figure out elevations can also be used to determine other continuous distributions, such as temperature or population density (see *Smooth Surfaces* in Chapter 1). With such phenomena, the notion of "height" becomes rather vague, of course. When describing the vertical dimension of these intangible distributions, the terms "magnitude" or "intensity" are more appropriate than "height."

Although the idea is the same as that behind elevation, such distributions may be difficult to visualize. With some of them—precipitation, temperature, or air pressure, for instance—a value naturally exists at every location. But such distributions as population density or land values are contrived in the sense that values don't exist at specific locations. Still, the cartometric techniques we use to determine all these continuous distributions are essentially similar.

Measuring the vertical component of a continuous surface is quite different from measuring the height of discrete objects. To appreciate the three-dimensional character of a continuous distribution, you need to "look down" through the surface to its base. It may not be necessary to view the whole distribution simultaneously, however. Sometimes knowing the value at only one location is enough.

One problem with computing a continuous surface's height is that map symbols don't usually show absolute magnitude information directly at all points. Thus, you'll often need to predict a feature's intensity at a given point using information from other map locations. Usually, the best way to find this information is to look at isolines. (We discussed these useful lines under *Isoline Maps* in Chapter 7.)

When a point falls on an isoline, you can determine its value directly. Few points, however, fall on the relatively small sample of mapped isolines. Thus, most isoline maps yield magnitude information only indirectly. To obtain the value at a non-isoline position, you must either **interpolate** between values provided by surrounding isolines or **extrapolate** from values provided by distant isolines. When you use these procedures, you really have two closely related magnitude determination problems: to find the position of some known value, and to find the value at some known position.

You can solve the first problem, **finding the position of a known value**, graphically by using a right triangle based on known data. Imagine, for instance, that the value for which you're seeking a location is an elevation of 520 meters. Find the isolines above and below that value. Use the map distance separating those two isolines to form the base of your triangle (**Figure 16.4A**). Then use the difference between lower and upper valued isolines to determine the triangle's height. On this right triangle, plot the desired height of 520 meters, and draw a horizontal line (parallel with the base) through this point. Finally, draw a vertical line through the point at which this horizontal line intersects the hypotenuse of the triangle. This line will intersect the base of the triangle at the map position at which the value is 520 meters.

342

You can solve the same problem numerically. To do so, first determine the contour interval, which in this case is 600 – 500 = 100 meters. Next, determine what proportion of 100 meters the value of 20 meters represents (20/100 = 1/5 = 20%).

You now know that the elevation of 500 meters lies 20 percent of the distance from point A (500 meters) to point C (600 meters). You can now plot this position on the map.

A slightly modified procedure is required if the value whose position you seek lies beyond the range of isolines depicted. To solve this extrapolation problem graphically, you form a triangle as before, but in this case you use data provided by the two higher (or lower) isolines (**Figure 16.4B**). Then, by assuming that the form of the terrain surface continues unchanged beyond the known isoline position, you can predict a second triangle. This second triangle provides the basis for the graphic solution, as Figure 16.4B demonstrates. As before, this graphic solution can be modified to produce a numerical solution.

Your second task is to **find the value at some known position**. The graphic solution to this problem is similar to the previous one. The only difference is that to determine the height value, you first draw a perpendicular line from the triangle base to the hypotenuse and then extend a horizontal line from this point (**Figure 16.5A**)

The numerical solution is also similar to the previous one, except that you now form a ratio between the point-to-contour distance (shown as P in the figure) and the contour-to-contour distance, multiply the contour interval by this proportion, and add the resulting value to the lower contour.

The graphic solution to finding elevation at a point by extrapolation is much like the one you used to find a known value's position by extrapo-

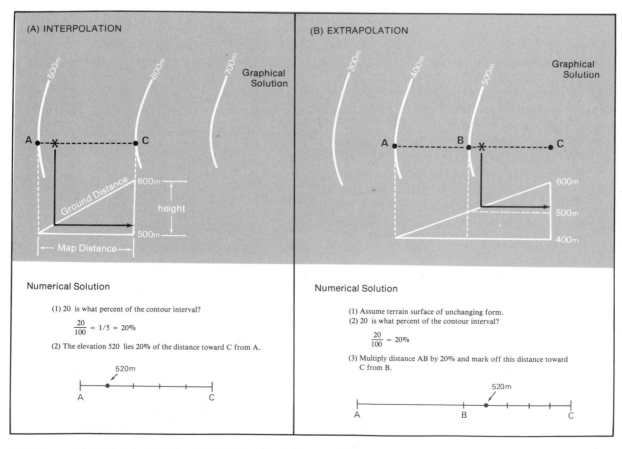

16.4 The map location at which the elevation is a given value can be determined through a process of interpolation (A) or extrapolation (B). Here we are answering the question: "At what position along line AC is the elevation 520 meters?"

lation (**Figure 16.5B**). You construct a predicted triangle with which you can determine the desired elevation. Again, the numerical solution is a modification of the graphic one.

SECONDARY SPATIAL CONCEPTS

We've seen how we can use cartometric procedures to obtain precise information about location (Chapter 11), direction (Chapter 12), distance (Chapter 13), and height (in the preceding section). We can now use these primary spatial elements as a foundation from which to build still higher-level spatial concepts. Included in this category are measures of area, volume, density, and spatial change. These geographic properties are derived from the primary elements and are somewhat more conceptual in nature. They, in turn, can be used to formulate still higher-order abstractions.

In this section, we'll see how we can use cartometrics to make accurate computations of a variety of secondary spatial elements. We'll begin our discussion with the concept of region.

Region

The name given to a geographic area is **region**. Some regions are thought of as being uniform or homogeneous within their borders. There are two types of uniform regions. Some, such as political units, are truly homogeneous within their legally defined borders. Politically, there is no difference between the central and border areas of Colorado, for instance.

But some regions are uniform only in concept. In reality, such a region may be quite different at its core than at its periphery. The thickness of an oil slick, for example, will vary between its

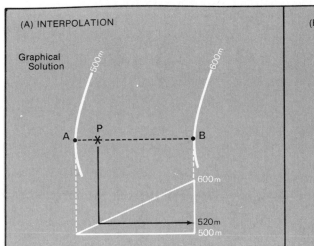
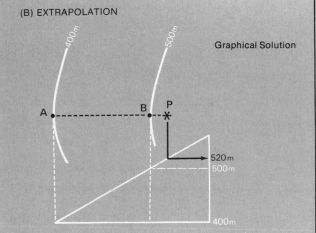

16.5 We can find the elevation at a given map location through interpolation (A) or extrapolation (B). Here we want to find the elevation at point P.

344

conceptually defined borders. Regions may also be defined functionally. An example of a functional region might be the commuting area of a city or the customer region around a bank.

The process of defining the extent of non-uniform regions, called **regionalization**, is central to the way we think about and deal with our surroundings. Our geographic vocabulary is enriched by concepts such as the South, corn belt, disaster area, climatic zone, and so forth.

Although abstractions of this sort can be useful, they also can mask the underlying reality. For example, once we define a non-uniform region, we tend to relate to it as if it were uniform. Thus, disaster benefits may go to those within a certain region and be denied to those outside. Yet the

region boundary may separate potential claimants by only a few feet on the ground. (See **Box 16.2** for some other problems of blurry boundaries.)

Centroid

The concept of center or **centroid** is commonly associated with geographic features and regions. You may want to find the **center of area** of a lake, for example. You can think of this as the lake's "balance point" or **center of gravity**.

If you cut the lake out of a map, and find the point where it balances on the tip of a pencil, you will have found the lake's center of gravity (**Figure 16.6A**). Mathematically, you can find the same point by calculating the **bivariate mean** of

---

BOX 16.2
THE PLACE IS HERE, ITS NAME SAYS THERE: AN ISLAND OF BLURRY BOUNDARIES

MINEOLA, N.Y.—Nassau County's designated county seat is Mineola. Government agencies and their official documents all dutifully list it on their addresses.

But they're wrong. The court, legislative and executive buildings are actually in Garden City. Which, despite its name, is not a city but an incorporated village. . . .

Even native islanders are bewildered by the quirks that can confound 911 dispatchers, mail carriers and map makers. For many residents, their own community identity suffers split personalities. . . .

The dyslexic gazetteer here has many bewildering quirks. Leonard's of Great Neck, a popular catering hall, is actually in University Gardens. The State University of New York at Farmington is about a mile from its namesake.

Five Towns College is not now, and never has been, in the Five Towns, though it originally planned to be. None of the so-called Five Towns, by the way, are really towns. . . .

Nassau Point is in eastern Suffolk County, far from Nassau. The L.I.R.R.'s Sea Cliff station is actually in Glen Cove. East Islip is in the western half of Islip Town and is south of Central Islip. . . .

Such oddities can have consequences. The Nassau and Suffolk police monitor address and phone changes on their border to keep people in the right 911 system. . . .

Long Island's mix-ups are rooted in politics and history. Modern Long Island is an artificial construct of suburban and rural Nassau and Suffolk, ignoring the adjacent urban boroughs of Queens and Brooklyn that share the same island. . . .

"Isn't it amazing we ever get the mail delivered?" asked a Post Office spokesman, Tom Gaynor, adding that his agency usually overcame the Island's hurdles. . . .

(Bruce Lambert, *New York Times*, August 10, 1997)

the lakeshore coordinates (x-y, latitude-longitude, SPC, UTM). The bivariate mean is defined as the average x-coordinate and the average y-coordinate of the lake boundary.

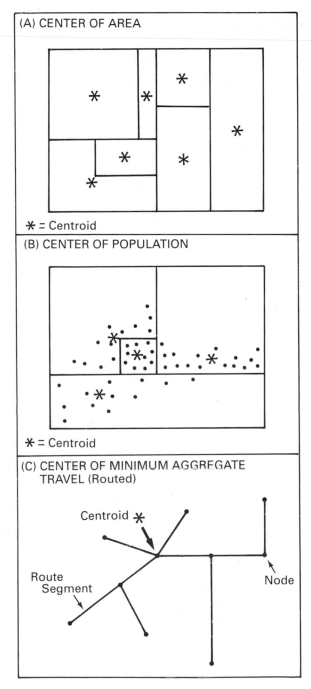

PART II
Map Analysis

The center of area isn't an appropriate centroid in all situations, however. For instance, knowing the center of area of New York State doesn't help you understand the distribution of the state's people. Indeed, the center of area falls in a relatively low population area. In this case, the **center of population** would be more meaningful (**Figure 16.6B**). You could find the center of population by calculating the bivariate mean of the x-y coordinates for the homes of all state residents.

In still other situations, neither of these centroids may be appropriate. If, for example, your aim is to find the best location to build an ambulance center, you need to find the center of **minimum aggregate travel** to the client population. In this case, you'll want to find the location that will minimize travel time along the road system (**Figure 16.6C**). This is a daunting task to perform manually but is easily handled with a computerized map analysis system.

Circumference

The boundary length of a geographic feature or region is often of interest. You can calculate this **circumference** using any of the distance measuring techniques discussed in Chapter 13. If high accuracy is desired, or the task requires a good deal of measuring, circumference calculations are best performed using a digitizer and spatial analysis software (see *Cartometrics* in Chapter 19).

Area

The size of a two-dimensional figure or region is called its **area**. You can think of an area in locational terms as a non-linear collection of adjacent cells or pixels that share a common defining characteristic. Or you can think of area in object-oriented terms as a figure or region enclosed by a boundary or edge. In either case, you can measure direction and distance in two directions from a point lying within an areal feature.

When you want to know how much area lies within a region's boundaries, you may obtain this figure in several ways. Visual estimation will suffice if you need only a rough approximation. But if you need a more precise value, you should rely on more rigorous computational methods. Depending on the situation, you can take one of

16.6 It is sometimes useful to compute the center of area (A), center of population (B), or center of minimum aggregate travel (C).

346

three approaches: graphic counting, instrumental, or mathematical. Let's look at these three area–computation methods in more detail.

Graphic Counting Methods

The simplest and most common techniques for computing area are graphic counting methods. There are two variations, although the idea is similar in both cases.

One procedure is to superimpose a **square grid** on the map (**Figure 16.7A**). To determine the area of the region, add up the grid cells that fall fully within the region, and then total the cells which fall partially within the region. Add the number of full cells to one-half the partial cell total. Finally, multiply the resulting sum by the cell area.

The second graphic counting technique is known as the **dot planimeter** method. Over the map, you superimpose a grid made up of alternating open and solid dots (**Figure 16.7B**). Next, count all the dots that fall entirely within the region. To this total, add the number of either open or solid dots falling on the region boundary. Multiply the result by the unit area value repre-

sented by each dot to obtain the region area in ground units (such as square kilometers or miles).

With both these methods, the smaller the cell size or dot unit value, the more accurate the area computation. But this greater accuracy is attained at the expense of more computational effort. Thus, you should choose a cell size or dot unit value based on how much accuracy you need.

Instrumental Methods

Sometimes it's most convenient to compute area by using instrumental (**mechanical/electronic**) methods. This is particularly true if you have areas with intricate boundaries, or a large number of areas to compute.

With one approach, you take advantage of the raster technology of electronic scanners (see *Electronic Imaging* in Appendix B). You can do so directly using the raster data generated by electronic scanners in remote sensing. Since these data are formatted in a grid of cells, called pixels, you can use an electronic implementation of the graphic counting technique discussed in the previous section to calculate the area of features.

First you must identify the features on the image. You can do so the traditional way, identifying features by eye and outlining them by hand. But this quickly becomes taxing if you have many images to process. In that case, it may be easier to use electronic image classification methods (see *Automated Feature Identification* in Chapter

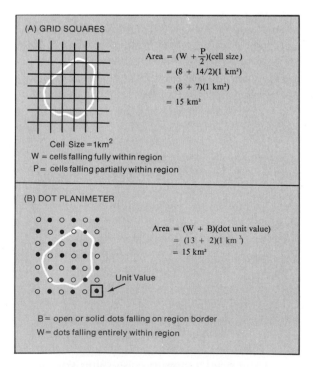

(A) GRID SQUARES

$$Area = (W + \frac{P}{2})(\text{cell size})$$
$$= (8 + 14/2)(1 \text{ km}^2)$$
$$= (8 + 7)(1 \text{ km}^2)$$
$$= 15 \text{ km}^2$$

Cell Size = 1 km^2
W = cells falling fully within region
P = cells falling partially within region

(B) DOT PLANIMETER

$$Area = (W + B)(\text{dot unit value})$$
$$= (13 + 2)(1 \text{ km}^2)$$
$$= 15 \text{ km}^2$$

Unit Value

B = open or solid dots falling on region border
W = dots falling entirely within region

16.7 You can use graphic counting methods involving cells (A) or dots (B) to determine the area of a polygon.

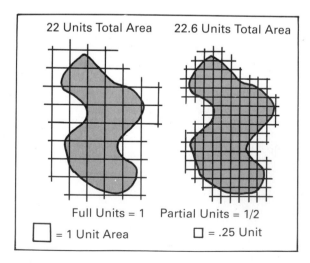

22 Units Total Area   22.6 Units Total Area

Full Units = 1   Partial Units = 1/2

☐ = 1 Unit Area   ☐ = .25 Unit

16.8 When cell–counting methods are used to compute area, smaller cells yield more accurate results but involve more data processing.

24). Once features such as lakes, wetlands, or forests are classified automatically through image processing, the software totals the pixels in each class and multiplies the result by the ground size of a pixel. The accuracy of the result is a function of the accuracy of the original classification and the size of a pixel. Smaller pixels produce more accurate results but also entail more data processing (**Figure 16.8**).

Notice that reducing a pixel's width by half increases the data by a factor of four. Of the satellite-based electronic scanner systems in widespread use, SPOT yields square pixels of 10 meters (black-and-white) and 20 meters (color infrared), while Landsat yields square pixels of approximately 30 meters with the Thematic Mapper (TM) and 80 meters with its Multispectral Scanner (MSS). (See Appendix B: *Remote Sensing of the Environment.*) The ground size of these pixels ranges from .025 acres (SPOT black-and-white) to 1.576 acres (MSS). You will have to decide which, if any, of these levels of spatial resolution is appropriate for your area computation needs.

If you don't have access to field-scanned electronic imagery, you can still take advantage of electronic cell-counting by using a laboratory scanner (**Figure 16.9**). Desktop models that scan page-sized images or graphics with a resolution from 300 to 1,200 dots per inch (dpi) are widely available. They come in both color and gray-scale models.

Much more expensive (but higher-resolution) film scanners are available for use with 35-mm. slides and other high-quality images. Large-format models that scan at high resolution are available for use with full-size printed sheet maps, such as topographic quadrangles.

Once your image map is scanned, you may still need to classify the data before you compute area. If you scan a line map such as a soils map or topographic quadrangle, however, you may be able to skip this classification step. The reason is that the more sophisticated high-resolution scanners can often be calibrated to recognize up to a dozen colors. These scanners can automatically separate features such as lakes and urban areas as long as they appear as distinct map symbols. This means you merely tally the pixels of appropriate color to obtain an area calculation. This technique is so fast and effective that it often pays to scan maps on which you have first hand-colored target features in distinct colors.

Notice that these electronic cell-counting procedures have an all-or-nothing character at the pixel level. You have feature pixels and non-feature pixels, but no in-between pixels representing boundary cases as you had with graphic counting methods (see previous section). In theory, the cross-boundary cases considered in graphic counting methods should produce a better result. The increased accuracy, however, is probably too slight to justify the manual labor required.

Electronic methods have all but displaced a mechanical instrument called a fixed-arm **polar planimeter** (**Figure 16.10**). Polar planimeters are much slower and less accurate than modern electronic methods, but the devices are still widely available. Thus, if you don't have access to electronic instruments, you may want to try your hand at using one of these polar planimeters.

You should begin by setting up the device with the fixed arm anchored off to the side of the region to be measured. This set-up lets you move the tracing point freely around the region boundaries. Then, trace the outline of the region in a

16.9 Electronic scanning devices are now common laboratory equipment and can be used to generate data for area computation by cell–counting.

348

clockwise direction. The dial will tell you the number of revolutions made by the recording wheel. It is a good idea to trace the outline several times to obtain an average reading.

Older, strictly mechanical instruments provide the area in square centimeters or square inches. This means your final step when using these instruments will be to convert this figure into ground units, using the map scale. More modern, computerized polar planimeters make the needed conversions automatically and display the results in a digital readout.

Mathematical Methods

A third way to compute a region's area is to use mathematical methods. If the region is a simple geometric shape such as a square, rectangle, or triangle, you can precisely determine its area with geometric calculations. Such **mensuration methods** are based on the area formulas you were required to memorize in grade school but may well have since forgotten (**Figure 16.11**). When only limited information is available, you can use more elaborate methods involving trigonometric functions. (See a basic textbook on trigonometry for the appropriate formulas.)

Most geographic regions, of course, aren't squares, rectangles, or triangles. Even so, you can often calculate their areas using **simple geomet-**

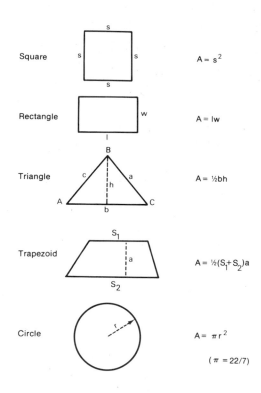

16.11 You can determine the area of simple geometric figures using mensuration methods.

ric figures. Suppose, for instance, that you want to know the area of a tract of land shaped like a plane polygon (a figure made up of a number of straight sides). You simply divide the polygon into a combination of squares, rectangles, and triangles, and then compute the sum of the areas of these simpler geometric forms.

If the tract has an irregular or curved border, you can use a modification of the "simple figures" approach, called the **strip method (Figure 16.12)**. With this technique, the first step is to position a series of equally spaced parallel lines over the region's outline. Make sure that there are lines touching the extremes of the region.

Next, construct "give-and-take" lines perpendicular to the parallel lines. Areas falling to the inside and outside of the give-and-take lines should be approximately equal. Measure the length of the strips between the give-and-take lines, and add these figures.

Now, by multiplying the total strip length by the strip width, you will have the map area of the region. Using the unit area value determined by the map scale, you can convert the map area to

16.10 Use of a polar planimeter for computing the area of a mapped region requires tracing the region's outline with the instrument's cursor and converting the resulting map reading to ground units.

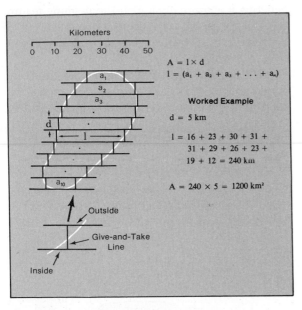

Kilometers

0   10   20   30   40   50

a_1
a_2
a_3

d

l

a_{10}

Outside

Give-and-Take
Line

Inside

$A = l \times d$
$l = (a_1 + a_2 + a_3 + \ldots + a_n)$

Worked Example

$d = 5$ km

$l = 16 + 23 + 30 + 31 +$
$\quad 31 + 29 + 26 + 23 +$
$\quad 19 + 12 = 240$ km

$A = 240 \times 5 = 1200$ km^2

16.12 It is convenient to use the strip method when computing the area of complex figures, especially if an electronic scanning device can be used to determine strip lengths automatically.

ground area units. Obviously, the more closely spaced the parallel lines, the greater the computational effort, but also the greater the accuracy of your results.

If you have available a string of (x, y) coordinate pairs describing the vertexes of a region's boundary, you can also use this information to calculate the tract's area. The idea is to find the areas of trapezoids formed by projecting the line segments bounding the region upon one of the pairs of coordinate axes. Although this would be tedious if done by hand, it is a simple matter to create a computer program based on the method of coordinates which will quickly and effortlessly compute the area of the region.

The computer-based coordinate approach is particularly appropriate when the tract's boundary is irregular or involves a large number of vertexes. With curved boundaries, increasing the number of vertexes improves the accuracy of area estimation. The problem is to balance accuracy with the added cost and computational effort associated with increasing sample sizes. Clearly, by establishing vertexes only at those positions on the boundary where major directional changes occur, you can approximate the figure's area most efficiently. Mechanical digitiz-

ing machines ease the chore of converting a region's map boundary to the appropriate numerical form for area computation by high-speed digital computer (**Figure 16.13**).

Area Distortion

One problem with making measurements of any kind on maps is that the map's geometry may not be true. This is often the case when making area computations. In general, all the area determination methods we've discussed so far will provide an accurate measure of a region's extent only if the region is relatively small (less than a country or state) and if the map is in parallel perspective from a vertical vantage point. If the map is in central perspective, the scale will change from one part to another, making area computations difficult and usually inaccurate. Oblique central perspective maps are especially difficult to use in computing area.

When the region extends over long distances, earth curvature also becomes a factor in determining area. If you plan to make area computations on a map of the world or other large region, you must be careful to use a map which preserves area. This may be easier said than done, for few flat maps of the world have areas everywhere correctly represented. What you must look for are maps based on **equal–area** or **equivalent** projections. On these maps, the property of equal area is attained by adjusting the scales

16.13 You can use an automated line-following digitizing machine to convert graphic map information into spatial coordinates.

350

along the meridians and parallels (or any other right-angle axes). The result is proportionate distortion of the latitude-longitude grid, which generally increases toward the map's margins (see Figure C.7 in Appendix C: *Map Projections*).

The property of equal area is so difficult to come by that there is only one perspective projection which possesses it. This is the cylindrical projection, which is discussed in Appendix C (see Figure C.17). Since on this projection the meridians are parallel rather than converging as in reality, the spacing between parallels grows shorter as distance from the equator increases. Except for this lone perspective projection, all other equal-area maps are based on non-perspective or modified projections.

The equal-area map is especially useful in mapping statistical variables when it is important to show the variation in a spatial distribution. Equal-area maps also play a role in land-use or similar mapping in which a measure of the area occupied by some distribution is crucial to map interpretation. The property of equivalence is perhaps more useful than any other for general-reference maps, since map study usually involves making comparisons in which the relative size of areas and densities is important, if not essential.

Volume

As we've seen, the size of two-dimensional objects is fully defined by the concept of area. The size of three-dimensional features, in contrast, is defined by the concept of **volume**. A volume can be thought of as a three-dimensional grouping of points, or as an area rotated or projected through the third dimension. In either case, direction and distance can be measured in three dimensions from a point lying within a volumetric feature.

Some volumetric features are uniform in character. Uniform volumes, like regions, may be truly homogeneous or only conceptually homogeneous. The legally bounded air space of the United States is a truly homogeneous volume. The smog layer over a metropolitan area is a conceptually homogeneous volume, since it varies in thickness and density from its core to its periphery.

Volumes can also be functional in character. A smoke plume and the thermal discharge into a lake from a power generating plant are examples. Although such a volume may be homo-

geneous, it is more likely that the defining feature will change intensity within functionally defined borders. In other words, a smoke plume will vary from light to dense smoke.

It is easier to compute the volume of some geographic features than others. The simplest features to deal with are those that can be conceived of as having one flat surface. For instance, a lake (which has a flat top), the landform surface (which has a flat bottom), and average annual precipitation (which has a 0-value datum) are volumes which satisfy this criterion.

The usual way to compute the volume of something such as annual precipitation within a

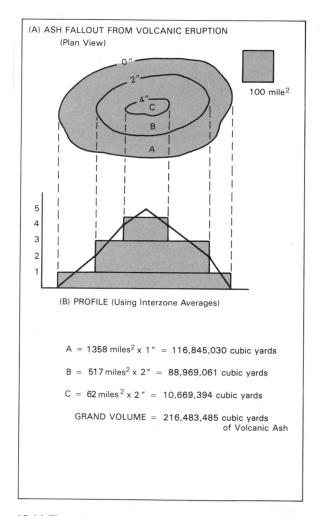

(A) ASH FALLOUT FROM VOLCANIC ERUPTION
(Plan View)

100 mile^2

(B) PROFILE (Using Interzone Averages)

A = 1358 miles^2 x 1″ = 116,845,030 cubic yards

B = 517 miles^2 x 2″ = 88,969,061 cubic yards

C = 62 miles^2 x 2″ = 10,669,394 cubic yards

GRAND VOLUME = 216,483,485 cubic yards
of Volcanic Ash

16.14 The volume of a feature with a flat surface, which has been mapped with isolines, can be computed using the method of ordinates. The procedure involves determining the volume associated with each inter-isoline zone and adding these values to obtain the grand total.

region is to use the **method of ordinates**. With this technique, you first determine the average ordinate (or height) of the feature within the region. This may be estimated visually, or it may itself be the result of detailed computations.

Once you have the average ordinate, multiply this value by the area of the region. If, for instance, the average annual precipitation within a square kilometer region is .76 meter (29.92 inches), the total volume of precipitation that normally falls in one year would be 1,000 x .76 = 760,000 cubic meters (26,828,000 cubic feet). If a volumetric distribution has been mapped with isolines, you can use the values and the area between the lines to compute volume (**Figure 16.14**).

If more than one region is involved, or if you want to use subregions to obtain the volume of a region, simply repeat the above procedure for each region and add the results. In this case, the average ordinates for the individual areal units will form a three-dimensional histogram. Clearly, the smaller these areal units are, relative to the size of the overall region, the more accurate the volume determination. But smaller units can also mean more computational effort.

The volume of a feature with a flat surface can also be computed using an **equation method** based on calculus. Before you can use this technique, the surface must be defined in the functional form $z = f(x,y)$, where z is the vertical dimension and x and y are the two horizontal dimensions (see *Trends and Cycles* in the next chapter for further discussion of mathematical functions).

Forming this equation may strike you as a troublesome task, but computers simplify it for you. At most large computer installations (such as university computer centers), you will find a program which will take a sample of (x,y,z) coordinates and generate an equation of the form $z = f(x,y)$. Programs to compute the volume for a region under such a surface are usually available at the same facilities.

Although this equation method may seem more sophisticated and involved than your needs dictate, it is the most effective approach if many computations must be made and if your information is already in computer-compatible form (that is, on punch cards, magnetic tape, or punch paper tape).

When geographic features are fully bounded by irregular surfaces (in other words, with no flat surface), you can use the same methods, but the computations are more involved. The method of ordinates will require a lower as well as an upper average value for each region; otherwise, the computational procedure is the same. Similarly, the equation method requires that equations for both the upper and lower surfaces be available.

Density

You can use the concepts of area and volume to help define a third spatial concept, that of **density** or texture. You might say that suspended particulates in the smog reached a maximum of 10 parts per cubic centimeter, that the population of the United States is 50 people per square kilometer, or that there is an average of three farm houses along each mile of rural road in central Iowa. In each case, you are expressing the quantity of an environmental feature per standard dimensional unit (volume, area, length). You derive the measure of density, then, by relating some feature to a unit of space.

The spatial unit used most often to compute densities of map distributions is area. Although a count of discrete point features, such as people or houses, provides the basis for most measures of density, you don't have to restrict yourself to point features alone. You can convert a line network to a density distribution, for example, by relating route length to area subdivisions such as counties or states.

Likewise, you can compute the drainage density of a river basin by forming a ratio between the total length of all channels to the basin's area (defined by the drainage divide). Since drainage density is a function of the amount of surface runoff, you can gain an understanding of climate and permeability of subsurface materials by comparing drainage densities of different river systems on maps.

You can also compute the density of areal units such as counties by relating them to larger regions, such as states. For instance, Nevada has 19 counties in an area of 111,000 square miles (287,490 km.²) for a density of 1.7 counties per 10,000 square miles (25,900 km.²), while Rhode Island has five counties in an area of 1,210 square

352

miles (3,134 km.²) for a density of 41 counties per 10,000 square miles. Consequently, the density of counties in Rhode Island is 41/1.7 = 24 times that of Nevada.

Since density computations soon become laborious, and since for many purposes you need only a rough estimate, it's helpful to use **density templates** if you must make many density readings. But because the necessary templates are rarely available, it's usually up to you to make a set matched to the map scales and graphic patterns you're using. (An example set of templates for determining contour line spacing is shown in Figure 16.17.)

With these keys as a guide, you can determine the approximate density of a distribution in any region on a map. If the observed density falls between template values, you can obtain a density estimate by simple interpolation.

The spatial units (usually area) are held constant in density computations so that you can study variation in the frequency with which some phenomenon occurs. Obviously, if density measures are to be meaningful, areas must be correctly portrayed in all regions of the map being analyzed. This means that you shouldn't compute densities from maps which distort area (see *Area Distortion* earlier in this chapter) unless you compensate for the distortion in your computations.

Density is sometimes taken as a crude guide to average **accessibility**, particularly in the case of communication networks. The density of bus routes, for instance, might be viewed as an indicator of the quality of bus service.

In contrast, density is sometimes used as a guide to **crowding** when territory or living space is considered. Thus, some people believe population density to be inversely related to environmental quality.

Obviously, this density indicator of access or crowding is an average figure and will provide an unfair impression of conditions when phenomena are variably distributed. In addition, we must consider the nature of the mapped features and their communication linkages. For example, highway network densities are naturally greater than railroad network densities. Similarly, people in highly industrialized societies such as the United States will generally cause greater pollution per individual than will people from less industrialized societies.

Spatial Change

In addition to area, volume, and density, there's another secondary spatial concept of great importance to map users—the **spatial change** which occurs from one point to another. The vertical change in ground surface has a major influence on human spatial behavior. Likewise, changes in socio-cultural phenomena over a region can profoundly affect the way we relate to the environment.

To help communicate spatial change concepts, we use various labels. We speak of roads as having a gentle, moderately steep, or steep roadbed, depending on the terrain traversed. We say that there is a sharp rise in temperature as we cross from a cold to a warm air mass. A lake bottom is said to drop off rapidly from shore. In each case, we are expressing the spatial change of a surface in three dimensions (although often only sections or profiles of the three-dimensional feature are illustrated).

To clarify this concept, let's begin by analyzing spatial change in two dimensions. In a two-dimensional context, spatial change is referred to as "slope."

Slope

The vertical change in the land surface, when taken over a given horizontal distance—along a road or stream, for instance—is known as its **slope**. Slope can only be computed between two points; it doesn't exist at a point. If we want to know the slope at a specific location, therefore, we must pick out two points, one on each side of our location, to use in computing the slope. Although we generally use the term "slope" to refer to the amount of rise or fall of the ground surface, the concept is equally applicable to the spatial change of any phenomenon.

We usually describe slope with such adjectives as gentle, moderate, or steep. These subjective designations are of limited use, however, because they can take on quite diverse meanings for people under different conditions of age, fitness, or stress. You can express slope more precisely if you use numerical terms. You simply form a ratio between the vertical distance (**rise**), as determined by the map symbols, and the horizontal distance (**run**) as determined through the map scale.

You may state this ratio in several ways. The easiest method is to express it as a **simple fraction (Figure 16.15A)**. Thus, in this example, a rise of 15 meters (49.2 feet) over a run of 300 meters (984.25 feet) yields a slope of 1/20.

Or you can express the slope as a **percent (Figure 16.15B)**. With this method, you must determine the number of vertical units to every 100 units of horizontal distance. To do so, multiply the slope expressed as a decimal fraction by 100. In the example, the slope of 1/20 is equivalent to the decimal .05; therefore, the slope is five percent.

And, finally, you can express the slope in units of angular measure, or **degrees (Figure 16.15C)**. This third method is based on the fact that the slope value as a simple fraction is the trigonometric tangent of the slope angle. Consequently, you can look up the slope angle in a table of trigonometric functions. You find the angle as a decimal number, and the table gives you the angle in degrees (Table E.5, Appendix E). In the example, the angle whose tangent is .05 is 3°. Notice that an angle of 45° would represent a 100% slope. If trigonometric tables aren't available, you can calculate the approximate slope angle with reasonable accuracy for angles up to 20° by multiplying the slope value by the constant 57.3°.

The slope concept is based on a surface which shows a constant spatial change. Such surfaces have a linear form. Deviation from a linear surface within the distance over which spatial change is computed will result in misrepresentation of slope. While the actual slope of a curved surface will vary in steepness, computations will yield a constant slope value.

The greater the distance over which slope is computed and the more curved the surface, the greater the slope misrepresentation. This factor may become critical when a relatively poor sample of contour lines is used in computing slope values.

So far, we have limited our discussion of spatial change to two dimensions. Sometimes, of course, we are interested in spatial change in three dimensions. In such cases, the computations are more involved, but the concept is still simple. When we move into three dimensions, we use the term "gradient" rather than "slope."

Gradient

The slope of a **surface**, rather than a line, is known as its **gradient**. "Gradient" is a little more specific than slope, however, because it means *the maximum spatial change away from a point which occurs on a surface*. In other words, while any downhill road has a slope between any two points along its distance, it may not follow a **gradient path**. It represents a gradient path only if from every point along its course it traces the steepest route down the hill.

When you want to know the maximum amount of a surface's spatial change at a point, you'll need to determine gradient. This process is a bit more complicated than computing slope. Actually, two calculations are necessary. In addition to the slope's magnitude, you also have to compute the gradient's direction (or azimuth). For this reason, we use the term "partial slope" to refer to slope in a single direction, in contrast to two-dimensional slopes which have no directional restriction.

To explore the concept of slope in three dimensions, it's convenient to think of the geographic surface in terms of the mathematical function $z = f(x,y)$. A partial slope measure serves as a quantitative expression of this surface's steepness or flatness in a given direction from any point on the surface. If the partial slope of $z = f(x,y)$ is computed with respect to x, treating y as constant, the result is the partial slope of

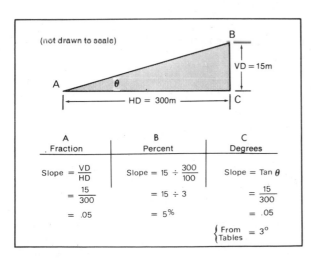

16.15 The slope of a surface between two points can be specified as a fraction (A), as a percentage (B), or in degrees (C).

354

f (or z) with respect to x, and is known as the **x–slope**. Likewise, if x is held constant, the partial slope in the y-direction is termed the **y–slope**.

The rate at which the height (or z) variable is changing at a location (x,y) depends on the direction we move away from the point. Although the partial slopes (x-slope, y-slope) represent the particular directional slopes in the x and y directions respectively, partial slopes can be computed in any other direction as well. In general, the directional slope of f in any direction is the rate of increase of z along that direction.

The gradient of a spatial function is defined as the maximum rate of change of the function at any location (x,y). By using the right-angle x and y axes of a square grid, you can calculate the numerical magnitude of the gradient at any grid intersection with the following equation:

$$G\ (x,y)\ =\ \sqrt{(x\text{-slope})^2 + (y\text{-slope})^2}$$

You can then find the azimuth of the spatial gradient by using the equation

$$\theta\ =\ \text{arctangent}\ \frac{x\text{-slope}}{y\text{-slope}}$$

where θ is the angle in degrees off the north (or vertical) base line, and arctangent (sometimes called arctan) is shorthand for "angle whose tangent is...."

By making repeated gradient computations, it is possible to derive a **slope zone map** from data representing a continuous surface such as the landform (**Figure 16.16A**). These slope zone maps have proven to be useful tools in the hands of land use planners and resource managers. They have been used successfully in runoff modeling, urban development (some cities have a slope-zone ordinance), logging, and farming.

Gradient computations become tedious if they must be repeated frequently. For this reason, professionals who create slope zone maps usually rely on computers or special optical devices to make the necessary computations.

If appropriate slope zone maps (or the methods used by professionals to produce them) aren't at hand, you can still come up with a crude slope zone map quickly and cheaply using a **graphic template method**. To do so, you first

make templates of contour lines which have the spacing necessary to represent each slope zone class you have chosen to isolate (**Figure 16.17**). Next, compare each of these contour line templates with the contour map itself. Each map region which matches a template can then be outlined and the zone appropriately symbolized according to the key you have chosen. Obviously, it is important for your graphic templates to be properly matched to the map scale and contour interval.

Like gradient computations, gradient azimuth computations are tedious if not done by computer. If such computations have been made, however, it is possible to create a **gradient vector map (Figure 16.16B)**. When working with

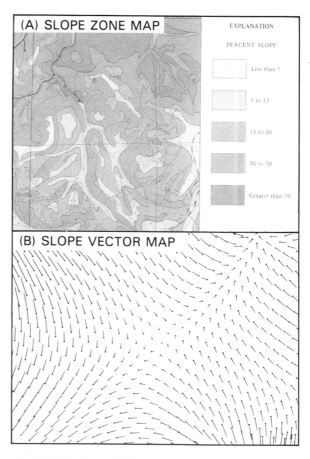

16.16 Gradient magnitudes can be used to create slope zone maps (A) which are useful land use planning and management tools. Gradient azimuths can be used to generate gradient vector maps (B) which outline ridge lines and basins and suggest patterns of flow associated with surfaces.

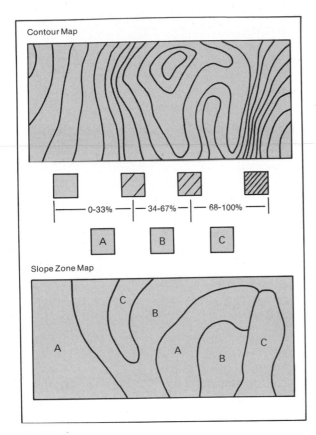

16.17 Slope templates make it convenient to convert an isoline map into a slope zone map.

terrain, such a map is useful in defining watersheds. With non-terrain data, surface gradient zones and breaks between zones may be suggestive of movement or flow of ideas, goods, or forces. Thus, a gradient vector map of barometric pressure may help to explain the pattern of winds.

CONCLUSION

In this chapter, we first talked about fundamental spatial elements and then saw how we could use these elements to build secondary spatial concepts. However useful this cartometric analysis might be in its own right, it's even more important in providing the foundation for higher-level spatial concepts. Among these are the notions of form and structure, which we'll explore in the next chapter.

SELECTED READINGS

Avery, T.E., "Stereograms, Shadow Heights, and Area," in *Interpretation of Aerial Photographs*, 3rd ed. (Minneapolis: Burgess Publishing Co., 1977), pp. 63-80.

Buttenfield, B., and Dribble, K., *Formalizing Cartographic Knowledge* (Santa Barbara, CA: NCGIA, 1995).

Clarke, J.I., "Morphometry from Maps," in Dury, G.H., ed., *Essays in Geomorphology* (London: Heinemann, 1966), pp. 235-274.

Dickinson, G.C., "Measurement of Area," Chapter 9 in *Maps and Air Photographs* (London: Edward Arnold Publishers, Ltd., 1969), pp. 132-141.

Dury, G.H., "Geometric Analysis," in *Map Interpretation*, 4th ed. (London: Pitman & Sons, Ltd., 1972), pp. 163-177.

Earickson, R.J., and Harlin, J.M., *Geographical Measurement and Quantitative Analysis* (New York: Macmillan College Publishing Co., 1994).

Eyton, J.R., "Rate-of-Change Maps," *Cartography and Geographical Information Systems*, 18, 2 (April 1991), pp. 87-103.

Gatrell, A., *Distance and Space: A Geographical Perspective* (Oxford: Clarendon Press, 1983).

Gierhart, J.W., "Evaluation of Methods of Area Measurement," *Surveying and Mapping*, 14 (1954), pp. 460-469.

Lawrence, G.R.P., "Measurements from Maps," and "Map Analysis," Chapters 9 and 10 in *Cartographic Methods*, 2nd ed. (London: Methuen & Co., Ltd., 1979), pp. 82-104.

Maling, D.H., *Measurement From Maps: The Principles & Methods of Cartometry* (New York: Pergamon Press, Inc., 1988).

Moellering, H., and Kimerling, A.J., "A New Digital Slope-Aspect Display Process," *Cartography and Geographic Information Systems*, 17, 2 (1990), pp. 151-159.

Neft, D.S., *Statistical Analysis for Areal Distributions*, Monograph Series No. 2 (Philadelphia: Regional Science Research Institute, 1966).

Pawling, J.W., "An Arithmetic Method of Determining Elevation Changes on Aerial Photographs," *The Professional Geographer*, 12, 5 (September 1960), pp. 10-12.

Proudfoot, M., *The Measurement of Geographic Area* (Washington, DC: U.S. Bureau of the Census, 1946).

Strandberg, C.H., "Aerial Photographic Measurements," in *Aerial Discovery Manual* (New York: John Wiley & Sons, 1967), pp. 51-57.

Thrower, N.J.W., and Cooke, R.U., "Scales for Determining Slope from Topographic Maps," *The Professional Geographer*, 20, 3 (May 1968), pp. 181-186.

Wolf, P.R., *Elements of Photogrammetry, With Air Photo Interpretation and Remote Sensing*, 2nd ed. (New York: McGraw-Hill, 1983).

Also see references in Chapters 17 and 18.

355

PART II
Map Analysis

CHAPTER 17
FORM AND STRUCTURE

EDGE

SHAPE

    Shape Indexes
    Shape Distortion
    Profiles

ORIENTATION

COMPOSITION

    Homogeneity
    Diversity
    Community

ARRANGEMENT

    Arrangement in Point Patterns
        Dispersion
        Spacing
    Arrangement in Line and Area Patterns

CONNECTIVITY

    Routed Paths
    Unrouted Paths

DISCONTINUITY

TRENDS AND CYCLES

HIERARCHY

CONCLUSION

SELECTED READINGS

The facts are available to all, but the patterns they form depend upon the point of view of the observer. Surely the patterns are as valid as the facts themselves, because they make rational and comprehensible a way of life which has too often been considered erratic and strange....Though the pattern is made up of facts, it differs from them as an assembled machine differs from a dismantled one.

—Walter Prescott Webb, *The Great Plains*

17
CHAPTER SEVENTEEN
FORM AND STRUCTURE

In the previous chapter, we developed a language of primary spatial elements and secondary spatial concepts. The aim was to find terms that would help us think more rigorously and systematically about the spatial character of the environment. We now need to use these basic conceptual tools to separate the environmental whole into its constituent parts. The first step is to isolate and describe the geographic features we see. This will entail describing the frequency with which we encounter different phenomena in space and the way various aspects of the environment are bonded together.

We can begin by recognizing that the vast complexity of our surroundings results from the simultaneous arrangement of like and unlike features and the interconnections and associations among phenomena. We're particularly interested in knowing where change occurs and in understanding spatial variation among features. Indeed, it's not the distribution of features so much as variation in these distributions from place to place that is of the greatest interest.

When we look at the landscape, or a map, our attention is naturally drawn to its internal organization, or the way its elements are spatially organized relative to each other. We call this structural organization **spatial order** or **pattern**. In defining what we mean by pattern, we find it necessary to relate the location of each feature to the others separately and collectively. We'll look more closely at these aspects of environmental structure in this chapter.

EDGE

As we saw in the introductory chapter of this book, people perceive the environment as a collection of objects. Fundamental to this object–oriented approach to our surroundings is the concept of **edge** or **boundary**. Much of our success as a species is a consequence of this boundary–making, for it's an efficient way to process information. Many of our failures come from the same source, however, as is clear in political boundary conflicts around the world.

For map analysis purposes, it's important to recognize that edge-making is an abstraction. It's an attempt to separate similar from dissimilar things. There's not much problem when this separation is obvious, as in defining the edge of a cement road. But when we define the edge between climate or soil zones, the level of abstraction is much greater. These latter edges are imposed rather than found. Thus, they're more conceptual than factual.

For all its problems, edge-making does help us clarify and simplify an otherwise confusing environment. It is central to map analysis in general. Our responsibility is to remember that boundaries come more from us than from the environment. They're an artifact of the way we think. Line maps carry this to the extreme by representing everything in a skeletal, edge-emphasized form. As map users, we want to become adept, first, at seeing as many edges as possible and, then, looking beyond the edges to the reality that is mapped.

SHAPE

The form of a line, area, or volume feature is called its **shape**. The quality of shape is what gives each geographic feature its distinctive character. We say that a region is compact, elongated, or irregular in shape. With volumetric features, we talk of lenticular (lens-shaped) clouds, basin lakes, and thin coal seams.

Important as the shape of geographic features is for map users, it's an elusive concept to communicate. The outlines or external surfaces of environmental features take so many forms that we can't conveniently attach labels to them all. But we have named a number of simple geometric figures, and we frequently refer to these through comparison. Thus, we might say that features are somewhat circular, roughly triangular, or approximately rectangular in shape. The actual association between the **empirical shape** (the shape observed on a map) and a **standard** (or known) **shape** may be difficult to state in words, however, and even harder to conjure up from someone's verbal description.

While this verbal, descriptive technique for treating shape suffices for many map use purposes, it is so subjective that little agreement is found between different map users or with a single user in varying circumstances. Thus, several other, more objective indexes for defining shape have been devised.

Shape Indexes

One objective method of viewing shape is to state in numerical terms the relationship between a standard two-dimensional shape and an empirical shape. If you want an idea of the circularity of an empirical shape, for example, you can superimpose the unknown shape on a circle of approximately the same area and compute the correspondence between the two figures mathematically. If you repeat the procedure using other standard shapes, you can then discuss the empirical shape's characteristics in an objective, systematic way.

Although an unlimited number of mathematical procedures could be devised, one example should make the procedure clear:

$$\text{Shape Index} = 1 - \left[\frac{\text{area (E and S)}}{\text{area (E or S)}} \right]$$

where the empirical shape is represented by E and the standard shape is represented by S.

To compute this shape index, first find the area in which the two shapes (E and S) overlap. Form a ratio between that area and the total area covered by either one or the other shape (E or S). Then subtract this value from 1 so that the shape index will range from 0 when there is perfect coincidence between the two shapes to 1 when there is no relationship.

In **Figure 17.1**, the empirical shape and the standard shape both have an area of 25 sq. km. The area covered by both shapes (E and S) is 23.28 sq. km., while the area covered by either E or S is 27.05 sq. km. Thus, the shape index = 1 – 23.28/27.05 = .14. This fairly low index value suggests that the empirical shape is quite close to a circle. If the index were 0, that would mean that the figure actually was a circle.

It's not uncommon to find indexes as low as 0, especially when determining the shape of cultural features (those produced by humans). The upper index value of 1, however, provides a limit which is never really obtained in practice, for it would mean that the figures didn't overlap at all, and the whole point of this method is to superimpose one figure on another.

In some situations, we would prefer to focus directly on shape compactness rather than comparing empirical shapes with standard shapes. Compactness of shape is considered desirable for many types of bounded space, in part because compact regions are most efficiently serviced and defended. Partitioning of space into compact units for administrative and political purposes also conveys a sense of fairness (see the discussions of gerrymandering under *Census* in Chapter 2 and *Redistricting* in Chapter 19).

A **compact shape** is one in which all points on the boundary are as close as possible to the center. The circle is the most compact figure, because its boundary is equidistant from its center point. This means that the sum of travel distances from its border to its center is minimized. The length of its boundary (perimeter) relative to its area is also minimal. For these reasons, shape compactness indexes all use the circle in some way as a standard reference figure.

One such shape compactness measure is known as the **figure attribute index**. With this technique, objective compactness indexes are derived by forming ratios between such basic figure attributes as area, perimeter, length of longest axis, and the radiuses of the largest inscribing or smallest circumscribing circle. For example, the ratio of a shape's area (A) to its perimeter (P) can provide a useful shape index. If this ratio is first modified by multiplying the perimeter by a con-

stant, then we can readily compare the resulting value with a circle. The shape index would become:

$$\text{Shape Index} = 2\left[\frac{A}{2.82P}\right]$$

With this index, a circle would receive an index value of 1. The more elongated and irregular the shape, the closer to 0 its index value would be. As an example, refer back to Figure 17.1. Since the region illustrated in that figure has a perimeter of 24 km., it would have a shape index of

$$2\left[\frac{25}{2.82 \times 24}\right] = .74.$$

When measuring shape compactness, it is important to keep in mind that the shapes of many natural and cultural features don't appear compact on the map but are, in fact, functionally compact, and vice versa. Function is more a matter of landscape configuration and resource distribution than of distance in miles or direction in degrees. A region that looks compact on a planimetric map may in fact be split into two very different functional regions by a high mountain range. Likewise, a region with a very irregular outline, such as an urban area, may be functionally compact in terms of travel time when we consider the road hierarchy.

The examples of standard shape and shape compactness which we've discussed in this section are fairly primitive compared to the more mathematically sophisticated procedures which have been proposed.* But they do illustrate several attributes of all numerical indexes which you need to weigh before putting too much faith in their infallibility. Due to all the decisions you must make when determining shape compactness or comparing empirical with standard shapes, a given environmental feature can have several index values. As if this weren't troubling enough, more than one shape can also have the

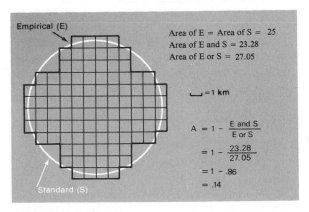

Empirical (E)

Area of E = Area of S = 25
Area of E and S = 23.28
Area of E or S = 27.05

⌐_⌐ = 1 km

$A = 1 - \dfrac{E \text{ and } S}{E \text{ or } S}$

$= 1 - \dfrac{23.28}{27.05}$

$= 1 - .86$

$= .14$

Standard (S)

17.1 The standard shape method makes it possible to compare the shapes of different regions numerically.

*For further discussion of statistical shape indexes, see Moellering, H., and Rayner, J.N., "The Dual Axis Fourier Shape Analysis of Closed Cartographic Forms," The Cartographic Journal, *Vol. 19, No. 1 (1982), pp. 53-59.*

same index value. In sum, the indexes devised to date don't make a unique assignment of number to shape. Despite these drawbacks, however, shape indexes are still useful in many map analysis situations, especially if they're simple, unit free, independent of the figure's size, and intuitively appealing.

Shape Distortion

There is little point in trying to determine the shapes of environmental features from their map portrayal unless they are truly represented. For shapes to be preserved, there can be no angular deformation in the cartographic representation. In other words, all angles on the earth's surface must be transformed into angles of equal size on the map. Maps of small regions in parallel perspective from a vertical vantage point meet this condition. They can be thought of as being **shape–preserving (conformal)** transformations of the earth's geometry.

But many large-scale maps don't preserve shapes. In addition, maps in central perspective from any vantage point (standard aerial photographs, for instance) show some, but not all, angles correctly. On a standard vertical photograph, the only directional relations that are true are those toward features from the principal point.

On small-scale maps covering large regions, shapes are preserved only in those special cases in which a conformal map projection has been used. Even then, the term "conformal" is somewhat misleading. It's not really possible to represent all angles over long distances correctly everywhere on a flat map of a large portion of the curved earth's surface. To do so would be to produce a completely undistorted map, which is impossible (see Appendix C: *Map Projections*). It is possible, however, to preserve certain angles, such as those within very small areas, and it is this preservation of angles on a global projection which we call conformality.

How will you know if a global projection is conformal? Look for two features. First, intersections in the latitude-longitude grid will all form right angles, as on the globe. Second, the scale will be the same in all directions from any point, although it may vary from point to point. Thus, a number of circular objects on the earth will project as circular objects on a conformal map,

but the mapped circles will be of varying sizes. In other words, a conformal map can't also be equivalent (size-preserving). Furthermore, the fact that angles are supposed to be shown correctly doesn't mean that it is always possible to measure them correctly on the map, as you can see in **Figure 17.2**. As a matter of fact, the shape-preserving quality of conformal projections may lead to confusion in map use, since for large regions shape distortion often exceeds that found on many non-conformal maps.

The only perspective projection possessing truth of angles is the **stereographic projection** (see Figure C.16B in Appendix C). All other conformal projections are of the non-perspective or modified type. The most famous (or infamous) modified projection is the **Mercator**. As explained under the heading *Projection Modifications* in Appendix C, the Mercator projection is a modified cylindrical form designed specifically to aid in navigation. In the normal aspect of the Mercator, meridians are parallel straight lines. This means that to maintain the same scale in all directions from each point, the parallels must be progressively farther apart with increasing distance from the equator (see Figure C.20B). Due to the tremendous scale distortion in high latitudes, this projection is rarely extended beyond 80° north or south latitude. But even at latitudes of less than 80°, the misrepresentation of area can cause serious map use confusion. On Mercator maps, for instance, Greenland appears larger than South America, while in fact South America is by far the larger.

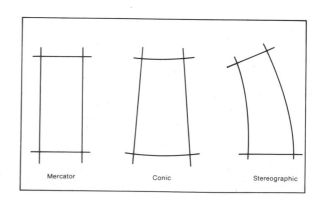

17.2 The shape of large features can be severely distorted by the projection used to create a map. On shape-preserving projections, latitude-longitude lines will intersect at right angles.

Conformal map projections are especially well suited for maps on which angular relationships and shapes are to be studied in the process of map use. It is understandable, therefore, that topographic, meteorological, and military maps as well as navigational charts are based on conformal projections. Users of such maps put up with distortion of area in order to have the truth of shape they need.

The infamy of Mercator's extremely valuable projection has come about through its indiscriminate use for non-navigational purposes, particularly in the schools and mass media. No other projection has been abused as much as the Mercator. For years it has served as the primary map base, even for studying spatial distributions in middle and high latitudes, which would be much more appropriately represented by an area-preserving rather than a shape-preserving projection.

Profiles

So far in this section we have concentrated on the shape of two-dimensional figures. But what about the shape of a three-dimensional surface such as the continuous landform? Surfaces of this type are often portrayed using the isoline method (see *Isoline Maps* in Chapter 7). But even skilled map users often find it difficult to visualize the third dimension of a geographic distribution on the basis of isoline information alone. If you encounter similar difficulties, you can benefit by following the method used by these professionals to supplement isoline data. Their strategy is to construct a **profile** between chosen points. This profile will dramatically show undulations of the mapped surface (**Figure 17.3**).

The simplest way to construct a profile on the basis of isoline information is to follow these steps:

1. Draw a straight line on the isoline map between the points of interest. This is called the **profile line**.

2. Determine how many isoline intervals separate the highest and lowest valued isolines which cross or touch the profile line, and add two to this number.

3. On a sheet of paper (or some other medium), draw as many equally-spaced parallel lines as you determined in Step 2 above.

You can save yourself some work by using commercial graph paper for this purpose.

4. Orient the paper so that the bottom line in the set of parallel lines is aligned immediately above the profile line.

5. Label the horizontal lines with isoline values, beginning at the bottom line with the lowest value (one interval below the lowest-valued isoline crossed by the profile line) and proceeding to the top line with the highest value (one interval above the highest-valued isoline crossed).

6. From every point at which the profile line is crossed or touched by an isoline, draw a perpendicular line to the horizontal line having the same value.

7. Draw a smooth, natural curve through all the points at which the perpendiculars intersect the proper horizontal lines. Remember that continuous geographic distributions are usually smooth rather than angular as the profile might suggest. If you're constructing a profile of the terrain surface, you should take local landform conditions into account in modifying the profile. Smoothing off sharp angles in the profile is usually justified.

A profile line doesn't have to be straight, of course. With a little extra work, you can profile a stream bed or hiking trail as well (**Figure 17.4**). To do so, follow these steps:

1. Determine and clearly mark on the map the desired profile line.

2. Same as Step 2 in the previous example.

3. Measure the length of the profile line (following the procedure described under *Determining Distance* in Chapter 13), and draw a line of this length on a sheet of paper. This is called the construction line.

4. Beginning at one end of the profile line, measure the distance to its first contact with an isoline, and mark off this distance from the end of the straight line you constructed in Step 3.

5. Repeat Step 4 until you reach the end of the profile line.

6. Parallel and adjacent to your construction line, draw as many equally-spaced lines as

you determined in Step 2. (Using graph paper will save time.) Label these lines from bottom to top as you did in Step 5 of the previous example.

7. From each point of contour contact on the straight construction line, extend a perpen-

dicular line to the horizontal line of the same value.

8. Draw a smooth curve through the points at which the perpendiculars intersect the appropriate horizontal line, as you did in the previous example.

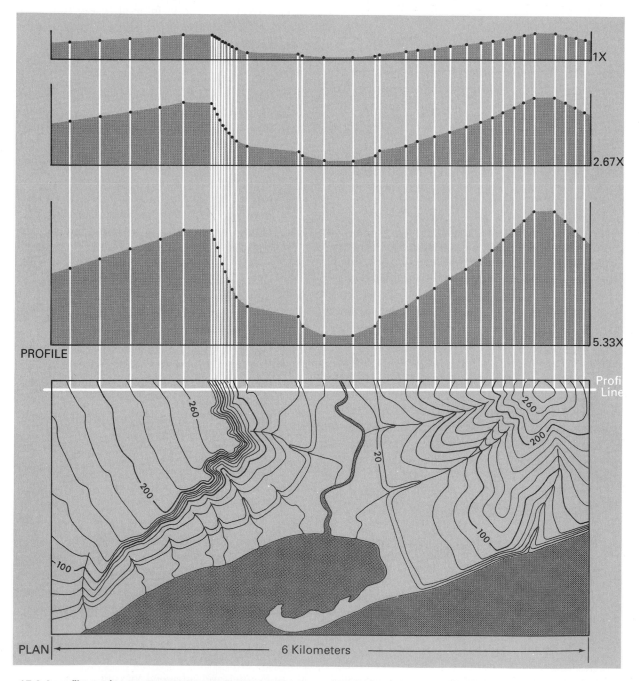

17.3 A profile can be constructed from an isoline map along any desired line. It is difficult, however, to choose the vertical component so that the profile gives the same impression of landform variation which the observer would receive in the field.

The profile's horizontal scale is set by the map scale. It may seem logical to make its vertical scale proportionate to the horizontal scale. Yet when this is done in constructing a terrain profile, the effect is invariably disappointing. We discussed the reason in Chapter 5. As we learned there, the vertical aspect of the topographic surface is numerically insignificant when compared to the horizontal aspect. Since terrain variation is so important to people's lives, you will have to expand the vertical dimension of your profile to make it realistic. Such exaggeration has the effect of steepening and lengthening the hillsides.

The spacing of the parallel horizontal lines used to construct a profile controls the scaling of the vertical dimension. To exaggerate minor features, you increase the spacing; to de-emphasize features, you decrease the spacing (see Figure 17.3). When dealing with a region of large relief, you may find it necessary to de-emphasize the mountain peaks somewhat while exaggerating the foothills to make the profile look natural.

Scaling the vertical component of non-topographic profiles is complicated by the fact that the magnitude units aren't comparable to those making up the horizontal dimension. The units used to measure population density, for example, bear no natural relation to the ground units measured in kilometers or miles. This means that in a technical sense there is no such thing as vertical exaggeration with non-topographic profiles. There is, however, such a thing as alternately emphasizing or de-emphasizing aspects of the profile by altering the spacing of the horizontal construction lines. You will have to take special care that you don't end up with a false impression of a distribution based solely on the way a profile is constructed.

Profiles based on isolines don't provide a perfect reconstruction of a surface, of course. This fact is especially obvious in the case of topographic profiles based on contour lines. As we saw in Chapter 5, contour lines represent sample transects from which we must infer the complete terrain surface. If contour lines are optimally placed with respect to the landform configuration, our inferences will be improved. If they're poorly situated, however, our inferences will be poor.

As further explained in Chapter 5, the spacing of contour lines is determined by the size of the contour interval. The larger this interval, therefore, the fewer the number of construction

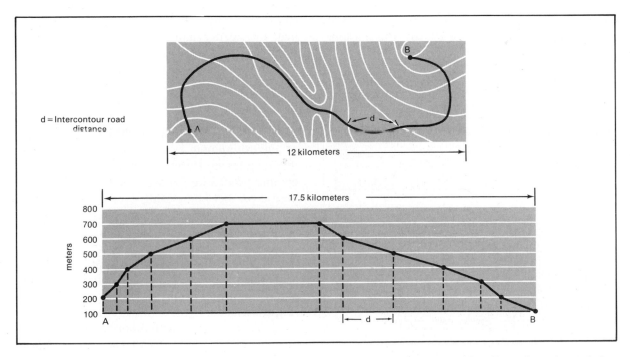

17.4 The line along which a profile is constructed needn't be straight. For example, the profile of a road can be made by scaling inter-contour road distances along the horizontal axis.

364

lines you will have available to make up a profile and the less topographic detail you will be able to come up with. The smaller the interval, the fewer the topographic features that can elude the contour samples. Be careful that you don't mistake a variable contour interval for a constant one and thus fail to adjust the spacing of your profile construction lines.

Profiles have a number of practical uses beyond providing a dramatic picture of the vertical aspects of geographic distributions. For instance, topographic profiles are used to plan the routing of roads, railroads, pipelines, and canals. When it comes time to determine the earth–moving needs of such projects, profiles are used to compute the volume of material involved in making landform cuts and fills.

Terrain profiles also provide a way to see what environmental features would be visible from a given vantage point (**Figure 17.5A**). This information, known as intervisibility or **difilade**, can be invaluable when orienting yourself in the field. It can also be used in the laboratory to determine whether a certain geographic feature would be visible from a possible building site, thereby saving you a trip into the field.

If profiles are constructed in several directions from a selected location (or set of locations, such as a trail), hidden areas on the ground can be plotted on the map (**Figure 17.5B**). This masking

of hidden areas in two dimensions has many uses, especially in land use management. For instance, land use activities deemed incompatible with an overall management plan can be hidden from view as much as possible. Thus, trails and campgrounds in a wilderness region might be built so that the visual impact of non-wilderness activities, such as clear-cuts, garbage dumps, and quarries, is minimized.

ORIENTATION

Our discussion of shapes leads naturally to a consideration of feature **directionality** or **orientation**. Although the orientation of a line is obvious, areas and volumes may also have a definite orientation if one extent is greater than the other(s). The directionality of an individual feature and of features within a region as a whole are both of interest, since feature orientation commonly is linked with environmental processes and, therefore, may help explain the landscape's structure and character. Landforms, for example, are often aligned with bedrock structure or with the direction of glacier movement. The micro-climate on south slopes may be warmer and drier than on north slopes, leading to very different biotic association on the two sides of the same ridge. Likewise, west slopes may be steeper and more dissected than east slopes in regions in which intense storms move from west to east, causing greater erosion on the windward side. We'll explore such topics in Part III: *Map Interpretation*.

In the meantime, it would be helpful to have a systematic way to analyze the orientation of environmental features. Perhaps the most revealing form of orientation analysis is a simple graphic procedure. To use this method, superimpose a parallel line grating over the map. Count the number of times features such as roads or contour lines are crossed by the grating lines (**Figure 17.6**). Then rotate the line grating slightly, and repeat the procedure. Eventually, enough orientation data will be generated to plot a **star diagram** (**Figure 17.6A**) or a **histogram** (**Figure 17.6B**).

Since a feature with no orientation bias will plot as a circle on the star diagram and as a horizontal line on the histogram, you can use these as standards against which to judge the orientation

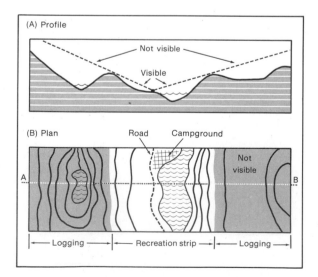

17.5 Topographic profiles (A) can be used to determine the intervisibility of landscape features (B).

bias of environmental features. Strongly oriented features will have pronounced spikes and depressions coinciding with their strongest and weakest directionality, respectively. Thus, either graph tells us something about both the direction and degree of feature orientation.

Counting intersections of the line grating with map features is a tedious task, of course. Therefore, those lacking access to a computer which has been programmed to carry out these computation chores automatically are likely to favor shortcut methods. The most obvious of these, and the one we used in Figure 17.6, is to use only a small sample of grating rotations. In the extreme, it may suffice merely to look at the map pattern and determine by eye the grating orientation which produces the most and least number of intersections.

Graphic and visual analyses aren't sufficient for all purposes, however, since they don't provide compact summary measures which we can compare statistically with other such measures. For this purpose, we need a statistical test of ori-

entation uniformity. A number of these tests have been proposed but can't be fairly evaluated in the limited space available here. For more information on these measures, statistical references should be consulted.*

COMPOSITION

The internal makeup of a distribution is its **composition**. The composition of environmental features may show homogeneity, diversity, or community. Let's look briefly at these three aspects of composition.

For a discussion of statistical tests of uniformity of orientation, including an evaluation of references concerning the topic, see: Dale, M.L., and Ballantyne, C.K., "Two Statistics for the Analysis of Orientation Data in Geography," Professional Geographer, Vol. 32 (1980), pp. 184-191; and Spurr, B.D., "Comments on 'Two Statistics for the Analysis of Orientation Data in Geography'," Professional Geographer, Vol. 35, No. 1 (1983), p. 87.

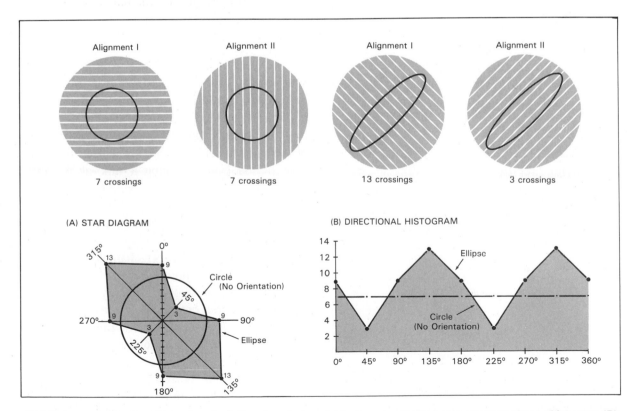

17.6 You can graphically analyze the orientation of environmental features by plotting a star diagram (A) or a histogram (B) of the number of times they are intersected by a parallel line grid oriented at different angles.

366

Homogeneity

The consistent dispersion of a single feature is called environmental **uniformity**, or **homogeneity**. A corn field, a pine plantation, and a uniform grid of city streets are examples of uniformity. Point, line, and area features each may be arrayed in homogeneous fashion (**Figure 17.7A**). Uniformity can occur in size, shape, orientation, dispersion, connectivity, and so forth. When a break in homogeneity occurs, we call it a discontinuity (see *Discontinuity* later in this chapter).

Diversity

The opposite of homogeneity is **diversity**, or **heterogeneity**. Instead of a uniform dispersion of a

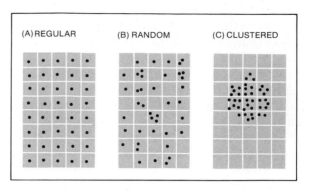

17.8 A pattern of point features can be characterized by its degree of dispersion as being more regular than random (A), random (B), or more clustered than random (C).

single feature, we see a mix of features (**Figure 17.7B**). The concept of **biodiversity** is widely used to refer to the mix of species in an area. A similar pluralism can exist with respect to a variety of features. House types, agricultural crops, and employment opportunities are just a few examples of distributions to which we might apply the concept of diversity.

Community

When diversity exists, but there are strong dependent relations among the assemblage of features, it is called a **community**. In a community, one feature interacts with and affects the others. Ecologists have long recognized this concept of association among a mix of features. Foresters talk, for example, about the maple-beech-birch-hemlock complex in a northern hardwood forest. Urban planners are sensitive to the "sense of community" that exists in different parts of a city. Such terms as habitat, ecosystem, live-zone, biome, and phylogenetic region all relate to this concept of community.

If you see a certain mix of features occurring repeatedly over a region, there's a good chance that some interaction among them exists. But you should make this assumption with caution. Spurious correlations among features are common, since proximity or juxtaposition needn't mean there is any functional relation among features.

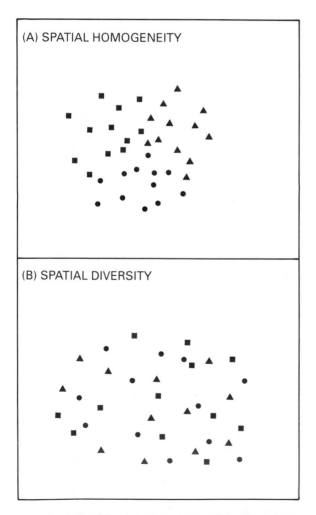

17.7 The composition of features in a region will fall someplace on a gradient from homogeneous (A) to diverse (B).

TABLE 17.1

Observed Frequency of Occurrences in 40 Quadrants

| | Number of Individuals (x) in Each Quadrat | | | | | | |
	x = 0	x = 1	x = 2	x = 3	x = 4	x = 5	x = 6
MAP A	0	40	0	0	0	0	0
MAP B	11	21	5	2	1	0	0
MAP C	30	1	1	1	2	4	1

ARRANGEMENT

Measures of orientation and composition are useful for many purposes, but they tell us nothing about structural relations within a pattern. This spatial **arrangement** of features is a fourth spatial concept we want to consider. The concept of arrangement has at least two main subcomponents—dispersion and spacing.* To clarify these terms, it is convenient to look first at the distribution of point features. Later we can look at arrangement in line and area patterns.

Arrangement in Point Patterns

Point features are in theory dimensionless. Thus, if we use them to demonstrate what is meant by spatial arrangement, we can focus solely on interpoint direction and distance relations and not have to deal with the added dimensions which characterize linear, areal, and volumetric features. Let's begin with the concept of dispersion.

Dispersion

The spread of a set of points with respect to some region is called **dispersion**. A dispersion is said to be **uniform** when there is equal spacing between points—that is, when each point is as far away from its neighbors as possible. Triangular

*Arrangement is thought by some to have a third subcomponent, called **localization**, which has to do with variations in the relative frequency with which features occur from one subdivision of a region to the next. For more information on this topic, see: Joseph, A.E., "On the Interpretation of the Coefficient of Localization," Professional Geographer, Vol. 34 (1982), pp. 443-446, and Yuill, R.S., "The Coefficient of Localization—An Addendum," Professional Geographer, Vol. 35, No. 3 (1983), pp. 338-339.*

and square grids (or lattices) of points are most uniform (**Figure 17.8A**). If, for example, the subsurface structure in an oil field were homogeneous, oil wells would likely be evenly dispersed to minimize drilling costs yet maximize areal coverage.

When points tend to be grouped into one or two small segments of space, a **clustered** dispersion results (**Figure 17.8C**). For instance, if an oil company can lease surface rights only to a few small parcels of land over an oil field, it may decide to drill a number of wells together in each parcel and angle the pipes out in different directions under the surrounding area.

When there is no apparent order in a dispersion, it is said to be **random** (**Figure 17.8B**). Even in random patterns, there is likely to be some clustering and some regularity, but not enough so that the dispersion as a whole looks either clustered or regular.

Several quantitative methods have been devised to detect non-randomness in spatial distributions. One of these is called **quadrat analysis**. To apply this technique, you must first superimpose a regular (preferably square) grid over the distribution to be analyzed. For this purpose, an arbitrary 5 x 8 = 40 cell grid has been superimposed on each distribution in Figure 17.8. The size of this grid may be crucial, as we shall see.

With the grid in place, tally the number of population occurrences (x) falling within each grid cell (or quadrat). The data for Figure 17.8 are given in **Table 17.1**. You are now in a position to compare the observed number of individuals per quadrat with the number of individuals per quadrat which would be expected if the population were distributed randomly in space.

To make this comparison, you must calculate two statistics. The first is the **arithmetic mean** (average) of the quadrat values or counts. The mean is defined as the sum of the quadrat values (Σx) divided by the number of quadrats (n). The second statistic required is the **variance**, which is defined as the average of the squared deviations of the individual quadrat values from their means. We may write this symbolically as

$$\text{Variance} = \frac{\Sigma(x - \overline{x})^2}{n}$$

Through experimentation, researchers have found that, for a random distribution, the variance of quadrat values about their arithmetic mean is equal to the mean itself. Therefore, the ratio of the variance and mean for a random distribution is equal to 1. For the variance-mean ratio to be close to 1, the pattern must meet three conditions: (1) Only a few quadrats will have no population occurrences. (2) A large number of quadrats will have an intermediate number of occurrences. (3) A few quadrats will have a relatively large number of occurrences.

Non-randomness in a map pattern can occur in two ways. If the observed distribution is characterized by large numbers of both empty quadrats and quadrats containing many individuals, we can say that the distribution is clustered. Since with such a pattern the variance between quadrat values will be greater than the mean of quadrat totals, the variance-mean ratio will become larger than 1. Thus, large variance-mean ratios indicate that individual population occurrences are clumped together in space. When such clumping occurs, we say that the pattern is more clustered than random.

At the opposite extreme from clustering, population elements may be spaced in a more regular than random manner. With these regular distributions, the vast majority of quadrats will contain an intermediate number of individuals. Since, with such a pattern, the variance between quadrat values will be less than the mean of quadrat totals, the variance-mean ratio will be less than 1. Therefore, small variance-mean ratios can be taken as an indication of pattern regularity.

As a rule, the greater the deviation from 1 in the variance-mean ratio, the more pronounced the degree of non-randomness. We can test the intuition we used in classifying the three distributions illustrated in Figure 17.8 by computing the variance-mean ratio for each pattern. To do so, we can use the variance formula which, in **Box 17.1**, has been rewritten in a form more convenient for use with a calculator.

Although this formula may look formidable, there are only a few simple computations which have to be made. We need only compute the sum of the quadrat values (Σx), the square of the sum of the quadrat values [$\Sigma x)^2$], and the sum of the squares of the quadrat values (Σx^2). These computations, based on the data listed in Table 17.1, are also shown in Box 17.1. Since the same number of quadrats (40) and the same number of population occurrences (40) are associated with each distribution, several terms will be identical from one distribution to the next.

The final step is to compute the variance-mean ratio for each pattern. If we recall that a value of 1 indicates a random distribution, while larger values indicate clustering and smaller values suggest regularity, our previous intuition is confirmed. Map A has a variance-mean ratio of 0.0, indicating a high degree of regularity in its pattern. The ratio of 0.9 for Map B is so close to 1 that the pattern can be said to be essentially random. The ratio for Map C is 3.64, which suggests substantial clustering of its pattern. Special statistical tests are available to tell you how significant (in a statistical sense) the difference is between each of these variance-mean ratios and the expected ratio of 1 for a random pattern. If these tests of statistical significance are of interest to you, the selected readings at the end of the chapter will provide the information.

One criticism of the variance-mean ratio is that the terms "random," "more clustered than random," and "more regular than random" are somewhat deceptive. They refer to the distribution curve of the data (quadrat frequency plotted on a graph against number of occurrences per quadrat). They don't refer to the spatial pattern of individuals on the ground from one quadrat to the next, as you might expect. Since the relative location of quadrats having different numbers of population occurrences isn't considered in the computations, the resulting measure of dispersion is of a non-spatial nature.

Another criticism of the variance-mean ratio is that its ability to detect non-randomness depends on the quadrat size used in the analysis. In an apparently clustered population, the use of quadrat analysis will show randomness, clustering, and regularity as the size of the quadrats is steadily increased. The most marked demonstration of clustering occurs when the quadrats have

an area about the same size as the area of the spatial grouping of population elements. Larger and smaller quadrats may produce vastly different results.

This relation between quadrat size and the ability to detect clustering can be put to good use. Merely by resampling the distribution several times with quadrats of different sizes, you can determine at what scale grouping occurs. This ability is important because it lets you detect non-

Box 17.1 Variance–Mean Ratio Computations

MAP A

$\Sigma x = (0 \times 0) + (1 \times 40) = 40$

$\Sigma x^2 = (1^2 \times 40) = 40$

$(\Sigma x)^2 = 40^2 = 1600$

$\dfrac{(\Sigma x)^2}{N} = \dfrac{1600}{40} = 40$

$\text{variance } (\delta^2) = \dfrac{\Sigma x^2 - \dfrac{(\Sigma x)^2}{N}}{N - 1}$

$= \dfrac{40 - \dfrac{1600}{40}}{40 - 1}$

$= \dfrac{0}{39} = 0$

$\text{mean } (\bar{x}) = \dfrac{\Sigma x}{N} = \dfrac{40}{40} = 1.0$

$\dfrac{\text{variance}}{\text{mean}} = \dfrac{0}{1} = 0$

MAP B

$\Sigma x = (0 \times 11) + (1 \times 21) + (2 \times 5) + (3 \times 2) + (4 \times 1) = 40$

$\Sigma x^2 = (1^2 \times 21) + (2^2 \times 5) + (3^2 \times 2) + (4^2 \times 1) = 75$

$(\Sigma x)^2 = 40^2 = 1600$

$\dfrac{(\Sigma x)^2}{N} = \dfrac{1600}{40} = 40$

$\bar{x} = \dfrac{\Sigma x}{N} = \dfrac{40}{40} = 1.0$

$\dfrac{\text{variance}}{\text{mean}} = \dfrac{.897}{1.0} = .9$

$\delta^2 = \dfrac{\Sigma x^2 - \dfrac{(\Sigma x)^2}{N}}{N - 1}$

$= \dfrac{75 - \dfrac{1600}{40}}{40 - 1}$

$= \dfrac{75 - 40}{39} = \dfrac{35}{39}$

$= .897$

MAP C

$\Sigma x = (0 \times 30) + (1 \times 1) + (2 \times 1) + (3 \times 1) + (4 \times 2) + (5 \times 4) + (6 \times 1) = 40$

$\Sigma x^2 = (1^2 \times 1) + (2^2 \times 1) + (3^2 \times 1) + (4^2 \times 2) + (5^2 \times 4) + (6^2 \times 1) = 182$

$(\Sigma x)^2 = 40^2 = 1600$

$\dfrac{(\Sigma x)^2}{N} = \dfrac{1600}{40} = 40$

$\bar{x} = \dfrac{\Sigma x}{N} = \dfrac{40}{40} = 1.0$

$\dfrac{\text{variance}}{\text{mean}} = \dfrac{3.64}{1.0} = 3.64$

$\delta^2 = \dfrac{\Sigma x^2 - \dfrac{(\Sigma x)^2}{N}}{N - 1}$

$= \dfrac{182 - \dfrac{1600}{40}}{40 - 1}$

$= \dfrac{142}{39} = 3.64$

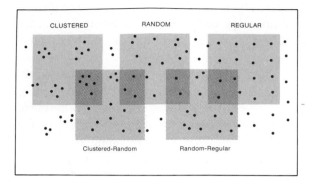

17.9 A spatial trend in a point pattern can give a false notion of dispersion. The zones of clustering, randomness, and regularity that we see here would be masked if a single dispersion measure were computed for the pattern as a whole.

randomness in a distribution when visual inspection alone may reveal no sign of clustering. In other words, the human eye seems to use a built-in quadrat size in judging pattern dispersion.

A third criticism of quadrat measures of dispersion is that the statistic represents an average or summary judgment. A single term is used to categorize the whole pattern. When there is a change or trend in a pattern over the region, therefore, measures of dispersion may have little meaning (**Figure 17.9**). The best thing to do in such cases is to divide the region into subregions within which the pattern is relatively homogeneous. Then we can say, for instance, that the pattern is random in one half of the region and regular in the other.

Even if we're willing to dismiss these criticisms, we must realize that the mere demonstration of non-randomness in a distribution is of limited interest. But once we know the scale or scales at which non-randomness occurs, we can relate this information to other environmental features occurring at these same scales. Such comparisons may lead to insights about spatial processes. We'll return to this subject in Part III: *Map Interpretation*.

Spacing

A second component of spatial arrangement is **spacing**. We can define spacing as the locational arrangement of objects with respect to each other (rather than relative to some area, as with the concept of dispersion). Thus, spacing is inde-

pendent of any boundary one might draw around the points.

Spacing has two additional characteristics. We can speak of the average distance of objects from their neighbors. Or we can look at the degree to which distances between neighboring objects deviate from the average.

The average distance of objects from their neighbors is called **mean** or **average spacing** (**Figure 17.10A**). To compute this statistic, we first have to calculate the distance between all pairs of points using the distance theorem (see *Determining Distance by Coordinates* in Chapter 13). For each point, then, we can determine which point is the nearest neighbor, the second nearest neighbor, and so on.

The distance from a point to its nearest neighbor may be **reflexive**. In other words, if point A is the nearest neighbor of point B, then point B may also be the nearest neighbor of point A. Usually, however, point B will have some other nearest neighbor, and the relationship between A and B won't be reflexive.

The average spacing (r) is computed by summing the nearest-neighbor distances (r_i) and

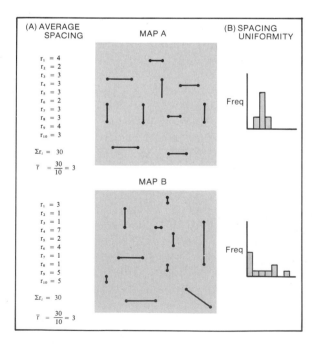

17.10 Average spacing (A) and spacing uniformity (B) are two components of spacing in point patterns.

dividing the total by the number of paired points (n). This may be written symbolically as

$$\bar{r} = \frac{\sum_{i=1}^{n} r_i}{n}$$

This average spacing statistic can be compared with the expected mean nearest–neighbor distance associated with a random distribution to provide a simple estimate of the distribution's dispersion. To do so, we compute the density of points (d). If a regional boundary doesn't enclose the distribution of points naturally, we will have to determine where this boundary should go. We can do this by calculating the area on the basis of the minimum and maximum x and y coordinates of the points. On the basis of the density of points we have observed within this region, we can then figure out what the expected mean distance to the nearest neighbors would be if the points were randomly distributed. This statistic $(\bar{r}_d)$ is computed using a factor $(.5 \sqrt{d})$, which has been derived by researchers who have studied many random point patterns.

An index of randomness, or departure from randomness, is given by the ratio between actual mean distance and expected mean distance. This may be written symbolically as

$$R = \frac{\bar{r}}{r_d}$$

where

R = 0 implies maximum clustering (or concentration)

R = 1 indicates randomness, and

R = 2.1419 implies maximum dispersion (uniformity).

Applying this formula to the three patterns in Figure 17.8, we obtain the data and results shown in **Box 17.2**. These computations agree quite favorably with those determined using the quadrat analysis technique.

When we use mean spacing methods, we end up with one number which represents the entire distribution. This number doesn't tell us everything we might want to know about the distribution. To obtain a more complete idea of the pattern, we must also be aware of a second characteristic of spacing. This second aspect of spacing, called **spacing uniformity**, is defined as the deviation of inter-point distances (ri) from their average value. At one extreme, the spacing between all pairs of nearest neighbors might be the same, and equal to the mean spacing (see

Box 17.2 Nearest–Neighbor Statistic Computations

MAP A

$$\sum_{i=1}^{40} r_i = 240$$

$$d = \frac{40}{30 \times 48} = \frac{40}{1440} = .028$$

$$\bar{r} = \frac{\sum_{i=1}^{40} r_i}{40} = \frac{240}{40} = 6$$

$$\bar{r}_d = \frac{.5}{\sqrt{d}} = \frac{.5}{.167} = 2.994$$

$$R = \frac{\bar{r}}{r_d} = \frac{6}{2.994} = 2.004$$

MAP B

$$\sum_{i=1}^{40} r_i = 148$$

$$d = \frac{40}{1440} = .028$$

$$\bar{r} = \frac{148}{40} = 3.7$$

$$\bar{r}_d = 2.994$$

$$R = \frac{3.7}{2.994} = 1.24$$

MAP C

$$\sum_{i=1}^{40} r_i = 80$$

$$d = \frac{40}{1440} = .028$$

$$\bar{r} = \frac{80}{40} = 2.0$$

$$\bar{r}_d = 2.994$$

$$R = \frac{2.0}{2.994} = .67$$

372

Figure 17.10A). On the other hand, the same mean spacing might be the result of averaging a wide range of nearest–neighbor distances (**Figure 17.10B**).

In other words, arrangements of points with similar degrees of spacing uniformity can have different average spacings. Uniform spacing doesn't guarantee a uniform dispersion. Thus, statistics based on mean spacing values must be interpreted carefully.

Arrangement in Line and Area Patterns

We can view the arrangement of line features much as we did point feature arrangements. The concept of dispersion can be meaningful if we consider orientation of the lines. We might also specify dispersion of a line arrangement by first subdividing the region and then making a tally of total line length within each subdivision.

Areas can also be grouped together to form a pattern. As we saw under *Mosaic Surfaces* in Chapter 1, an arrangement of different areas (the United States, for instance) is called a mosaic. Obviously, various areas within the same mosaic can differ widely. Consider the pattern of states in our country. There is a striking difference between the irregularity of the shapes of states on the east coast and the rectangularity of states in the West and Midwest. In addition to the assortment of shapes, a mosaic can also be defined by the variations in size, orientation, and compactness of the areas it includes.

These terms—size, shape, orientation, and compactness—are useful when we describe areas. But in characterizing a large mosaic such as the United States, it can become tedious and confusing to define every state with each of these descriptive terms. We may gain more insight into the total character of a mosaic if we represent each area by its center, or centroid (see *Centroid* in Chapter 16). In other words, we could place a dot in the middle of each state and then study this distribution of points. In this way, we might gain a good picture of the mosaic as a whole. There are a few problems with this approach, however. There may be a question of how representative of its region each centroid is. Also, it may be difficult to determine the center of an area that isn't relatively compact.

CONNECTIVITY

Another aspect of pattern is its **connectivity**. Environmental features are linked to like and unlike objects through a variety of connections. Roads, rivers, bus lines, airline routes, and a host of other connections link one place with another. Although near things are more likely to be functionally associated than distant things, juxtaposition alone doesn't ensure connectivity. For example, there may be no communication between adjoining countries despite their common borders. In contrast, places separated by great distance in space may be closely linked, as people who draw drinking water from a river discover when a toxic chemical spill occurs far upstream.

Routed Paths

Routed networks, consisting of places (**nodes**) and links, provide the most obvious evidence of spatial connectivity. Some networks are **totally connected**: In other words, all pairs of places are linked by the most direct route (**Figure 17.11A**). These networks are efficient because direct movements are possible in the greatest degree. Other networks are only **partially connected**; that is, linkages between some pairs of places pass through at least one additional place and are thus devious or indirect (**Figures 17.11B and C**). These networks are relatively inefficient for the traveler because they require indirect movements. Airline "hubs" are a familiar example of

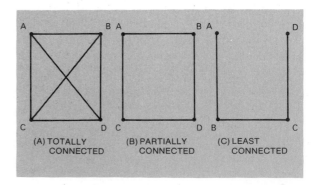

(A) TOTALLY CONNECTED

(B) PARTIALLY CONNECTED

(C) LEAST CONNECTED

17.11 Nodes are far more accessible in a totally connected network (A) than in partially or least connected networks (B and C).

partially connected networks: You often find yourself going out of your way to get to a regional hub such as Atlanta or Minneapolis to make "connections" to your destination.

Circuit networks, which have more than one possible path between some pairs of places, are the most connected (**Figure 17.12A**). Least connected are the **branching** (tree) networks, which have only one possible path between pairs of places (**Figure 17.12B**). When encountering these networks, your curiosity should be aroused so that you seek explanations for why some networks are more connected than others, and what influence these connections will have on communication and hence on other location patterns. Consider, for example, the economics of an airline company's routing system.

There are a number of measures of connectivity we may use to compare networks with one another and to relate a network's connectivity to the flow of goods and services. One such measure is devised by forming a ratio between the actual number of segments between nodes in a network and the maximum possible for a network linking that number of nodes. Often this ratio is multiplied by 100 to provide a measure of the percentage connection in a network. Written in symbolic form:

$$\text{Percent connection} = \frac{A}{P} \times 100$$

where A represents the actual links and P represents the possible links.

To make use of this connectivity index, we need a simple way to determine the maximum possible number of links in a network. We can do so quite readily by counting the number of nodes (n) in the network and then using a formula. The problem is that the formula varies with the type of network. There are three types of networks and hence three different formulas.

In the first type of network, links are symmetric (movement occurs in both directions), and links can't cross one another without defining a new place. This form is typical of road or railroad networks that don't have one-way segments, overpasses, or underpasses. With such a network, the formula $3(n - 2)$ defines the maximum possible number of links between n places (**Figure 17.13A**).

In a second type of network, links are still symmetric, but they can cross one another without defining a new place. A network of airline routes is a good example, since routes don't link

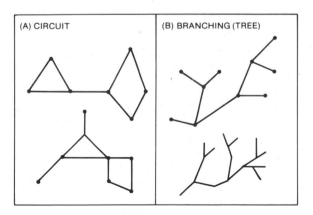

(A) CIRCUIT   (B) BRANCHING (TREE)

17.12 Circuit networks (A) are generally more connected than branching networks (B).

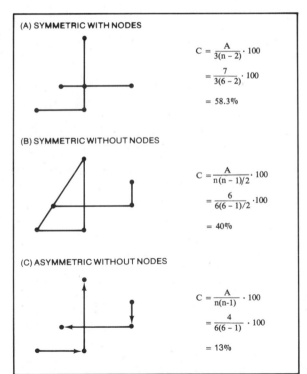

(A) SYMMETRIC WITH NODES

$$C = \frac{A}{3(n-2)} \cdot 100$$
$$= \frac{7}{3(6-2)} \cdot 100$$
$$= 58.3\%$$

(B) SYMMETRIC WITHOUT NODES

$$C = \frac{A}{n(n-1)/2} \cdot 100$$
$$= \frac{6}{6(6-1)/2} \cdot 100$$
$$= 40\%$$

(C) ASYMMETRIC WITHOUT NODES

$$C = \frac{A}{n(n-1)} \cdot 100$$
$$= \frac{4}{6(6-1)} \cdot 100$$
$$= 13\%$$

17.13 By computing the percentage connectivity of different types of networks, we can objectively compare their spatial accessibility.

374

up in mid-air. Overpasses and underpasses in a road network fall in this category as well. With this sort of network, the maximum number of links between n places is given by the expression n(n-1)/2 (**Figure 17.13B**).

A third kind of network is characterized by asymmetric links, such as one-way streets, and by links which cross one another without defining a new place, as with overpasses or underpasses along a limited-access highway. With such a network, the formula n(n-1) defines the maximum possible number of lines between n places (**Figure 17.13C**).

Rather than study the connectivity of a network as a whole, you might want to change your focus and determine the connectivity of a particular place with respect to the total network. You may do so, quite simply, by counting the linkages to or from a place. Obviously, in a completely connected network there will be no difference in the connectivity of the various places. In partially connected networks, however, there usually will be variation in the connectivity of individual places: Those with many links will be highly connected to the system, while those having few links will be weakly connected. The next step, of course, is to explain why connectivity varies as it does. Here, again, is the type of question we'll discuss in Part III: *Map Interpretation*.

Unrouted Paths

Not all movement or communication takes place along clear-cut paths. In addition to routed linkages, there are many environmental connections which aren't constrained to routes. These unrouted linkages can be relatively difficult to detect. The functional association between a television station and its home viewing audience is of this type. Another example is non-point pollution by farm chemicals in a watershed, since runoff eventually carries the contamination to the river. Linkage along such invisible but ubiquitous connections can be just as strong as with the more obvious physically routed systems.

One form of invisible route that has special meaning is the **least–effort path** from one location to another. To visualize this path, it's helpful to build a three-dimensional terrain model. Then place a drop of water on the highest point and observe the path the water drop takes in seeking equilibrium. If contour traces were etched into the model surface, you would see the water move downhill along a least-resistance path at right

17.14 The gradient path traces out the least–effort route on an isoline surface. If isolines are parallel, the gradient path is straight (A). Otherwise the gradient path traces out a curved route (B).

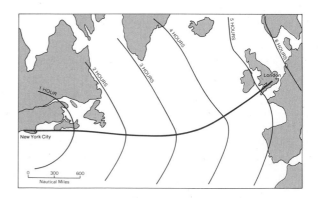

17.15 The gradient path between New York City and London in terms of flying time is based on the pattern of prevailing winds.

angles to the contours (**Figure 17.14A**). This is to be expected, of course, since the maximum gradient is at right angles to the contour lines. The water merely traces the **gradient path** (or steepest slope route) from high to low points on the landform.

Terrain surfaces aren't usually of linear form, of course. This means that single-azimuth gradient paths aren't all that common, since if water is to flow down a complex terrain surface along a gradient path, its course direction must be altered so that contours are crossed at right angles (**Figure 17.14B**). Errors are minimized when constructing gradient paths on linear surfaces because the initial gradient azimuth can be extended over the map surface without adjustments. With complex terrain surfaces, however, gradient–path construction errors are directly proportionate to the distance and angle between the existing contour lines. You can reduce construction errors somewhat by interpolating **guide contours** between the contour lines on the map.

Gradient paths can also be plotted on non-terrain surfaces with useful results. For instance, the minimum-time airline route between two cities can readily be plotted if a time-surface map based on either end point is available. **Figure 17.15** shows such a plot for the route between New York City and London. You can see that the

route has been extended across the Atlantic Ocean from New York City so that each isoline is crossed at a 90–degree angle.

Sometimes you may want to determine a path that doesn't exceed a specified maximum slope angle. Suppose, for example, that a road or canal can't exceed a grade of five degrees. If you have a contour map available, one way to define this path is to set a pair of dividers at a map distance equal to the contour interval divided by the tangent of the maximum allowable slope angle. This procedure is illustrated in **Figure 17.16**.

The first step, assuming that your origin is located on a contour line, is to place one foot of the dividers at this lower elevation point and the other foot on the next higher contour line. Mark this second point; then rotate the lower foot of the dividers to the next higher contour line, while keeping the other foot stationary. Mark this third point. Continue the process until you reach the contour line which lies at or just below the elevation of your destination point. Finally, connect the points, including origin and destination, with line segments.

Three things can happen. First, the maximum slope line may intersect the destination contour between the origin and the destination point (**Figure 17.17A**). This means that a straight-line course from origin to destination will fall within

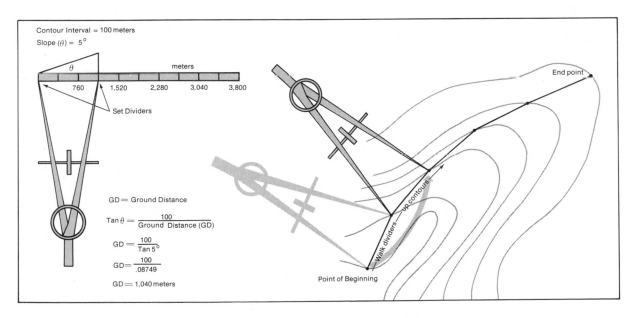

17.16 You can determine the maximum slope path by walking pre-set dividers up the slope.

376

acceptable slope limits. When this happens, you may have a great deal of flexibility in choosing the actual route to take.

The second possibility is that the maximum slope line will connect directly with the destination point (**Figure 17.17B**). Thus, there will be no flexibility in route location. Such cases are rare.

The greatest frustration comes when the maximum slope line intersects the destination contour beyond the destination point (**Figure 17.17C**). This means that a relatively indirect course must be taken between origin and destination to meet the maximum slope restriction. This last case explains the prevalence of "switchbacks" on steep mountain hiking trails and roads. Government regulations often specify the maximum slope permissible for such routes.

DISCONTINUITY

Places at which the environment changes abruptly are of special interest in map analysis. If we equate information with uncertainty, as is done in communication theory, then **discontinuity** holds more information than continuity. The reason is simple. If we understand a continuous feature at one location, we probably understand it at others. But our explanation of continuity is inappropriate at the point of discontinuity. We need a new understanding.

It turns out, as we saw in the *Edge* section earlier in this chapter, that we naturally focus on edges. Discontinuities are edges in the broadest

sense of the concept. Thus, a sudden change in a river course, street pattern, or species diversity naturally attracts our attention (**Figure 17.18**). These locations are important because they suggest a shift in influence from one environment-forming mechanism to another. Since processes can change with time, these breaks in continuity often indicate spatial development during different historic periods.

You should learn to spot functional as well as geometric discontinuities in the environment. Falls in a river constitute discontinuity for a person in a canoe, as anyone who has had to make a difficult portage can attest. Similarly, airports,

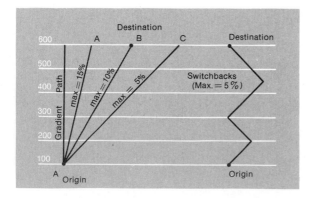

17.17 Routes laid out with a maximum slope restriction may end up in a series of switchbacks on steep slopes.

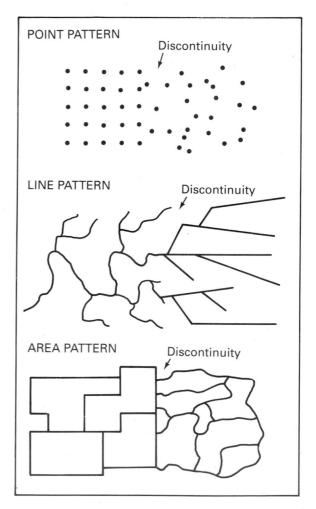

17.18 Breaks in continuity in point, line, and area distributions hint of underlying changes in environment–forming processes.

train stations, bus stops, and boat landings are discontinuities, since at these points one form of mobility is abandoned in favor of another. Your understanding of the environment grows richer as you become more sensitive to these breaks in continuity.

TRENDS AND CYCLES

A **trend** refers to a feature's tendency to increase or decrease with time or distance (see *Pattern of Change* in Chapter 1). When the feature is tangible, such as the landform, the spatial trend in the surface can be seen directly. Intangible spatial trends, such as the drop in average temperature

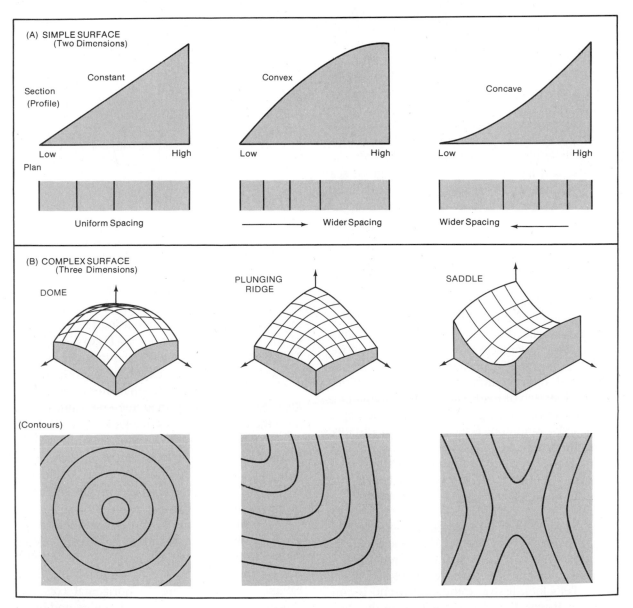

17.19 The ground surface occurs in many different forms. Two-dimensional profiles and plan contour projections of simple surfaces are shown in A, while three-dimensional oblique views and plan contour projections of more complex surfaces are shown in B.

378

from south to north in the northern hemisphere, or increasing land values toward the center of a city, must be experienced.

Some of the simpler and more distinctive spatial trends have been named. We use the terms **constant** (or **linear**), **convex**, or **concave** to describe the form of a ground surface profile and the terms **dome**, **plunging ridge**, or **saddle** to describe the spatial character of the terrain surface (**Figure 17.19**). The spacing of isolines (contour lines, in the case of Figure 17.19) provides the cues necessary to identify the terrain's form. Although there are specific bounds to the meaning of each term, the ground surface rarely falls neatly into one category or another. Thus, an element of subjectivity is usually involved in classifying the irregular ground form into a named spatial trend category.

In contrast to trends, **cyclical** phenomena have a repetitive character. Some cycles are primarily temporal (for example, traffic patterns, the rise and fall of tides, and the change of seasons). Others are primarily spatial. The linear array of population centers along a highway and the ups and downs in the landform as you cross terrain dissected by watercourses are examples of spatial cycles.

Distinctively cyclical shapes aren't named as such but, rather, are characterized in terms of two essential parameters. One parameter is the **period**, or length of cycle (**Figure 17.20**). Period is commonly related to some basic time or distance unit (seconds or miles) and stated in terms of frequency. Thus, we might say that hills are encountered with high, medium, or low frequency along a certain stretch of road. The second parameter is **amplitude**, or the height of the highs and depth of the lows. Amplitude is measured as the distance from the base line (0 value) of the cycle.

Those who require more rigorous specifications of spatial trends and cycles may prefer to rely on mathematical methods. For example, an equation in two dimensions of the form y = f(x), where x is the horizontal axis and y is the vertical axis, can be fitted to a profile. Since the equations for trends and cycles are slightly different in character, we will consider them separately.

Let's look first at trends. If a trend is constant, or **linear**, the equation will be of the form y = a + bx, where b is the slope of the line and a is the value of y when x = 0 (**Figure 17.21A**).

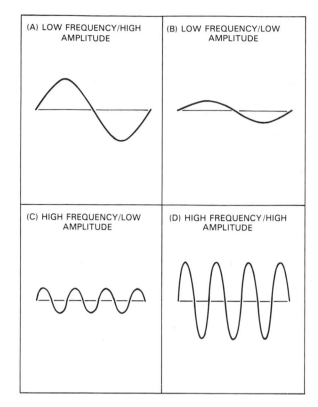

17.20 Changing the period and amplitude of a cycle can produce profiles or surfaces with very different shapes.

More complex profiles will require that x be raised to higher exponents. A profile which increases in value at an increasing rate might be of the form $y = a + bx + cx^2$ (**Figure 17.21B**). This type of trend is called a **quadratic trend**, because a second-order exponent is required.

Similarly, a profile that increases, then decreases, and then again increases in value might have the equation $y = a + bx + cx^2 + dx^3$ (**Figure 17.21C**). We call such a trend a **cubic trend**, because a third-order exponent is needed in its definition. In general, the larger the exponents used in an equation, the more complex the form of the profile.

To fit equations to surfaces rather than to profiles requires the addition of a third dimension (z) to the formulation. The basic functional relation then becomes z = f(x,y), where z is the vertical axis and x and y are the horizontal axes. We can still speak of linear, quadratic, cubic, and higher-order surfaces, of course (**Figure 17.22**). The only difference with the equivalent profiles is that the surface equations are complicated by the use of an extra dimension. Not all the cubic terms (x^3, x^2y, xy^2, y^3) need be found in a cubic trend, however. One suffices to establish the order of the surface.

Now let's consider equations for defining cycles. In theory, any profile can be fully described trigonometrically by a series of **sine (sin)** and **cosine (cos)** terms of different amplitudes and frequencies.* As **Figure 17.23A** shows, simple profiles require relatively simple trigonometric equations, but the equations for complex profiles can become very involved. As with trend equations, the trigonometric equations which fit a line to a two-dimensional profile can be extended to fit a surface to a three-dimensional form such as the terrain surface (**Figure 17.23B**).

Equations are extremely useful in describing profiles and surfaces in quantitative terrain studies. The tedious computations required to fit the equation to the data are avoided by using fitting software, which is widely available for personal computers. You merely enter a sample of elevation data with their locational coordinates into a computer program according to instruc-

....
Except for relatively smooth profiles, however, it's usually not practical to compute all the equation terms necessary to achieve a perfect fit. In practice, we use an approximating equation which accounts for a certain proportion of the profile's variance.

tions. Once equations describing the landforms of different regions are at hand, they can readily be manipulated and compared.

Spatial trends and cycles are interesting because they suggest that the environmental controls operating when a pattern was structured weren't the same throughout the region (a topic to which we'll return in Part III: *Map Interpretation*). But trends and cycles can also cause problems when we try to determine other pattern characteristics. If the structure of a pattern varies within an area, for example, the computed density for that area will represent an average number. This average density value for a variably distributed phenomenon tends to be too low or too high as an indicator of conditions within a given subregion. The average state population density for the United States will under-represent that of small, populous states such as New Jersey and over-represent that of large, sparsely populated states such as Wyoming.

....

HIERARCHY

The last aspect of pattern we will discuss is the **hierarchy** of features. Since environmental phenomena differ in size or importance, we can arrange them in a hierarchy. Sometimes this fact is more apparent in the environment than on a map, for maps tend to lump things together and

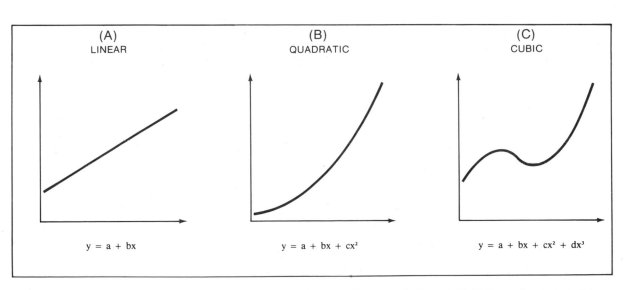

(A) LINEAR	(B) QUADRATIC	(C) CUBIC
$y = a + bx$	$y = a + bx + cx^2$	$y = a + bx + cx^2 + dx^3$

17.21 Two-dimensional trends can be defined by equations in two variables (x,y). Terms with higher–order exponents are needed when fitting equations to more complex curves.

380

simplify, which masks hierarchical differences. A map may show all roads as thin black lines, for instance, while in reality the roads form a hierarchy from gravel lanes to super highways.

On the other hand, maps sometimes show hierarchies more clearly than the environment does. All railroad tracks look pretty much the same. A map, however, might show railroads in terms of a hierarchy of high to low traffic. Such a map would quickly tell you which tracks accommodated 100 trains a day and which were used by only one train a week.

Regardless of whether environment or map provides the needed information, hierarchies are everywhere. Take, for instance, hierarchies of **point phenomena**. We could have a hierarchy of seedling, shrub, sapling and tree. Or we might speak of a hierarchy of silt, sand, pebble, rock, and boulder. Notice that in each case the dividing line between sub-classes is rather vague or arbitrary. These are examples of ordinal measurement (see *Measurement Level* in Chapter 2), since items are ranked, but the difference between ranks isn't numerically defined.

Other examples of hierarchy in point phenomena are more quantitatively defined. For instance, oil wells or mines vary widely in output. This continuous range in production can be divided so that we speak of small, medium, or large

producers. Likewise, our national capital is more important than our state capital, which in turn is more important than our county seat.

Linear phenomena, such as roads and rivers, are also arranged in hierarchies. In descending order of quality, we have limited–access, federal, state, and county highways. The Mississippi River is bigger than the Missouri, which in turn is larger than the Yellowstone. Other communication networks possess a similar hierarchy of linkages.

One way to analyze the hierarchical structure of line networks is to look at the relationship between segments at different levels of hierarchy in the network. To do so, it is first convenient to label each level. Segments of streams which have no tributaries are said to be of the **first order**. When two first-order segments join, they form a **second order** stream, and so on. In general, the junction of two network segments of the same order creates a segment which is one higher. When two segments of different orders join, it doesn't cause a change.

Your first step in analyzing a network hierarchy is to identify the order of each segment (**Figure 17.24A**). Colored pencils are useful in differentiating between orders. Once each segment in a network has been classified by its order, your next step is to make a tally of segments falling into each category. This tally will permit

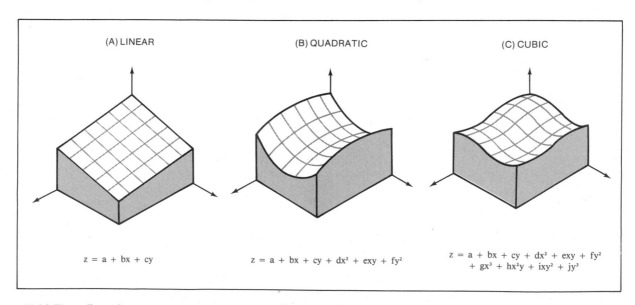

(A) LINEAR $z = a + bx + cy$

(B) QUADRATIC $z = a + bx + cy + dx^2 + exy + fy^2$

(C) CUBIC $z = a + bx + cy + dx^2 + exy + fy^2 + gx^3 + hx^2y + ixy^2 + jy^3$

17.22 Three-dimensional trends (surfaces) can be defined by equations in three variables (x, y, z). As with two-dimensional equations, terms with higher–order exponents are required to fit more complex surfaces.

you to calculate the **bifurcation ratio (R_b)**, which is defined as the ratio of line segments of one order to the number of line segments of the next higher order. Written symbolically, the bifurcation ratio becomes:

$$R_b = \frac{N_0}{N_0 + 1}$$

where N_0 is the number of line segments of any order and $N_0 + 1$ is the number of line segments of the next higher order. As an example, the bifurcation ratio between first and second order stream

segments could be found for the drainage basin illustrated in Figure 17.24 by computing the ratio:

$$\frac{\text{No. of 1st order streams}}{\text{No. of 2nd order streams}} = \frac{24}{7} = 3.4.$$

The results of these computations and others in the same drainage system are shown in **Figure 17.24B**. You could compare these results with statistics from other drainage basins to study the nature of different stream systems. The next step would be one of interpretation: You might want to explain any differences that emerge in terms of such factors as geology and climate.

Like point and linear features, **areal phenomena** also exhibit hierarchies. The territories of animals, for instance, can be ranked. A rabbit will spend its whole life within a territory of only a few acres, while a deer may have a life territory of several square miles and a wolf a territory of hundreds of miles. Thus, if something happens to restrict the habitat, the wolf will be the first to perish, then the deer, and finally the rabbit. Although you may see all three animals at the same spot, you won't understand how they can all survive together unless you recognize this hierarchy of territories.

Areal hierarchies aren't usually as obvious as point or linear hierarchies. Due to the increasing extent of area from lower to higher order regions, different ranks occur at different scales. Therefore, the rank of an areal phenomenon is often not

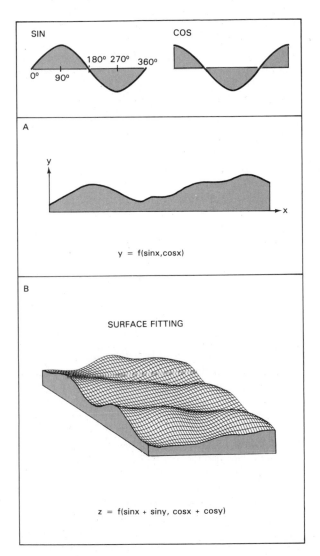

17.23 Trigonometric equations made up of sine and cosine terms can be used to describe a profile (A) or a surface (B) mathematically. The more complex the surface, the greater the number of terms required in the equation.

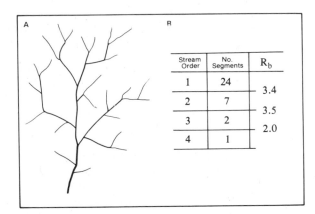

Stream Order	No. Segments	R_b
1	24	
		3.4
2	7	
		3.5
3	2	
		2.0
4	1	

17.24 The bifurcation ratio of a branching network provides an objective measure of its hierarchical organization.

apparent unless you make a concerted effort to view the environment from the perspective of several spatial scales. This is particularly true if a rank is **legally** rather than physically determined, since there may be no overt evidence to suggest its proper rank. Taxes, for example, are legally administered in a hierarchy based on area. We pay income taxes to the federal government, sales taxes to the state, and property taxes to the county. Such hierarchical levels aren't immediately obvious, yet if we ignore any one of them we will be in trouble!

The rank of **volumetric phenomena** is even more obscure, probably because many volumes have the appearance of areas. This is true of lakes, for instance, since we usually see only the surface. Yet a lake with a large surface may hold less water than one which is smaller in surface area but deeper. In many cases, as in pollution control and water supply evaluations, it is crucial to view lakes in terms of their volumes rather than their areas.

The nature of a hierarchy is simplest to visualize if you first break it into its component distributions. You can then analyze each component separately. In your state, for example, there may be a random dispersion of major cities, a slightly regular dispersion of secondary service centers, and a highly regular dispersion of rural market towns. Likewise, interstate highways may be randomly positioned, state highways more regular than random, and county roads still more regular than state highways. When the hierarchy of urban locations or highways is superimposed, the rather simple component patterns create an extremely complex composite distribution. If you separately analyze the individual hierarchical levels of a pattern in this way, however, you must exercise extra caution in your interpretation. For, in reality, the components aren't independent entities but, rather, fit together into one system.

CONCLUSION

In this chapter, we've looked at the form of features and the patterns these features make in our surroundings. The spatial concepts discussed here should greatly enhance your map analysis skills. But there's still more to map analysis. Next, we must move our focus from the internal structure of distributions to spatial associations among patterns. This external pattern correspondence is the topic of the next chapter.

SELECTED READINGS

Barber, G.M., *Elementary Statistics for Geographers* (New York: John Wiley & Sons, 1988).

Boots, B.N., and Getis, A., *Point Pattern Analysis* (Newbury Park, CA: Sage Publications, Inc., 1988).

Boyce, R.R., and Clark, W.A.V., "The Concept of Shape in Geography," *Geographical Review*, 54 (1964), pp. 561-572.

Clarke, J.I., "Morphometry from Maps," in Dury, G.H., ed., *Essays in Geomorphology* (London: Heinemann, 1966), pp. 235-274.

David, P., *Data Description and Presentation*, Science in Geography, 3 (London: Oxford University Press, 1974).

Davis, J.C., and McCullagh, M.J., eds., *Display and Analysis of Spatial Data* (New York: John Wiley & Sons, 1975).

Dury, G.H., "Geometric Analysis," in *Map Interpretation*, 4th ed. (London: Pitman & Sons, Ltd., 1972), pp. 163-177.

Ebdon, D., *Statistics in Geography*, 2nd ed. (New York: Basil Backwell, Inc., 1985).

Haggett, P., and Chorley, R.J., *Network Analysis in Geography* (London: Edward Arnold Publishers, Ltd., 1969).

Lee, D.R., and Sallee, G.T., "A Method of Measuring Shape," *Geographical Review*, 60, 4 (1970), pp. 555-563.

Lewis, P., *Maps and Statistics* (New York: Halsted Press, 1977).

McCullagh, P., *Data Use and Interpretation, Science in Geography*, 4 (London: Oxford University Press, 1974).

McGrew, J.C., and Monroe. C.B., *An Introduction to Statistical Problem Solving in Geography* (Dubuque, IA: Wm. C. Brown Publishers, 1993).

Moellering, H., and Rayner, J.N., "The Due Axis Fourier Shape Analysis of Closed Cartographic Forms," *The Cartographic Journal*, 19, 1 (1982), pp. 53-59.

Nagy, G., and Wagle, S., "Computational Geometry for Geography," *The Professional Geographer*, 32, 3 (1980), pp. 343-354.

Neft, D.S., *Statistical Analysis for Areal Distributions*, Monograph Series No. 2 (Philadelphia: Regional Science Research Institute, 1966).

Niemi, R., and Sullivan, J., *Quantitative Applications in the Social Sciences*, Sage University Paper Series (Beverly Hills, CA: Sage Publications, dates vary).

O'Brien, L., *Introducing Quantitative Geography: Measurement, Methods and Generalized Linear Models* (London: Routledge, 1992).

Rogers, A., *Statistical Analysis of Spatial Dispersion* (London: Pion, 1974).

Selkirk, K., *Pattern and Place* (Cambridge: Cambridge University Press, 1982).

Taylor, P.J., *Quantitative Methods in Geography: An Introduction to Spatial Analysis* (Boston: Houghton Mifflin Co., 1977).

Wilson, A.G., and Kirby, M.J., *Mathematics for Geographers and Planners* (NY: The Clarendon Press, 1980).

Also see references in Chapters 16 and 18.

CHAPTER 18

PATTERN COMPARISON

Phenomena intersect; to see but one is to see nothing.
—Victor Hugo, *The Toilers of the Sea*

18

CHAPTER EIGHTEEN

PATTERN COMPARISON

In our search for spatial order in the previous chapter, we compared geographic distributions with themselves—a sort of self-correlation procedure. Our focus was the **structural analysis** of a distribution. We can also compare geographic distributions with one another to determine their **spatial association**. As one thing in our environment changes, so do others in a consistent way. Indeed, relations between phenomena bind the environment together into systems or communities of features. When spatial elements interact, their dimensional character influences the geographic pattern which results. Therefore, we need to consider possible combinations of point, linear, areal, and volumetric features.

If we can determine where and how environmental features change together through space, we may receive clues to help explain why this spatial association occurs. (Such explanation is the subject of Part III: *Map Interpretation*.) When we can describe how environmental features vary together in a regular way, we can often make predictions. We can anticipate the effect of some event before it takes place in our experience—we can see behind the hill or over the ridge.

It's difficult to imagine, however, that our surroundings will ever be totally predictable. Furthermore, the ability to predict implies a rather profound and rare knowledge of our environment. Thus, predictions are always guesses—but guesses that will become increasingly "lucky" as you learn more about your world.

What, then, are you looking for? What creative suspicions should you nurture? Prior experience and knowledge enhance your chances of perceiving relationships. With practice, you learn to suspect interesting and important associations. This pattern and relation seeking ability is a creative act. To perceive order in a seeming chaos of events, you must make an active search, based on faith that relationships are there to be found.

TYPES OF CORRESPONDENCE

Your search will be more fruitful if you recognize that spatial correspondence can take several different forms. Skilled map analysts make a distinction between two basic types of spatial association. The first of these is cross–correlation.

Cross–Correlation

Perhaps the simplest case of spatial cross–correlation is one in which there is some spatial coincidence between two sets of **discrete** (separate) events (**Figure 18.1A**). The more closely paired the individual features are, the greater the strength of the suggested in–place association.

The suspicion that there is a relationship between separate things which are located close together is usually supported. In some cases the relation is direct. Fishers who realize that underwater features such as weed beds, logs, and rocks provide protection for fish are likely to have the best "luck."

But the relation may be indirect. Just because two things are regularly found together at the same location doesn't guarantee a meaningful relationship between them. Both features may be related to a third phenomenon and unrelated to each other directly. At certain times, trophy fish might be caught along the edge of weed

beds because this is where the small fish (their food) are found, not because large fish prefer to live close to weeds.

A second form of spatial association occurs when two or more **continuous** (everywhere present) variables change in intensity at the same time (**Figure 18.2A**). When environmental features vary together in this way, we say that they **covary**. The degree of association is strongest in a positive sense when the variables reach their peaks and valleys at the same locations. The association is strongest in the negative sense when one variable peaks where the other bottoms out, or vice versa. When there is no systematic relation between intensities, we can assume a weak or nonexistent spatial association between the variables.

Lag Correlation

When analyzing association between distributions, you need to be watchful for spatially **lagged relations**. These occur where there is a regular correspondence between two patterns, but one is shifted systematically to the side in one direction or another.

Perhaps the most familiar lagged correlation occurs with routed phenomena such as rivers. Conditions downstream correlate best with events upstream. In other words, there is a downstream lag.

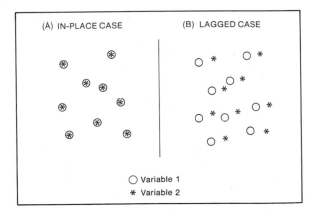

18.1 Spatial coincidence between discrete distributions is often used as an indicator of their degree of association, but it is important to distinguish between the in–place (A) and spatially lagged (B) cases.

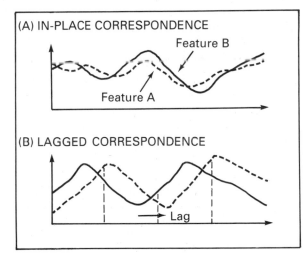

18.2 Spatial correspondence between continuous distributions, here shown in profile, is often determined by the degree to which their intensities covary. Both in–place (A) and lagged (B) relations should be recognized.

Unrouted phenomena can also reveal lag correlation relations. **Figure 18.1B** shows two patterns of discrete points. If north is at the top, you can see that shifting variable 1 slightly northeast will bring the two patterns into perfect spatial coincidence.

Lagged relations are simplest when only one direction is involved, as in the previous figure. For instance, the best place for catching large fish consistently might be in deep water close to weed beds. Similarly, paper mills might be found upwind of zones of air pollution, and farmsteads on the Great Plains might be found downwind of shelterbelts.

Lagged relations are more complex when several directions are involved, which is commonly the case. Thus, lake water quality is correlated with the characteristics of the landscape in the surrounding watershed. Soils, terrain slope, precipitation, vegetative cover, agricultural practices, urban development, and other factors all make a contribution.

Continuous distributions also exhibit lagged associations, as illustrated in **Figure 18.2B**. The same problems related to lagged association in discrete patterns pertain here. It's easy to miss this type of correspondence if only a small portion of the pattern is under study. For example, what would you think the correlation was between the variables in Figure 18.2B if you had data only for the right one-fourth of the profile?

MEASURES OF CORRESPONDENCE

Once you've sorted out the type of correspondence between distributions, you can focus on the strength of the correlation. For generations, map users have defined the degree of association between mapped patterns by using subjective visual judgments. The method continues to be popular, largely because it's so natural and easily performed. You might describe relations between two mapped patterns as having a "high correlation," a "poor correspondence," or "a moderate association." Since the meaning of such phrases isn't clear, however, other people won't know exactly what you mean.

Visual judgments of spatial association are easiest to make when the patterns being compared are superimposed one on the other. It makes little difference whether the two patterns are printed on the same map, or if one is constructed on a clear medium which is overlaid on the other pattern.

It's not always possible, however, to superimpose the patterns. Thus, it may be necessary to compare maps in a side-by-side arrangement—a chore which requires looking from one map to the other while keeping track of the relative spatial positions of features on the respective maps. This job is simplified, of course, if the maps to be compared are of the same scale and orientation. When this isn't the case, it may be worth your effort to rescale (enlarge or reduce) and reorient one of the maps to bring the two into closer physical format.

A third method for comparing maps visually is to view them in time sequence, as when they're alternately projected on a screen. Although the relative effectiveness of this technique isn't known, the method is increasing in popularity as computer map displays become more widespread. In some ways, time-sequence comparisons are similar to the overlay method.

Many quantitative measures of spatial association have been devised over the years. Each was designed to capture the essence of some logical, intuitive way of comparing patterns for a specific purpose. Some of these measures have become so popular that they're used in many disciplines to serve an even broader range of purposes. Indeed, there's such a diversity of ways to make map comparisons that it's hard to know which should be used when and what the results mean. In the remainder of this section, we'll shed light on this problem by seeing which approaches are most appropriate in which situations. We'll organize our discussion around three topics—the form of correspondence relations, the number of variables being computed, and the measurement levels achieved in the data.

Form of Relation

The correspondence relations between continuous environmental variables can take many forms. Linear relationships are the easiest to detect. In this case, the variables either increase or decrease together at a constant rate, or one increases while the other decreases. The simplest way to test for linearity is to create a graph, called a **scatter diagram**, by plotting values of one variable against those of the other (**Figure 18.3A**).

Non-linear (or curvilinear) relations are more complex than linear ones and aren't as easy to detect, yet many environmental relations are of this form. Increasing fertilizer applications to a field beyond a certain point, for example, may continue to increase crop yield but at a decreasing rate (**Figure 18.3B**). This is the familiar **diminishing returns** relation. If fertilizer applications are carried too far, the soil will become so toxic that yields will begin to decrease (**Figure 18.3C**).

With most common measures of spatial association, it's assumed that the variables being compared are linearly related. Although in some cases this assumption of linearity is valid, in many other instances it's not. When linearity is assumed but not met, measures of spatial association based on a linear relation between variables may be invalid. For example, a coefficient of spatial association may indicate little or no correlation when a scatter diagram suggests that there is a strong relationship, albeit a non-linear one, between the variables. This situation is illustrated in Figure 18.3. In examples B and C in this figure, you can see that changes in the independent variable (A) don't produce equal changes in the dependent variable (B) throughout the value range of the former. Thus, the relationship is non-linear, and linear correlation measures will be inappropriate.

If you want to analyze two map patterns for spatial association, and if you find a non-linear relation between the patterns, you should use one of the non-linear correlation methods devised for this purpose. Standard references on spatial analysis provide the information necessary to apply these techniques (refer to *Selected Readings* at the end of the chapter).

Number of Variables

Most common measures of spatial association are appropriate for simultaneously comparing **two variables**. In some cases, this is enough. But we must often compare more than two variables at a time. To do so using two-variable methods would require comparing all possible pairs of variables individually, an approach which is both inefficient and ineffective. It is also somewhat naive to believe that pairs of variables can be meaningfully analyzed in isolation.

A much better approach is to compare patterns simultaneously. Numerous quantitative methods of **multivariate spatial association** are available for this task. Some involve determining the correspondence of each pair of variables while holding the others constant. These measures are referred to as **partial correlation coefficients**.

Other multivariate measures of spatial association involve **ranking** a set of independent variables in terms of their statistical influence on the dependent variable. For instance, you may wish to correlate crop yield with various environmental factors. Through such analysis, you may find that soil fertility has a 60 percent influence, slope has a 25 percent influence, and all other factors have an influence of 15 percent. This means that 85 percent of the crop–yield variation can be explained by variation in only two environmental factors—soil fertility and slope.

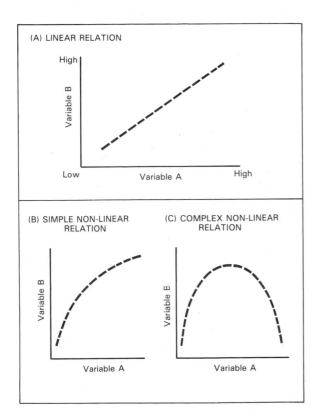

18.3 Continuous distributions can covary linearly (A) and non-linearly (B and C). Non-linear relations range from simple (B) to complex (C).

388

When the number of patterns representing independent variables that you wish to correlate with a single dependent variable is large—say greater than 10—you may use special numerical techniques. Most of these require an immense number of computations and therefore are practical only when high-speed computers are available. The techniques go by various names, including cluster analysis, factor analysis, and multi-dimensional scaling. But the result is essentially the same regardless of the procedure used. You end up with a sorting of the independent variables into groups representing different dimensions or factors of the spatial association arrangement. The individual dimensions are also ranked in terms of their degree of influence on the dependent variable, as was true with each variable in the multiple correlation analysis mentioned above.

Still another type of multivariate spatial association measure has been devised to facilitate the simultaneous comparison of two sets of variables. Thus, a set of maps depicting aspects of the cultural environment might be correlated with a set of variables from the physical environment. The results of the correlation analysis would be a ranking of cultural and physical variables in terms of their degree of contribution to the overall spatial variation in the two sets of patterns.

For the most part, the multivariate measures of spatial association we've been discussing go well beyond unaided visual judgments. Therefore, they provide valuable tools for the sophisticated map user. But they're also non-intuitive. Thus, someone who isn't knowledgeable about the mathematics used and the variables under study may find the results difficult to interpret. For these reasons, the use of multivariate map comparison methods is generally restricted to skilled environmental scientists who are willing to put up with the procedures' inconvenience to gain the insight they may provide.

Measurement Levels

Correlation measures are designed to be used with data that attain certain levels of measurement (see *Measurement Level* in Chapter 2). Different correlation models are available for use with nominal, ordinal, and interval-ratio data.*

Thus, before performing a correlation analysis, we must determine the measurement level reflected by the data and then choose a correlation model accordingly. In the following sections, we'll discuss examples appropriate for each of the measurement levels attained in mapped data. Let's begin with nominal data.

Nominal Data

We are often interested in the relationship between mapped phenomena which are different in *nature* rather than in *degree*. For instance, we may wish to compare soil types with the vegetation pattern, or to correlate climate zones with the pattern of land use. Such information is strictly **nominal**, for in each case we are comparing two entirely different things.

Imagine, for example, that we wish to obtain an objective measure of the degree of association between vegetation cover and ground slope zones in a portion of the driftless region in

18.4 Notice the spatial correspondence between forest cover and ground slope (shown by close contour spacing) on this portion of the Barneveld, Wisconsin, 1:24,000 USGS topographic quadrangle.

For statistical purposes, interval and ratio data are treated as equals. The results of map analyses based on these two data types may have different implications for the map user, however. See: Muehrcke, P.C., "Concepts of Scaling from the Map Reader's Point of View," The American Cartographer, Vol. 3, No. 2 (1976), pp. 123-141.

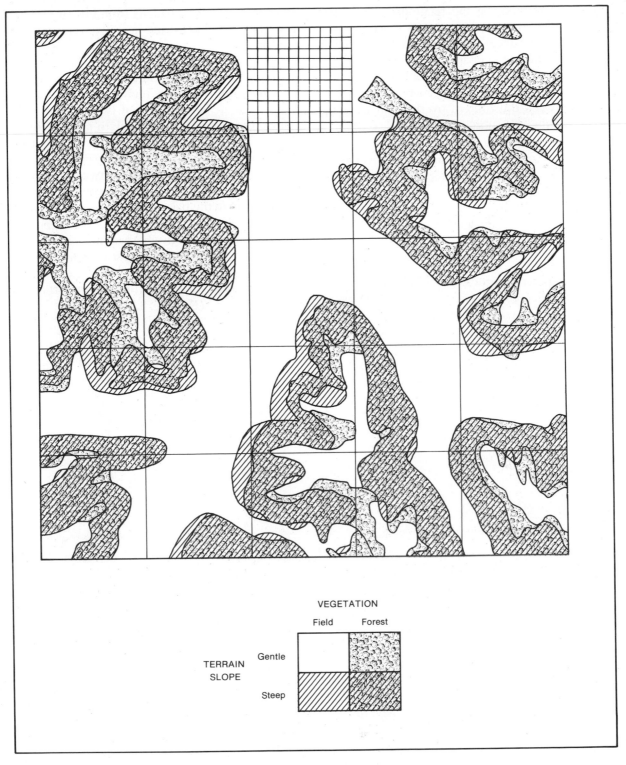

VEGETATION

Field   Forest

TERRAIN
SLOPE   Gentle

Steep

18.5 This map represents a four-way classification of Figure 18.4, based on forest–cover and ground–slope relations. For data tabulation purposes, the map has been divided into a 5 x 5 grid, and each of these 25 grid cells has been further divided into a 10 x 10 grid (100 cells).

390

southwestern Wisconsin (**Figure 18.4**). One approach to studying the relationship between these variables of classification is to compute a **coefficient of areal correspondence**, based on the proportion of overlap of the vegetation type (A) and ground slope (B) subregions (**Figure 18.5**). The coefficient is computed by forming a ratio between the zone of overlap and the total extent of the two subregions:

$$C_1 = \frac{\text{Area where regions A and B overlap}}{\text{Area covered by either region A or B}}$$

$$= \frac{(\text{A and B})}{(\text{A or B}).}$$

The computed coefficient will range in value from 0 (when there is no overlap) to 1 (when there is perfect correspondence) (**Figure 18.6**).

Let's now apply the above procedure to a practical problem. If we place a square grid of 2,500 cells (50 rows by 50 columns) over the map in Figure 18.4, and then tabulate the land status within each cell (**Table 18.1**), we find that:

(a) $\dfrac{\text{cells in steep forested land}}{\text{cells in forested or steep land}} = \dfrac{926}{1,288} = .72$

and

(b) $\dfrac{\text{cells in gentle slope fields}}{\text{cells in fields or gentle slope}} = \dfrac{1,212}{1,574} = .77$

In other words, there is a 72 percent correspondence between wooded land and steep slopes, while there is a 77 percent correspondence between fields and gentle slopes.*

Ordinal Data

In many situations, we can extract data from maps at an **ordinal** measurement level. With ordinal values in hand, we can study the relationship between two variables by comparing the respective ranks of the paired items.

....

For computational details, consult statistical references such as those provided at the end of this chapter.

Look again at the data in Table 18.1. This time, let's rank the quadrats from low to high on the slope-steepness and forest-cover variables (**Table 18.2**).

Notice that for tied ranks (that is, where two quadrats have the same value), an average of that rank and the next higher rank is used for each quadrat. For example, if two quadrats possessed the same value tie for sixth rank, a rank of 6.5 would be assigned to each, and no rank 6 or rank 7 would be used.

If there's a relationship between the rankings of slope steepness and forest cover, it may not be apparent in the paired rank listing in Table 18.2. But if we arrange the ranking of slope-steepness values from low to high and then plot forest-cover ranks against these values on a scatter diagram, the relationship between the variables is clear: Forest cover increases in linear (direct) proportion to slope steepness (**Figure 18.7**).

Table 18.1 Forest Cover—Ground Steepness Tabulation

Quadrat	Steep Fields	Forested Steep	Forested Gentle	Gentle Fields
1	9	45	4	42
2	8	45	8	39
3	—	—	—	100
4	—	26	11	63
5	9	30	10	51
6	8	34	12	46
7	7	61	4	28
8	1	3	1	95
9	—	69	15	16
10	2	29	43	26
11	3	26	38	33
12	9	43	14	34
13	5	80	2	13
14	—	19	3	78
15	13	38	12	37
16	3	29	3	65
17	—	33	1	66
18	19	39	8	34
19	5	13	2	80
20	7	30	5	58
21	1	61	4	34
22	10	23	—	67
23	3	54	8	35
24	2	55	12	31
25	—	41	18	41
Total	124	926	238	1212
Percent	5%	37%	9.5%	48.5%

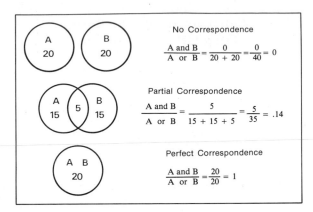

18.6 The coefficient of areal correspondence provides a simple measure of spatial association which varies between 0 (no overlap) and 1 (complete overlap).

For there to be a perfect linear correspondence between the two variables, the scatter diagram would have to form a straight line. Since there are some deviant points in our scatter dia-

PART II
*Map
Analysis*

gram, we must conclude that the spatial association between forest cover and slope steepness isn't perfect. We can interpret these results to mean that we'll find some steep slopes devoid of forest as well as some gentle slopes that are forested.

To quantify the degree of correlation between the rankings of forest cover and slope steepness, we can compute a **rank correlation coefficient**. The following reasoning is used in devising such a measure. If n regions (quadrats in this case) are ranked according to two variables (X and Y), the correlation will be perfect only if all the paired regions are ranked equally. Therefore, it is logical to use the various differences (d_i) between ranks of paired regions as an indication of the disparity between the two sets of rankings. A perfect correlation would be obtained when d_i = 0 for all d_i's. The larger the paired differences, then, the less perfect the association between the

Table 18.2 Paired Rank Listing of Forest Cover—Ground Steepness Data

Quadrat (i)	Steep	Rank X	Forest	Rank Y	(X_i-Y_i) d_i	d_i^2
i = 1	54	8	49	13	5	25.
2	53	9	53	11	2	4.
3	0	25	0	25	0	0.
4	26	21	27	20	1	1.
5	39	14	40	16	2	4.
6	42	12	46	15	3	9.
7	68	3	65	5.5	1.5	2.25
8	4	24	4	24	0	0.
9	69	2	84	1	1	1.
10	31	19	72	3	16	256.
11	29	20	64	7	13	169.
12	51	10.5	57	10	.5	.25
13	85	1	82	2	1	1.
14	19	22	22	22	0	0
15	51	10.5	50	12	1.5	2.25
16	32	18	32	19	1	1.
17	33	15.5	34	18	2.5	6.25
18	58	4	47	14	10	100.
19	18	23	15	23	0	0.
20	37	17	35	17	0	0.
21	62	5	65	5.5	.5	.25
22	33	15.5	23	21	5.5	30.25
23	57	6.5	62	8	1.5	2.25
24	57	6.5	67	4	2.5	6.25
N = 25	41	13	59	9	4	16.
					Total	637.

392

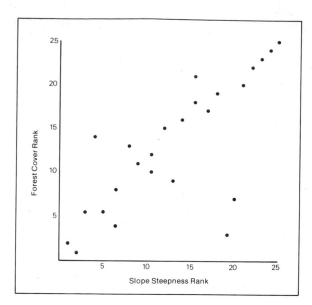

18.7 The relation between forest cover and slope steepness is clarified by plotting their rank correspondence on a scatter diagram. The relation shown here is linear and positive.

two variables. In order to avoid the problem of negative d_i's canceling out positive ones in determining the total magnitude of discrepancy, differences in paired ranks should be squared.

We can compute a rank correlation coefficient based on the above reasoning by substituting the appropriate values in the formula given in **Box 18.1**. This coefficient of rank correlation is known as Spearman's rho (ρ).* The coefficient will range from 0 when there is no rank association between the two variables to 1 when there is a perfect correlation between the rankings (**Figure 18.8**). The sign of the coefficient will be positive (+) when there is a direct correspondence between the ranked variables and negative (–) when there is an inverse relationship. In other words, there can be perfect negative correlation just as there can be perfect positive correlation between the ranked variables.

The computations required to determine the rank correlation between forest cover and slope steepness are also provided in Box 18.1. The deviations between paired X and Y rankings

....
Another rank correlation measure is Kendall's tau (τ). For computational details, consult a standard statistical reference such as the ones identified at the end of this chapter.

**Box 18.1
Calculations for the Rank
Correlation Coefficient
(Spearman's Rho)**

_____

IOWA COUNTY FOREST-SLOPE EXAMPLE

$$r_s = 1 - \frac{6\sum\limits_{i=1}^{n} d_i^2}{n^3 - n}$$

$$= 1 - \frac{6\sum\limits_{i=1}^{25} d_i^2}{25^3 - 25}$$

$$= 1 - \frac{6\,(637)}{15625 - 25}$$

$$= 1 - \frac{3822}{15600}$$

$$= 1 - .245$$

$$= .755$$

and the squares of these values, both of which are used in computing the rank correlation coefficient, are found in Table 18.2. The computed rank correlation value of .755 represents a fairly high degree of correlation between the two variables and compares favorably with the previously computed .72 coefficient of areal correspondence for

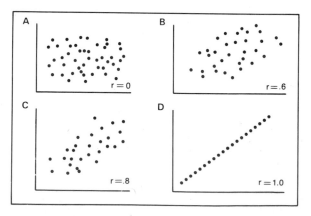

18.8 The strength of rank correlation between a low of 0 and a high of 1 is revealed by the dispersion of points on a scatter diagram.

the same data. Thus, our rank correlation measure also seems to meet our intuitive expectations of what we want an index of spatial association to show.

Interval-Ratio Data

Sometimes we can obtain mapped data for two variables at **interval** or **ratio** measurement levels. When this is the case, we can determine the degree of spatial association between the two patterns by using data values directly, thus avoiding the loss of information that occurs when raw values are converted to ranks or classes.

The first step is, again, to plot a scatter diagram. Rather than use rankings as in the previous example, however, we can use the raw information itself. The results of such a plot, using the data provided in Table 18.2, are shown in **Figure 18.9**. The plotted values in this second scatter diagram appear in an arrangement different from the first, but the forest–cover and slope–steepness values are still roughly proportional. In general, then, there is a tendency for small slope-steepness values (X) to be associated with small forest-cover values (Y) and for large slope values to be associated with large forest-cover values. The points also appear to be scattered on both sides of a straight line which can be used to approximate the trend between the two variables. This

suggests that in the region under study, forest cover and slope steepness are linearly related.

All this comes as no surprise, since our rank correlation analysis told us the same thing. What we want next is an objective measure of the degree to which the variables are linearly related. Such a measure of association should, of course, be independent of both the choice of origin and the measurement units used for the two variables (X and Y). It also shouldn't change if different numbers of values are used in its computation.

All these factors have been incorporated in the **coefficient of determination** (r^2). **Box 18.2** gives the formula, expressed in a form convenient to use with calculators.

Box 18.2 Formula and Calculations for the Coefficient of Determination (r^2)

IOWA COUNTY FOREST-SLOPE EXAMPLE

$$r = \frac{n\,\Sigma xy - \Sigma x\,\Sigma y}{\sqrt{[n\,\Sigma x^2 - (\Sigma x)^2]\,[n\,\Sigma y^2 - (\Sigma y)^2]}}$$

$$= \frac{25(57,812) - (1049)(1154)}{\sqrt{[25(53,959) - (1049)^2]\,[25(65,596) - (1154)^2]}}$$

$$= \frac{1,445,300 - 1,210,546}{\sqrt{[1,348,975 - 1,100,401]\,[1,639,900 - 1,331,716]}}$$

$$= \frac{234,754}{\sqrt{(248,574)\,(308,184)}}$$

$$= \frac{234,754}{\sqrt{76,606,529,616}}$$

$$= \frac{234,754}{276,779} = .85$$

$$r^2 = [.85]^2 = .72$$

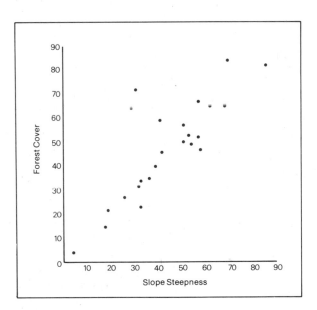

18.9 A plot of actual forest–cover values against slope–steepness values reveals a fairly strong spatial correlation between the phenomena.

Values of r^2 are similar to those for the rank correlation coefficient. They can range from +1, representing a perfect correlation in a directly proportionate sense, to –1, representing a perfect correlation in an inversely proportionate sense. At either extreme, points of the scatter diagram will lie on a straight line. An r^2 value of 0 is interpreted as meaning that there is no statistical rela-

394

tion between the two variables. In general, the strength of the relation between variables is given by the magnitude of r^2, whereas the sign of r^2 indicates whether the values of Y tend to increase or decrease with an increase in the values of X.

An example problem will demonstrate how simple it is to put the rather complicated-looking formula for r^2 into use. If you study the formula, you will see that only a few pieces of information are needed—the sum of the X and Y values (symbolized Σx and Σy), the sum of squares of the same values (Σx^2 and Σy^2), the square of the sums of the X and Y values [$(\Sigma x)^2$ and $(\Sigma y)^2$], the sum of the products of the X and Y values (Σxy), and the product of the sums of the X and Y values ($\Sigma x \Sigma y$). The results of performing each of these arithmetic operations are shown in **Table 18.3**.

Once you have this information, you are ready to compute the coefficient r^2. The substitutions of numerical values into the previous formula and subsequent arithmetic procedures are provided in Box 18.2. The computations indicate that $r^2 = .72$. This coefficient of determination value can be interpreted to mean that 72 percent of the variation in forest-cover values can be accounted for by variation in slope-steepness values. Or, put another way, there is a fairly high degree of spatial association between the two variables. This conclusion is in keeping with previous findings using nominal and ordinal data.

DIFFUSION PATTERNS

So far in this chapter we have treated environmental distributions as static phenomena. In many cases, this assumption is justified, and the pattern comparison methods we have discussed will produce meaningful results. But sometimes we are less interested in static pattern structure than in the pattern of spatial growth or **diffusion**. For distributions which are spatially dynamic by nature, we need to take a different perspective.

The first step in dealing with dynamic phenomena is to determine whether the features are discrete or continuous. Let's look first at discrete entities.

Table 18.3 Data for Computing the Coefficient of Determination

Quadrat	Steep Slope X	X²	Forest Y	Y²	XY
i = 1	54	2916	49	2401	2646
2	53	2809	53	2809	2809
3	0	0	0	0	0
4	26	676	27	729	702
5	39	1521	40	1600	1560
6	42	1764	46	2116	1932
7	68	4624	65	4225	4420
8	4	16	4	16	16
9	69	4761	84	7056	5796
10	31	961	72	5184	2232
11	29	841	64	4096	1856
12	51	2601	57	3249	2907
13	85	7225	82	6724	6970
14	19	361	22	484	418
15	51	2601	50	2500	2550
16	32	1024	32	1024	1024
17	33	1089	34	1156	1122
18	58	3364	47	2209	2726
19	18	324	15	225	270
20	37	1369	35	1225	1295
21	62	3844	65	4225	4030
22	33	1089	23	529	759
23	57	3249	62	3844	3534
24	57	3249	67	4489	3819
n = 25	41	1681	59	3841	2419
Total	1049	53,959	1154	65,596	57,812

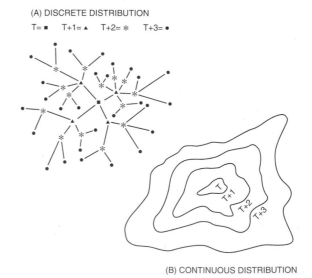

18.10 Diffusion patterns may be the result of new occurrences of discrete features (A) or the spread of continuous phenomena (B).

Discrete Entities

Sometimes patterns are made up of discrete entities. Examples include trees killed by Dutch Elm disease, people who have tested positive for the AIDS virus, and the household locations of automated breadmaking machines. New occurrences of discrete phenomena tend to "pop up" in scattered fashion, creating a "pox–like" pattern (**Figure 18.10A**). The diffusion of ideas, styles, jokes, diseases, and products all follow this pattern.

Although the scatter's density tends to diminish from the distribution's point of origin, there are striking exceptions. The global movement of machines, products, and animals (including people) can broadly scatter new occurrences in these patterns. Take the dispersion of cholera described in **Box 18.3**, for instance. In this case, airline meals picked up in Peru spread the disease from South America to California. The functional link between these two places wouldn't be obvious by looking at a dispersal pattern on a map.

Continuous Phenomena

Like discrete features, continuous phenomena often have a dynamic character. Examples include forest fires, oil slicks, and toxic chemical plumes in the groundwater. The dispersal or growth of these phenomena exhibits a spreading pattern (**Figure 18.10B**). The leading edge of these patterns may be quite ragged and discontinuous, however.

Given enough time, a continuous feature may break up and, eventually, disintegrate. For instance, forces exerted by tides, currents, and wind will cause an oil slick to separate into smaller patches. Other examples include the radioactive atmospheric plume that came from the Soviet Union's power plant disaster at Chernobyl and the dust plume created by the 1991 explosion of the Philippine volcano Mount Pinatubo. In both cases, the distribution gradually dispersed and settled out of the atmosphere as the plume circulated around the earth.

When working with diffusion maps, you will quickly realize that discrete entities are often mapped in continuous fashion. For instance, cartographers may use a continuous area symbol to show the spread of gypsy moths, killer bees, or similar discrete entities. In such cases, they are

BOX 18.3 DON'T DRINK THE WATER

And you thought airline food couldn't get any worse? The cholera epidemic in South America has touched Los Angeles: at least 39 passengers and crew members who arrived last month on an Aerolineas Argentinas flight from Buenos Aires have come down with the disease; one died. Los Angeles health officials, who are still trying to locate other passengers, suspect that airline meals taken on at a stop in Lima were tainted. Other major carriers now are taking special precautions. While American Airlines has eliminated green salads and fresh seafood from its South America menus, Varig copes by loading its planes with extra food from safer sources in Brazil, Chile and Argentina.

(*Time*, March 9, 1992)

exercising cartographic license. This change in dimension from discrete feature to continuous symbol is a common simplification strategy (see *Simplification* in Chapter 3). The continuous representation is designed to help you see the overall pattern, since distracting details have been eliminated.

Your task when faced with any sort of diffusion map is to ascertain the dispersal or growth mechanism that lies behind the pattern you see. Professionals use a variety of numerical modeling strategies in diffusion studies, and computer software is available to help in these endeavors. But the high level of statistical expertise required to work with these models falls beyond the scope of this book. For our purposes here, it is sufficient that you take two steps when analyzing diffusion maps. First, imagine what factors contributed to the pattern's current form. Then, predict what form the pattern is likely to take in the future.

HOLISTIC MAP ANALYSIS

In the past three chapters, we've discussed many aspects of map analysis. We began (in Chapter 16) by seeing how we could use fundamental spatial elements to build secondary spatial concepts. Next (in Chapter 17), we used these elements and concepts to describe the structure of mapped patterns. Finally, in this chapter, we discussed correspondence relations between patterns.

Each of the cartometric, pattern structure, and pattern comparison terms we introduced is a way to mold the world into more understandable form. We can think of these items in our geographic vocabulary as a set of spatial filters through which we force our experience. By focusing our attention in this way, we can ask more penetrating questions and find more satisfying answers in the course of map study.

Cartometric, form, pattern, and spatial association measures are similar in that they all give the appearance of precision and authority. The impression evoked by these numerical indexes can create the illusion that map analysis procedures are objective and absolute when in fact they're not.

One problem is that the information that's mapped, or the information that's easiest to retrieve from cartographic representations, is related more to physical than functional space. Yet it's functional space that is most directly related to human spatial behavior. What this means is that even the best map analysis based on physical data, while providing insight into the character of physical space, may be of little direct value in understanding our behavioral space. Just because something is mapped, or because some aspect of a map is easy to analyze numerically, doesn't mean that the results will be of much interpretative value when we're confronted with environmental problems.

Another difficulty with using the results of map analysis is that map makers tend to emphasize the most static aspects of the environment. Furthermore, cartographic representations are themselves primarily static. We treated both these factors in Chapter 8. When we try to analyze these static maps using the measures of spatial pattern structure and association introduced in the past three chapters, we often run into trouble. Since spatial distributions aren't static as they appear on most conventional maps, we can't expect the measures we use to analyze only one or two patterns to be temporally meaningful.

Thus, our ability to analyze how pattern structure or association has evolved is limited. We're being asked to analyze static maps with static measures as a basis for drawing conclusions about a dynamic world. In the process, we find that techniques which satisfy mapping convenience can actually make analyzing maps in a meaningful way more difficult.

A third problem with most map analysis procedures is that we can't perform them independently of the map scale. Since spatial organization takes place at a wide range of scales in our surroundings, there is a similar range of scales within which spatial distributions and their generating processes can be observed and analyzed. By studying the environment at only one scale, we may miss crucial things happening at other scales. In addition, our conclusions may be meaningful only at the scale of that particular map.

CONCLUSION

Despite the caution that is warranted when performing map analysis, the techniques discussed here and in previous chapters play an important role in map study and use. Although we isolated various analytical procedures and treated them separately, this was strictly a matter of convenience. In reality, they collectively form the basis for an integrated map analysis methodology. You'll gain an appreciation of their integrated, complementary character when we take on the task of interpreting maps in Part III: *Map Interpretation*.

Before moving on to map interpretation, however, there are several other issues related to map analysis that need our attention. One is the topic of computer software for map analysis. The other is the subject of map accuracy. We will tackle map analysis software first.

SELECTED READINGS

Clark, W.A.V., and Hosking, P.C., *Statistical Methods for Geographers* (New York: John Wiley & Sons, 1986).

Dunteman, G.H, *Introduction to Multivariate Analysis* (Beverly Hills, CA: Sage Publications, 1984).

Griffith, D.A., *Spatial Regression Analysis on the PC: Spatial Statistics Using SAS* (Washington, DC: AAG, 1993).

Griffith, D.A., and Armheim, C.G., *Multivariate Statistical Analysis for Geographers* (Upper Saddle River, NJ: Prentice-Hall, 1997).

Griffith, D.A., Armheim, C.G., and Desloges, J.R., *Statistical Analysis for Geographers* (Englewood Cliffs, NJ: Prentice-Hall, 1991).

Haining, R., *Spatial Data Analysis in the Social and Environmental Sciences* (New York: Cambridge University Press, 1990).

Johnston, R.J., *Multivariate Statistical Analysis in Geography* (New York: Longman, Inc., 1980).

Niemi, R., and Sullivan, J., *Quantitative Applications in the Social Sciences*, Sage University Paper Series (Beverly Hills, CA: Sage Publications, dates vary).

Odland, J., *Spatial Autocorrelation* (Newbury Park, CA: Sage Publications, Inc., 1988).

Shaw, G., and Wheeler, D., *Statistical Techniques in Geographical Analysis* (New York: John Wiley & Sons, 1985).

Walford, N., *Geographical Data Analysis* (New York: John Wiley & Sons, 1995).

Also see references in Chapters 16 and 17.

CHAPTER NINETEEN

GIS AND MAP ANALYSIS SOFTWARE

INTRODUCTION

STAND-ALONE PACKAGES

- Cartometrics
- Address Matching
- Route Finding
- Statistical Mapping
- Terrain Analysis
  - Elevation Determination
  - Surface Profiles
  - Slope and Gradient
- Spatial Optimization
  - Route Selection
  - Site Selection
  - Redistricting

GEOGRAPHICAL INFORMATION SYSTEMS (GIS)

- Data Conversion
- Search Window
- Buffer
- Overlay
- Modeling
  - Value-Free Measures
  - Value-Laden Measures

GPS-DRIVEN APPLICATIONS

- Navigation
- Precision Farming

CONCLUSION

SELECTED READINGS

The computer . . . can be asked by us to "think the unthinkable"
and the previously unthought.
—Alvin Toffler, *The Third Wave*

19

CHAPTER NINETEEN

GIS AND MAP ANALYSIS SOFTWARE

Computers love numbers and equations. Thus, to the great joy of map users, map analysis is now largely automated. A variety of commercial products is available to perform most common map analysis chores. As we discussed in Chapter 9: *Software for Map Retrieval,* these products require a fully-configured computer system and some computer literacy on the part of the map user.

The basic computer system needed for map analysis must be more robust than that used for mere map retrieval. The hardware must be more powerful. The software must be expanded to include analytical functions. And the database must be structured with extensive cross-referencing among different data entries.

No matter what product vendors say, we're still far from the point at which any single package can be a one-size-fits-all solution. Making map analysis easy and inexpensive enough for a novice working on entry-level computer hardware means you can't begin to satisfy the needs of professional users. Conversely, making it powerful enough to please a skilled professional with a high-end computer configuration means you're going to overload low-end hardware and bury the novice in confusing options. Given this situation, the market is filled with a multitude of products targeted at different market segments.

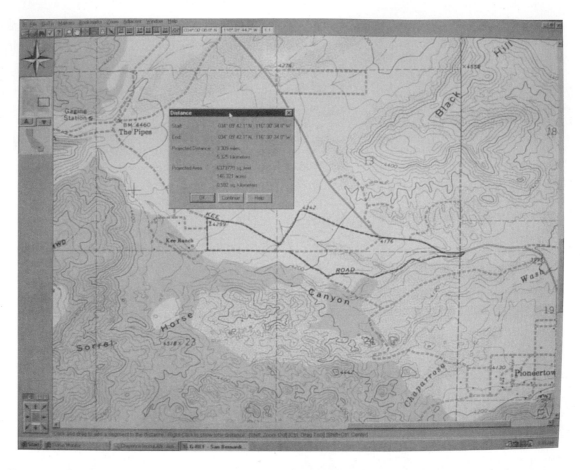

19.1 Simple two-dimensional cartometric analysis is both quick and accurate when using a software-database bundle such as *Earthvisions G-REF—U.S. Terrain Series,* which is designed specifically for position, direction, distance, and area analysis.

STAND-ALONE PACKAGES

The most direct way to enlist computers in map analysis is to attack one problem at a time. The idea is to do one thing well. Software designed to solve a specific problem is generally simpler, easier to use, and less expensive than multifunctional programs.* In most cases, software packages that stand alone also place the least demands on data-

Many packages that began as single-function software now are multifunction, so distinctions between the two categories of software are blurred. Competition between vendors contributes to "option creep" as each tries to gain market share by outdoing the functionality of the other's program. The result is bloated software that demands more computer resources to operate effectively.

base design and computer hardware. Individual software packages range widely in both scope and depth, as we'll see in the following examples.

Cartometrics

Computers are admirably suited to search a database for information and perform analyses such as those outlined in Chapter 16: *Cartometrics.* At the simplest level, for example, computer software for two-dimensional cartometric analysis could help you determine latitude-longitude coordinates of a position, the distance between two cities, the direction from a plane crash site to the nearest road, and the size of an urban area. As an example, the inexpensive package of *G-REF* software and *U.S. Terrain Series* data by Earthvisions*

Earthvisions, Inc., 655 Portsmouth Ave., Greenland, NH 03840-9967, 603-433-9397, www.earthvisions.com.

is well-suited to these tasks (**Figure 19.1**). After calling up the relevant portion of a USGS topographic quadrangle on your computer screen, you merely point, click, drag, or trace to perform the desired cartometric chores. This is both quicker and more accurate than traditional manual methods. But a computer system can go far beyond these simple analysis tasks.

Software for three-dimensional cartometric analysis is also available.* You might use this software to determine the volume of water in a reservoir, the size of a mineral deposit, or the amount of earth removed in a quarrying operation. To do so, of course, you also need a three-dimensional database. We discuss this topic in further detail under *Terrain Analysis* later in this chapter.

Address Matching

Position finding (see Chapter 14) is one of the most basic tasks we perform with maps. In the parlance of the computer age, we call this **address matching**. We're using "address" here in the broadest sense of the term. Any spatial identifier will do, such as latitude-longitude coordinates, geographic names, house numbers, ZIP-codes, and telephone area codes. To support effective address matching, we need a database that includes cross-references among as many of these locational aliases as possible.

We have several needs for address matching. We'd like to give an address and have the computer show its location on a map. Alternatively, we'd like to point to a map and have the computer give the address. A few products have either **address-to-map** or **map-to-address** capability; but most software has both capabilities (**Figure 19.2**).**

Address-matching software serves many needs. Of special importance is providing emergency services. Fire, ambulance, and police personnel benefit by being able to pinpoint the location of a distress call. Their next concern is

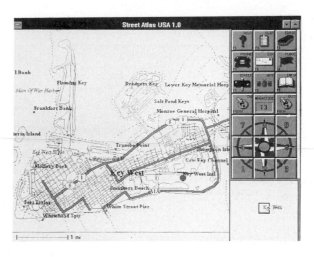

19.2 *Street Atlas USA* draws on a massive street-level cartographic database for the entire United States on a CD-ROM.

reaching the location as quickly as possible, which is a routing issue.

Route Finding

In many cases we want to go beyond position finding and determine the route between places. Computer programs that provide this capability build upon an address-matching functionality.* Route-finding software varies in sophistication, depending on the type of information and extent of cross-referencing included in its database (**Figure 19.3**). These databases have become broader with each new software version. But keeping large databases up to date is difficult and expensive, so choose your vendor carefully. Competition in this market is fierce, and the cheapest software is usually not the best buy.

Depending on the software you're using, you start the program by entering the street address, ZIP code, or latitude-longitude of your origin and destination. The package will then automatically determine the shortest travel route, taking into consideration one-way streets, overpasses, freeway exits, and speed settings for seven types of roads or streets. Some software can also read your travel agenda and then sort the order of stops to minimize travel distance or time. In addi-

---

Representative of this software is a package called Surfer *(Golden Software, Inc., 809 14th Street, Golden, CO 80401-1866, 303-279-1021, www.golden.com/ golden/).*

**The software discussed in Chapter 9 under* You-Are-Here Maps *and* Here-It-Is Maps *have an address-matching capability. Check the footnotes in those sections for titles and vendors of this type of software.*

Again, refer to software products and vendors mentioned in Chapter 9 under You-Are-Here Maps *and* Here-It-Is Maps.

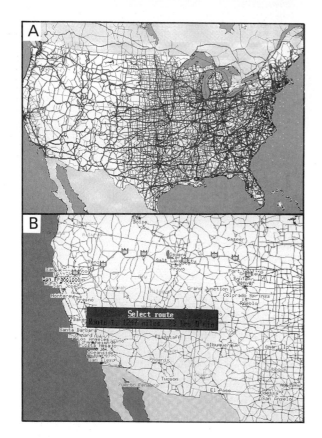

19.3 *Microsoft Automap* **lets you work with a map display and menu bar to determine the best route between places (A) and then highlights your selected route (B).**

tion to displaying the travel route, it can generate written directions and provide distance and travel time information (**Figure 19.4**). It can even estimate fuel requirements.

Statistical Mapping

Software for cartographic analysis of statistical data is available in several levels of sophistication. At the simplest level, some spreadsheet vendors now provide some mapping capability with their products.* Many other vendors market carto-

Spreadsheets such as Microsoft Excel *now come with limited statistical mapping features. More comprehensive add-on cartographic and statistical databases from outside vendors greatly enhance spreadsheet mapping capabilities. One such value-added product is* Maps and Data for Microsoft Office 95/97 *(MaconUSA, 214 Lincoln Street, Allston, MA 02134, 800-903-3127, www.maconusa.com).*

Time		Road	For	Di	Towards
00:00	DEPART New Orleans (Lousiana)	I10	3 mile	E	Mobile
00:04	At Arabi stay on the	I10	84 mil	E	Mobile
01:35	At Gulf Hills stay on the	I10	21 mil	E	Mobile
01:58	At Moss Point stay on the	I10	25 mil	E	Mobile
02:25	At Tillmans Corner stay on th	I10	65 mil	E	Mobile
03:39	At Ensley stay on the	I10	3 mile	E	Tallahasse
03:43	At Ferry Pass stay on the	I10	200 mi	E	Tallahasse
08:47	Turn off onto	I75	39 mil	S	Gainesvill
09:28	At Alachua stay on the	I75	73 mil	S	Gainesvill
10:47	Turn off onto	Florida Tpk	40 mil	E	Pompano Bc
11:30	At Winter Garden stay on the	Florida Tpk	172 mi	E	Pompano Bc
14:37	Turn off onto	I95	8 mile	S	W Palm Beac
14:46	At N Palm Beach stay on the	I95	6 mile	S	W Palm Beac
14:52	At W Palm Beach stay on the	I95	7 mile	S	Pompano Bc
15:00	At Greenacres City stay on th	I95	28 mil	S	Pompano Bc
15:31	At Pompano Beach stay on the	I95	21 mil	S	Ft Lauderda
15:58	At Ives Estates stay on the	I95	1 mile	S	Miami

Quickest route from New Orleans to Miami
Time 16 hrs 18 min. Distance 885 miles.

19.4 *Microsoft Automap* **will generate a written itinerary with directions and mileage data in addition to displaying your selected route.**

graphic and statistical databases that can be used with common spreadsheets.* In both cases, maps are usually restricted to the "value by area" type that we call choropleth maps (see Chapter 7: *Statistical Maps*).

More specialized stand-alone statistical mapping software is also available. These packages usually provide a choice of analysis and display methods (**Figure 19.5**).** You can expect to find such features as proportional point symbols, stepped surfaces (choropleth and 3-D histograms), and smooth surfaces (isolines and fishnets). We discussed these methods in Chapter 7.

And, finally, you can find statistical mapping capabilities in general-purpose software marketed to the business community. You may hear these packages referred to as **business geographics** software. More commonly, however, they get the

Examples of software that let you map spreadsheet data are MapLinx *(IMSI, 1895 Francisco Blvd. East, San Rafael, CA 94901, 800-833-4674, www.imsisoft.com) and* Business Map *(Environmental Systems Research Institute, Inc., 380 New York Street, Redlands, CA 92373-8100, 909-793-2853, www.esri.com)).*

**MapViewer *(Golden Software, Inc., 809 14th Street, Golden, CO 80401-1866, 303-279-1021, www.golden.com/golden/),* MapInfo *(One Global View, Troy, NY 12180, 800-327-8627, www.mapinfo.com),* Proximity *(Decisionmark Corp., 200 Second Ave., S.E., Cedar Rapids, IA 52401, 800-365-7629, www.decisionmark.com).*

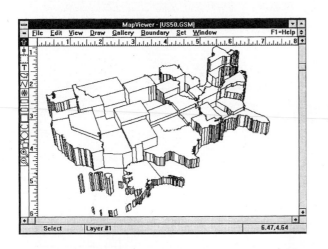

19.5 You can easily manipulate and display statistical data in a variety of map forms using software such as *MapViewer*.

GIS (geographic information systems) label.* We discuss this important category of analytical mapping software under *Geographical Information Systems (GIS)* later in the chapter.

Terrain Analysis

Printed maps are inherently two-dimensional, so it makes sense that they best facilitate analysis of horizontal measurements of position, distance, and direction. But what if we need to consider the third environmental dimension, as in measuring elevation, altitude, or depth? This three-dimensional analysis has always been more challenging, because it requires extracting information from quantitative symbols such as contour lines or using some other surface-rendering method.

But mapping software and three-dimensional digital databases now greatly ease the task of three-dimensional map analysis. We'll use a ter-

---

*Atlas GIS *and* ArcView *(Environmental Systems Research Institute, Inc., 380 New York Street, Redlands, CA 92373-8100, 909-793-2853, www.esri.com),* Compass *(Claritas, Inc., 1525 Wilson Blvd., Arlington, VA, 800-284-4868),* On Target Mapping-Technology that Delivers *(On Target Mapping, 1051 Brinton Road, Pittsburgh, PA 15221, 800-700-6277, www.otmapping.com.),* IDRISI *(The IDRISSI Project, The Clark Labs for Cartographic Technology and Geographic Analysis, Clark University, 950 Main St., Worcester, MA 01610-1477, 508-793-7526, www.idrisi.clarku.edu).*

rain example to illustrate this point, but anything that's mappable with quantitative symbols can be handled in the same fashion. Thus, the more general term "surface analysis" may be more accurate than "terrain analysis" to describe this method.

Software for digital-terrain analysis must be coupled with a database of elevation values.* This is usually a DEM (see Figure 5.19) or its equivalent.** The software makes all terrain calculations based on values in the DEM or TIN sample. Although many terrain-analysis applications are possible, all begin with determining the elevation at one or more locations.

Elevation Determination

Some software, such as *ArcView Spatial Analyst* and *ArcView 3-D Analyst*, lets you determine the elevation at a location by pointing and clicking the mouse. These programs have to be quite sophisticated because they must interpolate between known data points to answer your query (see *Spatial Prediction* in Chapter 2). If you find yourself frequently needing to determine elevations, it's easy to justify the extra cost of this software.

Surface Profiles

Most terrain-analysis software will let you create a terrain profile. The least-sophisticated packages may restrict the profile to rows or columns in the DEM. But the better-featured software, such as *ArcView Spatial Analyst*, will let you choose any two locations as the endpoints of a profile (**Figure 19.6**). The software may also allow you to define a complex profile, as along a road or river.

Examples of terrain-analysis software include Surfer *(Golden Software, Inc., 809 14th Street, Golden, CO 80401-1866, 303-279-1021, www.golden.com/golden/) and* ArcView Spatial Analyst *and* ArcView 3D Analyst *(Environmental Systems Research Institute, Inc., 380 New York Street, Redlands, CA 92373-8100, 909-793-2853, www.esri.com).*

**A triangulated irregular network (TIN) is used by some terrain-analysis software. Whereas a DEM approximates the terrain surface with a square grid of the same values, a TIN captures the surface with a network of triangular facets of varying size and shape, depending on the roughness of the surface. Each facet has a constant slope. A TIN is considered a more efficient way of storing terrain data than a DEM, but it is more difficult to create and its use requires more sophisticated software.*

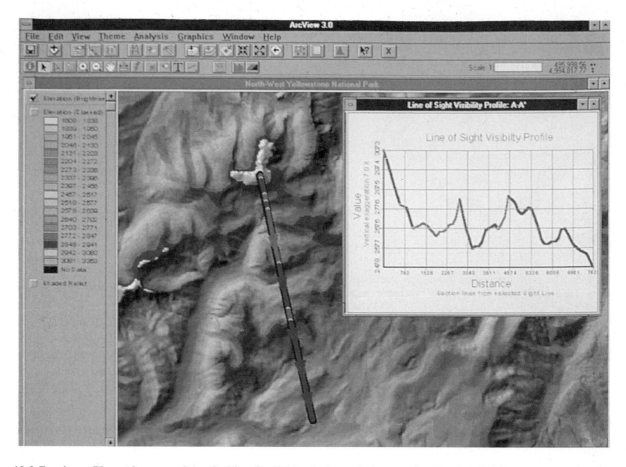

19.6 Terrain profiling software such as *ArcView Spatial Analyst* can do in seconds what it takes hours to do manually. Repetitive, point-and-click terrain profiling is also an excellent way to gain a feel for the landscape surface.

A digital-terrain profile is handy for making related calculations, such as the amount of cut and fill needed in a road construction project. You can also compute the intervisibility between different locations, which is useful in selecting sites with special views (potential building sites) or hiding sites having a noxious character (such as quarries or clearcuts).

Slope and Gradient

You can use terrain-analysis software to determine the steepness and direction of ground slope at any given location. Repeat the calculations, and you can trace the gradient (least-effort path) that water or eroded soil will take. Make enough calculations and you have a runoff map, from which you can define watersheds.

The angle at which the sun strikes the landscape has an important influence on vegetation. It also is critical in orienting solar collectors for heating purposes. Each benefits from slope and gradient analysis.

Automated slope analysis has other applications as well. Construction in mountainous areas is commonly restricted according to ground slope. Thus, it is desirable to produce slope-zone maps quickly and accurately. Similarly, slope data are critical inputs to erosion and stormwater runoff models used in managing such activities as agriculture, logging, and urban development.*

Spatial Optimization

We often want to do something in the environment in the best way possible. Doing so requires

---

See, for example, the watershed modeling package Geo-STORM (Innovative Systems Developers, Inc., 5950 Symphony Woods Road, Columbia, MD 21044, 800-803-5554).

an optimization strategy with respect to certain spatial factors. Since such a procedure can involve a great deal of computation, it is easiest done with the help of computer software and spatial databases. Here, as examples, we consider procedures for selecting optimal routes, sites, and territories.

Route Selection

How to best get from one place to another is a common environmental question. We discussed the simple "here to there" case previously under *Route Finding*. Here we explore the more complex situation in which we must choose a route to connect a number of locations involving pickup and delivery of varying amounts of goods.*

This is a typical problem for truckers. Let's take the case of a dairy plant. To be competitive, management must minimize production expenses, including the cost of trucks, driver wages, and truck maintenance. Looking at the supply side, the crucial raw material is fresh milk. It is perishable, bulky, and low in value for its weight. It is produced in different amounts and grades by farmers scattered across the landscape. Road conditions, bridge capacity, and traffic volume also vary from place to place.

So how is a milk truck to be routed to client farmers and back to the plant in order to minimize capital investment in trucks, driver time, and truck maintenance? Routing software tackles this task. Spatial inputs include a digital description of the transportation network and the location, volume, and grade of farm production. The computer searches all possible alternatives to come up with the optimal path sequence for the given conditions (available time, trucks, etc.). The route can then be plotted on a map, making it easy for a driver to follow (**Figure 19.7A**). When a farm goes out of business or a new farm becomes a client, the software can quickly recalculate an adjusted optimal route.

Site Selection

Where to best locate something in the environment is also a common concern. The list includes factories, sawmills, smelters, communication towers, airports, warehouses, retail businesses, hospitals, schools, churches, police/fire/ambulance stations, government buildings, residences, and other human constructions. The position we choose often has a crucial impact on the effectiveness, the efficiency, and even the ultimate survival of our establishments.

Some sites depend primarily on local conditions. An ideal airport site might be within 20 miles of the city boundary, have at least four square miles of nearly level land, be within two miles of an expressway, and be at least three miles from a waterfowl area or other site (such as a landfill) that might attract birds. You can think of many other examples where this same logic is appropriate. Problems of this type are best tackled with the aid of GIS software (see later in this chapter).

Other sites depend primarily on access or connections to distant places. This would be the case with a factory. Rarely are suppliers and clients at the same locations, and usually there's more than one of each. Furthermore, supplies and products are seldom moved in a straight line "as the crow flies" but, rather, routed along roads, railroads, and rivers.

To maximize product or service delivery under these conditions, the costs (time, effort, money, and skill) of moving inputs and outputs along transportation routes must be factored into site selection (**Figure 19.7B**). Local access to an expressway, railroad, or airport might be critical. Make a good choice and the establishment thrives. Make a poor choice and the establishment frustrates its clients and eventually fails. When these locational failures continue to operate, it is either at the expense of elevated product costs or through the support of a bail-out subsidy. In either case, the consumer pays for the bad site selection.

Many vendors offer site selection software, databases, and services.* This is a major growth area in business consulting. Your local yellow pages will locate at least several such firms. The payoff can be immense, since a good site can save

_____

A good example of routing software is ArcView Network Analyst *(Environmental Systems Research Institute, Inc., 380 New York Street, Redlands, CA 92373-8100, 909-793-2853, www.esri.com).)*

_____

Compass (Claritas, Inc., 1525 Wilson Blvd., Arlington, VA, 800-284-4868), On Target Mapping-Technology that Delivers *(On Target Mapping, 1051 Brinton Road, Pittsburgh, PA 15221, 800-700-6277, www.otmapping.com),* ArcView Spatial Analyst *(Environmental Systems Research Institute, Inc., 380 New York Street, Redlands, CA 92373-8100, 909-793-2853, www.esri.com).)*

A

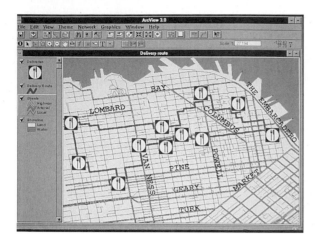

B

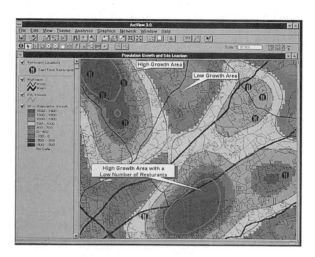

19.7 Routing software such as *ArcView Network Analyst* greatly eases the task of moving vehicles efficiently between a number of locations (A). Selecting a good site for a new restaurant is illustrated here (B) using *ArcView Spatial Analyst*.

much of the operating expense that would result from a poor location.

Redistricting

Our final example of spatial optimization is the need for creating territories or districts for management purposes. Businesses, for instance, try to establish marketing and sales territories so as to minimize costs and maximize profits. Schools need to determine districts from which to draw their student populations. To help bring peace to warring gangs or nations, someone must negotiate boundaries perceived to be fair to former combatants.

Another reason we create territories is for political redistricting purposes. Democratic societies are founded on the premise of equal representation. Since there are fewer politicians than voters, however, political districts must be created so that there is one representative per "x" number of voters.

One interesting result of population change through time is that inequities develop among voting districts. In the United States, an attempt is made after every 10-year census to create new, more equitable districts. This process, called **reapportionment,** is largely guided by informal, common-sense rules designed to ensure fairness. These rules state, for example, that districts should be contiguous, spatially compact, and equal in population. There is also a sense that "communities" shouldn't be split into separate districts. According to the Voting Rights Act, as amended in 1982, every effort should be made to create districts that give ethnic minorities a chance to elect their own representatives.

At the heart of reapportionment is a **redistricting map.** For decades, such maps have been created manually, using pencil and paper and requiring an encyclopedic knowledge of census data. Partisan manipulation of district boundaries to ensure re-election of incumbent

19.8 The technical aspect of redistricting is simplified by software that automatically recomputes district statistics after each boundary change.

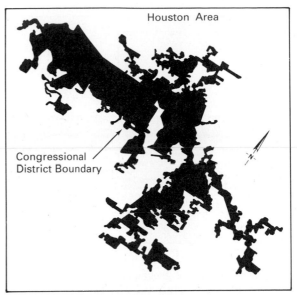

19.9 This bewildering shape is Congressional District 29, centered on Houston in Harris County, Texas. This modern-day example of gerrymandering is the product of electronic redistricting methods.

politicians, called **gerrymandering**, has been common practice.

Things changed with the 1990 census. Anyone with a powerful personal computer or workstation loaded with a **redistricting software program,*** TIGER files representing census unit boundaries, and census data detailing block-by-block demographics can now design a redistricting plan. As blocks are added or subtracted from a district on a display monitor, population totals and racial percentages are instantly recomputed **(Figure 19.8)**. Compactness, contiguity, and completeness reports can be generated automatically. While redistricting after previous censuses often left imbalances of tens of thousands of people between districts, current plans commonly show deviations of less than 10 people.

But electronic redistricting doesn't seem to have changed human nature. The new districts may meet population balance and racial restric-

tions with greater accuracy than would be possible if created by hand. But the process may still involve intricate manipulation of district boundaries to serve partisan political ends. **Figure 19.9,** for example, is a blatant illustration of modern-day multicultural gerrymandering.

GEOGRAPHICAL INFORMATION SYSTEMS (GIS)

Stand-alone software for map analysis has a negative side. Since each vendor introduces its own special jargon and procedures, learning to use a new package can be a major chore. Data format requirements also differ among software packages. These different standards cause data compatibility conflicts when you try to analyze the same information with more than one software package.

Frustration with the problems of stand-alone software has led to development of integrated map-analysis packages, called **geographical**

**For information on redistricting software, contact Election Data Services, 1225 I Street, Washington, DC 20005, 202-789-2004.*

408

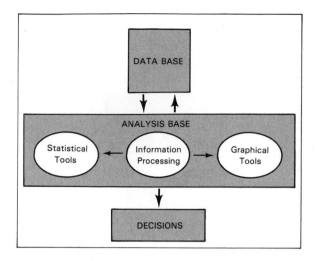

19.10 In an automated geographical information system (GIS), a database is integrated with powerful statistical and graphical tools of analysis to provide maps and other information needed in making environmental decisions.

information systems (GIS).* A GIS aims to facilitate environmental data-handling by melding the processes of data collection, storage, manipulation (both numerical and graphical), and representation into a single integrated system (**Figure 19.10**). Ideally, the map user would face no data-handling barriers and have the option of manipulating and representing data in all known ways. In practice, GIS software is still limited in functionality and becomes rapidly more demanding and difficult to use as its functionality grows.

Most of the analytical techniques we've discussed in this and previous chapters are now included in geographical information systems. In the remainder of this chapter, we'll consider

....
Perhaps the most ambitious, unique, and widely used system for GIS development is ARC/INFO. This system is marketed by the Environmental Systems Research Institute (ESRI), 380 New York Street, Redlands, California 92392, 909-793-2853, www.esri.com. More display-oriented software includes: Atlas GIS and ArcView (also by ESRI), Compass (Claritas, Inc., 800-284-4868), On Target Mapping-Technology that Delivers (On Target Mapping, 1051 Brinton Road, Pittsburgh, PA 15221, 800-700-6277, www.otmapping.com.), IDRISI (The IDRISSI Project, The Clark Labs for Cartographic Technology and Geographic Analysis, Clark University, 950 Main St., Worcester, MA 01610-1477, 508-793-7526, www.idrisi.clarku.edu).

some additional map-analysis applications of GIS technology.

Data Conversion

A great deal of data processing may be required to make data inputs to geographical information systems compatible. When maps of different scales and projections are scanned or digitized, the resulting data are recorded in arbitrary machine coordinates. These locational data have to be converted to a common reference system before they can be integrated (**Figure 19.11**). Terrestrial coordinates, such as latitude and longitude, are usually chosen for this purpose.

With a fully developed GIS, conversion among all common reference systems is facilitated. Provision is made for thematic data manipulations, such as standardizing values to make them suitable for subsequent statistical analysis. The aim is to remove the data incompatibility problems that so often plague people who work with environmental data.

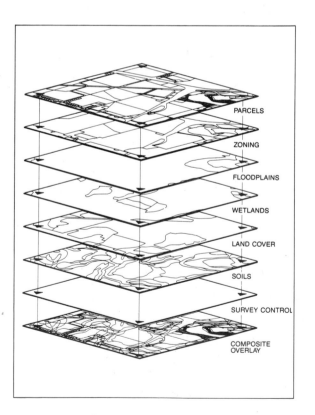

19.11 Environmental data which have been attached to a common terrestrial reference system can be stacked in layers for spatial comparison and analysis.

Search Window

In theory, digital databases are seamless.* That is, they extend continuously in all directions from a point. When you want to see a particular region or analyze data within a certain area, you must open a viewing or searching **window**. You may do so in several ways.

One way to specify a **viewing window** is to give a position and a search radius (**Figure 19.12A**). For example, you might instruct the computer to show the region within 50 miles of a resort town. Alternatively, you might specify the borders of a rectangular viewing window by giving its southwest and northeast corners (**Figure 19.12B**). In the same fashion, you might create a less regular viewing window by specifying key border points (**Figure 19.12C**).

Search windows are defined the same way as viewing windows. But, in this case, the program goes beyond displaying a map to performing some numerical operation on the data within the specified region. Someone looking for a new business location might want to know, for example, how many people live within a certain distance of a street intersection.

Buffer

Environmental decision makers are often interested in the zone, called an **offset** or **buffer**, surrounding features. To protect water quality, for example, environmental specialists might create a buffer along lakes and streams within which logging is prohibited. Likewise, rural zoning law may mandate that agricultural pesticides can't be used within 200 yards of a drinking-water well. Zoning laws may specify that buildings and other constructions (such as fences) must be offset at least 25 feet from the center of the street or highway. In each example, GIS technology lets us see the buffer (**Figure 19.13**).

GIS technology also lets us inventory features falling within a buffer. Thus, we can determine the number of acres in which logging or

The database may be seamless, but the maps used to build the database were not. It can be frustrating to discover the displayed map is based on parts of three printed maps differing by decades in their original production dates. So map borders do live on as database artifacts.

pesticide-based agriculture can't be practiced. If we want to know how much agricultural land or

PART II
Map Analysis

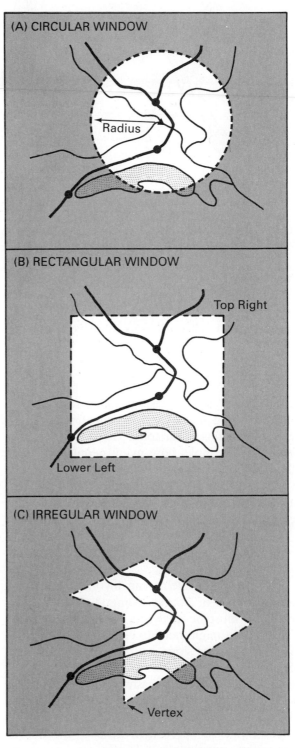

(A) CIRCULAR WINDOW

Radius

(B) RECTANGULAR WINDOW

Top Right

Lower Left

(C) IRREGULAR WINDOW

Vertex

19.12 GIS users must create a window within which to display or analyze information held in the database.

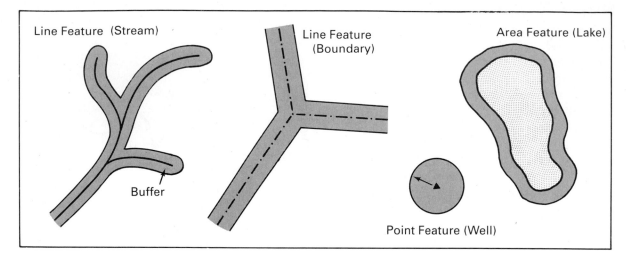

Line Feature (Stream)

Buffer

Line Feature (Boundary)

Area Feature (Lake)

Point Feature (Well)

19.13 Buffering, which involves simple proximity analysis with respect to points, lines, and surfaces, is one of the most useful GIS options.

how many board feet of lumber are to be taken from production by the buffer, we have to super-impose the buffered features on the appropriate resource maps. This brings us to the issue of map overlay.

Overlay

To carry out their decision-making responsibilities, environmental specialists must often consider combinations of variables. They might need to know, for example, how many people live in a floodplain or how many acres of an endangered species' habitat were destroyed by forest fire. To answer such questions, they must determine the extent of overlap between two distributions (**Figure 19.14**). The process is called **map overlay,** although it is carried out numerically in an automated GIS.

Overlay problems can involve more than two features, of course. Sometimes dozens of variables must be analyzed. Highway planners, for example, might need to consider such factors as terrain-surface slope, soil, vegetation, land-parcel configuration, groundwater, and location of rivers and lakes. Progressive overlay of maps showing each variable would reveal those corridors most suitable for highway construction. Further analysis could then be used to choose the optimal corridor (see *Spatial Optimization* earlier in this chapter).

The **U.S. GAP Analysis Program** offers an example of how overlay procedures can be applied. The aim of this program is to determine what types of ecosystems are protected fully, moderately, or not at all. This information is revealed by overlaying maps of vegetation, terrestrial vertebrate distribution, and land ownership/management status. The overlay method displays gaps in biodiversity protection, pinpointing priority areas on which to focus future conservation protection efforts.

Even multiple-variable overlay procedures don't satisfy the needs of all land-information professionals. Despite the many repetitive calculations involved, overlay analysis is nothing more than the simple manipulation of raw data values. What we need is a modeling procedure that lets us weight individual variables to form composite measures. Let's consider these more sophisticated products of GIS analysis next.

Modeling

Higher-level thought processes lead to attempts to model environmental situations and processes. For instance, we might simulate atmospheric dispersion of radioactive gas from a damaged nuclear power plant under different weather conditions. Such information would be useful in planning evacuation routes in case of an accident. This modeling activity involves selecting variables perceived to be relevant and giving each of them a priority rating or weight.

The **weighted-composite indexes** resulting from this activity have a meaning quite different from that of the simple analytical measures we discussed previously. There is even a vast difference in the subjectivity of composite-variable analysis. To clarify the implications of weighted-composite analysis, we'll look first at relatively value-free measures which represent the objective extreme, and then consider the more subjective case of value-laden measures.

Value-Free Measures

Some composite measures derived through GIS analysis are technologically weighted and, therefore, relatively value free. Environmental sensitivity, sustainability, or vulnerability measures are of this type. The computation and mapping of land **trafficability** measures also fall into this class (**Figure 19.15**). Here, vehicle weight, traction, and dimensions are used with environmental measures of slope steepness, ground firmness, soil greasiness when wet, vegetation size and density, and other factors to determine the potential for cross-country vehicular movement. Although trafficability maps are primarily of military interest, they are also of use in disaster relief operations, logging, and agriculture. A farmer planning a spring planting schedule might want to know, for example, how great an implement load each field could support in light of its soil and slope characteristics and recent weather conditions.

There are two main concerns with maps based on weighted-composite measures of the type suggested here. One is that the data used as inputs can vary greatly in quality. Soil, vegetation, slope, and similar distribution maps are themselves highly conceptual and generalized in nature. Composites made with these inputs can be only as good as the poorest component map—and may actually be worse due to the compounding effects of errors.

The second concern is also of conceptual origin. What is the proper weight to be given each variable? In other words, how much should each variable contribute to the composite index? This is a matter of judgment. The farmer, for instance, in deciding whether to risk moving heavy equipment into a field where it might get bogged down

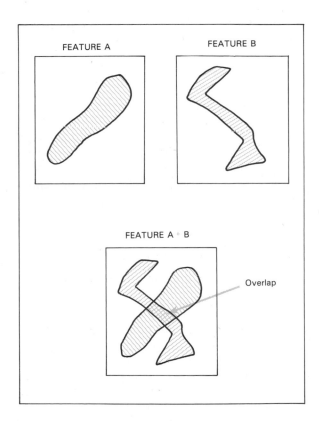

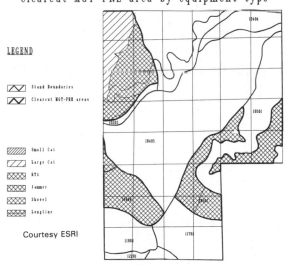

Clearcut MGT-PRE area by equipment type

Courtesy ESRI

19.14 The extent of overlap between two or more distributions can be determined through a procedure called map-overlay analysis.

19.15 A land trafficability map can be generated with a GIS by considering vehicle characteristics together with a host of potentially influential environmental factors.

412

TOPOLOGICAL OVERLAY OF VEGETATION AND SLOPE
TO PRODUCE SUITABILITY MAP

vegetation

slope

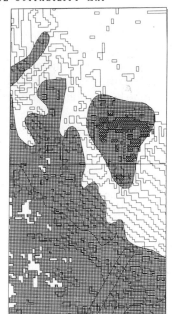

composite   Courtesy ESRI

19.16 A partitioning of land into zones most suitable for different uses involves values concerning which features are to be preserved, modified, and destroyed.

and further delay spring planting, has to determine whether recent weather conditions should override inherent soil characteristics or whether the latter is really the key factor.

The elements to consider in trafficability don't all have an environmental basis, of course. For instance, the farmer may have to factor into the equation the technical capability of a newly purchased tractor or the economic risk of not making enough profit to pay for the tractor if planting is delayed. Comments and jokes among neighbors pose a social risk. Ultimately, the trafficability decision comes down to a matter of how conservative the farmer wants to be.

Value-Laden Measures

As the previous examples suggest, weighting variables in a relatively value-free context may involve judgments concerning a variety of physical, economic, social, and technological factors. These judgments can be refined as knowledge of the factors improves. Thus, once the farmer learns the

capabilities of the new tractor, determining trafficability of each field under different weather conditions will be enhanced.

Many weighted composites, however, involve human values as well. For instance, land-information specialists may use a GIS to partition a region into zones most suitable for urban, recreational, industrial, agricultural, and waste-disposal uses. When the results of such an analysis are displayed, we have a **land-suitability map (Figure 19.16).***

To create such a map involves weighting all sorts of physical and human variables. No matter how hard the analyst tries to be objective, the final composite measure will reflect values placed on such environmental factors as clean air, pure water, undisturbed soil, and healthy natural vegetation. Likewise, it will reflect values placed on such human factors as health, individual rights, taxation, and profit making. The land-suitability map represents a balance between the values placed on natural and human factors. As such, it is as much the product of current environmental perception as of environmental conditions.

Care is needed when using maps based on value-laden composite measures. If different indexes were created at different times, by people of different cultural backgrounds, or for agencies with different responsibilities, the variable weightings and therefore the index values might well be different. To clarify this point, we need only look at how greatly values can change from one time to another. Just 25 years ago in the United States, for instance, it was legal to dump toxic industrial wastes into lakes and streams; asbestos was being used to insulate school buildings; cars burned leaded gasoline; and nuclear power plants were thought to be the answer to high energy costs.

Since GIS's powerful analysis capabilities facilitate suitability index mappings, we can expect to see such maps increasingly used to benefit land management and planning. But there is also the danger that the scientific appearance and computer mystique of these index maps may be misleading. We mustn't forget that, although these maps look like others of the composite-vari-

Other composite-variable models include those that address issues of sustainability, susceptibility, desirability, and accessibility.

**JOHN DEERE GREENSTAR™ COMBINE
YIELD-MAPPING SYSTEM**

19.17 With precision farming, you farm soils rather than fields. GPS technology monitors your crop yields, letting you know how much fertilizer, seed, and pesticides to apply. The aim is to minimize waste and environmental contamination while maximizing yields and, therefore, profits.

able type, they differ in their fundamental conception and are far more value-laden. It is disconcerting to think that the site so carefully chosen for a toxic waste dump based on today's values may be considered a hazard by the Environmental Protection Agency (EPA) when judged by the values of tomorrow. The landscape is already littered with such mistakes, and, unfortunately, we are likely to see still more.

GPS-DRIVEN APPLICATIONS

We're moving map analysis from the laboratory into the field with the help of GPS technology (see Chapter 15: *GPS and Maps*). We do so by using a GPS receiver to determine the coordinates of our current position, and then using these coordinates to display our position, route, and destination. We can also use GPS technology to attach locational coordinates to data being gath-

ered as we traverse the landscape, thereby producing a geocoded database directly in the field. We may later use this geocoded database to guide environmental activities. Let's look at two GPS-driven applications.

Navigation

We introduced the idea of linking GPS to maps for navigation purposes in Chapter 9. Land, water, and air navigators have all discovered the power of this GPS-driven application of digital-mapping technology. In each case the procedure is the same.

First, you use a GPS receiver to determine your coordinate position. A computer then uses these coordinates to search a digital cartographic database held on a CD-ROM. Since the corners of each map were geocoded when the database was created, the software can locate the map within whose borders you're located. This map is then displayed with your position marked.

If you preprogrammed a desired route into your computer or GPS unit, you can display this path. The screen will not only show your progress (where you've been) but will also indicate the path you plan to take to your destination. By using this "progress" report, you can make route corrections as you go.

Likewise, if you enter a destination, the software can compute and display alternate routes based on your instructions. Common options include the shortest, fastest, or most scenic path. The GPS receiver can then update your position as you move toward your destination.

Precision Farming

A more complex linking of GPS positioning and map analysis is illustrated by site-specific or precision farming (**Figure 19.17**). In this promising application of GPS technology, you attach a GPS unit, computer, and crop-yield monitor to your harvesting equipment. As you harvest your crop, the system geocodes the yield data every meter or so, producing a precise yield map of the field.

The next step is to produce an equally detailed soils map of the field and to map other significant factors, such as past management practices, ground slope, and groundwater table. The yield map is then analyzed in relation to these other maps. This analysis is best accomplished with the aid of GIS software.

From this analysis will emerge a crop management plan. During the next cropping season, you use this plan to guide soil preparation, planting, and chemical applications (lime, fertilizer, herbicide, pesticide, fungicide, etc.). You guide these activities with equipment that has a computer and GPS capability. Your GPS unit keeps track of where you are in the field and what optimum mix of treatments is called for at that location. Since treatments may vary from one location to the next, your equipment must be capable of variable rate applications. It may even be effective to use different seed hybrids in different parts of a field.

What you've done is switch from farming fields to farming individual soils in a field. The economic benefit is that precision farming minimizes expenses while maximizing profits. The environmental benefit is that applications of chemicals that go beyond crop needs are minimized and, therefore, aren't left in the landscape to contaminate air, soil, water, and living things.

CONCLUSION

Map-analysis software is growing in scope and depth almost daily. The computer software, databases, and hardware are expensive and take skill to use effectively. Yet once you've performed map analysis with automated methods, it's hard to imagine ever again doing map analysis manually. Electronic methods let you perform activities, such as cartographic modeling, that aren't practical to accomplish any other way.

Unfortunately, automated methods can't compensate for poor data. Much of the information used by environmental decision makers isn't of high quality. Problems related to data quality are bad enough when they are known. But when they go unrecognized they can lead to mistakes and confusion. Thus, in the next chapter, we'll take up the issue of map accuracy.

SELECTED READINGS

Berry, J.K., *Spatial Reasoning for Effective GIS* (Fort Collins, CO: GIS World, 1995).

Chou, T.H., *Exploring Spatial Analysis in Geographic Information Systems* (Santa Fe: On Word Press, 1997).

Christman, N., *Exploring Geographic Information Systems* (New York: John Wiley & Sons, 1997).

Clarke, K.C., *Analytical and Computer Cartography* (Englewood Cliffs, NJ: Prentice-Hall, 1990).

Cromley, R.G., *Digital Cartography* (Englewood Cliffs, NJ: Prentice-Hall, 1992).

ESRI, *Understanding GIS: The ARC/INFO Method* (Redlands, CA: Environmental Systems Research Institute, 1990).

Heit, M., and Shortreid, A., eds., *GIS Applications in Natural Resources* (Fort Collins, CO: GIS World Inc., 1991).

Hoffman, E.K., and Teeple, J., *Computer Graphics Applications* (Belmont, CA: Wadsworth Publishing, 1990).

Huxhold, W.E., *An Introduction to Urban Geographical Information Systems* (New York: Oxford University Press, 1991).

Johnson, A.I., et al., eds. *Geographic Information Systems and Mapping: Practices and Standards* (Philadelphia: American Society for Testing & Materials, 1992).

Laserna, R., and Landis, J., *Desktop Mapping for Planning and Strategic Decision Making* (San Jose, CA: Strategic Mapping, 1990).

Maguire, D.J., Goodchild, M.F., and Rhind, D.W., *Geographical Information Systems: Principles and Applications* (New York: John Wiley & Sons, 1991).

Moellering, H., ed., "Analytical Cartography," Special Content Issue, *Cartography and Geographical Information Systems*, Vol. 18, No. 1 (January 1990).

Morrill, R.L., *Political Redistricting and Geographic Theory* (Washington, DC: Association of American Geographers, 1981).

Orr, D.M., *Congressional Redistricting: The North Carolina Experience* (Chapel Hill: Department of Geography, University of North Carolina, 1970).

Taylor, D.R.F., ed., *Geographic Information Systems: The Microcomputer and Modern Cartography* (New York: Pergamon Press, 1991).

Tomlin, C.D., *Geographic Information Systems and Cartographic Modelling* (Englewood Cliffs, NJ: Prentice-Hall, 1990).

415

PART II
*Map
Analysis*

CHAPTER 20
MAP ACCURACY

INTRODUCTION

TRUTH OR EFFECTS?

Accuracy or Precision?
Types of Accuracy
 Positional Errors
 Conceptual Effects
 Generalization Effects
 Factual Errors
 Timeliness

COMMUNICATING MAP ACCURACY

Active Mapping Strategies
 Adjust Map Scale
 Adjust Generalization
User-Oriented Strategies
 Symbols and Notations
 Legend Disclaimer
 Reliability Diagram

DIGITAL RECORDS

Geographic Database
Cartographic Database
Data Lineage

MAP COMPOSITING

Map Overlay
Cartographic Modeling

LIABILITY ISSUES

Map Maker Responsibility
Map User Responsibility

CONCLUSION

SELECTED READINGS

For every problem there is a solution: simple, neat, and wrong.
—H.L. Mencken

Thinking they were in Canada, and not the area which is now Maine,
the McKinnon Brothers settled at the head of the Mattagash River.
Oral history says they stopped where they did because one of the women had to pee.
In truth, it may have been inaccurate maps.
—Cathie Pelletier, *The Funeral Makers*

20

CHAPTER TWENTY

MAP ACCURACY

Mapping, like architecture, is an example of functional design. Unlike free-form art, which takes geometric liberties to create special effects, a map is expected to be true to the location and structure of our surroundings. Indeed, our willingness to let maps "stand in" for the environment is due to this adherence to reality. We can thus take advantage of the convenience maps offer in a wide variety of situations.

All representation involves distortion, of course. You either deal directly with reality, or you deal indirectly with a fake version of reality. Fakes by nature are unreal and, therefore, distorted. Since maps are a form of representation, they're no exception. What, then, do we mean by adherence to reality in mapping?

The term **map accuracy** is widely applied when addressing maps' true-to-reality nature. Map accuracy turns out to be a rather complex topic, especially since maps are increasingly made from digital data taken from existing maps. In this chapter, we'll consider what we mean by map accuracy, how accuracy information is conveyed to the map user, and how electronic mapping adds to our accuracy concerns.

TRUTH OR EFFECTS?

Beware of the trap of thinking the map can be the territory. Those building spatial databases (see later in this chapter) by scanning or digitizing maps, and those using computer analysis to extract details from these cartographic databases, need to stop and reflect on the nature of mapping. If you want truth, you should embrace reality directly. If you want the convenience of maps representing reality, then you should consider what it means to map.

Cartographic abstraction lets us escape the complexity of the environment and look at a simplified, scaled-down version of our surroundings. This abstracted representation may be useful for many purposes, but we don't pretend it is true. In fact, we revel in its abstractness, because that is what frees us from the tyranny of our sensory reality.

418

Map abstraction helps us to be objective and analytical. It lets us see the effects of playing out countless "what if …?" scenarios. What would the environment look like if we did this? If we did that? It is these effects that make mapping such a powerful thought and communication tool.

Our big concern must be to compensate for the distorting or untruthful aspects of abstraction. This is true of all forms of representation. It's this distortion in mapping that is the focus of this chapter on map accuracy.

Accuracy or Precision?

First, we must address possible confusion of the terms "accuracy" and "precision." **Accuracy** means fidelity to the truth. How well, for example, do measured map coordinates conform to the true coordinates of a position? It sounds simple. But which datum do we use to establish true coordinates? Obviously, truth in this case is defined relative to some agree-upon standard.

Precision is more complicated. It's often used synonymously with accuracy, but there is an important distinction between the two. Precision has three meanings:

- the number of digits expressed in a measurement
- the repeatability of measurements or the agreement among measurements
- the rigor and sophistication of the measuring process.

All three meanings focus on the method of measurement and the reporting of measured values.

Be careful when using the terms "accuracy" and "precision," even though many people use them interchangeably. The topic of map accuracy is confusing enough without the added problem of sloppy language usage. Analyzing what is meant when you see or hear the term "accuracy" or "precision" will help you deal with the subject more effectively.

Types of Accuracy

Many subjects that seem simple turn out, upon closer inspection, to be surprisingly complex. This is the case with map accuracy. The more you think about the topic, the more facets you discover. Rather than treat map accuracy as a single issue, we'll approach the topic from the perspec-

tive of types of accuracy. We'll discuss five aspects of map accuracy: positional errors, conceptual effects, generalization effects, factual errors, and timeliness. It is these five components, when combined on a given map, that we refer to as **map accuracy**.

Positional Errors

We depend on maps, most of all, to give us the location of things. In many cases, what we mean by location is the horizontal position of an object. We might speak, for example, about the latitude and longitude of a feature. But, since we live in a world of three physical dimensions, location also has a vertical component. Thus, we speak of the elevation of the land surface, or the altitude of an aircraft or spacecraft. Any consideration of map accuracy should include reference to one or both of these aspects of position.

Many maps produced in the United States include the marginal notation, **"This map complies with National Map Accuracy Standards."** To learn what this comforting statement really means, read the explanation in **Box 20.1**. Here you'll find that, as far as National Map Accuracy Standards (NMAS) are concerned, map accuracy is a statistical notion; it is defined in both horizontal and vertical terms; it decreases progressively as map scale decreases; and horizontal accuracy pertains only to "well-defined points." Since only a few points on a sample of map sheets selected from each mapping project are actually tested to see if the project meets National Map Accuracy Standards, even the accuracy of most well-defined points is unknown. And, since map accuracy is statistically defined, the standards say nothing about the accuracy you can expect to find with respect to a specific point.

If you feel National Map Accuracy Standards are a bit vague about how close a map feature is to its ground location, you're on even shakier ground with maps that don't meet National Map Accuracy Standards. There is simply no way to ascertain the accuracy of data taken from non-standardized maps. We can expect, however, that the larger the map scale, the more reliable the plotted positions of features will be.

Conceptual Effects

The second aspect of map accuracy is called **conceptual accuracy**, because it concerns features

BOX 20.1 UNITED STATES NATIONAL MAP ACCURACY STANDARDS

With a view to the utmost economy and expedition in producing maps which fulfill not only the broad needs for standard or principal maps, but also the reasonable particular needs of individual agencies, standards of accuracy for published maps are defined as follows:

1. **Horizontal accuracy.** For maps on publication scales larger than 1:20,000, not more than 10 percent of the points tested shall be in error by more than 1/30 inch, measured on the publication scale; for maps on publication scales of 1:20,000 or smaller, 1/50 inch. These limits of accuracy shall apply in all cases to positions of well-defined points only. Well-defined points are those that are easily visible or recoverable on the ground, such as the following: monuments or markers, such as bench marks, property boundary monuments; intersections of roads, railroads, etc.; corners of large buildings or structures (or center points of small buildings); etc. In general, what is well defined will also be determined by what is plottable on the scale of the map within 1/100 inch. Thus, while the intersection of two roads or property lines meeting at right angles would come within a sensible interpretation, identification of the intersection of such lines meeting at an acute angle would obviously not be practicable within 1/100 inch. Similarly, features not identifiable upon the ground within close limits are not to be considered as test points within the limits quoted, even though their positions may be scaled closely upon the map. In this class would come timber lines, soil boundaries, etc.

2. **Vertical accuracy**, as applied to contour maps on all publication scales, shall be such that not more than 10 percent of the elevations tested shall be in error more than one-half the contour interval. In checking elevations taken from the map, the apparent vertical error may be decreased by assuming a horizontal displacement within the permissible horizontal error for a map of that scale.

3. **The accuracy of any map may be tested** by comparing the positions of points whose locations or elevations are shown upon it with corresponding positions as determined by surveys of a higher accuracy. Tests shall be made by the producing agency, which shall also determine which of its maps are to be tested, and the extent of such testing.

4. **Published maps meeting these accuracy requirements** shall note this fact on their legends, as follows: "This map complies with National Map Accuracy Standards."

5. **Published maps whose errors exceed those aforestated** shall omit from their legends all mention of standard accuracy.

6. **When a published map is a considerable enlargement** of a map drawing (manuscript) or of a published map, that fact shall be stated in the legend. For example, "This map is an enlargement of a 1:20,000-scale map drawing," or "This map is an enlargement of a 1:24,000-scale published map."

7. **To facilitate ready interchange and use of basic information for map construction** among all federal map making agencies, manuscript maps and published maps, wherever economically feasible and consistent with the uses to which the map is to be put, shall conform to latitude and longitude boundaries, being 15 minutes of latitude and longitude, or 7.5 minutes, or 3-3/4 minutes in size.

U.S. BUREAU OF THE BUDGET

Issued June 10, 1941
Revised April 26, 1943
Revised June 17, 1947

Source: Thompson, *Maps for America*, p. 104

BOX 20.2 VEGETATION ON STANDARD TOPOGRAPHIC MAPS

Many of the intricate vegetation patterns existing in nature cannot be depicted exactly by line drawings. It is therefore necessary in some places to omit less important scattered growth and to generalize complex outlines.

Types

The term "woodland" is generally used loosely to designate all vegetation represented on topographic maps. For mapping purposes, vegetation is divided into six types, symbolized as shown, and defined as follows:

▲ **Woodland (woods-brushwood).** An area of normally dry land containing tree cover or brush that is potential tree cover. The growth must be at least 6 feet (2 m.) tall and dense enough to afford cover for troops.

▲ **Scrub.** An area covered with low-growing or stunted perennial vegetation, such as cactus, mesquite, or sagebrush, common to arid regions and usually not mixed with trees.

▲ **Orchard.** A planting of evenly spaced trees or tall bushes that bear fruit or nuts. Plantings of citrus and nut trees, commonly called groves, are included in this type.

▲ **Vineyard.** A planting of grapevines, usually supported and arranged in evenly-spaced rows. Other kinds of cultivated climbing plants, such as berry vines and hops, are typed as vineyards for mapping purposes.

▲ **Mangrove.** A dense, almost impenetrable growth of tropical maritime trees with aerial roots. Mangrove thrives where the movement of tidewater is minimal—in shallow bays and deltas, and along riverbanks.

▲ **Wooded marsh.** An area of normally wet land with tree cover or brush that is potential tree cover.

Density

Woods, brushwood, and scrub are mapped if the growth is thick enough to provide cover for troops or to impede foot travel. This condition is considered to exist if density of the vegetative cover is 20 percent or more. Growth that meets the minimum density requirement is estimated as follows: If the average open-space distance between the crowns is equal to the average crown diameter, the density of the vegetative cover is 20 percent.

This criterion is not a hard-and-fast rule, however, because 20 percent crown density cannot be determined accurately if there are irregularly scattered trees and gradual transitions from the wooded to the cleared areas. Therefore, where such growth occurs, the minimum density requirement varies between 20 and 35 percent, and the woodland boundary is drawn where there is a noticeable change in density. A crown density of 35 percent exists if the average open space between the crowns is equal to one-half the average crown diameter.

Orchards and vineyards are shown regardless of crown density. Mangrove, by definition, is dense, almost impenetrable growth; crown density is not a factor in mapping mangrove boundaries.

(continued...)

Box 20.2 *continued*

Areas

On 7.5- and 15-minute maps, woodland areas covering 1 acre (0.4 ha.) or more are shown regardless of shape. This area requirement applies both to individual tracts of vegetation and to areas of one type within or adjoining another type. Narrow strips of vegetation and isolated tracts covering areas smaller than the specified minimum are shown only if they are considered to be landmarks. Accordingly, shelterbelts and small patches of trees in arid or semiarid regions are shown, whereas single rows of trees or bushes along fences, roads, or perennial streams are not mapped.

Clearings

The minimum area specified for woodland cover on 7.5- and 15-minute maps—1 acre (0.4 ha.)—also applies to clearings within woodland. Isolated clearings smaller than the specified minimum are shown if they are considered to be landmarks.

Clearings along mapped linear features, such as power transmission lines, telephone lines, pipelines, roads, and railroads, are shown if the break in woodland cover is 100 feet (30 m.) or more wide. The minimum symbol width for a clearing in which a linear feature is shown is 100 feet at map scale. Clearings wider than 100 feet are mapped to scale.

Landmark linear clearings 40 feet (12 m.) or more wide, in which no feature is mapped, are shown to scale. Firebreaks are shown and labeled if they are 20 feet (6 m.) or more wide and do not adjoin or coincide with other cultural features. The minimum symbol width for a firebreak clearing is 40 feet at map scale; firebreaks wider than 40 feet are shown to scale.

Source: Thompson, *Maps for America*, pp. 70-71

---

that are mental **abstractions** rather than concrete objects with clearly defined edges. Soil, wetland, and forest boundaries meet this criterion. They all have boundaries that are transitional and difficult to find in the field (see *Type of Feature* in Chapter 1).

To appreciate what we mean by conceptual accuracy, read the material concerning vegetation mapping on standard topographic maps provided in **Boxes 20.2 and 20.3**. Notice that the definitions of vegetation type, density, vegetated areas, and clearings are all human creations. The intricacy of the pattern to be mapped, the map scale, and the importance assigned to features all enter the cartographic judgment of what and how the mapping should be carried out.

Obviously, the accuracy of conceptual boundaries such as those surrounding forested areas on topographic maps means something quite different from the accuracy of discrete features, such as roads, on the same map. National Map Accuracy Standards for positional accuracy don't apply to these conceptually defined features.

Generalization Effects

Even environmental features that are well-defined, such as roads, rivers, or coastlines don't get mapped in all possible detail. These linear features and edges of areal features are smoothed in their map representation. We call this loss of detail **line generalization**. The degree of generalization is proportionate to a feature's spatial detail, and inversely proportionate to map scale **(Figure 20.1)**. Thus, on a state highway map, a high-speed expressway is likely to be less generalized than a low-speed county road.

Generalization causes a displacement of features as smoothing cuts off natural irregularities. But is this shift of a linear feature's position

422

BOX 20.3 WOODLAND BOUNDARY ACCURACY ON STANDARD TOPOGRAPHIC MAPS

Clearly defined woodland boundaries are plotted with standard accuracy, the same as any other well-defined planimetric feature. If there are gradual changes from wooded to cleared areas, the outlines are plotted to indicate the limits of growth meeting the minimum density requirement. If the growth occurs in intricate patterns, the outlines show the general shapes of the wooded areas. Outlines representing these ill-defined or irregular limits of vegetative cover are considered to be approximate because they do not necessarily represent lines that can be accurately identified on the ground. The outline of a tract of tall, dense timber represents the centerline of the bounding row of trees rather than the outside limits of the branches or the shadow line.

In large tracts of dense evergreen timber, sharp dividing lines between different tree heights may be shown with the fence- and field-line symbol. Published maps containing fence-line symbols that represent fences and other landmark lines in wooded areas bear the following statement in the tailored legend: "Fine red dashed lines indicate selected fence, field, or landmark lines where generally visible on aerial photographs. This information is unchecked."

Woodland is not shown in urban-tint areas, but it is shown where appropriate in areas surrounded by urban tint if such areas are equivalent to or larger than the average city block.

Mangrove is shown on the published map with the standard mangrove pattern and the green woodland tint. Breaks in the mangrove cover usually indicate water channels that provide routes for penetrating the dense growth.

Source: Thompson, *Maps for America*, pp. 71-72

an example of positional error? Is a map of the world on a postage stamp best critiqued in terms of its generalization errors? We think not.

To say abstraction is error misses the point. We might better think in terms of generalization effects, not generalization errors. In this way we focus our attention on the power of cartographic abstraction rather than dwell on inevitable distortions. And, as you've probably guessed by now, U.S. National Map Accuracy Standards make no attempt to address generalization effects.

Factual Errors

Sometimes features are left off a map by mistake. A lake or town may have been overlooked by the cartographer.* In other cases, features found on the map don't exist in the environment. Sometimes a name or symbol is misplaced on the

---

*Features left off the map on purpose by the cartographer for design reasons aren't included in this "overlooked" feature category.

map. At other times a feature has disappeared from the environment, but its map symbol persists. Still other errors occur when a feature is misclassified by its map symbol, as when a railroad is shown as a road. These are all examples of **factual errors**. Errors of this type can be minimized by thorough map editing but, given the complexity of mapping, it isn't practical to eliminate them altogether. Since map makers rely on data from diverse sources, mistakes can be made at many levels. Cartographers rely on feedback from map users to keep from repeating mistakes in subsequent map editions.

The previous comments refer to mapped features, such as roads, towns, or rivers. Image processing, on the other hand, yields a pixel-by-pixel classification, not an object-oriented categorization (see *Image Classification* in Chapter 24). Mistakes in classifying pixels represent a special type of factual error, sometimes called **attribute error.** Most pixels falling in a feature such as a lake may be classified correctly, but pixels falling partly on the shoreline may be misclassified. Pixels within a lake that fall on a boat or weedbed may also be misclassified, since they won't exhibit the spectral characteristics of open water.

We must assess factual or attribute errors differently from positional errors. In contrast to positional errors, which vary in size, factual errors either occur, or they don't occur. If factual errors were known, they would be corrected as a matter of professional pride. In the case of misclassification errors on image maps, a report of the average number of attribute errors counted on similar maps is sometimes given. Thus, testing may show that pixel classification is subject to an approximate error rate of, say, 15 percent.

Timeliness

One thing that contributes to factual errors is the fact that environmental features change through time (also see Chapter 8: *Time and Maps*). The map may have been correct when made but since then become outdated. Or the map may have been out-of-date at the time of production. This happens when the map maker isn't aware that features have been added or deleted from the environment since data for mapping were gathered.

Problems of timeliness increase when maps and other sources of information used in mapping aren't properly dated. The map may have been compiled, unknowingly, from information collected at significantly different times. The growing use of digital information records in mapping invites problems of this sort, because it is common for the source date of these records to be lost in the computer process (see Chapter 19: *GIS and Map Analysis Software*).

COMMUNICATING MAP ACCURACY

Understanding types of map accuracy is one thing, but conveying a sense of the accuracy to a map user is quite another. The aim in mapping should be to provide as much information as possible so that map users can make reasonable accuracy assessments. The map maker may do so in either an active or passive way. We'll discuss both of these options.

Active Mapping Strategies

One approach is to design the map so that it adequately reflects available data. When cartogra-

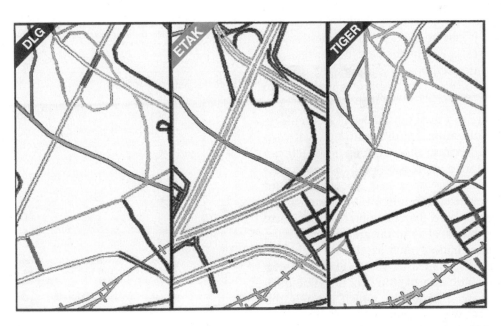

20.1 Cartographic databases from different sources can vary dramatically in their spatial detail. This variation in feature detail may reflect the generalization level of the original map. It may also be due to map scanning or digitizing.

424

phers take this active approach, they do so in two ways. The first strategy is to adjust the map scale to accommodate the data they have available.

Adjust Map Scale

It takes lots of high-quality data to make a detailed, large-scale map. If sufficient data aren't available to justify mapping at a given scale, then a reduction in map scale may solve the problem. The reason is that symbols of a given size cover more ground area as map scale diminishes (see *Exaggeration* in Chapter 3). Furthermore, there is less map space for symbols as the map scale decreases. Ultimately, then, a scale can be found to match the nature of available data.

Unfortunately, map makers are often reluctant to produce maps at scales commensurate with poor data. This is especially true if data are inadequate for only part of the region to be mapped. The result is that many maps are larger in scale and show more detail than they should. Many other maps include at least some regions for which data are inadequate. In this case, the quality of the representation varies from place to place across the map.

Adjust Generalization

The alternative to adjusting map scale is to adjust the generalization level of map symbols so that it matches the nature of available data. The smoothing technique is particularly useful for this purpose, since it can be used to adjust the detail of linear features as well as the edge of area features. But the other methods of cartographic abstraction are also effective (see Chapter 3: *Map Abstraction Process*).

Be sure to watch for the use of different levels of generalization for different layers of map information, because this mapping approach can leave a deceptive impression of map accuracy. As a rule, all variables on a map should be about equally generalized. Frequently, however, cartographers depict base information (rivers, political boundaries, roads, etc.) in far greater detail than thematic information, such as climate, soils, and vegetation. As a map user, you're likely to think that the thematic information is of the same quality as the base information, which is rarely the case. The best way to counteract this problem is to ignore base feature details as best you can, and be careful not to draw conclusions about theme

information that exceeds the accuracy of the mapped data.

User-Oriented Strategies

You can't always count on map makers taking an active role in communicating the nature of available data through map design. They are at least as likely to take a passive role, shifting the burden of assessing map accuracy to the map user. When map makers take this passive approach, they warn map users about the accuracy of mapped data in a "truth-in-advertising" sense. They may do so in three ways—with special symbols and notations, legend statements, and reliability diagrams.

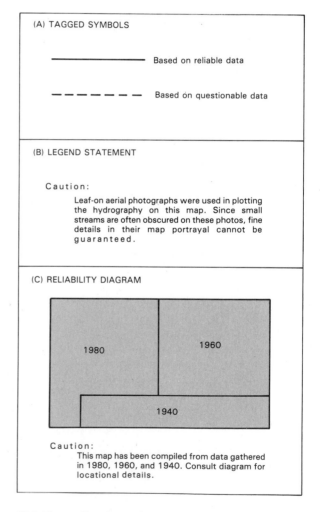

20.2 The quality of map data is often indicated by tagged symbols (A), legend statements (B), or reliability diagrams (C).

Symbols and Notations

The most direct way cartographers warn map users is with special **tagged symbols**, which indicate that there are problems with the data. They may make line symbols broken instead of solid, for example (**20.2A**). On topographic maps, they may use dotted supplemental contour lines and dashed form lines (see Chapter 5: *Landform Portrayal*). Another design strategy is to make the clarity or sharpness of symbols increase with better quality data. Weak data would be portrayed with blurred or fuzzy symbols.

A method almost as direct as using tagged symbols is to add notations to map areas in which accuracy may be a concern. A note, such as "This region was not field checked" serves this purpose. On aeronautical charts, it's common to find notations of this sort, especially to warn that the general magnetic declination information given on the map may be subject to local disturbance.

Legend Disclaimer

Sometimes a statement in the map legend is the only indicator of map accuracy (**Figure 20.2B**). The statement, "This map meets National Map Accuracy Standards," is an example of this approach. Of course, you have to know what such a statement means (see *Positional Errors* earlier in this chapter). Remember, there are no rules saying that you must be warned of an inaccurate map.

A legend disclaimer is commonly found on commercial maps that use government maps as a base. For example, someone may enhance nautical charts with bearing and distance information and then market this value-added product. You're likely to find the statement, "This map is for reference only and should not be used for navigational purposes." The aim, of course, is to avoid lawsuits resulting from accidents attributed to the map. It's a curious kind of message, however, since the map is clearly intended for navigational use.

The most common types of legend statements report the date of map production and source of the data. The date is especially useful if the mapped region is undergoing rapid change. The source of data gives a hint of its reliability, since some data-gathering organizations have better reputations than others for doing professional work. Data from promotional and private-survey groups should be viewed with suspicion.

Reliability Diagram

A third device for communicating map accuracy to the user is a **reliability diagram**. This is a simple outline map showing variation in source data used to produce the map (**Figure 20.2C**). It may appear in the legend or as an inset near the map margin. The date and source of the data used in mapping are usually provided. You're left to draw your own conclusions about the impact these data may have had on the map representation.

The problem with a reliability diagram is that you must first spot that it's there and then pay attention to what it suggests. Although it seems straightforward enough, in practice few map users probably gain much from this passive approach. This raises questions about the sufficiency of the warning, especially in this age of product liability lawsuits.

DIGITAL RECORDS

Throughout this book, we've stressed the growing importance of electronic technology and map use. Computers work with numbers, not written or pictorial documents. Ideally, these numbers would come directly from field data-gathering. In fact, considerable progress has been made in developing electronic sensors that can generate digital records in the field. But for some time there will also be a need to convert existing tabular, textual, and pictorial information into the digital form computers require. The implications of each of these approaches with respect to map accuracy deserve our consideration

Geographic Database

The most direct way to gather environmental data in digital form is to carry electronic sensors into the field. Automated stations for monitoring air quality, for example, could be set up at different locations within an urban area. Likewise, an electronic positioning system could be carried down a highway in a vehicle, providing coordinate information as it moved along. A person could walk around the boundary of an area burned by a forest fire and collect coordinate data for this border using a hand-held positioning device. In each case, data artifacts resulting from the method of information gathering and reporting are minimized.

426

When information is gathered directly in the field in this way, it is called **geographic data**. Collectively, these data form **geographic databases**. In view of rapid developments in electronic sensing technology, we can expect a growing proportion of data for electronic mapping to be entered directly in databases from field sites in the future.

Cartographic Database

In the meantime, a great deal of information is still being gathered in traditional format by non-automated methods and must be converted into computer-compatible form before it can be used in electronic mapping and analysis. Furthermore, vast amounts of historical and basic reference information central to the successful operation of automated mapping exist in the form of written reports, tables, and graphic records (photographs, maps, charts).

Converting existing maps into digital form is one of the major challenges in modern mapping. Even with modern devices, such as digitizers and scanners, the conversion task is overwhelming. Expending vast amounts of time, energy, and money doesn't guarantee that a reliable **cartographic database** will be created.

The distinction between geographic and cartographic databases is significant. Data extracted from a map differ from geographic data to the extent that cartographic abstraction distorts geographic reality (see Chapter 3: *Map Abstraction Process*). In addition, digital data won't be more accurate than the maps that are digitized or scanned. Since existing maps are often inaccurate, this can be a serious problem (**Figure 20.3**).

These problems often show up at the edge of adjacent map sheets. It's common for those building digital databases to "fudge" their way through the situation by performing an **edge-matching** operation. This entails displacing mismatched features on each map sheet until they join at the edge (**Figure 20.4**). From the map user's standpoint, it would be nice if these edge matches were tagged so that they were apparent in subsequent mapping, but this is rarely done.

Although these problems of abstraction, inaccuracies, and edge matching can have a profound impact on the quality of cartographic databases, they aren't the only difficulties. Additional irregularities occur in the process of converting maps to digital form. Technical errors may occur, for example, during digitizing and scanning.

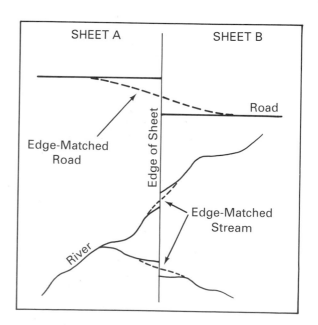

20.3 This illustration shows the difference between the first and second version of the World Data Bank II for a portion of Columbia.

20.4 When features on adjoining map sheets don't line up, it's common in database building to perform a generic edge-matching operation.

Editing, formatting, and structuring problems may arise during database creation.

Data Lineage

A big danger with cartographic databases is that we may forget the **lineage** of the data. By lineage, we mean the origin of the source data and subsequent manipulations that may affect the data's accuracy. Because maps vary so greatly in quality, it's critical to preserve a database's pedigree so that we can trace it to its origins.

Data lineage standards for cartographic databases arc in place in some countries. They have a "truth-in-labeling" character, which is intended to help you judge their "fitness-for-use" in your mapping application. Thus, there is no absolute accuracy standard specified.

What the standards do is outline how database lineage should be documented. These "data about data" are called **metadata**. At present, adherence to metadata standards is voluntary, however. We're left to rely on the professionalism and ethics of the people converting the map to digital form.

MAP COMPOSITING

One advantage of working with electronic maps is that you can manipulate and combine environmental information almost at will. You can thus tailor a map to serve your needs. In the simplest case, you might search for areas with certain characteristics, such as steep hills and forest. A more complex problem would be to determine how susceptible individual farm fields are to erosion. In both cases, a compositing of environmental features is required to obtain the desired information. Therefore, it's important that you consider the accuracy of the resulting map composite.

Map Overlay

When maps are superimposed to show relationships between patterns, the process is called **map overlay**. Imagine, for example, that you want to build a country home but must adhere to environmental regulations. These are the restrictions: Your home must be in a an area zoned for recreation, it can't be on a slope greater than 15 degrees, and it must be within 500 feet of a high-

way. The overlay procedure would indicate acceptable building sites (**Figure 20.5**).

You need to be concerned, of course, with the accuracy of each map used in the overlay process. Some errors in the individual layers may cancel each other out. Usually, however, such errors are additive. Unfortunately, as you saw in the previous section, inaccuracies in database layers are rarely known. Thus, you're wise to treat these overlay maps with caution. They are suitable for making general assessments, but you shouldn't risk much on their site-to-site validity.

Cartographic Modeling

Overlay problems are minor compared to those associated with cartographic modeling (see *Modeling* in Chapter 19). Cartographers use the modeling technique to produce suitability, trafficability, susceptibility, and similar maps. To make such a map, they must make three decisions. First, they select a limited number of environmental variables. Second, they give each variable a weight according to its importance. Third, they link these weighted scores arithmetically to form a composite index value. They then map this index value.

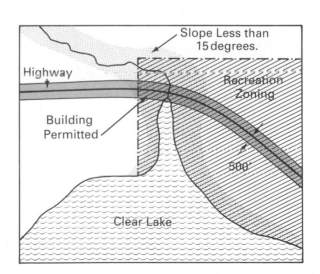

20.5 A map overlay operation is commonly used in electronic mapping to determine areas having a special combination of feature characteristics.

428

All these decisions affect the accuracy of maps produced by cartographic modeling. Thus, the accuracy of maps representing each selected variable, the validity of the weights assigned to each variable, and the soundness of the linking arithmetic all contribute to the quality of the resulting map. The problem is that we can't test the map's accuracy in any of the ways we use with conventional maps. We have invented no device that can measure trafficability or any other modeling index.

At best, we have to be satisfied with some form of **sensitivity** or **stability analysis**. To perform such an analysis, we alter, just slightly, each decision made to produce the map. Then we note how different the new map is from the original. Big differences with slight changes suggest that the map isn't very stable and could be an artifact of the modeling process. You should have little confidence in using a map of this type except for the most general, regional applications.

On the other hand, if slight changes in modeling inputs have little effect on the resulting map, you can have confidence that the representation is probably not an artifact of the method. You can use this type of map for more specific purposes than an unstable representation.

LIABILITY ISSUES

Map accuracy is a concern for both the map maker and map user in a society quick to sue. You compound your problems if you are both map maker and user, as is often the case when working with digital maps. The question is to what degree you place yourself at legal risk when making and using maps. Let's consider map liability issues from the perspective of both maker and user.

Map Maker Responsibility

The interpretation of liability law makes the responsibility of the map maker quite clear. In essence, "every reasonable effort" must be made to ensure map or cartographic database quality. What is reasonable is judged by contemporary professional standards.

Additionally, the map maker must inform or warn map users of potential problems and hazards in using the product. We discussed ways this can be done in the earlier section on *Communicating Map Accuracy*.

Map User Responsibility

The legal responsibility of the map user is less well-defined than that of the map maker. But the same advice holds true, especially if careless map use on your part has the potential to harm someone else. If your business is to market map-use products, then your responsibility to conduct yourself professionally is increased.

Speaking ethically rather than legally, you probably have no business using maps if low skill on your part could harm others or the environment. You especially have an obligation to get beyond "map-as-territory" blinders (see *Truth or Effects?* earlier in this chapter).

CONCLUSION

This discussion of map accuracy isn't meant to scare you away from using maps. As we've noted, maps are abstractions, and abstraction by its nature involves distortion. This is the paradox of cartography. We're using a distorted representation to make accurate decisions about spatial issues.

Inaccuracies are the price we must pay to obtain the convenience of map abstractions. Since accuracy problems can't be eliminated, or we would have no map, we must learn to live with them.

Each time you use a map, you should evaluate its accuracy in light of the task at hand. You'll want to ask, "Can I live with the accuracy of this map in this situation?" Or, "What special care should I take if I use this map for this purpose?" Such questions will be even more important as we move to our next topic—map interpretation.

SELECTED READINGS

Buckner, B., "The Nature of Measurement, Part II: Mistakes and Errors," *Professional Surveyor* (April 1997), pp. 19-22.

Buckner, B., "The Nature of Measurement, Part IV: Precision and Accuracy," *Professional Surveyor* (July-August 1997), pp. 49-52.

Chrisman, N.R., "A Diagnostic Test for Error in Categorical Maps," *Proceedings of AUTO-CARTO 6* (Baltimore, MD: American Congress on Surveying and Mapping, 1991), pp. 330-348.

Chrisman, N.R., "The Accuracy of Map Overlays: A Reassessment," *Landscape and Urban Planning*, 14 (1987), pp. 427-439.

Congalton, R.G., and Green, K., *Assessing the Accuracy of Remotely Sensed Data: Principles and Practices* (Boca Raton, FL: Lewis Publishers, 1997).

Evangelatos, T.V., "Digital Geographic Interchange Standards," in D.R.F. Taylor, *Geographical Information Systems: The Microcomputer in Modern Cartography* (New York: Pergamon Press, 1991), pp 151-166.

Frans, J.M, et al., "Visualization of Data Quality," in A. MacEachren and D.R.F. Taylor, eds., *Visualization in Modern Cartography* (New York: Pergamon Press, 1994), pp. 313-331.

Goodchild, M., and Gopal, S., eds., *Accuracy of Spatial Databases* (London: Taylor & Francis, 1989).

Guptill, S.C., and Morrison, J.L., eds., *Elements of Spatial Data Quality* (London: Elsevier Science Ltd., 1995).

Hopkins, L.D., "Methods of Generating Land Suitability Maps: A Comparative Evaluation," *Journal of American Institute of Planners*, 43, 4 (1977), pp. 386-398.

Lanter, D.P., *Problems of Lineage in GIS*, Technical Paper 90-6 (Santa Barbara, CA: National Center for Geographic Information and Analysis, 1990).

Lodwick, W.A., Monson, W., and Svoboda, L., "Attribute Error and Sensitivity Analysis of Map Operations in Geographical Information Systems: Suitability Analysis," *International Journal of Geographical Information System*, 4, 4 (1990), pp. 413-428.

MacEachren, A.M., *Some Truth with Maps: Primer on Symbolism and Design* (Washington, DC: AAG, 1994).

Monmonier, M., *How to Lie With Maps*, 2nd ed. (Chicago: University of Chicago Press, 1996).

Montgomery, G.E., and Schuch, H.C., "GIS Data Quality," in *GIS Data Conversion Handbook* (Fort Collins, CO: GIS World Books, 1993), pp. 131-146.

Thompson, M.M., *Maps for America*, 3rd ed. (Washington, DC: U.S. Geographical Survey, 1988).

Unwin, D.J., "Geographical Information Systems and the Problem of 'Error and Uncertainty'," *Progress in Human Geography*, 19, 4 (1995), pp. 549-558.

Veregin, H., *Taxonomy of Error in Spatial Databases*, Technical Paper 89-12 (Santa Barbara, CA: National Center for Geographic Information and Analysis, 1989).

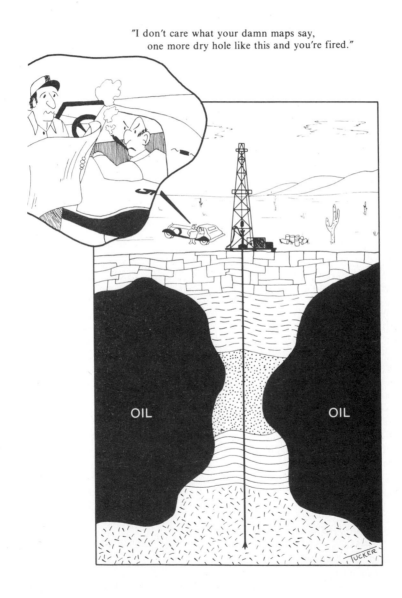

III
PART THREE
MAP INTERPRETATION

You practice interpretation every day. When you notice that things seem to form a pattern, you ask yourself, "Why?" If you come into class and find everybody crowded into one corner, you'll be struck by this unusual arrangement of students. You can describe their grouping as a clustered distribution, but that won't explain why they're clumped over there. Are they looking at something fascinating or trying to hide from something terrible? Has there been an accident or a great discovery? Your curiosity will likely be aroused to find the answer.

When you interpret a map, you do the same thing. You notice unusual or interesting patterns and seek explanations for them. The difference is that in map interpretation there is a buffer between you and your environment. Features and distributions are generalized and symbolized. Thus, the answers to your questions will not often be immediately obvious. The map can include only enough clues to provide you with touchstones, starting points for discovery. Maps are springboards for the imagination, trigger devices to set you questioning and inspire you to search for answers.

As we emphasized in our discussion of map reading (Part I), the relationship between reality and its map representation is not one to one. It requires a creative effort to move from the static, simplified map to the vibrancy and detail of the environment. And, as the cartoon at the beginning of this section suggests, even a skill in map reading does not guarantee success in interpretation. The distinction between map reading and interpretation is analogous to the difference between reading a book for its obvious story line and interpreting the book's symbolism to discover what the author was trying to show. With a book or a map, one must learn to "read between the lines."

Intuition is an important part of map interpretation, just as it is in interpreting a book, a poem, or a painting. Therefore, the validity of your inferences depends on your ability to let the map serve as a surrogate for your environment. As your mental map improves, so will your skill at interpretation.

You can approach map interpretation in two ways. You can look at one map and seek explanations for the patterns you see. Or you can compare several maps from different periods and speculate on what processes might have produced the changes that have taken place over time.

Even if you use just one map, you are looking at time as well as space. Present environmental forms are the result of past environmental processes. Since these "results" are what maps depict, map interpretation rests upon inferences about the past. Thus, time should never be overlooked as a possible factor in map interpretation. When a pattern differs from one place to another, it may be due to varying conditions in different areas at the same time, or it may be due to the fact that the patterns developed under the same conditions but at different times.

432

It is also important to be aware that a variety of different processes can lead to the same result. This is known as the **principle of equifinity**. There may be a lack of trees in an area, for example, because the climate isn't conducive to vegetation, or because there has been a forest fire, or because the trees have been cut down. The map interpreter must decide which of these or other possible explanations applies in a particular case.

The opposite is also true. A single process can end in a number of different results. The process of building a city, for instance, can lead to a wide variety of city patterns.

Map interpretation, then, is a complex, creative act. Everything you have learned so far about map reading and analysis will be put to use. In fact, everything you have learned throughout your life will be helpful. For interpretation requires an understanding of more than maps. You must also have some knowledge of the features depicted on the map. To interpret a vegetation map successfully, you need to know something about vegetation. To explain the pattern of soils on a map, you must know a number of things about the area, such as its climate, bedrock geology, and whether it has been glaciated.

Obviously, it is impossible to include all these potentially important factors on one map. The resulting portrayal would be cluttered and complex beyond human comprehension. Consequently, interpretation requires going beyond the map itself and seeking additional information elsewhere. The best source of such information may be other maps. Many patterns will become clear as you compare one map to another and study the patterns of related phenomena.

As you gain proficiency in map interpretation, you'll be amazed at your ability to generalize from situation to situation. The explanation of some small detail of the environment will often provide the basis for understanding many other features in the surrounding area as well. Similarly, the clues you use to explain phenomena in your local area can help you to understand things in other parts of the world and even on other planets.

As you study maps, you'll discover that certain features and patterns are repeated over and over, because there are relatively few fundamental processes molding the environment. You should therefore expect your map interpretation ability to grow at an ever increasing rate.

Map interpretation is a skill that comes with practice, a skill that can't really be taught in a book.

All we can do here is to give examples of interpretation and describe some general procedures that might be used. For convenience, we'll deal first with the interpretation of physical features (Chapter 21) and then with human phenomena (Chapter 22). Since the environment is in reality an integrated system, we'll then look at the interaction between the physical and human realms (Chapter 23). Perhaps the ultimate challenge is provided in our discussion of image map interpretation in Chapter 24. Finally, in Chapter 25, we'll discuss the need to balance imaginative map interpretation with common sense.

The examples of map interpretation given in these chapters are by no means exhaustive. They merely represent a selection of interpretative situations and problems you may encounter. As you go through them, you'll notice that there are a few basic methods which are used repeatedly. Also, since the interpretation of a map often requires finding other maps to study and compare, many of these examples use other maps in the explanation.

Interpretation is open-ended. Comprehension is never complete. Each new experience you have, in every facet of life, will give you new understanding and allow you to extract new meaning. If you have ever reread a book years later, you found that you gained different insights from it than you did the first time, because you had grown. So it is with a map. The more you bring to it, the more you will gain from it.

Of all the aspects of map use, interpretation requires the most from the map user. You must give all of yourself. Every subject you have studied, every experience you have ever had, every thought process you have mastered, contributes to your interpretation of a map. Interpretation is the most demanding of all map use endeavors.

It is also the most exciting. You can spend hours lost in an interesting map, just as you can in a good book. Everyone loves a mystery, they say, and a map is as enthralling as any detective story. Hidden within that pattern of map symbols is the very essence of the environment. The map interpreter's challenge is to search out those buried meanings, to piece together the fragments of mapped information and come up with a picture of vibrant, ever-changing reality. Once you have met that challenge and discovered the rewards of interpretation, you'll look at all maps in a new way, picking out intriguing patterns and asking yourself, "Why?"

CHAPTER TWENTY-ONE
INTERPRETING THE PHYSICAL ENVIRONMENT

INTRODUCTION

PHYSICAL FORCES

LITHOSPHERE

Continental Drift
Michigan Basin
Closed Depressions

ATMOSPHERE

Precipitation in Washington State
Sunshine

HYDROSPHERE

Stream Types
Stream Patterns

BIOSPHERE

Flora
Climatic Influences
Slope Orientation Effects
Fauna
Individual Animal Maps
Species Range Maps
Migratory Route Maps

CONCLUSION

SELECTED READINGS

One of the best paying professions is getting ahold of pieces of country in your mind, learning their smell and their moods, sorting out the pieces of a view, deciding what grows there and there and why....This is the best kind of ownership, and the most permanent.

—Jerry & Renny Russell, *On the Loose*

21

CHAPTER TWENTY-ONE

INTERPRETING THE PHYSICAL ENVIRONMENT

No place on earth has escaped the influence of our species. Even the antarctic ice fields contain fallout from our atomic weapons testing, mute testimony to the pervasiveness of our imprint on the earth's surface. Despite the far-reaching extent of human influence, however, we probably still don't influence the physical environment nearly as much as the physical environment influences us. With this in mind, we will begin our discussion of map interpretation with the physical setting.

Immediately we are confronted with a serious difficulty, however. The physical environment is far too detailed and complex to take on as an integrated whole. Environmental scientists usually circumvent this apparent impasse by decomposing the physical environment into its component systems and then studying each in turn. This serves as a useful map interpreting strategy as well. As a first step, we can view the environment not as a unit but as a composite of four great spheres. As we saw in Chapter 1, these are known as the lithosphere (land surface), the atmosphere, the hydrosphere (water surface), and the biosphere.

These physical realms aren't independent of one another, of course. Nor is one dependent on the next in simple, systematic fashion. Eventually, therefore, we'll have to overcome these convenient but artificial divisions and see the physical environment as a single, fully interrelated entity.

One way to do so is to focus on basic physical forces, such as gravity, heat, and pressure. These forces are felt through action of environmental agents, such as water, wind, fire, and ice. Since these physical forces and agents influence all aspects of the environment, they serve as a unifying theme.

The challenge of interpreting the physical environment isn't easily met. We're fortunate, however, in having the benefit of centuries of observation and research to bring to bear on the problem. Believable theories have been put forth explaining all four physical realms, introducing such concepts as erosional cycles, biological evolution, and climatic periodicity. Properly applied, these theories are a great help in effective map interpretation. Let's draw on this outside information now to see how much insight we can gain from even a simple map of the physical setting.

PHYSICAL FORCES

Natural features are complex expressions of the host of underlying forces at work in the physical realm. **Centrifugal** forces due to earth rotation, for example, have caused a slight flattening of the earth at the poles of rotation and a bulge at the equator. **Gravitation** holds us and our atmosphere on earth. It also is the cause of avalanches, rockslides, water running downhill, and the crashes of malfunctioning aircraft. **Pressure** transforms ice into a pliable state so that glaciers flow. Differences in atmospheric pressure produce winds. **Heat** causes matter to expand, giving rise to circulation patterns in the earth, oceans, and atmosphere. **Sunlight** is the primary source of heat on earth and is needed by plants, which become food for animals. **Magnetism** causes orientation in mineral crystals as molten earth cools and solidifies into rock.

These few examples illustrate some effects of physical forces. Since they all work together, of course, it's difficult to identify cause-effect relations between a feature and only one of these forces. Tectonic activity, for example, is expressed as earthquakes, volcanoes, and drifting continents. Heat, gravity, pressure, and centrifugal forces all play an obvious part in each of these features. Sunlight and magnetism are probably involved as well.

Physical features are sculpted by **agents** of these basic environmental forces. These agents include ice, fire, moving water, and wind. These are often called erosional agents, because they act collectively to cause landform erosion and depo-

sition. As we shall see, they also exert a strong influence on the other physical realms.

LITHOSPHERE

The most prominent aspect of the physical environment is the land surface upon which we live. Its changing form is everywhere evident. It also provides the stage upon which other aspects of the physical environment operate. For these reasons, understanding the landform is fundamental to interpreting the physical environment from maps.

To understand the present landform, we must consider the great forces of land building and destruction. Volcanic processes force molten rock to the surface from deep within the earth. The solid crust of the earth is folded and faulted by the stress set up by tectonic (land shifting) processes. Less dramatic but equally powerful land forming agents are wind, water, and glaciers. Land is continually being torn down by erosional processes and built up by depositional processes.

Textbooks on physical geography, geology, soils, and geomorphology cover these topics in detail. In addition, most map interpretation textbooks and manuals have focused the greatest attention on landforms. We won't be so exhaustive here. The few examples which follow are intended only to demonstrate the scope of landform interpretation from maps.

Continental Drift

The mere shape of environmental features is often a major clue to understanding them. It usually takes more than the observation of form, however, to explain why things look the way they do. Complex spatial processes may underlie the creation of what appear to be simple shapes.

One dramatic map interpretation case which led from observing form to finding causes concerns the shape and configuration of continental land masses. Soon after the Atlantic Ocean was mapped during the age of exploration in the 16th century, the parallelism of opposing shores attracted the attention of map readers. North and South America seemed to fit up against Europe and Africa, as if these great land masses had broken apart during some past age.

436

Early observers, among them Francis Bacon, were impressed enough with this observation to speculate about its meaning. Their theories were vague and brief, however, possibly because the idea that continents might fit together seemed, at the time, so outrageous. But by the 1800s enough evidence was accumulated to support the idea that the continents once fit together in a single central land mass, which subsequently broke up and dispersed to become the separate continents of today (**Figure 21.1**). This radical theory was called **continental drift**, a term descriptive of the notion of floating land masses.

Incredible as the idea of large-scale lateral displacements of the continental masses was, by the early 1900s the theory was well formulated. Most people, including environmental scientists, still chose to ignore or ridicule it, however. Finally, in the 1960s, after nearly four centuries of

research and debate, the notion of continental drift became the accepted explanation for the present shape and position of continents. It remains only for scientists to elaborate the details of the process, as they are currently doing.

We can gain insight into the nature of map interpretation by looking at the evidence which provided an explanation for Bacon and other observers of the early 1600s. They were seeking confirmation of a single supercontinent. They found it by matching environmental features cross-continentally. For example, rock types, fossils, and magnetic orientation at the time of bedrock solidification found in southeastern South America matched those found along the southwestern tip of Africa. Similar matching of features occurred on other continents as well.

But if the single supercontinent theory was true, there should also be some evidence that the

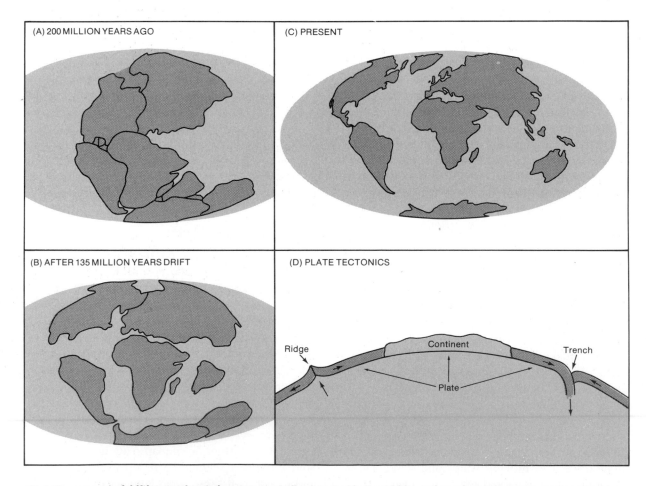

21.1 The concept of drifting continents became generally accepted in the 1960s, and as a bonus the pattern of earthquakes and volcanic activity was largely explained as well.

continents were adrift. Continental movement would have to be associated with severe stress in the earth's crust. Land masses acting like giant ships plowing through a sea of rock not only would cause major disturbances in the surface layer but would have to be driven by some monumental force. The evidence was clear once scientists knew what to look for and had the technology to make the search possible.

Studies of rock density (through the use of gravity readings) confirmed the suspicion that the continents were lighter than the material upon which they floated. Mountain building occurred along the leading edge of continents and at spots where land masses collided. Volcanic and earthquake activity was also concentrated along the forward edge of land masses. It wasn't until mid-ocean trenches and rifts (mountain ranges) were discovered, however, that the mechanism behind the whole process was revealed (**Figure 21.1D**).

We now know that the earth's surface is circulating vertically as well as horizontally. Molten rock emerges from deep within the earth along the mid-ocean rifts and returns to the earth's depths along the mid-ocean trenches. Both zones are active volcanic and earthquake regions. Between the rifts and trenches, the continents are floating like giant disks or plates, giving rise to the term **plate tectonics,** which is currently more popular with scientists than the term "continental drift." Thus, beginning with Bacon's speculations on a map of continental outlines, we have come up with a theory of a dynamic earth. Not only have we explained the shape and configuration of the earth's land masses, but as a bonus we can in large part account for the geographical distribution of tectonic and volcanic activity as well.

Michigan Basin

For the concept of continental drift to be believable, we must accept the fact that earth-molding processes have gone on for hundreds of millions of years. This ability to think of landform building processes in terms of a geologic time scale is crucial in understanding how the terrain has developed. Changes which are imperceptible during our lifetime can result in gross alterations of the landform when accumulated over millions of years. To clarify this notion of geologic time still further, let's take as an example the interpretation of a landform map of the Great Lakes region. The question for the map interpreter is why the region is shaped as it is.

If you look closely at the line map in **Figure 21.2A**, you will notice a curious thing. There is a rough symmetry about the central part of the southern peninsula of Michigan. Specifically, there appear to be concentric rings of remarkably similar features. Lake Michigan on the west is matched by Lake Huron on the east. The Door Peninsula, Garden and Stonington Peninsulas, Manitoulin Islands, and the Bruce Peninsula form the second ring. These features are flanked by Lake Winnebago and Green Bay on the west and Georgian Bay and Lake Simcoe on the east.

This remarkably circular pattern of nested features is a map interpreter's dream. Not only is there order to the landforms, but the elements of the topography are intimately related. This means that if we can explain only one of the rings, or even one feature such as a lake or peninsula, the chances are that we will have found the key to the entire structure.

We can begin our interpretation of the Great Lakes region by studying its topography, as depicted in **Figure 21.2B**. This admittedly "exaggerated" illustration looks much as if a number of different-sized saucers have been piled on top of one another, from largest at the bottom to smallest at the top of the stack. The circular pattern of peninsulas and islands represents erosional remnants of the edges of these saucer-like strata, while water bodies occupy the belts of lower land which lie between the saucer rims. But what could have caused these saucer-shaped layers of rock?

If there is a structural explanation, this can easily be confirmed by studying a map of the region's geology. Therefore, let's turn next to the geologic map and cross-section in **Figure 21.2C**. This figure reveals that the geologic structure is that of a **basin**. Geologically speaking, the entire region was inundated for millions of years by some prehistoric ocean. During this period, thick beds of sediments were deposited in layers of sand, mud, and seashells. With time, these horizontal sediment layers were slowly transformed into beds of sedimentary rock (sandstone, shale, and limestone), which subsequently were warped up at their margins, forming a giant basin structure. The uplifted edges of the structure were

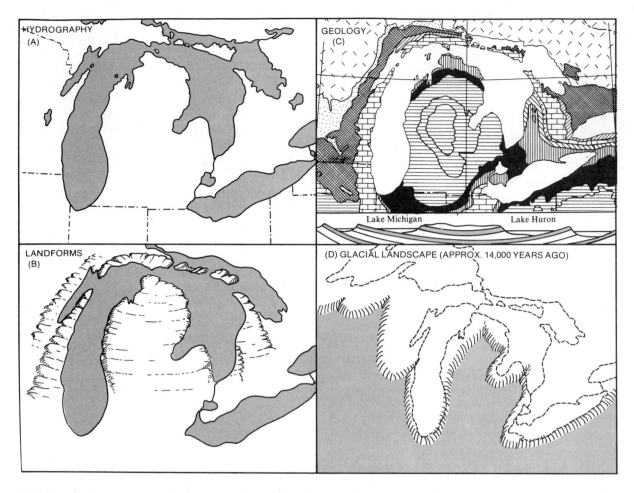

HYDROGRAPHY (A)

GEOLOGY (C)

Lake Michigan   Lake Huron

LANDFORMS (B)

(D) GLACIAL LANDSCAPE (APPROX. 14,000 YEARS AGO)

21.2 The Michigan Basin (A) provides an excellent example of how landforms (B), geology (C), and glacial activity (D) are all interrelated.

then eroded, leveling out the whole region. The rate of erosion varied with the strength of the alternate rock layers, however. Beds of weaker rock eroded the most, leaving lowlands separated by intervening high belts (cuestas) of more resistant rock.

But this scenario still doesn't explain how the Great Lakes were formed. The missing scrap of information we need is the fact that a thick continental ice sheet moved through this region on at least four occasions. According to the glacier theory, the region was molded by immense forces of moving ice several miles thick. The last glacier (which melted only some 12,000 years ago) gouged out the Great Lakes and, by alternately scouring and depositing material, disrupted the region's surface form in countless other ways (**Figure 21.2D**). The effect was to disguise the basic geologic structure in some places and accentuate it in others.

Closed Depressions

We are likely to find evidence of structural basins on many maps because they are rather common regional features. The pattern will rarely be as well marked, however, as it is on the small-scale map of the Great Lakes region we just looked at. More commonly, the map sheet will cover only a small portion of such regional features, in which case the overall pattern usually will remain a mystery. Many landform features, however, are small enough to be seen in their entirety even on large-scale topographic maps. To demonstrate how useful such features are in piecing together the nature of the local landform, let's take a detailed

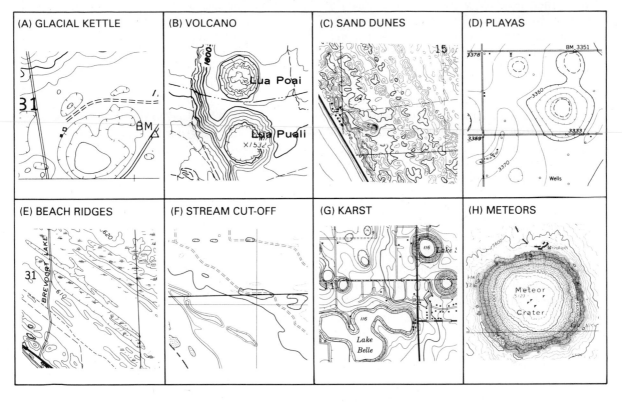

21.3 Small closed depressions on contour maps can be attributed to one of several sources. Thus, it's usually quite easy to surmise what has caused this unique landform.

look at one of the more distinct features, the **closed depression**. This feature is easy to spot because it is symbolized on most topographic maps by hachured contours (**Figure 21.3**). (For more on hachured contours, see *Special Contours* in Chapter 5.)

Closed depressions are transitional features in the landform, since natural erosional forces work both toward filling them with material from surrounding high areas and toward cutting a surface drainage outlet. In the interim period, the depression is likely to fill with water, especially where subsurface drainage is poor and annual precipitation high.

Thus, when you see a closed depression on a map, your first response should be that this probably represents a relatively young landscape feature. Most likely, the depression can be attributed to one of five natural factors: The area was recently glaciated; it is volcanically active; it is the result of wind action; it was affected by the movement or dissolving action of water; or it was sub-

ject to a meteor attack. Let's take a look at each of these possible situations.

1. **Recent glaciation.** The debris left behind by melting ice sheets creates a thoroughly disrupted drainage pattern. The poorly drained surface is frequently covered by marshes in low spots and by steep-sided depressions, called **kettles**, which form when a buried chunk of ice melts and causes local subsidence. There isn't enough precipitation to cause the water flowing out of these swamps and depressions to cut a natural channel, and not enough time has elapsed for the depression to fill with erosional material. The example in **Figure 21.3A** is taken from Michigan's Upper Peninsula.

2. **Volcanically active area.** Volcanoes are characterized by a dome-shaped feature, called a **cone**, with a central depression on the summit. The example in **Figure 21.3B** is taken from Hawaii. These central depressions may

be formed in three ways. First, they may be created by the subsidence which follows the cooling or withdrawal of melted rock (magma) in the central portion of a lava dome. These depressions are called **sinks**. Second, they may be produced by the explosive action which throws solidified magma out of the central portion of cinder cones. Such depressions are called **craters**. Or, finally, they may be formed when an explosive eruption blows out a large mass of a previously solidified volcanic dome. These explosion craters are called **calderas.**

3. **Wind action.** Wind-blown sand deposits are common in coastal and desert regions. Due to the way in which sand is laid down by the wind, the surface of a sand dune landscape is usually highly irregular, although the individual dunes may be smooth and regular. Surface drainage is often poorly developed or nonexistent due to a combination of factors which may include dry conditions, the porosity of the sand, and the shifting character of the dunes themselves. The resulting ridge and valley configuration commonly contains an irregular scatter of rather finely textured closed topographic depressions. This is evident in **Figure 21.3C**, which is taken from the north shore of Lake Michigan just west of the Straits of Mackinaw. Once stabilized by vegetation, these depressions may be far more persistent than the coasts or dry conditions which contributed to their formation. Thus, the factors associated with sand dune formation may not appear on the same map sheet as the dunes themselves.

In dry climates, with little vegetation to protect the land surface from the scouring effect of winds, soil loss can lead to depressions called **playas**. The example in Figure **21.3D**, taken from the southern high plains of west Texas, is dominated by these **deflation basins**, which show up as depression contours. Notice the build-up of sand dunes on the downwind (southeast) side of the playas.

4. **Water action.** Sand dune formations are often associated spatially with beach ridges. These ridges are created when a lake level drops, then stabilizes long enough to create new beach deposits, then drops again, and so on. Under certain conditions, the resulting land-

form consists of a series of narrow, roughly parallel low sand ridges interspersed with long, linear depressions. Due to the sand or gravel make-up of beach ridges, and their relatively low relief, shallow closed depressions often persist. **Figure 21.3E** is taken from the same area as Figure 21.3C. As with sand dunes, the coast which led to the formation of beach ridges may be so distant that it doesn't presently appear on the same map sheet.

Water action also may produce closed depressions in broad, flat valleys due to shifts in riverbed location. The shift may occur during floods, or it may be the result of stream meandering over many years. In either case, the old, **cut-off stream channels** can be isolated by subsequent streambank ridge-building, and show up on maps as depression contours (**Figure 21.3F**). Since these are usually rather shallow depressions, supplemental contours are sometimes used to indicate their position.

Although these features result from water-transported sand, water can transport minerals in solution as well as in suspension. Caverns commonly form in regions of limestone beds through the dissolving action of infiltrated surface water. This can be seen in **Figure 21.3G**, taken from Florida. As large quantities of carbonates are removed in solution by the downward movement of water, the surface loses its natural support and eventually collapses, causing a surface depression which is known as a **sink**, or **sinkhole**. If the limestone bed is shallow, there may be so much general subsidence that, in time, scattered depressions will merge with their neighbors.

5. **Meteors.** Most depressions can be accounted for by one of the four situations we have discussed. Sometimes, however, a depression may have some localized cause. One such local depression is a **meteor crater**, which is produced by the impact of a meteor hitting the earth. **Figure 21.3H**, taken from Arizona, illustrates such a feature. If the force is great enough, the rim of the crater may actually be elevated above the surrounding surface. The ability to recognize meteor craters will grow more crucial as maps of our moon and the other planets become more commonplace.

For all the above closed depression examples, the map tells you only that the condition exists. It doesn't tell you why. This is where interpretation of the physical evidence comes in.

Exercise caution, however, in interpreting this map feature, because it may not be created by physical forces at all. People also create closed depressions (excavations, gravel pits, quarries, open pit mines, and so on); we will return to this topic in *Influence of Human Factors* in Chapter 23.

ATMOSPHERE

We can't proceed very far in our interpretation of the landform unless we consider weather processes and climate. Sometimes the imprint of atmospheric forces is so strong that we can surmise past climatic conditions merely by studying the present form of the land surface. For instance, the presence of glacial landforms signals at least one prolonged cold period in the past.

Weather and climate are also influenced by the configuration of the landform surface. Mountains and valleys may block and channel general air flow patterns, significantly altering local conditions. Temperature, precipitation, humidity, winds, and barometric pressure can all be affected.

Precipitation in Washington State

For our first example of how weather patterns may be interpreted from maps, consider the distribution of precipitation in Washington state (**Figure 21.4A**). How can this varied pattern be explained?

The key here is the fact that the pattern changes so abruptly from one area to the next. This implies that local rather than regional climatic controls are in force. Indeed, precipitation in much of the state is known as **orographic**, meaning that it is related to mountains. A map of precipitation is in fact a rather good substitute for a map of the mountains (**Figure 21.4B**), although it is necessary to understand the general atmospheric factors which are operating as well.

The precipitation-producing mechanism is most developed in the winter months when pre-

vailing westerly winds carry moist air inland from the Pacific Ocean and force it to flow over several mountain ranges (**Figure 21.4C**). Rising air on the west side of these ranges is cooled, causing cloud build-up and even precipitation if the drop in temperature is great enough.

After crossing the mountain crest, the air descends the east side of the ranges, warming in the process. Since this warming air is capable of picking up moisture, the east (or rain shadow) side of the mountains tends to be relatively dry.

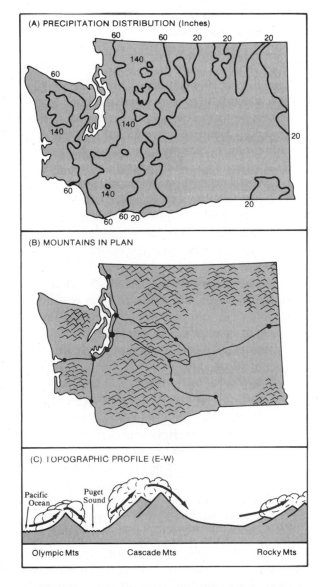

21.4 Relations among landforms, prevailing winds, and orographic precipitation are well illustrated in Washington state.

442

These wet and dry climatic belts are characteristic of the Pacific Northwest.

The pattern of precipitation, therefore, is related directly to the configuration of the various mountain systems in respect to the westerly air flow. Since the moisture-laden air passes over the coastal mountain barrier first, the potential for precipitation is greatest in this region. In local areas of the Olympic Mountains, the rainfall can reach 500 cm. (197 in.) per year. This pattern is muted on the map, however, because the southern portion of the coastal range is relatively low in elevation when compared to the Olympic Mountains to the north.

A second topographic barrier is provided by the Cascade Mountains. This range is fairly uniform in height from north to south. As a result, the Cascades receive about the same amount of precipitation throughout their north-south extent. Mt. Baker and Mr. Ranier stand out as exceptions, however, because they are so much higher than the rest of the range.

The Cascades also extend across the northern part of the state to the western extreme of the Rocky Mountains. Despite the height of these mountains, they receive far less orographic precipitation than either the coastal ranges or the Cascade front. The same is true for the Blue Mountains (a remnant of the Rockies) in the southeastern corner of the state. The reason for this drop-off in precipitation is that the air rapidly becomes drier as it moves inland.

For people living in the Puget Sound lowland, the actual amount of precipitation isn't as meaningful as the ratio between cloud cover and precipitation. Seattle, for example, receives only about 76 cm. (30 in.) of precipitation a year, which is approximately equivalent to that received by a Midwestern city such as Chicago. Why, then, does Seattle have the reputation of being the wettest city in the United States? The explanation is that the Puget Sound lowland, although drier than the higher coastal belt, is likely to be blanketed by clouds which are backed up from air masses being forced over the Cascades to the east. The effect of day after day of cloud cover and drizzle is to give the impression that Seattle receives far more precipitation than it really does.

Sunshine

Another climatic condition which we can interpret from maps is the amount of sunshine. This example is especially apropos, since diminishing supplies of fossil fuels have led to increased interest in the sun as an alternate energy source. Although it has been said that solar energy is everywhere available and free, this is only partly true. The amount of solar energy which reaches different parts of the earth varies immensely, and the cost of collecting it in sufficient amounts varies in direct proportion to the amount received. Thus, if we can determine the amount of solar energy reaching the earth across the United States, we will know to a large degree where it is practical to install solar energy collectors.

This problem is fairly complex. First of all, the amount of solar energy reaching our location on earth is determined by two factors. One factor is the duration of sunshine. This depends on the length of day, which is related to the latitude of our location. The higher the latitude, the longer the summer days and the shorter the winter days.

But the length of day is only one aspect of solar energy potential. The other factor is the angle of the sun above the horizon. The higher the latitude, the lower the average annual sun angle. The average in Miami, Florida, is 64°15', while in Seattle, Washington, it is only 42°24'. Sun angles also change on a diurnal cycle. The reason sun angle differences are important is that the lower the angle is, the farther the sun's rays have to travel through the atmosphere to reach the earth's surface. Since the atmosphere absorbs, reflects, and scatters the sun's rays, the amount of solar energy eventually reaching a location on the earth is inversely related to the amount of atmosphere which must be traversed.

The distance a sun's ray must travel through the atmosphere to reach our position also depends on our altitude. Denver is a mile higher in elevation than San Francisco and other coastal cities. Since the atmosphere is densest near sea level, this difference in elevation alone can have a substantial influence on the amount of solar energy which reaches the earth.

By accounting for length of day, sun angle, and elevation, we could make a map of solar energy potential in the United States. This map would

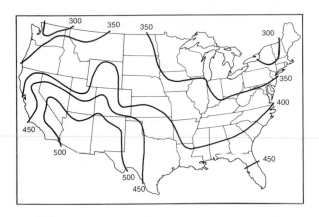

21.5 Average daily solar radiation actually received at the ground surface on an annual basis (measured in langleys).

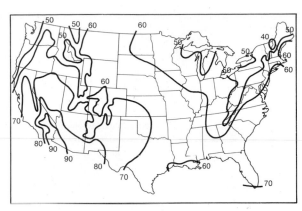

21.6 The annual percentage of possible sunshine received at different locations in the United States varies dramatically.

show a progressive decrease in potential solar energy from south to north, which is what we should expect. We might also expect mountainous regions to be exceptions to the systematic pattern of east-west energy potential zones. As anyone who has ever received a high-altitude sunburn knows, the thin, less polluted atmosphere at mountainous locations lets more solar energy reach the earth than is the case at lower elevations. Despite this added solar energy potential, mountains are rather cool because they lose their heat to the atmosphere quickly, and the temperature naturally drops with increased altitude (at a rate of 3.3°F. with every 1,000 feet).

Our imaginary map of solar energy potential doesn't give the whole picture, however. It would bear little resemblance to a map showing the average annual solar radiation which was actually received at the earth's surface (**Figure 21.5**). The reason is that length of day, latitude, and altitude factors provide a measure of *potential*, not actual, hours of sunshine. Clouds, dust, and air pollutants may obscure the sun for much of the day, substantially reducing the amount of solar energy recorded at a spot on the ground.

If the average number of sunshine hours actually received is related to the potential sunshine hours for locations across the United States, the result is a map of the annual percentage of possible sunshine (**Figure 21.6**). This is really a cloud cover map in reverse. In other words, a place which falls in the 70 to 80 percent sunshine class would experience cloud cover 20 to 30 percent of the time.

But why is the cloud cover pattern so irregular? This is a good question for the map interpreter. To answer it, we have to know what meteorological conditions lead to cloud production, persistence, and movement.

The best place to begin is with the large air masses which move over the United States and control the daily weather pattern (**Figure 21.7**). Air masses that have a maritime source carry a great deal of moisture. As Figure 21.7 indicates, these systems influence the west, gulf, and east coasts of the country. In contrast, air masses that have a continental source are relatively dry. These form in Mexican deserts and in northcentral Canada.

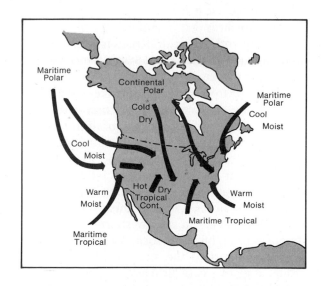

21.7 The weather in different parts of the United States is influenced by different air mass source regions.

444

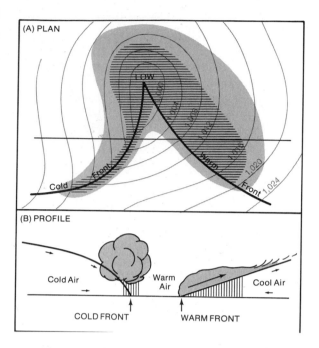

(A) PLAN

LOW

Cold Front

Warm Front 1.024

(B) PROFILE

Cold Air

Warm Air

Cool Air

COLD FRONT

WARM FRONT

21.8 Cyclonic storms occur along the margins of large air masses.

The majority of cloud activity in the United States is a direct result of the movement of these air masses. Clouds form when moist air is uplifted into cooler zones of the atmosphere, causing water vapor to condense. This uplifting may be caused by an air mass being forced over a mountain range, as we saw in the previous Washington state example. Or it may be caused by other air masses. Cool air is denser and heavier than warm air. Consequently, when air masses from the north sweep down over the United States, they displace warmer air moving from the south. The cool air masses move from west to east like a series of giant whales (**Figure 21.8**). Friction with the earth's surface slows the movement of the heavy, cool air, creating a steep temperature-pressure gradient, called a **cold front**, along the forward edge of the air mass. The warmer and lighter air lying in the path of the cold front is forced up over the cold air mass, creating heavy clouds and sometimes violent but usually short-lived storms (thunderstorms, blizzards, tornadoes).

In contrast to the steep gradient on the leading edge of a cool air mass, friction with the ground draws out the temperature-pressure gradient along the slower-moving tailing edge of the air mass. Because lighter warm air moves across the country faster than cool heavy air, moist air from the south often pushes up the gentle back slope of cold air masses, creating a **warm front**. This front is characterized by light to heavy clouds and gentle but steady (often lingering for days) precipitation.

We see, then, that frontal weather patterns are based on the same uplift principle as orographic clouds and precipitation. The big difference is that frontal systems are mobile. The fronts don't follow the same track each time they cross the country. This makes the influence of frontal cloud patterns on the amount of solar energy more difficult to predict than the impact of orographic patterns.

To complicate things further, clouds also form when air near the ground is heated and then uplifted by **convection currents**. Local thunderstorms are often created in this fashion. The greater the potential for evaporation and transpiration, and the higher the temperature, the more likely that convection cloud patterns will influence the solar energy received at the ground. The eastern half of the United States—and the southeastern states in particular—are therefore most affected by convection cloud cover.

By putting the forces of orographic, frontal, and convection uplift together, we can now explain why the map of received solar energy deviates as it does from the map of potential solar energy. Moist air moving in from the ocean is forced over the mountains in the Pacific Northwest, New England, and the western mountain states, forming cloud cover. The entire country is swept by frontal cloud systems, with the greatest cloud cover occurring in the eastern half of the country due to the moist gulf coast air that moves inland. Since the southwest and plains states are missed by most of the moist air flows, these regions are relatively dry with clear skies prevailing.

Before we can take this knowledge of solar energy distribution and apply it to home heating, we must consider several other factors. First, we should know the monthly distribution of solar energy, since we are concerned primarily with the winter season. Places may receive the same total amount of solar energy in different ways. Seattle residents, for example, see only half the sunshine which is enjoyed by the residents of

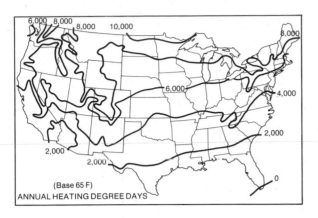

21.9 A map of annual heating degree-days.

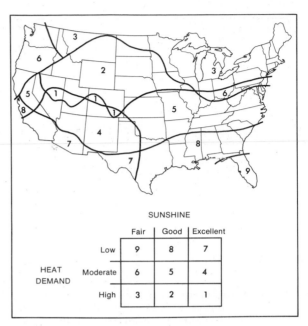

21.10 The practicality of solar home heating at the present time depends upon available solar radiation as well as annual heating degree-days.

Schenectady, New York, during the crucial heating month of January, although both cities receive the same average annual amount of solar energy.

The second factor in applying solar energy to home heating is the temperature of a region. How much heat will it take to bring house temperatures up to a comfortable level? A standard measure called **heating degree-days** has been devised to answer this question. Heating degree-days are the number of degrees (Fahrenheit) by which the average temperature for a day falls short of 65°F. If the average temperature on a given day is 50°F., for instance, that day contributes 15 degree-days to the heating season. A map of accumulated heating degree-days for the average heating season provides a useful indication of predicted fuel consumption, heating system capacity, and desirable amounts of insulation (**Figure 21.9**).

The fewer heating degree-days accumulated during the average heating season, the more practical solar heating becomes in light of current technology. When we compare Seattle and Schenectady on the basis of heating needs, we see that Schenectady requires about 2,000 more heating degree-days. Such great heating needs in Schenectady may mean that solar heat isn't practical there, even though it receives twice as much solar radiation in January as Seattle does.

The final step in determining solar home heating potential is to combine heating degree-day information with the solar energy received at a site. A map of these combined factors is shown in **Figure 21.10**. This map gives a fair idea of whether solar heating is a practical alternative to conventional methods of home heating at the present time.

Two things about this map warrant special mention. One is that the information has been highly generalized in order to present a national picture. Solar home heating will be practical in many local areas not indicated in the general map pattern. Of course the reverse is also true.

The other thing to remember is that this map will change as engineers come up with more efficient designs for solar energy collectors. This point raises an interesting question: Are resources such as energy part of the physical environment, or are they culturally derived? The answer is that both are true. Our notion of what constitutes a resource depends on our ever-changing needs and technology. What this means for the map interpreter is that resource maps should be viewed as cultural perceptions rather than unbiased reflectors of the physical realm. Resource maps are constantly changing as we change.

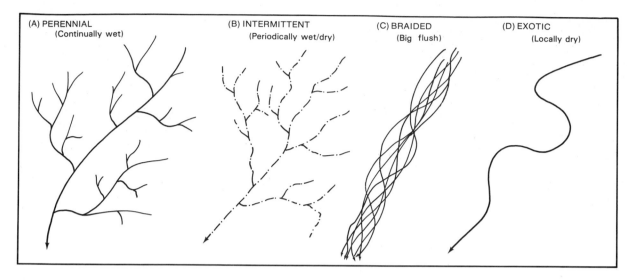

21.11 The types of streams found on a map can be clues to the local climate. Perennial streams (A) occur in humid regions. Intermittent streams (B) are found in regions which are alternately wet and dry. Braided streams (C) result when major discharges are followed by low water levels. Exotic streams (D) indicate a locally arid area.

HYDROSPHERE

The vast majority of the earth's surface is covered with water. Oceans, lakes, and streams dominate the global scene. Although the pattern formed by these water features is relatively static, the water itself is perpetually changing in physical state and geographical position. It is freely transformed from a liquid to a solid to a gas as it moves from the oceans to the land and the atmosphere. This continuous series of interchanges is called the **hydrologic cycle**.

In addition to their importance to agriculture, recreation, and other human uses, hydrographic features provide useful locational references. Merely by studying the hydrography, the alert map interpreter can come up with valuable information about a region. For example, we can tell a great deal about a region's climate, underlying rock type and structure, topography, and erosional processes by examining the types of streams on a map.

Stream Types

Humid regions are characterized by streams which flow throughout the year. These **perennial streams** are symbolized on standard maps by solid lines and in blue if color is used (**Figure 21.11A**).

In dry regions, streams flow sporadically, and the streambed is dry for part of the year. On large-scale topographic maps, these **intermittent streams** are depicted with broken lines to distinguish them from perennial streams (**Figure 21.11B**).

A special type of intermittent stream is the **braided stream** (**Figure 21.11C**). These multiple-channel streams are created when the water flow can't transport the full load of soil and gravel that washes into the streambed during periods of rapid runoff. For this reason, braided streams commonly flow out of arid mountain regions. Since material is deposited in the broad, shallow bed after each major storm, the main stream channel is forced to change position frequently. The result is a complex network of intertwined channels. Map representations of these streams are often purely symbolic, of course. We wouldn't expect to find the streams forming the braided system in the exact locations shown on the map.

Unfortunately, map makers aren't always careful to differentiate between perennial and intermittent streams. For instance, the Pantano River is depicted on the city map of Tucson, Arizona, with no indication that its streambed is dry most of the year. Such misleading symbols may cause no problems for local residents and others knowledgeable about the region. But outsiders who haven't learned to use caution in interpreting maps may be led to expect something quite different from what exists in the environment. Those careless enough to buy land "sight unseen" after looking at the blue river on the map, for example, are often appalled to discover ugly stretches of dirt instead of the scenic water view they imagined.

Even when intermittent streams are symbolized on a map, we still have no direct way of telling how frequently and under what conditions the streambed actually carries water. In extremely dry areas, maps that show numerous streams which are rarely filled with water may have the effect of "the boy who cried wolf." People camp in dry streambeds, not realizing that a storm far upstream could flood them out with no warning.

We must also be careful not to make hasty judgments about a region's climatic conditions on the basis of perennial streams which originate in distant humid regions. These **exotic streams** can be identified by the fact that there is little evidence of drainage within the local area (**Figure 21.11D**). Large portions of rivers such as the Columbia, Rio Grande, and Colorado are in fact transient streams.

Stream Patterns

Gaining insight into climatic conditions on the basis of stream type is just one benefit of interpreting hydrography from a map. In addition, mapped streams display an intriguing variety of drainage patterns. These patterns reflect an order and regularity in nature. The drainage network can tell us a great deal about the topography and the type and structure of the underlying bedrock.

Take, for instance, the **dendritic** drainage system. This tree-branching system is the most common type (**Figure 21.12A**). It is characteristic of regions in which resistance to erosion (both vertically and horizontally) is relatively uniform. When such a drainage pattern is evident, then, we can be fairly sure that it has developed on a thick bed of rather homogeneous material. This material may either be hard or resistant bedrock or unconsolidated debris such as volcanic ash or glacial deposits.

Notice how streams in the dendritic drainage pattern converge at more acute angles as the volume of stream flow increases. This convergence factor is common to many natural trans-

portation systems, such as blood vessels in your body or veins in a leaf. Thus, whenever major streams converge at right or obtuse angles, there is probably some functional explanation. Perhaps the structure of the bedrock is the cause. Or perhaps there has been a major local tectonic or erosional event, such as faulting or glaciation.

A slight variation of the dendritic pattern is the **parallel** drainage system. Here the stream network is strongly oriented in a single direction, with minor as well as major streams flowing roughly parallel with each other (**Figure 21.12B**). Obviously, it would take some special force to induce water to run off the land in this consistent way. Usually it is a general inclination or slope of the land that is responsible. But parallel drainage can also result from the scouring action of continental ice sheets, from internal geologic structures such as parallel folds or ridges, or from parallel faults.

On some maps you will find a **trellis** drainage system, which has a strong parallel orientation in one direction and a secondary parallel orientation at right angles to the first (**Figure 21.12C**). Even major streams converge almost at right angles. Such stream behavior is caused by internal geologic structure. Trellis drainage forms along parallel folded rock strata or along bands of rocks of different resistance. This pattern is characteristic of the ridge and valley region of Pennsylvania and West Virginia.

Sometimes you will find a river system oriented strongly in two directions, with individual river segments running approximately at right angles to each other (**Figure 21.12D**). This is known as a **rectangular** drainage pattern. It is characterized by successive reversal of stream direction and by smaller streams converging perpendicularly with larger ones. To create such a pattern, the underlying bedrock must exert a powerful influence on the hydrography. You will usually discover that two systems of joints or faults in a resistant rock structure are responsible. Since the fault lines are weaker than the rest of the rock, streams erode valleys along them. Every so often a stream will jump abruptly from the fault of one system to a fault of another.

Another type of drainage system is the **radial** pattern (**Figure 21.12E**). With this system, a number of streams flow outward in different directions, suggesting the presence of a

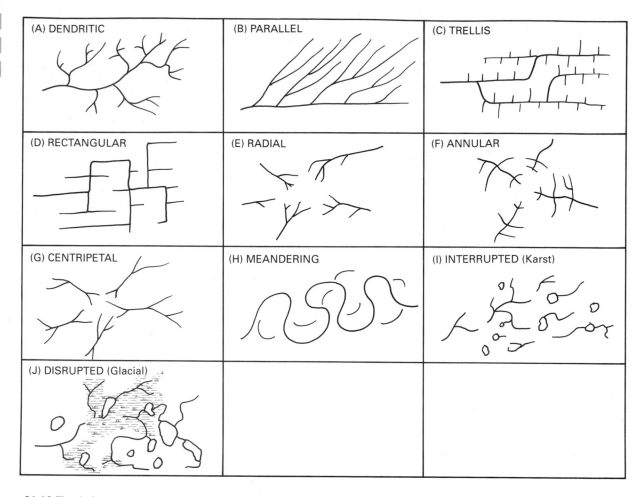

21.12 The drainage pattern found on a map may reveal a great deal about the region's geology and topography. Map interpretation involves imagining what landforms might lead to these different geometrical configurations.

central hill or mountain. If the streams are roughly parallel, the landform is probably made up of relatively homogeneous volcanic or igneous rock. Drainage from a volcano is usually of this type.

An **annular** drainage pattern is similar to a radial one except that it is made up of concentric rings (**Figure 21.12F**). In this case, the controlling landform is probably a **structural dome**. Such a dome is made up of uplifted beds of rock of varying resistance. When eroded at different rates, these strata control stream flow and direction.

A radial but converging drainage pattern, with streams flowing inward from several directions, indicates the presence of a landform depression (**Figure 21.12G**). This **centripetal** pattern is sometimes seen in well-formed volcanic craters, but it is probably most common in the western United States where former lakes have evaporated under arid conditions, leaving huge depressions.

Throughout this discussion of drainage systems, we've assumed that streams occupy valley positions, but we've made no mention of these valleys' form. It's usually difficult to determine valley form from the stream pattern alone. There is a major exception, however—a **meandering** stream system such as that in **Figure 21.12H**. Such streams give the impression that they are wandering aimlessly, without topographic restriction. The crisscrossed paths taken by the stream at previous times support this observation. Meandering streams occur on plains, on deltas, and in tidal marshes. The greatest topographic relief in the region is frequently the natural levee built up by sediment deposits along the present and past stream banks.

We could go on indefinitely with examples of how environmental information can be deciphered from drainage patterns. Our aim, however, is only to give an idea of how to interpret drainage systems, not to provide complete coverage of the subject. Two more examples, each representing a unique drainage system, will suffice.

First, consider a map of a region in which the hydrography is **interrupted (Figure 21.12I)**. Isolated stream segments, drainage into but not out of lakes, and a roughly dendritic pattern with few small tributary streams all characterize this type of drainage system. The explanation of such an odd pattern, regardless of where it is found, is always the same. Interrupted drainage develops on limestone or dolomite beds through the dissolving action of water on the formation. Consequently, streams can disappear into subterranean caverns, often not re-emerging until they have traveled underground for a considerable distance. The term **sinkhole** or **karst** drainage is sometimes used to describe this unusual stream pattern. Regardless of the name we give them, these streams are frustrating to try to canoe or fish.

The second special drainage system is the **disrupted** pattern illustrated in **Figure 21.12J**. This map shows an area of many swamps and lakes and of streams wandering around with no apparent orientation. In regions with this type of drainage, the water looks lost—as if it is having trouble finding its way to the nearest ocean. And that is exactly the problem. Inevitably, a disrupted drainage pattern signals a stream system which is relatively new, speaking in terms of geological time. The water hasn't yet had time to adjust itself to the topography and carve out a path toward the sea. Such patterns are usually formed with the retreat of continental glaciers. Thus, much of the northcentral and northeastern United States exhibits this type of drainage pattern.

BIOSPHERE

The examples we have given so far have demonstrated the interdependence of the landform, the atmosphere, and the hydrosphere. The biological realm further exemplifies the relationship of different aspects of the physical environment to one another. Plants and animals have evolved in close association with their inorganic surroundings, as well as with each other. Specialization and adaptation to different physical settings are pronounced. In both the plant and animal communities, there is a great range in size and form. At one extreme are whales and redwoods, at the other countless varieties of invisible microorganisms.

Because of their high degree of environmental sensitivity, both plants and animals provide powerful clues for interpreting the physical setting from maps. Plant types reflect soil moisture conditions. Animal populations suggest nearby water sources. The vigor of plants and animals reflect mineral nutrients in soil and water. Climate conditions are indicated by the existence of certain species of plants and animals. Thus, understanding the workings of the biosphere is a major step toward becoming a skilled map interpreter.

Not only has the biosphere emerged in close association with the surrounding physical environment, but it has altered other physical realms as well. The **atmosphere** is changed by plants taking in carbon dioxide and giving off oxygen and water vapor through transpiration. Animals, in turn, use oxygen and give off carbon dioxide. Plant cover also has a cooling effect on the ground surface. When these factors are combined, the impact can be substantial. For instance, large-scale irrigation projects may significantly alter the local climate. Likewise, large desert regions may be caused by animals overgrazing the land, stripping away the native vegetation.

The **landform** can also be changed by plant and animal life. The accumulation of a litter of organic matter and the gripping power of plant roots protect the ground surface from natural erosional processes. When the accumulation is large enough, and geologic processes have had time to do their work, the result can be beds of coal, oil pools, and peat bogs. Minerals concentrated in the skeletons of animals can alter the landscape, too. Thick limestone deposits, coral reefs, and beaches made of seashells are all powerful reminders of the impact of animal life on our environment.

Even the **hydrography** is influenced by the biosphere. The effect may be direct, as when beaver build dams on lakes and streams. Or it may be more indirect. For instance, vegetative cover can hold precipitation long enough for it to soak into the ground, preventing rapid runoff. Plant and animal life also keeps the soil porous so that

450

water can percolate through it rather than running off the surface. When runoff is reduced, streams change from erratic flows supported by surface sources to uniform flows supported by ground-water sources.

It is evident, then, that interpreting the biosphere means considering the total physical environment. An example first from the plant and then from the animal community should further demonstrate this fact. These examples stress both direct and indirect effects of the atmosphere on the biosphere. But even when the other spheres aren't mentioned directly, keep in mind that they are influencing and being influenced by the biosphere as well.

Flora

A variety of ecological factors influence vegetation characteristics and distributions. These include climate, topography, soil, plant-animal interaction, and disturbance events (fire, disease, etc.) We will look at examples of several of these influences.

Climatic Influences

The relationship between vegetation and climate couldn't be more direct. In some classifications, vegetation zones are even used to define climatic types. All plant life depends on two things: (1) enough water to meet the plant's immediate needs and to compensate for moisture transpired in the form of water vapor, and (2) a temperature range which favors cell reproduction and growth.

These two factors—precipitation and temperature—are interdependent. The higher the temperature, the greater the potential for evaporation of soil moisture and transpiration of plant fluids. Higher temperatures diminish the effectiveness of precipitation. Wind speeds up the processes of evaporation and transpiration, while high humidity reduces them. What all this means is that precipitation alone isn't always a good index of the type of vegetation that will be found in a region.

The most prominent vegetation zones occur with latitude. Temperature decreases as latitude increases, causing the lush, dense vegetation of the tropics to give way step by step to the stunted, slow-growing vegetation of the arctic region. Between these extremes lies a variety of vegetative associations which are fairly easy for a trained eye to recognize (**Figure 21.13A**). The serious map interpreter will have to make reference to textbooks on forestry, systematic botany, and biogeography to gain a full appreciation of these vegetative associations.

As Figure 21.13A shows, the systematic north-south latitude zonation of vegetation is disrupted in the mountainous regions of the United States. This is because of the progressive cooling which occurs as altitude increases. The effect is the same as with the cooling at higher latitudes. Thus, a vertical stratification of life zones in high mountains may be roughly equivalent to latitude zonations.

An example of these altitudinal life zones for the southwestern United States is shown in **Figure 21.13B**. These southwestern mountains can be quite dramatic on a map, for they show up as lush vegetative islands in a sea of surrounding sagebrush.

Slope Orientation Effects

Altitude zonation is only one aspect of the pattern of vegetation in mountainous regions. In a region of hills, it isn't uncommon to find one slope heavily forested and the next grass-covered. The area may actually take on a striped appearance when seen from a vertical vantage point (**Figure 21.14A**). These stripes will usually be oriented in an east-west direction.

How do we explain this alternate banding of grass and forest? Winds, bedrock, and soils can all influence vegetation, but none of these is likely to produce such a consistent east-west orientation to the bands of trees and grass. There is another possibility, however—the sun. Since the sun is located south of the United States, its rays strike the ground at steeper angles on southern than on northern slopes. The topographic profile in **Figure 21.14B** demonstrates why this is so. The greater the sun angle, the less the sun's energy is spread over the ground.

These differences in solar energy can easily lead to significant local, or **micro**, climatic variations. Greater solar energy on southern slopes leads to increased potential for evaporation and transpiration. The effect is to make south slopes drier than north slopes. Since grass is more tolerant than trees to dry environments, south slopes support grassland rather than forest cover. The

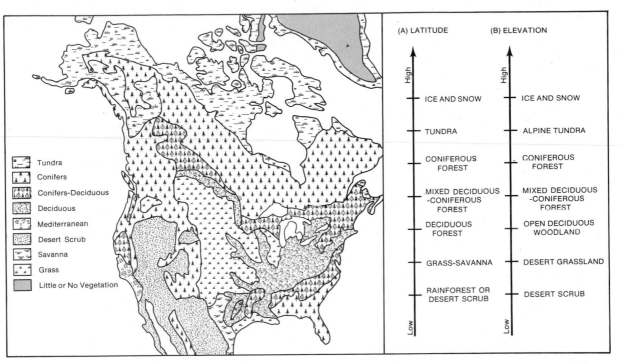

21.13 General vegetative regions in the United States are determined primarily by topographic and latitudinal controls. Regions depicted on this small-scale map are highly generalized.

less the annual precipitation and the higher the temperatures in a region, the more pronounced the effect of slope orientation is likely to be.

Fauna

Most animals feed directly on plants or on plant-eating animals. Thus, maps of plants and animals are closely related. One can rarely be interpreted properly without reference to the other.

Spatially, the primary difference between plants and animals is their mobility. Plants move about primarily through their offspring: Wind, water, and animals carry seeds to distant places. Otherwise, plants are fairly well rooted in space.* For this reason, plants make good map subjects. They are likely to be found where maps show them to be. (We're speaking here in the collective rather than the individual sense, however. Maps of individual plants are rarely made, with the exception of large-scale landscape models.)

Exceptions must be made, of course, for such vegetative features as plankton floating in the ocean currents.

21.14 In many regions, north slope vegetation is much lusher than that found on south-facing slopes.

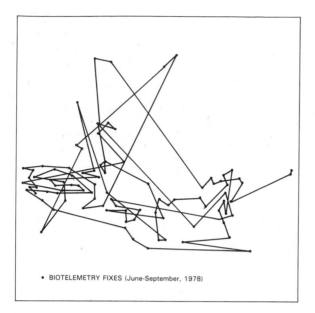

21.15 Time composite plot of the movements of a cow elk which was tagged with a radio transmitter.

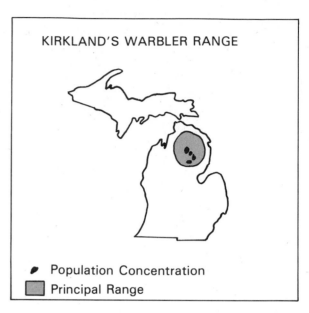

21.16 Range map of Kirkland's warbler, taken from L.M. Sommers, ed., _Atlas of Michigan_ (Lansing: Michigan State University Press, 1977).

In contrast, animals are highly mobile. Most have a diurnal pattern of movement, and many also exhibit a seasonal migration pattern. In the extreme case of some mammals (whales), birds (ducks), fish (salmon), and reptiles (turtles), the annual migration cycle may span several thousand miles.

Animal mobility raises problems for the map maker and map interpreter alike. Maps of animal populations usually have a strong temporal bias. This is easily demonstrated by studying three standard types of animal maps.

Individual Animal Maps

The first type of map we will consider shows the movement of an individual animal (**Figure 21.15**). Increasing use of radio telemetry by wildlife researchers in animal tracking studies has made such maps rather common.* Movements of individual whales, turtles, birds, and elk have been

In telemetry research, an animal is captured and fitted with a radio transmitter. After the animal is released, the radio signals can be used by a researcher equipped with an appropriate radio receiver to plot the animal's movements. It is assumed, of course, that the animal's routine hasn't been affected by the whole process.

made visible by plotting telemetry data over a base map.

This type of map is difficult to interpret, however. Part of the problem is the loss of environmental context due to cartographic abstraction. In the case of Figure 21.15, we may gain useful insights by comparing the elk's movements with landforms, vegetation, water sources, roads, and other features found on maps. But functionally more meaningful may be factors which don't appear on typical maps, such as seasonal availability of food supplies, changing weather conditions, predators, human disturbances, and the presence of other members of the same species.

Thus, this type of map may have little but historical validity for times other than when it was made. You might say that such maps risk being too time-specific to be generally useful. Furthermore, we have no idea how representative the monitored animal was of species behavior in general at the time. We also can't be certain that the behavior of the animal carrying the radio transmitter wasn't affected by the research process itself.

Species Range Maps

Considering the problems associated with mapping individual animal movements, it may seem logical that the mapping of species would be more useful. But even these highly generalized maps of animal populations may bear little resemblance to present reality. The species range map is a good example (**Figure 21.16**). Range is defined as the region inhabited at some time by a species. When we translate this concept into map symbols, we draw a boundary to segment space into range and non-range. Presumably, we'll find a species on one side of that boundary and not the other.

Since species range has an areal dimension, we need to interpret the range's location, size, shape, and orientation. If we use the range of Kirkland's warbler as our example (see Figure 21.16), we find that less than 500 breeding pairs occupy the entire area. Furthermore, species densities within the range vary markedly. Thus, if we randomly checked a dozen sites within the range boundary, we probably wouldn't see the target species.

This is understandable given the abstract nature of the species range concept. The range boundary was generalized from a scattering of past sighting locations and is somewhat biased toward regions of high accessibility and visibility. The species range was probably changing (most likely contracting) during the time that sightings were gathered. Thus, there is a historical lag or friction factor built into the location of the range boundary.

In addition, we need to consider many of the same factors as when interpreting individual animal maps. Studies pinpoint several factors affecting the number of birds and the shape and location of the range. These factors include: the availability of young jack pine from five to 15 feet in height, human disturbance, and the presence of parasite cowbirds (which lay their eggs in warbler nests). There is far more to it than that, of course. The Kirkland warbler is a migratory species, yet the map depicts only the summer (breeding) range. Little is known about its migration route, but it is believed to winter in the Bahamas. Conditions along the migration route and on the wintering grounds may be critical to the species' distribution. We would need a map of the annual range to fully grasp the spatial dynamics of the bird's life cycle.

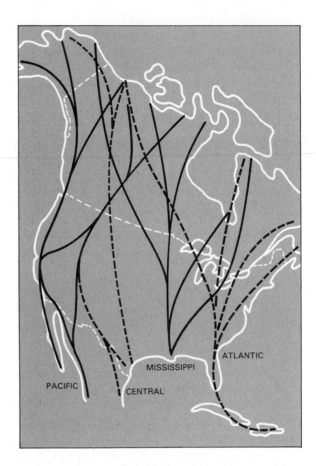

21.17 The routes taken by migratory birds in North America have been classed into four flyways: Atlantic, Mississippi, Central, and Pacific. A host of environmental factors contribute to these general patterns.

Migratory Route Maps

Migratory route mapping further illustrates the unique character of fauna maps. Consider the map of migratory bird flyways in **Figure 21.17**. After millions of observations, scientists concluded that migration routes could be generalized into four paths. These have been labeled the Atlantic, Mississippi, Central, and Pacific flyways. The migration route taken by an individual bird can be classified by one of these labels.

Clearly, we are dealing here with a highly conceptualized map. At this level of abstraction, it is the general pattern, not the route of an individual bird, which is relevant. The map indicates that flyway boundaries are only vaguely defined, with a great deal of interaction occurring among the separate flyways. This interaction is most pronounced on the northern breeding grounds. From

454

about latitude 45° southward, the flyways become much more distinct. The spatial complexity of the flyways also tends to decrease from east to west.

Why do we have this flyway pattern? Its north-south character undoubtedly reflects a seasonal adjustment to food supplies and weather conditions. The individual migration routes further represent adjustments to such environmental factors as the landform configuration, suitable resting sites, and prevailing winds. On a species by species basis, limiting factors such as parasites, disease, and predators also help explain why some locations are chosen over others for breeding and wintering.

CONCLUSION

As we have seen, effective map interpretation requires that we draw heavily on our own knowledge and experience. This may not be easy, for the complexity and detail of the physical environment are boundless. Although some relationships may be rather obvious, or at least susceptible to logic and reasoning, others take a trained eye to decipher—or even to detect. Consequently, a formal environmental science education is basic to interpreting maps of the physical environment. Each discipline mastered permits you to glean more information from even your favorite old aerial photograph or topographic map.

In map interpretation, we aren't interested only in the physical environment, of course. Even more important is the fact that the physical setting provides us with a diversified home. People have modified and adapted to this environment in countless ways. Indeed, evidence of human engineering rather than physical features dominates the surroundings of the many people living in urban areas. Thus, we must also learn to find explanations for the patterns which dominate this humanized world. This brings us, in the next chapter, to a discussion of ways to interpret the human environment.

SELECTED READINGS

Blair, C.L., and Gutsell, B.V., *The American Landscape: Map and Air Photo Interpretation* (New York: McGraw-Hill Book Co., 1974).

Broecker, W.S., "The Ocean," *Scientific American,* 249, 3 (September 1983), pp. 146-160.

Burchfiel, B.C., "The Continental Crust," *Scientific American,* 249, 3 (September 1983), pp. 130-142.

Cloud, P., "The Biosphere," *Scientific American,* 249, 3 (September 1983), pp. 176-189.

DeBruin, R., *100 Topographic Maps Illustrating Physiographic Features* (Northbrook, IL: Hubbard Press, 1970).

Dury, G.H., *Map Interpretation,* 4th ed. (London: Pitman & Sons, Ltd., 1972).

Furley, P.A., and Newey, W.W., *Geography of the Biosphere* (London: Butterworths, 1983).

Gersmehl, P.J., "Maps in Landscape Interpretation," *Cartographica,* Monograph 271, 18, 2 (Summer, 1981), pp. 79-114.

Goudie, A., *The Nature of the Environment,* 3rd ed. (Boston, MA: Blackwell Publishers, 1993).

Gregory, K.J., ed., *Earth's Natural Forces* (New York: Oxford University Press, 1992).

Ingersoll, A.P., "The Atmosphere," *Scientific American,* 249, 3 (September 1983), pp. 162-174.

Lisle, R.J., *Geological Structures & Maps* (New York: Pergamon Press, 1988).

Lobeck, A.K., *Things Maps Don't Tell Us: An Adventure Into Map Interpretation* (New York: Macmillan Publishing Co., 1956).

MacMahan, H., *Stereogram Book of Contours* (Northbrook, IL: Hubbard Press, 1972).

Manning, R., *Grassland: The History, Biology, Politics, and Promise of the American Prairie* (New York: Penguin Putman Inc., 1997).

Miller, V.C., and Westerback, M.E., *Interpretation of Topographic Maps* (Columbus, OH: Merrill Publishing Co., 1989).

Murphy, J.B., and Nance, R.D., "Mountain Belts and the Supercontinent Cycle," *Scientific American,* 266, 4 (April 1992), pp. 84-91.

Scott, R.C., *Essentials of Physical Geography* (St. Paul, MN: West Publishing Co., 1991).

Shelton, J.S., *Geology Illustrated* (San Francisco: W.H. Freeman & Co., 1966).

Siever, R., "The Dynamic Earth," *Scientific American,* 249, 3 (September 1983), pp. 46-53.

Strandberg, C.H., *Aerial Discovery Manual* (New York: John Wiley & Sons, 1967).

Sullivan, W., *Landprints: On the Magnificent American Landscape* (New York: The N.Y. Times Book Co., Inc., 1984).

Wanless, H.R., *Aerial Stereo Photographs* (Northbrook, IL: Hubbard Press, 1973).

Wilson, J.T., "Continental Drift," in *Scientific American Science in the 20th Century,* Special Issue, 3, 1 (1991), pp. 114-129.

Wood, E.A., *Science From Your Airplane Window,* 2nd ed. (New York: Dover Publications, 1975).

CHAPTER TWENTY-TWO

INTERPRETING THE HUMAN ENVIRONMENT

INTRODUCTION

HUMAN FORCES

Administrative Factors
Technological Factors
Cultural Factors
Economic Factors

HUMAN FEATURES

Institutions
    Census Districts
    Land Tenure Systems
    Zoning Policy
    Incentives
Work
    Producing Goods
        Agricultural Fields
        Manufacturing Plants
    Providing Services
Shelter
    Urban-Rural Fringe
    Ethnic Neighborhoods
Transportation and Communication
    Road Form
    Street Network
Recreation
    Sports Facility
    Urban Park

SELECTED READINGS

22

CHAPTER TWENTY-TWO

INTERPRETING THE HUMAN ENVIRONMENT

Although the physical environment sets the stage for human activity, we spend most of our lives in an environment of our own making. This human landscape is intimately entwined with the physical realms, yet it remains mostly the product of the human mind and hand.

To interpret map patterns, we must often search for clues in the human realms. Yet much of the needed information may not be expressed directly on the map. The logic underlying decisions made by politicians and other administrators is often better explained by psychologists, sociologists, and historians than by environmental scientists such as geographers. The role of environmental perception in influencing spatial behavior is crucial. Thus, map interpretation of human features, which must be based on other human variables, is usually difficult. The task is further complicated by the fact that the social and cultural mechanisms underlying human organization and communication aren't well understood.

Because of our lack of knowledge in this area, human factors are probably responsible for more patterns than we realize. To become effective in recognizing these features, we'll have to discipline ourselves rigorously in interpreting the human environment from maps. One way to do so is to isolate forces that underlie human activity and see how they have contributed to the pattern of human occupance on the landscape.

HUMAN FORCES

When we examined the physical environment in Chapter 21, we looked first at the forces that molded the environment. We can apply the same strategy to our human surroundings. In doing so, we can classify human activity into four broad realms: administrative, technological, cultural, and economic (**Figure 22.1**). After introducing these human forces, we'll discuss several examples of human features that reflect adjustment to each force.

22.1 The human landscape is molded by a mix of technological, cultural, economic, and administrative forces.

Administrative Factors

The complex workings of human societies require structure at all levels. Indeed, that is the essence of civilization. Since the job of managing falls on the governmental sector, it is understandable that bureaucratic and administrative factors will strongly affect the character of the human landscape. Later in this chapter (see *Institutions*), we'll consider map interpretation examples of census district, land tenure, zoning, and incentive programs. In each case, we'll discover that administrative factors are the core force behind these mapped patterns.

Technological Factors

The design of tools and machines is in part a matter of function and in part a matter of human imagination and aesthetics. Our technological inventions leave a unique imprint on the pattern of human activity viewed on a map. Furthermore, this imprint changes almost as readily as technology itself. We can tell a great deal about a society's technological development by interpreting a map of its human landscape (see **Box 22.1**). Later in this chapter (see *Work* and *Transportation and Communication*), we'll use examples of agricultural fields, manufacturing plants, and road forms to demonstrate the environmental impact of technological forces.

Cultural Factors

Administrative and technological factors are primarily responsible for many human landscape characteristics. But these factors alone are insufficient to explain the pattern of human activity, because they don't account for the variety of social and cultural forces which guide our lives. Attitudes, values, aesthetics, styles, heritage, and wealth are just a few of the many cultural factors which influence our work and leisure activities. These factors are expressed in such diverse human features as the geometry of street grids and the segmentation of a city into ethnic neighborhoods. We'll examine these features later in this chapter (see *Shelter* and *Transportation and Communication*).

Economic Factors

Accountants like to point out that, in general, all human activity is governed by economic viability. There are exceptions, of course, since we make errors in judgment, attach nonmonetary value to things, and forego economic considerations altogether if entertainment is our goal. But it is probably fair to say that our environmental behavior reflects at least the perception of economic prudence. It is natural, then, that the character of the human landscape will represent adjustments to these economic factors. We'll explore these adjustments in more detail through the example of urban-rural fringe later in this chapter (see *Shelter*).

HUMAN FEATURES

The administrative, technological, cultural, and economic forces we've discussed influence the form in which human features appear in the landscape. We can classify human features in terms of the human needs that create them. Thus, human features emerge in response to our need for (1) institutions, (2) work, (3) shelter, (4) transportation and communication, and (5) recreation. Let's look at each of these feature types and the forces that helped mold them. These few examples are only intended to provide ideas on how a skilled map interpreter might proceed. Countless other traces of human behavior on the landscape would be equally instructive.

BOX 22.1 TECHNOLOGY SPURS AGRICULTURE

When humans first walked on this globe we were **gatherers**. A nomadic way of life was necessary to acquire an adequate food supply.

Probably by accident, we discovered that buried seeds and nuts sprouted and grew into plants that bore fruit. **Farming** began. We became shepherds as animals were domesticated. Herds and flocks were maintained beside our plants.

Humankind began to change and improve that which we grew. We grafted one plant to another. We kept seeds from the best plants and offspring from the finest animals. Without realizing it, we changed the gene pool to improve our quality of life.

In the 1850s Gregor Mendel carefully collected and dusted pollens of his garden peas and discovered he could change the color of blossoms, the location of fruit and the quality of a plant. Dominant and recessive genes were discovered—as was **hybridization**. Mendel's research was put into agricultural practice with the commercialization of hybrid seed corn in the early 1900s.

Through selective farming, special varieties were developed. Here in Wisconsin a single cabbage plant survived in a field. A university professor dug it up, nurtured it, and we had a cabbage resistant to root rot. A gene was being "farmed," but no one called it that.

Through the discovery of DNA and RNA the concept of moving genes from one species to another became a reality. Today **"farmed" genes** are commonplace and dozens of plant species have been patented.

Some plants now have resistance to specific pesticides, others grow a virus to destroy certain insects when they feed, and others have new or more genes to allow the plant to resist disease or stress.

Transgenic animals provide vaccines, and mediums for testing research to cure both human and animal problems.

From artificial insemination to super ovulation and embryo transplants we are moving beyond hybrid livestock to **cloning**.

Just as the caveman buried a nut, today we can plant a specific gene into bacteria, and harvest a specific new crop.

With this concept, we've been able to grow human insulin, develop a vaccine for hoof and mouth disease, and produce proteins and hormones to solve human problems and improve animal productivity.

This is a new kind of farming, not with a wooden stick or a 30-foot chisel plow behind a diesel tractor—but it is farming! It is **planting, nurturing, growing and harvesting**. It is using our God-given talents and skills to improve our way of life for an ever-increasing human population.

A few decades from now, the wondrous and awesome genetic engineering concepts which we are beginning today will be as common as a flat of identical petunias. But it is also safe to predict that new biological concepts only dreamed of today will create potential dilemmas for our grandchildren.

While we certainly must have legal safeguards on biological sciences, we can't afford artificial political barriers based on emotional rhetoric.

(Russel Weisensel, director, Wisconsin Agri-Business Council, from Jan. 22, 1990, *Wisconsin State Journal,* emphasis added)

Institutions

People have created a variety of institutions to protect, guide, and nurture their spatial behavior. Many of our buildings serve our desire for education, police, military, health, religion, finance, planning, judicial, and other services. Governmental organization, taxation, and regulation contribute still more structures to the environment.

But it is the **policies** established by these institutions, not the structures themselves, that have the greatest impact on the human landscape. To gain more insight into this administrative impact, we'll discuss examples of census districting, land tenure, zoning, and government incentive programs.

Census Districts

One example of how institutional policies influence mapped patterns is the way that census information is gathered and represented. The shape, size, and configuration of political units can have a particularly strong influence on the appearance of thematic maps. In the United States, for instance, a large amount of information is reported by county (**Figure 22.2**). These political regions create problems in map interpretation, because geographical distributions are masked by the way information has been collected.

Consider again the cancer mortality maps we discussed in the *Introduction* (see Figure I.9). While the maps give a general regional impression, explanatory factors have been disguised by the fact that information was pooled by county before mapping. To interpret the pattern of cancer deaths portrayed by these maps, we need to look within the counties themselves. Whatever is responsible for the deaths is likely to be a detached factor—something as isolated as a single factory emitting pollution, perhaps—rather than a county-wide phenomenon.

To find explanations for cancer deaths, therefore, we might want to look at such factors as industrial plants, the eating habits of specific ethnic groups, or municipal water pollution. Take St. Louis County in Minnesota as an example (**Figure 22.3**). The explanation for the high cancer rate here can probably be found in only a small portion of the county. The city of Duluth and the northern iron mining towns might be good places to start searching for causes.

459

PART III
*Map
Interpretation*

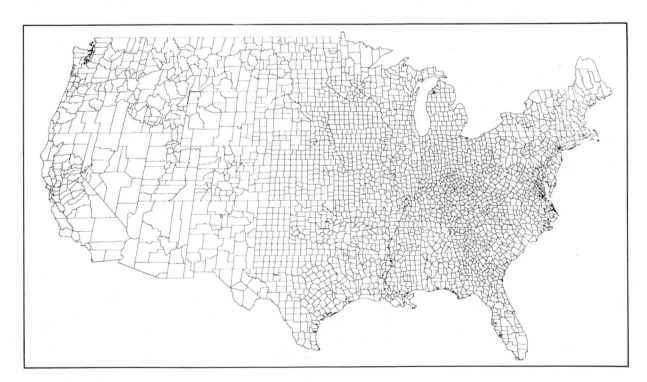

22.2 Much census-type information is collected by county political unit in the United States. Maps based on these data will directly or indirectly reflect this pattern of counties.

460

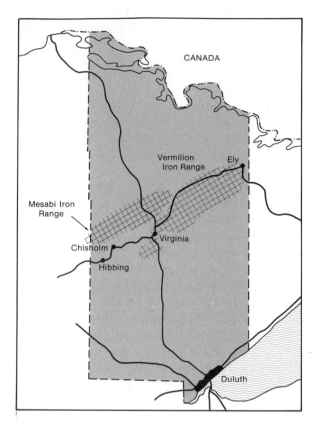

22.3 Data aggregated by political unit will mask variation that occurs within the region (St. Louis County, Minnesota).

Land Tenure Systems

Human habitation patterns are often best explained by the land ownership policy used when the land was settled. The correspondence between the two is greatest in relatively flat regions, of course. But the system of land ownership can greatly influence human settlement patterns regardless of the natural setting. Therefore, it isn't uncommon to find two or more contrasting patterns of settlement adjacent to one another even in regions of quite homogeneous topography (see **Box 22.2**).

The most widespread land ownership system in the United States is the U.S. Public Land Survey (USPLS). According to this system (as we saw in Chapter 11), land was partitioned into fairly well-surveyed squares prior to European settlement. Thus, in the vast regions in which the USPLS was used, you will find that the roads, fields, and political boundaries all reflect the character of this square grid system. Roads follow the

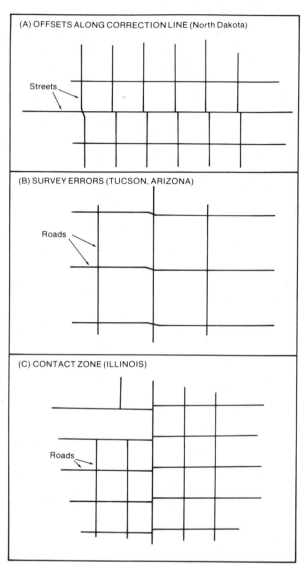

22.4 Artifacts of the USPLS land partitioning system are often exposed in maps of the human environment.

section lines; buildings are close to the roads; and woodlots are located at the center of the sections (as far as possible from the wood-burning stoves in the farmhouses).

Even special characteristics of the USPLS can be seen in the pattern of cultural features. For instance, we saw in Chapter 11 that USPLS surveyors compensated for earth curvature by readjusting the southern boundary of every fifth township. This offsetting of lines is often strikingly apparent in sudden, seemingly meaningless jogs in the road (**Figure 22.4A**).

BOX 22.2 IF YOUR HEAD IS IN THE CLOUDS AND YOUR EYES ON THE GROUND

A flight across the United States looks like nothing so much as a giant geometry lesson. There are rectangles, circles and spirals everywhere you turn.

In *Taking Measures Across the American Landscape* (Yale, 1996), a book of aerial photographs by Alex S. MacLean and landscape analysis by James Corner, it's obvious that America makes much more sense from the air (which is the way many travelers see it) than from the ground. And there's a good reason why that's so.

Early European settlers molded the landscape around the belief that Platonic geometrical forms had divine properties. They treated the American land like a piece of giant graph paper, Denis Cosgrove, a British geographer, writes, transferring their maps "from parchment or paper to the ground itself."

There is legislation lurking behind most of America's large geometrical features. The big squares all over the Midwest date back to the Land Ordinance Act of 1785, which divided the land west of the Alleghenies into 36-square-mile townships, and then subdivided those into one-square-mile plots, regardless of topography.

After the Homestead Act of 1862, farmhouses came to be spaced at regular intervals in the grid and each one was protected by a rectangular woodlot. It was the perfectly geometric, perfectly democratic, perfectly isolationist solution to land settlement. This pattern isn't evident from the ground, but it becomes apparent from the air.

In fact, the land was laid out in such strict linear patterns and over so great a territory that corrections had to be made for the curvature of the earth. American legislators altered the grid—periodically making a tiny jog in the straight line between plots—so the grid could catch up with the curved lines of latitude and longitude. Every four townships, or every 24 miles, there would be a "slippage," a dogleg in the road.

And what about those circular fields in the West? Sometimes as vast as a mile in diameter, these circles were created with the aid of survey instruments, and today they are kept in shape by long-armed sprinklers or centrally located wells that pump water up from aquifers below. Because the water comes from a central point, the perfect green circle is maintained, much the way the pencil of a compass traces a circle around its central needle.

Of course, geometry hasn't overwhelmed geography completely. You know those wavy, meandering lines that snake through the rectangles? Those are called rivers.

(Sarah Boxer, *The New York Times*, August 31, 1997)

Survey errors may also be glaringly obvious in the road pattern (**Figure 22.4B**). An even more confusing break in the settlement pattern occurs along lines at which adjacent grid systems come together (**Figure 22.4C**). What happened in this case was that surveyors starting from different points simply weren't able to make their lines meet where they were supposed to.

Although the pattern of the USPLS dominates the United States, other land ownership systems have also exerted a strong influence on the look of the American landscape. The irregular patchwork pattern of the "metes and bounds" system is especially prominent in the eastern and southwestern states because these regions were settled prior to the USPLS (see Figures 11.15A and

462

11.15B in Chapter 11). The regular "long lot" system can be seen in the scattered locations of French settlement (see Figure 11.15C). The characteristic form of land division produced by each of these systems is difficult to miss, particularly on an image map. In each case, the pattern is explained by historical rather than natural factors.

One of the most intriguing stories told by the pattern of land ownership comes from the Black Hills of South Dakota. This region falls well within the part of the country controlled by the USPLS and was settled by Europeans long after the USPLS was in effect. Then why is the Black Hills region segmented by the unsystematic metes and bounds system as well as the systematic USPLS (**Figure 22.5**)?

For an explanation of this apparent paradox, we must consider historical factors. The Black Hills area was originally set aside as an Indian reserve. Once gold was discovered there, however, there was no stopping the stampede of white settlers into the region. Mining claims were established, and supporting towns, farms, and ranches sprang up according to the common metes and bounds system. Years later, the land was systematically surveyed by the USPLS, but the scattered mining towns, with their unsystematic settlement, remained as they were. Today the two systems coexist in a jumble of land parcels confusing enough to frustrate the most skilled map user. Here again, human rather than physical forces provide the key explanation of the habitation pattern.

Zoning Policy

A third way institutional policies affect the pattern of human habitation is zoning policy. Human activity in an organized society is generally structured by laws designed to ensure a sensible land use pattern. The common aim is to optimize the long-term good for the greatest number of people while minimizing damage to the physical environment. Often these goals are contradictory, of course; thus, a compromise is sought. Depending on your point of view, you might feel that people usually come out ahead in this conflict or that the

(A) LAND USE/COVER MAP

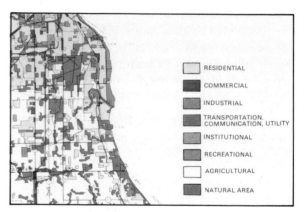

RESIDENTIAL
COMMERCIAL
INDUSTRIAL
TRANSPORTATION, COMMUNICATION, UTILITY
INSTITUTIONAL
RECREATIONAL
AGRICULTURAL
NATURAL AREA

(B) ZONING MAP

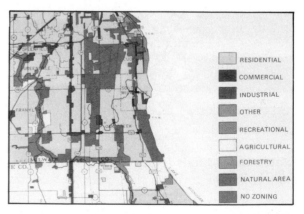

RESIDENTIAL
COMMERCIAL
INDUSTRIAL
OTHER
RECREATIONAL
AGRICULTURAL
FORESTRY
NATURAL AREA
NO ZONING

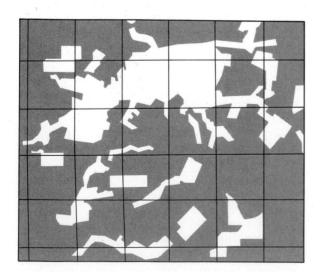

22.5 The post-USPLS metes and bounds pattern of land ownership in the Black Hills of South Dakota begs for explanation.

22.6 The spatial mix of residential, recreational, industrial, commercial, and agricultural land uses (A) reflects zoning policies designed to keep human activities in their desired place (B).

physical environment usually wins. In truth, people and their physical surroundings win or lose this struggle together, since ultimately there is only one environment.

As a map interpretation problem, consider the land use map in **Figure 22.6A**. The spatial mix of residential, industrial, commercial, recreational, and agricultural land uses defies interpretation if we consider physical factors alone. The geometric pattern of land uses and the abrupt breaks from one land use class to another seem to implicate human factors as strong influences.

If a zoning map (**Figure 22.6B**) is brought into the picture, the explanation for the land use pattern becomes much clearer. Admittedly, zoning policy reflects a concern for various aspects of the physical setting. But it is also sensitive to human needs, including food production, shopping, journey to work, recreation, clean air and drinking water, and high-quality residential areas. Planners do the best they can under difficult conditions to zone for land uses which will serve all these often-conflicting needs. Explaining the reasoning behind individual zoning decisions is a challenge for even the most adept map interpreter.

Incentives

With growing frequency, government is influencing the structure of the human landscape through incentive programs. Consider, for example, the incentives that were used by state governors to woo General Motors Corporation to locate its new Saturn auto manufacturing plant in their state. These incentives included tax breaks, low-interest loans, buildings, transportation facilities, land, state-sponsored training, and a host of other enticing "perks."

Thus, the Saturn plant's eventual location in Tennessee reflects administrative factors as much as market considerations and sources of raw materials. When this scenario is multiplied countless times, the resulting pattern of manufacturing facilities may be impossible to interpret from the map unless we consider the influence of administrative controls.

Work

Most adults spend roughly a third of their life working. Clearly, then, a large proportion of human features on the landscape will be related to employment. In looking at work-related map features, we find that economic and technological forces have the strongest impact. But cultural attitudes and governmental regulations can also affect the environment of employment.

There are two types of work-related map features, those related to producing goods and those related to providing services. The landscape imprint varies markedly between the two. Let's look first at employment that involves producing goods.

Producing Goods

Some goods-producing industries focus on harvesting and extracting natural resources. These industries include fishing, logging, and mineral extraction. Agriculture and grazing represent modified versions of these resource-related activities. Other industries are associated with processing these raw materials. Examples are canning, smelting, and refining. Still other industries are involved in manufacturing and assembling finished products. Work in all these production industries tends to have a major impact on the landscape. Signs of many such activities are visible from satellites orbiting 500 miles above the earth. We'll consider examples from agriculture and manufacturing.

Agricultural Fields. Earlier in this chapter, under the heading *Land Tenure Systems*, we saw how the pattern of land ownership influences a host of human activities. Sometimes, however, what at first glance seems to result from land parceling by the government actually reflects technological rather than governmental factors.

Consider **Figure 22.7**, for example. The prominent feature in this satellite image map is a circular field pattern. Is this unique pattern the result of some deviant system of circular land division? If we weren't careful, we might be tempted to think so. In reality, however, it indicates a rotating central-pivot sprinkler system used by farmers to irrigate their fields (**Figure 22.8**). As this example demonstrates, the pattern of human activity viewed on a map may be influenced as strongly by our tools and equipment as by our governmental structures.

Ultimately, the circular field pattern has to be more economical than some other form, or the products produced by this agricultural practice

464

22.7 A circular field pattern is one of the most prominent features on many satellite image maps of dry farmlands in the United States.

wouldn't be competitive in the marketplace. Thus, economic forces are at play here, too. If this competitiveness is achieved through some kind of government subsidy or incentive program, of course, then administrative forces are also operating.

Manufacturing Plants. The location of manufacturing plants also represents the strong influence of technological factors on the character of the human landscape. Changing technology in many industries has made it more economical to produce with large facilities than with small ones. Advances in transportation and electronic communication have further enhanced this trend. One result is that the density and distribution of manufacturing plants have in many cases adjusted to changing technological forces over the years.

Let's look at cheese factories as an example. **Figure 22.9** shows their changing distribution in southwestern Wisconsin over the past 80 years. The most obvious characteristic of this

22.8 Central-pivot irrigation systems are in widespread use in areas where precipitation isn't sufficient during the growing season.

22.9 The changing distribution of cheese factories in southwestern Wisconsin reflects an adjustment to such technological factors as transportation, refrigeration, and the economies associated with automated milk processing equipment.

changing pattern is its decreasing density. This centralization of facilities can be attributed to a number of factors, including farm electrification; milk refrigeration; improved roads; larger, faster, refrigerated trucks; and large, automated processing facilities. If we compared a series of maps representing conditions throughout the time span shown in Figure 22.9, many of these factors would be evident. We would still have to bring supplementary information to the map interpretation task, of course.

Providing Services

In a modern industrial society, a large proportion of people work in service industries. These include a variety of wholesale, retail, distribution, communication, and marketing enterprises. They also encompass education, social services, banking, advertising, finance, and health care.

Structures associated with the service industry tend to be modest compared to goods-producing industries. The reason is that service-related businesses are more decentralized. They are serving people after all; thus, they tend to locate close to their clients. There are exceptions, of course. These are particularly evident in cen-

tral city high-rise structures and in industrial parks, filled with home offices showcasing the wealth of large corporations.

Technological and economic forces are somewhat less important in molding the "service landscape" than they are with production industries. On the other hand, cultural and administrative forces tend to assume a bigger role in creating the pattern of service industries in the environment.

Shelter

Not everyone is working, but most people do live in some sort of shelter. Indeed, of all built features, residential construction probably takes up the greatest portion of the environment. In part this is due to its dispersed nature, but it is also a function of the tremendous number of people living on the earth's surface. The pattern of housing is influenced by the full mix of human forces (administrative, technological, cultural, and economic), as we'll see in examples of the urban-rural fringe and ethnic neighborhoods.

Urban-Rural Fringe

The concentration of population in urban areas is a good illustration of how we adjust our behavior to a variety of factors. In this case, the aesthetic reasons for having a home in the country must be balanced against the convenience of living in the city. What you will generally see on a map, especially if a city is growing rapidly and has a robust economy, is a sharp contrast at the rural-urban fringe (**Figure 22.10**). In part, this contrast is due to economics associated with mass construction. Builders find it most economical to build up an area completely while the necessary equipment and labor are at hand. Isolated building projects are far more costly.

Likewise, utilities can be provided more economically to dense clusters of consumers than to widely scattered sites. A septic system and drilled well may add $10,000 to $20,000 to the cost of a country home, while the urban dweller might receive these services for less than $200 annually. Environmental protection laws may also require that country homes be located on land parcels of at least five acres, in contrast to the 1/3-acre city lot, adding further to the cost of these utilities.

465

PART III
*Map
Interpretation*

466

Services are also more economically provided to consumers living in high density. Fire, ambulance, and police protection services cost more at scattered locations than in urban areas. The same can be said for such services as garbage collection and snow removal.

As a final note, local government commonly bears responsibility and expense in conjunction with providing utilities and services to the governed. For these reasons, government generally tries to control the situation through restrictive zoning, which further accentuates contrasts in the human landscape at the urban-rural fringe.

Ethnic Neighborhoods

A second example of residential activity can be seen in the clustering of individuals of similar ethnic background in city neighborhoods. As **Figure 22.11** illustrates, the stark geometric character of the pattern of these ethnic neighborhoods hints strongly of human rather than physical controls.

Overt government districting or zoning might be suspected as the cause of ethnic concentration in some countries, but not in the United States. If governmental factors are responsible here, they are likely to be expressed in subtle ways. They may show up, for instance, in the

provision of services which encourage concentration and in bureaucratic red tape which discourages movement into other neighborhoods.

Indeed, cultural factors most likely have had the biggest influence on the creation and perpetuation of ethnic neighborhoods in U.S. cities. Cultural forces can encourage movement into and discourage movement out of these ethnic zones. High on the list of positive influences is cultural continuity. New immigrants face less cultural shock by joining people who share their ethnic heritage. Faces, churches, stores, jobs, and language will all be familiar. Community support is also available. It makes for a much easier transition for an immigrant to start life in a new, unfamiliar country by settling first in an ethnic neighborhood.

On the negative side, the behavior of outsiders can discourage people from leaving their socially comfortable neighborhoods. Sometimes there is overt prejudice, as when people refuse to rent or sell housing to others. Or the behavior may take the more subtle form of making people feel uncomfortable socially when out of their neighborhoods.

The reasons that ethnic neighborhoods develop and persist are obviously very complex. But the influencing factors almost always are of

22.10 The fringe of an expanding city commonly looks like a jigsaw puzzle of rural and urban parcels. The abrupt edge of developed land is a consequence of a variety of economic factors.

22.11 The partitioning of this portion of Milwaukee, Wisconsin, into ethnic neighborhoods is a spatial manifestation of a host of social influences on immigrant settlement.

human origin. The map interpreter thus should concentrate on cultural factors when attempting to explain such patterns in the human landscape.

Transportation and Communication

Ideas, goods, and people move along networks of transportation and communication, bonding together the diverse aspects of the human environment. The result is a multicomponent web of wires, rails, roads, and pipes crisscrossing the landscape. Less obvious is a superimposed maze of ship, airline, and telecommunication links. The form, density, and variety of transportation and communication services to and from a location say a great deal about the nature of the human landscape.

Road Form

Roads serve as a good illustration of how technology affects the structure of the human landscape. Although the overall highway network may reflect an adjustment to the physical setting, specific details of the road pattern, such as the degree of curvature at bends and intersections, is based mostly on technological factors.

When hiking and horse-drawn-wagon trails were improved to handle cars, traffic was still slow enough so that sharp turns were acceptable. In today's residential areas, too, traffic is of low enough speed and volume so that roads may be built with sharp (often right-angle) turns. But modern high-volume, high-speed highways are built along more serpentine lines. Whether a road curves sharply or gently, it appears, depends mostly on historical factors, automotive design, and road building technology. This is evident in the fact that many roads are periodically modernized to handle increasing traffic speeds (**Figure 22.12A**). When such modernization has occurred, you can often detect traces of previous roadbeds, especially on an image map.

The angles at which roads converge also suggest technological controls. With slow traffic, right-angle intersections are common. Faster traffic is accommodated by less acute angles of convergence at intersections. This feature reaches its extreme with the modern cloverleaf interchange (**Figure 22.12B**).

The combined effect of road curvature and convergence angles is a fair indication of road sta-

tus. Progressive smoothing of road forms is apparent as we move up the ranking of county, state, federal, and interstate highways. County roads are the most sensitive to the physical geography. At the other extreme, interstate highways are built to rigid federal specifications concerning curvature and grade (slope) and therefore may be imposed

467

PART III
Map Interpretation

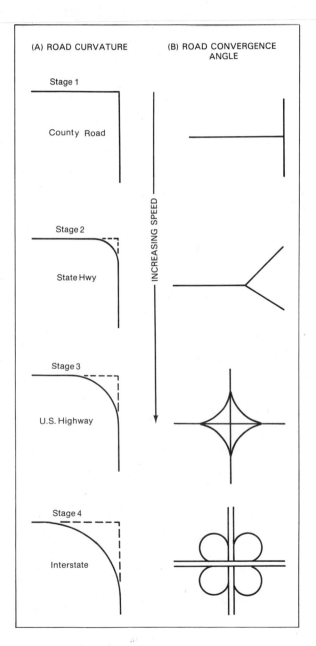

22.12 Road curvature and convergence angles seen on maps are useful clues in determining traffic volume and speed along associated routes.

468

Street Network

If street networks were determined only by the natural landscape, we would expect to find square or rectangular street grids in flat regions and irregular grids in hilly areas. But here is another case in which human factors frequently override physical ones. A square street grid has such a strong cultural tradition in the United States that it isn't always restricted to flat regions.

A classic example of this triumph of geometry over reason can be seen in the city of Houghton, Michigan (**Figure 22.13**). A rectangular street system has been superimposed on a hillside with a 10 to 15 percent slope, despite the resulting inconvenience. Considering what a hairraising experience it is to drive down this hill in snowy weather, "inconvenience" may well be an understatement! Such cities as Houghton underline the point that a rectangular grid cannot be taken as proof of level topography.

At the other extreme, irregular street grids may not reflect an adjustment to the physical environment, either. During European settlement of the United States, streets usually were aligned with features in the natural environment, such as rivers,

lakes, or mountain ranges (**Figure 22.14A**). Then, from shortly after the settlement period until World War II, cities tended to be built on a rectangular grid system with a north-south alignment (**Figure 22.14B**). After the war, there was another substantial change. The suburbanization phenomenon which began at that time, and which continues today, introduced still another pattern of streets. In the new suburbs, the rectangular grid was often replaced by winding streets and cul-de-sacs (**Figure 22.14C**). The break in systems is so abrupt that it is frequently possible to outline the pre-World-War-II city from the growth which followed.

Sometimes you can put this information to use when you arrive in an unfamiliar city. The street pattern on a map may tell you where to look for new homes, historical buildings, slums, hotels, and so on. You can't always be sure, of course, whether human or physical determinants have had the strongest influence. But it is often useful to know that street patterns may be a result of human rather than physical forces.

Recreation

People spend their leisure time in many ways that leave an impression on the landscape. Sometimes people build elaborate recreational facilities. At

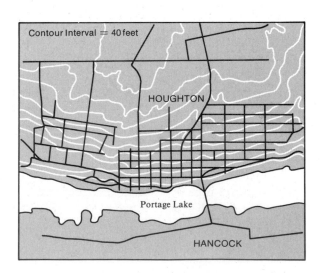

22.13 Rectangular street patterns are not always restricted to flat terrain, as this map of the street pattern in Houghton, Michigan, illustrates.

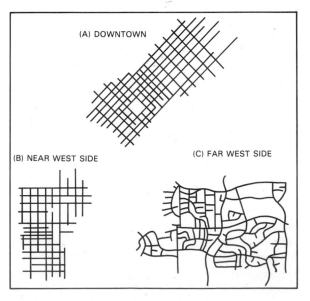

22.14 The changing geometrical character of the street grid in Madison, Wisconsin, documents historical factors in city building.

other times, they merely designate an area as a place for recreation. In both cases, cultural forces are the prime determinant of the form these features take. Let's look at an example of each type of feature.

Sports Facility

Recreational activities are often focused on a structure such as a coliseum, stadium, amusement park, sports arena, racetrack, bowling alley, skating rink, or swimming pool. Many of these structures have characteristic shapes, making them easy to recognize on image maps (**Figure 22.15**).

Sometimes nearby features provide helpful information in determining the function of a recreational facility. A horse or dog racing track, for instance, will have kennels or stables which may show up on an image map.

Also, to be economically feasible, most sports facilities depend on packing visitors in like sardines. Thus, they are usually accompanied by parking lots that are enormous relative to the size of the building itself—another useful clue on an image map.

Other recreational features, such as fairgrounds, amusement parks, golf courses, and dirt-bike courses, exhibit features of various shapes and sizes that give useful hints. With golf courses, for example, the configuration of sand traps, greens, and fairways produces a unique pattern.

As noted earlier, cultural forces are predominant in molding the form of sports facilities. People's ideas concerning aesthetics and leisure at the time these features are built strongly influence their character.

Urban Park

The more diffuse recreational opportunities offered by city parks distinguishes them in the landscape from sports facilities (**Figure 22.16**). Both the location and form of city parks reflect people's attitudes about the need for general recreational areas scattered throughout populated areas. Trees and grass tend to dominate. Usually a distinct pattern of paths or trails is evident, although they appear to go no place in particular. There commonly is evidence of structured activity as well. This may appear in the form of a swimming pool, playground equipment, baseball diamond, or tennis court. Often there will be a fountain or artificial pond.

Notice that both types of recreational features we've discussed are replicated widely through the human landscape. Also note that their location is associated with concentrations of people. The physical setting is not as important as access to potential visitors. We'll return to this subject in the next chapter, in which we'll consider how the physical and human realms influence one another.

22.15 Sports facilities often have a very recognizable shape and are surrounded by large parking lots.

22.16 Urban parks are usually dominated by grass and trees, but also are crisscrossed with paths and dotted with dedicated sports areas.

470

SELECTED READINGS

Archer, J.C., and Shelley, F.M., *American Electoral Mosaic* (Washington, DC: Association of American Geographers, 1986).

Clay, G., *Close-Up: How to Read the American City* (Chicago: The University of Chicago Press, 1980).

Earle, C., Mathewson, K., and Kenzer, M.S., eds., *Concepts in Human Geography* (Lanham, MD: Rowman & Littlefield Publishers, Inc., 1996).

Fisher, J.S., *Geography & World Development*, 5th ed. (Englewood Cliffs, NJ: Prentice-Hall, 1995).

Garreau, J., *The Nine Nations of North America* (New York: Avon Books, 1981).

Hamnett, C., ed., *Social Geography: A Reader* (London: Edward Arnold, 1996).

Hardwick, S.W., and Holtgrieve, D.G., *Patterns on Our Planet* (New York: Macmillan Publishing Co., 1990).

Hart, J.F., *The Look of the Land* (Englewood Cliffs, NJ: Prentice-Hall, 1975).

Hartshorn, T.A., and Alexander, J.W., *Economic Geography*, 3rd ed. (Englewood Cliffs, NJ: Prentice-Hall, 1988).

Heat-Moon, W.L., *PrairyErth* (Boston: Houghton Mifflin Co., 1991).

Heat-Moon, W.L., *Blue Highways: A Journey into America* (Boston: Little Brown and Co., 1982).

Jackson, J.B., *Discovering the Vernacular Landscape* (New Haven: Yale University Press, 1984).

Jackson, R.H., and Hudman, L.E., *Cultural Geography: People, Places and Environment* (St. Paul, MN: West Publishing Co., 1990).

Johnson, H.B., *Order Upon the Land: The U.S. Rectangular Land Survey and the Upper Mississippi Country* (London: Oxford University Press, 1976).

Jordon, T.G., and Rowntree, L., *The Human Mosaic*, 5th ed. (New York: Harper & Row, Publishers, 1990).

Klett, M., et al., *Second View: The Photographic Survey Project* (Albuquerque: University of New Mexico Press, 1984).

Knowles, R., and Stowe, P.W.E., *North America in Maps* (London: Longman Group, Ltd., 1976).

MacLean, A.S., and Corner, J., *Taking Measures Across the American Landscape* (New Haven, CT: Yale University Press, 1996).

Manners, I.R., and Mikesell, M.W., eds., *Perspectives on Environment* (Washington, DC: Association of American Geographers, 1974).

Meining, D.W., *The Interpretation of Ordinary Landscapes: Geographical Essays* (New York: Oxford University Press, 1979).

Raitz, K.B., and Hart, J.F., *Cultural Geography on Topographic Maps* (New York: John Wiley & Sons, 1975).

Richardson, B.F., *Atlas of Cultural Features: A Comparative Study With Topographic Maps and Aerial Photographs of Man's Imprint on the Land* (Northbrook, IL: Hubbard Press, 1973).

Riffel, P.A., *Reading Maps: An Introduction to Maps Using Color Aerial Photography* (Northbrook, IL: Hubbard Press, 1973).

Schlereth, T.J., *Reading the Road: U.S. 40 and the American Landscape* (Knoxville, TN: The University of Tennessee Press, 1997).

Watts, M.T., *Reading the Landscape of America*, revised ed. (New York: Collier Books, 1975).

White, P.T., "This Land of Ours—How Are We Using It?", *The National Geographic Magazine*, 150, 1 (July 1976), pp. 20-67.

CHAPTER TWENTY-THREE

INTERPRETING ENVIRONMENTAL INTERACTIONS

We must allow for the possibility that we can only understand something
truly by knowing its future, its fruits, its consequences.

—Frederick Turner, *A Field Guide to the Synthetic Landscape*

23

CHAPTER TWENTY-THREE

INTERPRETING ENVIRONMENTAL INTERACTIONS

In the previous two chapters, we divided the environment into broad physical and human realms and noted that many features are primarily the result of physical or human forces. The reality, of course, is much more complex. "Pure" examples of physical and human features make up only a small portion of our richly-featured surroundings. Cause-effect interactions between the two realms are the rule. Through our examples of map interpretation in Chapters 21 and 22, we have hinted at the many interactions which occur between the physical and human realms.

In this chapter, we'll view these interactions more directly. We'll focus first on human influences on the physical realm. Then we'll consider physical influences on human activities. Finally, we'll look at the environment as an integrated whole.

INFLUENCE OF HUMAN FACTORS

People are engineers. No place on earth has fully escaped their influence (see **Box 23.1**). Many changes wrought by people are too subtle to be captured by map makers' gross generalizations. But other human factors have had more obvious effects on the form of the natural environment. To simplify our discussion of the human impact on natural features, we've divided the physical environment into five parts—the atmosphere, hydrography, land surface, vegetation, and wildlife—so that we can consider each separately.

BOX 23.1   PEOPLE MAKE A DIFFERENCE

The true wilderness—the great woods and clear rivers, the wild swamps and grassy plains which once were the wonder of the world—has been largely despoiled, and today's voyager, approaching our shores through the oiled waters of the coast, is greeted by smoke and the glint of industry on our fouled seaboard, and an inland prospect of second growth, scarred landscapes, and sterile, often stinking, rivers of pollution and raw mud, the whole bedecked with billboards, neon lights, and other decorative evidence of mankind's triumph over chaos. In many regions the greenwood not converted to black stumps no longer breathes with sound and movement, but is become a cathedral of still trees; the plains are plowed under and the prairies ravaged by overgrazing and the winds of drought.

(Peter Matthiessen, *Wildlife in America*)

Impact on Atmosphere

Human impact on the atmosphere is reflected in shifting, rather elusive map patterns. The impact's extent is influenced by natural atmospheric processes, giving the pattern of human influence an irregular, dynamic character. Sharp breaks are rare; transitions or gradients are the rule. The temperature, composition, and movement of the atmosphere have all been altered by human activity. The evidence is often captured in image maps and can be made apparent through thematic mapping, using sensor data gathered at selected observation sites.

Temperature mapping in the lower atmosphere reveals several effects of human activity. The alternating removal and planting of vegetation in farming causes micro changes in surrounding air temperature. In cities, heat absorption by large-scale constructions built of such material as concrete or asphalt, when combined with heat discharge through the burning of fossil fuels, can create an urban "heat island" several degrees warmer than the surrounding air (**Figure 23.1**). Water bodies of human construction, such as the reservoirs along the Missouri River and the widespread flooding associated with rice farming, can also create local temperature anomalies.

Movement of air can also be altered by human activity, particularly by elevated constructions. Buildings and other obstructions interfere with the natural air flow. Shelterbelts, for example, have been purposefully planted to protect buildings and crops from the effects of wind. A thermal infrared image map will show warmer (lighter) streaks on the lee side of these artificial wind barriers. (See *Thermal Infrared Imaging* in Appendix B for more information about these remotely sensed images.)

Perhaps the most widespread impact of human activity has occurred with respect to the **composition** of the atmosphere. The proportion of gases and suspended particulates has been affected. The level of water vapor, carbon monox-

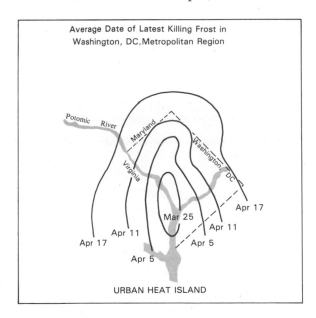

Average Date of Latest Killing Frost in Washington, DC, Metropolitan Region

Potomic River

Maryland

Virginia

Washington, DC

Mar 25

Apr 17

Apr 11

Apr 5

Apr 11

Apr 17

Apr 5

URBAN HEAT ISLAND

23.1 Heat absorption by building materials and heat discharge from the burning of fossil fuels may be sufficient to create an urban "heat island" several degrees warmer than the air temperature in the surrounding region.

474

ide and dioxide, and ozone have all been altered by the burning of fossil fuels in homes, factories, smelters, and automobiles. Suspended particulates have also been increased by the burning of fossil fuels, bomb testing, and ore smelting. Devegetation associated with construction, grazing, and farming further exposes the atmosphere to wind-blown particulates.

To appreciate how we can affect the atmosphere when it seems so immense relative to the scale of human activities, it may help to study **Figure 23.2**. This diagram shows the extent of the atmosphere compared to earth curvature, as seen from the vantage point of a space shuttle orbiting the earth at 150 miles altitude. If the layer doesn't look very thick relative to the size of the earth, you are right. But that isn't all. Only a thin zone of the atmosphere next to the earth can sustain human breathing. In fact, if you traced the earth in this diagram with a fine pen, your line would be thicker than the breathable atmosphere. It should now be clear why the activities of over five billion people on earth have an impact.

Initially, the effect of human activity on the composition of the atmosphere is localized. But due to the nature of atmospheric circulation, the effects soon extend around the globe. For instance, there has been discussion for some time that human activity may be contributing to a general **global warming.** Evidence is still weak, if not contradictory, and the mechanism is being hotly debated. But the concern is that carbon dioxide emissions generated by our industrial society are trapping heat that normally would escape the atmosphere. This is called the **greenhouse effect**. Although average temperature increases currently forecast seem small—up to two or three degrees—even this slight change could have an immense impact on agricultural practices and yields around the world.

Our most recent concern is that some of the chemicals we have created are contributing to **ozone depletion** in the atmosphere. The main culprit seems to be chlorofluorocarbons (CFCs), which are widely used in refrigeration and aerosol sprays. These CFCs break down into a byproduct called chlorine monoxide (ClO). Evidence is overwhelming that this chlorine monoxide is eating away the stratospheric ozone layer that shields life on earth from the sun's hazardous ultraviolet rays. When an **ozone hole** first showed up over the Antarctic each spring in the late 1980s, there was concern among scientists, but no general alarm. The situation changed dramatically in the winter of 1992, however. The reason was that a second hole opened, but this time it was over the Northern Hemisphere, and the threat received widespread public attention.

Impact on Hydrography

Maps document humans' impact on the hydrography better than their impact on the atmosphere. This is because hydrographic features are less

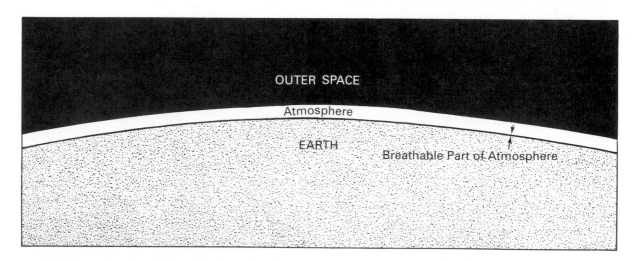

23.2 Although the atmosphere extends from the earth in a band several hundred miles deep, a layer less than four miles thick is breathable.

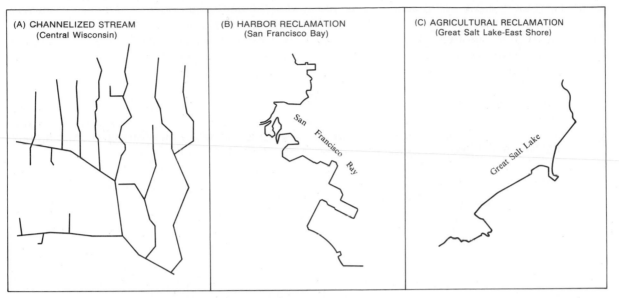

23.3 Evidence of human impact on the form of hydrographic features is common, even on relatively small-scale maps. Here the effects of stream channelization (A), harbor dredging and filling (B), and agricultural land reclamation (C) are shown.

dynamic and more tangible in nature. Human effects on both the form and composition of these features are subjects for map interpretation.

Form of Hydrography

The horizontal structure of drainage systems and the shorelines of open water bodies tend to be irregular and rather subdued in form. Only rarely do abrupt changes or angular shapes occur naturally.* Likewise, streams (with the exception of the trellis and annular drainage patterns discussed under *Stream Patterns* in Chapter 21) wander along in irregular fashion and converge at angles much less than 90 degrees. Thus, when a map shows angular hydrographic features that don't seem to fit the natural pattern, it is a good bet that human engineering has been a contributing factor. A channelized stream or an irrigation ditch is a good example, for only the human hand produces such drainage angularity in regions of flat topography (**Figure 23.3A**).

Similarly, it is often possible to spot places where marsh or open water has been either dredged and filled or diked and drained. In both

When they do, they are usually caused by the structural characteristics of the underlying bedrock. There may be a large fracture or fault in the rock, or different types of rock may be joined together.

cases, a regular (usually angular) shoreline is created. If the shoreline area is built up with marinas, airports, or warehouses, there is a good chance that the reclaimed zone has been filled (**Figure 23.3B**). On the other hand, agricultural land, instead of being filled, is normally drained and diked, in which case drainage ditches should be evident (**Figure 23.3C**).

Human impact on the hydrography doesn't always express itself as sharp angles. Human influences sometimes appear quite natural, as in the case of reservoirs created by damming free-flowing rivers. Even when a reservoir isn't identified on your map, you may be able to determine its location by its characteristic form. Reservoirs have a distinctive hand-shaped (or **palmate**) outline, with fingers pointing up the valleys which have been flooded (**Figure 23.4A**). In addition to this finger-like shape, a reservoir will have an irregular shoreline, because erosional forces have had only a short time to work toward smoothing it out.

Map interpretation goes beyond mere identification of features, of course. Thus, once a hydrographic feature is identified as a reservoir, we naturally begin to wonder about its function. Why was it built where it was? What purpose does it serve? Is it used for power generation, irri-

476

gation, navigation, urban water supply, or recreation? Since these uses are to some degree compatible with one another, multiple use of reservoirs is the rule. Other map features, as well as knowledge of the region's climate and land use, will provide helpful map interpretation clues.

Unfortunately, not all human impacts on the hydrography which show up as natural forms are as easy to spot as reservoirs. Consider the case of a natural lake which has had its level artificially raised by a dam or lowered as a result of water removal for irrigation, industrial, or drinking purposes. Except for the dam itself (when one is present), the shoreline is likely to look quite natural (**Figure 23.4B**). Associated features, such as aqueducts, pipelines, canals, or power plants, may pro-

vide the only solid evidence of human influence. Lacking these clues, the only way to determine the extent of human impact may be to compare current maps of the region with those made at earlier dates.

If an image map is at hand, you may be in luck, however. If a devegetated, or lighter-toned, band around the shoreline is visible on such a map, this is a good indication that the water body has been altered to serve human needs. Unless the dammed water body is located in an extremely humid region, it will fill to its highest level during the period of peak runoff (usually in the spring in the United States), and the water surface will then be lowered as water evaporates and is used for human purposes. The fluctuating water level leaves a strip of land devoid of vegetation and sometimes of a different photographic tone. This is especially true in the western states, due to the collection of mineral salts on the exposed rocks and soil. The width of the exposed strip is also a good clue to the steepness of the banks along the shoreline. Narrow bands occur along steep slopes, while wide bands indicate gentle slopes.

In general, when interpreting hydrography from maps, you will find that human disturbance is considerably less obvious on the vertical than on the horizontal structure of features. This is understandable, because maps tend to give a flattened view of the environment. But interpretation of the vertical component of the hydrography can still be rewarding. Angular navigation channels dredged in a harbor bottom may be evident in the bathymetric data. Dams and locks along streams are indications that the depth, gradient (and therefore velocity), and flood cycle have all been altered. Maps depicting a drop in the ground water table may indicate that more water is being extracted for agricultural, industrial, or residential purposes than is being added through precipitation.

Water Quality

Human impact on hydrographic features goes far beyond their geometric form, of course. More important in many ways are people-induced changes in water composition or quality. These influences generally appear on thematic maps in a subdued, irregular pattern which reflects natural dispersion processes.

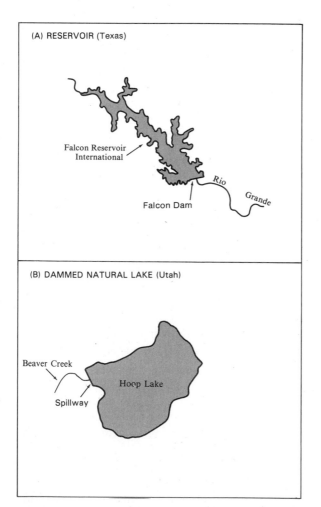

23.4 The shape of reservoirs (A) and dammed lakes (B) on maps provides evidence of human impact on a region's hydrography.

Surface waters, for example, have been contaminated by industrial pollutants (cleaning agents, energy generation and manufacturing byproducts, heat), agricultural chemicals (fungicides, pesticides, herbicides, fertilizers), and products associated with urban living (road salt, sewage, petroleum products). Sediment from construction, ore processing and handling, and agricultural runoff represent additional surface water pollutants. Initially, the effects of these human impacts on water quality tend to show up on maps as localized plumes of contamination (**Figure 23.5A**). But with time, the pattern becomes nearly as dispersed and general as in the case of atmospheric contaminants discussed earlier in this chapter.

Ground water quality has also been affected by human activities. The pumping of water from reservoirs below major coastal cities such as Los Angeles and Houston, for example, has led to salt water invasions and contamination of these fresh water supplies. Toxic chemicals dumped or spilled on the ground surface have in many areas also entered the ground water system. Cities across the country now commonly report traces of volatile organic compounds (VOCs) in drinking water pumped from deep wells (**Figure 23.5B**). The problem for the map interpreter faced with determining the origin and dispersion pattern of these toxic agents is that considerable underground movement and

(A) SURFACE WATER CONTAMINATION

(B) GROUND WATER CONTAMINATION

Source

30ppm
20ppm
10ppm

• Test wells

⌒ Probable extent of contamination (parts per million)

23.5 Human impact on water quality shows up on maps as plumes of contaminants which disperse through surface water bodies (A) and ground water reservoirs (B).

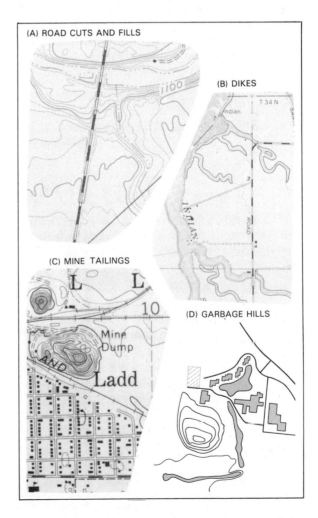

(A) ROAD CUTS AND FILLS

(B) DIKES

(C) MINE TAILINGS

(D) GARBAGE HILLS

23.6 Human constructions have altered the form of the land surface in many ways that show up on maps. Here, the effects of road fills (A), dikes (B), mine tailings (C), and garbage hills (D) are depicted.

478

dilution has occurred since they entered the hydrologic system.

Impact on Land Surface

Direct human effects on the form of the land are usually only of local extent. But the results can still be dramatic, as the dredging and filling of San Francisco Bay or the reclamation of the Great Salt Lake suggest. Other human constructions include road fills, dikes, mine tailings, dredge spoils, and "hills of garbage" (**Figure 23.6**).

The landform is also modified by direct human **excavations**. These may be of minor proportion, as in hill terracing or agriculture, strip mining, and road cuts. Other features, such as open pit mines, gold dredgings, rock quarries, and gravel pits, are quite prominent (**Figure 23.7**).

An indirect form of human excavation which is appearing on maps with increasing fre-

quency is land subsidence. Local subsidence due to cave-ins following underground excavations has long characterized areas in which ores, coal, or salt are mined. More recently, regional subsidence due to the pumping of oil, brine, and fresh water from subterranean reservoirs has become evident (**Figure 23.8**). Fortunately, the effects of regional subsidence for the most part are measured in centimeters rather than meters. But even subsidence of this magnitude can have a severe impact on the stability of human constructions.

The astute map interpreter will find other indirect effects of human activity on the landform. Erosion, for instance, has been decreased by planting vegetation to stabilize the surface of sand dunes and to reduce the force of winds on agricultural fields. Conversely, soil erosion has been increased by farming and forestry practices which lay the soil bare to the effects of wind and water. Ocean beach erosion has been increased by shoreline construction that disrupts currents. Dams built upstream from the coast lessen silt discharge and contribute to erosion.

Increased erosion in one region leads to increased sedimentation in others, of course. Thus, deposition in deltas, river channels, and lakes has been increased by human activities. In

(A) OPEN PIT MINE (Arizona)

(B) GOLD DREDGING (Oregon)

23.7 Human excavations of the land surface can be seen on maps in many forms. Here, an open pit copper mine (A) and gold dredging spoils (B) are shown.

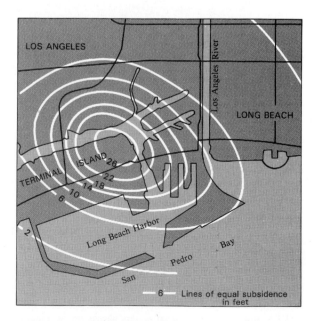

23.8 General subsidence of the ground surface has occurred in many regions due to the pumping of oil, brine, or water from underground reservoirs.

extreme cases, shoreline constructions are actually designed to enhance beach-building processes.

More subtle than outright excavation and construction processes are human effects which alter the composition of the landform. The soil layer, for example, is readily affected by human activities. Farming, tramping, and repeated removal of organic litter result in compaction, a loss of humus, and a change in soil color, texture, and permeability. These effects show up to some degree on image maps but for the most part must be surmised on the basis of those human activities which are apparent.

Indeed, a general problem when interpreting maps is that the human impact on landforms may appear rather insignificant if it is apparent at all. On large-scale maps, the actual form of landscape features modified by human activity can sometimes be determined directly. But because landform alterations by human activity are relatively small compared to common map scales, such features are usually depicted abstractly on line maps, using point symbols. When this is done, it is up to you to imagine what these artificial features look like in reality. You will have to draw on past experience and memory if your interpretation is to be valid.

Impact on Vegetation

Vegetation mapping poses special interpretation problems, because we can focus either on native species (natural vegetation) or exotic species (introduced by people). Thus, we can alternately approach the map interpretation activity from the perspective of disturbed natural vegetation or its reverse, vegetation added or planted by humans. In either case, we can glean evidence of human impact on both the form (distribution) and composition (ecology) of vegetation. We will consider each of these two factors in turn.

Spatial Pattern of Vegetation

The most obvious examples of human impact on vegetation include the clearing of trees and the planting of crops. As we noted in Chapter 20, boundaries between vegetation zones tend to be irregular and vaguely defined in nature. Thus, sharp, geometric boundaries or edges are significant clues to human impact on the natural landscape. Examples include woodlot borders in

agricultural regions; fence lines between heavily grazed and lightly grazed rangelands; cleared right-of-ways for roads, fences, and pipelines; and the border of clearcut zones in forested areas (**Figure 23.9**). When natural vegetation is sparse, the most obvious edge may be that of the farm fields themselves. This is particularly true in regions in which crops are irrigated (see Figure 22.8 in Chapter 22).

One imprint of human activity which may be easily overlooked is vegetative regrowth following logging or agricultural land abandonment. Close inspection will often reveal a patchwork pat-

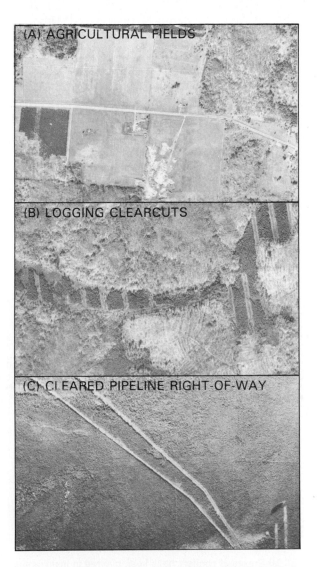

(A) AGRICULTURAL FIELDS

(B) LOGGING CLEARCUTS

(C) CLEARED PIPELINE RIGHT-OF-WAY

23.9 Vegetation is typically altered by humans in a simple geometric pattern, as can be seen in these photos of agricultural fields (A), logging clearcuts (B), and a cleared pipeline right-of-way.

480

tern of different aged stands of trees, reflecting the land tenure pattern (see *Land Tenure Systems* in Chapter 22). Since changing farming practices and logging activities have affected most forested regions of the country, there is a good chance that the evidence will be visible. Sometimes the regrowth of fields and cleared land will contain entirely different species than are found in the nearby woods (see the next section, *Species Composition*).

Another sure indication of human interference in the physical environment is a regular pattern of trees. Orchards are so obvious that their human origin can hardly be overlooked. Although most planted trees aren't of the orchard variety, they still tend to be located in rows and are therefore quite easy to spot. Sometimes the effect of tree planting is highly localized, as in the case of shelterbelts, fence rows, wind-breaks, and urban landscaping. When large plots have been forested artificially, mechanical equipment that plants seedlings in rows is often used. Even when the crown cover over these plots is complete, a certain regularity is usually apparent on an image map (**Figure 23.10**).

In some situations, of course, it takes rigorous map interpretation to detect human interference on the distribution of vegetation. A case in point is the irregular forest pattern shown in

Figure 23.11A. Close study reveals that the irregular unforested area was created by the strip mining of outcroppings from horizontal beds of coal. The cleared areas follow the contours of the land, producing a palmate pattern much like that created by a reservoir in similar terrain.

Another example which fits this irregular pattern model is the ridgetop and valley-bottom arrangement of farmland in southwestern Wisconsin (**Figure 23.11B**). As a third example,

(A) STRIP MINE

(B) RIDGE AND VALLEY FARMS

(C) VEGETATION KILL ALONG HIGHWAY

23.10 Groves of conifers have been planted in many areas in an attempt to prevent soil erosion, shelter wildlife, and generate wood products. The parallel row structure persists even in mature stands of trees, as this vertical photo indicates.

23.11 Human impact on vegetation doesn't always leave a regular geometric imprint, as these examples of strip mining (A), farmland clearing (B), and drowning due to drainage disruption (C) indicate.

the disruption of natural drainage due to roadbed construction often drowns vegetation along one side of the highway in an irregular kill pattern (**Figure 23.11C**).

At first glance, the controlling factor in each of these three examples appears to be natural, because there is so much irregularity in the distribution. Closer scrutiny, however, reveals that human influence is the cause of the mapped pattern.

Species Composition

In addition to changing the form of natural vegetation, people often alter the types of species that grow. These changes are less obvious on maps, but they are just as important. The impact may be direct, as in the case of selective logging, in which certain species are removed and others are allowed to remain. At least in the short term, even clearcut logging changes species composition, because the species that regrow are different from those that existed before logging took place.

Another direct influence on the composition of vegetation is the planting of "desirable," often exotic, species in reforestation efforts. To appreciate this fact, we must be able to detect not only differences between geometric patterns of vegetation on maps but differences between species as well. It may not be too hard to differentiate between broad groups such as conifers and deciduous trees (see Figures 23.9 and 23.10). But to separate individual species, such as oak or pine, takes skilled map interpretation.

Less direct effects on species composition are caused by the grazing of domestic livestock. Cattle, goat, sheep, and horses all tend to forage for different species. Over the long run, their grazing can greatly alter the mix of plant species in a region. Thus, image maps of rangelands where different grazing practices are in force often show dramatic vegetation changes on opposite sides of fence lines.

The management of wildlife species for nuisance control, income (from meat, fur, feathers, and so on), or sport can have effects on vegetation similar to those brought about by livestock grazing. Management practices by definition are designed to manipulate species' composition and density. Efforts intended to increase, decrease, or maintain a constant population all have very different vegetative consequences. Plant species can

be eliminated or encouraged unintentionally as a result of the way we treat different animals. These effects are usually rather subtle as far as mapping goes, but they do show up on high-quality image maps in many instances.

Fire suppression is another example of indirect human impact on plant species composition. Some species thrive on fire, others are fire-intolerant, and still others are indifferent to fire. Thus, fire suppression by humans in an attempt to "protect" forests, grasslands, and buildings can't help but alter natural species composition in the long run. The effects tend to be subtle, however, and may go undetected unless we carefully compare maps from several dates.

Air pollution resulting from human activity is still another case in which species composition can be indirectly changed. Along urban streets, sugar maples which are dead or dying due to the effects of auto exhaust can be readily spotted on large-scale image maps, especially those created in the near infrared portion of the spectrum (see Appendix B: *Remote Sensing of the Environment*). Sometimes vegetation kill is severe but localized, as it is near ore smelters which spew toxic wastes into the atmosphere. In other cases, as with acid rain, the impact on vegetation is more general and widespread. In all these instances, the map interpreter has to deal with a **spatial lag effect**, whereby vegetation change occurs downwind of the pollution source (**Figure 23.12**).

Some of the most far-reaching indirect effects of humans on vegetation have to do with introduced diseases and insect pests. Dutch elm disease is a good example. The beetle which carries the disease from one tree to the next was inadvertently brought to North America from Europe. Since its introduction, the American elm has completely disappeared from some areas, and its numbers have been greatly reduced in many others. Loss of one species is a gain for others, of course, and quickly leads to fundamental changes in species composition. To a large degree, then, vegetative composition is of human making in the sense that it reflects ongoing adjustments to disturbances wrought by people.

Impact on Wildlife

As with plants, people both support and destroy wildlife. Species which are compatible with

482

human activities thrive, while those in conflict perish. Species considered to be "good" or "desirable" are artificially stocked (from special rearing facilities) and protected. Out-of-favor species are put on varmint "hit lists" or, in extreme cases, bountied. Exotic species are introduced to take over niches vacated by extinct species or to fill perceived gaps in the ecosystem. As a result of these human manipulations, some intentional and others inadvertent, species distribution and migration patterns have undoubtedly been affected.

Species Distribution

Human impact on the distribution of animal populations is particularly difficult to interpret from maps. One reason is the mobility of animals. Ranges of animals are constantly expanding and contracting in response to a host of environmental factors. To complicate matters still more, the spatial proximity of features on maps may suggest cause-and-effect relations when there are none.

Consider, for example, a map showing distribution of a big-game species, such as elk in Washington state (**Figure 23.13A**). At first glance, the map seems to suggest that elk prefer forested mountain areas. In reality, however, elk were originally plains animals. To explain the current distribution of elk populations, we must consider several human factors not visible on the map. First of all, it is crucial to recall that by the early 1900s the slaughter of wildlife which followed European settlement of this country had left only remnants of former elk herds. The few herds which survived did so only because they were located in wild or otherwise inaccessible areas. Elk had vanished completely from the state of Washington.

In the 1930s, Washington state began to bring in animals from other western areas. These restocking programs, along with realistic game management practices, led to a rebuilding of herds, but in a pattern quite different from that of pre-European settlement. The emerging pattern of elk distribution had to reflect the realities of the new age, which were several. First, the large, conspicuous nature of the beasts and the vast quantities of prime meat that they carried attracted poachers. At the same time, most farmers weren't interested in re-establishing this competitive species but, on the contrary, considered elk, with their immense appetites, to be incompatible with agricultural activity. The nightmare of elk-vehicle accidents scared highway planners into

IMPACT OF TOXIC SMELTING FUMES

CONISTON, ONTARIO

Drift

Site of Nickel Ore Smelter

Generalized zone of apparent devegetation on 1/250,000 topographic map.

0   2   4
Miles

23.12 The map interpreter soon learns that vegetation disturbance caused by air pollution commonly occurs far downwind of the source of the contaminant.

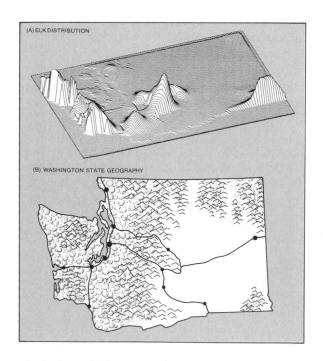

(A) ELK DISTRIBUTION

(B) WASHINGTON STATE GEOGRAPHY

23.13 The apparent spatial association between wildlife and environmental factors can be deceptive. Here, we compare elk density (A) in Washington state with the distribution of mountains and forests in the region (B).

building expensive elk-proof fences, which further contained expansion of the species. The influence of these human factors combined to force elk to live in the relatively remote, forested mountain regions of the state (and of the whole West, for that matter).

These historical determinants help explain the general correlation pattern between the map of elk populations in **Figure 23.13A** and that of forests, mountains, and human activity in **Figure 23.13B**. But we still haven't accounted for some major details in the mapped pattern of elk distribution. In particular, the mountains of the north, northeast, and northcentral areas appear to be void of elk. To explain this discrepancy, we must understand the elk management policy of state game officials. To keep crop damage by elk at an acceptable minimum level, as well as to keep elk from invading zones set aside for other large-game species such as deer, elk distribution is rigidly controlled by harvesting "stray" animals. This is done in conjunction with annual hunting seasons, designed to keep elk density within the carrying capacity of the natural habitat.

If you were especially observant, you might also have noticed that there are three "holes" or vacant zones in the elk distribution. These empty spots are anomalous because they occur (in two cases) in high mountain areas and (in the third case) in heavily forested coastal lowlands, where we would expect elk to be. The explanation in the first two cases is that the vacant areas coincide with national park boundaries (Mt. Ranier and Olympic). In the third case, the empty zone coincides with an Indian reservation. It's not that elk have been kept out of these areas but, rather, that no information was available for these three regions. The map maker simply chose to leave blank zones on the map rather than speculating what elk population might be in these areas. Therefore, your explanation of this aspect of the elk distribution rests with your map reading skill. Once you understand how the map was created, you can identify these empty zones as mere artifacts of the mapping process, not observable aspects of the environment.

Migration Routes

In Chapter 21, we saw that a crucial aspect of the range of many animal species is their migration route between breeding and wintering grounds.

These routes have in many cases been altered by human activity. Migratory fish such as salmon, for example, may be hatchery-reared hybrids from distant natural stocks. The natural breeds may have long since perished due to human activity. Yet the current crop of hatchery-raised fish will return to that faraway place to spawn, simply because that's where they were released when young. Their migration route may take them up dredged rivers, polluted with urban and industrial waste, over dams via fish ladders, into the hands of sport and commercial fishers, over old (natural) spawning grounds which have been inundated (and therefore destroyed) by reservoirs, and onto new spawning beds that are being choked with runoff from agricultural, mining, and logging areas. In sum, the migration pattern is largely a human creation that requires a historical perspective to decipher. The choice of which stream will have a spawning run is decided more by humans these days than by the fish themselves.

A second example of human impact on migration patterns is provided by the Canadian goose. Natural migration routes, as well as summer and winter habitats, were long ago altered by human activity. Much of the habitat of the Canadian goose was destroyed outright to make way for farms, cities, factories, and transportation facilities. Other areas were contaminated beyond use. But some habitat was preserved, recreated, or created in the form of the U.S. Wildlife Refuge System. Additional habitat was produced through protection and artificial feeding in parks and other preserves. Agricultural crops such as wheat and corn provided a vast new food supply.

The birds have been "short-stopped" going both north and south (**Figure 23.14**). This was done on the northbound migration by establishing breeding flocks of wing-clipped birds on refuges in certain northern states. It was accomplished on southbound migration by providing plentiful agricultural food supplies on or near refuges in the central tier of states (for example, Illinois in the Mississippi Flyway and Colorado in the Central Flyway). The result is a much shortened migration route for many geese and a multitude of problems, including breeding failures, crop damage, pollution of park waters, and irate southern sport hunters.

Indeed, goose populations are now managed in much the same way as domestic animals.

484

Sport hunting is the primary management tool keeping goose populations at current levels and goose distributions in the present pattern. Hunting season length and bag limits are liberalized by waterfowl managers when populations increase and are restricted in years of stability or decline. Thus, the current migration pattern is to a great extent controlled by people. Again, you need a solid historical perspective to interpret contemporary map patterns.

Forcefulness of Human Intervention

The human landscape reflects our attempt to control nature. It is easy to forget that our designs and constructions are imposed against the collective might of powerful natural forces. If not constantly maintained, human features quickly become temporary. We can accept this fact when we see ancient ruins. But it comes as a shock to visit a building abandoned in the last half century and

23.14 Short-stopping Canadian geese on their northern and southern migrations, with the help of the U.S. Wildlife Refuge System, has become common practice.

find it collapsed, rotting, and overgrown with vegetation. With a little study, most landscapes show decay and abandonment of human features from earlier times. Many of these features can be seen on maps, especially image maps, making them useful tools for historians and archaeologists.

The forcefulness of human intervention on the landscape exhibits a wide range. At one extreme, people share in a co-creation arrangement with nature. They plant seeds, remove brush and vines that are choking desirable species, prune trees, divert water for irrigation, and nurture endangered species. More forceful intervention occurs in single-crop agriculture, which requires destroying native species, or in building that involves gathering and assembling natural materials. Still more forceful intervention occurs in construction projects that introduce asphalt, cement, metal, glass, plastics and other foreign materials into the natural setting. When you look at a map, it helps to see features from this perspective, since some features are much more temporary than others.

Nature isn't the only healer of landscapes. Human hands can mend as well as destroy. The rapidly growing field of **restoration ecology** addresses this issue. Increasingly, a walk in a woods, wetland, or prairie is really a trip to a "restored" environment. When damage is severe, as in mining, reclamation may require smoothing the terrain, establishing watercourses, restoring vegetation, and restocking animals. If carefully planned and executed, these restored environments may actually appear to be natural areas on contemporary maps.

Healing need not be restricted to human damage. Forest fires, insect pests, hurricanes, mudslides, earthquakes, floods, and other natural events can significantly alter the landscape. People commonly mobilize a restoration effort after such events.

INFLUENCE OF PHYSICAL FACTORS

Just as humans have modified the physical environment, physical features influence human activity in many ways. Water supplies, soil fertility, mineral resources, vegetation, climate, and steepness and elevation of the land all powerfully affect our lives. Even when we appear to have overcome these environmental influences, our pattern of habitation demonstrates the price we have had to pay.

To a large degree, human patterns reflect the form of the physical landscape. Thus, a map of human features in the hands of a skilled map interpreter can effectively mirror the natural setting. What people are doing in a region and how they are doing it can be useful clues to the natural environment.

Human Settlement

People are basically opportunists. Some settle where they can best exploit forests, fertile soils, pure water, abundant supplies of fish and game, and rich mineral resources. Others settle where they can best facilitate the transportation and processing of these raw materials and the distribution of finished products. Still others settle where they can provide the most attractive recreational facilities. And, finally, some people work at structuring the settlement process so as to most efficiently provide the services required by a human society. In each instance, the physical setting influences the spatial character of human settlement. Several examples will clarify this point.

Location of Cities

A great deal can be said about the location of cities on the basis of their scatter across a map. Cities which are uniformly spaced over the landscape, for example, tend to be based on broadly distributed resources, such as forests, grasslands, or soils. The cities in this case provide governmental, financial, commercial, and marketing services for the dispersed population.

Clustered cities, on the other hand, suggest a concentration of resources, usually of a mineral or fossil fuel nature. Settlement associated with iron ranges, gold veins, and oil fields fall into this category (**Figure 23.15**). Often the cities persist long after the mineral deposits (at least those that can be profitably exploited) have been depleted, and it is important for the map interpreter to be alert to that possibility.

Linear patterns of cities tend to be associated with natural transportation routes. This is particularly true in remote areas. The pattern of cities

in the Amazon Basin, for example, exhibits strong linearities due to the influence of the Amazon River and its tributaries. The cities strung along the Rocky Mountain front in Colorado further exemplify the linear city pattern that develops through the influence of the natural environment.

Finally, cities scattered randomly across the landscape often owe their location to an initial transportation or communication advantage. Thus, you will find cities at the entrance of mountain passes (Denver), at the mouth of rivers (New York City), next to deep harbors (San Francisco), at the confluence of rivers (Pittsburgh), at rapids or falls in rivers (Niagara Falls), at the end of large bodies of water (Chicago), and so forth. The common factor in each case is the influence of a prime physical site at the time of settlement. Although the initial advantage of the site may no longer be important, the cities may persist through momentum of their own making.

A region of sparse settlement surrounded by dense human activity might catch your eye. A likely explanation has to do with an inhospitable physical setting. Factors that should come to mind are rough terrain, poor soil, and lack of water.

Urban Landscapes

Patterns within urban areas may also be explained by aspects of the physical environment. Settlers frequently aligned the street system with such

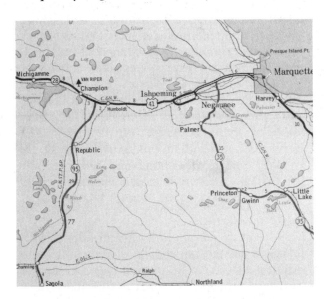

23.15 The clustering of towns on the Marquette iron range on the Upper Peninsula of Michigan is typical of mining settlements.

486

natural features as a bay or lakeshore. The effects of this early method of street orientation can still be seen in the downtown sections of such cities as Detroit, New Orleans, and Seattle.

As cities have expanded, their street networks have adjusted to many obstacles. Swamps, lakes, rivers, and rough terrain have all had considerable effect on the street systems of our cities. Indeed, the street network alone is often enough to give major clues to the nature of the physical environment. The pattern of light and dark (created by the lights from street lamps, homes, and businesses) seen from an airplane flying over a city at night begs for such explanation.

The land use pattern within cities is another aspect of the urban landscape which often reflects adjustment to physical factors. Industrial land use is generally tied most closely to the terrain and hydrography. For heavy industry, a broad, flat area is ideal. Residential land use, in contrast, tends to be least sensitive to the physical setting. Houses are built on flat areas if land is available but can also be built up steep slopes if necessary. In fact, slopes may be preferred for the view they afford. Recreational land uses commonly occupy old landfills and zones prone to flooding but may be chosen for their aesthetic appeal as well. The map interpreter who is able to put map clues together and to sort out probable physical influences on the land use pattern has in effect conjured up a picture of the physical setting from evidence of human activity.

Agricultural Land Use

The pattern of agricultural land use, like that of urban land use, can be greatly influenced by aspects of the physical environment. This is true of the type of crops grown in an area. It is also true of the structure of farm fields used to raise these crops. We will look at examples of both these factors.

Type of Crops

Let's begin by considering a map of agricultural practices along the shores of Lake Michigan (**Figure 23.16A**). This map reveals that a wide variety of products is grown in this Midwestern region. It also indicates that there is a definite grouping of crop types on opposite shores of the lake. Apples are grown west of the lake, while such crops as peaches, grapes, and blueberries are raised east of the lake. At the northern end of the lake, cherries are grown along both shores. Why, we may wonder, is fruit-growing clustered along the shores of the lake in the first place? And why are different types of fruits grown on different sides of the lake?

The answer to the first question is found in the special type of climate caused by the lake. Water bodies influence climate by warming up more slowly than land in warm periods and cooling down more slowly than land in cool periods. Through constant mixing and circulation, the mass of water in a lake serves as a great reservoir of solar energy. Thus, winter temperatures are generally warmer along the shores of a large lake, while summer temperatures are cooler. The result is a moderation in temperature extremes. The moderate winter serves the fruit trees' need for a cold dormant period but isn't so cold that blossom buds and other delicate plant tissue are damaged. Large bodies of water are also likely to increase the average annual precipitation and reduce the range in monthly precipitation. Of special importance for this example is the fact that the incidence of late spring frosts is greatly reduced at the vulnerable blossoming stage of the fruiting cycle. Together, these conditions create a climate conducive to growing fruit in the middle latitudes.

This lake effect explains why fruit-growing is clustered near the shores of Lake Michigan. But it doesn't provide insight into the distribution of crops around the lake. To explain why different fruits are grown on opposite shores of the lake, we must refer to the general weather pattern of the Great Lakes region.

Notice that with the exception of cherries in the north, only hardy fruits such as apples are successfully grown on the west side of the lake, while less hardy crops, such as peaches and grapes, are grown to the east. This suggests that the moderating lake effect is greatest to the east, which in turn implies that the prevailing winds are probably coming from the west. Temperature, precipitation, and humidity profiles taken across Lake Michigan confirm this suspicion (**Figure 23.16B**). These profiles show that the east shore is more moderate than the west, and both are more moderate than inland locations. From these statistics, the climatic effect of Lake Michigan

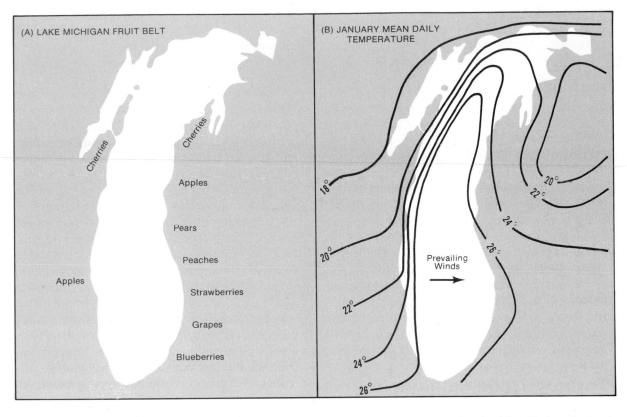

23.16 Agricultural practices around the shores of Lake Michigan are influenced by the moderating lake effect on the local climate.

appears to be rather subtle. Still, its influence on agriculture in the region is substantial.

At first glance, cherries appear to be an exception to the upwind-downwind thesis because they are grown on both sides of the lake. But the pattern of cherries can be explained by the fact that Wisconsin's Door Peninsula is itself under the lake effect of Green Bay, which lies to the west

Field Structure

The physical environment is a primary factor in determining not only the type of crops grown but the shape of farm fields as well. If land is flat, it's simplest for the farmer to make rectangular fields of fairly uniform size and orientation. On rough terrain and land segmented by a stream network, farmers often create fields of irregular shape, size, and orientation. In areas of mixed landform types, therefore, the field pattern may clearly identify the different terrain features. Notice in Figure **23.17A**, for example, how the pattern of farm fields sharply defines two parallel beach ridges.

Similarly, a drainage system which might otherwise be indistinguishable or obscure may be made obvious by breaks in the field pattern (**Figure 23.17B**).

Even when field shapes don't reflect the form of the topography, the manner in which the fields are cropped might. Contour plowing and strip cropping can sometimes create a vivid picture of the terrain. In the case of contour plowing, farmers work the land parallel with the terrain slope to minimize runoff and erosion. On detailed, low-altitude image maps, individual rows will often be evident even when the crops are mature and fully cover the ground surface.

Contour strip cropping is even easier to spot. With this conservation practice, farmers plant alternate strips of row and cover crops along the terrain contour. This method helps preserve light soils in hilly, erosion-prone regions. During most of the growing season, the crops in adjacent strips look different from one another on an image map. Texture and color changes follow

488

the maturation cycle of the plants. Even in winter, fields may be distinguishable by debris left after the harvest.

In some regions, contour farming is so prevalent and landform features so localized that the terrain looks as though it has been portrayed with layer tints. The drumlin region of Wisconsin is an excellent example (**Figure 23.18**). In most cases, however, the contour pattern is fragmented, and we are left to piece together sometimes diverse clues in conjuring up an image of the topography. This often involves looking beyond the rows and crop strips to the drainage, forest, and highway patterns.

The absence of contour farming on an image map is a good indication that the area is characterized by relatively flat landforms. This isn't always the case, however, because contour farming is usually voluntary, requiring foresight and extra work on the part of the farmer. Therefore, the presence of contour farming on a map is an almost certain indicator of hilly terrain.

Transportation-Communication Networks

If the natural realms were homogeneous, we might expect transportation and communication networks to be rather uniform in structure. Of course, this isn't the case. The natural setting presents a variety of encouraging and discouraging influences, and these are reflected in the form of transportation and communication networks on maps.

Generally, we want to move goods, people, and ideas as quickly and with as little effort as possible. To accommodate this desire and because of the high cost of constructing route linkages, we build direct communication routes wherever possible. These tend to be paths of least resistance; that is, they take advantage of features which minimize route cost and avoid barriers.

Some types of communication systems are more sensitive to the natural environment than others, of course. A map of hiking trails will tell us far more about the physical setting than one of airline routes. In decreasing order of sensitivity to local conditions, we might make the following ranking: hiking trails, county roads, state highways, federal highways, railroads, interstate highways, pipelines, high tension powerlines, microwave relay systems, and airline routes.

Directness isn't the only goal in constructing transportation and communication networks, however. Most interesting paths are sometimes as desirable as least resistance paths. Scenic routes and routes providing access to features of unique natural interest or beauty are found in many regions. Since the goals underlying the location of

23.17 The pattern of agricultural fields may reflect major adjustments to the natural setting. The effects of beach ridges (A) and hydrography (B) illustrate this fact.

23.18 Contour strip cropping represents one attempt to adjust agricultural activity to the physical environment.

these recreation-oriented routes differ markedly from those associated with the construction of day-to-day linkages, their structure can also vary dramatically. Indeed, in many instances, recreation-oriented routes seem to seek out and, therefore, reflect the complexity of the landscape.

Be careful not to leap to simplistic explanations of communication networks. The natural realms are so interrelated that it may be impossible to sort out the major environmental influence.* Human values (reflected in construction policy) and engineering potential also must be considered, and these change over time. And, finally, to justify the expense of building a communication network, there must be something to communicate. Thus, in the Canadian north there are few roads in part because construction is expensive but also because there is little perceived need. All factors go hand in hand and must be carefully weighed before coming to any conclusions about why the network appears as it does on the map. With this general background, let's now look at specific examples of the influences of topographic and hydrographic factors on communication and transportation networks.

Topographic Influences

The most obvious physical influence on the structure of transportation networks is the topography, including the configuration of land and water bodies. Road builders not only seek a direct route when linking places; they also try to avoid rough terrain. When there's no alternative, they thread the roadbed along the landform as best they can to minimize grade (steepness) and curves. Thus, when you see a highway network made up of irregular segments, you can expect topography in the region to be relatively rough. This is the case in the western half of the map in **Figure 23.19**. Conversely, in flat terrain, roads should be relatively straight or gently curving. This is true of the highway structure in the eastern half of the map.

The site as well as the general structure of transportation networks can be related to the landform. It is most practical in hilly regions to establish transportation routes along ridgetops and in valleys. This was more true in the past than it is today, and it's more true with railroads than with roads.

In extreme situations, such as in rugged mountain areas, the terrain may severely control all communication networks. An isolated mountain pass demonstrates how great this topographic influence can be. It's not uncommon to find pipelines, roads, railroads, and powerlines all constricted to a narrow strip of land as they cross a high mountain range and then dispersing widely on either side of the pass. Simply because there are several types of communication systems together, however, doesn't mean that there is a natural cause. It may merely have been more economical and convenient to construct them together, as when powerlines are built along roads.

Hydrographic Influences

The influence of hydrographic features on transportation networks can be twofold. On one hand, transportation is facilitated by navigable rivers and lakes. The siting of large cities along these hydrographic features provides ample evidence of this impact. Water bodies link human settlements by providing a relatively inexpensive

---

The Cascade and Appalachian Crest hiking trails, for example, are located where they are because of the attractiveness of the environment as a whole, not because a single aspect was especially important.

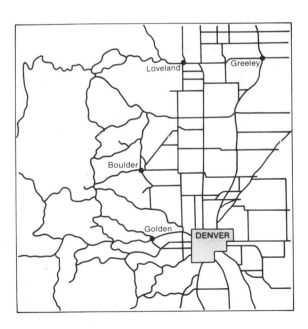

23.19 A sharp break in the road pattern occurs along the Rocky Mountain front in Colorado (taken from the Colorado state highway map, 1963).

490

means of transportation, since no roadbed need be built and maintained.

On the other hand, hydrographic features serve as barriers to land-based transportation. Consider the case of large lakes and bays. Only four east-west bridges cross the San Francisco-San Pablo Bay complex. Yet this water body extends 60 miles (97 kilometers) north-south and is surrounded by high population density. Similarly, there are no bridges across Chesapeake Bay from Annapolis, Maryland, to Norfolk, Virginia, a distance of 150 miles (241 kilometers). Countless other examples should immediately come to mind.

More subtle, perhaps, but equally important with respect to the development of communication linkages, is the influence of rivers. This is especially true as rivers grow larger or are contained in a broad and active floodplain. Although the transportation network in the southcentral United States may appear equally connected everywhere, closer inspection reveals the tremendous barrier created by the Mississippi River (**Figure 23.20**). There are only four bridges between Memphis, Tennessee, and Baton Rouge, Louisiana, a straight-line distance of approximately 400 miles (645 kilometers). Clearly, it's more convenient to travel by road or railroad north-south than east-west in this region.

23.20 The Mississippi River is clearly a barrier to east-west travel. Only four bridges are found in the 400-mile-long stretch between Memphis and Baton Rouge.

Wetlands represent still another hydrographic influence on the communication network. An extreme example is provided by the Okeefenokee Swamp along the Florida-Georgia border. Although it extends approximately 80 miles (129 kilometers) in a north-south direction, it is crossed from east to west by only one road. This is in direct contrast to the density of the road network in the surrounding region. We must also consider its status as a national wildlife refuge, however, since during the past several decades the policy has been not to build roads through these protected places.

FEEDBACK RELATIONS

We've seen that the human and physical realms are by no means independent entities. There's a great deal of interaction between them. Thus, many landscape features result from a blending of physical and human forces. Some human features reflect a strong impact of physical factors, and the impact of human forces can be seen in some physical features.

Yet, even when we include these "impact" features, we still haven't accounted for much of the landscape. The reason should be obvious. The environment is a single entity characterized by complex interrelations. It was to serve our convenience that we simplified this whole into separate realms and forces. The environment, of course, remains as complex and detailed as ever, in spite of how we view it.

Although our simplified treatment provides insights, there's a chance it may foster a relatively superficial impression. To be effective map interpreters, we need to put the pieces back together, like parts of a jigsaw puzzle, to create a meaningful picture of the environment. We need to move beyond cause-effect interactions to consider more complex feedback relations. For nothing is the result of one cause or even a handful of causes (see **Box 23.2**). The cycle of give-and-take between environmental factors rarely ends after a single exchange. A change in one factor is likely to lead to changes in others, which in turn change the first factor, and the cycle continues. The active feedback between physical and human factors is diagrammed in **Figure 23.21**.

BOX 23.2 BEYOND CAUSE-AND-EFFECT TO FEEDBACK RELATIONS

Today, when a problem arises we immediately seek to discover its causes. However, until now even the most profound thinkers have usually attempted to explain things in terms of a relative handful of causal forces. For even the best human minds find it difficult to entertain, let alone manipulate, more than a few variables at a time. In consequence, when faced with a truly complicated problem—like why a child is delinquent, or why inflation ravages an economy, or how urbanization affects the ecology of a nearby river—we tend to focus on two or three factors and to ignore many others that may, singly or collectively, be far more important.

Worse yet, each group of experts typically insists on the primal importance of "its own" causes, to the exclusion of others. Faced with the staggering problems of urban decay, the Housing Expert traces it to congestion and a declining housing stock; the Transportation Expert points to the lack of mass transit; the Welfare Expert shows the inadequacy of budgets for day-care centers or social work; the Crime Expert points a finger at the infrequency of police patrols; the Economics Expert shows that high taxes are discouraging business investment; and so on. Everyone high-mindedly agrees that all these problems are somehow interconnected—that they form a self-reinforcing system. But no one can keep the many complexities in mind while trying to think through a solution to the problem.

Urban decay is only one of a large number of what Peter Ritner, in *The Society of Space*, once felicitously termed "weave problems." He warned that we would increasingly face crises that were "not susceptible to 'cause and effect analysis' but would require 'mutual dependence analysis'; not composed of easily detachable elements but of hundreds of cooperating influences from dozens of independent, overlapping sources."

(Alvin Toffler, *The Third Wave*)

Sometimes there is **positive feedback,** whereby one thing increases activity in another. A few people discover a clean, quiet town for vacations or retirement, and as the news spreads people show up in increasing numbers. When a new insect pest is introduced to a region, breeding and predator problems slow population increase. But as pest numbers increase, breeding becomes easier and predators have less effect, so the population grows at an increasing rate.

Not all feedback is positive, of course. With **negative feedback**, one factor decreases the activity of another. Draw too many people into a small vacation or retirement town and it becomes congested, noisy, and polluted. Its attraction may be so diminished that it is abandoned as a vacation or retirement haven. As insect pests increase in numbers, they exhaust their food supply, and the population falls. Spreading too much fertilizer

on a field poisons the soil and actually reduces crop yield.

The previous examples all deal with direct feedback relations. Indirect feedback between environmental features is even more common. In this second case, the effects pass from one feature to another. For instance, using toxic pesticides on crops may increase the yield, but the residue may get into the drinking water supply and cause health problems. Similarly, an industry may achieve a competitive market price for its product by contaminating the air, water, soil, or workers with polluting industrial byproducts. Thus, the true cost of the product has been hidden. In particular, clean-up costs have been shifted away from the product to some other sector of society. The "bill" still must be paid, however.

The environmental effect of cost-shifting deserves our attention. To use an analogy, the

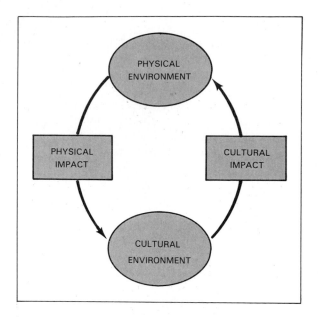

23.21 The physical and cultural realms influence each other in an active feedback relationship, making up what we think of as the environmental system.

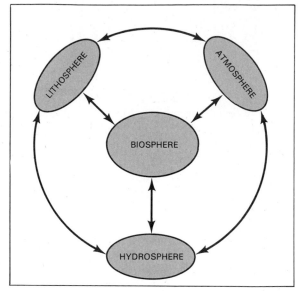

23.22 The subsystems of the physical realm are highly interdependent. A change in one affects all the others, something we must keep in mind as global population growth and industrialization increase the risk of environmental destruction and contamination.

retail price of a bottle of liquor is only a small fraction of the expense of dealing with its consumption if we consider its contribution to lost wages, decreased productivity, health problems, traffic accidents, and family abuse. The cost of these effects has merely been transferred from the product price and is covered by using resources extracted from society as a whole.

The true cost of environmental activity is something the map interpreter should seek to track down. Who or what pays when a ski resort, a highway, or a large manufacturing plant is built at a location? What form does the payment take, and at what cost? Has the true cost been shifted in a way that disguises the effect or amount? By addressing these questions, your insight into the nature of environmental feedback relations will be greatly enhanced.

The mix of positive and negative feedback relations quickly becomes complicated beyond comprehension. It's impossible to think of all the environmental ramifications of a simple action. Consider what happens, for example, when a start-up factory in a small town is successful. As the industry grows, it requires more workers, more houses, more roads, more schools, more police protection, and more health care. The effects are more pollution, congestion, crime, and so on. The small town is transformed in countless ways as each new addition affects all others.

It's relatively easy to see that feedback relations play a key part in the evolution of the landscape. It's more difficult to grasp the scope and depth of their impact. Although this is an overwhelming task, it will seem more achievable if you take it in steps. First, work on rebuilding the physical subsystem; then tackle the human subsystem. Finally, put these physical and human subsystems together. Let's go through these steps now, beginning with the physical subsystem.

Physical Subsystem

In Chapter 21, we divided the physical realm into four component subsystems and treated each in relatively independent terms. We saw, however, that to interpret maps effectively it is essential to view the physical realm as a single, integrated system. Although the biosphere tends to be the most interconnected with the others, to some degree every sphere is related to every other. These relations are diagrammed schematically in **Figure 23.22.**

In considering this figure, it's useful to develop a concrete example. Picture, for instance, the structure of the landform surface as shown by contour lines on a topographic map. How did the landform come to have this particular form?

What you see on the map is the current state of an endless struggle among earth building and erosional forces. Earth building occurs through uplift and deposition and is a matter of geology. Erosion, on the other hand, represents the combined effect of forces from the different physical realms. Differential heating and cooling, precipitation, and wind are factors contributed by the atmosphere. Biotic components include the digging of animals, the uprooting of trees, the expansion of roots in rock cracks, and the stabilizing effects of vegetation. Wave action, currents, running water, moving ice, and the dissolving action of water add a hydrologic dimension. In fact, all these activities are occurring simultaneously or in various feedback sequences.

Maps are intended to help us understand these complex relations. Unfortunately, individual maps suffer the same drawback as other means of indirect communication: They take things out of context. But maps do preserve spatial relations. Thus, by studying maps representing a variety of topics, you can, in a sense, put the environment back together, piece by piece. Indeed, maps serve this endeavor well.

Human Subsystem

Earlier in this chapter, we explored the influences of administrative, technological, cultural, and economic factors on the structure of the human landscape. For the most part, we treated the effect of each of these factors independently. As we saw in several instances, however, an independent treatment of human factors is unrealistic. We must approach the human landscape in integrated fashion, as shown in **Figure 23.23**, if we are to be effective map interpreters.

The question of economic viability can be used to illustrate this point. When looking at an image map of an agricultural region, we may well conclude that agriculture is being practiced because it is the most economical use of the land. But the concept of what is economical is very complex. Without government price supports, crop quotas, low-interest loans, tax shelters,

research, and education, for example, the crops being grown quite likely couldn't be raised for a profit when sold at current market prices. In other words, it isn't the free marketplace but administrative factors which figure most prominently in what is economical at any given time.

Technological factors also play an important part. The farming methods practiced today might not have been possible a decade ago before the invention of critical agricultural machinery.

Human factors, too, help define what is economical. People must be willing to buy farm products at a price which includes a reasonable profit margin for all those involved in the raising, processing, distributing, and marketing system. Changing eating habits can create or destroy a market for farm products in a very short time.

Thus, this example shows the combined influence of administrative, technological, and cultural factors on what we think of as economic behavior. Each of the factors we have looked at in this chapter is similarly intertwined with all the others. And all these factors are also interwoven with the great spheres of the physical environment, as we shall see in the next chapter when we study the interpretation of image maps.

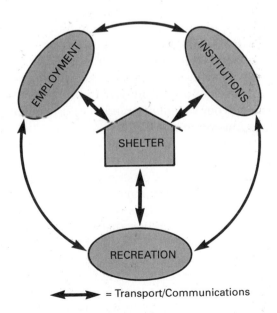

23.23 The landscape is structured by a complex mix of highly interdependent features associated with human behavior.

BOX 23.3 THIS PRECIOUS PLANET

Whole-earthers have been telling us for decades to view this planet as a single system. Thirty years ago Rachel Carson wrote that people who kill bugs in cornfields with pesticides may also kill the birds that eat the bugs, not to mention the humans who drink the water that runs off the field. Somehow, though, scientists have become increasingly fascinated with ever more specialized studies of Earth, often ignoring hypotheses about linkages among air, soil and water. Eric Barron, director of Penn State's Earth System Science Center, puts it this way: "Oceanographers study water and ignore the atmosphere above it. When the water evaporates and forms a cloud that makes rain, it becomes the purview of a meteorologist. If that rain falls on land, it becomes civil engineering. If it percolates down, that's geology. If it affects vegetation, it's biology. If it becomes snow it's something for a polar expert."

Now, two problems that affect every part of Earth—global warming and holes in the ozone layer—are forcing scientists to think macro, toward one complete ecological system. Help comes from the encompassing views offered by satellites. Computers help, too, but Earth's ecology is so complex that all the computers in the world couldn't contain sufficient information to analyze it.

(Claudia Glenn Dowling, "This Precious Planet," *Life*, Vol. 15, No. 4 (April 1992), p. 31)

All Together

As a final map interpretation step, you need to reintegrate the physical and human realms to view the environment as a single functional unit (see **Box 23.3**). Such a view requires you to think holistically. This type of intuitive thinking yields hunches, feelings, and "gut reactions" at a subconscious level. One way to bring these feelings to your conscious mind is to use a communication vehicle such as language, numbers, or pictures.

You can use the diagram in **Figure 23.24** to guide you in this process. It should help you reintegrate the environmental pieces discussed in this and the previous two chapters. The diagram is tacit recognition that understanding the whole environment depends on knowing how its parts fit together. Therefore, the figure provides a parts checklist. Use it as a way to remind yourself to analyze an environmental feature or setting thoroughly. When this task is still new to you, or when you are faced with a new and strange interpretation challenge, you may find the checklist invaluable. But as you gain exper-

tise, you will be able to perform the task intuitively, without overt reference to the checklist.

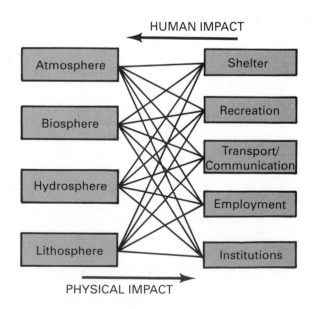

23.24 Ultimately, we must think of the environment as a whole. A checklist of physical and human factors can be a helpful analytical tool.

CONCLUSION

The challenge of map interpretation is that everything in the environment is related to everything else. Some relations between physical and human factors are direct, immediate, and obvious. Others are indirect, develop over the long term, and are difficult to detect. But whatever the nature of these relationships, together they bond us with the environmental system.

Ultimately, as we saw in the last section of this chapter, we must integrate all that we know about physical and human processes if we're to realize the full power of map interpretation. Even then, the map leaves much unsaid. We also need a vivid imagination if we are to obtain a rich, detailed picture of the environment from a few map features. In the next chapter, we'll see how our map interpretation skills can be applied to the holistic representations provided by image maps.

SELECTED READINGS

Barrow, C.J., *Land Degradation: Development and Breakdown of Terrestrial Environments* (New York: Cambridge University Press, 1991).

Bateson, G., *Mind and Nature: A Necessary Unity* (New York: Bantam Books, 1980).

Botkin, D.B., et al., eds., *Changing the Global Environment: Perspectives on Human Involvement* (New York: Academic Press, Inc., 1989).

Brody, H., *Maps and Dreams* (New York: Pantheon Books, 1981).

Cotton, W.R., and Pielke, R.A., *Human Impacts on Weather and Climate* (Fort Collins, CO: Aster Press, 1992).

DeBlij, H.J., *The Earth: A Physical and Human Geography*, 3rd ed. (New York: John Wiley & Sons, 1987).

Gersmehl, P.J., *The Language of Maps* (Indiana, PA: National Council of Geographic Education, 1991).

Goudie, A., *The Earth Transformed: An Introduction to Human Impacts on the Environment* (Boston, MA: Blackwell Publishers, 1997).

Goudie, A., ed., *The Human Impact on the Natural Environment*, 4th ed. (Boston, MA: Blackwell Publishers, 1994).

Goudie, A., ed., *The Human Impact Reader: Readings and Case Studies* (Boston, MA: Blackwell Publishers, 1997).

Heat-Moon, W.L., *Blue Highways: A Journey into America* (Boston: Little Brown and Co., 1982).

Levine, A.D., *Love Canal: Science, Politics, and People* (Lexington, MA: Lexington Books, 1982).

Maboganje, A., *The State of the Earth* (Boston, MA: Blackwell Publishers, 1997).

Mainquet, M., *Desertification: Natural Background and Human Mismanagement* (New York: Springer-Verlag, 1991).

Martin, C., *Keepers of the Game: Indian-Animal Relationships and the Fur Trade* (Berkeley: University of California Press, 1978).

McCormick, J., *Acid Earth: The Global Threat of Acid Pollution,* 2nd ed. (London: Earthscan, 1989).

Middleton, N., *The Global Casino: An Introduction to Environmental Issues* (London: Edward Arnold, 1995).

Neal, P., *Greenhouse Effect and Ozone Layer* (London: Dryad Press, 1989).

Raitz, K.B., "Irrigation on Topographic Maps," *Journal of Geography,* 78, 3 (1979), pp. 82-93.

Stern, P.C., Young, O.R., and Druckman, D., eds., *Global Change: Understanding the Human Dimensions* (Washington, DC: National Academy Press, 1992).

Turner, B.L., ed., *The Earth as Transformed by Human Action* (New York: Cambridge University Press, 1990).

Vale, T.R., *Plants and People: Vegetation Change in North America* (Washington, DC: Association of American Geographers, 1982).

Vale, T.R., and Vale, G.R., *U.S. 40 Today: Thirty Years of Landscape Change in America* (Madison: University of Wisconsin Press, 1983).

Van Andel, T.H., *New Views on an Old Planet: A History of Global Change*, 2nd ed. (Cambridge: Cambridge University Press, 1994).

495

PART III
Map Interpretation

CHAPTER TWENTY-FOUR

IMAGE MAP INTERPRETATION

INTRODUCTION

NON-VERBAL THOUGHT AND COMMUNICATION

KEYS TO IMAGE INTERPRETATION

Shape
Tone
    Conventional Photos
    Photo-Infrared Imagery
    Thermal Imagery
    Radar Imagery
Color
Size
Shadow
Pattern
Site and Situation
Texture
Context
    Date and Time
    Region
    Imaging Method

SCALE GRADIENT

INTERPRETATION STRATEGY

Checklist
20 Questions
Quotas
Meaning

MENTAL TEMPLATES

AUTOMATED FEATURE IDENTIFICATION

Image Classification
Theme Extraction
Promising Future

SELECTED READINGS

> It is a hieroglyphical and shadowed lesson of the whole world.
>
> —Sir Thomas Browne

CHAPTER TWENTY-FOUR

IMAGE MAP INTERPRETATION

From our point of view as map interpreters, we can think of conventional line maps as value-added products. The cartographer has helped us by labeling environmental features by category, so that we see different symbols for roads, buildings, water, and so forth. If the meaning of a symbol isn't obvious, we merely look it up in the map's legend. With the feature identification task so simplified, we can devote our attention to problems of interpretation.

The convenience of conventional line maps does have a price, however. For one thing, a cartographer has determined what in the environment to represent on the map, and what symbols to use for this purpose. One potential problem is that these abstraction decisions may not suit your needs. However frustrating it may be, you must make do with the cartographer's filtered version of the environment, unless you have access to an image map.

Another problem is that the map abstraction process is costly. It demands time, labor, and capital. For this reason, line maps commonly aren't available at large scales or frequent intervals. Image maps often serve as a substitute for line maps in these situations.

So, for these reasons, it's helpful to learn to interpret image maps. They will prove the ultimate test of your map interpretation ability. You'll be dealing with an image made up of raw tones, textures, and forms. These images contain a detailed record of the environment at the time of image creation.

Despite conventional wisdom, image maps don't constitute a complete document of the environment, however. What they do contain depends on sensor sensitivity (spectral, spatial, radiometric) and vantage point. Within the constraints set by these factors, image maps usually provide less of a cartographic buffer between reality and map user than do line maps.

Thus, the person using an image map is in a conceptual sense closer to the environment than when using line maps. There has been less cartographic intervention in the character of the representation.

498

The fact that you must first "read" an image complicates your interpretation task. In contrast to line maps, on which features are symbolized and identified in a legend, image reading is based on visual cues that become clear through tonal variation alone.

It is this tonal contrast that leads first to visual detection, next to visual differentiation, and finally to feature recognition. The image interpretation process is the same in contexts as diverse as medical, astronomical, and geographical imaging. The same visual cues form the basis for interpretation in each case. Thus, image map interpretation is a subset of image interpretation in general.

The image map interpretation process has been applied successfully to many fields. These include agriculture, forestry, geology, meteorology, archeology, oceanography, soil science, ecology, civil engineering, planning, and military intelligence. (In fact, many of the advances in image interpretation first occurred in the military.) But the procedures are perfectly general in application and can be used in a wide variety of arenas.

NON-VERBAL THOUGHT AND COMMUNICATION

Image interpretation may seem strange to the novice, because we've come to rely on a word-based thought process, in which everything in the environment is first classified and labeled. Because language is based on labels for generic cases, it encourages us to think in stereotypes, prototypes, and typical forms.

In contrast, the tonal variation of image maps at first may seem incomprehensible. We're forced to conjure up features for ourselves, and then try to identify what we're seeing. Most of us have had little formal training in this type of picture-based thinking and, therefore, feel more comfortable with word-based thought. But with some

24.1 Even a novice can usually identify some features on a conventional aerial photo at a glance. See how you do.

guidance and experience, you'll be amazed at how much you can learn from an image map.

Expert image map interpreters appear to work effortlessly, with no apparent rules. They "just know" what something is at a glance. If you look at **Figure 24.1**, you can experience this for yourself. If you instantly recognize a road, house, river, or some other feature, you know that "expert" feeling of just knowing. If asked how you knew the identity of a feature, you might first say, "I just knew." If questioned further, you probably could come up with a list of reasons to support your answer.

In fact, expert image interpretation requires that you meld conscious analytical and unconscious holistic thinking into a single, integrated approach. Perhaps most important, experts have learned to use the image as a trigger to dredge up tacit knowledge from their subconscious. They are able to imagine how things they have experienced in day-to-day living might look when viewed from a distant vantage point, particularly one that is highly oblique or vertical, with little feature profile information to provide familiar cues.

While such expert skills don't come automatically, there are strategies that will help you learn them. First, you may need to enrich your language of spatial terms. The checklist of keys to feature identification in **Figure 24.2** provides a useful spatial vocabulary. You can use these terms as tools to pick meaningful features out of the image.

This list is equally well suited to all forms of image interpretation. Only the meaning of the cues differs from field to field. Thus, what you see on an aerial photo as a dark patch of evergreen trees in a lighter-toned deciduous forest, a radiologist might see as a dark clump of cancer cells against a background of healthy tissue.

KEYS TO IMAGE INTERPRETATION

In the following discussion, we'll consider each of the keys to image interpretation separately. Ultimately, however, we must recognize that these keys address aspects of a whole feature. It's when we integrate all these keys into simultaneous perceptions that we move from novice to expert image interpreters.

Shape

An object's shape is the most fundamental clue to identifying it. Our eye is by nature drawn to the edge of features. Indeed, our brain has a special mechanism for processing these edges.

When interpreting an image map, first decide if a shape is likely of natural or human origin. Natural features tend to have irregular shapes. In contrast, features resulting from human activity tend to have simple geometric forms (sharp angles, smooth curves, regular patterns).

This division into natural vs. human is only a general guideline, however. Natural features can sometimes have regular shapes, as is the case with a smooth sandy coastline, a river running along a

24.2 The standard keys to image interpretation provide a convenient checklist when you have trouble identifying a feature on an image map.

500

fault line, or vegetation stopping abruptly at a break between bedrock types.

Conversely, human activity can sometimes result in deceptively irregular patterns, as when a strip mine follows an outcrop of coal along a valley, or a farm field conforms to a fertile soil region in otherwise infertile soils. Perhaps most deceptive of all features created by people are those influenced by natural environmental processes, such as wind or water currents. With acid rain, for example, the pattern of vegetation damage is a consequence not only of the pollution source, but also of wind, soil alkalinity, precipitation, and other patterns.

Tone

Tone refers to the degree of lightness or darkness of an object. Although all colors exhibit some level of tone, we'll focus here on the achromatic gray-tone range from black to white. Other aspects of color, called hue and saturation, provide the basis for another interpretation key (see *Color,* later in this chapter).

Next to shape, tone is the most important visual cue, because it creates contrasts which are fundamental to detection and discrimination. The human brain has a special mechanism for detecting tonal variation.

The meaning of tone varies considerably from one type of medium to another. Let's look first at tonal variations on conventional photos.

Then we'll compare these with tone on photo-infrared, thermal, and radar images.

Conventional Photos

In a conventional photograph, tone is determined by the amount of **reflectance**. An object's reflectance depends, first, on its surface characteristics and, second, on how it is positioned in the environment.

A smooth, shiny surface is highly reflective. The reflected energy leaves the surface at the same angle as it arrives from its source but in the opposite direction (see the left diagram in **Figure 24.3**). We can think of these shiny surfaces as mirror **reflectors** (it helps to recall the flash you see when light reflected from glass or metal strikes your eye).

In contrast to mirror reflectors are objects with rough surfaces that scatter or diffuse light in many directions (see the middle diagram in **Figure 24.3**). These **diffuse reflectors** appear about the same tone no matter what the angle of incoming light or position of the sensing device (camera or electronic scanner).

A third type of reflection occurs when objects are close together and thus create special reflection effects. For instance, light reflecting from water may bounce off a metal boathouse and be directed back to your eye, creating an unusually bright spot in the landscape or image (see the right diagram in **Figure 24.3**). These are referred to as **corner reflectors**.

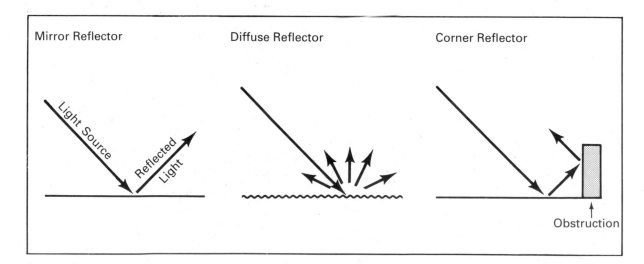

Mirror Reflector   Diffuse Reflector   Corner Reflector

Light Source
Reflected Light
Obstruction

24.3 Image tones depend on features' reflective character. Some features reflect in mirror fashion (left diagram). Some reflect diffusely (middle diagram). And, in some cases, light bounces off several features (right diagram).

Highly reflective objects will usually appear light toned (although they can assume a full range of tones from light to dark depending on the orientation of the light source and the sensor relative to their position). Highly absorbent objects almost always will appear dark toned.

Sand, dry soil, and rock tend to appear light in tone on a conventional photo, while wet soil usually appears dark. Roads made of cement and gravel usually appear light, whereas blacktop roads appear medium gray. Water usually is dark, but may be lightened by aquatic vegetation or suspended sediments. Buildings vary widely in tone depending on roofing material.

Vegetation is rarely white or black, but varies in tone from light to dark depending on type. Conifers (needle-leaf, evergreen) tend to be darker than broad-leaf deciduous vegetation. Grass varies in tone with the seasons more than evergreen shrubs and trees. Farm crops are especially prone to vary in tone through a seasonal cycle of growth, maturation, and dormancy.

It's important to note that tone may be more than a simple matter of reflectance. Tone also depends on the position of the sun and the sensing device (camera or electronic scanner). Thus, a highly reflective surface such as a lake may appear black on one part of an image and white on another, depending on where the light is reflected relative to the sensor's position (**Figure 24.4**). Tone is therefore not completely reliable as an interpretation cue.

Photo-Infrared Imagery

You'll see different tonal variations on photo-infrared images from what you see on conventional photos. For one thing, the longer wavelengths of infrared energy are absorbed by water more completely than the shorter wavelengths of visible light energy. The result is that hydrographic features such as lakes and streams tend to appear dark gray to black on photo-infrared images. Also, you won't find the mirror reflection from water bodies that are common on conventional aerial photos.

24.4 Tone isn't a reliable indicator of feature type, as this photo shows. Note how lakes vary in tone from white to black across the image as you scan from left to right.

502

An even more pronounced difference between conventional photos and photo-infrared images is the appearance of vegetation. As you can see in Figure B.4 in Appendix B, vegetation is much more reflective in the photo-infrared waveband than in the visible waveband. Due to this extra energy, vegetation appears lighter on a photo-infrared image than on a conventional aerial photograph (**Figure 24.5** and **Figure 24.6**).

More important, differences in vegetation types lead to more pronounced tonal variation on photo-infrared images than on conventional photos. In particular, conifers tend to be darker than deciduous trees. This fact makes it possible to distinguish between these broad groups, if not to differentiate within groups.

Thermal Imagery

Interpreting tone on thermal scanner imagery is even less intuitive than it is with photo-infrared images. On thermal imagery, lighter tones are associated with warmer objects, darker tones with colder objects (**Figure 24.7**).

On thermal images, an object's tone is related to three characteristics: (1) its **thermal capacity** (the amount of energy it can store); (2) its **conductivity** (its resistance to heating or cooling); and (3) its **inertia** (the rate at which it gains or loses heat).

Water, for example, has low conductivity but high thermal capacity and inertia. In contrast, rock has moderate conductivity and capacity but low inertia. Thus, water features tend to be warmer (lighter) than land features at night, but cooler (darker) than land features during the day when the sun is shining.

What makes matters even more confusing is that tone reversal between features may occur diurnally, or throughout the day. For instance, a lake may look darker than the surrounding land on a thermal image taken at noon, but lighter than the land on a nighttime image. In this case, the two features will appear the same temperature (therefore tone) twice a day (morning and evening). These times are referred to as **thermal crossover** points (**Figure 24.8**).

Similar tone variations occur with changes in the seasons. Again, not all features heat up and cool down at the same rate. Water, for example, heats more slowly in the spring and cools more slowly in the fall than the surrounding land. To avoid misinterpretation, we must be aware of the

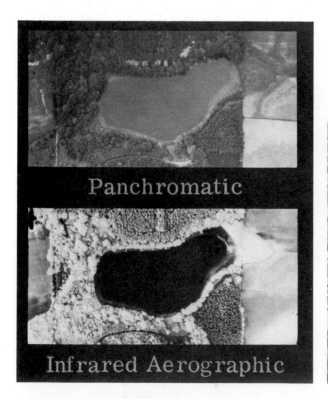

24.5 Note the tonal contrast between these normal (top) and infrared (bottom) black-and-white photos (Three Sisters Lake in Michigan's Saginaw Forest).

24.6 This black-and-white print of a color infrared photo of the Madison area in Wisconsin was taken from an altitude of 20 kilometers. The darker the red on the original, the darker the gray tone.

(A) THERMAL PLUME

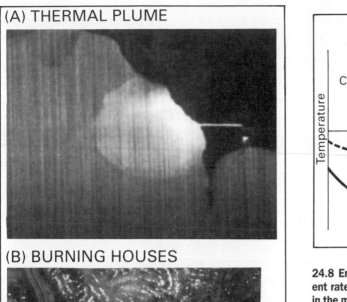

(B) BURNING HOUSES

24.7 Thermal infrared imagery makes it possible to distinguish between warm and cold features, as you can see by the thermal plume from a power generating plant (A) and burning houses in the Oakland Fire (B).

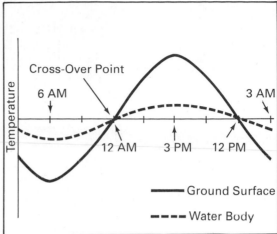

24.8 Environmental features change temperature at different rates from day to night, resulting in a thermal crossover in the morning and evening when they appear the same tone.

seasonal effect on tonal relations between land and water.

A variety of contextual factors can also contribute to tonal variations in a thermal image. Rain, for example, can cause fine tonal streaking, even though thermal waves readily penetrate this weather phenomenon. Other curious tonal effects are discussed later in this chapter under *Shadow*.

Radar Imagery

Several factors cause tone on a Side Looking Airborne Radar (SLAR) image to vary. First, SLAR tonal variation depends on the surface character relative to microwave-energy reflection. Rough surfaces scatter microwave signals, resulting in mid-range tones. Smooth surfaces (mirror reflectors) reflect microwave energy with strong directional characteristics. Thus, these surfaces may appear light or dark depending on the sensor's position (**Figure 24.9**).

When smooth surfaces and highly reflective objects are close together, they may serve as corner reflectors, creating a very high-intensity SLAR signal. When studying radar images, be careful of bright spots created by corner reflectors. Because these spots tend to be disproportionately large, you may be tempted to think an object is bigger than it is.

Second, tonal variation on SLAR images depends on a surface's orientation relative to the SLAR sensor. Surfaces at right angles to incoming microwaves will send back the strongest signal, while those oriented away from outgoing microwaves will be relatively weak. Areas blocked from the outgoing radar signal will appear black (see *Shadow*, later in this chapter).

Color

For most people, the word "color" means red, green, blue, and so forth. Technically, the sensation of red or any other "color" is caused by the dominant wavelengths of visible spectral energy received by our eye. The term "hue" refers to this

504

24.9 This SLAR image of the area south of Flagstaff, Arizona, shows a great amount of environmental detail. Notice the characteristic black radar "shadows."

spectral aspect of the phenomenon we call color.*

The hue of features on natural-color image maps is one of the most straightforward interpretation cues and can be a very helpful aid. What surprises novice interpreters, however, is the weakness or washed-out nature of image color. The richness and intensity of color aren't nearly so great on an image as on the ground. Colors become more and more muted with increasing distance between the sensor and the ground. We experience this effect in day-to-day activity, where views of distant landscapes lack crisp color definition. It's also obvious to anyone who has looked out an airplane window that color decreases with distance. But it still comes as a shock to find that color cues in natural-color images leave much to be desired.

....
*Another aspect of color is a sensation called **saturation**, **purity**, or **chroma**. These terms refer to the "brightness" or "intensity" of a hue. Thus, one feature might be described as bright red, another as dull red.

We also experience color degradation under reduced light conditions. Notice how colors in your surroundings seem to come alive at dawn and fade at dusk. At night, we live in a monochrome world of gray tones (see *Tone*, earlier in this chapter). Maybe it's for this reason that we so readily accept a gray-tone photograph as a true representation of our surroundings. When you interpret an image map, it's important to note how a gray-tone image has transformed the rainbow of landscape hues into its monochrome representation.

The color of features on image maps isn't always natural. When images are created from energy recordings beyond the visible-light waveband, there is no such thing as natural color. In these cases, any coordination between image color and the environment is arbitrary. This explains why the adjective **false-color** is applied to these images.

Since humans are most sensitive to the red portion of visible light, red is commonly used in creating false-color images. The choice of red as the dominant hue ensures that we can see the maximum amount of image detail.

You'll find the most dramatic example of false-color technology in color photo-infrared images. Here, red is used to represent electromagnetic energy just beyond visible red wavelengths. Since in this zone healthy vegetation is highly reflective, the red component of these images represents plant health. Deciduous trees will generally be brighter red than conifer species. Roads, buildings, and parking lots look blue. Water appears black, unless contaminated with sediments or supporting considerable plant life.

False-color thermal, passive microwave, SLAR, and Doppler radar images are found in all variety of colors. Since choice of color is arbitrary, it's up to you to determine this information from the image legend. Once you've done so, you can interpret color as an indicator of energy strength within the associated waveband. Different environmental features will have different spectral responses and will thus be represented by different colors.

Size

An object's size can be an important identifying clue. The problem is that image maps are available in a variety of scales. Thus, the same-sized object may turn out to be a house on a large-scale image and a farm field on a small-scale image.

You can usually solve this problem by finding some feature on an image, such as a house or road, whose size on the ground is standard. You can then compare your target feature with one of these features of known size.

If you can't find a feature of standard size on an image, then you'll have to determine the image scale. As with conventional line maps, the scale is defined as the ratio of image distance to ground distance (see Appendix A: *Map Scale*). Once you know the image scale, you can easily determine the ground size of an object on the image.

Avoid taking a shortcut here. Low-contrast images, and objects which contrast little with their background, can make it difficult to determine an object's image size. Although you may feel a scale check is too much effort, it is time well spent. Novice interpreters often ignore size considerations altogether, or make unjustified size assumptions. But unless you make at least a rough size approximation, you risk becoming hopelessly confused in identifying features.

Shadow

The shadows cast by environmental features are important cues in image interpretation in several respects. On conventional photos, the tone of a shadow is usually darker than the tone of an object. Objects that occur within shadows reflect little light energy and will be harder to discern than similar objects not in shadows. In this respect, shadows hinder feature recognition.

But shadows can make it easier to recognize objects, too. A shadow gives a vertical profile of an object, indicating the object's shape. For instance, on a vertical image map, a water tower might appear as a circle. You could have trouble distinguishing it from a round building, tank, or pool. The water tower's shadow would provide the information needed to identify it. Likewise, you can use shadow information to differentiate between conifer and deciduous trees.

On non-photographic images, shadows have a different meaning. On thermal images, "shadows" may represent the cooling that occurs when sunlight is blocked. For instance, although

clouds won't be visible because the long thermal wavelengths easily penetrate them, the "cool" shadow of clouds may indeed be noticeable. This can be particularly confusing on images taken when a scattering of isolated but dense clouds is present.

Similarly, the cooling effect of wind can cause tonal streaking of the image. Leeward areas tend to be warmer than windward areas. The resulting pattern can be intricate and confusing since it is related to objects' height and density as well as to wind speed and direction.

On radar images, shadows represent areas in which microwave energy from the sensor was blocked. These shadows are completely black, unlike the somewhat transparent shadows on conventional photos (see Figure 24.9). Radar shadows are cast from raised objects in a direction perpendicular (at right angles) to the flightline of the sensor vehicle (see Figure B.9). The lower the sensor vehicle and the higher the relief, the longer the shadows.

Shadows can have a curious effect on the interpretation of relief features. In order to see raised features and maximize the relief effect, you must view the image with the shadows falling to your lower-right. In other words, you want to face the source of illumination. To do otherwise is to risk getting the impression that raised objects are depressed, and vice versa. This apparent reversal of relief is called the **pseudoscopic effect** (see Figure 5.4).

The people who produce image maps have established conventions which unwittingly encourage relief reversal. The problem arises because images taken in the northern hemisphere are commonly labeled along their north edge. Since in this hemisphere the sun is usually located to the south, holding these images with the labeling at the top means that the shadows fall away, not toward, the observer. The likely consequence is relief reversal. To overcome this possibility, it is good practice to rotate an image until the relief effect is maximized before you interpret the image. Once you determine the image's date, try to ignore the position of the labels.

Pattern

Repetition of certain general forms or relationships is characteristic of many environmental fea-

505

PART III
Map Interpretation

506

tures. This spatial arrangement creates a pattern, which can be a helpful aid in recognizing objects.

Pattern is valuable because it signals some underlying environmental process. Pattern represents order, and order has a cause. If we can figure out what process led to the pattern, our image interpretation will be facilitated. Since natural processes lead to different types of pattern than human processes, it is convenient to separate the impact of these two factors for purposes of discussion.

Natural processes usually result in more irregular patterns than those of human origin. Natural patterns are created by the great physical, chemical, electromagnetic, gravitational, and biological forces of nature. Some of these earth-molding forces, such as volcanic, tectonic, and biological growth processes, build new landscapes. Other processes, such as erosion (by the action of gravity, wind, water, and ice), biological decay, and chemical dissolution, tear down these landscapes. The environment reflects a historical tension between these construction and destruction processes.

Examples of natural patterns abound. Glaciers and lava flows, for instance, reflect movement in their spatial structure (**Figure 24.10A**). Beach ridges along a water body whose surface level has dropped display growth rings that are easily recognized (**Figure 24.10B**). Sand dunes, even when covered with forest, exhibit a characteristic wind-blown pattern (**Figure 24.10C**). A

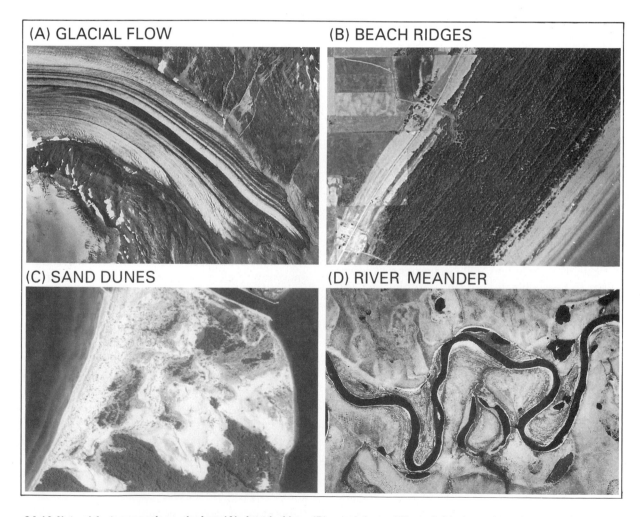

(A) GLACIAL FLOW

(B) BEACH RIDGES

(C) SAND DUNES

(D) RIVER MEANDER

24.10 Natural features such as glaciers (A), beach ridges (B), sand dunes (C), and river meanders (D) are often easy to identify by their characteristic pattern on image maps.

meandering river in a broad, flat valley, with its cut-off meanders and ox-bow lakes, is equally easy to spot (**Figure 24.10D**).

In contrast to these natural patterns, human patterns tend to have a simple form, with sharp angles, straight lines, and smooth curves. These arrangements can be traced to the effects of technological, political, economic, and social forces. The result is such recognizable patterns as street grids, farm fields, orchards, trailer courts, mine tailings, auto junkyards, and countless other arrangements.

Patterns of human origin aren't always so uniform, however. Sometimes human activity is purposefully guided along irregular courses in an attempt to make life more interesting or natural.

This happens with golf courses, for example, and with upscale residential subdivisions.

More commonly, human activity that takes on an irregular structure has been influenced by the natural environment. For instance, a strip mine may follow the mineral outcrop around the sides of a valley (see Figure 23.11A). Or a road may follow the irregular ridge or valley line in a region of highly dissected terrain.

Site and Situation

The relation of an object to surrounding features can provide useful hints to its identity, and may be the only way to recognize some objects. Many environmental features are closely linked and therefore occur in association with each other.

For example, factories and warehouses are often served by a railroad. Thus, you can differentiate a factory from a similarly-sized school, which would rarely be located near a railroad (**Figure 24.11**).

Likewise, you can distinguish high schools from grade schools on an image map by looking at surrounding features. Near high schools, you'll find football fields, baseball diamonds, running tracks, and parking lots for students and teachers. Near grade schools, you'll see playground equipment, open playing fields, and parking for teachers only.

Vegetation types are also found in association with certain landscape forms. You can guess, for instance, that trees near the tree line on a Colorado mountain are spruce or fir, while those at lower altitude are oaks or aspen.

Anticipation is fundamental in human communication because it speeds up the process. Written and spoken language is rife with errors and omissions, yet we're able to understand by using context to anticipate details. Likewise, the geographical situation provides a means of anticipating what to look for on an image map.

For example, we would expect to find a storage area for boats along a lakeshore. Thus, a boat storage shed near a freeway will be more difficult to identify than one located near a lake. Likewise, a ferris wheel stored in a farm field will be harder to recognize than one in an amusement park.

In some cases a feature may not be visible, but its location can be predicted on the basis of

507

(A)FACTORY

(B) SCHOOL

24.11 You can use the relations between site and situation to determine the function of buildings, such as a factory (A) and a school (B).

508

24.12 The pattern of roads, tanks, powerlines, and well sites on this small-scale photo all suggest an oil field, even though the pumps themselves aren't obvious.

context. Animal trails converging on a watering trough or spring in a dry landscape might be clearly visible on an image, for example, even though the source of water isn't evident. The pattern of roads, tanks, and well sites that suggest an oil field may all be visible, even though the oil pumps themselves aren't distinguishable (**Figure 24.12**).

So far we've considered site and situation cues only where there is a connection between a site and its situation. The reverse condition can also yield insights. If there appears to be no connection between a feature and its surroundings, we can guess that the setting will provide relatively little interpretative information. We can thus conclude that the feature is connected at a more regional level than that of the image. Examples include roads, pipelines, powerlines, railroads, communication transmission towers, and similar features that serve a regional rather than a local purpose.

Texture

Many environmental features are too small to be perceived individually on an image map. Together, however, their shape, size, arrangement, shadow, and tone combine to give a clear pattern of tonal variation. The frequency of tonal change is referred to as texture (see Figure 23.10).

Texture may range from coarse (in the case of mature trees with broad crowns) to fine (in the case of grass). As an image's scale becomes smaller, the texture of a given feature grows progressively finer. Eventually, of course, smaller scales will cause the feature's texture to disappear.

This relationship between texture and scale is a key factor in image interpretation. When using texture as an interpretation clue, the first step is to determine image scale. Then imagine what size an object must be to create a given texture at that scale.

Texture is an excellent aid in identifying crops and vegetation types. The texture of corn is quite different from that of alfalfa. Similarly, spruce and pine trees have different textures.

Context

It is best to approach image interpretation with as much information as possible about when and how the image was created. This information will enhance the efficiency as well as the effectiveness of the interpretation process. It will help you to anticipate and to project, to draw on a storehouse of information not found on the image itself.

Thus, before you interpret an image, you should know when the image was created, the environmental character of the region, and the method used to create the image. Let's look at each of these factors in detail.

Date and Time

The environment is constantly changing. Features commonly change through the cycle of seasons. What appears as a light tone in the spring may be a dark tone in the summer and a light tone again in the fall. Thus, it's crucial to know the date of the image.

It may also be important to know whether the image was taken during the day or night. On conventional photos, for example, shadow length is directly related to the time of day the image was taken. Long shadows may indicate high objects, but they may also be the result of a low sun angle.

On thermal images, the time of image creation is even more significant than on conventional photos. The reason is that thermal images don't depend on sunlight and, therefore, can be taken at any time of day or night. In addition, environmen-

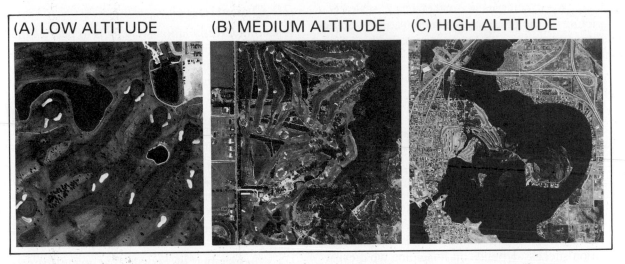

24.13 Large-scale images provide the best feature detail (A), but small-scale images are more useful for studying regional patterns in the landscape (C). Notice how the appearance of the golf course changes as the photo scale changes.

tal features heat up and cool down through a diurnal cycle as well as a seasonal cycle. These cycles vary from one feature to another. This differential temperature change can cause the thermal crossover phenomenon discussed earlier in this chapter (see *Thermal Imagery*).

Region

The location of a region depicted on an image map can provide vital clues to the interpreter. Both the natural and human environment vary from one region to another.

A region's climate is of particular importance because it is closely related to the nature of landforms, soils, hydrography, plant and animal life, and land use. Cultural regions are also significant, because the pattern of human activity can differ markedly from place to place.

Imaging Method

The same feature can appear very different from one image to another, simply because of the many variables of remote sensing. These variables include the vantage point and resolution (spatial, spectral, radiometric) of the sensor.

Before interpreting an image, then, you must determine how the image mapping method has represented the environment. On one image, light tone will mean one thing, while on a different image it will mean another. This is particular-

ly true of false-color images (photo-infrared, thermal, microwave), on which red, for example, might represent vegetation, heat, or microwave reflectance.

SCALE GRADIENT

Earlier (see *Size*), we discussed image scale. We noted that scale is important in identifying features because it determines the apparent (or image) size of an object.

Scale also is important in image interpretation for other reasons. Large-scale image maps are easiest to interpret because they provide details familiar from our daily experience. On these images, we have strong visual cues such as contrast differences, shadows, size, shape, and texture to help distinguish between features (**Figure 24.13A**). Indeed, large-scale images can appear so realistic and familiar that you almost feel you are there.

This familiarity is quickly lost as image scale decreases. The smaller an image's scale, the fewer environmental details are visible (**Figures 24.13B** and **24.13C**). There is a progressive loss of cues, such as shadows, and a general degradation of feature definition. As the small features that make up most of what we see in day-to-day living disappear, the image perspective becomes less and less familiar.

510

What emerges at smaller image scales is a picture of the relations between features—something we may not be aware of in daily living. Size, pattern, site, and situation cues become more important in recognizing features as image scale decreases.

INTERPRETATION STRATEGY

Image interpretation draws on a wide range of skills. The most successful interpreters are those with keen powers of observation and a rich and varied environment experience. Image interpretation success depends on imagining what everyday features might look like if viewed from an elevated, distant vantage point. Here are several strategies to help you polish your image interpretation skills.

Checklist

The keys to feature recognition which we've been discussing can serve as your conceptual tools. When you consciously apply them to an image map, they will help you distinguish features and see their graphic characteristics. These keys will extend and enrich your image analysis vocabulary.

When you want to identify a feature on an image map, run down the list of keys in Figure 24.2. You'll be surprised at how easily this triggers ideas. The identity of many features will become apparent well before you reach the end of the checklist.

What you're doing here is getting in touch with the tacit knowledge you've acquired over your lifetime but have lost to your subconscious. Your goal is to use the image to help you remember.

Guard against using only size, or shape, or any other cue by itself or in combination with only one or two other cues. These keys only represent concepts we can use to stimulate the way we think about the environment. The environment is a single whole, in which everything occurs simultaneously. Objects can best be recognized by integrating information from all of the interpretation keys.

20 Questions

A second interpretation strategy is to play a game similar to "20 Questions." Ask yourself, first: Is the feature primarily of natural or human origin?

If the feature is primarily human, does it reflect agriculture, recreation, mineral exploitation, forestry, or transportation (pipelines, railroads, roads, airports, canals, power transmission, telecommunication)? Does it represent residential, commercial, or industrial forces?

If natural, does the feature reflect the atmosphere, biosphere, lithosphere, or hydrosphere (lakes, rivers)? Or does it represent the combined effect of these spheres (such as climate)?

Remember, of course, that many features are the result of physical impact on human activity, human impact on physical features, interactions between human and physical forces, or complex feedback relations between the physical and human realms.

Quotas

Patience is also of paramount importance in image interpretation. You must guard against leaping to conclusions at the first hint of a feature's identity.

A good strategy for creative, productive thought is to set an idea quota. For example, you might set yourself a quota of three ideas. You would then refrain from coming to a judgment until you've come up with three possible interpretations. These possibilities may be as off-the-wall as you like, because your only goal at this point is to meet the quota.

Once you've used intuition to meet your quota, it's time to release the power of analytical thinking. Analyze the pros and cons of each idea. Eliminate any idea that doesn't stand up to rational scrutiny. This will leave you with the most plausible interpretation or, at worst, several possible identifications. Go back to your checklist if you want more insight.

Now let's test this quota strategy. Study **Figure 24.14**. Before reading further, make up a list of possible explanations for the strip of missing vegetation running from left to right near the top of the photo. After you've filled your quota of ideas, go back and logically determine which is

24.14 This aerial photo was taken in the Snoqualmie Pass area of Washington's Cascade Mountains. Can you identify the wide, treeless linear feature running from left to right near the top of the photo?

the most plausible. After you're satisfied with your answer, check the footnote at the bottom of the page.*

....
The straight-line geometry of this target feature suggests it is a human creation. Your quota of ideas might include such guesses as pipeline, international boundary, road, canal, powerline, clearcut logging, railroad, and so forth. Notice that the target feature ignores terrain and has no connection to other features on the image. It seems merely to pass through the region. Since it doesn't make sense to log such a narrow, long strip of land, clearcut logging can be assigned a low probability. Since roads, railroads, and canals are all evident elsewhere on the photo and look quite different from our target feature, these also get a low probability. Roads can be seen crossing the target feature at will, so an international boundary is also unlikely. This leaves a powerline as the most likely idea. Indeed, the feature is a right-of-way for high-tension powerlines. Look closely and you'll see shadows from the towers that hold up the wires. You can even see some of the powerlines.

Meaning

Often you'll recognize a feature on an image map but have no ready answer for why it is found where it is. This is particularly true when the feature is of human origin, since its location will be influenced by political, social, technological, and economic forces. To decipher the meaning of such features, it helps to understand human motivation, especially how people use the land.

Consider, for example, the image provided in **Figure 24.15**. A large marsh with a number of ponds is evident. The rectangular shape and regular spacing of the ponds suggest a human origin. But why would people spend valuable resources making ponds in a marsh? No roads or trails to the ponds are evident, so it is unlikely that people use the ponds for recreation. The ponds are obviously not needed as a source of irrigation or domestic water. So what happened here?

The answer is obvious if you're tuned in to modern wetland management ideas. The ponds

512

24.15 The regular shape and pattern of these wildlife ponds, dug in a wetland area, provide useful interpretation cues.

24.16 Sometimes features, such as this pond in a gravel pit, are the consequence rather than the aim of human activity.

were made with the aid of special "wildlife funds" in an attempt to improve waterfowl habitat. This activity is intended to compensate for the widespread destruction of wetlands due to urban growth, industry, and agriculture.

Notice how our explanation came from focusing on the question "Why would people spend scarce resources building ponds in a marsh?" It's easier to explain a cultural feature if you remember that people have reasons for doing what they do at different locations. It takes time, energy, and money to create visible impressions on the landscape. Thus, little that you see of human origin on an image map "just happened."

Something similar can be said for physical features. You can usually find evidence of the work of wind, gravity, sunshine, precipitation, and so on to aid in your explanation.

Beware, however, of bi-product features. Novice image interpreters often have trouble explaining coincidental features, such as a pond in a gravel pit. In **Figure 24.16**, for example, the pond (the dark feature in the top-center of the image) wasn't the aim but, rather, the consequence of mineral extraction activity.

Always consider the possibility that the feature you're studying is best explained by some related activity. Sometimes, as in the case of a cleared strip through a forest for a powerline right-of-way, the associated activity (in this case,

the powerline) may not even be visible at the image scale.

MENTAL TEMPLATES

It's easier to recognize something familiar than something new. Once you've identified a feature on one image, then, you'll recognize it much more quickly next time.

Classes of features have distinctive characteristics. Once you've seen one trailer park, you have in a sense seen them all. These class prototypes are stored in your brain as **visual templates**, to later be recalled and matched to image features under scrutiny.

Thus, as you practice image interpretation, it's a good idea to take advantage of successful identifications. After you've recognized a feature, go back and review in your mind the information that led you to this conclusion. Become conscious of the decision path you followed. By doing so, you'll make it easier to identify the same category of features next time. Also, your decision-making will become more and more intuitive as you assess your successful strategies.

The value of experience is that it shifts the feature identification threshold from conscious (analytical) to unconscious (intuitive). The more experience you have, the more intuitive you will become and the fewer analytical cues you'll need to trigger an identification.

Even the novice will holistically recognize familiar features, of course. Similarly, experts have to become more analytical when they encounter an unfamiliar feature. Thus, the relative importance of analysis and intuition in feature identification will vary from situation to situation.

Remember that the smaller the image scale, the fewer the interpretation clues. As you progress from novice to expert, therefore, you'll be able to work with smaller and smaller scale images.

Mental template building will help you increase your image interpretation skill rapidly with experience. But you always face the problem of encountering something you've never before seen. To get around this lack of direct experience, you can train with the aid of feature templates. **Figure 24.17A** shows a variety of such templates taken from images, and **Figure 24.17B** shows sketches of image forms that can also serve as templates. More such templates can be found in standard image interpretation texts. By studying these and similar examples, you'll build your store of generic mental templates.

AUTOMATED FEATURE IDENTIFICATION

With a little practice, most people can become proficient image interpreters. The trick is to stimulate and nurture our intuitive mind so that it generates a range of creative ideas, which we then evaluate through rational thought. This process of idea generation and evaluation that is so characteristic of human intelligence does have limitations, however. It takes time, and it is restricted by the sensitivity of the human eye.

Due to increased demand for environmental monitoring through remote sensing, human interpreters have been overwhelmed in recent years by the volume of image maps, especially those generated by satellites. It is understandable that people have turned to machines for help. The machine of choice is the electronic computer.

Image Classification

The most dramatic examples of automated image interpretation fall in the realm of image classification. Software for image classification is now available for computers of all sizes. Smaller computers are slower and more restricted in the size of image that can be handled, of course.

The basic requirement for automated image classification is a powerful microcomputer. A graphics workstation is preferred. Whatever computer configuration is used, the image must first be available in digital form. Increasingly, digital imagery comes directly from electronic scanners. But existing images can also be converted to digital form in the laboratory, using a video recorder, electronic still camera, film recorder, or scanner.

24.17 As you gain experience in image interpretation, you build up a storehouse of useful mental feature templates, which greatly speed the process.

514

All image processing programs available commercially today manipulate only the tonal value of individual pixels, usually in several different wavebands at the same time. The image classification logic is far more sophisticated in some programs than in others, and their classification accuracy varies accordingly.

Two approaches are used in image classification programs. The first, called **density slicing**, entails looking for natural groupings in a frequency plot of tones, and placing class boundaries between these groupings (**Figure 24.18**). Since no information other than that on the image is used in density slicing, the technique is commonly called **unsupervised classification**.

Although the results of density slicing can be dramatic, the technique suffers from the problem that environmental features aren't always the same tone in different locations on an image. Lakes illustrate this point well, since they may be light-toned in one part of an image and dark-toned in another, depending on the positions of the sun, the sensor, and the reflectivity of the water surface (see Figure 24.4).

A more sophisticated approach to image classification is to combine image tone information with a sample of feature identifications made in the field. The idea is to go to the environment, determine the landcover at a selection of sites, and then look at the tone of the image at those locations. A plot of tones at the selected sites for known landcovers can then be used to assign tones at other sites to their probable feature classes (**Figure 24.19**). Since field information is used to inform or "train" the classifier, this procedure is known as **supervised classification**.

The best programs for desktop computers can achieve 80 to 90 percent landcover classification accuracies using multispectral satellite imagery of 30-meter spatial resolution and a map-

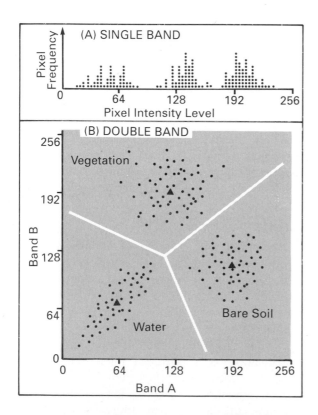

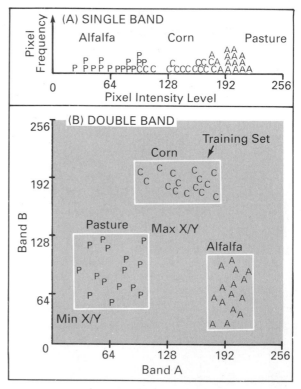

24.18 When the computer searches for natural groupings in the tone of pixels, the process is called density slicing or unsupervised classification. Here density slicing is illustrated using tonal data from a single band (A) and data from two bands plotted against each other (B).

24.19 When field data are used to determine the tone of known features, the computer can produce what is known as a supervised classification. Here supervised classification is illustrated using tonal data from a single band (A) and by plotting data from one band against another (B).

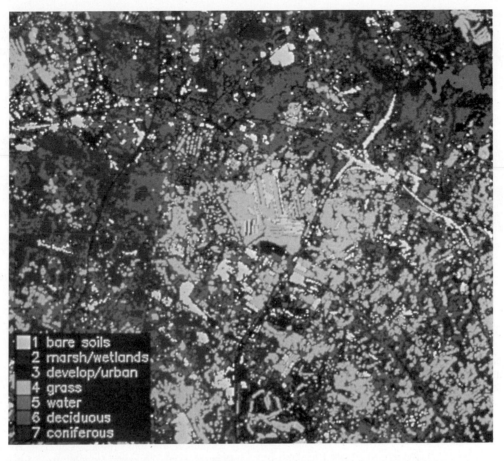

1 bare soils
2 marsh/wetlands
3 develop/urban
4 grass
5 water
6 deciduous
7 coniferous

24.20 This map was produced quickly with the aid of automated image classification procedures and is useful for many purposes. The actual classification accuracy isn't known, however, so there is reason for caution. (This is a black-and-white reproduction of a color original.)

ping scale of 1:100,000. If multispectral imagery of 10-meter spatial resolution is used, similar results can be achieved at a mapping scale of 1:24,000. **Figure 24.20** is a typical map based on automated image classification procedures.

Notice the phrase "landcover classification" in the previous paragraph. Existing image classification programs identify such features as vegetation zones, bare soil, crop types, water bodies, urban areas, and so forth. They don't identify schools, beaver dams, railroads, and other individual features.

Each pixel in the image is classified separately on the basis of its tonal characteristics. Complexes of these classified pixels make up the classification zones on the image. The result is primarily descriptive and relatively insensitive to the functional nature of classified features. You might learn that a feature is a water body, but have no

indication whether it is used for stock watering, human drinking, fish breeding, waterfowl nesting, or sewage treatment. In other words, true interpretation that gets at the "why?" aspect of the image is missing.

Theme Extraction

If you can be satisfied with a general classification of landcover, then automated procedures may serve your needs. It is currently possible, for example, to extract various landcover themes from an image using a desktop image classification system. You can see what is covered with water, what is land, what part of the land is covered with vegetation of a certain type or density, and so on (**Figure 24.21**).

You may want, for instance, to estimate Iowa corn yield prior to harvest. In this case, a

516

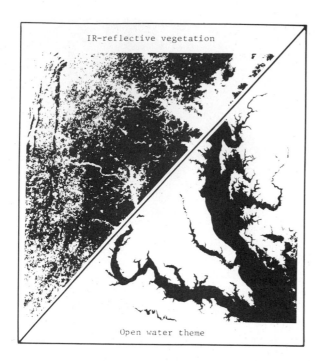

24.21 Image processing methods have been used to extract themes from the Landsat imagery illustrated in Figure B.21 in Appendix B (upper Chesapeake Bay area).

theme extraction that isolates the acreage in corn would be ideal. You would then merely add up the pixels classified as corn, multiply the total by the pixel size in acres, and multiply that figure by the estimated corn yield per acre.

Promising Future

To date, automated feature identification has relied solely on tonal variations in multiband imagery, ignoring the other interpretation keys that people find so useful. Furthermore, such automation has emulated only the analytical side of human thought, neglecting the intuitive, holistic side. Massive numbers of calculations made at very high speed have been used as a substitute for human intelligence.

Despite these shortcomings when compared to human interpreters, automated methods are useful in classifying landcover and landscape types, and hold promise for feature identification as well. Major advances can be expected as we learn to use the other keys to image interpretation in conjunction with tone.

Even greater breakthroughs can be anticipated when we learn to use the intuitive side of human intelligence in concert with the analytical approach taken currently. Chess-playing computers have led advances in this hybrid information processing environment with spectacular results. The best computer programs can now beat the world's top chess players. Can image-interpreting computers be far behind?

SELECTED READINGS

Arnold, R.H., *Interpretation of Airphotos and Remotely Sensed Imagery* (Englewood Cliffs, NJ: Prentice-Hall, 1997).

Avery, T. E., *Interpretation of Aerial Photographs*, 4th ed. (Minneapolis: Burgess Publishing Co., 1985).

Avery, T.E., and Berlin, G.L., *Fundamentals of Remote Sensing and Airphoto Interpretation*, 5th ed. (Englewood Cliffs, NJ: Prentice-Hall, 1992).

Blair, C.L., and Gutsell, B.V., *The American Landscape: Map and Air Photo Interpretation* (New York: McGraw-Hill Book Co., 1974).

Blair, C.L., Frid, B.R., and Day, E.E.D., *Canadian Landscape: Map and Air Photo Interpretation*, 3rd ed. (Toronto, ON: Copp Clark Pitman, 1990).

Brugioni, D.A., "The Art and Science of Photoreconnaissance," *Scientific American* (March 1996), pp. 78-85.

Buisseret, D., ed., *From Sea Charts to Satellite Images: Interpreting North American History through Maps* (Chicago: The University of Chicago Press, 1990).

Conway, E.D., and the Maryland Space Grant Consortium, *An Introduction to Satellite Imagery Interpretation* (Baltimore: The Johns Hopkins University Press, 1997).

Denegre, J., ed., *Thematic Mapping from Satellite Imagery* (London: Elsevier Applied Science Publishers, Ltd., 1988).

Doane, J., *America: An Aerial View* (New York: Crescent Books, 1978).

Drury, S.A., *A Guide to Remote Sensing: Interpreting Images of the Earth* (New York: Oxford University Press, 1990).

Editons Technip, *Photo Interpretation*, Paris, France (bimonthly journal that provides detailed discussion of several interpretation problems in each issue).

El-Baz, F., "Space Age Archaeology," *Scientific American* (August 1997), pp. 60-65.

Erickson, J., *Exploring Earth from Space* (Blue Ridge Summit, PA: TAB Books, Inc., 1989).

Frohn, R.C., *Remote Sensing for Landscape Ecology* (Boca Raton, FL: Lewis Publishers, 1997).

Hock, T.K., and Brown, E.D.R., *Geographical Interpretation Through Photographs* (London: George Allen & Unwin, 1972).

Jensen, J.R., *Introductory Digital Image Processing: A Remote Sensing Perspective*, 2nd ed. (Upper Saddle River, NJ: Prentice-Hall, 1996).

Lillesand, T.M., and Kiefer, R.W., *Remote Sensing and Image Interpretation*, 3rd ed. (New York: John Wiley & Sons, 1994).

Muller, J.P., *Digital Image Processing in Remote Sensing* (London: Taylor & Francis, 1988).

Rabenhorst, T.D., and McDermott, R.D., *Applied Cartography: Introduction to Remote Sensing* (Columbus, OH: Merrill Publishing Co., 1989).

Stephens, N., *Natural Landscapes of Britain from the Air* (New York, Cambridge University Press, 1990).

Stone, K.H., "A Guide to the Interpretation and Analysis of Aerial Photos," *Annals of the Association of American Geographers*, 54, 3 (September, 1964), pp. 318-328.

Ungar, S.G., *The Earth's Surface Studied from Space* (Oxford: Pergamon Press, 1985).

Verbyla, D.L., *Satellite Remote Sensing of Natural Resources* (Boca Raton, FL: Lewis Publishers, 1995).

Wanless, H.R., *Aerial Stereo Photographs* (Northbrook, IL: Hubbard Press, 1973).

Williams, J., *Geographic Information from Space: Processing and Application of Geocoded Satellite Images* (New York: John Wiley & Sons, 1995).

Wood, E.A., *Science from Your Airplane Window*, 2nd ed. (New York: Dover Publications, Inc., 1975).

Also see references in Chapter 4 and Appendix B.

517

PART III
*Map
Interpretation*

CHAPTER TWENTY-FIVE

MAPS AND REALITY

INTRODUCTION

THE NATURE OF MAPS

What Makes Maps Popular?
Cartographic Artifacts
The Missing Essence
Imaginative Map Use

THE MAP AS REALITY

Abuse
Propaganda
Degraded Environmental Image
Abstract Decision Making

REALITY AS A MAP

SURVIVAL

We Are Human
Living With Map Limitations

SELECTED READINGS

It is not down on any map: true places never are.

—Herman Melville, *Moby Dick*

25
CHAPTER TWENTY-FIVE
MAPS AND REALITY

...the very best map-reader ha[s] to suffer some severe shocks when he comes face to face with reality.

(Josephine Tey, *The Man in the Queue*, p. 138)

This observation about map use, disquieting though it may be, is as important as anything we have learned about maps. Our ultimate aim, after all, is not to understand maps. Maps are just one means to our real goal—to understand the world.

If we don't look beyond map symbols to the reality they represent, we may defeat our purpose and end up with a warped view of our surroundings. The gravest accusation we can make of maps is that they may taint our judgments about the environment. In this chapter, then, we will look at the hazards of putting too much faith in maps, of not realizing their limitations, and of forgetting to look beyond symbols to the real world. We will begin by taking a closer look at the nature of maps.

THE NATURE OF MAPS

By now you have a good idea of the many things maps can do. But to use maps wisely, you must also realize what they can't do, for maps are useful only within certain limits. As you explore the nature of maps, you'll discover that the very things that make maps so valuable hold their own built-in dangers.

What Makes Maps Popular?

In scrutinizing the nature of maps, the obvious question is, "What accounts for their widespread popularity?" There are four main factors.

Maps are convenient to use. They are usually small and flat for ease of storage and handling. Thus, they bring reality into less unwieldy proportion for study.

Maps simplify our surroundings. Without them, our world often seems a chaos of unrelated phenomena, a mass of meaningless events. The selection of information found on a map, on the other hand, is clear at a glance. The world becomes intelligible.

Maps are credible. They claim to show how things really are. The coordination between symbol and reality seems so straightforward that we're comfortable letting maps "stand for" the environment. When we manipulate maps, we expect the results to apply in our surroundings. Maps, even more than the printed word, impress people as authentic. We tend to accept the information on maps without question.

And, finally, **maps have strong visual impact.** Maps create a direct, dramatic, and lasting impression of the environment. Their graphic form appeals to our visual sense. It's axiomatic that "seeing is believing" and "a picture is worth a thousand words."

These factors combine to make a map appealing and useful. Yet these same four factors, when viewed from a different perspective, can be seen as limitations.

Take **convenience.** It's what makes frozen dinners popular. When we buy processed foods, we trade quality for easy preparation. Few would argue that the result tastes like the real thing made from fresh ingredients. The same is true of maps. We gain ease of handling and storage by creating an artificial image of the environment. This distortion of reality is bound to make maps imperfect in many ways.

Simplicity, too, can be seen as a liability as well as an asset. Simplification of the environment through mapping is nothing but an illusion which appeals to our limited information-processing ability. By using maps, we avoid confronting reality in its overwhelming and confusing natural state. But the environment remains unchanged. It's just our view of it that lacks detail and complexity. If we can understand map information at a glance, it's because maps are such crude models of our surroundings. Yet it's the environment, not the map, that we want to understand.

You should also question the **credibility** of maps. The map maker's invisible hand isn't always reliable or rational. Some map features are distortions; others are errors; still others have been omitted through oversight or design. So many perversions of reality are inherent in mapping that the result is best viewed as an intricate, controlled fiction. Maps are like statistics: People can use them to show whatever they want. And once a map is made, it may last forever, although the world keeps changing. For all these reasons, a map's credibility is open to debate.

Nor should you overrate maps' **visual impact.** To create a vivid, lasting impression, maps must have a strong figure-ground organization. Just about the only maps that meet this condition are thematic maps, which stress a few features (figure) at the expense of many (ground). Even these maps may not make as great an impression as you think. (Try drawing a map of your state. Although you've seen one dozens of times, chances are you can't recreate it perfectly.)

Also, be careful not to confuse maps' visual impact with proof or explanation. Just because a map leaves a powerful effect doesn't make it meaningful. Simply because map features are close together doesn't mean they're related. For explanations you must look beyond maps and come face to face with the real world. And when you do so, as Josephine Tey pointed out in the quote beginning this chapter, you're in for some shocks.

Cartographic Artifacts

One shock you have to face is that much of what you see on a map doesn't exist in reality. Many map features are pure cartographic fiction—the result of the mapping process. The first time you realize this, you may react as indignantly as Huck Finn did while on a balloon trip with Tom Sawyer. When Huck commented that they were flying over Illinois, Tom asked how he could be sure. Huck replied:

"I know by the color. We're right over Illinois yet. And you can see for yourself that Indiana ain't in sight."

"I wonder what's the matter with you, Huck. You know by the *color*?"

"Yes, of course I do."

"What's the color got to do with it?"

"It's got everything to do with it. Illinois

is green, Indiana is pink. You show me any pink down there, if you can. No sir; it's green."

"Indiana *pink*? Why, what a lie!"

"It ain't no lie; I've seen it on the map, and it's pink."

You never see a person so aggravated and disgusted. He says:

"Well, if I was such a numskull as you, Huck Finn, I would jump over. Seen it on the map! Huck Finn, did you reckon the states was the same color out-of-doors as they are on the map?"

"Tom Sawyer, what's a map for? Ain't it to learn you facts?"

"Of course."

"Well, then, how's it going to do that if it tells lies? That's what I want to know."

(Twain, *Tom Sawyer Abroad*, pp. 42-43)

Huck's question is a good one: How can a map give you facts if it tells lies? The answer is central to an understanding of maps. To tell the truth, a map *must* lie. As you saw in Chapter 3, *Map Abstraction Process*, elaborate generalization is required to transform reality to a map. This process is a helpful way to organize and reduce the detail of our world. But each stage of this transformation process adds map features which bear little or no relation to reality. The danger is that these effects will so dominate the map that you'll mistake them for aspects of the environment.

Most map readers aren't as naive as Huck. Few of us expect a map's colors to be the same on the ground or a tree's symbol to look like its leafy real-life counterpart. It's obvious that colors and other symbols are **artifacts** of the mapping process and have nothing to do with the environment. Yet even sophisticated map users can mistake cartographic artifacts for real geographical features, as a few examples will show.

Image maps, created from photos, are a good example, since many people don't think of them as maps at all. Photos, they reason, can't contain misleading artifacts because they show the environment exactly as it is. This is one of the biggest map misconceptions. Photos, like all maps, contain distortions and artifacts of the methods used to make them.

For one thing, atmospheric and light conditions can alter tones and textures on photos. As you saw in Chapter 4, this problem is especially clear on mosaics, made by fitting several photos together. Figure 4.14, a mosaic of high-altitude photos, shows the mottled effect of different tones and textures. Notice, too, that some lines joining the photos are unnoticeable, while others stand out clearly. If you don't realize how the map was made, you could confuse these method-produced designs with real environmental patterns. Like Huck, you could expect to see in reality what was only a cartographer's technique.

Even on a single image map, features can vary dramatically in tone. A lake in one corner of a photo may appear as a light tone, for example, while a similar lake in another corner appears dark. You might jump to the conclusion that these variations indicate different water depths, turbidity levels, or algae growth. But if the map's other lakes show the same light-to-dark trend, you can assume that light reflection, not water quality, provides the explanation.

Other artifacts are caused by flaws in the mapping or photographic process. It's common, for instance, to find streaks across an image map. For you, the map user, it doesn't matter whether these streaks are caused by the film, camera, development, or reproduction. The effect is the same. You just want to be sure you don't come up with some exotic interpretation for a feature which doesn't even exist.

You can't anticipate every possible artifact. The best defense is to learn to recognize the effects of various mapping methods. Whenever you look at a map, review the transformations required to make it. Envision these methods' impact on the map's appearance. This will keep you from reading into reality something which exists only on the map.

The Missing Essence

The fact that many things on maps don't exist in reality, troublesome though it is, is only one side of the coin. Even more serious is the fact that many things in reality are missing from maps. Indeed, it seems to be the most beautiful and humanizing parts of our lives which are absent from map abstractions. In his *Diary* (November 10, 1860), Thoreau laments the inadequacy of a map:

How little there is on an ordinary map! How little, I mean, that concerns the walker and the lover of nature. Between the lines indicating roads is a plain blank space in the form of

522

a square or triangle or polygon or segment of a circle, and there is naught to distinguish this from another area of similar size and form. Yet the one may be covered, in fact, with a primitive oak wood, like that of Boxboro, waving and creaking in the wind, such as may make the reputation of a county, while the other is a stretching plain with scarcely a tree on it. The wauling woods, the dells and glades and green banks and smiling fields, the huge boulders, etc., etc., are not on the map....

By condensing geographical relations into symbols, we make the environment easy to study, but we also make it sterile. The essence of life, that which is most crucial, rarely is found on a map. In *Travels With Charley* (p. 71), Steinbeck records which highways he took on his cross-country trip and adds:

I can report this because I have a map before me, but what I remember has no reference to the numbers and colored lines and squiggles.

Maps seldom capture life's vivid, meaningful experiences—the touches, sounds, smells, and linkages between people and their surroundings. The price of losing these traits is that we may forget the relation between an object and its map symbol.

An example occurred at a meeting of geographers, who were shown an animated map of traffic accidents. Lights flashed periodically to show the location and severity of crashes. The audience learned to anticipate the pattern, breaking into laughter when the screen "lit up" with the havoc caused by drinking drivers each Friday and Saturday night.

What happened here? These weren't callous people. If they came across a bloody accident, the last thing they would do is laugh. The problem, then, must be with the map. Somehow, when traffic crashes were transformed into map symbols, the pain and horror of the reality was lost.

Thus, this incident casts doubt on our ability to translate from map symbol to reality. It also raises questions about the compassion of decision makers. If insensitive people use maps to make plans and policies, you have reason to be concerned. This problem is critical, for as our society grows more impersonalized, the need for more humanistic decision making increases. Before making judgments which will affect the environ-

ment and other people, it is vital to reconstruct a map's "missing essence." The best way to do so is through imaginative map use.

Imaginative Map Use

To gain the most from maps, you must be willing to stretch your imagination, allowing symbols to conjure up their full meaning in your mind. Map symbols are meaningless in themselves. They are meant to direct your thought beyond the map to the environment. Here, for example, is what an imaginative map reader saw in one line symbol:

Finally, there was the fact that this was a frontier region. That meant far more than a line on a map. It meant all the treachery, the corruption, the bravado, and the watchfulness of such a confrontation.

(Drummond, *Cable Car,* p. 73)

Every symbol holds such hidden meanings if you look for them. It's up to you to step from map to real world—and a giant step it is. Getting at realities beneath appearances is never easy. Can you imagine a map which evokes images of disaster less than the "disaster map" in **Figure 25.1**? At a glance, you'd never know it portrays floods, tornados, and other disasters. The matter-of-fact symbols don't begin to show the devastated fields, shattered towns, homeless people, and ruined lives caused by these disasters. It takes a vast imaginative leap to look at such symbols and picture reality.

One person who has perfected the technique of using imagination to look beyond map symbols is the armchair traveler. Before travel was as widespread as it is today, writers often remarked that those who had never traveled could have exciting journeys by map. In *Don Quixote* (Vol. 3, p. 80), Cervantes commented that one can "journey all over the universe in a map, without the expense and fatigue of traveling, without suffering the inconveniences of heat, cold, hunger, and thirst."

A map can inspire an imaginative person to enter the reality it depicts. Joseph Conrad (*Heart of Darkness*, p. 33) has noted the imaginative appeal of maps:

Now when I was a little chap I had a passion for maps. I would look for hours at South America, or Africa, or Australia, and lose myself in all the glories of exploration. At that

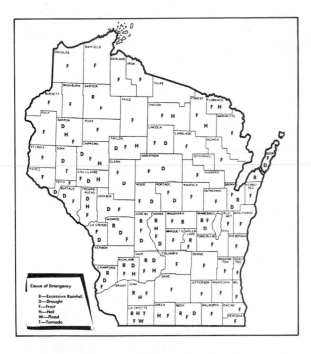

25.1 This map shows the 68 counties in Wisconsin which were designated "disaster areas" because of crop loss in 1974. Note how hard it is to achieve a visual impression due to the poor graphic design.

time there were many blank spaces on the earth, and when I saw one that looked particularly inviting on a map (but they all look that) I would put my finger on it and say, "When I grow up I will go there."

The fact that even blank spaces can generate excitement underscores the imagination's power to give maps depth. As Aldo Leopold put it:

> To those devoid of imagination, a blank place on the map is a useless waste; to others, the most valuable part.

In *Deliverance*, James Dickey (pp. 7-8) also suggests a map's ability to evoke more than the composite of its symbols. In the novel, some friends plan a trip down a river which will soon be obliterated by a new dam. For Ed, the narrator, the map has a power and vitality—almost a life of its own.

> "When they take another survey and rework this map," Lewis said, "all this in here will be blue...."
>
> I leaned forward and concentrated down into the invisible shape he had drawn, trying

to see the changes that would come, the nighttime rising of dammed water bringing a new lake up with its choice lots, its marinas and beer cans, and also trying to visualize the land as Lewis said it was at that moment, unvisited and free.... I looked around the bar and then back into the map, picking up the river where we would enter it....

The author's wording gives life to the map; we can almost see the river running. By using such phrases as "looked into the map," Dickey suggests that a map isn't just something at which you glance but something *into which* you can see. For Ed, the map holds an unknown dimension, wonder, and excitement. He can see a crooked blue line on paper and at the same time a raging river. As he studies the map, he sees even more (p.13):

> It [the map] was certainly not much from the standpoint of design. The high ground, in tan and an even paler tone of brown, meandered in and out of various shades and shapes of green, and there was nothing to call you or stop you on one place or the other. Yet the eye could not leave the whole; there was a harmony of some kind. Maybe, I thought, it's because this tries to show what exists. And also because it represents something that is going to change, for good. There, near my left hand, a new color, a blue, would seep upward into the paper, and I tried to move my mind there and nowhere else and imagine a single detail that, if I didn't see it that weekend, I never would; tried to make out a deer's eye in the leaves, tried to pick up a single stone.

This ability to let your imagination carry you from map to reality is the sign of skilled map use. Once you have this knack, maps will be truly beautiful and useful to you, evoking images and emotions beyond the printed paper or computer screen. But if you lack the imagination to move from a map's abstract image to the concrete world, you will never realize the map's full value.

THE MAP AS REALITY

We began this book with the statement that maps mirror the world. Therefore, we suggested, the better your knowledge of maps, the wiser your spatial behavior. If we carry this analogy further, we see that some cautions are built in. A mirror is a useful tool, but it shows only a piece of reality. No one would confuse its reflection with the real thing. Yet a surprising number of people treat maps' reflection of the world as if it were reality.

Substituting maps for reality encourages a mechanical rather than humane view. A statement such as "the explosion wiped the town off the map" ignores the fact that a real town has suffered. Such fuzzy thinking can cause a confusion of cause and effect. How often do you hear people speak of "the changing map" when they're referring to a changing world? They see maps as actors rather than reflectors of the world. This viewpoint suggests that if we could keep maps from changing, we could keep the world from changing—or that by changing a map, we could change the world.

The extremes to which such faulty reasoning can carry us are portrayed in the novel *Catch-22*. The men in a bomb squadron have been ordered to bomb Bologna the next day. They stare pleadingly at the bomb line on the map, as if that mapped line were itself to blame.

> "I really can't believe it," Clevinger exclaimed to Yossarian in a voice rising and falling in protest and wonder. "It's a complete reversion to primitive superstition. They're confusing cause and effect. It makes as much sense as knocking on wood or crossing your fingers. They really believe that we wouldn't have to fly that mission tomorrow if someone would only tiptoe up to the map in the middle of the night and move the bomb line over Bologna. Can you imagine? You and I must be the only rational ones left."
>
> In the middle of the night Yossarian knocked on wood, crossed his fingers, and tiptoed out of his tent to move the bomb line up over Bologna.
>
> (Heller, p. 117)

The next morning the men consult the map. Sure enough, it shows that Bologna has been captured. The mission is canceled, and everyone is happy.

The outcome here is a pleasant one. Usually, though, you get in trouble when you substitute maps for reality. Sometimes the result is merely inconvenience and narrow-mindedness. But the consequences can be far more serious, as you will see.

Abuse

When you treat maps as reality, it becomes easy to view the environment in impersonal, machine-like terms. Environmental features are dwarfed on maps. People are invisible. The cultural environment (farms, cities, roads) looks like a child's board game. The world is reduced to an unchanging background against which you play out your life. If you don't remind yourself how limited maps are, you can lose sight of that "missing essence" which is found on no map but only in reality.

In *I Was a Savage*, a Nigerian educated in the United States describes his eagerness to return to his people and share the wonders of maps. To his surprise, his father was less than enthusiastic:

> Maps are liars, he told me briefly. . . . The things that hurt do not show on the map. The truth of a place is in the joy and the hurt that come from it. I had best not put my trust in anything as inadequate as a map, he counseled.
>
> (Prince Modupe, p. 147)

Many preliterate people share this distrust of maps, and with good reason. Maps separate you from the environment. If you see yourself as part of your environment, you know you can't harm it without harming yourself. If you reduce your environment to symbols on a map, however, you're more apt to abuse it. You can then misuse maps just as you can mutilate a person's photo while you wouldn't think of injuring the real person. There's an important difference, though: When you paint a mustache on a political poster, the politician doesn't suffer. But when your behavior results from abusive map use, reality may bear the consequences.

When environmental decision makers treat a map as mere symbols and disregard the real-life emotions it represents, the results can be disastrous. City planners, for instance, may be tempted to build a new freeway along the line that looks straightest and most convenient on the map. But the route may disrupt thousands of people's lives or the ecology of an area where an endangered animal species lives. Thus, it might be better to take a more roundabout path, along which there are no homes or animals facing extinction. The map way isn't always the best way.

It can't be overstressed that the reason for studying maps is to understand the real world, not the map world. When you make plans based on maps, it's not the map but reality which stands to gain or lose. This fact may seem obvious. Yet time and again, people draw map boundaries for a project without regard for the people or region to be affected. Subdivisions are constructed, dams built, neighborhoods "renewed," all without due thought for those who will suffer.

This is also one of the tragedies of war. Many people die needlessly because the way that looked simplest on the map wasn't the wisest way in the field. A commander may study a map, decide that a certain spot would make a good observation point, and give the order to march. While peering at symbols on a map, it's convenient to ignore such things as terrain or climate or morale. Yet these factors will influence the soldiers who must obey the orders. While it takes only a second to put that X on the map, it may take millions of dollars of equipment, weeks of time, and a terrible toll of lives to carry out the mission.

People who surround themselves with maps are liable to arrive at cold strategies, untempered by feelings, if they forget who or what will bear the consequences of their decisions. In *The Naked and the Dead* (p. 567), Norman Mailer describes such an unimaginative map reader. Major Dalleson, making strategy decisions with maps during the war, "had a picture for a moment of the troops moving sullenly along a jungle trail, swearing at the heat, but he couldn't connect that to the figures on the map. An insect crawled sluggishly over his desk and he flicked it off." As casually as this, as casually as he brushes an insect from his desk, a decision is made and people's fate decided.

Major General Cummings, another *Naked and the Dead* character, wanted to reduce reality to mere "figures on the map." He was frustrated that soldiers' emotions kept his plans from being as effective in real life as in theory. At one point (p. 277), Cummings threw down his pencil and "stared with febrile loathing at the map board by his cot. By now, it was a taunt to him." He could control the map world but not the reality.

War encourages military officers to substitute maps for reality. Miles from the battlefield, surrounded by "complete" map intelligence, they find the consequences of their actions easy to ignore. To make a few lines on a map is painless. To visualize the soldiers and their loved ones, the landscapes and ecosystems whose doom is sealed by those mapped lines is another matter. How different it would be if the decision makers were there when their decisions were carried out!

Even the soldiers who carry out these decisions aren't always in direct touch with reality, as an article about bomb crews over Vietnam tells us:

> The maps used by the crews show almost no place names. One general said that kept the maps uncluttered. It also keeps them impersonal. The targets are given code numbers and are marked by intersecting map coordinates. "For all you know," one pilot said, "you could be bombing New York City."
>
> "As far as losing any sleep over what we're doing, how many people we kill ... we never get to see the damage," said Captain Crook, whose home is in Memphis.

(*The New York Times*, October 13, 1972, p. 12)

4-7   © 1977 by NEA. Inc. T.M. Reg. U.S. Pat. Off.

"Hopkins, I see you just as a pin in our western sales territory ... not as someone who deserves a raise!"

526

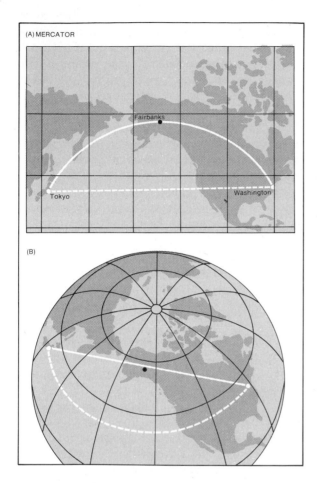

(A) MERCATOR

Fairbanks

Tokyo   Washington

(B)

25.2 A map projection which distorts earth relations can be a convincing propaganda aid. Here, the great circle route between Washington, D.C., and Tokyo is contrasted with a small circle route.

In this case, technology has removed military personnel from the reality of fighting and killing and made possible warfare by remote control. The bomb crew, with only their maps to go by, need never face the destruction they have caused.

> For the crewmen, sitting in their air-conditioned compartments more than five miles above the steamy jungle of South Vietnam, the bomb run had been merely another familiar technical exercise. The crew knew virtually nothing about their target and they showed no curiosity. Only the radar-navigator, who in earlier wars would have been called the bombardier, saw the bombs exploding, and those distant flashes gave no hint of the awesome eruption of flames and steel on the ground.... A crewman said that bombing South Vietnam from a B-52 was like "delivering the mail."

Likewise, the media referred to the Persian Gulf War as the "Nintendo war" and praised "smart" bombs for their "surgical strikes." As *Newsweek* (January 28, 1991) described it:

> It all seemed effortless, antiseptic and surreal: casualties were very light, at least among the attackers, and the high-tech gadgets in America's multibillion-dollar arsenal seemed to work with surgical lethality. Like a day at the office, one pilot said.

Map abuses are by no means solely responsible for war's atrocities. But we can trace many military difficulties to maps' insensitivity to crucial human and environmental features—and to map users' failure to take this missing essence into account.

All maps aren't equally insensitive, of course. Since some types represent reality better than others, decisions based on one map won't be the same as those based on another. Image maps, for instance, show much more information than conventional line maps and therefore aren't as likely to be abused. The consequences of military actions are also more evident on an image map, providing more information for decision making.

Propaganda

Most people who abuse maps in decision making do so out of ignorance rather than malice. But another danger of treating maps as reality is that map makers can deliberately mislead us. Such propaganda is common, especially on advertising, political, and religious maps. Since all maps distort reality, what could be easier than to make this distortion serve a special propaganda theme? And unless we know enough to question every map, how would we suspect anything was wrong?

We've seen, for example, that all map projections distort some combination of distance, direction, area, shape, or earth continuity. Thus, it's a simple step for map makers to use projections to suit their own ends. Take the case of Gerald Ford's trip to the Orient when he was President of the United States and campaigning for re-election. His political opponents complained that this was a tax-supported campaign junket disguised as a diplomatic trip. As evidence, they trotted out a Mercator projection (which makes compass lines straight). They used it to suggest that Ford didn't fly straight to Tokyo.

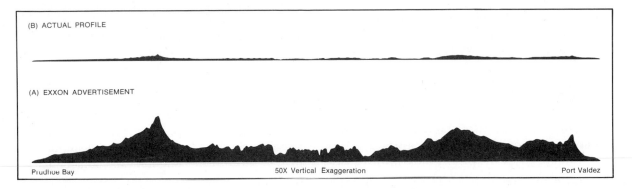

(B) ACTUAL PROFILE

(A) EXXON ADVERTISEMENT

Prudhoe Bay   50X Vertical Exaggeration   Port Valdez

25.3 By exaggerating the vertical dimension 50 times in this ad showing the Alaska pipeline, Exxon may have gained sympathy and thereby made eventual customers more tolerant of higher gasoline prices.

Instead, they charged, he flew far out of the way—as far as Alaska—to make a political speech (**Figure 25.2A**). In reality, the shortest route from Washington to Tokyo (a great circle) actually cuts across Alaska north of Fairbanks, where Ford made his speech on a normal refueling stop. He didn't fly out of the way at all. This fact is revealed on a map which shows great circles as straight lines (**Figure 25.2B**). The Republicans were the victims of map propaganda, and few voters realized it.

Map makers can also distort maps in the vertical dimension. Note the Exxon ad in **Figure 25.3A**. The oil company's aim was to win over Alaska-pipeline skeptics. It wanted to show that it was taking care to preserve the environment despite the difficulties of building its pipeline in mountainous regions. Of course Exxon wanted to make these difficulties seem as monumental as possible. It did so dramatically—by exaggerating the vertical dimension 50 times in the relief profile. When we compare this magnification of relief with the actual profile (**Figure 25.3B**), the false impression passed along to the public is obvious. In fairness to Exxon, it did have to overcome major topographic obstacles to build the pipeline. The question is whether the ad was designed to make the high price of North Slope oil more acceptable when it was marketed in the lower 48 states.

In the same way, map makers can manipulate the vertical component when mapping non-topographic distributions. Such distributions include, for example, per-capita income, incidence of alcoholism, and population density. The problem is that there's no way to equate figures

for such distributions with physical-distance measures on a map's horizontal scale. The only rule for adjusting the vertical dimension is to make maps "look right." The result may be biased mapping. It's not hard to imagine, for example, that if the forces opposing family planning paid a map

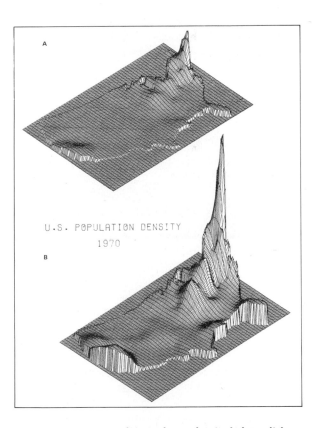

U.S. POPULATION DENSITY
1970

25.4 Using the same data and mapping technique, it is a simple task to make the United States appear sparsely settled on one hand or densely settled on the other.

528

maker to show population density, the result might look like **Figure 25.4A**. In contrast, a map of the same data, paid for by forces for zero population growth, might resemble **Figure 25.4B**. Both maps are correct, of course, since there's no true vertical dimension to such a map. Still, these are unmistakable examples of persuasive cartography. Before you use three-dimensional maps of non-terrain surfaces, then, be sure to consider possible effects of the map maker's bias.

Another type of propaganda involves disproportionate symbols. As we've seen, map makers must make symbols overly large. Otherwise, the symbols wouldn't show up at reduced map scales. In propaganda mapping, map makers carry this normal aspect of cartographic abstraction to extremes. Imagine that a resort wants to show that nearby lakes have excellent fishing. Which of the maps in **Figure 25.5** better conveys this idea? Both maps use the same number of symbols. But the map with the larger symbols suggests you would actually be alleviating a serious overcrowding problem by catching a few!

National Car Rental Agency evidently learned the effectiveness of symbol size exaggeration, for it changed its ad from **Figure 25.6A** to **25.6B**. There's no denying that the second ad gives a more impressive picture of the company's scope. The remarkable thing is that the first ad is less effective even though it shows more car rental locations (check Florida, for example).

Insurance companies, too, often deliberately exaggerate symbol size on their maps. Their purpose is to show that no matter where you are when you need help, there will always be an agent nearby. How better to give this impression than to show agents shoulder to shoulder across a map of the country? Yet if you have an accident, you soon realize that agents aren't standing shoulder to shoulder on the ground. You could wait a long time for assistance, especially in less populous regions.

Map simplification can also be used for propaganda purposes. **Figure 25.7** shows two maps of illegal West Bank settlements. Both maps come from the same weekly news magazine. One map depicts 16 settlements, while the other shows 30 settlements. Which is correct? The truth, revealed deep in the magazine's text, is that there were 45 illegal Israeli settlements in the West Bank region when these maps were made in the mid-1980s. The legend, at the least, should have provided this

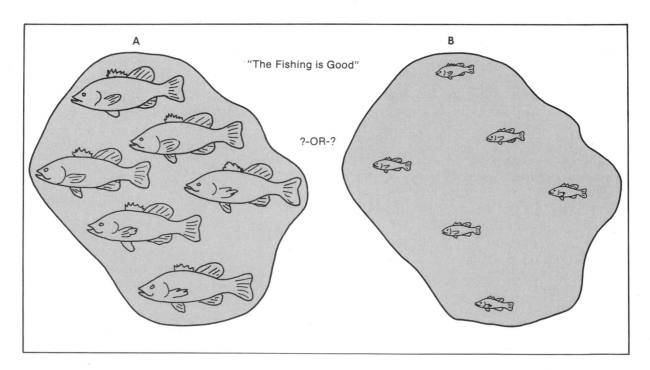

25.5 The psychological impact of map design may entice people to stay at a fishing resort. In this case disproportionate symbols are used to create different impressions.

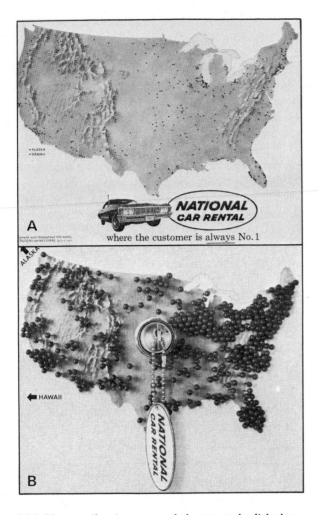

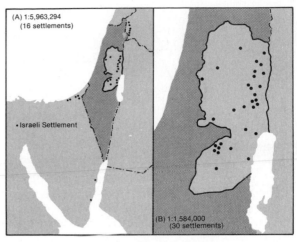

25.7 The need for map simplification can easily be used to create a propaganda effect. Here West Bank settlements on maps of two scales are shown (examples taken from a weekly news magazine in the mid-1980s).

25.6 Disproportionate map symbols may make it look as though car rental agencies are crowding each other off the land.

information. The makers of these maps, however, clearly favored the Israeli cause and thus played down the illegal settlements. You should never overlook the possibility for such political bias in mapping.

It pays to be especially cautious of novel or artful advertising maps, because they are invariably more eye-catching than factual. Consider the propaganda effect of **Figure 25.8**, taken from a Wisconsin Dells travel guide. The map was printed at a scale of one inch to 56 miles so that distance units could be matched with the 55-mile-per-hour speed limit. If we could travel at the maximum speed limit under all conditions at all times, the map scale could be stated in time-distance units as one inch to one hour. But we

can't possibly travel 55 miles per hour on all roads under all conditions. Furthermore, roads don't lead from all places directly to the Wisconsin Dells. Thus, the idea of drawing equally spaced travel rings around the Dells is absurd. The average travel time to the Dells from Traverse City, Michigan, for example, is 10 hours under the best conditions, not four hours as the map suggests. These deceptive travel times may lure tourists to set off on a much longer trip than they expect.

A more subtle form of map propaganda is the use of symbols which have suggestive powers beyond their factual role. Colors in particular are often manipulated on maps to produce the desired psychological response. Red symbols, for instance, are used to attract our attention to threats, action, or danger. On battle zone maps of Vietnam, red was commonly used to depict the enemy when support for our side was needed. Conversely, red was used to represent our side when there was a need to convince Congress or the constituents of our successes.

Color is a favorite propaganda tool because of the unconscious associations it can evoke. Warm colors (red, orange, yellow) are said to stimulate the mind, to invite interaction. Map makers frequently use them as interior decorators do—to elicit feelings of pleasure, happiness, and comfort. In contrast, cold colors (blue, purple, black) are believed to have a depressing effect on the mind.

530

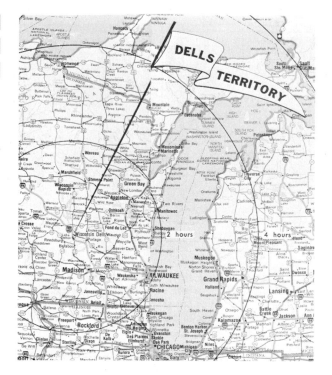

25.8 On this deceptive map, travel time to the Wisconsin Dells is shown by concentric circles spaced two hours' driving time apart. But distance is measured "as the crow flies," not as the car travels.

They are used on maps to create a moody, negative reaction. Even the bright, lively character of warm colors can be muted by mixing in some gray. The success of such use of color is open to question, of course. Some people are undoubtedly affected more than others. Judging from the maps they produce, however, advertisers believe the technique has merit.

Design as well as color can be manipulated to evoke the desired response. Notice the layout of the map in **Figure 25.9A**. Ordinarily a map—or any picture with so much black at the top—would be considered poor design, because it seems top-heavy, unbalanced. On this 1970s-era map from *Time* magazine, however, the intent was to show white-ruled South Africa being hemmed in by black-ruled countries, and the map's design helps to give that impression. South Africa looks threatened, overcome by ominous forces. If we interchange the black and white colors, a different mood is created (**Figure 25.9B**). The design slips into balance, and the feeling of menace disappears.

This is by no means an isolated incident. The same design trick was used repeatedly in mapping the Vietnam war. The maps were meant to show

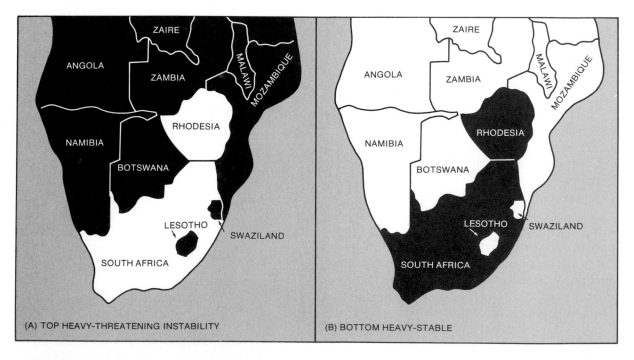

25.9 The visual balance of map symbols can be modified to create different impressions. Having black at the top and white at the bottom (A) is less stable visually than the reverse (B).

how the Communists were threatening from the north to take over American-controlled provinces in the south. Again, map makers created an impression of sinister foreboding by using black at the top of the map. (This ploy, obviously, works only with regions oriented in a north-south direction).

Whether we realize it or not, map makers are constantly molding our attitudes. Of course, they aren't the only people guilty of propaganda. But the effect of map propaganda is especially insidious because so many people believe that maps are neutral and unbiased. The consequences are often dramatic: A year's vacation is ruined, or a retirement nestegg is spent on a land parcel in the swamp.

The best way to avoid being victimized is to make a deliberate search for maps used as propaganda. Any magazine or newspaper contains a wealth of examples. Once you learn to sort out normal distortion from cartographic trickery, you'll be amazed at how often map propaganda occurs. You should be especially suspicious of any map produced by a special-interest group to support its point of view.

Degraded Environmental Image

Another result of treating maps as reality may be to hinder us from experiencing a rich, full life, as Steinbeck (*Travels With Charley*, p. 23) reminds us:

> For weeks I had studied maps, large-scale and small, but maps are not reality at all—they can be tyrants. I know people who are so immersed in road maps that they never see the countryside they pass through, and others who, having traced a route, are held to it as though held by flanged wheels to rails.

You would be wise to adopt Steinbeck's suspicion of maps as complete records of reality. As he notes, a map represents only a few of many truths. Its purpose is to help us see more, but if you expect too much of it, it may keep you from seeing anything.

> There are map people whose joy is to lavish more attention on the sheets of colored paper than on the colored land rolling by. I have listened to accounts by such travelers in which every road number was remembered, every mileage recalled, and every little countryside discovered. Another kind of traveler

requires to know in terms of maps exactly where he is pin-pointed every moment, as though there were some kind of safety in black and red lines, in dotted indications and squirming blue of lakes and the shadings that indicate mountains.

(*Travels With Charley*, p. 70)

By realizing a map's limitations, Steinbeck found his cross-country trip far more satisfying than his friends who were slaves to maps. For him, a map was useful as a framework for his memories. Maps enhanced rather than detracted from his enjoyment because he was wisely aware that "maps are not reality at all."

Abstract Decision Making

Although there are dangers in treating maps as reality, at times such a viewpoint has advantages. Decision makers who deal with emotional issues (and pressure groups) may find it easier to do their jobs when they can work with symbols. Our values and feelings are less aroused when working with abstractions than when confronting ugly or distasteful issues directly. Thus, an objective, removed position may be desirable; otherwise, short-term satisfaction might compromise the long-range good.

In *Night Flight*, Saint-Exupéry describes a decision maker who has learned that only by treating maps as reality can he do his duty. The character Riviére has the job of tracing the flights of pilots who carry the mail at night. In the pioneering days of air mail delivery depicted in this novel, such flights involved great hazard, and Riviére knows that each time he sends a plane into the darkness, he risks a pilot's life. As he stares at the map with the air lines traced in red, he muses (p. 48):

> "On the face of it, a pretty scheme enough— but it's ruthless. When one thinks of all the lives, young fellows' lives, it has cost us! It's a fine, solid thing and we must bow to its authority, of course; but what a host of problems it presents!" With Riviére, however, nothing mattered save the end in view.

For a moment Riviére has allowed his imagination to make the leap from the cold, solid "face" of the map to the reality it symbolizes. To accomplish "the end in view," however, he must veer abruptly from this reality and think of the map as an

531

532

abstract thing. Otherwise, he couldn't keep sending pilots into such danger. He would be better off, perhaps, would suffer less, if he were a more unimaginative map reader.

Map readers are, in a way, like doctors, who must put emotional distance between themselves and their patients. Otherwise, tragic cases may impair their judgment. Some doctors succeed so well that patients complain they're treated as diseases or broken bones, not as the frightened people they are. We would hope our doctors would strike a balance between emotion and rationality. When we use maps to make decisions which affect other people, we must achieve just such a balance. Overly emotional decisions are as undesirable as overly insensitive ones. When we need to transcend our human limitations, maps can provide a useful counterbalancing perspective.

REALITY AS A MAP

We've seen how dangerous it is to treat maps as reality. Just as dangerous is the mistake of treating reality as if it were a map—of thinking that the world is laid out in map-like form. How many people look down at the earth from an airplane and say, "It looks exactly like a map"? Such a statement is comparable to gazing at the Grand Canyon and remarking, "It looks just like a postcard"; this attitude strips an incredible sight of its grandeur. Likewise, when we view the world as a map, the land becomes a thing—fragmented, split, weakened, drained.

To see the earth as a map is to reduce it to a skeleton of its true self. Consider the old Pan Am advertisement shown in **Figure 25.10**. The text states:

> We're the only U.S. airline that can honestly promise you the world. . . . It's true for the simplest of reasons: we're the only airline that flies to all parts of the world from America. 84 cities in 58 countries on 6 continents. . . .

The accompanying map dramatizes the absurdity of such ad copy. Pan Am, even in its heyday, obviously couldn't fly you to "all parts of the world," since thousands of cities, hundreds of countries, and one of the seven continents were unvisited by the airline.

25.10 This Pan Am ad from the mid-1980s has the effect of reducing the environment to a mere skeleton of its true self.

Regrettably, this confusion of maps and reality isn't an isolated incident. We all know people who claim to have visited nearly every state in the nation; when pressed, they admit that all they saw of many states was an airport or freeway. Even business executives who cross the United States hundreds of times may be familiar with little more than the views from Holiday Inns. Although the *map* says they're in a distant state, in *reality* they may as well be at the Holiday Inn in their home town.

Marlowe, Joseph Conrad's narrator in *Heart of Darkness* (p. 48), describes the map-like way we often view an unfamiliar environment:

> Next day I left that station at last, with a caravan of sixty men, for a two-hundred-mile tramp.
>
> No use telling you much about that. Paths, paths, everywhere; a stamped-in network of paths spreading over the empty land, through long grass, through burnt grass, through thickets, down and up chilly ravines,

up and down stony hills ablaze with heat; and a solitude, a solitude, nobody, not a hut.

To maintain his sanity in the African jungle, Marlowe reduces the environment to a series of connected pathways, like lines on a map. The abundance of plant and animal life between those paths he dismisses as "empty land."

Many people simplify the world this way when thrust into an unfamiliar setting. But it's a bad habit to develop. With this map-like conception of reality, it's easy to lose your orientation. Whatever is unknown becomes, as it did for Marlowe, a wilderness to be avoided.

"Wilderness" doesn't have to be the backwoods kind, of course; for some people, a trip to the central city is as adventuresome as a journey to the Yukon. We fear what we don't understand. If we would stop infusing our world with the structure of a map and explore its true variety, we might find many of our fears unfounded.

Reality may often remind you of a map, but the world has a wonderful complexity which is lacking on maps. Symbols of any kind hold reality at bay. To best deal with your environment, ask yourself what processes produced the map-like structure and what relation this pattern has to the rest of your surroundings.

The error of treating reality as a map can affect your whole perception of yourself and your world. The following warning about photographs applies to all types of maps:

> [P]hotography as art has had a lot to do with the way we perceive the world and react to it, and to some extent the accepted image of our environment is one that the art of photography has given us.
>
> They (photographers) have taught us a way to look at the world, and in turn, we see the world their way.
>
> And that is the rub. The curious thing about images of the environment is that they inevitably structure reality. Our perception is trained by them. . . .
>
> In architecture and urbanism the photograph has become as valid as the thing itself.
>
> (Ada Louise Huxtable, *The New York Times*, Nov. 25, 1973, Section 2, p. 26)

So it is with a map-like view of reality. Such environmental images are no more objective than photographs; they reflect the way *we* view the world.

SURVIVAL

The deficiency of both the "map as reality" and "reality as map" attitudes is that they separate you from your environment. They encourage you to ignore the interrelationships upon which your quality of life and your survival depend.

Maps are a metaphor for a limited kind of experience. Mapped qualities may have as little relation to the world as a telephone number to its subscriber. You must place maps in perspective as a limited communication device, only one of many. To put too much emphasis on maps is to screen out much of what is crucial to environmental behavior.

Rather than see the environment as map makers do, biased by the tools of their profession, take an omniscient viewpoint. Unite yourself and the environment in all phases of experience. Only when you see the whole environment as one system, as events separate but united in time and space, will you appreciate all that maps have to offer. While viewing a map, you can then bridge the distance between you and the environment and look *into* rather than *at* map symbols.

This task of visualizing mapped features in all their depth won't be simple. It will take effort and experience. The job will be hardest when you're sitting in an environmentally controlled room scrutinizing artificial map symbols, far removed from the phenomena under study and the procedures used to create the map. In addition, your job is complicated by an obvious but often overlooked fact: We all are human.

We Are Human

Mapping, as a communication process, is influenced by human shortcomings throughout. We, map maker and map user alike, are fallible. We crave simplicity; we are strong in some areas and weak in others; we are biased in many ways; and our integrity, judgment, and insight are never beyond question. We are human, and the mapping process is built around this fact.

Every map is a reflection of a myriad of decisions made by the map maker. It's not a copy but a semblance of reality, filtered by the map maker's motives and perceptions. The map is partly a representation of reality and partly a product of its maker. The map maker's knowledge, skill, and

534

integrity all enter the map design. If 10 map makers were given the same mapping task, the results would vary widely. Some of their maps would be effective and pleasing, while others would fail to communicate or would actually mislead.

But the blame for poor map communication doesn't rest entirely with the map maker. You, the map user, approach maps with the bias of your experience, motives, and skill. Your biggest danger is that you'll see what you want to see or anticipate seeing. You can guard against this tendency by keeping an open mind.

Sometimes the penalty for being a human link in the cartographic process is disaster. A pilot misreads a map, and an airplane crashes. Deadly accidents occur when drivers miss their freeway exit and try to turn back. Soldiers are bombed by their own comrades when map coordinates are misunderstood.

Luckily, the price of misusing maps is usually more frustrating than disastrous for most of us. And even this frustration can be reduced if you understand the nature of maps. There's no way to eliminate human failings or map limitations, but once you know they exist you can learn to live with them.

Living With Map Limitations

You've seen how maps' abstract, generalized nature introduces the potential for error and abuse. Yet these same qualities are what make maps so valuable for showing the big picture. If a map's strengths are also its weaknesses, the opposite is true as well. A map is remarkably useful as long as you don't ask it to do things for which it wasn't designed. You mustn't, for instance, ask a map to be the same as reality; if it were, it would lose its unique clarifying function.

One problem with maps is that they are rarely tailored to the requirements of the individual user. Therefore, they are seldom perfect for specific needs. Most map makers have only a vague idea of who will use their maps. But you can learn to live with this map weakness, too. Maps are available in infinite variety. You can save yourself grief by finding the best map available for each situation, rather than using one map for all purposes.

If you're aware of map limitations, it's usually easy to make up for them. It makes sense to

bring as much experience and information as possible to bear on map interpretation. The best navigators are those who augment map information with all the direct "ground truth" they can. Pilots don't land their planes or dock their ships with maps; they rely on direct visual or instrumental contact during those final, crucial moments. Part of using maps shrewdly is knowing when to go beyond them.

Every map represents just one way of looking at reality. If one map doesn't serve your needs, don't become disenchanted with all maps. Perhaps you can find another map which better fits your requirements. Or maybe you need to supplement your map or turn to another source of information. But if you give up on maps entirely, you are cheating yourself, for at some other time they may be exactly what you need. You must strike a balance between too much faith and not enough faith in maps.

In this chapter, we have stressed that maps are incomplete, limited, and often faulty. But maps needn't be perfect to be useful, as Alvin Toffler points out in *Future Shock* (p. 6):

> Even error has its uses. The maps of the world drawn by the medieval cartographers were so hopelessly inaccurate, so filled with factual error, that they elicit condescending smiles today when almost the entire surface of the earth has been charted. Yet the great explorers could never have discovered the New World without them. Nor could the better, more accurate maps of today been drawn until men, working with the limited evidence available to them, set down on paper their bold conceptions of worlds they had never seen.

Those old maps, so pitifully lacking, served an indispensable function by moving us the next step to something better. Our still-flawed maps of today serve the same purpose. We are on a long path toward understanding the world, and every new map, imperfect though it may be, carries us one step closer to our goal.

SELECTED READINGS

Boggs, S.W., "Cartohypnosis," *Scientific Monthly*, 64 (June 1947), pp. 469-476.

Gersmehl, P.J., "Maps in Landscape Interpretation," *Cartographica*, Monograph 27, 18, 2 (Summer, 1981), pp. 79-114.

Henrickson, A.K., "The Map as an 'Idea': The Role of Cartographic Imagery During the Second World War," *The American Cartographer*, 2, 1 (April 1975), pp.19-53.

Keates, J.S., "Symbols and Meaning in Topographic Maps," *International Yearbook of Cartography*, 12 (1972), pp. 168-180.

Monmonier, M., *How to Lie With Maps* (Chicago: University of Chicago Press, 1991).

Monmonier, M., *Maps, Distortion & Meaning*, Resource Paper No. 77 (Washington, DC: Association of American Geographers, 1977).

Muehrcke, P.C., "Beyond Abstract Map Symbols," *Journal of Geography*, 73, 8 (November 1973), pp. 35-52.

Muehrcke, P.C., "Map Reading and Abuse," *Journal of Geography*, 73, 5 (May 1974), pp. 11-23.

Muehrcke, P.C., and Muehrckc, J.O., "Maps in Literature," *Geographical Review*, 64, 3 (July 1974), pp. 317-338.

Pickles, J., ed., *Ground Truth: The Social Implications of Geographic Information Systems* (New York: The Guilford Press, 1995).

Quam, L.O., "The Use of Maps in Propaganda," *Journal of Geography*, 42, 1 (January 1943), pp. 21-32.

Ristow, W.W., "Journalistic Cartography," *Surveying and Mapping*, 17, 4 (October-December 1957), pp. 369-390.

Speier, H., "Magic Geography," *Social Research*, 8, 3 (1941), pp. 310-330.

Robinson, A.H., "The Image and the Map: The Cartographic Problem," paper presented at the IGU-ICA Joint Session, Montreal, Canada, August 16, 1972.

Robinson, A.H., and Bartz-Petchenik, B., *The Nature of Maps: Essays Toward Understanding Maps and Mapping* (Chicago: University of Chicago Press, 1976).

Tyner, J.A., "Persuasive Cartography: An Examination of the Map as a Subjective Tool of Communication," unpublished Ph.D. dissertation, Department of Geography, University of California, Los Angeles, 1974.

Vernon, J., *The Garden and the Map* (Urbana: University of Illinois Press, 1973).

Wood, D., and Fels, J., "Designs on Signs: Myth and Meaning in Maps," *Cartographica*, 23, 3 (1986), pp. 54-103.

Wright, J.K., "Map Makers Are Human: Comments on the Subjective in Maps," *Geographical Review*, 32, 4 (October 1942), pp. 527-544.

535

PART III
Map Interpretation

APPENDIX A

MAP SCALE

INTRODUCTION

EXPRESSING SCALE

CONVERTING SCALE

DETERMINING SCALE

SCALE PROBLEMS

SELECTED READINGS

"How much further?"

"We've got a hairpin, a thumbnail, and a breathmint to go, according to this map...."

—Erma Bombeck

APPENDIX A

MAP SCALE

Maps are always smaller than the environment they represent. The reduction factor is known as the scale of the map. To use maps effectively, you'll need to convert measurements from map units to ground units. As you might expect, an understanding of map scale is central to performing this task. In this appendix, we'll explore the map-scale abilities needed to become a skilled map user.

EXPRESSING SCALE

Map scale is always given in the form, "This little on the map represents that much on the earth's surface." We can state this relation between map and ground distance in two ways—with respect to a linear measurement, or with respect to an areal measurement.

Linear Scale

The relationship between the map and the ground can be expressed in terms of a linear measurement in three ways—with a word statement, a fraction, or a graphic scale.

Word Statement

The most familiar way to express scale is to use a descriptive phrase or **word statement**. We say that there are so many "centimeters to a kilometer" or "inches to the mile." At first it may be confusing to find that one map indicates scale as "one centimeter to the kilometer" and another as "one kilometer to the centimeter." This lack of standardization should cause little trouble, however, since the shorter measure obviously refers to the map while the larger measure refers to the earth.

A more serious problem is the mixture of distance units, such as centimeters and kilometers, in the same word statement. All the time we're using the map, we must consciously keep these different units in mind. The alternative is to use the same unit throughout—to say, for instance, "one centimeter to 200,000 centimeters" rather than "one centimeter to two kilometers." The advantage of this procedure is that the units themselves then become irrelevant and can be put from our minds. Instead of "one centimeter to

538

200,000 centimeters," the scale might just as well be given as "one inch to 200,000 inches"; it makes no difference in the way we use the map.

Convenient as this method is, though, it introduces an even bigger problem. We have a hard time visualizing what 200,000 centimeters or inches mean in terms of ground distance. It's the same trouble we always have when we try to conceptualize very large numbers. Thus, we're probably better off with our original way of expressing scale. By using larger units of measurement, we eliminate unimaginably huge numbers. The result, regrettably, is that we must learn to think in terms of fractions and multiples of kilometers or miles.

Fraction (Ratio)

A simpler way to describe scale is with a **representative fraction** (**RF** for short). We may also think of this fraction as the **ratio** between map and ground distance. We can write it either as 1/63,360 or 1:63,360. The numerator is always 1 and represents map distance, while the denomi-

nator indicates distance on the ground. Both map and ground distance must be given in the same unit of measurement. The advantage of having identical units on the top and bottom of the fraction is that map measurements may be made in centimeters, inches, or whatever unit you choose.

Graphic Scale

A third way to show map-ground relations is to use a **graphic scale**. The simplest of these, called a **bar scale**, looks like a small ruler printed on the map. We usually read this scale from left to right, beginning at 0. Sometimes the scale is extended to the left of the zero point, using smaller markings (**Figure A.1A**). This allows us to determine distance not only in whole units but also in fractions of units.

The marks on the bar scale are arranged so as to provide whole numbers of kilometers or miles of ground distance. This means that the marks won't represent whole numbers of centimeters or inches—there will almost always be some fraction left over. In other words, although

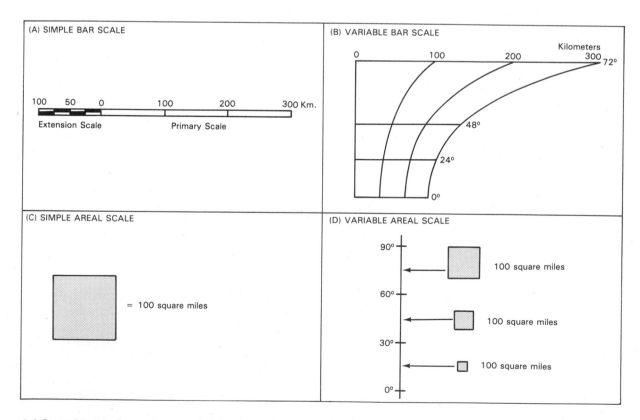

A.1 Several types of graphic scales are found on maps. Shown here are a simple bar scale (A), a variable bar scale (B), a simple areal scale (C), and a variable areal scale (D).

the bar scale *looks* like a ruler, its markings will not coincide with those on your ruler. (Rare exceptions would be a scale of 1:100,000, since at this scale one kilometer on the ground would equal exactly one centimeter on the map, and 1:63,360, since one inch on the map would then be equivalent to one mile on the ground.)

The bar scale has three features which make it especially useful. First, if the map is enlarged or reduced using some method of photocopying, the bar scale changes size in direct proportion to the map. The word statement and representative fraction, on the other hand, lose their meaning when the map changes size. Second, both kilometers and miles can be shown conveniently on the same bar scale. And finally, the bar scale is easy to use when figuring distance on a map, as we see in Chapter 13.

When maps show the whole globe, the scale may vary significantly from one part of the map to another. In such cases, the map maker sometimes replaces the standard bar scale with a **variable graphic scale**. An example of this type of bar scale, taken from a Mercator projection, is given in **Figure A.1B**. Notice that the scale changes systematically in both the north-south and east-west directions. To use such a scale, first decide in what latitude-longitude zone you want to make a distance determination, and then check the scale to see what distance units to use. In effect, you are working with a rubber ruler which can be stretched or shrunk to match the local map scale.

Areal Scale

Although map scales are usually given in linear units such as miles or kilometers, map users are often interested in the size of things in acres or square miles. If the map scale is given in linear units, a conversion to areal units is possible but tends to be a laborious process. Alternatively, the map scale may be given directly in areal units. For example, a word statement might read: one square inch to four square miles (equivalent to a linear scale of 1/126,720).

By far the most common way to show the size of areal units is with the graphic scale. A simple graphic areal scale generally consists of a labeled square or circle of appropriate size (**Figure A.1C**). Variable graphic areal scales consist of a series of squares or circles of different sizes positioned in a latitude-longitude framework (**Figure A.1D**).*

CONVERTING SCALE

If the map maker has been at all conscientious, you will find the scale depicted on the map somewhere. At times, however, it may be in the wrong form to best serve your purpose. Therefore, you may often want to make conversions between a word statement, RF, and graphic scale.

You may, for instance, have a map with a word statement and wish to know the RF. The first thing to remember with any scale conversion is that the ratio is always map distance (numerator) to ground distance (denominator). Suppose that the word statement is three inches to 10 miles. In converting it to an RF, the ratio would be 3"/10 mi. But you can't have a representative fraction with different units on its top and bottom. So you must convert miles to inches—no problem if you just remember that there are 63,360 inches in a miles. Thus:

$$3"/10 \text{ mi.} = 3/10 \times 63,360 = 3/633,600.$$

Remember, too, that the numerator of an RF is always 1.** So in this case you will also have to reduce the numerator from 3 to 1 by dividing numerator and denominator by 3.

$$3/633,600 = \frac{3/3}{633,600/3} = \text{an RF of } 1/211,200.$$

Figure A.2 illustrates some other word statement to RF conversion problems.

Sometimes you may find yourself in the opposite situation. You know the RF but want to know how many miles to the inch or inches to the

---

The distortion ellipses sometimes drawn on map projections to help viewers understand the degree and pattern of distortion represent a form of areal scale (see Figure C.12 in Appendix C).

**Hint: In grade school you learned to "reduce fractions" by dividing the numerator and denominator by the same number, since that procedure didn't change the fractional relationship. Thus, you reduce 6/12 to 1/2 by dividing both the top and bottom of the fraction by 6.*

1″ to 3 miles

$$\frac{1″}{3\text{ mi.}} = \frac{1″}{3 \times 63,360″} = \frac{1}{190,080}$$

5″ to 8 miles

$$\frac{5″}{8\text{ mi.}} = \frac{5″}{8 \times 63,360″} = \frac{5″}{506,880″} = \frac{5/5}{506,880/5} = \frac{1}{101,376}$$

15″ to 1 mile

$$\frac{15″}{1\text{ mi.}} = \frac{15″}{1 \times 63,360″} = \frac{15/15}{63,360/15} = \frac{1}{4,224}$$

.2″ to 5 miles

$$\frac{.2″}{5\text{ mi.}} = \frac{.2″}{5 \times 63,360″} = \frac{.2″}{316,800″} = \frac{.2/.2}{316,800/.2} = \frac{1}{1,584,000}$$

A.2 Converting a word statement to a representative fraction involves manipulating the terms so that the numerator is 1 and both numerator and denominator are in the same units.

mile the map scale represents. If it is miles to the inch that you need, then you merely divide the denominator of the RF by the number of inches in a mile, or 63,360. If it is inches to the mile that you wish, divide the denominator of the RF into 63,360. Similarly, if you want to know kilometers to the centimeter, divide the denominator of the RF by the number of centimeters in a kilometer, or 100,000; if you want centimeters to the kilometer, divide the RF denominator into 100,000.

Some common RF to word statement conversions are provided in **Figure A.3**. Additional conversions can be made indirectly by adding the numbers given in this figure. If the scale of a map is 12 miles to an inch, for example, and you want to know the RF, you can proceed as follows:

$$\begin{array}{l} \ 8 \text{ miles to an inch is } 1{:}506{,}880 \\ +\ \underline{4 \text{ miles to an inch is } 1{:}253{,}440} \\ \ 12 \text{ miles to an inch is } 1{:}760{,}320 \end{array}$$

Or, if the RF is 1:79,200 and you need the number of miles to an inch, just reverse the process:

$$\begin{array}{l} \ 1{:}63{,}360 = 1.00 \text{ mile to an inch} \\ +\ \underline{1{:}15{,}840 = .25 \text{ mile to an inch}} \\ \ 1{:}79{,}200 = 1.25 \text{ miles to an inch} \end{array}$$

Actually, most maps are made at a few common scales. You can therefore save a lot of bother if you figure out beforehand the correspondence between commonly used units of map and ground distance. The best idea is to make your own scale conversion table to which you can refer whenever you need it. This table might take the form shown at the top of Figure A.3.

Sometimes you may want to create a graphic scale from a word statement or representative fraction. There are really two solutions to this problem. You must decide whether you want even units of map distance or of ground distance. Rarely can you have both at once.

Imagine that you have a map with a scale of 3/4 mile to an inch, or 1:47,520. You might want a graphic scale with even inch divisions, since it would then be easy to make measurements on the map with a ruler. You would simply draw a line and divide it into inches, each representing 3/4 mile on the ground (**Figure A.4A**).

Or you might prefer even miles, because that would facilitate ground distance computation. Since an inch equals 3/4 mile, 1/3 inch equals 1/4 mile, and each mile equals 1-1/3 inches. So you would mark off 1-1/3 inch intervals on your graphic scale (**Figure A.4B**).

RF	In. to Miles	Miles to In.	Cm to Km	Km to Cm
1:1,980	32	.03125	50.50	.0198
1:3,960	16	.0625	25.25	.0396
1:7,920	8	.125	12.626	.0792
1:15,840	4	.250	6.313	.1584
1:31,680	2	.5	3.156	.3168
1:63,360	1	1.00	1.578	.6336
1:126,720	.5	2.00	.789	1.2672
1:253,440	.25	4.00	.3946	2.5344
1:506,880	.125	8.00	.197	5.0688
1:1,013,760	.0625	16.00	.0986	10.1376

Worked Examples

(1) How many inches to the mile when RF = 1:24,000?

Solution:

$$\frac{2.64}{24,000 \overline{)63,360.00}}$$

(2) How many miles to the inch when the RF = 1:24,000?

Solution:

$$\frac{.3798}{63,360 \overline{)24,000.0000}}$$

(1) How many cm to the km. when RF = 24,000?

Solution:

$$\frac{4.17}{24,000 \overline{)100,000.00}}$$

(2) How many km to the cm. when RF = 24,000?

Solution:

$$\frac{.24}{100,000 \overline{)24,000.00}}$$

A.3 Converting a representative fraction to a word statement.

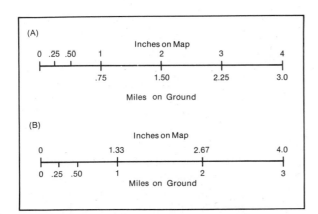

A.4 A graphic scale can be divided so that either the map units are whole numbers (A) or the ground units are whole numbers (B). (Caution: These bar graphs are not drawn to scale.)

You'll have no trouble doing this if your ruler is marked with 1/3 inch increments. But not all rulers are. When you make graphic scales, you will often run into this problem of trying to divide a line into segments which aren't found on your ruler. The thing to do then is to fall back on an old trick of plane geometry concerning the relation of parallel lines.

Let's use our previous example and assume that you want to make a graphic scale with 1-1/3 inches to a mile. First you must decide how long to make the graphic scale. Because it would be convenient if your scale showed an even number of inches as well as miles, keep adding 1-1/3 inches until you come up with an even number. (If you don't arrive at an even number within a reasonable amount of time, abandon this method and

542

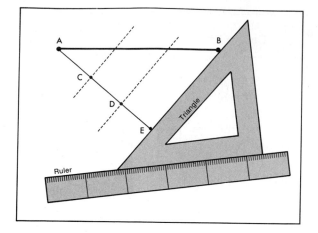

A.5 A line can be divided into equal segments using a triangle and straightedge.

choose an arbitrary length for your graphic scale.) If you add 1-1/3" + 1-1/3" + 1-1/3", you get an even four inches, which represents three miles. So four inches is a good length for your graphic scale. Draw a four-inch line, and label it AB (**Figure A.5**).

Now draw a second line at an acute angle from your first line. It doesn't matter exactly where you draw it, but an angle of less than 75 degrees will be most convenient. Next, starting at point A, mark off three equal divisions on this second line, say at one-inch intervals. Label these points C, D, and E. Then connect points B and E with a line.

Now place a right triangle along line BE and a ruler along the bottom of the triangle, as shown in Figure A.5. Slide the triangle along the ruler to point D, and draw a line from D up to line AB. Slide the triangle to point E, and draw another line to AB. What you have done is to draw a series of parallel lines which neatly divide your graphic scale into thirds. Since your original line was four inches long, each of those thirds is 1-1/3 inches.

DETERMINING SCALE

It's a good feeling to know that, no matter what sort of map scale you encounter, you can change it to the type of scale you want. But what if you come across a map with no scale depicted at all? This happens more often than you might expect. You may want to know the scale of an air photo,

for instance, or of a photocopied portion of a map on which no scale has been shown.

You can figure out the scale on your own if you know the ground distance between any two points on your map. Then you just measure the distance between those same two points on the map. The ratio of map to ground distance will be the map's scale.

How, though, do you find the ground distance you need? There are several ways. One method is to use some terrestrial feature whose length is known.

Determining Scale With a Terrestrial Feature

Some features have standard dimensions. If you can identify one of these on your map, and if you can be sure that it's shown in proportional size, then you can easily figure out the map scale. A regulation U.S. football field, for example, can be assumed to be 100 yards long. If the map distance of the field is .5 inch, then .5 inch on the map represents 100 yards on the ground. To determine the map scale, we merely convert yards to inches and reduce the numerator to 1:

$$\frac{.5"}{100 \text{ yd.}} = \frac{.5"}{100 \times 36"} = \frac{.5"}{3,600"} =$$

$$\frac{.5/.5}{3,600/.5} = \text{an RF of } 1/7,200.$$

Determining Scale With Reference Material

If you can't find a feature of standard dimensions on your map, you can still determine scale if you turn to other reference material, such as gazetteers, distance logs, or atlases. From these sources, you should be able to find out the distance of something on your map—the length of a lake, say, or the dimensions of a political boundary, or the distance between two prominent features such as cities. With this information in hand, you can compute the map scale as was done above when we used a feature of standard dimensions.

You can follow the same procedure to determine the scale of **global maps**. Here you make use of the fact that the earth's circumference is approximately 25,000 statute miles (the actual figure is 24,901.92 statute miles). If, for example, a world map extends the length of an eight-inch textbook page, you find the map's scale as follows:

$$\frac{8" \text{ page (map distance)}}{25,000 \text{ miles (ground distance)}} =$$

$$\frac{8"}{25,000 \text{ miles} \times 63,360"} =$$

$$\frac{8"}{1,584,000,000"} =$$

$$\frac{8/8}{1,584,000,000/8} =$$

an RF of 1/198,000,000 or a word statement of 198,000,000 ÷ 63,360 = 1 inch to 3,125 miles.

Determining Scale With Latitude-Longitude Lines

It isn't always convenient or even possible to find a feature such as a football field or a lake of known length on your map. But on many maps, especially those of small scale, latitude-longitude lines are shown. Thus, you can determine scale by finding the ground distance between these lines.

Finding the ground distance between latitude lines is quite simple, since a degree of latitude varies only slightly from pole to equator. The first degree of latitude north or south of the equator extends 110.567 kilometers (68.703 statute miles), while a degree of latitude adjacent to the North or South Pole covers 111.699 kilometers (69.407 miles). Thus, the variation in a degree of latitude from equator to pole is only 1.132 km. or .704 mile. This discrepancy is so small that for many purposes it can be ignored. We say that a degree of latitude is equivalent to a degree of longitude at the equator, which is **69.172 miles**, regardless of where on earth the degree of latitude is found. (If you need a more precise measure of the length of a degree of latitude, refer to Table E.6 in Appendix E.)

In order to use this information in determining map scale, you must be able to find at least two parallels on your map. Let's say you find two latitude lines separated by an increment of two degrees and a map distance of five inches. To find the ground distance between these parallels, you multiply the number of degrees separating them by the length of a degree. Thus, 2° × 69.172 = 138.344 statute miles. Now you can form a relation between map distance and ground distance, yielding 5"/138.344 miles = 5"/138.344 × 63,360" = 5"/8,765,475" = an RF of 1/1,753,095 or a word statement of 1,753,095 ÷ 63,360 = 28 miles to the inch.

Unfortunately, two parallels are not always shown on a map. You can still compute the map scale, however, if two meridians are shown. The trouble is that longitude lines are not as consistent as latitude lines. Because meridians converge at the poles, a degree of longitude varies from 111.321 kilometers (69.172 miles) along the equator to 0 kilometers at either pole (see Table E.7 in Appendix E). This means that the distance between longitude lines depends on the mapped region's latitude. Luckily, there's a simple functional relationship between latitude and longitude: Longitude changes as the cosine of the latitude. (You'll find the cosine you need in Table E.5 in Appendix E.) To find the length of a degree of longitude, you multiply the length of a degree of latitude (111.321 kilometers or 69.172 miles) by the cosine of the latitude. This relationship can be written symbolically as

Longitude = cos (latitude) × 111,321 km.

or

Longitude = cos (latitude) × 69,172 miles.

Now how can you use this equation to determine map scale? Although the procedure may at first seem complex, it is actually straightforward if viewed as a series of simple steps. You begin by measuring the map distance between two longitude lines. Suppose you find that lines spanning 1/2° of longitude on the map are 10 inches apart. To determine ground distance between these two longitude lines, first find the latitude of the region on the map. Then check the table of cosines in Appendix E to find the length of a degree of longitude at this latitude. Suppose the latitude is 45°N. In this case,

1° longitude = cos (45°) × 69.172
= .7071 × 69.172
= 48.9 miles

Thus, you know that one degree of longitude at 45°N covers a ground distance of 48.9 miles. But since the measured map distance spanned 1/2° rather than 1° of longitude, the ground distance in this problem would be half the computed figure, or .5 x 48.9 = 24.45 miles.

You now have all the information necessary to find the map scale. Simply form a ratio between map and ground distance, obtaining 10"/24.45 miles = 10"/24.45 x 63,360" = 10"/1,549,152" = an RF of $\boxed{1/154,915}$ or a word statement of 154,915 ÷ 63,360 = approximately 2.5 miles to the inch.

Determining Scale by Comparison

If you aren't able to determine the scale with any of the above methods, you might try comparing your scaleless map with other maps of the same region which do have their scales identified. It should be possible to place any map along a continuum between maps of known scales. This procedure is only approximate, but sometimes a rough idea of a map's scale is all you need.

SCALE PROBLEMS

We often compare maps according to the relative size of their scales. **Small-scale** maps result when map distance is small relative to ground distance—that is, when the scale ratio is small; on **large-scale** maps, the map-ground ratio is large.

Since map distance is always stated in the numerator of the RF as 1, it follows that the smaller the denominator (the closer to a 1 to 1 ratio), the larger the scale will be. Thus, a map scale of 1:20,000 is twice as large as a scale of 1:40,000. If that sounds backwards, remember that the RF is a fraction, and 1/2, after all, is a larger proportion (or piece of the pie) than 1/4.

Common as it is to classify maps by their scales, there is no general agreement as to where the class limits should be set. If we sort maps into two groups—large and small scale—then 1:1,000,000 would be a likely dividing point between the two. Atlas, textbook, and wall maps of continental coverage would then fall into the small-scale group, while topographic, cadastral, and other sheet maps would be in the large-scale

class. If a more detailed three-way grouping is used, maps with scales of 1:1,000,000 and smaller (16 or more miles to the inch) would probably be classed as small-scale and those of 1:250,000 and larger (four or less miles to the inch) as large-scale. Maps ranging in scale between these extremes would then be referred to as medium-scale. Any such classification, of course, is arbitrary and shouldn't be given meaning beyond the organizational convenience it provides.

It's often useful to know the relation between map scale, map size, and ground coverage. You may, for instance, want to know the relationship among ground areas shown on four maps of equal size but of different scales. The rule, as **Figure A.6** shows, is that ground area changes as the square of the linear distance. Although Map C is two times the scale of Map A, it depicts a ground area only 1/4 as great ($2^2 = 4$). Conversely, Map B is 1/3 the scale of Map D, yet it shows a ground area which is nine times as large. In other words, a map's ground coverage varies inversely with the square of any scale change. Or, stated symbolically:

$$GC = 1/\text{scale change}^2.$$

If a map's scale is increased by a factor of four, then, the area that can be shown on a map of the same size decreases to 1/16 the original value ($GC = 1/4^2 = 1/16$).

Let's see how we can use this information.

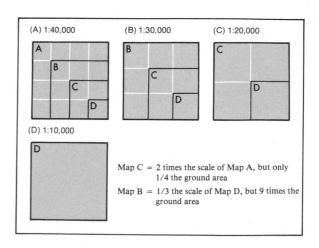

A.6 The ground coverage of a map changes in inverse proportion to the square of the map scale. Cutting the map scale in half increases the ground coverage by a factor of four.

Problem 1. Using a photocopy machine, you reduce a map with a scale of 1:90,000 to 45 percent its original size. What will be the scale of the reduced map? Remember that, although the map distance will be reduced to 45 percent, it will still represent the same ground distance.

Answer:

$$\frac{1}{90,000} \times \frac{.45}{1} =$$

$$\frac{.45}{90,000} = \frac{.45/.45}{90,000/.45} = 1/200,000$$

Problem 2. On one map, with a scale of 1:100,000, the distance between two cities is .7 cm. On a second map, the distance between the same two points is .5 cm. What is the scale of the second map?

The solution involves equating distance on the first map to distance on the second. Answer:

$$(.5 \text{ cm.}) (X) = .7 \text{ cm. } (100,000)$$
$$.5X = 70,000$$
$$X = 70,000/.5$$
$$X = 140,000$$

Problem 3. On a map with an RF of 1:100,000, there is a rectangular reservoir measuring 12 by 5 centimeters. What is the area of the reservoir in square kilometers?

The key is to recall that there are 100,000 centimeters in a kilometer. Therefore, the map scale is one cm. to the km.

Answer:

$$12 \text{ cm. } \times 5 \text{ cm.} = 60 \text{ cm.}^2$$

Since 1 cm.² on the map = 1 km.² on the ground, 60 cm.² = 60 km.².

Problem 4. On the first of two maps, a square parcel of land measures 2.7 cm. by 2.7 cm. On the second map, whose RF is 1:30,000, the same parcel of land occupies 1/9 as much area as on the first map. What is the RF of the first map, and what is the area of the parcel of land in square meters?

The best way to solve this problem is to begin with a picture. **Figure A.7** shows that the second map is of smaller scale than the first map, since it covers the same ground area with only 1/9 the map area. Remembering our scale changing rule (GC = 1/scale change²), we know that area changes as the square. Thus, it would take a linear change of 1/3 to produce an area change of 1/9, since 1/3² = 1/9. This means that 2.7 cm. on the first map is equivalent to 1/3 x 2.7 = .9 cm. on the second map.

In other words, a given distance on the first map (X_1) represents 1/3 times the same distance on the second map (X_2). Or, written symbolically, $X_1 = 1/3 \times X_2$. Since we know that the RF of the second map is 1/30,000, then $X_2 = 1 \times 30,000 \times 30,000$. To find X_1, we merely multiply X_2 by 1/3. So the RF of the first map is 1/30,000 x 1/3 = 1/10,000.

The area of the parcel of land can be determined using either .9 cm. at the scale of 1:30,000 or 2.7 cm. at the scale of 1:10,000. Using the latter RF, and letting S represent the length of a side of the land parcel, we get:

$$S = 2.7 \text{ cm. (map distance) } \times 10,000 \text{ cm.}$$
$$(\text{ground distance}) = 27,000 \text{ cm.}$$

We then transfer this value into the formula for obtaining the area of a square:

$$\text{Area} = S^2$$
$$= (27,000 \text{ cm.})^2$$
$$= 729,000,000 \text{ square cm.}$$

Since there are 10,000 square centimeters in a square meter, 729,000,000 square centimeters = 72,900 square meters.

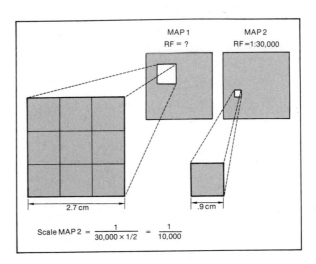

A.7 A graphic representation of Scale Problem 4 (see text).

These problems, ranging from simple to complicated, demonstrate the far-reaching usefulness of the map scale. They show only a few of the many ways you can manipulate scale information to solve problems involving distance relations. We usually think of the scale as the index of how much detail the map portrays. But, as these varied examples have illustrated, the map scale's utility extends far beyond that.

SELECTED READINGS

Dickinson, G.C., *Maps and Air Photographs* (London: Edward Arnold Publishers, Ltd., 1969), pp. 99-107, 142-148.

Espenshade, E.B., "Mathematical Scale Problems," *Journal of Geography,* 50, 3 (March 1951), pp. 107-113.

Greenhood, D., *Mapping* (Chicago: University of Chicago Press, 1964), pp. 39-53, 180-184.

Hodgkiss, A.G., *Maps for Books and Theses* (New York: Pica Press, 1970), pp. 37-43, 169-170, 239-242.

Keates, J.S., *Cartographic Design and Production*, 2nd ed. (New York: John Wiley & Sons, 1989), pp. 5-6.

Lawrence, G.R.P., *Cartographic Methods*, 2nd ed. (London: Methuen & Co., Ltd., 1979), pp. 1-6.

Map Uses, Scales, and Accuracies for Engineering and Associated Purposes, ASCE Committee on Cartographic Surveying (New York: American Society of Civil Engineers, 1983).

Quattrochi, D.A., and Goodchild, M.F., *Scale in Remote Sensing and GIS* (Boca Raton, FL: Lewis Publishers, 1997).

Robinson, A.H., et al., *Elements of Cartography,* 6th ed. (New York: John Wiley & Sons, 1995).

U.S. Army, Chapter 4 ("Scale and Distance") in *Map Reading*, FM 21-26, Department of the Army Field Manual, 1969, pp. 4-1 to 4-4.

Wolf, P.R., *Elements of Photogrammetry* (New York: McGraw-Hill Book Co., 1983), pp. 120-127, 414-416.

Also see references in Chapter 13.

APPENDIX B

REMOTE SENSING OF THE ENVIRONMENT

INTRODUCTION

SPECTRAL SIGNATURES

RECORDING METHODS
Photography
Black-and-White Photography
True Color Photography
Infrared (IR) Black-and-White Photography
Infrared (IR) Color Photography
Film-Filter Combinations
Electronic Imaging
Thermal Infrared (IR) Imaging
Passive Microwave Imaging
Active Microwave Imaging
Plan Position Indicator
Side Looking Airborne Radar
Space Imaging Radar
Doppler Radar
Multiband Sensing

RECORDING STATIONS
Low-Altitude Stations
Mid-Altitude Stations
High-Altitude Stations
Space Stations
Weather Satellites
Geostationary Satellites
AVHRR Satellites
Manned Space Flights
Mercury, Gemini, and Apollo
Skylab
Space Shuttle
Earth Resources Satellites
Landsat
SPOT
IRS
Next-Generation Sensors
High-Resolution Imagery
Hyperspectral Imagery
Commercialization of Space
Image Detail

PICTURE PROCESSING
Image Enhancement
Map Use Changes

SELECTED READINGS

APPENDIX B

REMOTE SENSING OF THE ENVIRONMENT

All objects which have a temperature above 0° Kelvin (-173° Centigrade or -459.4° Fahrenheit) emit and reflect **electromagnetic energy** in the form of waves. The range in **wavelengths**, as measured by the distance between successive crests of a wave, is immense (**Figure B.1**). This continuum from short to long waves is referred to as the **electromagnetic spectrum**.

Differing wavelengths have vastly different properties. Actually, it is a portion of the spectrum, or **spectral band**, rather than a specific wavelength, whose characteristics we can identify. The most important of these bands have been named (although in reality definite boundaries don't exist). At the short end of the spectrum are deadly gamma rays, which are about one billionth of a millimeter long, while at the long end of the spectrum are useful radio waves, which are about 10 kilometers (6.2 miles) long (**Figure B.2**). Between these extremes, from short to long, fall X-ray, ultraviolet, visible light, infrared (IR), and microwave energy.

Figure B.2 provides insight into how little of our environment we see with our eyes. Visible light energy falls in the spectral range of .4 to .7 micrometers. A micrometer, or micron (abbreviated μm) is a millionth part of a meter. Obviously, then, visible light occupies only an infinitesimally small portion of the spectrum. Yet until a relatively few years ago, we have been preoccupied with the visible aspects of our surroundings. How incredibly narrow our view of the world has been!

The primary source of visible light is energy emitted from hot objects. This fact is evident when a heated piece of black iron progressively changes hue from red to orange to yellow to white. A secondary source of visible light is energy which is reflected from objects but which originated with such hot sources as the sun, lightbulbs, or flares. Moonlight is a good example of reflected light.

The characteristic color of objects as seen by the human eye is primarily the result of selective reflection of sunlight in the spectral range of visible light. Thus, an object appears green because it reflects green wavelengths and absorbs blue and red wavelengths (**Figure B.3**). The characteristic light

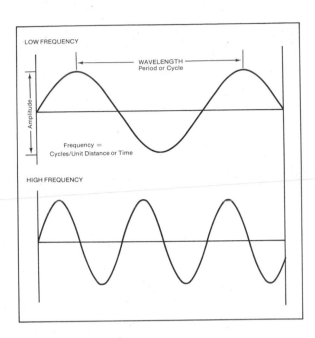

B.1 Electromagnetic energy occurs in the form of waves of different lengths.

reflectance curves for most environmental phenomena are more complex than indicated by this simple example, of course. In addition, the curves extend into the invisible portion of the spectrum. Here, emission as well as reflection of electromagnetic energy is a contributing factor.

SPECTRAL SIGNATURES

Typical reflection-emission curves for several environmental features are illustrated in **Figure B.4**. Note that these curves have been extended beyond the visible light portion of the spectrum. Also notice that each curve is distinctly different in form. In fact, the reflection-emission curves for environmental features are so distinctive that they are referred to as **spectral signatures**. The signature analogy is apt, for every object's curve, like each person's handwriting, is unique.

The spectral signature of an object is in part a function of its reflection and emission properties. Smooth, shiny features are highly reflective, while rough, dark objects are highly absorbent. Cold objects emit little energy, while hot objects are highly emissive.

Spectral signatures are also a function of incoming energy from the sun. Water vapor, carbon dioxide, ozone, and solid particles (dust, pollen) in the atmosphere absorb or block (scatter) energy of certain wavelengths. Other wavelengths pass through the atmosphere in what are called the visible, thermal, and microwave **windows.**

The effect of these atmospheric windows is that people have formulated their environmental images on the basis of highly selected electromagnetic energy. Until very recently, the unaided human eye has been the primary data-gathering device. Considering that environmental phenomena have been identified and defined accordingly, our perspective on our surroundings is extremely biased. There is far more to the world than meets the eye!

RECORDING METHODS

Although people have relied primarily on their own eyes to learn about the environment, they haven't done so exclusively. Even thousands of years ago, there were many indirect methods of collecting environmental information. Expeditions were sent to distant places to gather information. Atmospheric phenomena were used to predict storms. The behavior of animals provided an indicator of critical yet imperceptible environmental factors, such as poisonous water holes.

But such methods of gathering data remotely provide information only for specific sites. Remote sensing capable of yielding an overall picture of the environment is relatively recent—dating back only to the early 19th century. Once begun, though, the development of recording media, instruments, and methods has been rapid. We are now inundated with a vast array of remotely sensed images of our surroundings. The best known of these is the photograph.

Photography

The development of cameras and photographic emulsions began in the early 1800s. While at first the visible light portion of the spectrum was reduced to shades of gray, later photography not only came close to duplicating the multi-color sensing capability of the human eye but also

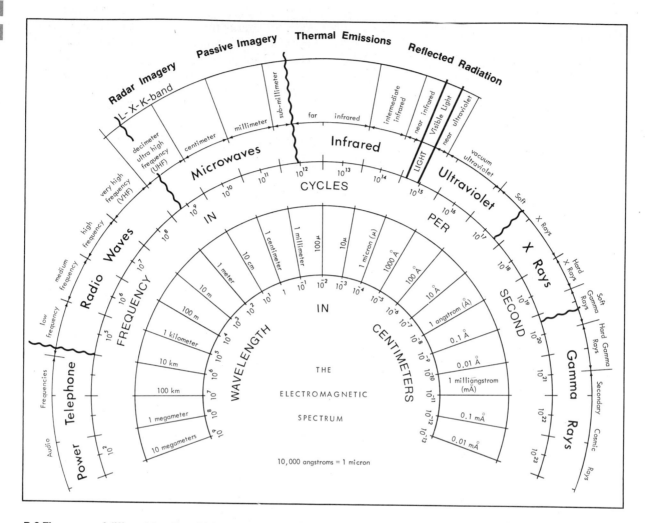

B.2 The waves of different lengths which make up the electromagnetic spectrum have been divided into named wavebands, such as microwave, infrared, and visible light waves.

extended our sensing capability into the near-invisible portions of the spectrum at both ends of the eye's sensitivity range. In addition to broadening our image of the environment, these variably sensitive films, when combined with filters for blocking out unwanted wavelengths, made it possible to focus on different aspects of visible and near-visible light energy.

The look of a photograph depends on a number of factors. One factor is the type of camera used. In taking aerial photos for mapping purposes, photographers usually use the familiar kind of camera which produces individual pictures (or frames). Aerial mapping cameras are specially designed so that they will use large-sized (9" x 9") film. Larger film makes it possible

to include more detail on the photo and to minimize spatial distortion. Such cameras are so large and heavy, however, that they must be used in a fixed position; therefore, it is also common to use smaller hand-held cameras which take 70-millimeter (mm.) film.

The kind of lens used is as important to the look of the photo as the type of camera. The same camera will take quite different photos, depending on whether a wide-angle, normal, telephoto, or fish-eye lens is employed. Interesting panoramic photos can be created if the camera is rotated on a fixed pivot while exposing the film.

While the spatial character (or geometry) of a photo is determined mainly by the nature of the camera and its lens, the photo's quality (or

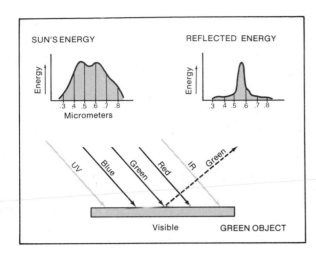

B.3 The color of an object depends on which visible wavelengths are reflected and which are absorbed. Here a green object is shown.

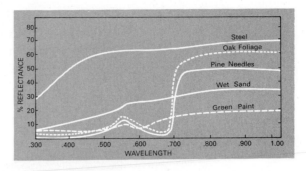

B.4 The spectral signatures of different terrestrial objects vary considerably over the visible and photographic infrared wavebands.

resolving power) is primarily a function of the film emulsion characteristics. Film emulsions are made up of one or more (in the case of color film) layers of light-sensitive silver salts. The individual salt crystals (or grains) are packed into a dense mosaic (see Figure 4.3 in Chapter 4: *Image Maps*). When the film is exposed to light reflected from the ground, each crystal responds to light according to an all-or-nothing principle. Those crystals struck by sufficient light change their chemical make-up, while those not activated by enough light remain unaltered.

The grain size in film is usually so small that it is imperceptible. This fact explains why photos appear to be continuous in tone rather than mosaicked, as you might expect from the previous comments. But these fine-grained emulsions require relatively good light conditions and long exposures, both of which are difficult to maintain in environmental remote sensing. If we increase the grain size, the light-gathering power of individual crystals is increased, which in turn increases the film speed and reduces required exposure time. The cost, however, is loss of detail: These coarse-grained films often have a fuzzy appearance. It is the same loss of image clarity which results when a photo is excessively enlarged; eventually the individual grains become so large that they are visible. Slow-speed film may also show increased image blurring due to movement of the aircraft carrying the camera.

Black-and-White Photography

Standard black-and-white (B & W) photographs are based on film emulsions which normally record energy in the .3 to .7 micrometer range (**Figure B.5A**). This is essentially the visible spectrum. In fact, because of its sensitivity to visible light, black-and-white film is often called **panchromatic** (meaning "light-sensitive") film. There is, however, some extension of film sensitivity into the shorter invisible wavelengths; and, unfortunately, these shorter blue light and ultraviolet wavelengths are badly scattered by the atmosphere, reducing the clarity of the photo. This explains why black-and-white photos taken from commercial airliners flying at 35,000 feet are so often hazy. Luckily, atmospheric scatter can be greatly reduced by using a haze filter over the camera lens.

The greater the amount of light energy an object reflects through the camera lens onto the film, the lighter its tone on the final photographic print (see Figure 4.7). The moisture content, surface roughness, and natural color of objects all influence a feature's tone on a B & W photo. Moist soils, marshlands, and newly plowed fields tend to be darker than surrounding features, while human constructions such as roads and buildings tend to appear lighter.

This does not mean that dark tones always indicate objects of low reflectance, however. Highly reflective features will appear dark if energy reflectance away from the camera occurs (see Figure 4.9). Thus, the same feature can appear on B & W photos in many different tones, depending on the position of the light source, the orientation of the object, and the position of the camera.

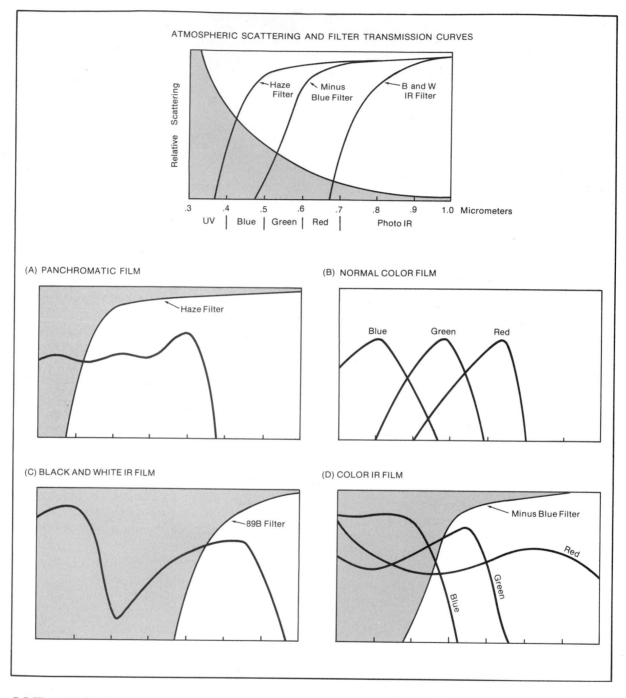

ATMOSPHERIC SCATTERING AND FILTER TRANSMISSION CURVES

Relative Scattering

Haze Filter

Minus Blue Filter

B and W IR Filter

.3   .4   .5   .6   .7   .8   .9   1.0   Micrometers

UV | Blue | Green | Red | Photo IR

(A) PANCHROMATIC FILM

Haze Filter

(B) NORMAL COLOR FILM

Blue   Green   Red

(C) BLACK AND WHITE IR FILM

89B Filter

(D) COLOR IR FILM

Minus Blue Filter

Red

Blue

Green

B.5 Film emulsions are manufactured to have different spectral sensitivities. Film sensitivity can itself be modified through use of light-blocking filters.

Standard black-and-white photos have been put to many uses. The Forest Service uses them in making timber inventories and in mapping national forests. They are used by the United States Geological Survey (USGS) for topographic and photo mapping in its quadrangle series (see Chapter 5). The Soil Conservation Service uses them for mapping soils and agricultural activities. They are also used widely for road building, recreation, forestry, and planning purposes. Indeed, by far the largest amount of remote sensing has been done using standard black-and-white photography. These photographs have provided the basis for most of the image maps which have been made in the past half century. (Image maps are discussed in detail in Chapters 4 and 24.)

True Color Photography

For a long time after its development in the 1930s, color film was little used in mapping. For one thing, color film is more expensive than conventional black-and-white film. This is because it contains three separate layers of light-sensitive (panchromatic) emulsion with special dyes, each sensitive to a different portion of the visible spectrum (**Figure B.5B**). Special film processing requirements add further to the cost. In addition, early color film had poor resolution capabilities.

Image clarity of color film has improved so dramatically in recent years, however, that it is comparable in quality to black-and-white film. In fact, color photos are usually easier to read than black-and-white photos, because they provide an added dimension from which to draw conclusions: they capture the colors uniquely associated with special landscape features. It is visually easier to distinguish subtle differences between color tones than between shades of gray.

Color is especially revealing of the condition of objects, such as the stage of a crop in its maturation cycle. For such applications as vegetation and soils classification, geologic mapping, and surface water studies, using color photos has proven simpler and more accurate than working from equivalent black-and-white images alone. Despite its extra cost, therefore, color film is rapidly growing in importance for remote sensing of the environment.

Infrared (IR) Black-and-White Photography

Some black-and-white film has its sensitivity extended beyond the visible portion of the spectrum into the longer **near-infrared** wavelengths (.7 to .9 micrometer range). When this film is used in conjunction with a filter which blocks wavelengths shorter than .7 micrometer, only the reflected solar energy in the photographic IR band is recorded (**Figure B.5C**).

Photographs produced by the longer wavelengths of near-infrared energy have several advantages over conventional B & W photos (see Figures 24.5 and 24.6). For one thing, IR photos have improved smoke and haze penetration because the severe atmospheric scattering that occurs in the visible and ultraviolet regions of the spectrum is eliminated by the filter used. As a result, IR photographs generally have a higher spatial resolution.

Infrared photos also have tonal characteristics quite different from those produced with standard panchromatic film. Water appears dark due to its better absorption of near-infrared energy than visible light energy. In contrast, vegetation tends to appear in bright tones on an infrared photo because maximum reflectance from vegetation occurs in this spectral band. Maximum spectral difference between broadleaf and coniferous species is also found in the photographic IR region.

These characteristics of IR photography can greatly increase the speed and reliability of image reading, analysis, and interpretation. An object may not be discernible on an ordinary B & W photo because it blends in with the background tones, yet the same feature may stand out in sharp tonal contrast on B & W infrared film. Thus, B & W infrared film has a number of specialized applications. Foresters, for example, find the tonal variation on infrared photos useful in distinguishing one type of forest cover from another. Black-and-white infrared photos are also valuable in indicating land-water boundaries, mapping water courses, studying tidal incursion, and investigating soil moisture.

Infrared Color Photography

During World War II, military researchers developed color infrared film. This special film was sensitive in the near-infrared (.7 to .9 micrometers) as well as the visible light spectral range (**Figure B.5D**). One of the best reflecting materials in this wavelength zone is the cellular structure in the leaves of plants. Generally speaking, the healthier the vegetation, the brighter the reflectance. This property turned out to be extremely useful for the military, since on a photograph produced with color IR film, artificial camouflage materials could be distinguished from live, healthy vegetation. Because color infrared film is used for this purpose, it is sometimes called **camouflage detection film**. It is also known as **false-color film**, since the spectral sensitivities of the dye lay-

554

ers in the film bear no relation to the natural colors of environmental features. The explanation for this lack of natural color association can be seen by comparing the spectral sensitivity curves for normal color and IR color film shown in Figure B.5. Clearly, the blue, green, and red layers of color IR film have been shifted toward the longer wavelengths. When a minus blue filter is used, the blue, green, and red dyes which make up color IR film are primarily sensitive to the green, red, and photo IR wavebands, respectively.

An environmental feature that is highly absorbent of photo IR energy, such as clear water, appears dark blue or black on color IR photos. Less absorbent features such as buildings and unhealthy vegetation appear blue or blue-gray. The most obvious aspect of color IR photos is that healthy vegetation, which is highly reflective of near-infrared energy, appears bright magenta-red rather than green. The cut vegetation, green paint, and rope netting used to conceal military installations are recorded on camouflage detection film in pinkish to bluish tones, in stark contrast to the background of bright reds produced by the surrounding healthy vegetation.

Although the first important applications of color infrared film were in military reconnaissance, many other uses in vegetation, geologic, and urban studies have been found. The film is now used for such applications as crop inspection, tree-growth inventories, and damage assessment of diseased flora. Plant diseases can often be detected on color infrared photographs well before they would be visible to the unaided eye.

Geologists have found color infrared photos useful, too, in locating near-surface structural features such as faults, fractures, and joints. These features can be detected because they often collect water, encouraging lusher vegetation growth than in the surrounding area. Color infrared film also enhances boundaries between soil and vegetation and between land and water, making it useful for map makers. In addition, the film is valuable for urban mapping because it shows a sharp contrast between vegetation and cultural features, and because the long infrared wavelengths penetrate smog easily.

Film-Filter Combinations

As we've mentioned, film emulsions can be made sensitive to any portion of the visible and near-vis-

ible spectrum desired. It is also possible to restrict the recording capability of film emulsions which are sensitive over a broad spectral band. This can be accomplished by placing a filter in front of the camera lens. The filter will absorb a certain portion of the spectrum, preventing the electromagnetic energy of these wavelengths from reaching the emulsion.

Figure B.6 shows how it's done. The first curve illustrates the spectral sensitivity of a commonly used black-and-white aerial film (Kodak Tri-X). The second curve shows the spectral transmission characteristics of a commonly used filter (Wratten 12). The third curve demonstrates the manner in which this filter modifies the **effective sensitivity** of the film. Other films and filters could be used to move the zone (or zones) of effective film sensitivity around in the visible and near-visible part of the spectrum.

Thus, different **film-filter combinations** can turn a general-purpose film into a highly-selective recording medium. It is possible to block unwanted spectral information from a photograph almost at will. In fact, normal color film is produced by building the appropriate filters into a three-layered emulsion, with the result that each layer is effectively sensitive to a different color (red, green, or blue).

Photography alone, however, doesn't provide a comprehensive method of remote sensing. For one thing, it hasn't been possible to make emulsions which are sensitive beyond 1.2 microns (near-infrared). This sets an upper wavelength limit which falls far short of our knowledge of the electromagnetic spectrum. At the other extreme, the lower limit of photography is determined by atmospheric scattering of electromagnetic energy of wavelengths shorter than .3 microns (ultraviolet). To overcome the limitations of photography, it was necessary to design special devices which worked on an electronic rather than a photographic principle. Electronic imaging devices were developed for this purpose.

Electronic Imaging

The limitations of photography were eventually circumvented by replacing standard photographic film (light-sensitive silver salt emulsion) with electronic scanners equipped with small energy detectors called **photocells**.* (See *Imaging Systems* in Chapter 4.) As the scanner-equipped aircraft or spacecraft moves along its flight path, the electromagnetic energy received from the earth is recorded line by line and cell by cell as an electrical impulse of varying strength (see Figures 4.1B, 4.1C, and 4.3).

In the case of **sweep** scanners, a continuous electrical impulse is recorded by a photocell for each waveband as the ground scene is scanned from side to side, and this signal is then sampled into discrete intervals to produce pixels (**Figure B.7**). In contrast, a **pushbroom** scanner directly records the signal pixel by pixel, since it has a photocell in its linear array for each pixel in the scan line. Multiband sensors require additional linear arrays of detectors. Modern **digital cameras** represent the latest form of electronic scanner. Since this device uses a two-dimensional matrix of photocells, the entire ground scene is captured at once.

Regardless of the method, the ground size of the pixel determines the **spatial resolution** of a scanner image. Smaller pixels yield greater image detail, but they also mean more data to transmit and process.

Pixel generation isn't the only sampling needed in electronic scanning. The electromagnetic energy associated with a pixel needs to be further sampled into discrete intensity levels (see Figure B.7). The number of levels determines the **radiometric resolution** of the scanner. These intensity levels are subsequently represented with proportional gray tones or color. Thus, the greater the number of levels, the better the image quality. Cruder, less expensive systems tend to have fewer image intensity levels, because more levels mean more data to record, transmit, and process.

The effect of electronic scanning is that of painting an image cell by cell and line by line, just

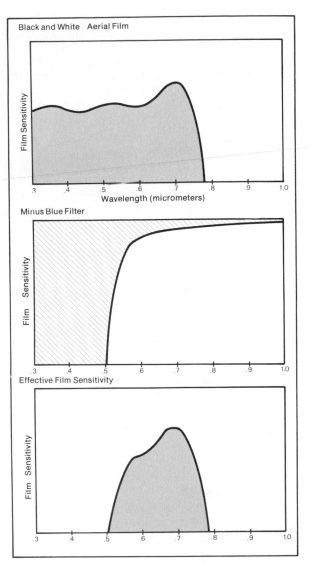

B.6 Filters over the camera lens can be used to change a film's effective sensitivity. Here a haze filter has been used to reduce the effects of atmospheric scatter in the blue wavelengths.

Charge Coupled Device (CCD) is the technical term for photocell. This solid-state electronic detector is also used in camcorders and electronic still "cameras." In these applications, however, a two-dimensional array of sensors is needed in order to capture the entire image simultaneously. Cost and technical considerations restrict the size of the CCD array used in these consumer devices, which explains the relatively coarse spatial resolution of video images.

as an image is created on a TV screen. Although sweep and pushbroom scanners operate differently, the images they create have the same basic structure (see Figure 4.4). Often scanner images are subsequently photographed.

Although scanner images are comparable to photographs in many respects, there are some basic differences. For one thing, the cell size of scanner images tends to be substantially larger than the grain size of photographic film. As a

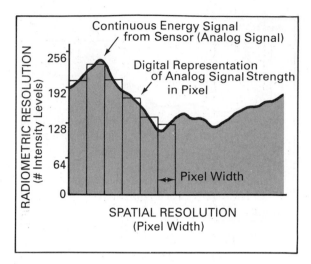

B.7 Electronic scanners sample electromagnetic energy in selected wavebands by pixel size and intensity level.

result, most scanner images have a fuzzy appearance unless reduced in scale, and the resolution of landscape detail is relatively poor. The large size of scanner cells also means that distinct lines, called **scan lines**, are visible in the image. Fortunately, as technology develops, the cell size has been progressively reduced, yielding images of improved clarity.

Another problem is that on scanner images taken from a moving aircraft, lines aren't always parallel. The normal scan line effect is thus accentuated still further. Again, with time, technological advances will surely eliminate this drawback of scanner images.

Despite these problems, electronic scanning devices have two major advantages over cameras. For one thing, scanners eliminate the need for film handling. Only an electronic connection between the sensor and image-processing facility is needed. As a result, scanners carried aboard unmanned spacecraft will gather data until there is an equipment malfunction or loss of power, which may not occur for many years. This electronic capability is so important when dealing with spacecraft that most satellites designed for earth monitoring have carried scanners set to record information in the spectral range open to photography.

Although the electronic characteristics of scanners are convenient when film handling would be awkward, it is the second advantage of scanning devices which is the most dramatic. This is the capability of scanners to record electromagnetic energy beyond the visible portion of the spectrum. Electronic scanners outperform cameras in terms of **spectral resolution**. In recent years, many scanner images have been produced in the thermal infrared and microwave parts of the spectrum. These image maps differ markedly from anything seen with the eye or camera.

Thermal Infrared Imaging

Scanners designed to record heat (or thermal infrared) energy usually operate in the 3.5 to 5.5 or 8 to 14 micrometer spectral range. This means that there is no dependence on light energy. *Ergo*, mapping can be done in any weather, at any time of day or night. The 3.5 to 5.5 band is used to detect relatively hot targets, such as volcanoes or forest fires, whereas the 8 to 14 band is used for general thermal mapping purposes when objects are expected to be somewhat cooler.

Resolution of landscape detail on thermal IR images tends to be inferior to photography. This is due in part to the use of longer wavelengths by heat-sensitive detecting devices. It is also due to the lack of adequate thermal contrast between many features and the background.

Thermal sensors receive reflected and radiated (emitted) infrared energy in about equal proportion during daylight hours. At night, however, sensing depends almost entirely on emitted energy. These factors must be considered in interpreting the tonal differences on thermal imagery (see Figure 24.7). The rate at which an object heats up and cools down, the form of its surface, atmospheric conditions before and during sensing, and the time and date that sensing takes place all lead to temperature difference. Complete **tone reversals** can occur. An object can appear as a light tone (relatively hot) on one image and as a dark tone (relatively cold) on another, depending on normal diurnal temperature changes or on changes from day to day or season to season.

To understand thermal IR imagery, it is crucial to be aware of the nature of these tone reversals. Water bodies, for instance, are colder (darker in tone) than neighboring soils and rocks during the day but hotter (lighter in tone) during the night. Similarly, damp ground (from either soil moisture, ground water, or precipitation) is darker (cooler) than dry ground during the daytime, due to evaporation, and lighter at night. Green vegetation is darker than soil on daytime images, due to transpiration, and lighter than soil on nighttime images. For these tone reversals to occur, obviously, there must be a **thermal crossover**—a time during which there is no difference in tone between land and water, wet and dry soil, or soil and vegetation. For most features, this crossover occurs just after dawn and sunset.

Still other factors can influence the temperature of environmental features and therefore their tone on infrared images. Clouds often create a mottled or patchy pattern of light (warm) and dark (cool) tones on the image. The effect is similar to the shadow pattern cast on the ground by scattered clouds on a sunny summer day. Rain can cause fine tonal streaking at right angles to the scan lines. Areas protected from the cooling effect of the wind will appear as light tone (wind) streaks or plumes downwind from obstructions.

Thermal sensing is growing rapidly in importance, especially since modern sensors are capable of providing absolute thermal values (within .1°C.) as well as indicating relative heat contrasts. The technique has been particularly useful in detecting thermal water pollution from power generating plants and industries which use water for cooling purposes. In addition, it is possible to determine the number of livestock or wildlife in a region, because the animals' body heat contrasts sharply with the temperature of the surrounding area.

Successful applications of infrared mapping also include the detection and delineation of potential geothermal energy areas, the edges of forest fires, the boundaries of ocean currents, and cold underground streams. Perhaps the most vital application of all is the measurement of heat loss through the roofs of urban dwellings. Considering the need for energy conservation, this fast and inexpensive way to see which buildings need more insulation is of great value.

Passive Microwave Imaging

Wavelengths in the one-centimeter to one-meter spectral range are called **microwaves**. One type of scanning sensor used to record energy in this portion of the spectrum is the **microwave radiometer**. It is called a **passive sensor** because it merely observes energy which already exists in the environment. It can detect three forms of energy: emitted energy related to the surface temperature of objects, transmitted energy of subsurface origin, and reflected energy during daylight. Radiometers differ from thermal sensors only in that they operate with longer wavelengths and sense electromagnetic energy with an antenna rather than a heat detection device.

The levels of energy recorded by a radiometer can either be converted to gray tones or assigned different colors. Interpretation of the image will vary accordingly. Due to the relatively weak energy signal in the microwave portion of the spectrum, radiometric scan lines tend to cover a larger ground area than is necessary with infrared scanners. The result is a reduction in image detail or resolution.

Passive microwave mapping can be put to many uses. Soil moisture conditions have been successfully monitored. The water content of snowpacks of non-uniform depths has been measured to predict the flood potential if a rapid melt should occur or to determine the water resources available the following summer. Other applications include the study of sea surface conditions and boundaries between ice and water. A variety of geologic uses also appears likely.

Active Microwave Imaging

All images of microwave energy aren't produced by means of passive recording. It's also possible to remotely sense the environment by first transmitting an electromagnetic signal (in the one-cm. to 30-cm. range) and then measuring the energy reflected back from the landscape. The strength of the returned signal can then be converted to gray tones. This is how **radar**, an acronym for "radio detection and ranging," works. It is called an **active sensor** system because it depends on energy generated by the sensing device rather than the environment.

Radar equipment is used to produce four types of maps: plan position indicator, side looking airborne radar, space imaging radar, and Doppler. Although radar is used in creating all four types of images, the methods used are vastly different, as are the resulting images. To clarify these differences, let's look at each in turn.

1. Plan Position Indicator. The most primitive application of radar in mapping involves sending out electronic impulses from a fixed position, such as an airport or weather station, through the use of a rotating antenna (transmitter). An electronic display scope, called a **plan position indicator (PPI)**, is then used to convert the return signals (possessing distance and direction information) to a graphic image (**Figure B.8**). The display screen is usually circular, with the transmitter-receiver position located at its center. Major features, such as aircraft in flight, severe storms, coastlines, and mountain ranges, show up on the screen in their true relative locations as light spots on a dark background. The screen is updated continuously by each sweep of the rotating antenna, making it possible to monitor even those features which are moving rapidly. PPI map displays are used routinely in airport traffic control and are often included in television weather programs to show approaching severe weather systems.

2. Side Looking Airborne Radar. A second and far more dramatic form of radar map is that created by a system called **side looking airborne radar (SLAR)**. An SLAR map is made up of successive parallel strips or scan lines out to one side of an aircraft's flight path (**Figure B.9**). An antenna on the airplane's belly directs short pulses of microwave energy, in the one cm. to 30 cm. range, in a narrow fan-shaped beam at right angles (called the **look direction**) to the aircraft's flight direction (azimuth). As each pulse strikes the landform, the back-scattered portion is returned to the aircraft antenna. As the airplane moves forward, the signal transmission-reception process is repeated, creating a continuous image of the ground area. Differences in the return signal strength, representing feature reflectance and orientation characteristics, appear on the SLAR image as proportional gray tones.

Thus, an SLAR image looks much like a conventional photo or scanner image (see Figure 24.9). But this appearance is deceptive. Imagery obtained by SLAR depicts the landscape in a far different way than does photography or passive scanning. Return signal strength depends primarily on object orientation with respect to the aircraft's position. Since radar signals travel in straight lines out from the aircraft, areas obscured by hills or other vertical features aren't illuminated by the radar signal. Radar shadows cast beyond

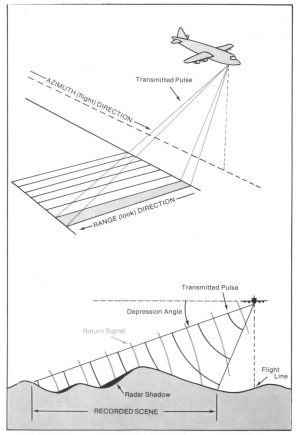

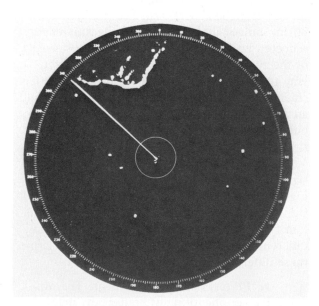

B.8 Light tones on a plan position indicator (PPI) show the location of radar obstructions such as terrain features.

B.9 Side looking airborne radar (SLAR) paints a picture of the landscape out to one side of the aircraft.

these obstructions appear extremely dark on the SLAR image.

Surface roughness relative to the radar pulse's wavelength will also alter an SLAR image's appearance. If the ground surface is rough, it will scatter the radar signal in all directions, returning only a small portion to the antenna. Such **diffuse reflectors** will appear as a dull gray spot on the SLAR image.

Smooth surfaces, on the other hand, will act like a mirror, reflecting the radar signal in only one direction. If such a mirror-like surface, called a **specular reflector**, happens to lie at a right angle to the radar beam, the energy returned to the antenna will be intense, creating a bright spot on the SLAR image. If the smooth surface lies at any other angle to the radar beam, however, no energy will be returned, and a dark spot will show up on the SLAR image.

Sometimes related horizontal and vertical surfaces (such as a building next to a parking lot) will work together to form a **corner reflector**. When this happens, a large proportion of the radar signal may be returned to the antenna, creating an intense light spot, far out of proportion to the object's size, on the SLAR image.

Other characteristics of the landform can also influence the gray shades that make up the SLAR image. One little-understood factor is the electrical property of surface materials. Another is the moisture content of soils. Still a third factor is the distance of a terrain feature from the airborne sensor. All these factors, combined with the impact of object orientation and roughness, create the fundamental differences between SLAR images and conventional photographs and scanner imagery.

The nature of the radar signal itself can also strongly influence the character of an SLAR image. One factor is the wavelength of the transmission pulse. Most available images have been acquired by Ka-band (.8 to 2.4 cm.), X-band (2.4 to 3.8 cm.), or L-band (15 to 30 cm.) systems. Images produced in these three bands differ among one another in that the longer wavelengths are better able to penetrate precipitation and terrain surface. These gains in image clarity may be offset, however, by the fact that the longer the wavelength of the transmission pulse, the coarser the resolution of ground detail.

A second aspect of the radar signal which influences the nature of an SLAR image is the **depression angle** between the aircraft and the ground feature which is returning a radar signal (see Figure B.9). The smaller the depression angle, the greater the radar shadow cast by relief features. Thus, small depression angles have proven quite effective in accentuating subtle vertical changes in the landscape. The problem is that the larger the radar shadows, the greater the chance that important features will be hidden within a dark zone on the image. In addition, the lower the depression angle, the lower the intensity of return signals from specular reflectors.

Only a few of the many properties of SLAR images are understood at this time. Yet it appears that SLAR has tremendous potential for mapping applications, especially in regions of perpetual cloud cover. Due to the low angle of the system's illumination source (particularly toward the horizon), SLAR images highlight even subtle relief features. This characteristic has proven valuable in detecting fractures, faults, stream patterns, and other features of significance in geologic studies. The technique is also useful in distinguishing between different urban land use zones and in detecting variations in vegetation type. Major advantages of the SLAR system are that it isn't dependent on an external energy source and that it provides an all-weather, day-or-night mapping capability.

3. Space Imaging Radar. Radar is also used aboard satellites and the space shuttle, where it is called **Space** (or **Shuttle**) **Imaging Radar (SIR)**. In this case, technical trickery, called **Synthetic Aperture Radar (SAR)** is commonly used to extend the "effective length" of the antenna. This extension enhances signal transmission and reception and, thus, image quality. SIR has shown dramatic ground penetration ability. This capability has led to a host of new remote sensing applications, especially in archaeology (see *Space Shuttle* later in this chapter).

4. Doppler Radar. One of the most important modern tools in severe storm detection and study is **Doppler radar**. It is similar to conventional radar discussed above in conjunction with plan position indicators. But Doppler radar has the added capability of detecting the movement and speed of objects, such as raindrops or ice particles, either toward or away from the sensor. It does so by measuring the frequency change (called **Doppler shift**) in a transmitted pulse caused by an object's motion.

Doppler radar sends out millions of microwave pulses a minute. When these signals bounce back from moving objects, a powerful computer is used to translate the frequency shift data for a given direction (azimuth) into a color-coded image on a video screen (**Figure B.10A**). The colors are coded for both wind speed and direction. Red, for example, might indicate maximum velocity away from the radar unit, while yellow might indicate maximum velocity toward the sensor. People trained to read and analyze Doppler radar images are able to detect patterns of air mass rotation which frequently spawn tornadoes or represent actual twisters in the making. When Doppler data for a number of azimuths are represented in spatial format, the result is a map such as those commonly seen in severe weather reports on TV (**Figure B.10B**).

Doppler radar has proved very useful in warning against severe storms. When compared with previous methods, the success in detecting tornadoes doubled (from 30 to 60 percent); false alarm rate was cut by 40 percent (from 63 to 25 percent); and the average warning time improved by a factor of 10 (from two to 20 minutes). Predicting where tornadoes will touch down has proven accurate within a kilometer with the use of Doppler radar. For these reasons, over the next decade Doppler is expected to replace conventional radar in regions susceptible to severe storms. It appears that we will be seeing a great deal more of this method for visualizing the wind.

Multiband Sensing

The electromagnetic spectrum is broad and rich in environmental information throughout its range. In the past several decades, we have learned to tune ourselves in to a variety of different channels, each of which gives us valuable insights into the nature of our surroundings. Interpretation problems which are difficult or impossible to solve when we are restricted to the information provided by a single spectral band are often simplified if we look at images from several portions of the spectrum.

To compare imagery from several spectral bands effectively, you must first compare what you see at a given position on one image with

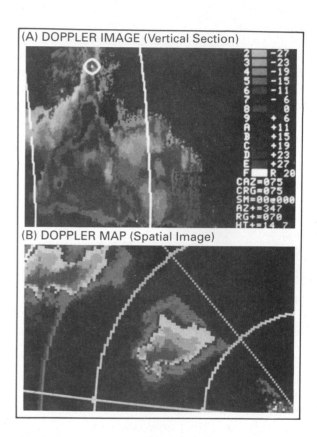

(A) DOPPLER IMAGE (Vertical Section)

(B) DOPPLER MAP (Spatial Image)

B.10 A vertical slice through the atmosphere in the form of a colored Doppler radar image has been reproduced here in black and white (A). The tones indicate combinations of wind speed and direction. When Doppler data are mapped, the areas of greatest storm intensity are easily seen (B).

what you see at the same location on each of the other images. Next, to understand what you are seeing, you must take into consideration the reflective-emissive characteristics of different environmental features in each spectral band. As you might imagine, this isn't always easy to do. It is difficult enough if the scale and geometry of the images being compared are identical; if they aren't, it is almost impossible.

The map maker's problem, then, is to capture the ground scene repeatedly in different

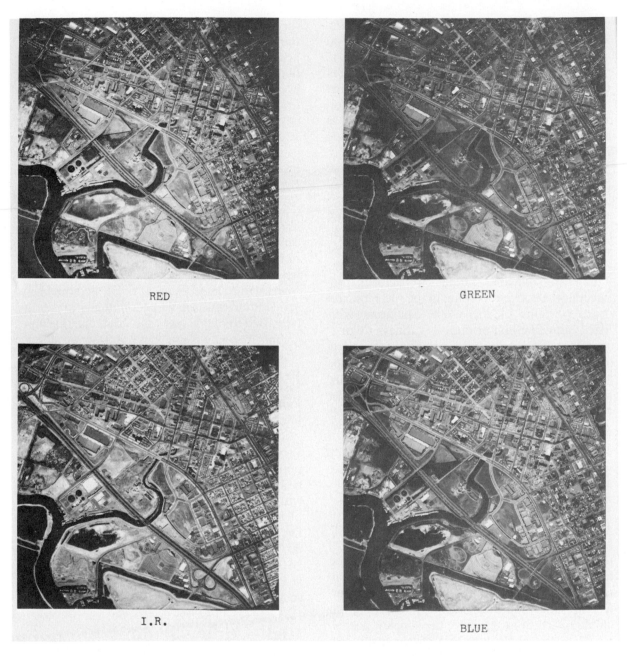

RED

GREEN

I.R.

BLUE

B.11 Multiband photography provides several map versions of the same scene (portion of Redwood City, California).

spectral bands so that the resulting images are geometrically identical. There is no practical way to do this using standard cameras and scanners. The only way for map makers to obtain the repeated coverage needed is to make a single overflight using special **multiband** (or **multispectral**) sensing devices. This special equipment records electromagnetic energy separately in several narrow spectral bands, thereby creating different images of the same ground scene simultaneously.

Such multiband sensing may be achieved either with photographic equipment or with scanners. Multiband photography is accomplished by arranging two or more mapping cameras side by side or by using a special multi-lens camera designed specifically for this purpose. The images of a ground scene taken simultaneously will differ only in respect to differences in the limited range of electromagnetic energy recorded on each. Each image will enhance certain aspects of the ground scene, based on the particular combination of film emulsion and filter used. What appears gray on one image might appear black on another, and white on the next (**Figure B.11**). In this way the different images can be tailor-made to complement one another to best advantage.

Multiband scanners are used for the same purpose as multiband camera systems. They can be adjusted so that they are sensitive to a number of different wavelengths from ultraviolet through thermal infrared. Thus, the images produced by these scanners have an even more flexible range than those produced by multiband photography.

Many full-color photos are actually produced by selective recording in the red, blue, and green portions of the visible spectrum with black-and-white film or optical scanners. Color is then added at the display or printing stage to create multiband results. Many colored image maps produced by the USGS and other agencies are put together by adding colors to black-and-white recordings from the visible light and near-infrared bands.

RECORDING STATIONS

The primary factor in determining the spatial character of a remotely sensed image is the position of the sensor (camera or scanner) with respect to the landscape being monitored. The height and orientation of the sensor in relation to the ground surface are both important factors. From any given altitude, vertical images have the simplest geometry. Therefore, their distortion characteristics are also the easiest to understand. Also from a given altitude, a narrow angle field of view produces images bearing less distortion than a wide field of view. To minimize distortion, in other words, a telephoto lens or short scan line is preferred over a wide-angle lens or long scan line.

Low-Altitude Stations

The most detailed remote sensing comes from low-altitude recording positions. Towers and balloons provided convenient sensing platforms in the 1800s, but these devices were superseded in the 20th century by light aircraft, particularly helicopters (although, curiously, the Goodyear Blimp is still used to photograph major sporting events). Thus, low-altitude pictures can be taken from a variety of vantage points. They usually cover a small ground area at extremely large scale (see Figure 22.15). It's possible, of course, to tilt the camera toward the horizon to obtain images which cover a larger ground area (see Figure 22.8).

Mid-Altitude Stations

Sensing at medium altitudes provides less environmental detail than that at low altitudes. But it has the advantage that more ground area can be covered in a single image at these medium image scales. Conventional aerial photography of the type used to obtain basic elevation data for topographic mapping is usually taken from an altitude of about two miles (see Figure 4.7). These photos are available in a standard 9" by 9" format. Systematic coverage of the United States in this format began in the 1930s and has been repeated in many areas at intervals of five to 10 years.

In 1987, the **National Aerial Photography Program (NAPP)** was established to develop a photographic database of consistent scale, orientation, and image quality.* The aim of this federal and state multiagency program is to provide complete coverage of the United States, updated every five years. The photographs are taken from 20,000 feet and are oriented to the format of USGS 7.5-minute quadrangles. Ten 9" x 9" images at 1:40,000 scale are needed for complete stereoscopic coverage of each quad.

High-Altitude Stations

If there is an advantage in taking pictures from several miles above the ground, then why not even higher? As a matter of fact, it is now quite common to take images from special aircraft flying at altitudes as high as 10 to 20 miles. Examples are the **National Aeronautics and Space Administration (NASA)** ex-spy plane, the ER-2, or the military U-2, U-R2, TR-1 and SR-71 (stealth) spy planes.

You can order NAPP products directly from the U.S. Geological Survey, EROS Data Center (EDC), User Services Section, South Falls, SD 57198.

The advantages of such high-altitude imagery are that relief distortion is minimal and a large ground area can be covered in a single photo. The resulting rapid, high-quality ground coverage suggests many potential mapping applications. The damage caused by earthquakes, floods, and droughts, for instance, can be monitored using high-altitude aircraft. Experiments involving forest resources, snow cover, crop yields, and many other environmental features are being conducted to determine additional uses of high-altitude photography. The USGS uses high-altitude pictures to make image maps and revise existing topographic quadrangles.

High-altitude black-and-white and color infrared photography in the United States was initially coordinated by the **National High Altitude Photography (NHAP)** program, begun in 1978. NHAP program specifications called for cloud-free stereographic coverage oriented with USGS 7.5-minute quadrangles. It takes three black-and-white and four color photos to cover a quadrangle. This federal multiagency program was superseded by NAPP in 1987 (see previous section), but NHAP photography is still available. Details of the NHAP program and specifications for photographs in the high-altitude photographic database are described in the USGS publication "The Sky's the Limit."

An illustration of the quality of high-altitude imagery is provided by the photo of the Madison, Wisconsin, region shown in Figure 24.6. This image map was made using color infrared imagery taken from an altitude of approximately 20 kilometers (13 miles). For most purposes, this image map is equivalent in geometry to the standard topographic quadrangle of the area, although the image map shows far more detail. Many uses of this imagery can easily be imagined.

Space Stations

The most recent sensing platforms have been provided by rockets and satellites. Images from a vantage point in space cover a relatively large ground area at a small scale. The scales—and therefore the environmental detail—of space imagery vary widely, depending on the distance between the spacecraft and earth when the images were created and on the make-up of the sensing device.

Weather Satellites

Satellites were used early for weather monitoring and prediction. The **meteorological satellites,** or **metsats,** tend to have rather coarse spatial resolution. But what their images lack in spatial detail they make up for in rapid repeat coverage. Two civilian meteorological satellite systems representing very different orbital and sensor characteristics are chosen for further discussion. Both systems are operated in a cooperative arrangement between the **U.S. National Oceanic and Atmospheric Administration (NOAA)** and NASA.

Geostationary Satellites. The broadest coverage imagery obtained from space is that from weather satellites positioned in orbit above the equator at an altitude of 35,680 kilometers (22,300 miles). These **Synchronous Meteorological Satellites (SMS),** or **Geostationary Operational Environmental Satellites (GOES),** maintain a "fixed" position with respect to the earth. When things are going well with GOES, North America is covered from both the southwest and southeast every half hour. GOES-6 failed in 1989, however, leaving only one satellite (GOES-7) in orbit until the launch of a replacement satellite (GOES-Next) in 1994.

From the height of SMS/GOES satellites, a single image covers millions of square miles of ground surface, making it possible to see the cloud pattern over the entire United States instantaneously (**Figure B.12**). By taking images every half hour, we can easily study the detailed movement of cloud patterns. This imagery has been used to produce some very dramatic video weather mapping, and is commonly seen on TV weather broadcasts. The resolution of ground details on weather satellite imagery is extremely poor, however. Consequently, the use of the imagery is essentially restricted to broad-scale atmospheric phenomena.

AVHRR Satellites. The NOAA series of weather satellites has now gone through several generations of technology. The most recent satellites carry an **Advanced Very High Resolution Radiometer (AVHRR)** in polar orbit. A ground swath 2,400 kilometers (km.) wide is covered by each satellite every 12 hours. Directly below the spacecraft, ground resolution is 1.1 km., and it decreases rapidly away from this point. This

B.12 A single image taken from a SMS/GOES weather satellite orbiting far out in space can cover the entire United States.

means a raw AVHRR image exhibits severe scale distortion. The images you see have usually undergone geometrical manipulation so that the spatial resolution is approximately 4 km. (**Figure B.13**).

Four or five spectral bands are recorded by the AVHRR sensor. One of these is in the visible zone, and the others are in the near-infrared and thermal infrared wavebands. The relatively poor resolution of AVHRR imagery is made up for by its broad coverage. Thus, it has proven useful in regional and even global studies. It seems particularly suited to monitoring vegetation changes and has been used to make dramatic global portraits of vegetation conditions.

Manned Space Flights

Extensive coverage of ground features has been obtained through NASA's manned space program.* Manned missions can be grouped into three phases: (1) Mercury, Gemini, and Apollo; (2) Skylab; and (3) the space shuttle. The mapping aspects of these three program phases differ greatly.

Mercury, Gemini, and Apollo. Although the main purpose of NASA's **Mercury, Gemini,**

Photographs acquired during the manned spacecraft program are available from the National Cartographic Information Center, U.S. Geological Survey, 507 National Center, Reston, VA 22092, 703-860-6045.

B.13 This AVHRR mosaic of the Great Lakes region shows the general structure of the physical landscape.

and **Apollo** programs wasn't to gather earth imagery from space, the astronauts in the last two of these programs did find time to take many photographs, albeit in a rather casual manner. When an astronaut observed an interesting ground scene and had time, he would simply point his camera out a window of the spacecraft and snap a picture.

The pictures taken during these manned space flights were often quite dramatic. But the equipment and manner used to gather the imagery limited the quality and extent of ground coverage obtained. For one thing, the position of the window on the side of Gemini spacecraft meant that only oblique views could be obtained. The first vertical photograph was taken from the unmanned Apollo 6 spacecraft.

Second, the cameras used in Gemini and Apollo missions were 70-mm. Hasselblads, not the precision mapping cameras which were being used at the time for high-altitude imagery. Up through Apollo 7, the cameras were all loaded with ordinary color film. Apollo 9, however, carried a bank of four 70-mm. cameras equipped with different film-filter combinations. Three of the cameras were used to produce black-and-white images in the green, red, and photo IR portions of the spectrum. The fourth camera was set up with color IR film and a minus blue filter.

A third factor which detracted from Gemini and Apollo imagery of the earth was that only the low and mid-latitude regions (35°N to 35°S) could be photographed because of the spacecrafts' oblique, near-equatorial orbits (**Figure B.14**). Within this low and mid-latitude zone, rather complete coverage could be obtained, since each ground path was offset by the amount the earth turned on its axis while the spacecraft was completing a circuit. The coverage was by no means systematic, however. To determine the coverage of a particular region, you must search through catalogs for each manned spacecraft mission. Considering that there are over 900 photos available from Gemini flights and over 1,400 photos from Apollo flights (6, 7, and 9), this search through the imagery catalogs is no simple chore.

Skylab. NASA's Skylab project initiated a much more ambitious project of obtaining spacecraft imagery than was true of the previous Mercury, Gemini, and Apollo flights. In May, 1973, the Skylab vehicle was placed in an oblique, near-equatorial orbit about 270 miles above the earth. The 100-ton laboratory was subsequently occupied on three occasions: the first mission (Skylab 1) from May 25 to June 22, the second (Skylab 2) from August 29 to September 25, and the third (Skylab 3) from November 16 to February 8.

In many respects, the ground coverage obtained on these missions was similar to that of the Gemini and Apollo projects. But there were some major differences as well. In addition to Hasselblad cameras, Skylab carried three sensor systems designed specifically for gathering earth resource data. One of these sensors was a fixed, multispectral camera. With this camera, designated S190A, high-quality images of the same ground scene were obtained simultaneously in six bands within the visible light and near-infrared zones of the spectrum (**Figure B.15**). The 70-mm. camera was equipped with a six-inch focal-length lens and contained black-and-white film with a green filter (sensitive between .5 and .6 micrometers), black-and-white film with a red filter (.6 to .7 micrometers), natural color film (.4 to .7 micrometers), black-and-white infrared film (.7 to .8 micrometers), experimental black-and-white film (.8 to .9 micrometers), and false-color infrared film (.5 to .88 micrometers). These 70-mm. films provided a ground resolution of approximately 24

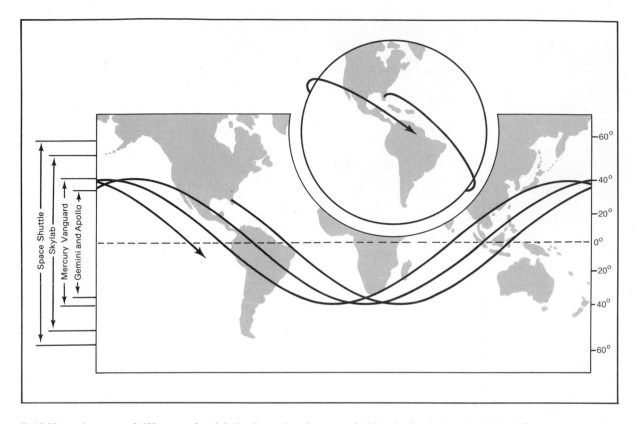

B.14 Manned spacecraft (Mercury, Gemini, Apollo, and early space shuttle missions) were placed in oblique, near-equatorial orbits, letting the astronauts see only the middle and low-latitude portions of the earth's surface.

to 68 meters (79 to 223 feet), depending on atmospheric conditions at the time the photo was taken and the quality of film processing.

Another sensor carried by Skylab was a high-resolution Earth Terrain Camera (S190B). This camera was equipped with an 18-inch focal-length lens and used three 114-mm. (5-inch) films: aerial color film (sensitive between .4 and .7 micrometers), color infrared film (.5 to .88 micrometers), and high-definition aerial black-and-white film (.5 to .7 micrometers). Depending on atmospheric conditions and film processing quality, these films provided a spatial resolution of approximately 10 to 38 meters (m.) (33 to 125 ft.)

The last sensor system carried aboard Skylab was a multispectral scanner (S192). Thirteen channels were used to provide a spectral coverage from .4 to 2.35 and 10.2 to 12.5 micrometers. The spatial resolution of this scanner was 80 by 80 m. (262 by 262 ft.) Despite the broad spectral range of the scanner, it was only operated during daylight hours

when the other sensors were being used. Many of the S192 images are of such poor quality that they haven't received wide public distribution.

Every image taken with Skylab's multiband camera covered a ground area of 163 by 163 kilometers (101 by 101 miles); images taken with the high-resolution camera had a ground coverage of 109 by 109 km. (68 by 68 mi.); and images taken with the multispectral scanner covered a ground swath 74 km. (46 mi.) wide. Each ground path of the satellite ranged from 50°N to 50°S and was repeated every five days, yielding successive images which make the study of seasonal changes possible. Catalogs are available to help you identify and obtain images of special interest. If you first want to get an idea of the quality of these photos, look up the *National Geographic* articles listed in the selected readings at the end of this appendix.

Space Shuttle. Environmental remote sensing from space entered a new era with the

B.15 These strips taken from Skylab photos of the San Francisco Bay area show many details of the physical and cultural environments.

launch of the manned space shuttle **Columbia** in 1981. Later, three additional shuttles, **Challenger, Discovery**, and **Atlantis** were put into service. Challenger exploded on takeoff January 28, 1986, and was replaced in 1992 by **Endeavour**. To date, approximately three dozen launches have been made.

Shuttle missions have originated at Florida's Kennedy Space Center, with orbits inclined from 25° to 60° from the equator. Thus, coverage has been limited to low and medium latitudes. Orbital altitudes also have been relatively low, varying from 225 km. to 300 km. Shuttle launches are supposed to be made from Vandenberg Air Force Base in California as well, but program recovery after the loss of Challenger has caused delays. Higher-altitude (545 km. or 339 mi.) orbits are planned for these missions. Vandenberg launches will also permit near-polar orbits, which will facilitate global coverage.

The space shuttle project was in part justified as a way of consolidating various civilian and military earth observation programs. Thus, imagery created on designated "military" missions is classified and unavailable to the public. But the space shuttle does have a scientific purpose which includes earth surveillance experiments. NASA's **Office of Space and Terrestrial Applications (OSTA)** is conducting a half dozen or so remote sensing experiments. Topics under evaluation involve geology, atmospheric pollution, meteorology, and marine biology.

The remote sensing project that has received the most attention is the **Shuttle Imaging Radar (SIR)** system. This is a sideways-viewing radar of the L-band (23-cm. wavelength) type. The sensor (SIR-A) was initially flown in 1981, and an upgraded version (SIR-B), incorporating several new features, was first flown in 1984. With SIR-B, the depression angle is selectable between 15° and 60°. This permits ground resolutions from 20 to 100 m. (66 to 328 ft.) while mapping a ground swath 25 to 60 km. (16 to 37 mi.) wide, depending on the shuttle's orbital altitude.

The space shuttle **Endeavour** first carried even more refined radar sensors in 1994. The **Spaceborne Imaging Radar (SIR-C)** sensor system used wavelengths of six (C-band) and 24 (L-band) centimeters. The same flight also carried an X-band (three centimeter) **Synthetic Aperture Radar (X-SAR)**.

The computer-processed SIR signals can be used to generate black-and-white images highlighting the terrain in sharp relief. These images can be further computer-processed and rendered in false colors to enhance features of interest. Indeed, the primary aim of the experiment is to see if it is possible to reveal geologic features such as faults, folds, and drainage patterns which could help scientists locate important mineral resources. Results indicate that SIR imagery can also be used to emphasize subtle differences in vegetation, soil moisture, and ocean waves.

It was expected that the SIR system would be able to penetrate vegetation to reveal the contours of the naked land. What wasn't expected was that the radar pulses are also able to penetrate dry, wind-blown sand to a depth of 5.5 km. (18 ft.) Thus, to everyone's surprise, one of the first SIR images of the Sahara desert exposed ancient river channels buried beneath the parched landscape (**Figure B.16**). Productive reservoirs of fresh water may thereby be located. The most publicized SIR application was the apparent discovery in 1991 of the lost city of Ubar, buried by sand in remote southern Oman.* According to legend, Ubar (known as Iram, the "city of towers" in Islam's sacred Koran) was destroyed during a disaster about A.D. 100, and was buried by sand. This led Lawrence of Arabia to call the city "the Atlantis of the Sands."

The shuttle's ability to return payload instruments safely and quickly to experimenters on the ground was supposed to greatly enhance scientific investigations. Unfortunately, the chaos at NASA following the loss of Challenger, and the slow pace of program recovery from that disaster, casts doubt on the future of the space shuttle as a remote sensing laboratory. Initiative seems to be moving toward strictly instrumental systems,

---

Expedition leaders Nicholas Clapp and George Hedges speculated the city may have been the earliest known shipping center for frankincense, possibly the source offered to Jesus by one of the wise men. If preliminary dating is correct, urban development occurred in the region about 3,000 B.C., about 1,000 years earlier than previously thought.

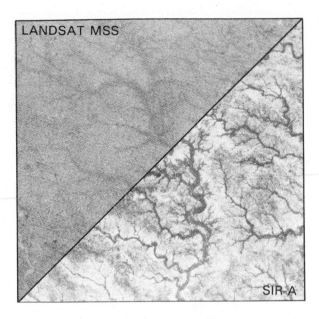

B.16 Shuttle Imaging Radar (SIR-A) images can highlight the subsurface terrain in sharp relief in some dry, sandy areas.

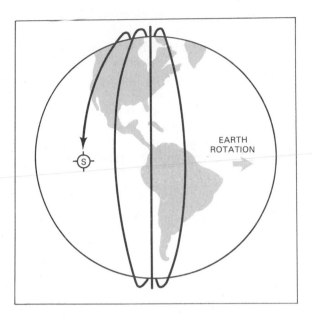

B.17 The near-polar orbit of early Landsat satellites made it possible to provide complete imagery of the earth's surface every 18 days.

which avoid the complications of transferring people to and from space.

Earth Resources Satellites

The rather haphazard, project-oriented coverage of manned spacecraft only hints at the potential of remote sensing from space. To obtain better insight into what systematic remote sensing holds for our future, let's look at three unmanned satellite-based systems currently in operation—Landsat, SPOT, and IRS.

Landsat. In the late 1960s, NASA began a program titled **Earth Resources Observation Systems (EROS)** to explore the potential for monitoring the earth from space. The first satellite was placed in orbit in 1972. Initially called the **Earth Resources Technology Satellite (ERTS-1)**, it was later renamed **Landsat-1**.* Subsequent launches in the Landsat series took place in 1975 (**Landsat-2**), 1978 (**Landsat-3**), 1982 (**Landsat-4**), and 1984 (**Landsat-5**). Technologically and func-

tionally, these five satellites represent two generations of environmental remote sensing from space.

The first three Landsat satellites made up an **experimental, first-generation** effort in environmental remote sensing from space. All three satellites were placed in circular orbit 917 km. (570 mi.) above the earth. A near-polar orbit was used so that the satellite could be synchronized with the sun and so that global coverage was possible due to earth rotation under the satellite (**Figure B.17**). The orbits of these early Landsats were timed so that the satellites would circle the earth roughly 14 times per day and would pass over the same spot on earth at almost the same hour every 18 days.* On each descending orbit (daylight pass from north to south), sensors carried aboard the spacecraft were capable of recording the ground scene over a strip 184 km. (115 mi.) wide (**Figure B.18A**). Each image (or frame) covers a 185-km. square ground area at a resolution of 80 m. (262 ft.). Sixty-four intensity

---

You may find reference to Landsat-A through D in the literature. NASA's early practice was to use a letter designation for the Landsat satellites before launching and then switch to a number designation once the satellites were functioning in orbit.

When Landsat-2 was launched in 1975, it was nine days out of phase with its predecessor. Thus, in the period between January, 1975, and January, 1978, when both satellites were operational, it was possible to generate successive and comparable imagery of a ground scene at nine-day intervals.

levels were use to record electromagnetic energy within each pixel.

Individual images form a grid which is referred to as the **Worldwide Reference System (WRS)**. The WRS indexing scheme consists of a global network of 251 paths (one for each ground track of the satellite) and 148 rows (corresponding to lines of latitude). You can refer to any one of these images by identifying the three-digit numbers for the intersecting path and row (**Figure B.19A**).

Due to the way the Landsat orbit is timed, lighting conditions at each site are the same on successive images, except for the slow seasonal drift in the angle of the sun and, possibly, different cloud cover. As a result, there is little difference in shadows from one picture to the next for a given ground scene. This makes it possible to spot any changes in terrestrial features since earlier visits of the satellite.

In the first three satellites, the same **Multispectral Scanner (MSS)** was flown as the primary sensor system.* This sensor produced four synchronous images of the same ground scene, each in a different waveband (**Figure B.20**). Two of the wavebands are in the visible light portion of the electromagnetic spectrum. One of these, called **band 4**, captures energy in the green (.5 to .6 micrometer) zone. This green band can be graphically rendered as a separate black-and-white image. Band 4 discriminates the depth and turbidity of water bodies. Thus, it emphasizes the movement of sediment-laden water and delineates areas of shallow water, such as shoals and reefs (**Figure B.21A**).

The other visible band, designated **band 5**, is in the lower red (.6 to .7 micrometer) zone of the spectrum. This red band can also be graphically represented as a black-and-white image. It emphasizes topographic and cultural features such as drainage patterns, roads, buildings, and parking

*A **Return Beam Vidicon (RBV)** television camera system was also carried aboard the first three Landsat satellites. Landsat-1 and Landsat-2 had three RBV cameras, each sensitive to a different wavelength (green, red, and near-IR), with a spatial resolution of 80 m. (identical to the MSS sensor). Landsat-3 carried two RBV cameras, each sensitive to the same visible waveband, with an improved ground resolution of 40 m. Unfortunately, these television cameras had mechanical problems, and relatively few images were ever released.

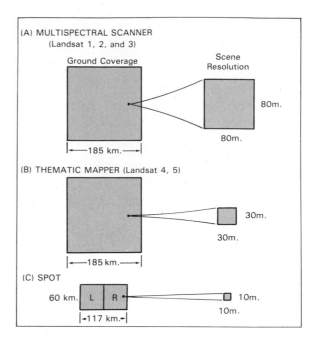

B.18 The ground coverage and spatial resolution of land resources satellite imagery vary from project to project.

lots (**Figure B.21B**). As a rule, this band gives the best general-purpose view of the earth's surface.

Two of the bands lie beyond the visible in the near-infrared portion of the spectrum. Both these bands can be portrayed as black-and-white images. The first of these, known as **band 6**, falls in the .7 to .8 micrometer range. It shows the best tonal contrasts, reflecting various land use practices. It also emphasizes vegetation, landforms, and the boundary between land and water (**Figure B.21C**).

The second near-infrared band, called **band 7**, falls between .8 and 1.1 micrometers. This band provides the best penetration of atmospheric haze and the best land-water discrimination. Like band 6, it emphasizes vegetation and landforms (**Figure B.21D**).

By ordering a complete set of black-and-white images from all four bands, you can see how the same region differs in appearance when filtered to green, red, and near-infrared wavelengths. These four MSS bands are also printed together in different combinations to produce a false-color composite. The composite image is created by exposing three of the four black-and-white images (one of the infrared bands is usually omitted) through different color filters onto color film. Red

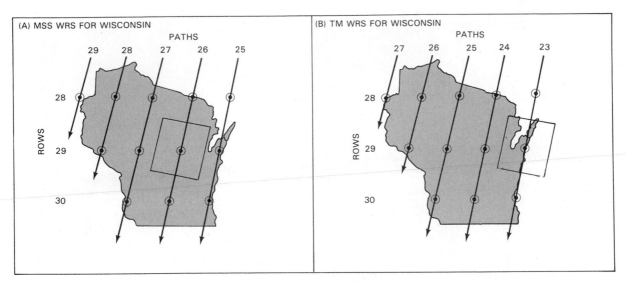

B.19 The Landsat Worldwide Reference System (WRS) is different for Landsat 1, 2, and 3 MSS imagery (A) than for Landsat 4 and 5 TM imagery (B).

is assigned to the near-infrared band; thus, vegetation appears red rather than green. The healthier the vegetation, the redder the image. Since water absorbs the sun's long wavelengths, clear water appears black on infrared photos. Sediment-laden water (highly reflective in band 4) is powder blue in color, while urban centers (highly reflective in band 5) usually appear blue or blue-gray.

Figure 4.8 shows a black-and-white version of a color composite of the same scene illustrated in Figure B.21. This composite was made by combining bands 4, 5, and 7. Although subtle tonal variations apparent on the color rendition aren't clear on this black-and-white reproduction, it still gives some idea of what the color composite reveals. Some of the features which are clear on the individual images have been obscured in making this composite. But other features not apparent in any one of the individual images emerge quite dramatically.

Between Landsats 2 and 3, a significant improvement was made in the MSS scanner so that the sensor on Landsat-3 was equipped with an additional (fifth) MSS channel, designated **band 8**. This fifth band was calibrated for thermal infrared energy. Its image resolution was 237 meters (778 feet), compared with the 80-m. (262-ft.) resolution of the other four spectral bands.

Band 8 didn't necessarily make recordings of the ground scene simultaneously with the other bands. It was principally designed to make recordings at night during the satellite's ascending orbit on the back side of the earth. Indeed, this nighttime sensing capability turned out to be one of the sensor's major advantages. In spite of its gross resolution, band 8 imagery is helpful in identifying agricultural crops and providing information on the thermal characteristics of rocks and soils. In addition, it is useful in monitoring volcanic action, geothermal activity, forest fires, and industrial thermal pollution.

After nearly a decade of research and development activity, the proof-of-concept phase for an **operational, second-generation** earth-sensing

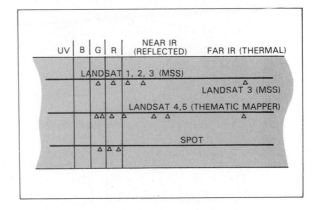

B.20 The spectral sensitivity of land resource satellite sensors varies from one project to the next.

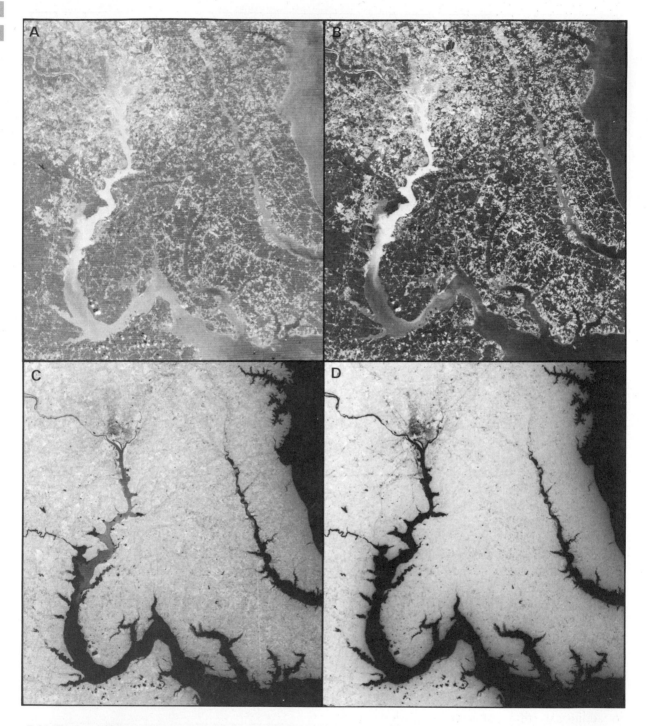

B.21 The four MSS bands of a Landsat-1 image (No. 1080-15192) show different aspects of the upper Chesapeake Bay area. Band 4 (A) is green; band 5 (B) is red; and bands 6 and 7 (C and D) are near-infrared.

capability was initiated in 1982 with the launch of Landsat-4. This satellite was placed in a 705-km. (438-mi.) high, near-polar orbit, making nearly total global coverage possible every 16 days. Landsat-4 soon malfunctioned and was replaced by an identical satellite, Landsat-5, in 1984.

Recognition of the performance limitations of the MSS sensor provided impetus for the design of an improved Landsat-4/5 sensor called the **Thematic Mapper (TM)**.* The design of the TM was strongly influenced by the technology of the first-generation MSS sensor, but it incorporates improvements which add substantially to its effectiveness (**Figure B.22**). Specifically, the new sensor increased spatial resolution to 30 m. (91 ft.) from the 80-m. (262-ft.) MSS capability (**Figure B.18B**). Spectral separation was expanded from the four MSS bands (five on Landsat-3) to seven channels (see Figure B.20 and **Table B.1**). Three of these channels (bands 1 to 3) are in the visible red, green, and blue portions of the spectrum; three channels (bands 4, 5, and 7) are in the reflected (near) infrared portion of the spectrum; and one channel (band 6) is in the thermal infrared (heat) portion of the spectrum. The thermal channel has a ground resolution of 120 m. (394 ft.), in contrast to the 30-m. resolution of the other channels. Radiometric sensitivity was improved, increasing signal quantitizing levels (gray tones) from 64 with the MSS to 256 with the TM. Through improved satellite guidance control and more precise positioning data, the data's geometric fidelity was also enhanced with the TM. And, finally, the ground processing capability for handling TM data was highly automated and streamlined over what was available for earlier MSS data.

The TM spectral bands were chosen primarily for vegetation monitoring. The one exception is band 7, which is included primarily for geologic applications. The size of pixels is 30 m. (ground resolution) in all but band 6, allowing landcover classification of areas as small as 6 to 10 acres (2 to 4 hectares). In contrast, with the MSS in earlier Landsats, it wasn't possible to classify fields of less than about 40 acres (16.2 hectares). It is expected that the TM sensor will make 1:100,000 thematic mapping possible. Even larg-

er-scale maps may be forthcoming if encouraging early research results are supported.

Due to differences between the MSS and TM sensors, their WRS for identifying and ordering images are incompatible. The Landsat-4 and Landsat-5 WRS indexing scheme defines a global network of 233 paths and 248 rows (in contrast to the 251 paths and 248 rows with Landsats 1 through 3). Refer to Figure B.19 for a comparison of the two systems. The earth coverage cycle also differs between Landsat-4/5 and earlier satellites in the series. With the first three satellites, the adjacent swath to the west was covered one day later, whereas with the last two Landsats the same swath is covered seven days later. This greater temporal discontinuity will hamper efforts to make regional image mosaics over short time spans.

Despite the cartographic promise of Landsat, the program has faltered badly due to lack of imaginative and forceful leadership. Even the TM sensor is technically far out of date, and little has been done to design and construct replacement satellites to carry on the series when Landsat-5 dies. After 13 years of operation, Landsat-5 is long past its three-year design life and only through inexplicable good fortune hasn't stopped working. Its loss would break the quarter-century continuity of the program.

Landsat-6, designed to last five years, suffered many delays. The final blow came when its launch failed in September, 1993, and the satellite was lost. Its new sensor system, called the **Enhanced Thematic Mapper (ETM)**, matched the existing multispectral capability of current Landsat satellites. But to this was added a 15-meter

---

To provide continuity with previous Landsat missions, a four-band MSS sensor similar to those flown before was also carried aboard Landsats 4 and 5. A new numbering system is being used to designate the four spectral bands of the Landsat-4/5 MSS, however. What are known as bands 4, 5, 6, and 7 on the previous MSS sensors are now labeled, respectively, as Landsat-4/5 MSS bands 1, 2, 3, and 4.

TABLE B.1

Thematic Mapper Bands (Landsat 4/5)

Band No.	Spectral Range	Name
1	0.45-0.52μm	Blue
2	0.52-0.60μm	Green
3	0.63-0.69μm	Red
4	0.76-0.90μm	Near IR
5	1.55-1.75μm	Mid IR
6	10.40-12.50μm	Thermal IR
7	2.08-2.35μm	Mid IR

B.22 Each of the seven bands of the Landsat Thematic Mapper provides different information about the environment. The bands can be put together in various combinations to accentuate particular features.

resolution panchromatic capability in the .5 to .9 micron range.

Construction of **Landsat-7** is proceeding, with a launch date scheduled for 1998. Plans are that it will carry two sensor systems. The main system, an enhanced version of the Landsat-6 sensor, is called the **Enhanced Thematic Mapper Plus (ETM+)**. The major change is to improve the spatial resolution of the thermal channel from 120 meters to 60 meters. The other Landsat-7 sensor is called the **Landsat Advanced Technology Instrument (LATI)**. Plans call for mid-infrared sensors of 30-meter resolution and a 10-meter resolution panchromatic band, but the design isn't fixed. Delays and changes could occur if history is a guide. If current satellites perish, and something happens to Landsat-7, there could be a gap in the program. If a data lapse threatens, some have speculated that a spare military sensor could be "borrowed" to fill the gap.

For more than a decade now, the trend in U.S. political philosophy has been that the government has no business providing services and subsidizing costs which the private sector is quite willing to underwrite. In this spirit, the cost of Landsat products was sharply increased, and a bill providing for phased Landsat commercialization was signed into law in July, 1984. At the time, a provision was made for basic data (but not necessarily sensor) continuity. Thus, the next Landsat satellites will be launched through a cooperative effort of government and chosen commercial interests.* Under this arrangement, NASA is designing Landsat-7 and its ground support system, and after launch NOAA will operate the satellite and process data. Eventually, total transfer to the private sector may occur. In the meantime, there are other "eyes" in the sky.

SPOT. Landsat isn't the only earth resources satellite program. The "commercialization of space" is well underway. The French have launched a series of land resources satellites known as the **Systeme Probatoire d'Observation de la Terre (SPOT)**.* SPOT-1 was placed in a sun-synchronous polar orbit at an altitude of 832 km. (517 mi.) on February 1, 1986. SPOT-2 was launched into an identical near-circular orbit on January 21, 1990, but is 180 degrees out of phase with SPOT-1. SPOT-3 was launched on September 23, 1993. All three satellites carry identical sensors.

The sensors aboard each satellite are two identical linear array imaging devices of the **pushbroom** type (see Figure 4.1), which can be operated simultaneously or independently. A scene can be generated in nine seconds with either sensor. These solid-state sensors are sensitive to one near-infrared and two visible (green, red) spectral bands optimized for vegetation differentiation and TM compatibility. A radiometric resolution of 256 intensity levels is achieved in each spectral band. The sensors are capable of operating in two modes: black-and-white (panchromatic) with a 10-m. (33-ft.) ground resolution, and multispectral (color infrared) with a 20-m. (66-ft.) spatial resolution (**Figure B.23**). The viewable image area with each scene is 60 x 60 km. (37 x 37 mi.). Deducting for a three-kilometer image sidelap, a single pass of the satellite covers a ground swath 117 kilometers (73 miles) wide (**Figure B.18C**).

SPOT can aim its sensors up to 400 km. (249 mi.) on either side of its ground track using pointable optics. As a result, each satellite can view the same ground scene at one to five day intervals, depending on the latitude. But it takes 26 days for a satellite to repeat its orbit pattern. Thus, this is the interval between views taken from a given vantage point for each satellite. Having two satellites in the same orbit but 180 degrees out of phase cuts this revisit time in half. Having a shorter revisit interval than Landsat permits SPOT to gather better ground coverage in heavily clouded areas and to monitor environmental phenomena of shorter duration (floods, fires, pollution, natural hazard damage, etc.).

The Earth Observation Satellite (EOSAT) Company, a partnership between Radio Corporation of America (RCA) and Hughes Aircraft Company, was chosen in 1985 as the commercial vendor for future Landsat operation and services. A decade later, EOSAT became Space Imaging EOSAT. For further information, contact: Space Imaging EOSAT, 9351 Grant Street, Thornton, CO 80229.

SPOT imagery is distributed from outlets in several dozen countries around the world. In the United States, address inquiries to SPOT Image Corporation, 1897 Preston White Drive, Reston, VA 22091-4368 (phone 703-620-2200; fax 703-648-1813).

B.23 This enhanced SPOT image of central Washington, D.C., shows the level of detail obtainable with this modern sensor. Data from the 10-meter resolution black-and-white band are commonly used to enhance the 20-meter resolution color bands.

SPOT also has a stereoscopic imaging capability (see *Stereo Photos* in Chapter 5). This permits 10-m. (33-ft.) landform contouring from stereopairs using conventional stereoplotting instruments. Indeed, SPOT data are of sufficient quality to support 1:100,000 topographic mapping, 1:50,000 topographic-map revision, and 1:25,000 thematic mapping. In a 1992 application, Air Force crews flying relief supplies into remote, potentially hazardous airfields throughout the former Soviet Union used black-and-white 10-m. SPOT images enhanced with terrain data. (Refer to Figure 5.30 to see the results of this type of overlay procedure.)

To provide continuity in SPOT imagery over the long term, planning is underway for subsequent satellite launches. Although SPOT-2 and -3 were identical to SPOT-1, design changes are in order for SPOT-4 and -5. Additional spectral bands at both 10-meter (panchromatic) and 20-meter (color) resolution are anticipated for SPOT-4. The satellite will also carry a new broad-coverage sensor with a 1-kilometer resolution. These changes would make imagery more useful for ocean and vegetation studies. Launch could come at any time. Plans call for SPOT-5 (year 2000 launch) to include a 5-meter resolution sensor.

In comparison with Landsat, SPOT has higher spatial resolution, more repetitive coverage, and the addition of stereoscopic imagery. Furthermore, the state-of-the-art linear array sensors are based on solid-state electronics, in contrast to the mechanical technology used in Landsat. This means that SPOT should be able to avoid the mechanical malfunctions which have plagued Landsat. It also means that SPOT can provide improved image geometry, something of great interest to map makers.

IRS. The **Indian Space Research Organization (ISRO)** joined the commercial remote sensing community in 1988 with the launch of its first earth resources satellite. With a series of successful launches in rapid succession, ISRO now has an impressive constellation of satellites orbiting in its **Indian Remote Satellite**

TABLE B.2

Indian Remote Satellite (IRS) Program

Satellite	Date	Sensors*	Type-Bands	Resolution
IRS-1A	1988	LISS-I	Multispectral-4	72.5 meters
		LISS-II	Multispectral-4	36.25 meters
IRS-1B	1991	LISS-I	Multispectral-4	72.5 meters
		LISS-II	Multispectral-4	36.25 metcrs
IRS-1C	1995	Pan	Panchromatic-1	5.8 meters
		LISS-III	Multispectral-4	23.5 meters
				70 meters (SWIR)
		WiFS	Multispectral-2	188 meters
IRS-P2	1996	LISS-II	Multispectral-4	36.25 meters

*See text for definitions of sensor terms.

(IRS) series (**Table B.2**). Space Imaging EOSAT distributes data from these satellites worldwide.*

The rapid succession of launches has allowed ISRO to respond to user needs with quick design changes. The IRS-1A and -1B satellites carried two versions of the **Linear Imaging Self-Scanning Sensor (LISS)**. LISS-I and -II were both four-band pushbroom sensors with the same spectral resolution (**Table B.3**). The spectral bands match the lower four bands of Landsat's Thematic Mapper sensor. The spatial resolution of LISS-I (72.5 meter) was roughly equivalent to Landsat MSS (80 meter) imagery, whereas LISS-II resolution (36.25 meters) approximated that of the Thematic Mapper (30 meters). Both sensors have a ground swath of 148 km., but it takes four LISS-II images to cover the ground area of one LISS-I image. Repeat coverage is 22 days at the equator, and less elsewhere.

IRS-C1 carries three sensors. The LISS-III has four spectral bands, but they differ somewhat from those of the earlier LISS sensors. The blue band was dropped, but the band 1 identifier was not reassigned. A short-wave infrared (SWIR) capability (band 5) with 70-meter pixels, similar to TM band 5, was added. LISS-III bands 2-4 have a

finer spatial resolution (23.5 meters) than earlier LISS sensors. This is roughly equivalent to multispectral SPOT imagery (20 meters). The LISS-III swath width is 145 km.

The Pan (panchromatic) sensor aboard IRS-C1, with its 5.8-meter spatial resolution and 70-km. ground swath, ushers in a new generation of advanced remote sensing devices. Pan images are

Space Imaging EOSAT, 9351 Grant Street, Thorton, CO 80229.

TABLE B.3

Spectral Characteristics of IRS Sensors

Sensor	Band	Spectral Range
LISS-I and -II	1	Blue-green, 0.45-0.52 µm
	2	Green, 0.52-0.59 µm
	3	Red, 0.62-0.68 µm
	4	Near-infrared, 0.77-0.86 µm
LISS-III	1	(Not included)
	2	Green, 0.52-0.59 µm
	3	Red, 0.62-0.68 µm
	4	Near-infrared, 0.77-0.86 µm
	5	Mid-infrared, 1.55-1.70 µm
WiFS	1	Red
	2	Near-infrared

578

B.24 The 5.8-meter resolution panchromatic imagery from India's IRS-1C satellite ushers in a new generation of advanced remote sensing devices that facilitate applications in urban areas. (Courtesy Space Imaging EOSAT.)

acquired simultaneously and are **coregistered** with LISS-III, so they can be merged into hybrid images having desirable characteristics of both parents. The fine detail of Pan imagery also makes possible a host of important new applications of remote sensing from space. Urban studies top this list (**Figure B.24**).

The **Wide Field Sensor (WiFS)** aboard IRS-C1 has 180-meter resolution, a 810-km. ground swath, and two spectral bands (red and near-infrared). This sensor provides regional imagery that falls between the spatial resolution of the Landsat MSS (80 meter) and NOAA's AVHRR (1.1 kilometer) sensors. WiFS provides repeat coverage every five days (compared to several times a day for AVHRR). The sensor was designed to monitor floods, droughts, forest fires, and other dynamic natural events covering broad areas.

ISRO has ambitious plans for the next few years. IRS-1D should be launched by early 1998. Its sensors duplicate those of IRS-1C. Soon thereafter ISRO plans to launch follow-up satellites with a 2.5-meter resolution panchromatic sensor and a 10-meter resolution multispectral sensor.

Next-Generation Sensors

A new generation of remote sensing devices is coming. Plans call for dozens of launches by private firms and government-private partners. The first of this new generation of satellites should be in orbit by early 1998. Two aspects of these new earth resources sensors are of special importance for mapping. One is a vast improvement in spatial resolution. The other welcome feature is a move toward larger numbers of more narrowly-focused spectral bands.

High-Resolution Imagery

The big news in the remote sensing industry is that a number of commercial satellites boasting 1-meter to 4-meter resolution panchromatic imagery and 4-meter to 10-meter resolution multispectral imagery are planned for launch in the late 1990s.* Some of these **high-resolution** sensors are likely to be generating imagery by the time this book is published. When satellites carry both panchromatic and multispectral sensors of different resolution, plans call for the images to be coregistered so that they can be merged into a hybrid display of superior characteristics.

This high-resolution imagery will open remote sensing to a wide range of new uses. Past applications of civilian space imagery were largely restricted to landcover and general thematic analysis. The spatial detail (shape, size, texture, pattern) that can be seen in high-resolution space imagery will make individual feature identification possible. This will make space imagery suitable for reference mapping, whereas cartographic use of imagery from prior generations of civilian space sensors was restricted to thematic mapping.

Hyperspectral Imagery

As the spatial resolution of imagery increases, so does the need for greater spectral resolution. While pixel size is crucial in identifying features by their spatial form, spectral resolution helps us identify objects by their composition. For technical reasons, space sensors to date have had only limited spectral resolution. Less than 10 broadly-defined spectral bands is the current standard.

But for some time researchers have been experimenting with airborne sensors having tens

*Vendors poised to launch high-resolution sensors include: Space Imaging, Inc, Thornton, CO; EarthWatch, Inc., Longmont, CO; Orbital Sciences Corporation, Dulles, VA; GDE Systems, San Diego, CA; and Space Imaging EOSAT, Thornton, CO. This list is tentative, of course. Mergers, drop-outs, and new faces characterize this rapidly-evolving market.

to hundreds of separate, narrowly-restricted spectral bands. Technical development has now progressed to the point where these **hyperspectral** sensors are ready for satellite launch. Once space-borne systems are operational, the huge volume of data generated will require development of powerful information processing strategies. This will require complex software engineering based on newfound understanding of effective use of hyperspectral data in image interpretation. This is a challenging task, since our current image-processing approach is usually based on using three or less broadly-defined spectral bands.

But once we build an infrastructure for using hyperspectral imagery, we can expect major improvement in our ability to interpret space imagery. When we use this imagery in conjunction with high-resolution sensors, we'll be able to determine surface properties as never before. Rather than identify bare rock, we'll see specific minerals and rock types. Rather than identify broad vegetation classes, we'll determine species. At the same time, hyperspectral imagery will add confidence to feature interpretations based primarily on spatial properties.

Commercialization of Space

SPOT and IRS are truly operational and commercialized systems. In contrast, Landsat still functions in part as an experimental program of the U.S. government bureaucracy. Rather than provide systematic coverage, as Landsat does, the SPOT and IRS systems are used to providing selective coverage upon demand by paying customers.

Per-image costs for SPOT, Landsat, and IRS are comparable, and considerably higher than early Landsat prices when the program was run solely under taxpayer subsidy by the U.S. government. It remains to be seen whether in the long run the private sector or some quasi-government organization can do better in the environmental remote sensing business. But it's clear that we've entered a new era, one in which environmental data are recognized to have value in the marketplace. This "data-for-sale" privatization has profound consequences for mapping.

How much spatial resolution in "off the shelf" satellite imagery can a free society tolerate? At what point does our right to know violate the right to privacy of others? These are difficult questions for individuals who need ready access to information if they are to make responsible decisions in a democratic society. They are difficult decisions for editors who must decide what information to publish and when it should be seen by the public. They are hard questions, too, for elected governments, which have the responsibility of protecting their citizens.

The Persian Gulf War in 1990-91 proved to be an interesting test for an emerging global "open sky" policy in remote sensing. In describing its coverage of the Gulf War, Landsat officials said their pictures showed "only sand," a refreshingly candid reference to its images' comparably poor spatial resolution. Officially, SPOT Image Corporation said it only sold pictures to people with security clearances. Of course, the actual dissemination of Landsat and SPOT images of the Persian Gulf region during the conflict may never be known. What we do know is that the print and broadcast media provided only highly censored images before, during, and after the war. The source, as well as the implications, of this censorship should be a point of debate.

Past issues related to image resolution are sure to be magnified by the new generation of five-meter and one-meter pixel imagery now coming on the market. Space imagery with one-meter resolution is comparable in detail to USGS digital orthophoto quadrangle imagery created from medium-altitude aerial photos (see Figure 4.15). Although these photos have a somewhat fuzzy appearance, you can still clearly see features with a width of two meters. Civilians have no experience dealing with problems associated with public access to timely imagery having this fine level of detail.

Image Detail

The overriding problem in remote sensing is to strike a working balance between image detail, coverage, and cost. We saw in the previous section that the trend in environmental remote sensing is to move to higher vantage points. Thus, for many purposes, images taken from high-altitude aircraft have replaced those from conventional low-altitude craft. More recently, images taken from space vehicles have superseded those taken from aircraft of all types.

There are advantages to be gained by moving to higher vantage points, of course. For one thing, a wider ground swath can be covered in a single pass of the sensor vehicle. In addition, relief distortion is greatly reduced in images taken from higher altitudes. But image quality is another matter.

If the same sensing system is used in every instance, image detail will diminish with increasing altitude. But the spatial resolution of environmental detail on a remotely sensed image doesn't always bear an inverse relationship to the distance of the sensor from the ground scene. Instead, better-quality sensors are often substituted for standard devices when sensing from higher altitudes. The size of the film grain or the scanner cell can be reduced, or the fidelity of the lens or other sensing equipment can be improved.

It is common knowledge that the quality of military satellite and high-altitude aircraft images far exceeds that available for civilian applications. When the military decides that its imagery no longer presents a security risk, it (or the sensor used) may be released for civilian use. If we're patient, then, remote sensing will eventually provide solutions to many current problems. Our wish may soon be reality, since the "next-generation sensors" discussed previously are a big step toward this end.

PICTURE PROCESSING

Just when you think you've mastered the intricacies of remote sensing, you're likely to encounter images that don't fit into any of the types you've learned. There are two possible explanations. First, enhancement may have been used to remove image distortions or selectively accentuate certain phenomena. Second, special techniques may have been used to extract wavelength information related to special themes from known image types. These two methods of **picture processing** are becoming increasingly popular because of their ability to improve the quality of image maps.

Image Enhancement

Despite the technical sophistication which has gone into the design and operation of remote sensing systems, the products of remote sensing often fall short of the ideal. We frequently seem to want more than we can get for the investment in time, money, and effort we are willing to make. This situation has encouraged the development of methods which make it possible to enhance certain aspects of an image after initial recording of information. A variety of these **image enhancement** techniques are now in use on an experimental or developmental basis. Most such procedures are performed by high-speed electronic computers. This means that the gray tones in the picture must be converted to a matrix of computer-compatible numerical values. While the data used to create scanner images are naturally in this form and can be processed directly, photographs must first be scanned by a device capable of converting gray tones to proportionate numbers on a cell-by-cell basis.

There is almost no limit to what can be done with an image available in computer-compatible numerical form. Probably the most obvious thing is simply to remove any geometrical distortion introduced by the information-gathering and display systems used to create the graphic. Sources of this distortion might be the central perspective geometry, instability in the sensor-carrying vehicle, or aberrations in the sensor equipment itself.

Sensor-produced effects which degrade the graphic quality of the image can also be removed by image processing. Scanner images usually require more upgrading than photographs. One problem is that scanner imagery involves transmitting signals which are subject to electronic interference or noise (similar to radio static or TV snow). Even when signal transmission is perfect, the resulting image is built cell by cell, line by line. These scan lines may become so visually dominant in a ground scene that they obscure important landscape detail unless they are muted through subsequent image processing.

Useful results can also be obtained by improving the thematic content of an image. One way to accomplish this is to accentuate the edges of features (**Figure B.25A**). This **image sharpening** or **edge enhancement** procedure creates a crisp edge between tonal zones, often to such an extent that the image assumes a three-dimensional or relief effect.

Another way to improve thematic content is to emphasize the contrast between tonal

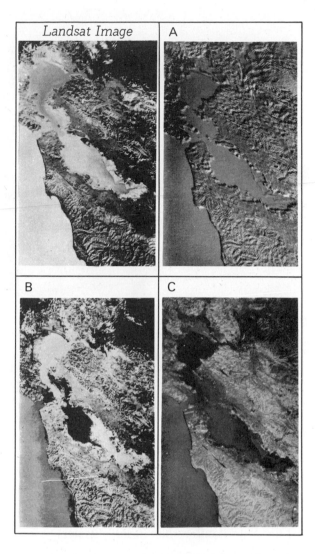

B.25 The thematic content of aerial photos and scanner imagery can be improved through a number of methods, including edge enhancement (A), band ratioing (B), and change detection (C).

was overexposed or underexposed when it was created.

A third content enhancement method is called **band ratioing (Figure B.25B)**. This procedure involves taking the gray scale value of the pixels in one Landsat band and dividing it by the value of the pixels in another band. The ratio value can then be assigned a new gray-scale level. Band ratioing improves tonal image quality by emphasizing classes of similarities and differences. Tone and color difference can be displayed much more precisely. In addition, the effects of shadows and different sun angles are minimized. The method has proven to be a key processing technique for petroleum and mineral geology work and in delineating the rural-urban fringe.

Change detection represents a fourth content enhancement procedure (**Figure B.25C**). The technique is extremely simple. Images of the same area taken at different periods merely have their identical picture elements eliminated. What remain are multispectral signatures which have shown change. This process can make familiar landmarks which haven't undergone any change, such as rivers or cities, disappear from the picture. Change-detection methods are useful in monitoring sedimentation changes, in showing seasonal differences in crops and other vegetation, and in studying changes in snow cover and lake ice.

Still another form of image enhancement entails combining several images into a composite image. The images to be combined may be of the same or of different types. Dramatic improvement in Landsat imagery is possible, for example, if it is combined with lower-altitude radar imagery. This is obvious in **Figure B.26**, which shows a portion of a Landsat scene of the San Diego, California, area. When hydrologic and vegetation information from the Landsat image is superimposed onto relief information from the radar scene, the overall image is much improved. Indeed, the composite image is far superior to the original Landsat image even though it is printed at a scale of 1:250,000—four times larger than the maximum scale recommended for Landsat imagery.

Image enhancement practices are sometimes carried so far that they isolate a class of environmental feature from the rest of the photograph or scanner image. When this result is the specific goal of picture processing, the procedure

zones on an image. The process involves assessing the distribution of tonal intensity on the original and then stretching the intensity range so that on the new image gray tones range from black to white. This **contrast stretching** technique is particularly useful on images with very little tonal range. The technique will frequently bring out information so subtle that it may not otherwise be visible. Contrast enhancement is especially useful when terrain reflectance is high, as in the case of ice caps, deserts, and snow-covered ground. It is also valuable if a picture

B.26 Radar enhancement of this Landsat image of the San Diego, California, area shows dramatic results.

is called **theme extraction** (also see *Theme Extraction* in Chapter 24).

The practice of theme extraction can begin well before a picture is ever recorded, of course. Highly selective remote sensing is possible by using various combinations of sensor, film sensitivity, filter, and vantage point. Alternatively, it is possible to extract certain aspects of the image after initial information recording (see *Image Classification* in Chapter 24). We may want to isolate a single class of feature—water bodies or forest, say—from other image features (see Figure 24.21). Or we may want to separate and emphasize different classes of information such as residential and commercial development within the image context itself, by giving each feature class a special tone or color (see Figures 24.18, 24.19, and 24.20). Many contemporary photo and scanner maps are the product of one or the other of these theme extraction processes.

Once one or more themes have been extracted from an image, it is sometimes desirable to reduce the visual complexity of the resulting image. One way to do this is by eliminating features which fall below a lower size threshold. Thus, regions smaller than 40 acres, for example, may be reclassed so that they fall into the same class as the surrounding area. Another method of reducing visual complexity is to smooth out fine

irregularities in the boundaries of each region in the picture.

Both these simplification methods have the effect of reducing the amount of information an image contains. This is apparent in **Figure B.27**. There are two possible advantages in throwing out information in this way. One is that small errors in theme extraction may be eliminated because they would tend to show up as irregularities in the image pattern. The other is that for certain purposes we might want to gain a general impression of the pattern rather than to study its details.

Map Use Changes

Picture processing holds tremendous promise for map users. It gives us an opportunity to use maps in an entirely new way. It also makes possible the widespread use of image maps. In the past, map users have had three main objections to image maps.

First, the imaging system seemingly introduced geometric distortion of such exotic origin that it was difficult to understand. These distortions can now be eliminated through picture processing so that photos and scanner images can share the desirable geometrical characteristics of parallel perspective maps.

Second, map users have charged that image maps presented information in a confus-

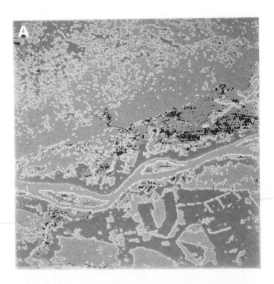

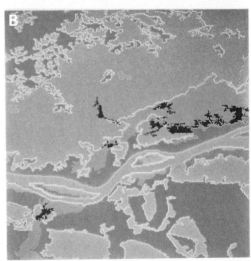

B.27 Image map classification can produce a cluttered, confusing pattern of spatial units (A). Simplifying through digital processing can have a powerful clarifying effect (B).

ingly indiscriminate way. This problem can now be circumvented by selective theme extraction in conjunction with simplification of the tonal pattern which results. In the extreme case, image maps can become indistinguishable from thematic line maps.

Finally, many people have preferred line maps over image maps because they found the former easier to read. This was because line-map makers had intervened between the environment and its representation by generalizing and identifying classes of information portrayed by map symbols. Picture processing now promises the same feature detection and identification service, a process which in the past was usually called **photointerpretation** (**photoreading** might be a better term).

Combining these three factors, picture processing brings image maps into a form which closely resembles that of parallel perspective line maps. Vastly more important in the long run, however, is the fact that picture processing techniques turn image maps into a truly dynamic map form. With images displayed electronically on a computer screen, map users can manipulate maps at will, generating an immense amount of information. At this time, it is difficult to imagine the eventual impact of picture processing, but it is certain to be beneficial. In a few years, we will be able to work with countless transformations of our original image, subsets of image information, and potentially infinite combinations of information from other images. This new ability to use maps interactively should advance our environmental understanding and reduce spatial behavior conflicts immeasurably.

We are entering a whole new dimension in map use. In the next generation, enhanced remotely sensed views of the environment will become the dominant map form. Image mapping has gone far beyond the black-and-white low-altitude photography which dominated for the 50 years leading up to the satellite era (which began about 25 years ago). We already have almost as many distinct image mapping methods as there are line mapping techniques. We also have an increasing number of hybrid image-based maps, on which special symbols for roads and other features have been superimposed on an image base. Map users now have to realize that a single remotely sensed image is no more valuable than a single line map. Rarely will either one be sufficient for all purposes. There is a multitude of images, each best suited for a different need. It is up to us to learn how to put each of these mapping methods to best use.

SELECTED READINGS

Campanella, R., "High-Resolution Satellite Imagery for Business," *Business Geographics* (March 1996), pp. 36-39.

Campbell, J.B., *Introduction to Remote Sensing,* 2nd ed. (New York: The Guilford Press, 1996).

584

Canby, T.Y., "Skylab, Outpost on the Frontier of Space" and "Skylab Looks at Earth," *The National Geographic Magazine*, 146, 4 (October 1974), pp. 441-469, 470-493.

Carleton, A.M., *Satellite Remote Sensing in Climatology* (CRC Press, Inc. 1991).

Chedin, A., *Microwave Remote Sensing of the Earth System* (Hampton, VA: A. DeePak Publishing, 1989).

Chien, P., "High Spies," *Popular Mechanics* (Feb. 1996), pp. 47-51.

Cook, W.J., "Ahead of the Weather: New Technologies Let Forecasters Make Faster, More Accurate Predictions," *U.S. News & World Report* (April 29, 1996), pp. 55-57.

Corbley, K.P., "Applications of High-Resolution Imagery," *Geo Info Systems* (May 1997), pp. 36-40.

Corbley, K.P., "Multispectral Imagery: Identifying More than Meets the Eye," *Geo Info Systems* (June 1997), pp. 38-43.

Corbley, K.P., "Regional Imagery: Wide Angle Advantages, Wide-Ranging Applications," *Geo Info Systems* (April 1997), pp. 28-33.

Evans, D.L., et al., "Earth from the Sky," *Scientific American* (Dec. 1994), pp. 70-75.

Hamit, F., "Where GOES Has Gone: NOAA's Weather Satellite Imagery and GIS-Marketed," *Advanced Imaging* (Nov. 1996), pp. 60-64.

Jensen, L.C., et al., "Side-Looking Airborne Radar," *The Scientific American*, 237, 4 (October 1977), pp. 84-95.

Land Satellite Information in the Next Decade, Conference Proceedings (Bethesda, MD: American Society of Photogrammetry & Remote Sensing, 1995).

Lillesand, T.M., and Kiefer, R.W., *Remote Sensing and Image Interpretation*, 3rd ed. (New York: John Wiley & Sons, 1994).

Nicolson, I., *Sputnik to Space Shuttle: The Complete Story of Space Flight* (New York: Dodd, Mead & Co., 1985).

Office of Technology Assessment, U.S. Congress, *The Future of Remote Sensing from Space: Civilian Satellite Systems and Applications* (Washington, DC: U.S. Gov. Printing Office, 1993).

Silverman, J., Mooney, J.M., and Shepherd, F.D., "Infrared Video Cameras," *Scientific American*, 266, 3 (March 1992), pp. 78-83.

SPOT User's Handbook (Reston, VA: SPOT Image Corporation, 1989)..

Uhlir, D.M., "Hyperspectral Imagery: On the Brink of Commercial Acceptance," *Earth Observation Magazine* (Feb. 1995).

Waters, T., "More than Skin Deep," *Earth* (Dec. 1994), pp. 50-55.

Webster, B., "Space Imagery: A Catalyst for New Business Opportunities," *Business Geographics* (July 1997), pp. 24-26.

Also see references in Chapter 4 and Chapter 24.

APPENDIX C

MAP PROJECTIONS

Strike flat the thick rotundity o' th' world!
—William Shakespeare, *King Lear*

APPENDIX C
MAP PROJECTIONS

More has been written about map projections* than all other facets of mapping and map use combined, yet people still find the subject to be the most bewildering aspect of map appreciation. Many people readily admit that they don't understand map projections. This ignorance can have unfortunate consequences. For one thing, it greatly hinders our ability to understand international relations in our global society. It also makes us easy prey for politicians, special interest groups, advertisers, and others who through ignorance or by design use map projections in potentially deceptive ways (see *Abuse* and *Propaganda* in Chapter 25). And, finally, by unknowingly using maps based on projections ill-suited for our purposes, we encourage and perpetuate the abuse of maps.**

The solution is education. Unfortunately, however, people tend to be more confused than enlightened by the detailed treatment of map projections found in many standard textbooks on maps. Authors tend to stress either the mathematical elegance of projections or the properties of long lists of named projections.

Yet what you as a map user need to know about projections is neither boring nor mathematically complicated. The secret is to look for similarities rather than focus on differences between projections. Many projections share common features. Once you recognize these, you can group the infinite variety of projections into a few types or families, each of which has a characteristic geometric distortion pattern. It's then quite simple to learn the special properties of interesting individual projections. Rather than trying to recognize a long list of projections by name, you should aim to gain a general understanding of the concepts and problems involved with each projection family.

By "projection" we mean the geometric transformation of the earth's surface into the map's surface.

**Major TV news programs commonly use maps designed to serve special compass-navigational needs as backdrops for discussing world events. The majority of wall maps sold at retail outlets for home and office display are also of this compass-navigational variety. It would be hard to make a worse choice of projection for either purpose.*

Before we discuss these major families, we can clarify the whole issue of map projections with a brief discussion of the logic behind them. Why are projections necessary? We'll begin our discussion with globes because they are, theoretically, the best projections of all.

GLOBES

Of all maps, globes give us the most realistic picture of the earth as a whole. Basic spatial attributes such as distance, direction, shape, and area are preserved; and proximity relations are maintained. Thus, globes facilitate the study of geographical relations. They represent the best possible map projection, because they include a minimum of spatial distortion.

Globes have a number of disadvantages, however. They do not permit us to view all parts of the earth's surface simultaneously. Nor are they very convenient, either from the standpoint of the map maker or the map user. They are bulky and do not lend themselves to convenient handling and storage, especially as the size and weight

increase. We can't carry globes around with us or stash them in the glove compartment of our car.

We wouldn't have these handling and storage problems if we used a baseball-sized globe. But such a globe would be of little practical value, since it would have a size reduction of approximately 1 to 125,000,000. Even a globe which is two feet in diameter (the size of a large desk model) still represents a 1 to 20,000,000 scale reduction. It would take a globe about 40 to 50 feet in diameter—the height of a four-story building!—to provide a map image of the scale used with state highway maps. A globe nearly 180 feet in diameter would be required to provide a map image equivalent to the standard 1:24,000-scale topographical mapping series in the United States.

Another problem with globes is that the instruments and techniques which are suited for studying spatial relations on spherical surfaces are relatively inconvenient and difficult to use. Computations on a sphere are far more complex than computations on a plane surface. (For a demonstration of the relative difficulty of making distance computations from plane and spherical coordinates, see Chapter 11.)

And, finally, globe construction is laborious and costly. High-speed printing presses have kept the cost of flat map reproduction to manageable levels but have not yet been developed to work with curved media. Therefore, globe construction is not suited to the volume of map production required for modern mapping needs.

It would be ideal if the earth's surface could be mapped onto a flat medium, such as a sheet of paper, since this would facilitate map production, handling, and storage. It would also provide us with an instantaneous view of all parts of the earth's surface. Unfortunately, the earth is not what is known as a **developable surface**. In other words, it cannot be flattened without distorting such geometrical properties as direction, distance, area, and shape. The continuity of the earth's surface also must be violated. Thus, all flat maps geometrically distort reality. It is impossible to transform a spherical surface that curves away in every direction from every point into a plane surface that does not exhibit curvature in any direction from any point. This is the map **projection problem**. There is no true solution, only approximate or near solutions.

588

NEAR GLOBES

Globes are produced commercially by first printing a flat map in gores (lune-shaped segments). With wetting and a little stretching, these gores are then wrapped around a spherical form (**Figure C.1**). Obviously, the more gores that are used, the less the amount of stretching required and therefore the less distortion involved. If the gores are fitted together without stretching, the result is a solid body resembling a globe, but not a true globe. As the number of flat gores used to construct such a **near globe** increases, the approximation becomes better and better until eventually it is visually indistinguishable from a true globe.

This near-globe technique provides an inexpensive and interesting way to bridge the gap between the true globe and the flat map, particularly when facets of other shapes are substituted for the flat gores. For example, a number of solids bounded by polygons (squares, pentagons, triangles) and known as **polyhedrons** can be used to form near globes. Regular polyhedrons appear to be the more preferred near globes, apparently because their facets are all the same size and shape, resulting in visual symmetry when spread out flat (**Figure C.2**).

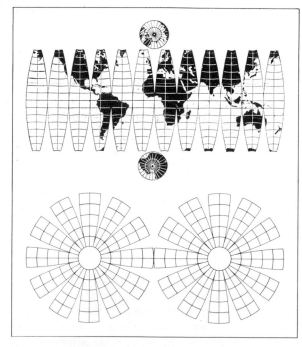

C.1 The use of gores in globe construction.

FLAT MAPS

By reversing the process of forming near globes using polyhedrons, the facets upon which subglobal maps have been projected can be laid out flat. Certain adjoining facets will then match along one or more of their common edges. The actual arrangement of the facets of a flattened near globe can vary considerably, resulting in different global patterns to suit individual needs.

Probably the most disturbing aspect of such world pictures is that they are always characterized by a number of interruptions or breaks in true earth continuity. To some extent, this lack of continuity can be reduced by using a single map projection, but the cost is to transfer the distortion to other spatial properties. But, then, no projection can provide a completely distortion-free representation of the spherical earth surface, for this is the projection problem.

Flattening Continuum

The concept of map projection is somewhat more involved than is implied in the previous discussion of near-globe flattening. Not one but a series of distorting transformations is required. The highly irregular earth's surface is initially transformed into a much simpler three-dimensional surface, and, through several additional steps, this derived surface is subsequently projected onto a plane.

This progressive flattening of the earth's surface is illustrated in **Figure C.3**. The first step is to project the earth's irregular surface onto a more regular imaginary surface known as the **geoid**. This is the surface that would result if the average level of the world's oceans were extended under the continents. It serves as the **datum**, or starting reference surface, for the elevation

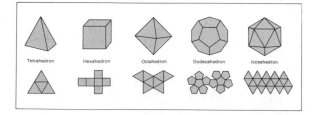

C.2 Rectangular polyhedrons in solid and flattened form.

C.3 The mapping process involves a progressive flattening of the irregular earth's surface.

data found on our maps (see "Absolute Relief Methods" in Chapter 5: *Landform Portrayal*).

The second step is to project the undulating geoid onto a still more regular oblate **ellipsoid**. (See Figure 2.1 in Chapter 2.) This new surface serves as the basis for geodetic and astronomic coordinates used by surveyors. It also serves as the datum for the common spherical coordinates of latitude and longitude found on our maps.

The third step is to project the oblate ellipsoid onto a still more regular **spheroid**. This produces the standard globe.

The fourth transformation—and the one most directly associated with the bulk of map projection activity—involves the mapping of the spheroid onto a **plane** surface. The greatest distortion of the earth's surface geometry occurs in this step. Thus, the results are also most dramatic.

Sometimes projection activity is carried a final step, in which one plane surface is transformed into another. This provides a convenient means for creating new projections by modifying existing ones. Photography could be used, for example, to turn a standard planimetric map in

parallel perspective into an oblique central perspective view. The possibilities are endless.

Correspondence Relations

You can gain an idea of the distortion effects of map transformations by considering correspondence relations between flat maps and the earth's surface. Three relations between map and reality are shown in **Figure C.4**. With the most desirable relation, each location on the earth's surface has one and only one corresponding point on the map. This **one-to-one** correspondence lets the map user shift attention from a feature on the earth to the same feature on the map, and vice versa, with equal facility. Unfortunately, this desirable trait can't be maintained for all points on world map projections.

To represent an entire spherical surface on a plane, the continuous spherical surface must be interrupted at some point or along some line. These breaks in continuity naturally form the map border on a world projection (see *Continuity* later in this chapter). Thus, a point, such as the North Pole, may become a circumscribing circle or a line as long as the equator. Such undesirable but unavoidable relations represent a **one-to-many** correspondence between earth and map space, since one point on the earth's surface has become a series of points on the map.

A third relationship between reality and map occurs when several locations on the earth's surface become a single location on the map. This **many-to-one** correspondence makes the transcription from map image to earth space confusing and is thus considered undesirable. In practice, however, such a correspondence is unavoidable because of the great scale reduction required between earth and map, and because symbols must be large enough to be seen. In fact, many-to-one correspondence between reality and its representation is what makes mapping possible.

CLASSIFYING PROJECTIONS

Potentially, there is an infinite number of map projections, each of which is better suited for some uses than for others. How, then, do we go about distinguishing one projection from another?

590

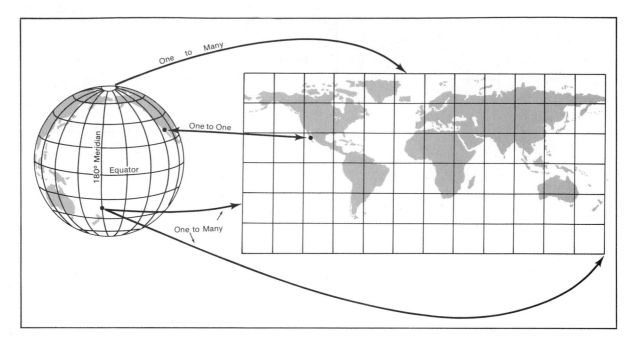

C.4 Correspondence relations between earth and map may take one of several forms. One-to-many and many-to-one relations are causes for concern, but cannot be avoided on global maps.

Our first step is to organize the unlimited variety of projections into a limited number of groups or families on the basis of shared attributes. Two approaches are revealing for those who use maps. One focuses on preserved spatial properties, such as shape, area, direction, distance, and continuity. The other focuses on the nature of the surface used in constructing the projection—a factor central to understanding the pattern of spatial distortion over the map surface. The two approaches go hand in hand, since the map user is concerned, first, with what spatial properties are preserved and, second, with the pattern and extent of distortion. Let's look, then, at both these projection classification schemes.

Preserved Properties

The accuracy with which we can extract distance, direction, area, shape, and proximity information from maps depends on how well these properties are preserved in the projection geometry. Obviously, they can't all be preserved at once or there would be no "projection problem" and hence no need for this appendix. Thus, for purposes of map analysis (detailed in Part II of this book), the most functionally meaningful classi-

fication of projections is one which focuses on preserved spatial properties. Let's discuss each property in turn.

Distance

For a map to be truly distance-preserving (equidistant), the scale would have to be equal in all directions from every point. This is impossible. Because of the stretching and shrinking which occurs in the process of transforming the spherical earth's surface to a plane, the stated map scale (see Chapter 13 and Appendix A for more information on scale) is true only at selected points or along particular lines. Everywhere else the scale of the map is actually smaller or larger than the given scale. Thus, the preservation of distance in a map projection is at best a partial achievement. The property of equidistance is not universal.

To grasp the basis of distance preservation on maps, we must first realize that there are in fact two map scales. One is the **actual** scale of the map at any point, which will tend to differ from one location to another. The other is the **stated** scale of the map. This concept is best visualized by imagining that the earth is first reduced to a globe of desired scale, and this globe is subsequently transformed into a flat map (**Figure C.5**).

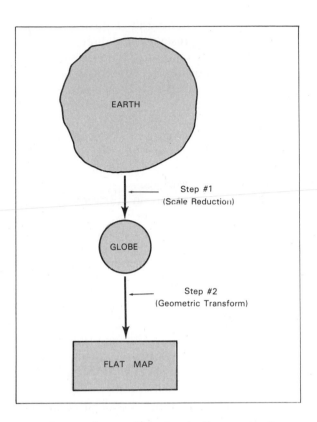

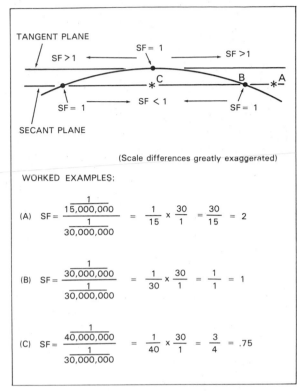

C.5 It is convenient to think of projection construction as a two-step process whereby the earth is first reduced to a globe of the desired scale and this globe is then transformed into a flat map.

C.6 Scale factors greater and less than unity (1.0) indicate that the actual scales are larger and smaller than the principal scales, respectively.

The scale of the globe is the fixed scale which is normally stated on the flat map, where it is referred to as the **principal** or **nominal** scale.

To understand the relation between the actual and principal scales, it is convenient to compute the **scale factor (SF)**, which is defined as follows:

$$SF = \frac{\text{Actual Scale}}{\text{Principal Scale}}.$$

If the actual and principal scales were identical, then the SF would equal 1.0. But since the actual scale varies from place to place, so does the SF. Scale factors of 2.0 and 0.75 on small-scale maps would mean that the actual scales were twice as large and 25 percent smaller than the principal scales, respectively (**Figure C.6**). On large-scale maps, the SF would vary only slightly from unity (1.0).

By nature, then, the scale factor varies from location to location in a map projection. But if

these variations are suitably arranged, it's possible to achieve some special distance-preserving qualities. These are discussed in detail under *Scale Error* in Chapter 13 and won't be pursued further here. Suffice it to say that the scale can be made true to and from a single point or along selected lines.

Clearly, the scale factor may be different in different directions. This directional variation provides a convenient basis for analyzing how projections distort shape, direction, and area. Let's turn to these properties next.

Shape

When angles are preserved in mapping, the projection is called **conformal** or **orthomorphic**, meaning "correct form or shape." Unlike the property of equidistance, the property of conformality is universal. But there is a qualification. Conformality applies only to directions or angles at points or in the immediate vicinity of points. It does not apply to areas of any great extent. Thus, even on shape-preserving maps, the shape of large regions can be greatly distorted.

To attain the property of conformality, the scale must be equivalent in all directions from a point; a circle on the ground will thus appear as a circle on the map. But to achieve this characteristic, it is necessary either to exaggerate or reduce the scale of the map from place to place. This means, of course, that the relative size of regions must also vary from location to location. While circles will always map as circles, their sizes will differ.

Conformal maps are best suited for tasks which involve plotting, guiding, or analyzing the motion of objects over the earth's surface. Thus, conformal projections naturally form the basis of navigational charts, topographic quadrangles, and maps used by meteorologists. They are also called for when the shape of environmental features is a matter of concern. (See *Shape Distortion* in Chapter 17 for further discussion.)

Direction

Whereas conformal projections preserve angles "in the small" (locally), there is also need to preserve angles "in the large" (globally). The class of projection which exhibits this latter property is called **azimuthal** or **zenithal** because its geometry is symmetrical about a central point.

Unfortunately, no projection makes it possible to represent correctly all directions from all points on the earth as straight lines on a flat map. But the SF distribution can be arranged so that certain types of direction lines are straight under special circumstances. Thus, direction-preserving, like distance-preserving, is not a universal property. (For further discussion, see *Round Earth* in Chapter 12.)

Area

When relative size of regions is preserved, the projection is said to be **equal area** or **equivalent**. There are no qualifications; this is a truly universal characteristic. The property of equal area is attained by adjusting scale along meridians and parallels (or any other right-angle axes). The scale factors must be arranged so that shrinkage in one direction from a point is compensated for by exaggeration in another direction. Equivalent world maps, therefore, display proportionate **compaction and elongation, shear,** or **skew**

in the latitude-longitude grid (**Figure C.7**). This distortion of shape, distance, and direction is usually most pronounced toward the map's margins.

The demands of achieving equidistance are such that the scale factor can only be the same in all directions along one or two lines, or from at most two points. Since the SF and hence angles around all other points will be deformed, the scale requirements for equivalence and conformality are contradictory. No projection can exhibit both universal properties.

Despite the distortion inherent in equal area projections, they are the best choice for tasks that call for area or density comparisons from region to region. (For more details, see the discussion under *Area Distortion* in Chapter 16.)

Continuity

To produce a flat, global projection, as we've seen, the earth's surface must be torn apart at some point or along some line. Although the resulting discontinuity is inevitable, where the map maker places that discontinuity is a matter of choice. On some maps, for example, opposite edges of the map are in fact the same meridian. Since this

Compaction-Elongation Type

Shear Type

Skew Type

C.7 Latitude-longitude quadrangles can be distorted in a number of area-preserving ways.

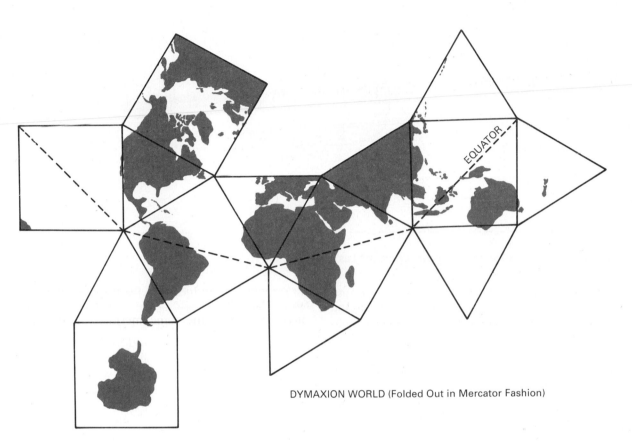

DYMAXION WORLD (Folded Out in Mercator Fashion)

C.8 Buckminster Fuller's famous Dymaxion Globe is actually a collage of 14 local map projections, and suffers severe continuity problems as a result.

means features next to each other on the ground are found at opposite extremes of the map, this is a blatant violation of proximity relations. It is also a source of potential confusion for map users.

Similarly, your map may show the north and south poles with lines as long as the equator. This means features adjacent to each other, but on opposite sides of a pole, will be far apart along the top or bottom edge of the map. They will also appear to be on the same side of the pole.

The issue of continuity is well-illustrated by the famous **Dymaxion Globe**, designed by Buckminster Fuller (**Figure C.8**). He set out to overcome the Mercator projection's area distor-

tion problem. To do so he used a non-symmetrical polyhedron, consisting of six square and eight triangular facets. In effect, Fuller created a collage of local map projections, with discontinuities between each of the map facets. In comparison to the Mercator projection, the result is to shift geometrical distortion from one spatial property (area) to another (continuity).

Projection Surface

As we explained earlier, we can take two primary, and interrelated, approaches toward understanding projections. So far we've explored the first

594

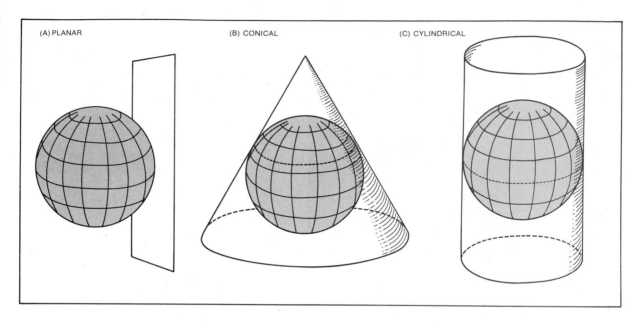

(A) PLANAR   (B) CONICAL   (C) CYLINDRICAL

C.9 Planes (A), cones (B), and cylinders (C) are used as map projection surfaces.

approach, based on the fact that spatial properties can to some degree, in certain combinations, and under special circumstances be preserved. To gain further insight into these conditions and to visualize the patterns of projection distortion, it is helpful to shift to the second approach and consider the nature of different surfaces used in constructing projections.

As a child, you probably played the game of casting hand shadows on the wall. You were actually making projections, and the wall was your **projection surface**. You discovered that the direction of the light source relative to the position of your hand influenced the shape of the shadow you created. But the projection surface also had a great deal to do with it. A shadow cast on a corner of the room or on a curved surface was quite different from one thrown upon the flat wall.

Many map projections are take-offs on this shadow-casting game. You can think of the globe as your hand and the final map projection as the shadow on the wall. To visualize this, imagine a transparent **projection generating globe** with the graticule (latitude-longitude grid) and continent outlines etched on it in black. Then suppose that we place this globe at various positions relative to a source of light and a projection surface (**Figure C.9**). This projection surface can either be a plane (flat) surface or a developable surface

(a curved form which can be flattened without distortion). There are only two developable surfaces—cones and cylinders. Consequently, there are three basic projection surfaces—planar, conical, and cylindrical. Depending on which type of projection surface we use and which way our light is shining, we will end up with different shadow maps cast by the globe.

Not all projections are produced this simply, however, since true-perspective, or geometrical, projections are rarely used. Non-perspective, mathematical projections are more common, because they can be designed to serve any purpose desired and can be readily produced with the aid of computers. Yet even these non-perspective, mathematical projections can usually be thought of as derivatives of one of the three basic projection surfaces—planar, conical, or cylindrical.

Case

Regardless of the type of projection surface which is visualized, it may bear either a **tangent** or a **secant** relationship to the globe (**Figure C.10**). In other words, the projection surface may either touch the sphere at a point (tangent case) or intersect the sphere along a line (secant case). The advantage of the tangent case is its simplicity. The secant cases's advantage is that it minimizes distortion, because there is greater contact (line rather than point) between the projection surface and the generating globe.

It is also possible to combine a series of projection surfaces into a single **complex case**. The result is even less distortion but with additional loss of simplicity, as shown in Figure C.10.

Aspect

The projection surface may be oriented to the sphere from any viewpoint (**Figure C.11**). When the projection surface is centered at any point along the equator, the resulting projection is said to be in **equatorial aspect.** Likewise, when the central point coincides with either pole, the resultant projection is said to be in **polar aspect**. Any other alignment of the projection surface to the sphere leads to a projection in **oblique aspect.**

Of these three projection aspects, the one which has the simplest geometry for a given family of projections is referred to as the **normal aspect**. The normal aspect of planar projections is polar; the normal aspect of conic projections is oblique; and the normal aspect of cylindrical projections is equatorial. Note, for example, the planar projections shown in Figure C.11. You can see at once why the normal aspect is polar, since its design is the least complicated of the three.

With cylindrical projections, the term **transverse aspect** is also used. This aspect occurs when the central line of the projection, which is the equator in normal aspect, is shifted 90 degrees so that it follows a pair of meridians (see Figure C.18A).

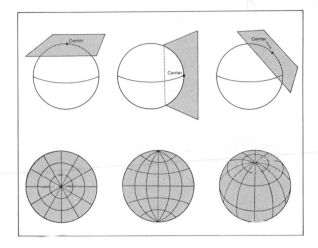

C.11 Polar, equatorial, and oblique aspects of the planar projection surface dramatically affect the appearance of the latitude-longitude grid.

The choice of different projection surface aspects leads to substantially different images of the earth's surface (again refer to Figure C.11). Yet the special properties of a given projection surface remain unaltered regardless of the aspect. This means that the geometrical character of a planar projection will be similar in the polar, oblique, and equatorial aspects.

Degree and Pattern of Distortion

Image distortion is an inevitable consequence of transforming the spherical earth's surface into a flat map. Ideally, the impact of this projection distortion would be minimized by centering and aligning each projection on the region of interest to the map user. This is generally impractical, however.* For one thing, the eventual audience of a map is rarely known. In addition, the diversity of map user needs would require more mapping flexibility than is feasible. Since you will not always be presented with an optimum projection solution, it is useful to know the error distribution characteristics of the various projections.

You can gain helpful clues to these error distribution characteristics by comparing the projected graticule image with its natural spherical form. Ask yourself several questions: To what

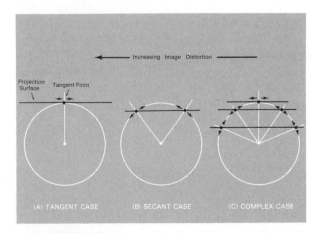

C.10 Tangent, secant, and complex cases of projection surfaces.

Computers promise to make it possible to choose, center, and align projections at will. But in the near future few map users are likely to enjoy this capability for other than the crudest outline maps.

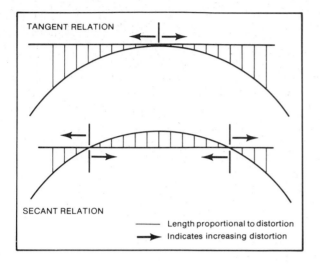

C.12 Different distortion patterns result when a curved surface is projected onto a plane in tangent and secant relations.

degree do meridians converge? Do meridians and parallels intersect at right angles? Do parallels shorten with increasing latitude?

Another way to visualize the nature of map distortion is to recall the relationship between a plane projective surface and the projection generating globe (**Figure C.12**). Obviously, there is minimal distortion around the zone of contact between the two surfaces. This explains why earth curvature may often be ignored without serious consequence when using flat maps for a local area. But as the distance from the contact zone increases, so does the degree of image distortion. By the time a projection has been extended to include the entire globe, therefore, image distortion may have a significant impact on map use.

Not all projections exhibit the same distortion pattern, of course. Tangent planes will contact the sphere at a point. Tangent cones will contact the sphere along a closed line or curve called a **small circle** (a circle smaller in diameter than the equator). Tangent cylinders will contact the sphere along a line or closed curve called a **great circle** (the greatest possible circle on the globe). A secant plane will contact the sphere along a small circle. Secant cones and cylinders will touch the sphere along two lines (both great and small circles in the former case, and only small circles in the latter case). Conic and cylindric developments have an advantage over projections onto a plane

since they increase contact between the projection surface and the generating globe. This provides a greater area of minimum distortion.

No matter what the projection aspect, the distortion pattern characteristic of a particular type of projection will hold true. Unfortunately, an indication of the degree and pattern of distortion is rarely found on published maps; thus, you will have to commit this information to memory.

As an aid, it helps to remember that the coincidence relations between the various projection surfaces and the sphere determine the nature of distortion found in projections based on those surfaces. Both the degree and pattern of distortion are of interest.

The **degree** of distortion can be visualized with the aid of familiar figures. Sometimes a human face is superimposed on the projection,

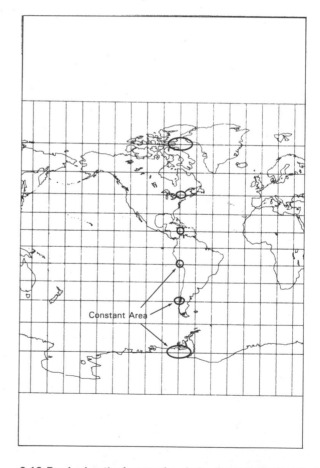

C.13 By viewing the image of a circle of constant ground area at different locations on a projection, we obtain a good impression of the extent and pattern of distortion.

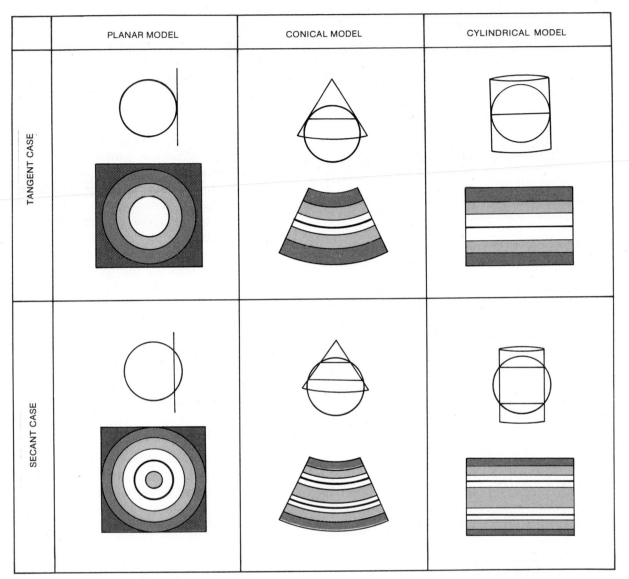

	PLANAR MODEL	CONICAL MODEL	CYLINDRICAL MODEL
TANGENT CASE			
SECANT CASE			

C.14 Distortion patterns are shown here for the tangent and secant cases of the basic projection surfaces. Darker tones equal greater distortion.

but more commonly the image of a circle of constant ground area is shown at different locations on the projection (**Figure C.13**). Variation in the size and shape of these circles reveals the degree and nature of distortion at different positions and provides clues to the **pattern** of distortion as well. A more direct way of showing the distortion pattern, however, is first to group the distortion values and then map these classes using proportional areal symbols (**Figure C.14**). The visual simplicity of the resulting pattern of distortion zones or bands facilitates later recall of the general pattern.

BASIC PROJECTIONS

We've seen that map projections can be grouped into families based on which projection surface was used—a plane, cone, or cylinder.* Consequent-

*Strictly speaking, very few projections actually involve planes, cones, or cylinders in a physical sense. Most, as mentioned earlier, are of abstract mathematical derivation. But even with these mathematical projections, it is conceptually useful to think of an implied projection surface.

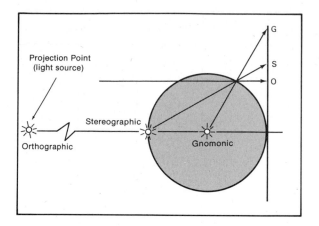

C.15 The three basic forms of planar projections are created merely by changing the projection point.

ly, with some stretch of your imagination, you can think of all projections as falling into one of three groups—the planar, cylindrical, or conical group.

If you remember your childhood shadow-casting game, you will recall that the projection surface was only one of the factors influencing the shape of the shadow you threw upon the wall. The other influence was the direction of the light source. Thus, there will be basic differences within each projection family, depending on where the imaginary light source is located.

Planar Family

Simple **planar** projections (sometimes called **azimuthal** projections) are created by projecting upon a plane tangent to the globe at any point. This family includes three basic named projections: orthographic (light source at infinity), stereographic (light source on the earth's surface opposite the tangent point), and gnomonic (light source in the center of the earth) (**Figure C.15**).

The **orthographic** projection is the type of view that would be gained by looking from a distant star back to earth (**Figure C.16A**). This projection came into vogue during World War II with the advent of the global perspective provided by the air age and is even more popular in today's space age. Projecting from the far side of the globe leads to the conformal **stereographic** projection, in which shape is preserved for small areas (**Figure C.16B**). Projecting from the center of the earth produces the **gnomonic** (or **central**) projection, which possesses the useful property that great circles are straight lines (**Figure C.16C**). Since a great-circle route is the shortest distance between two points on a sphere, the gnomonic projection is especially valuable as an aid to navigation (see *True Direction* in Chapter 12). The gnomonic projection is also useful for plotting seismic and radio waves.

Cylindrical Family

Simple **cylindrical** projections are made by projecting the graticule upon a cylinder of equal diameter to the projection generating globe and tangent to the globe along any great circle (normally the equator). This family includes the **cylin-**

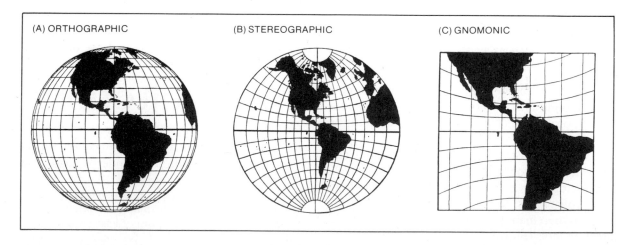

C.16 A comparison of the orthographic (A), stereographic (B), and gnomonic (C) projections in equatorial aspect illustrates the great differences in projection geometry.

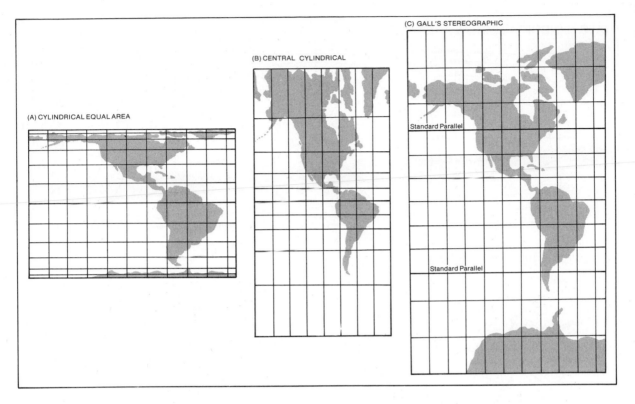

C.17 The three basic forms of cylindrical projections are created by changing the latitudinal scale in variable fashion.

drical equal-area (linear light source along the polar axis) (**Figure C.17A**) and the **central cylindrical** (light source at the center of the generating globe) (**Figure C.17B**). The whole world can't be projected onto the central cylindrical projection because the polar rays will never intersect the cylinder. The equal-area cylindrical projection, on the other hand, does include the entire world, albeit with major shape distortion in the polar regions. (In addition to severe latitudinal foreshortening, the poles must become lines as long as the equator.)

If the graticule is projected onto a secant cylinder (on which the globe is intersected by the cylindrical projecting surface at standard parallels of 45 degrees north and south latitude) from an equatorial light source, the result is **Gall's stereographic cylindrical** projection (**Figure C.17C**). This is an example of a **compromise projection,** because it has no special properties. Rather than preserving one spatial property at the expense of all others, it moderately distorts everything.

Different aspects of cylindrical projections possess widely varying graticule images. For instance, cylindrical projections in **normal** aspect may be recognized by such characteristic features as straight parallels of equal length (only one being of correct scale), straight meridians equally spaced and of equal length, right angle intersection of meridians and parallels, and an essentially rectangular complete projection image (see Figure C.17).

Transverse cylindrical projections are quite different from normal ones. In transverse position, the central axis of a cylindrical projection is any great circle formed by a pair of opposite meridians. The straight parallels and meridians characterizing the equatorial aspect become curves in transverse aspect (**Figure C.18A**).

The appearance of the **oblique** aspect of cylindrical projections differs significantly from both the normal and transverse aspects. The projected graticule is often symmetrical only at its central meridian, and sometimes does not even exhibit that degree of symmetry (**Figure C.18B**). The possibilities for variation are limitless.

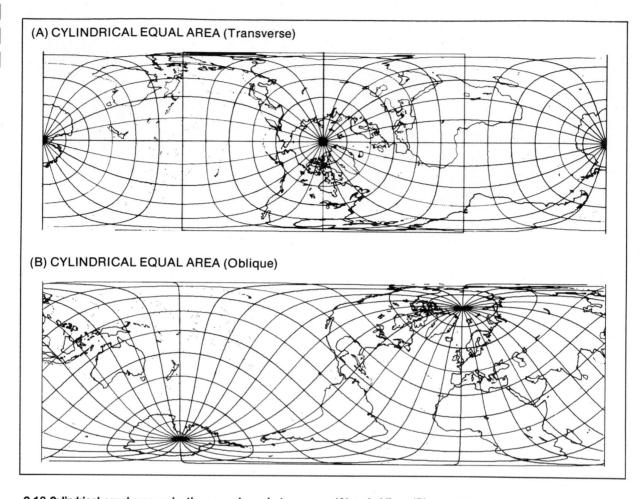

C.18 Cylindrical equal-area projections are shown in transverse (A) and oblique (B) aspects.

Map users seem to find appeal in the simplicity of cylindrical projections in their normal aspect. The rectangular graticule is easy to use—probably because of our familiarity with the x-y axes of the cartesian coordinate system (see *Abstract Frames of Reference* in Chapter 11). The normal aspect also seems quite natural (despite the fact that its meridians never come together, while in reality meridians converge at the poles). The horizontal parallels are especially convenient when it's necessary to make latitudinal comparisons.

Conic Family

The characteristics of conical projections are illustrated by the **central conical** projection. This projection is created by projecting the graticule onto a cone tangent to the generating globe along any small circle (usually a mid-latitude parallel—hence the name **standard parallel**). In normal aspect, parallels are projected as concentric arcs of circles, and meridians are projected as straight lines radiating at uniform angular intervals from the apex of the flattened cone **(Figure C.19A)**.*

Simple conic projections are of little interest in mapping, as their practical value is limited by their relatively small accuracy zone. For this reason, the secant case is most frequently used with conics, producing two standard parallels **(Figure**

These angular intervals are always less than what their annotations claim them to be. This is because the globe's 360 degrees, when projected onto the cone, are shrunk to accommodate the gap that occurs when a cone is rolled out (see Figure C.19).

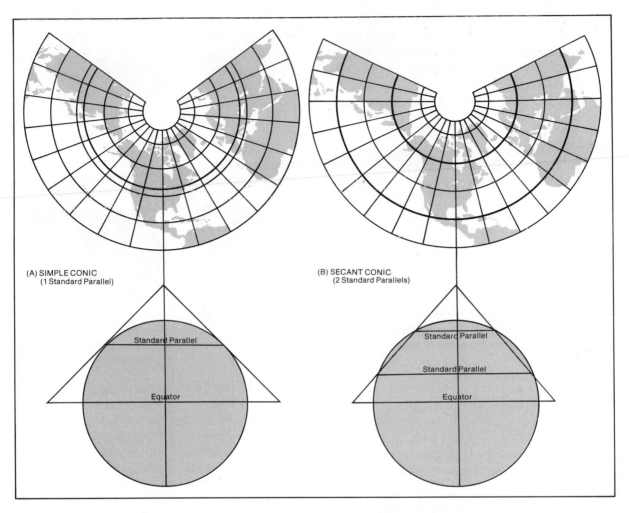

(A) SIMPLE CONIC
(1 Standard Parallel)

(B) SECANT CONIC
(2 Standard Parallels)

Standard Parallel

Standard Parallel

Standard Parallel

Equator

Equator

C.19 The tangent (A) and secant (B) cases of conic projections differ markedly in their distortion patterns.

C.19B). Even then, however, the scale of the map quickly becomes exaggerated with distance from the correctly represented standard parallels. Because of this problem, conic projections are best suited for maps of mid-latitude regions, especially those elongated in an east-west direction. The United States meets these qualifications and therefore is frequently mapped on conic projections.

PROJECTION MODIFICATIONS

The use of projection surfaces as a visualization technique has allowed us to organize projections according to planar, conic, and cylindrical develop-

ments. But strictly perspective projections constitute only a small portion of the vast array of projections which have been created by map makers. As mentioned earlier, there are also a variety of mathematical transformations or constructional modifications of the basic geometrical models. A number of purely mathematical developments of spherical surfaces are also used in map projections.

The reasons for using modified projections vary. Some modified projections have no special trait other than holding overall distortion to a minimum or presenting a pleasing visual image. For many purposes, a projection that "looks right" is more important than a projection that rigidly provides area, distance, shape, or direction fidelity. The need for this type of projection is satisfied by a group of specially designed compromise projections which preserve no spatial properties but which do not severely distort any of them either. Such projections include the **globular**, which is widely used in atlases, **Miller's cylindrical**, which allows the poles to be shown, and the **polyconic**, which is used for the standard topographic series of the United States.

For some purposes it is desirable to extend the sub-global coverage of direct geometrical projections so that a global image can be created. Thus, it is common to modify simple planar and conic projections so that they can show the entire world simultaneously, or to extend cylindrical projections to include the poles (a full 90° of latitude) conveniently. Special effects are often created by "splicing" the best "zones" from several different projections together into a super-projection, or by interrupting a global projection so that distortion is thrown into non-critical regions and important features such as the world's land masses are well imaged (**Figure C.20A**).

Still other projections are modified to a form which possesses some specific spatial quality, such as truth of shape, area, direction, or distance. The well-known **Mercator** projection belongs in this group. Navigators who used a magnetic compass needed a map on which compass bearings would appear as straight lines (see *The Navigator's Dilemma* in Chapter 12). Mercator solved their problem in 1569 by modifying a standard cylindrical projection. His solution was to expand the spacing of the parallels toward the poles. This latitudinal expansion was designed to be directly proportional to the meridional expansion which results from having equal spacing of the "convergent" meridians (**Figure C.20B**). The inevitable result is severe distortion of area at high latitudes.

PROJECTIONS AND COMPUTERS

Until digital computers became widely available in the 1960s, computing a map projection grid and plotting geographical details in the appropriate locations were long, tedious tasks. One consequence was that map makers had great incentive to use available projections rather than create

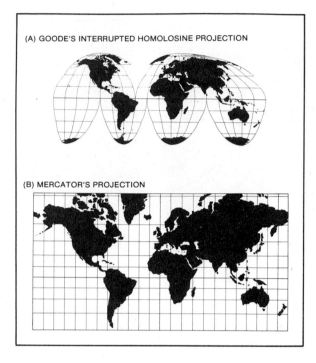

C.20 Basic projections can be modified to attain special effects or spatial properties.

new ones "from scratch." For the most part, available projections were those that were relatively easy to construct by hand. Usually this meant a projection in normal aspect, aligned so as to accommodate the largest possible user group. In short, projections seldom were tailored to the specific needs of the map user, because the extra costs couldn't be justified.

This situation has improved immensely in the age of computer-assisted mapping. Projections can now be tailor-made if three items are available: (1) a computer with a printing-plotting capability, (2) a projection program (set of instructions) which includes the mathematical definition (formula) for the desired projections, and (3) a digital cartographic database containing coastlines, political boundaries, and so forth.

If these three criteria are met, then projections can be created at will. Indeed, many of the projections used as illustrations in this book were constructed with computer assistance (see, for example, Figure C.18). Even relatively inexpensive microcomputers with crude printing attachments can be used to create map projections (**Figure C.21**).

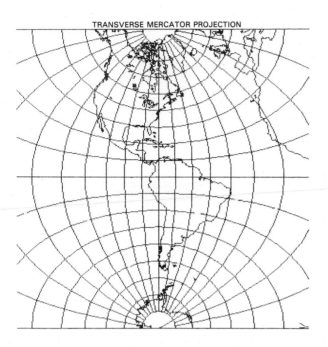

TRANSVERSE MERCATOR PROJECTION

C.21 Several projection program packages are available on disk for use with microcomputers. This projection plot was done using a crude dot matrix printer linked with a personal computer.

What computerization of projection construction means for the map user is that there will be less and less need to "make do" with an inappropriate projection. For one thing, a wider selection of projections will become available. Furthermore, it will increasingly be practical for map users to sit down before an electronic display screen and create their own projections. Most important, perhaps, will be the ability to manipulate projection parameters in search of the ideal projection base for a given application. This potential of automation can only be realized, of course, if map users are sophisticated enough concerning projections to take advantage of the opportunity computers provide.

CONCLUSION

Every map projection has its own particular virtues and limitations. These traits can be evaluated only in light of the purpose for which a map is to be used. You should not expect that the best projection for one situation will also be the most appropriate in another. Fortunately, the map pro-

jection problem effectively vanishes if the map maker has done a good job of using projection attributes and if you are careful to take projection distortion into consideration in the course of map use.

Since most map use takes place at the local level, where earth curvature is not an overriding problem for most day-to-day purposes, global map projections need not usually be a great concern. With regions as small as those covered by topographic map quadrangles in the United States, your main projection-related problem is that, while the individual sheets match in a north-south direction, they do not fit together in an east-west direction. Yet even this difficulty will not be a serious handicap unless you try to create a large map mosaic. In general, then, rather than to be solely concerned with the geometrical projection problem, it is important to devote your attention to the full array of image-distorting transformations required to make a map and to remember that map projection is one of many such mapping transformations.

SELECTED READINGS

American Cartographic Association, *Which Map is Best? Projections for World Maps* (Bethesda, MD: American Congress on Surveying and Mapping, 1986).

American Cartographic Association, *Choosing a World Map—Attributes, Distortions, Classes, Aspects* (Bethesda, MD: American Congress on Surveying and Mapping, 1988).

American Cartographic Association, *Matching the Map Projection to the Need* (Bethesda, MD: American Congress on Surveying and Mapping, 1991).

Bugayevskiy, L.M., and Snyder, J.P., *Map Projections: A Reference Manual* (London: Taylor & Francis, 1995).

Canters, F., and Decleir, H., *The World in Perspective: A Directory of World Map Projections* (New York: John Wiley & Sons, 1989).

Chamberlin, W., *The Round Earth on Flat Paper: A Description of the Map Projections Used by Cartographers* (Washington, DC: National Geographic Society, 1947), pp. 39-126.

Dent, B.D., *Cartography: Thematic Map Design,* 4th ed. (Dubuque, IA: Wm. C. Brown Publishers, 1996), pp. 24-48.

Hsu, M.L., "The Role of Projections in Modern Map Design," *Cartographica,* 18, 2 (1981), pp. 151-186.

Maling, D.H., *Coordinate Systems and Map Projections,* 2nd ed. (New York: Pergamon Press, 1992).

Pearson, F., *Map Projections: Theory and Applications* (Boca Raton, FL: CRC Press, 1990).

Richardus, P., and Adler, R.K., *Map Projections: For Geodesists, Cartographers and Geographers* (New York: American Elsevier Publishing Co., 1972).

Robinson, A.H., et al., *Elements of Cartography,* 6th ed. (New York: John Wiley & Sons, 1995), pp. 59-90.

604

Snyder, J.P., *Flattening the Earth: A Thousand Years of Map Projections* (Chicago: University of Chicago Press, 1993).

Snyder, J.P., *Map Projections—A Working Manual* (Washington: U.S. Geological Professional Paper 1395, 1987).

Snyder, J.P., and Voxland, P.M., *An Album of Map Projections* (Washington: U.S. Geological Survey Professional Paper 1453, 1989).

Snyder, J.P., and Steward, H., eds., *Bibliography of Map Projections* (Washington: U.S. Geological Survey Bulletin 1856, 1988).

Tobler, W.R., "A Classification of Map Projections," *Annals of the Association of American Geographers*, 52 (1962), pp. 167-175.

APPENDIX D

NAVIGATION INSTRUMENTS

"Curse thee, thou quadrant!" dashing it to the deck, "no longer will I guide my earthly way by thee; the level ship's compass, and the level dead-reckoning, by log and by line; *these* shall conduct me, and show me my place on the sea."

—Herman Melville, *Moby Dick*

D

APPENDIX D

NAVIGATION INSTRUMENTS

In our discussion of direction concepts in Chapter 12, we saw the need for objective direction-finding aids. Many such instruments have been invented over the centuries.

The best known and most widely used of these directional instruments is the **magnetic compass**. This simple device has served human path-finding needs for over a thousand years. In this appendix, we'll focus on the magnetic compass, discussing the different types which exist and the ways they are used to take direction readings. We'll also look at some modern direction-finding instruments—gyrocompasses, special radio transmitters and receivers, inertial navigators, and global positioning satellites. We'll discuss the characteristics and relative merits of each. To fully appreciate the value of these navigational aids, you may find it useful to review the material on direction in Chapter 12.

MAGNETIC COMPASS

The magnetic compass has three main parts—a **balancing needle** or **floating disk**, which has been magnetized so that it will align itself with the earth's magnetic field; a **jewel pivot** or **fluid**, which allows the needle or disk to float freely; and a dial, called a **compass card**, marked with the cardinal directions (**Figure D.1**). Some compasses also have a **damper button**, which locks the needle in place when the compass isn't in use and stabilizes the needle while the compass is being used. Sometimes a sighting device is also added for convenience. The case which encloses all these parts is known as the compass **housing**.

When you use a compass to find the direction to something, you are taking a compass **reading**. A reading is given as the angular difference between a direction or sight line and a north-south base line. Since the compass needle points to magnetic north, a compass usually gives you a magnetic read-

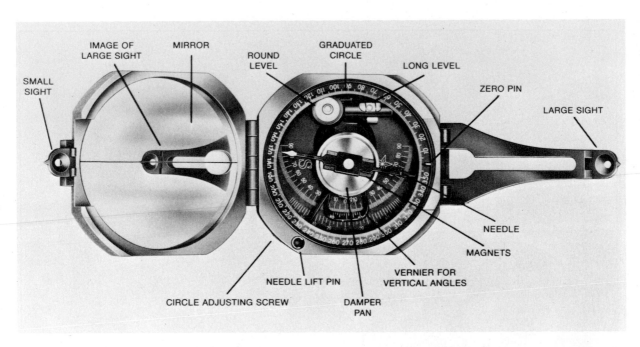

D.1 Basic components of a precision magnetic compass.

ing. Some compasses, however, can be adjusted for declination so that true readings can be made (see *Magnetic North* and *Declination* in Chapter 12).

Compass Types

Compass quality varies greatly, in rather direct relation to the price (currently $5 to $200). The wide range in prices and designs often confuses the compass user (**Figure D.2**). This need not be so, especially if you remember that there are really only three basic compass types. For convenience, we'll refer to these as Type I, Type II, and Type III, although many other names have been used.

Type I

On **Type I compasses**, a degree system is inscribed clockwise on the compass card (**Figure D.3A**). The magnetic needle operates independently of the compass card—a great advantage, since it means that you can achieve either magnetic or true readings. To find magnetic north, rotate the compass card slowly until north on the dial is lined up with the needle. With your compass set this way, you can take a sighting at any object and the reading on the compass will be a magnetic reading.

Suppose, for instance, that you want to find the direction to a distant tree. With the needle stabilized on north, face the tree and project an imaginary direction line (or **sight line**) from the center of the compass to the tree. You will now be able to read from the dial the number of degrees between magnetic north and the tree.

Your reading will, of course, be approximate. A more precise reading is possible if a sighting aid has been added to the compass. Sighting devices are of two forms. One type, resembling a standard raised gunsight, is mounted on opposite sides of the compass housing (**Figure D.2E**). Instead of peering over your compass to the tree, you simply rotate the sighting device until you can see the tree through it. You can then read the angle between the sight line and magnetic north. Readings are thus made easier and more accurate. Most Type I compasses don't include these raised sights, however, because they increase the cost and bulk of the compass and because approximate readings are usually good enough.

A second form of sighting aid is that found on special **orienteering compasses**. On these Type I compasses, the housing (consisting of a compass card, an orienting arrow, and a floating magnetic needle) is mounted on a transparent rectangular base (**Figure D.2A**). To use an orien-

608

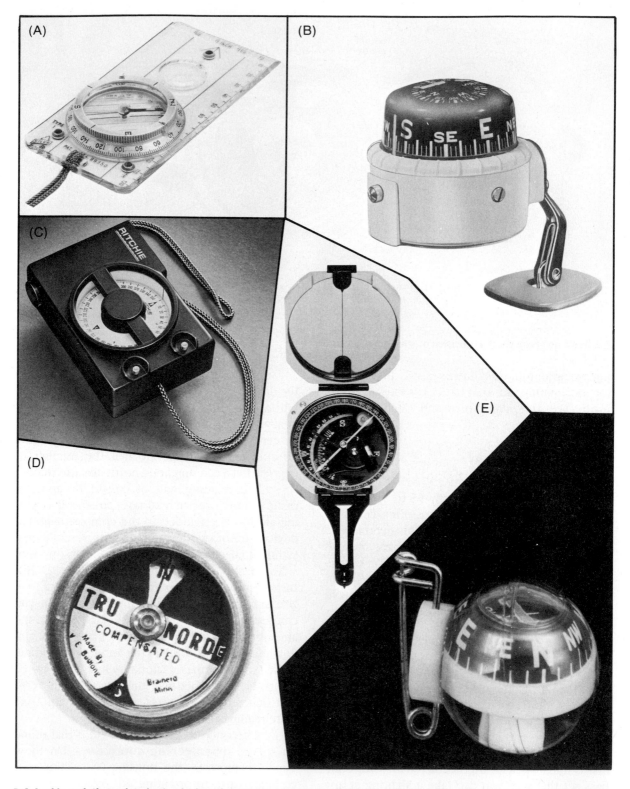

D.2 A wide variation exists in the design of magnetic compasses. Although they all work on the same basic principle, they are engineered to serve many specialized functions.

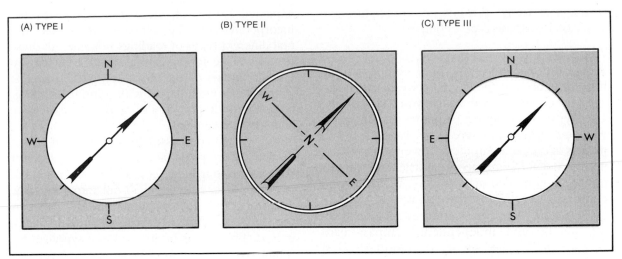

D.3 All magnetic compasses can be grouped into one of three basic types: Type I, Type II, or Type III.

teering compass, you merely aim the direction line, which is etched into the base, at your destination, and then rotate the compass housing until the orienting arrow is aligned with the magnetic needle. Now find the point on the compass card beneath the sight line. That point gives you the direction to your destination.

A major advantage of Type I compasses is that they allow you to make true as well as magnetic readings. To find true rather than magnetic north, first check the declination diagram or find the local magnetic declination on an isogonic map (see *Declination Diagram* in Chapter 12). Then rotate your compass card east or west until the needle points to the amount of declination for your area. If the local declination is 5°E, you will line up the needle with 5°E on the dial. Now when you take a sighting to an object, you will obtain a true reading, because you have compensated for magnetic declination. Therefore, a Type I compass is easy to use with maps, when a true reading is most useful, as well as in the field, when a magnetic reading is of the most use.

Type II

On the **Type II compass**, the magnetic needle and compass card are joined and work as a single unit (**Figure D.3B**). Consequently, you don't have to bother with aligning the needle and compass card, as you did with the Type I compass. As soon as the disk stabilizes and the arrow points to north, you're all set to make your sightings.

Magnetic readings are thus simplified—an advantage when you are in the field without maps.

But the Type II compass points only to magnetic north, not to true north. Therefore, it isn't well suited for use with maps oriented to true north, particularly if there is significant magnetic declination in the local area. To obtain a true reading, you'll have to add (or subtract) local declination to (or from) your reading; the compass won't do this for you, as the Type I compass did.

Lensatic compasses, available as military surplus items, fall into the Type II group, as do the common floating-dial compasses which are generally available to the public. Many people get by quite well with these inexpensive little compasses—which goes to show that we can usually tolerate less than absolute accuracy. Just be sure you know what you're buying. One brand of Type II compass carries the name "TRU-NORD" in bold letters above the word "Compensated" (see Figure D.2D). Customers who have a vague knowledge of declination may be taken in by this sales gimmick and believe that this brand of compass will give true north readings. Anyone who understands declination, however, won't be tricked. Type II compasses may sometimes be corrected so that they give true north readings for the area in which you buy them; as soon as you leave the area, though, readings will no longer be true. No compass will automatically give true readings wherever you are. The only way to obtain consistently true

610

readings is to go through the procedure we described with the Type I compass.

Type III

With either a Type I or Type II compass, you'll have to figure out the angle between true north and the object toward which you are sighting. The **Type III compass** computes the angle for you. You are going to have to pay for such convenience, of course: computers, however crude, cost money. But for some people, particularly surveyors and others who make a living with map and compass, the extra cost is worth it.

Type III, like Type I, compasses have a floating needle and independent compass card (**Figure D.3C**). They are, in fact, almost identical to Type I compasses except that they include a number of refinements which make them more useful. The first thing you'll notice about the Type III compass is that the degree system seems to be backward—west and east are reversed on the compass card (see Figure D.1). The manufacturer hasn't made a mistake; there is a good reason for this design.

To visualize the logic behind this counterclockwise degree system, imagine yourself with a Type I compass. Assume that you are facing north and that the needle on your compass is also pointing north. Now turn slowly to face the object whose direction you are seeking. Although the needle actually remains stationary, it will look as though it is moving around the compass card in the opposite direction from which you move. If you turn directly to the east, then, the needle will point due *west*. You can see how awkward it would be to substitute west for east mentally each time you made a reading. On Type III compasses, therefore, west and east have been switched on the compass card. If you hold a Type III compass and turn to the east, the needle will also point east, and you can read the angle directly off the point of the compass needle. No mental figuring is necessary.

The Type III compass is the most sophisticated, expensive, and versatile of the three types. Like the Type I compass, it can be set for local magnetic declination, thereby permitting true readings. While Type I compasses sometimes include a sighting device, Type III compasses always do. In addition, a damper button is usually included and precision craftsmanship can be expected. More than one degree system is often incorporated onto the compass card to make several different types of readings possible. All these features make for a very accurate compass. To take advantage of this accuracy potential, most professionals use a tripod with Type III compasses, just as photographers do with very expensive and sensitive cameras.

Type III compasses, in fact, are used almost exclusively by professionals. Cruiser or forester compasses (so named because foresters use them to plan timber-cutting lines) fall into this class. The best known example of a forester compass is the *Brunton Pocket Transit** (**Figure D.2E**); indeed, "Brunton" is often used as a synonym for "compass," like "Kleenex" for "tissue" or "Jeep" for "off-road vehicle."

Compass Readings

In addition to the problem of choosing between different types of compasses, much of the confusion surrounding compass use arises because of the different methods of making readings. Again, such confusion is needless, since there are only a few basic ways to read a compass. Any method of compass reading may be used with any compass type, although some mental conversions may be necessary if the compass card hasn't been designed for the reading form used.

Azimuth Reading

The most common method of compass reading is the **azimuth reading**. It gives direction in degrees as the horizontal angle measured clockwise from a north base line to any direction line (**Figure D.4A**). The reading can range from 0 degrees to 360 degrees and is written as 45°, 120°, and so forth.

Azimuths are named according to the north base line which is used. Thus, there are true, magnetic, and grid azimuths. An azimuth compass card may be found in the Type I, II, or III compass group.

Bearing Reading

A second compass reading method is the **bearing reading** (**Figure D.4B**). Like the azimuth reading, it gives direction in degrees as horizontal

**Brunton, East Monroe Avenue, Riverton, WY 82501, 307-856-6559.*

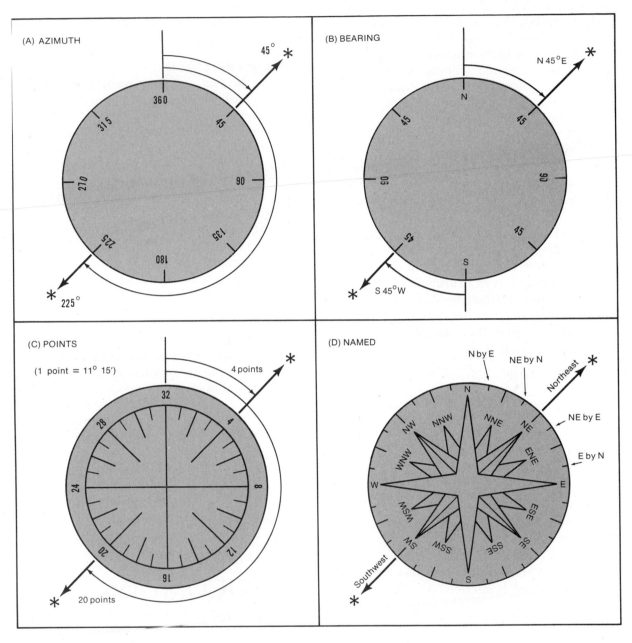

D.4 There are four basic ways to take direction from a magnetic compass. The face of the compass may be designed so that several types of readings can be made directly.

angles. The difference is that azimuth readings go through the whole circle up to 360 degrees, while bearing readings can range only from 0 degrees to 90 degrees. Bearing readings may be measured clockwise (eastward) or counterclockwise (westward) from either a north or south base line, whichever is closer to the direction line. To avoid ambiguity with this method, it's essential to give both a base line (north or south) and an orientation (east or west) in addition to the angular measure in degrees. Therefore, the bearing reading is written as N30°E (meaning 30 degrees east of north), S25°W (meaning 25 degrees west of the south base line), and so on.

A compass with a bearing compass card is frequently referred to as a surveyor's compass because it has long been preferred as a surveying instrument. But since surveyors often must convert bearings to azimuths in their recordkeeping, it's common for bearing information to be augmented with azimuth information on the compass card. When both bearing and azimuth degree systems are found on the same card, you can be quite sure that the compass is of the Type III variety.

"Azimuth" and "bearing," incidentally, are often used as synonyms for "direction." But strictly speaking, as we've seen, bearings go only to 90 degrees, while azimuths include all 360 degrees of a circle.

GPS vendors are especially prone to use the term "bearing" when they mean "azimuth." Thus, if a GPS receiver displays a bearing of 100°, you should interpret this as an azimuth notation. The correct bearing notation would be S80°E. Since standard usage of terms has clearly been ignored, your task is to grasp the concept rather than to dwell on the terminology.*

Point Reading

A third way to read a compass is with **point readings (Figure D.4C)**. This system was devised by early mariners, who used the winds to find their way. The first mariner's compass card had eight points, representing the directions of the principal winds. But eight directions, sailors found, weren't exact enough. So they split their compass card further—first into eight "half-points" and later into 16 more "quarter-points."

The mariner's compass thus came to have 32 points. The card, which looks something like a 32-petaled flower, is called a **compass rose**. Since the compass rose is inscribed on a floating disk, the mariner's compass belongs to the Type II group. With 32 equal divisions of 360 degrees, each point on the mariner's compass is equal to 11°15'. Therefore, a reading of three points between base line and direction line would be equivalent to an azimuth of 33°45'.

In modern times, the mariner's point reading system has been largely replaced by bearing and azimuth readings. Not only are they less awk-

*We gave the same advice earlier with respect to confusing usage of the terms "scale" and "precision." In each case your attention is best directed to the intended meaning of the terminology.

ward and confusing to use, but they are more accurate. On the mariner's compass, even quarter-points can only define direction to within 2°49'.

Named Directions

Azimuth, bearing, and point readings are all stated numerically. But the points of a mariner's compass may also be described verbally, using the common cardinal directions. **Figure D.4D** shows how it's done. The sizes of the compass rose points establish the priority system used to name direction. North and south have first priority; east and west have second; and northeast, northwest, southeast, and southwest have third. A **named reading** of the compass rose is therefore of the form NE (verbally read as "northeast"), ENE (read as "east, northeast"), etc. Each of these terms, of course, has a direct numerical counterpart in points or degrees.

Conversions

With so many schemes for specifying direction, sooner or later you'll want to convert one type of compass reading to another. When you do so, keep in mind both the declination diagram discussed in Chapter 12 and the relationship between the various compass reading systems. In **Figure D.5**, for example, the true azimuth of 85° converts to a true bearing of N85°E, a grid bearing of S85°E, and a grid azimuth of 95°, all of which may be roughly described by the named direction "east." It will be worth your while to practice making these reading conversions, since the skill will prove useful in both the field and lab.

GYROCOMPASS

As we have seen, the magnetic compass has many useful properties. It does, however, have some limitations as well. Metal objects and electrical disturbances can throw compass readings in error. Corrections have to be made for magnetic declination. At certain locations, the magnetic compass may actually point in the opposite direction from true north because of magnetic declination or deviation. Moreover, the magnetic compass can't be used near the magnetic poles, since the directive force of the earth's magnetic field is almost vertical in these regions. All these disadvantages can be traced to the fact that the

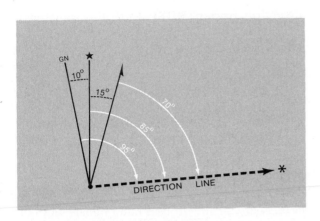

D.5 Compass readings based on true, magnetic, or grid base lines are easily converted from one form to another.

magnetic compass relies on the earth's magnetic field for directive force.

The problems of magnetic compasses can be averted by using a **gyrocompass**, an instrument that harnesses the earth's gravitational field and rotation for its directive force (**Figure D.6A**). The gyrocompass incorporates the properties of a rapidly spinning device called a **gyroscope**, which is little more than an elaborate top. It has three frames, each providing an axis of angular movement. One of its three axes, known as the spin axis, is forced by the pull of gravity and earth rotation to line up parallel with the local meridian. Thus, the gyrocompass indicates true north.

The gyrocompass has several advantages over the magnetic compass. For one thing, it seeks true north rather than magnetic north. It isn't affected by proximity to the magnetic poles or by local magnetic materials. It can be used when surrounded by steel, as it might be on a ship.

But gyrocompasses have some drawbacks, too. The ones in use today are large, complex instruments and hence are subject to mechanical failure. The services of a skilled technician are required for maintenance and repair. A gyrocompass also depends on an uninterrupted supply of electrical power. For these reasons, the use of gyrocompasses is usually restricted to aircraft and ships.

The gyrocompass situation may soon change dramatically, however, due to the miniaturation trend in modern electronics. Small electronic components use little power. Therefore, hand-held gyroscopes operated by batteries are

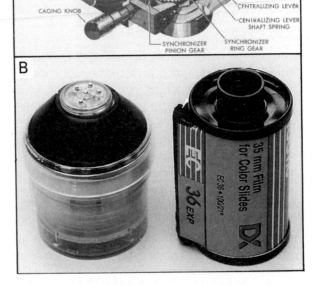

D.6 The gyrocompass has largely replaced the magnetic compass in modern navigation of large ships and planes (A) and will soon be available in inexpensive, portable models (B).

likely to be incorporated into products soon (**Figure D.6B**).* Once these devices are mass-produced, the ancient magnetic compass will lose much of its appeal.

ELECTRONIC NAVIGATORS

Dramatic progress has been made in applying electronics to navigational instrumentation during the past several decades. Gyrocompass technology was an early success, but it represents only the beginning of revolutionary developments in

---

A leader in hand-held gyroscope technology is Gyration, Inc., 12930 Saratoga Ave., Building C, Suite 6, Saratoga, CA 95070, 408-255-3016.

614

direction-finding aids. In recent years, computers, satellites, motion sensors, and radio transmissions have been combined with gyroscopes to produce a variety of powerful electronic navigators.* For the purposes of discussion, these can be grouped under the headings of radio transmitters and receivers, satellite positioning devices, inertial positioning systems, and flexible hybrid systems. Let's look at each in turn.

Radio Transmitters and Receivers

The use of radio signals to establish position is under rapid development. The advantages of such electronic position determination over traditional visual observation methods are that radio signals travel to great distances, function equally well in daylight or darkness, and can penetrate vegetative cover or fog as well as clear sky. Otherwise, the use of radio waves differs from conventional position fixing only in the methods of data collection and in the senses used.

There are several ways to fix position by radio waves. We may passively receive signals transmitted from distant stations, or we may actively send out signals and note the response. In the passive reception case, a **radiobeacon (RBn)** network, which transmits dot-dash signals in the medium frequency range, has been established for marine and air pilots. The sending units vary in type. The most common are **Non-Directional Beacons (NDBs)**, which send beams in all directions. Some radiobeacons are directional (transmitting along a fixed bearing) and others are rotational (revolving a beam of waves). Although standard RBns are of fixed position, sending units may be mobile. Mobile units have proven invaluable in tracking wildlife, locating plane crashes, and monitoring paroled criminals.

To make use of the sending unit's signal, it's necessary to have a receiving unit or **radio**

In the past, most navigation instruments were highly specialized devices designed exclusively for determining angles, distances, latitude, or longitude. Modern navigation devices, in contrast, are best described as "systems" in the sense that they are designed to take several of these measurements simultaneously and have the capacity to compute other data as well.

direction finder (RDF). An RDF is sometimes referred to as a **radio compass**, because it's an azimuthal instrument which can automatically determine the direction of the sending station. It either uses a directional antenna, or it makes use of two antennas (one rotational) which can convert the strength of an incoming signal to a bearing.

An example of an azimuth system is **Very High Frequency Omnidirectional Range (VOR)** technology, which provides en-route air navigation assistance around the world. A receiver on board an aircraft uses radio signals sent out from airport-based ground transmitters to determine the azimuth of the aircraft relative to the sending unit. The pilot can use the signal to track directly to the airport runway.

Since VOR equipment provides only directional information, there is still a need for a system that can provide range information. **Distance Measuring Equipment (DME)** provides this form of air navigation assistance around the world. This is a line-of-sight system, which limits its operation to less than 30 miles at ground level. Combined VOR/DME stations constitute the international standard for civil air navigation.

Technically sophisticated receiving units are capable of converting signals from one or several transmitting stations to both range and bearing readings. For example, automated range and bearing reading capability is available for mariners around the world with **Loran-C** (which stands for *long range navigation*) technology. Although Loran-C stations generally are focused along coastlines, there is also complete mainland coverage of the conterminous United States. With this system, synchronized signals must be received from at least two pairs of known points (in this case coastal transmitters). Each pair of stations consists of a **master**, which broadcasts a signal, and a **slave**, which receives and rebroadcasts the same signal, but with a certain time lag.

A Loran-C position determination involves a series of steps. First, the time between receiving the two signals from one pair of stations is converted to a parabolic line of position using a special **Loran-C chart (Figure D.7)**. Next, the same procedure is followed using the signals from the other pair of stations. The point at which the two

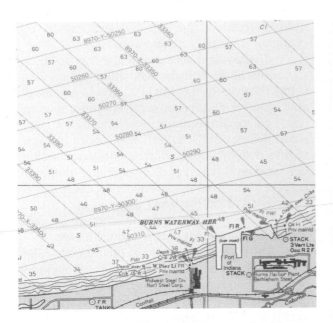

D.7 The parabolic lines of position shown on this portion of a Loran-C chart can be used to convert the signals from Loran radio signals into a position fix.

parabolic lines of position intersect on your Loran-C chart is your fix. More sophisticated Loran receivers possess the electronic means necessary to provide a direct digital readout of position coordinates.

Position-fixing systems entailing transmission as well as receipt of radio signals are of two forms. One type of equipment generates a directional radio wave which, when it strikes an object, is reflected back to a receiving unit. Examples are **radar** (*radio detection and ranging*), which works in the atmosphere, and **sonar** (*sound navigation ranging*), which works in water. With both systems, the distance to an object is determined from the time lag between signal transmission and receipt of the reflected wave. An object's bearing depends on the transmitting antenna's direction at the time the signal was sent out. The radar unit combines bearing and range information to paint a picture of your environment. By viewing the radar scope, you can see your position relative to surrounding objects (see Figure B.8 in Appendix B).

A second type of transmitting-receiving equipment is used to send out a radio signal which triggers one or more ground stations to respond with signals of their own. This is the basis of **shoran** (*short range navigation*). With this system, a signal from the primary sending unit elicits responses from two fixed transmitters.

Global Positioning System

Clearly, radionavigation based on ground transmitters represents a major advance over traditional methods of direction finding. But its potential is still limited by earth curvature, terrain obstructions, and the density of stations. Fortunately, these limitations are now being overcome by carrying radio transmitters into space aboard artificial satellites. By so doing, modern radionavigation is being combined with ancient celestial navigation principles to produce revolutionary space-age navigation procedures.

The most promising satellite-based radionavigation system is one developed by the U.S. Department of Defense (DOD). It's called the **NAVSTAR Global Positioning System (GPS)**,* and became fully operational in 1994. Its constellation consists of 24 orbiting satellites (21 plus three operating spares). The satellites are placed in six evenly spaced orbital planes. Thus, from any point on earth, four to seven satellites will usually be visible at all times (**Figure D.8**). Each satellite broadcasts precise time and position data concerning its orbital location.

The positional accuracy achieved with GPS receivers depends on a number of factors. Some have to do with the design of the system. Others have to do with operating conditions, as we'll see.

System Design

DOD officials designed two tiers of service into the system. Each satellite broadcasts unique signals of three types: protected or **Precision codes (P-codes)** at two frequencies (L1 and L2); **Coarse Acquisition (C/A or CA)** at one frequency (L1); and status information on satellite condition and orbital position (known as ephemeris and

---

When the former Soviet Union broke up in 1991, it was in the process of building a global satellite positioning system called GLONASS. This system was commissioned by Russia in 1996. The GLONASS constellation is now being used internationally. Instruments that can take advantage of both GPS and GLONASS signals are used in some precision surveys because this "satellite-rich" method achieves the highest possible positioning accuracy.

616

(A) TRANSMITTER SATELLITES

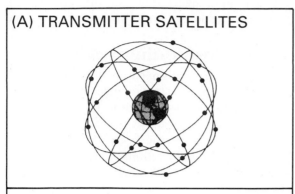

(B) RECEIVER

D.8 By receiving signals from the network of GPS satellites (A), you can use an inexpensive portable GPS receiver (B) to determine your latitude, longitude, and elevation with accuracies of 100 meters or so in each dimension.

almanac data).* All signals are synchronized to GPS time, called **Universal Time Coordinated (UTC)**, using precise atomic clocks.

In an attempt to frustrate code-breakers, an **anti-spoofing (A-S)** feature is invoked randomly to the P-codes. (C/A codes aren't affected by anti-spoofing efforts.) The altered signals are called Y-codes.

The military and other "authorized" parties have access to the more accurate P-code positioning and timing signals. This is called the **Precise Positioning Service (PPS)**. To achieve this higher accuracy, military receivers hold P-codes in memory. With both P-code frequencies available, dual-code military receivers can also

....
For a guide to GPS abbreviations, acronyms, and jargon, see Tables 15.1 and 15.2 in Chapter 15: GPS and Maps.

make corrections for signal delays caused by changing atmospheric conditions.

Civilians can access only the less accurate C/A codes in the **Standard Positioning Service (SPS)**. With only the single L1 frequency available, single-code civilian receivers must rely on less-accurate atmospheric modeling to estimate signal delays. The DOD further degrades this service by deliberately interfering with signal timing in a random way, so actual error at any time isn't known. This signal degradation process is called **Selective Availability (SA)**. There's also a risk of the DOD terminating signals to the public altogether in times of national security concern.

The DOD's efforts to keep accurate GPS technology out of the hands of potential enemies by providing two levels of service have largely failed. Ingenious ways to circumvent SA are now available. For example, specialized **codeless** receivers are now used by surveyors when they desire super accurate positioning. These receivers can use P-code information indirectly.

Similarly, a procedure called **differential GPS (DGPS)** can greatly improve positioning accuracy. This method uses a fixed-position receiver, located at a control station, in conjunction with a mobile unit (**Figure D.9**). Since the fixed receiver knows its location precisely from past measurements, it can tell to what extent current atmospheric conditions are affecting satellite signal reception. This information is then communicated by phone or radio to the local mobile unit, which is assumed to be working under similar atmospheric conditions. Line-of-sight between the fixed and mobile unit isn't necessary.

DGPS is of great value to surveyors and is becoming popular with air and water navigators (**Figure D.10**). Before long, inexpensive hand-held DGPS receivers will be available for recreational users as well. You can either set up your own multiple-receiver system, or you can receive correction data from one of a rapidly growing number of government or commercial DGPS utilities.

Operating Conditions

GPS positioning accuracy is also influenced by operating factors that go beyond receiver design and number. For example, changing atmospheric conditions can affect the speed at which signals travel. Signals of different frequencies will be affected differently. Signals can also be reflected

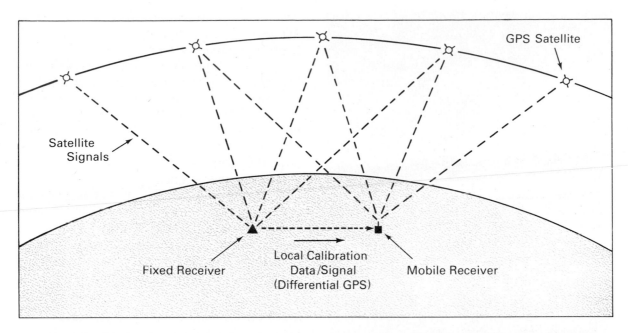

D.9 By using signals from several satellites, a mobile GPS receiver can quickly compute your latitude, longitude, and elevation coordinates. By using signal correction data from a receiver fixed at a known location, you can greatly improve the accuracy of your positioning.

from surrounding objects, causing both direct and indirect signal reception from the same satellite at a receiver. This is called the **multipath** problem.

Positioning accuracy is also affected by the number and geometric configuration of the satellites contacted. At least three satellites are needed to make a horizontal fix. A fourth satellite is necessary to make a vertical fix. Even more satellites improve accuracy. Widely-spaced satellites are said to have a strong geometry. Conversely, satellites bunched in the sky have a weak geometry. It's best to have signals reach your position at angles as close to 90° as possible.* In GPS jargon, the strength of satellite geometry is called **dilution of precision (DOP)**. Your GPS receiver may display either horizontal DOP or vertical DOP, or both. The expressions **Geometric Quality (GQ)** and **Geometric DOP (GDOP)** are also used to describe this phenomena. This infor-

mation lets you place more or less confidence in the accuracy of your unit's coordinate readings.

Another factor affecting positional accuracy is the time it takes to make a fix. A stationary receiver is more accurate than a moving one. If you can stay at one location and take repeated signals, your positioning accuracy is improved. Indeed, surveyors may occupy a point for several hours in an attempt to achieve the best possible accuracy.

Accuracy Potential

Taking all these factors into consideration, what positional accuracy is possible using GPS? If we adopt a 95% rule using the **circular error probable (CEP)** method, we can answer by giving the radius of a circle containing 95% of all possible fixes.* Using this concept, we can say that military

To understand the logic of this rule, refer to the triangulation diagram in Figure 2.2. Here you can see how much easier it is to determine the exact point where two sight lines cross when the angles approach 90°. Conversely, the intersection of sight lines that cross at small angles is difficult to pinpoint. Thus, wide sight-line angles lead to greater accuracy in determining the intersection point. The same principle holds for GPS fixes.

Beware of vendor hype. You'll see a wide range of numbers given for GPS receiver accuracy. These figures commonly represent the most optimistic case under the best of all conditions. Such luck is rare. The numbers also vary with the definition of accuracy used. CEPs of 50, 67, 95, and 99.9 percent are commonly reported. If vendors adopt a 50% rule, of course, their products may seem to the unwary to be more accurate. You must take care to judge the competition against the same standard.

618

D.10 Highly accurate DGPS receivers, such as this *OmniSTAR* unit, are portable enough to be carried into the field on foot.

GPS receivers can achieve horizontal accuracies of 21 meters and vertical accuracies of 28 meters. In other words, 95% of the fixes can be expected to fall within 21 meters horizontally and 28 meters vertically. In practice, greater accuracy is the rule rather than the exception.

Civilian GPS receivers are less accurate. They should give horizontal accuracies of 100 meters or less 95% of the time, and vertical accuracies of 140 meters with the same probability. Again, in practice greater accuracy is the rule.

Using DGPS, you can expect even a moderately expensive civilian receiver to give horizontal accuracies of 10 meters or less. This more than matches military specifications for GPS—a fact that has frustrated the DOD. Expensive codeless receivers used in surveying do even better. Horizontal accuracy under half an inch is possible with these complex devices. Receivers that use both GPS and GLONASS satellite constellations

can also achieve phenomenal accuracy.* Averaging DGPS fixes over several hours improves accuracy as well.

In the future, even casual users can expect better accuracy from GPS technology. The U.S government has promised to remove SA sometime in the next few years. Thus, civilians with inexpensive GPS receivers could receive positioning accuracies at least as good as the military enjoys now. The military may also provide civilians with a second signal frequency, making atmospheric corrections possible. DGPS will undoubtedly grow in popularity as hundreds of low-orbit communications satellites are launched in the next few years. As receivers gain more channels, GLONASS signals will likely be used more often to augment the limited GPS constellation.

Inertial Positioning Systems

Electronics has also breathed new life into the ancient position-finding method of dead reckoning, whereby current location is deduced from a record of directions and distances traveled from a known starting position (see *Dead Reckoning* in Chapter 14). The accuracy achieved in dead reckoning depends on the precision with which travel speed (velocity), time (from which distance can be calculated), and direction are measured. Technical improvements in clocks, compasses, and motion sensors through the years have greatly enhanced the accuracy of dead reckoning and have given impetus to a procedure known as inertial navigation.

Inertial navigation systems (INS) received their biggest boost when they were adapted for ships, submarines, modern aircraft, and missile guidance systems. Inertial navigation systems integrate gyroscopes, acceleration meters (for measuring differences in acceleration, from which velocity can be computed), and electronic computers. The result is a feedback system which provides constantly updated positional information. With position known, the direction and distance to a destination can be readily computed.

*The Russian GLONASS system has a horizontal accuracy within eight meters 95% of the time, and isn't degraded for non-military users. Differential GLONASS (DGLONASS) accuracies are one meter or less with the same probability.

Unfortunately, inertial navigation systems are expensive and not yet generally used outside military and large commercial applications. They also aren't foolproof: In 1983, the ill-fated Korean Air Lines Flight 007 carried three independent, cross-checkable inertial navigation units in its cockpit. Yet the Boeing 747 jumbo jet strayed 300 miles into Soviet airspace before it was shot down by a Soviet fighter, killing all 269 people aboard (see Box 14.3 in Chapter 14).

Inertial navigation principles are currently being applied to surveying applications in ground vehicles. In this case, distance is measured in wheel revolutions; otherwise the system is similar to that used in ships and aircraft. Since, with few exceptions, ground vehicles follow established roads, dead-reckoning procedures are used to collect data but not actually to navigate. The aim is to make an accurate determination of road position, not the route to be taken.

Recent adaptation of inertial navigation to automobile navigators is exciting news for the general map user. But land applications have proven more difficult than air and water systems. Any variation in traction between ground and wheel causes errors. Even small distance and direction errors early in a trip can lead to large errors later. These errors also add up as you move along. To make matters worse, digital maps aren't always accurate and up to date. For any combination of these reasons, your current position marker may soon "drift" off the road on your digital map display.

Vendors can improve accuracy through a "smart" or "augmented" dead-reckoning procedure. With this method, the device assumes you are always traveling along roads found on the digital map. The computer compares your computed location with the most logical map location at each turn (bend or intersection). If your position indicator strays off track due to an accumulation of small distance and direction errors, the system will get you back on the correct road on the display screen within a few turns.

Hybrid Positioning Systems

Major auto manufacturers are now showing interest in electronic navigation systems. Several after-market vendors also offer add-on units for cars and trucks. But problems persist. The accuracy of GPS technology suffers from poor satellite geometry and blocked signals. The accuracy of inertial technology in land applications suffers from cumulative errors and variation in wheel traction.

The obvious solution is to combine the two technologies. This is now being done. These **hybrid positioning systems** rely primarily on GPS technology. But when adequate satellite data aren't available, the unit switches to inertial technology. Once sufficient satellite data are again available, the unit shifts back to GPS technology. The result is constant and accurate positioning fixes under most conditions.

You can now expect to find a positioning option in at least the high-end models by most major automobile companies. Taxi fleets and emergency vehicles (police, fire, ambulance) in many cities now use positioning technology. In a growing list of cities, you can even rent a car equipped with some form of electronic navigator.

CONCLUSION

The magnetic compass has served as a useful navigational aid for many years and is still the practical instrument for direction finding when portability, low cost, and ease of use are critical factors. But times change, and electronic navigators are replacing the magnetic compass for many purposes. The cost of electronic systems is dropping, portability is increasing, and applications are expanding.

Devices which only a decade ago could be justified in only the largest ships and airplanes are now showing up in medium-sized craft. Electronic navigation devices for small planes and recreational boats are already used routinely, and units for highway vehicles are growing rapidly in popularity. Hand-held GPS receivers are now sold in most sporting goods stores and catalogs. Personal navigators of wristwatch size cannot be far in the future. The effort underlying these technological advances provides strong testimony to the value we place on direction-finding instruments. Only a few years ago, the positional accuracies we currently take for granted were beyond our wildest dreams.

620

SELECTED READINGS

Air Training Command, *Air Navigation*, AFM 51-40, NAVAIR DO-80V-49 (Washington, DC: U.S. Government Printing Office, 1973).

Bosler, J.D., and Hanson, R.H., "The Impact of VLBI and GPS on Geodesy," *Surveying and Mapping*, 44, 2 (1984), pp. 105-113.

Bowditch, N., *American Practical Navigator* (Washington, DC: U.S. Government Printing Office, 1972).

Dunlap. G.D., *Navigation and Finding Fish With Electronics* (Camden: NJ: International Maine Publishing Co., 1972).

Gardner, A.C., *A Short Course in Navigation* (New York: Funk & Wagnalls, 1968).

Henderson, R., *The Cruiser's Compendium: A Complete Guide to Coastal, Inland and Gunkhole Cruising* (Chicago: Henry Regnergy Co., 1973).

Large, A.J., "Satellite Plan Seen as Boon to Navigation," *The Wall Street Journal,* October 25, 1983, Section 2, pp. 39, 51.

Li, R., "Mobile Mapping: An Emerging Technology for Spatial Data Acquisition," *Photogrammetric Engineering & Remote Sensing*, 63, 9 (September 1997), pp. 1085-1092.

Monmonier, M.S., "Location and Navigation" in *Technological Transition in Cartography* (Madison: University of Wisconsin Press, 1985), pp. 15-45.

Naval Training Command, *A Navigation Compendium*, NAVTRA 1049-A (Washington, DC: U.S. Government Printing Office, 1972).

Shuldiner, H., "Here Now: Computerized Navigator for Your Car," *Popular Science*, 226, 6 (June 1985), pp. 64-67.

Snufeldt, H.H., and Dunlap, G.D., *Navigation and Piloting* (Annapolis, MD: Naval Institute Press, 1970).

Stewart, J.Q., and Pierce, N.L., *Marine and Air Navigation* (Boston: Ginn & Co., 1944).

Time-Life Books, *Navigation* (Chicago: Time-Life Books, 1975).

Also see references in Chapters 14 and 15.

APPENDIX E

TABLES

Table E.1
Random Numbers

79788	68243	59732	04257	27084	14743	17520	95401	55811	76099
40538	79000	89559	25026	42274	23489	34502	75508	06059	86682
64016	73598	18609	73150	62463	33102	45205	87440	96767	67042
49767	12691	17903	93871	99721	79109	09425	26904	07419	76013
76974	55108	29795	08404	82684	00497	51126	79935	57450	55671
23854	08480	85983	96025	50117	64610	99425	62291	86943	21541
68973	70551	25098	78033	98573	79848	31778	29555	61446	23037
36444	93600	65350	14971	25325	00427	52073	64280	18847	24768
03003	87800	07391	11594	21196	00781	32550	57158	58887	73041
17540	26188	36647	78386	04558	61463	57842	90382	77019	24210
38916	55809	47982	41968	69760	79422	80154	91486	19180	15100
64288	19843	69122	42502	48508	28820	59933	72998	99942	10515
86809	51564	38040	39418	49915	19000	58050	16899	79952	57849
99800	99566	14742	05028	30033	94889	53381	23656	75787	59223
92345	31890	95712	08279	91794	94068	49337	88674	35355	12267
90363	65162	32245	82279	79256	80834	06088	99462	56705	06118
64437	32242	48431	04835	39070	59702	31508	60935	22390	52246
91714	53662	28373	34333	55791	74758	51144	18827	10704	76803
20902	17646	31391	31459	33315	03444	55743	74701	58851	27427
12217	86007	70371	52281	14510	76094	96579	54853	78339	20839

Table E.2
Square Roots

n	$\sqrt{n}$	$\sqrt{10n}$	n	$\sqrt{n}$	$\sqrt{10n}$	n	$\sqrt{n}$	$\sqrt{10n}$	n	$\sqrt{n}$	$\sqrt{10n}$
1.00	1.00	3.16	2.10	1.45	4.58	4.30	2.07	6.56	3.20	1.79	5.66
1.02	1.01	3.19	2.12	1.46	4.60	4.32	2.08	6.57	3.22	1.79	5.67
1.04	1.02	3.22	2.14	1.46	4.63	4.34	2.08	6.59	3.24	1.80	5.69
1.06	1.03	3.26	2.16	1.47	4.65	4.36	2.09	6.60	3.26	1.81	5.71
1.08	1.04	3.29	2.18	1.48	4.67	4.38	2.09	6.62	3.28	1.81	5.73
1.10	1.05	3.32	2.20	1.48	4.69	4.40	2.10	6.63	3.30	1.82	5.74
1.12	1.06	3.35	2.22	1.49	4.71	4.42	2.10	6.65	3.32	1.82	5.76
1.14	1.07	3.38	2.24	1.50	4.73	4.44	2.11	6.66	3.34	1.83	5.78
1.16	1.08	3.41	2.26	1.50	4.75	4.46	2.11	6.68	3.36	1.83	5.80
1.18	1.09	3.44	2.28	1.51	4.77	4.48	2.12	6.69	3.38	1.84	5.81
1.20	1.10	3.46	2.30	1.52	4.80	4.50	2.12	6.71	3.40	1.84	5.83
1.22	1.10	3.49	2.32	1.52	4.82	4.52	2.13	6.72	3.42	1.85	5.85
1.24	1.11	3.52	2.34	1.53	4.84	4.54	2.13	6.74	3.44	1.85	5.87
1.26	1.12	3.55	2.36	1.54	4.86	4.56	2.14	6.75	3.46	1.86	5.88
1.28	1.13	3.58	2.38	1.54	4.88	4.58	2.14	6.77	3.48	1.87	5.90
1.30	1.14	3.61	2.40	1.55	4.90	4.60	2.14	6.78	3.50	1.87	5.92
1.32	1.15	3.63	2.42	1.56	4.92	4.62	2.15	6.80	3.52	1.88	5.93
1.34	1.16	3.66	2.44	1.56	4.94	4.64	2.15	6.81	3.54	1.88	5.95
1.36	1.17	3.69	2.46	1.57	4.96	4.66	2.16	6.83	3.56	1.89	5.97
1.38	1.17	3.71	2.48	1.57	4.98	4.68	2.16	6.84	3.58	1.89	5.98
1.40	1.18	3.74	2.50	1.58	5.00	4.70	2.17	6.86	3.60	1.90	6.00
1.42	1.19	3.77	2.52	1.59	5.02	4.72	2.17	6.87	3.62	1.90	6.02
1.44	1.20	3.79	2.54	1.59	5.04	4.74	2.18	6.88	3.64	1.91	6.03
1.46	1.21	3.82	2.56	1.60	5.06	4.76	2.18	6.90	3.66	1.91	6.05
1.48	1.22	3.85	2.58	1.61	5.08	4.78	2.19	6.91	3.68	1.92	6.07
1.50	1.22	3.87	2.60	1.61	5.10	4.80	2.19	6.93	3.70	1.92	6.08
1.52	1.23	3.90	2.62	1.62	5.12	4.82	2.20	6.94	3.72	1.93	6.10
1.54	1.24	3.92	2.64	1.62	5.14	4.84	2.20	6.96	3.74	1.93	6.12
1.56	1.25	3.95	2.66	1.63	5.16	4.86	2.20	6.97	3.76	1.94	6.13
1.58	1.26	3.97	2.68	1.64	5.18	4.88	2.21	6.99	3.78	1.94	6.15
1.60	1.26	4.00	2.70	1.64	5.20	4.90	2.21	7.00	3.80	1.95	6.16
1.62	1.27	4.02	2.72	1.65	5.22	4.92	2.22	7.01	3.82	1.95	6.18
1.64	1.28	4.05	2.74	1.66	5.23	4.94	2.22	7.03	3.84	1.96	6.20
1.66	1.29	4.07	2.76	1.66	5.25	4.96	2.23	7.04	3.86	1.96	6.21
1.68	1.30	4.10	2.78	1.67	5.27	4.98	2.23	7.06	3.88	1.97	6.23
1.70	1.30	4.12	2.80	1.67	5.29	5.00	2.24	7.07	3.90	1.97	6.25
1.72	1.31	4.15	2.82	1.68	5.31	5.02	2.24	7.09	3.92	1.98	6:26
1.74	1.32	4.17	2.84	1.69	5.33	5.04	2.24	7.10	3.94	1.98	6.28
1.76	1.33	4.20	2.86	1.69	5.35	5.06	2.25	7.11	3.96	1.99	6.29
1.78	1.33	4.22	2.88	1.70	5.37	5.08	2.25	7.13	3.98	1.99	6.31
1.80	1.34	4.24	2.90	1.70	5.39	5.10	2.26	7.14	4.00	2.00	6.32
1.82	1.35	4.27	2.92	1.71	5.40	5.12	2.26	7.16	4.02	2.00	6.34
1.84	1.36	4.29	2.94	1.71	5.42	5.14	2.27	7.17	4.04	2.01	6.36
1.86	1.36	4.31	2.96	1.72	5.44	5.16	2.27	7.18	4.06	2.01	6.37
1.88	1.37	4.34	2.98	1.73	5.46	5.18	2.28	7.20	4.08	2.02	6.39
1.90	1.38	4.36	3.00	1.73	5.48	5.20	2.28	7.21	4.10	2.02	6.40
1.92	1.39	4.38	3.02	1.74	5.50	5.22	2.28	7.22	4.12	2.03	6.42
1.94	1.39	4.40	3.04	1.74	5.51	5.24	2.29	7.24	4.14	2.03	6.43
1.96	1.40	4.43	3.06	1.75	5.53	5.26	2.29	7.25	4.16	2.04	6.45
1.98	1.41	4.45	3.08	1.76	5.55	5.28	2.30	7.27	4.18	2.04	6.47
2.00	1.41	4.47	3.10	1.76	5.57	5.30	2.30	7.28	4.20	2.05	6.48
2.02	1.42	4.49	3.12	1.77	5.59	5.32	2.31	7.29	4.22	2.05	6.50
2.04	1.43	4.52	3.14	1.77	5.60	5.34	2.31	7.31	4.24	2.06	6.51
2.06	1.44	4.54	3.16	1.78	5.62	5.36	2.32	7.32	4.26	2.06	6.53
2.08	1.44	4.56	3.18	1.78	5.64	5.38	2.32	7.33	4.28	2.07	6.54

Table E.3
Metric-English Distance Equivalents

METRIC	ENGLISH
1 millimeter (mm)	.03937 inch
2.54 mm	.1 inch
1 centimeter (cm) (10 mm)	.3937 inch
2.54 cm	1 inch
1 decimeter (dm) (10 cm)	3.937 inches
30.48 cm	1 foot (12 inches)
91.44 cm	1 yard (3 feet)
1 meter (m) (100 cm)	39.37 inches (1.094 yd.) (3.281 ft.)
1 decameter (10 m)	32.81 feet
1 hectometer (hm) (100 m)	328.1 feet
1 kilometer (km) (1,000 m) (100,000 cm)	.6214 mile (3,281 ft.) (39,372 in.)
1.609 km	1 statute mile (5,280 feet) (63,360 inches)

Table E.4
Metric-English Area Equivalents

METRIC	ENGLISH
1 cm^2	.155 inch^2
6.45 cm^2	1 inch^2
.092 m^2	1 foot^2
.836 m^2	1 yard^2
1 m^2	1.196 yard^2 (10.764 foot^2)
.405 hectare	1 acre (43,560 foot^2)
1 hectare (10,000 m^2)	2.471 acres
16.188 hectares	40 acres
1 km^2 (1,000,000 m^2)	.386 mile^2
2.59 km^2	1 mile^2 (640 acres)

Table E.5
Natural Trigonometric Functions

°	Sin	Cos	Cot	Tan	°	°	Sin	Cos	Cot	Tan	°
0	.0000	1.0000		.0000	90	23	.3907	.9205	2.356	.4245	67
1	.0174	.9998	57.290	.0175	89	24	.4067	.9135	2.246	.4452	66
2	.0349	.9994	28.636	.0349	88	25	.4226	.9063	2.144	.4663	65
3	.0523	.9986	19.081	.0524	87	26	.4384	.8988	2.050	.4877	64
4	.0698	.9976	14.301	.0699	86	27	.4540	.8910	1.963	.5095	63
5	.0872	.9962	11.430	.0875	85	28	.4695	.8829	1.881	.5317	62
6	.1045	.9945	9.514	.1051	84	29	.4848	.8746	1.804	.5543	61
7	.1219	.9925	8.144	.1228	83						
8	.1392	.9903	7.115	.1405	82	30	.5000	.8660	1.732	.5773	60
9	.1564	.9877	6.314	.1584	81	31	.5150	.8572	1.664	.6009	59
						32	.5299	.8480	1.600	.6249	58
10	.1736	.9848	5.671	.1763	80	33	.5446	.8387	1.540	.6494	57
11	.1908	.9816	5.145	.1944	79	34	.5592	.8290	1.483	.6745	56
12	.2079	.9781	4.705	.2126	78	35	.5736	.8191	1.428	.7002	55
13	.2249	.9744	4.331	.2309	77	36	.5878	.8090	1.376	.7265	54
14	.2419	.9703	4.011	.2493	76	37	.6018	.7986	1.327	.7535	53
15	.2588	.9659	3.732	.2679	75	38	.6157	.7880	1.280	.7813	52
16	.2756	.9613	3.487	.2867	74	39	.6293	.7771	1.235	.8098	51
17	.2924	.9563	3.271	.3057	73						
18	.3090	.9511	3.078	.3249	72	40	.6428	.7660	1.192	.8391	50
19	.3256	.9455	2.904	.3443	71	41	.6561	.7547	1.150	.8693	49
						42	.6691	.7431	1.111	.9004	48
20	.3420	.9397	2.747	.3640	70	43	.6820	.7313	1.072	.9325	47
21	.3584	.9336	2.605	.3839	69	44	.6947	.7193	1.035	.9657	46
22	.3746	.9272	2.475	.4040	68	45	.7071	.7071	1.000	1.0000	45
°	Cos	Sin	Tan	Cot	°	°	Cos	Sin	Tan	Cot	°

Table E.6
Variation in the Length of a Degree of Latitude
(measured along the meridian)

Latitude	Meters	Statute Miles	Latitude	Meters	Statute Miles	Latitude	Meters	Statute Miles
°			°			°		
0–1	110 567.3	68.703	30–31	110 857.0	68.883	60–61	111 423.1	69.235
1–2	110 568.0	68.704	31–32	110 874.4	68.894	61–62	111 439.9	69.246
2–3	110 569.4	68.705	32–33	110 892.1	68.905	62–63	111 456.4	69.256
3–4	110 571.4	68.706	33–34	110 910.1	68.916	63–64	111 472.4	69.266
4–5	110 574.1	68.707	34–35	110 928.3	68.928	64–65	111 488.1	69.275
5–6	110 577.6	68.710	35–36	110 946.9	68.939	65–66	111 503.3	69.285
6–7	110 581.6	68.712	36–37	110 965.6	68.951	66–67	111 518.0	69.294
7–8	110 586.4	68.715	37–38	110 984.5	68.962	67–68	111 532.3	69.303
8–9	110 591.8	68.718	38–39	111 003.7	68.974	68–69	111 546.2	69.311
9–10	110 597.8	68.722	39–40	111 023.0	68.986	69–70	111 559.5	69.320
10–11	110 604.5	68.726	40–41	111 042.4	68.998	70–71	111 572.2	69.328
11–12	110 611.9	68.731	41–42	111 061.9	69.011	71–72	111 584.5	69.335
12–13	110 619.8	68.736	42–43	111 081.6	69.023	72–73	111 596.2	69.343
13–14	110 628.4	68.741	43–44	111 101.3	69.035	73–74	111 607.3	69.349
14–15	110 637.6	68.747	44–45	111 121.0	69.047	74–75	111 617.9	69.356
15–16	110 647.5	68.753	45–46	111 140.8	69.060	75–76	111 627.8	69.362
16–17	110 657.8	68.759	46–47	111 160.5	69.072	76–77	111 637.1	69.368
17–18	110 668.8	68.766	47–48	111 180.2	69.084	77–78	111 645.9	69.373
18–19	110 680.4	68.773	48–49	111 199.9	69.096	78–79	111 653.9	69.378
19–20	110 692.4	68.781	49–50	111 219.5	69.108	79–80	111 661.4	69.383
20–21	110 705.1	68.789	50–51	111 239.0	69.121	80–81	111 668.2	69.387
21–22	110 718.2	68.797	51–52	111 258.3	69.133	81–82	111 674.4	69.391
22–23	110 731.8	68.805	52–53	111 277.6	69.145	82–83	111 679.9	69.395
23–24	110 746.0	68.814	53–54	111 296.6	69.156	83–84	111 684.7	69.398
24–25	110 760.6	68.823	54–55	111 315.4	69.168	84–85	111 688.9	69.400
25–26	110 775.6	68.833	55–56	111 334.0	69.180	85–86	111 692.3	69.402
26–27	110 791.1	68.842	56–57	111 352.4	69.191	86–87	111 695.1	09.404
27–28	110 807.0	68.852	57–58	111 370.5	09.202	87–88	111 697.2	69.405
28–29	110 823.3	08.862	58–59	111 388.4	69.213	88–89	111 698.6	69.406
29–30	110 840.0	68.873	59–60	111 405.9	69.224	89–90	111 699.3	69.407

Table E.7
Variation in the Length of a Degree of Longitude
(measured along the parallel)

Latitude	Meters	Statute Miles	Latitude	Meters	Statute Miles	Latitude	Meters	Statute Miles
° ′			° ′			° ′		
0 00	111 321	69.172	30 00	96 488	59.956	60 00	55 802	34.674
1 00	111 304	69.162	31 00	95 506	59.345	61 00	54 110	33.623
2 00	111 253	69.130	32 00	94 495	58.716	62 00	52 400	32.560
3 00	111 169	69.078	33 00	93 455	58.071	63 00	50 675	31.488
4 00	111 051	69.005	34 00	92 387	57.407	64 00	48 934	30.406
5 00	110 900	68.911	35 00	91 290	56.725	65 00	47 177	29.315
6 00	110 715	68.795	36 00	90 166	56.027	66 00	45 407	28.215
7 00	110 497	68.660	37 00	89 014	55.311	67 00	43 622	27.106
8 00	110 245	68.504	38 00	87 835	54.579	68 00	41 823	25.988
9 00	109 959	68.326	39 00	86 629	53.829	69 00	40 012	24.862
10 00	109 641	68.129	40 00	85 396	53.063	70 00	38 188	23.729
11 00	109 289	67.910	41 00	84 137	52.281	71 00	36 353	22.589
12 00	108 904	67.670	42 00	82 853	51.483	72 00	34 506	21.441
13 00	108 486	67.410	43 00	81 543	50.669	73 00	32 648	20.287
14 00	108 036	67.131	44 00	80 208	49.840	74 00	30 781	19.127
15 00	107 553	66.830	45 00	78 849	48.995	75 00	28 903	17.960
16 00	107 036	66.510	46 00	77 466	48.136	76 00	27 017	16.788
17 00	106 487	66.169	47 00	76 058	47.261	77 00	25 123	15.611
18 00	105 906	65.808	48 00	74 628	46.372	78 00	23 220	14.428
19 00	105 294	65.427	49 00	73 174	45.469	79 00	21 311	13.242
20 00	104 649	65.026	50 00	71 698	44.552	80 00	19 394	12.051
21 00	103 972	64.606	51 00	70 200	43.621	81 00	17 472	10.857
22 00	103 264	64.166	52 00	68 680	42.676	82 00	15 545	9.659
23 00	102 524	63.706	53 00	67 140	41.719	83 00	13 612	8.458
24 00	101 754	63.228	54 00	65 578	40.749	84 00	11 675	7.255
25 00	100 952	62.729	55 00	63 996	39.766	85 00	9 735	6.049
26 00	100 119	62.212	56 00	62 395	38.771	86 00	7 792	4.842
27 00	99 257	61.676	57 00	60 774	37.764	87 00	5 846	3.632
28 00	98 364	61.122	58 00	59 135	36.745	88 00	3 898	2.422
29 00	97 441	60.548	59 00	57 478	35.716	89 00	1 949	1.211
						90 00	0	0

Table E.8
Latitude-Longitude Values for the Largest City in Each State

CITY & STATE	LATITUDE		LONGITUDE	
Birmingham, Alabama	33°	25′N	86°	52′W
Anchorage, Alaska	61	20	149	55
Phoenix, Arizona	33	22	112	5
Little Rock, Arkansas	34	45	92	15
Los Angeles, California	35	12	118	2
Denver, Colorado	39	46	104	59
Hartford, Connecticut	41	53	72	45
Wilmington, Delaware	39	45	75	23
Miami, Florida	25	45	80	11
Atlanta, Georgia	33	45	84	21
Honolulu, Hawaii	21	20	157	50
Boise, Idaho	43	37	116	10
Chicago, Illinois	41	49	87	37
Indianapolis, Indiana	39	50	86	10
Des Moines, Iowa	41	37	93	30
Wichita, Kansas	37	35	97	20
Louisville, Kentucky	38	16	85	30
New Orleans, Louisiana	30	00	90	4
Portland, Maine	43	31	70	20
Baltimore, Maryland	39	22	76	30
Boston, Massachusetts	42	15	71	7
Detroit, Michigan	42	23	83	5
Minneapolis, Minnesota	45	00	93	10
Jackson, Mississippi	32	20	90	10
St. Louis, Missouri	38	40	90	10
Billings, Montana	45	47	108	29
Omaha, Nebraska	41	15	96	5
Las Vegas, Nevada	36	10	115	10
Manchester, New Hampshire	43	00	71	30
Newark, New Jersey	40	40	74	5
Albuquerque, New Mexico	35	6	106	40
New York, New York	40	40	73	58
Charlotte, North Carolina	35	14	81	53
Fargo, North Dakota	46	52	97	00
Cleveland, Ohio	41	30	81	45
Oklahoma City, Oklahoma	35	30	97	30
Portland, Oregon	45	29	122	48
Philadelphia, Pennsylvania	44	00	75	5
Providence, Rhode Island	41	52	71	30
Columbia, South Carolina	34	00	81	00
Sioux Falls, South Dakota	43	30	96	50
Memphis, Tennessee	35	8	90	3
Houston, Texas	29	46	95	21
Salt Lake City, Utah	40	46	111	57
Burlington, Vermont	44	30	73	15
Norfolk, Virginia	36	49	76	15
Seattle, Washington	47	36	122	20
Charleston, West Virginia	38	23	81	30
Milwaukee, Wisconsin	43	5	88	00
Cheyenne, Wyoming	41	8	104	47

Table E.9
Area of Quadrilaterals of 1° Extent

Lower Latitude of Quadrilateral	Area in Square Kilometers	Area in Square Miles	Lower Latitude of Quadrilateral	Area in Square Kilometers	Area in Square Miles
0°	12308.09	4752.16	45°	8686.89	3354.01
1	12304.44	4750.75	46	8533.30	3294.71
2	12297.14	4747.93	47	8377.07	3234.39
3	12286.21	4743.71	48	8218.17	3173.04
4	12271.63	4738.08	49	8056.69	3110.69
5	12253.39	4731.04	50	7892.69	3047.37
6	12231.56	4722.61	51	7726.18	2983.08
7	12206.05	4712.76	52	7557.23	2917.85
8	12176.94	4701.52	53	7385.85	2851.68
9	12144.23	4688.89	54	7212.17	2784.62
10	12107.89	4674.86	55	7036.18	2716.67
11	12067.92	4659.43	56	6857.93	2647.85
12	12024.41	4642.63	57	6677.51	2578.19
13	11977.30	4624.44	58	6494.94	2507.70
14	11926.61	4604.87	59	6310.33	2436.42
15	11872.35	4583.92	60	6123.64	2364.34
16	11814.57	4561.61	61	5935.01	2291.51
17	11753.24	4537.93	62	5744.46	2217.94
18	11688.41	4512.90	63	5552.08	2143.66
19	11620.06	4486.51	64	5357.88	2068.68
20	11548.24	4458.78	65	5161.97	1993.04
21	11472.95	4429.71	66	4964.38	1916.75
22	11394.19	4399.30	67	4765.19	1839.84
23	11312.01	4367.57	68	4564.44	1762.33
24	11278.21	4334.52	69	4362.18	1684.24
25	11137.44	4300.17	70	4158.56	1605.62
26	11045.08	4264.51	71	3953.53	1526.46
27	10949.38	4227.56	72	3747.24	1446.81
28	10850.36	4189.33	73	3539.73	1366.69
29	10748.06	4149.83	74	3331.05	1286.12
30	10642.47	4109.06	75	3121.29	1205.13
31	10533.66	4067.05	76	2910.51	1123.75
32	10421.62	4023.79	77	2698.75	1041.99
33	10306.39	3979.30	78	2486.14	959.90
34	10188.00	3933.59	79	2272.70	877.49
35	10066.48	3886.67	80	2058.51	794.79
36	9941.87	3838.56	81	1843.64	711.83
37	9814.18	3789.26	82	1628.17	628.64
38	9683.49	3738.80	83	1412.17	545.24
39	9549.80	3687.18	84	1195.70	461.66
40	9413.15	3634.42	85	978.84	377.93
41	9273.60	3580.54	86	761.67	294.08
42	9131.15	3525.54	87	544.21	210.12
43	8985.85	3469.44	88	326.60	126.10
44	8837.75	3412.26	89	108.88	42.04

Table E.10
Values of e^{-m}

m	0·0	0·1	0·2	0·3	0·4	0·5	0·6	0·7	0·8	0·9
0	1·00000	·9048	·8187	·7408	·6703	·6065	·5488	·4966	·4493	·4066
1	·3679	·3329	·3012	·2725	·2466	·2231	·2019	·1827	·1653	·1496
2	·1353	·1225	·1108	·1003	·0907	·0821	·0743	·0672	·0608	·0550
3	·0498	·0450	·0408	·0369	·0334	·0302	·0273	·0247	·0224	·0202
4	·0183	·0166	·0150	·0136	·0123	·0111	·0101	·0091	·0082	·0074
5	·0067	·0061	·0055	·0050	·0045	·0041	·0037	·0033	·0030	·0027
6	·0025	·0022	·0020	·0018	·0017	·0015	·0014	·0012	·0011	·0010
7	·00091	·00082	·00075	·00068	·00061	·00055	·00050	·00045	·00041	·00037
8	·00033	·00030	·00027	·00025	·00022	·00020	·00018	·00017	·00015	·00014
9	·00012	·00011	·00010	·00009	·00008	·00007	·00007	·00006	·00005	·00005

Table E.11
Ground Distance Error Due to Compass Reading Errors

Distance Traveled (Meters)	1°	2°	3°	4°	Angular Error 5°	6°	7°	8°	9°	10°
1,000	20	35	53	69	87	105	122	139	157	174
2,000	40	69	106	139	174	210	245	279	314	349
3,000	60	104	159	208	262	315	367	418	471	523
4,000	80	139	212	277	349	420	490	557	627	697
5,000	100	173	265	346	436	524	612	696	784	872
6,000	120	208	317	416	523	629	735	836	941	1,046
7,000	140	242	370	485	610	734	857	975	1,098	1,220
8,000	160	277	423	554	697	839	980	1,114	1,255	1,395
9,000	180	312	476	624	785	944	1,102	1,254	1,412	1,569
10,000	200	346	529	693	872	1,049	1,225	1,393	1,568	1,744
11,000	220	381	635	762	959	1,154	1,347	1,532	1,725	1,918
12,000	240	416	688	831	1,046	1,259	1,470	1,671	1,882	2,092
13,000	260	450	741	901	1,133	1,363	1,592	1,811	2,039	2,267
14,000	280	485	794	970	1,220	1,468	1,715	1,950	2,196	2,441
15,000	300	520	847	1,039	1,308	1,573	1,837	2,089	2,353	2,615

$$\left[\begin{array}{l} 1,000 \text{ m} = .6214 \text{ statute mile} \\ \quad 1 \text{ m} = 3.28 \text{ feet} \end{array}\right]$$

BIBLIOGRAPHY OF QUOTATIONS

Abbey, Edward, *The Journey Home* (New York: Dutton, 1977).

Bryant, Adam, "From an Airliner's Black Box, Next-to-Last Words," *The New York Times,* April 21, 1996.

Carroll, Lewis (Charles Dodgson), *Sylvie and Bruno Concluded* (London: Macmillan Co., 1893).

Cervantes, Miguel de, *Don Quixote of La Mancha* (Edinburgh: John Grant, 1902).

Conrad, Joseph, *Heart of Darkness and The Secret Sharer* (New York: The New American Library, 1960).

Dickey, James, *Deliverance* (Boston: Houghton Mifflin Co., 1970).

Drabble, Margaret, *The Waterfall* (New York: The New American Library, 1969).

Drummond, June, *Cable Car* (New York: Holt, Rinehart & Winston, 1967).

Heller, Joseph, *Catch-22* (New York: Simon & Schuster, 1961).

Hotchkiss, Noel, *A Comprehensive Guide to Land Navigation with GPS* (Herndon, VA: Alexis USA, 1995).

Huxtable, Ada Louise, *The New York Times* (November 25, 1973), Section 2, p. 26.

Lansing, Alfred, *Endurance* (New York: Avon Books, 1960).

Least Heat-Moon, William, *PrairyErth* (Boston: Houghton Mifflin Company, 1991).

Llewellyn, Richard, *How Green Was My Valley* (New York: Macmillan Co., 1940).

Lockridge, Frances & Richard, *The Devious Ones* (New York: J.B. Lippincott Co., 1964).

Mailer, Norman, *The Naked and the Dead* (New York: Holt, Rinehart & Winston, 1948).

Matthiessen, Peter, *Wildlife in America* (New York: Viking Press, 1959).

Nautical Chart, National Oceanic & Atmospheric Administration (NOAA), U.S. Dept. of Commerce.

Newsweek, material in issues dated January 22, 1973 & January 21, 1991 (page 12).

New York Herald, "Some Railway Map-Making" (*Inland Printer,* Vol. 15, 1895), p. 500.

The New York Times, material in the issue dated October 13, 1972.

Pan American Airways advertisement, "America's Airline to the World" (1978).

Patton, Frances Gray, *Good Morning, Miss Dove* (New York: Pocket Books, 1956).

Pelletier, Cathie, *The Funeral Makers* (New York: Macmillan, 1986).

Prince Modupe, *I Was A Savage* (New York: Frederick A. Praeger, 1957).

Rand McNally & Co., "Whatever Happened to Alice?" advertisement for the Rand McNally Atlas.

Russell, Jerry & Renny, *On the Loose* (New York: Ballantine Books, 1967).

Saint-Exupéry, Antoine de, *The Little Prince* (New York: Harcourt, Brace & Co., 1943); *Night Flight* (New York: The New American Library, 1961).

The San Francisco Chronicle, material in the issue dated August 24, 1967.

Snow, C.P., *Strangers and Brothers* (New York: Charles Scribner's Sons, 1960).

Steinbeck, John, *Travels With Charley* (New York: Bantam Books, 1963).

Tey, Josephine (Elizabeth Mackintosh), *The Man in the Queue* (London: Peter Davies, 1927).

Thompson, H.S., *Fear and Loathing in Las Vegas: A Savage Journey to the Heart of the American Dream* (New York: Random House, 1971), p. 169.

Thompson, M.M., *Maps for America,* 2nd Edition (Washington, DC: U.S. Government Printing Office, 1981).

Thoreau, Henry David, *The Journal of Henry D. Thoreau* (Thoreau's diaries), two volumes, edited by Bradford Torrey & Francis Allen (New York: Dover Publications, 1963), pp. 228-229.

Time Magazine, "Enlightenment—in Living Color" (June 26, 1978); "Explaining the Inexplicable" (September 19, 1983); "Don't Drink the Water" (March 9, 1992).

Toffler, Alvin, *The Third Wave* (New York: Bantam Books, 1981).

Toffler, Alvin, *Future Shock* (New York: Bantam Books, 1971).

Twain, Mark (Samuel Clemens), *Tom Sawyer Abroad* (New York: Charles L. Webster & Co., 1894).

U.S. News & World Report staff, *Triumph Without Victory: The Unreported History of the Persian Gulf War* (New York: Times Books, 1992).

Wolfe, Tom, in Gerald E. Stearn, ed., *McLuhan: Hot & Cool* (New York: The New American Library, 1969).

Wurman, Richard S., *Information Anxiety* (New York: Doubleday, 1989).

CREDITS

INTRODUCTION

Cartoon, modified version of cartoon by John Jonik, *Writers Digest* (August, 1975); Figure I.4, courtesy Register and Tribune Syndicate; Figure I.6, courtesy Eugene S. Sinervo (Sand River, MI); Figure I.7, after Peter R. Gould, *On Mental Maps,* Discussion Paper No. 9, Mich. Inter-University Community of Mathematical Geographers (Ann Arbor: Dept. of Geography, University of Mich., 1966); Figure I.9, from Thomas J. Mason, *et al., Atlas of Cancer Mortality for U.S. Counties: 1950-1969,* DHEW Publication No. (NIH) 75-780 (Washington, DC: U.S. Dept. of Health, Education, and Welfare, 1975).

PART I

CHAPTER 1

Figure 1.11B, graph from *Tide Tables 1979, High and Low Water Predictions, West Coast of North and South America*, National Ocean Survey (1978).

CHAPTER 2

Figure 2.5, after map *Time Magazine,* July 13, 1981; Figure 2.9, from color map in *Wisconsin State Journal;* Figure 2.12, from lake bottom contour plot using commercial software.

CHAPTER 3

Cartoon, courtesy Robert Tucker; Figure 3.7, data from map prepared by USDA; Figure 3.18, after map produced by USGS.

CHAPTER 4

Figure 4.8, courtesy EROS, USGS; Figure 4.11 courtesy National Cartographic Information Center; Figure 4.12 courtesy National Cartographic Information Center; Figure 4.13 courtesy Michael Thoma; Figure 4.16 courtesy ERDAS Inc. (Atlanta, GA); Figure 4.19 courtesy Michael Thoma.

CHAPTER 5

Figure 5.2, courtesy Rauda Scale Models (Seattle, WA); Figure 5.3, courtesy Hubbard Scientific Co. (Northbrook, IL); Figure 5.4, courtesy Warren Roll of the *Star-Bulletin* (Honolulu, HI); Figure 5.6, courtesy Alan Gordon Enterprises, Inc. (North Hollywood, CA); Figure 5.7, courtesy University of Illinois Committee on Aerial Photography; Figure 5.8A, courtesy Goodyear Aerospace; Figure 5.9, Courtesy National Geographic Society; Figure 5.11, from Christopher North, "Determining a Vertical Scale for Graphical Representation of Three-Dimensional Surfaces," Dept. of Geography, University of London, England (courtesy of the author); Figure 5.12, courtesy Hyacinth (Norcross, GA); Figure 5.14B, courtesy L. Batten, USGS/NMD/EROS; Figure 5.26, courtesy Hubbard Scientific Co. (Northbrook, IL); Figure 2.28, courtesy P. Yoeli; Figure 5.29A, courtesy Dynamic Graphics Inc.; Figure 5.30, courtesy Image Data Corp. (Pasadena, CA); Figure 5.31, courtesy Radian Corp.; Figure 5.32, courtesy Intergraph Corp. (Huntsville, AL).

CHAPTER 6

Figure 6.3A, courtesy Madison Convention Bureau; Figure 6.9, courtesy USDA; Figure 6.11, after map in William Bunge, *Theoretical Geography* (Lund, Sweden: C.W.K. Gleerup, 1962).

CHAPTER 7

Figure 7.6A, courtesy Wis. Natural History Survey and UWCL; Figure 7.6B, after map in R.L. Wesson and R.E. Wallace, "Predicting the Next Great Earthquake in California," *Scientific American,* Vol. 252, No. 2 (1985), p. 43; Figure 7.8, after map prepared by the National Weather Service; Figure 7.16, map prepared by Eugene Turner using data from the Los Angeles Community Analysis Bureau (Northridge, CA); Figure 7.18, courtesy Division of Research Statistics, Ohio Bureau of Employment Services, Columbus; Figure 7.19A, after Exxon Corp. advertisement; Figure 7.19B, after Waldo R. Tobler, "Cartograms and Cartosplines," paper presented at Workshop on Automated Cartography and Graphics in Epidemiology and Health Statistics (Washington, DC: Dept. of HEW, March 20, 1976).

CHAPTER 8

Figure 8.1, Landsat MSS images courtesy EROS, Dept. of the Interior; Figure 8.3, courtesy GTE Sylvania (Mountain View, CA); Figure 8.4, courtesy Dept. of Commerce, NOAA; Figure 8.6, courtesy *The Canadian Cartographer* (from M.S. Monmonier, "Class Intervals to Enhance the Visual Correlation of Choropleth Maps," Vol. 12, pp. 161-178); Figure 8.9A, courtesy National Geographic Society; Figure 8.11A, based on map in *USA Today,* published by Gannett Co., Inc. (Washington, DC); Figure 8.13, courtesy MIT Architecture Machine Group; Figure 8.14, courtesy Chrysler Corp. (Detroit, MI); Figure 8.15 and 8.16, courtesy Intergraph Corp. (Huntsville, AL).

CHAPTER 9

Figure 9.2 courtesy DeLorme Mapping, Inc. (Freeport, ME); Figure 9.3 and 9.4 from Designer clip-art files, Micrografx (Richardson, TX); Figure 9.3, courtesy Comwell Systems Inc. (Tempe, AZ); Figure 9.5, courtesy NOVA Development Corp. (Calabasas, CA), Figure 9.6, Software Toolworks (Novato, CA); Figure 9.7, courtesy Golden Software, Inc. (Golden, CO); Figure 9.8, courtesy ESRI (Redlands, CA); Figure 9.9, courtesy Wis. Dept. of Transportation; Figure 9.10, courtesy Engineering Design Systems (Dubuque, IA); Figure 9.11, courtesy Jet Propulsion Lab (Pasadena, CA); Figure 9.12, courtesy ETAK, Inc. (Menlo Park, CA).

PART II

Cartoon, courtesy United Feature Syndicate.

CHAPTER 11

Cartoon, courtesy United Feature Syndicate; Table 11.1, from Army Map Service Aid No. 6, "Map Intelligence," list ed. (1953); Figure 11.17, based on map published by U.S. Dept. of Interior, Bureau of Land Management; Figure 11.18, after illustration published in Thomas R. Beveridge, et al., *Topographic Maps of Missouri*, Information Circular No. 15 (Rolla, Missouri: State Dept. of Business and Administration, 1957); Figure 11.21, from *Ohio Land Subdivision*, p. 210; Figure 11.22B, see credit for Figure 11.18.

CHAPTER 12

Figure 12.3, courtesy Yerkes Observatory (Williams Bay, WI); Figure 12.9, data from map titled "Magnetic Declination in the United States—1990," courtesy USGS.

CHAPTER 13

Cartoon, courtesy Sierra Features Syndicate; Figure 13.1, courtesy U.S. Army (from *Map Reading*, FM 21-26, 1965); Figure 13.13, courtesy Maryland Dept. of Transportation; Figure 13.14, courtesy Alaska and North Carolina Depts. of Transportation.

CHAPTER 14

Cartoon, courtesy Cartoons by Johns; Figure 14.3C, photo courtesy Ranging, Inc. (East Rochester, NY); Figure 14.10, altimeter photo courtesy Peet Bros. Co., Inc. Ocean, NJ); Figure 14.12, map courtesy Standard Oil Division, American Oil Co.; Figure 13.13, Triptik courtesy American Automobile Association.

CHAPTER 15

Figures 15.1 through 15.7, courtesy Garmin Corporation (1200 E 151st St, Olathe, KS 66062);

Figure 15.8, courtesy Magellan Systems Corp. (San Dimas, CA), Figure 15.9, courtesy Lowrance Electronics (Tulsa, OK); Figure 15.10, courtesy ETAK, Inc. (Menlo Park, CA).

CHAPTER 16

Figure 16.9, photo courtesy Hewlett-Packard Corp. (Cupertino, CA); Figure 16.10, courtesy Keuffel & Esser Co. (Morristown, NJ); Figure 16.16A, base courtesy USGS.

CHAPTER 17

Figure 17.13, method from K.R. Cox, *Man, Location, and Behavior* (New York: John Wiley & Sons, 1972); Figure 15.15, after W. Wantz, "Transatlantic Flights and Pressure Patterns," *The Geographical Review*, Vol. 51, 1961, p. 206.

CHAPTER 19

Figure 19.1, Earthvisions, Inc. (Greenland, NH); Figure 19.2, courtesy DeLorme Mapping, Inc. (Freeport, ME); Figures 19.3 and 19.4, courtesy Microsoft Automap (www.microsoft.com/automap/); Figure 19.5, Golden Software, Inc. (Golden, CO); Figure 19.6 and 19.7, ESRI (Redlands, CA). Figure 19.9, after map published in Michael Tomasky, "Out-of-Bounds Lines?," *Harper's*, Vol. 284, No. 1702 (March 1992), pp. 56-57; Figure 19.11, after cover illustration, *Land Records Modernization*, Wis. Land Information Reports, No. 2 (Madison: University of Wis.-Madison, 1984); Figures 19.15 and 19.16, after maps created by ESRI (Redlands, CA), Figure 19.17, courtesy John Deere & Co. (Moline, IL).

CHAPTER 20

Figure 20.1, courtesy American Digital Cartography, Inc. (Appleton, WI); Boxes 20.1, 20.2, and 20.3, courtesy Morris Thompson, *Maps for America*, 2nd ed. (Reston, VA: USGS, 1982); Figure 20.3, courtesy Central Intelligence Agency.

PART III

Cartoon, courtesy Robert Tucker.

CHAPTER 21

Figure 21.1, after maps published in *Continents Adrift*, Readings from *Scientific American* (San Francisco: W.H. Freeman & Co., 1972); Figure 21.2B, after Armin K. Lobeck, *Things Maps Don't Tell Us* (New York: Macmillan Publishing Co., 1956); Figure 21.2C, after Great Lakes Basin Framework Study, Appendix 3, "Geology and Ground Water"; Figure 21.2D, after *Atlas* of *Mich.*, p. 28; Figure 21.3, courtesy USGS; Figure 21.10, after map found in D. Watson, *Designing & Building a Solar House* (Charlotte, VT: Garden Way Publishing, 1977), p. 12; Figure 21.13, map after "Natural Vegetation" map by A.W. Kuchler; Figure 21.15, courtesy Oregon Dept. of Fish and Wildlife; Figure 21.16, after map found in *Atlas of Mich.* (Lansing: Mich. State University Press, 1977); Figure 21.17, after maps found in J.P. Linduska, ed., *Waterfowl Tomorrow* (Washington, DC: U.S. Dept. of the Interior, 1964).

CHAPTER 22

Figure 22.5, after U.S. Forest Service map of the Black Hills; Figure 22.6, courtesy Wis. Coastal Management Program; Figure 22.8, courtesy Agricultural Journalism Dept., University of Wis.-Madison; Figure 22.9, data courtesy Wis. State Dept. of Agriculture; Figure 22.10, courtesy Milwaukee Map Service, Inc.; Figure 22.11, data courtesy U.S. Census Bureau.

CHAPTER 23

Figure 23.1, after C.A. Woollum, *Weatherwise*, Vol. 17, 1964; Figure 23.2, from photo published in Claudia Glenn Dowling, "This Precious Planet," *Life*, Vol. 15, No. 4 (April 1992), pp. 34-35; Figure 23.7A, courtesy USGS; Figure 23.7B, courtesy Oregon Dept. of Fish and Wildlife; Figure 23.8, data from Long Beach Harbor Dept.

CHAPTER 24

Figures 24.5, courtesy Environmental Research Institute of Mich. (Ann Arbor); Figure 24.6, courtesy NASA and EROS Data Center; Figure 24.7B, NASA-Ames Research Center Airborne Science and Application Program C-130 aircraft image; Figure 24.9, courtesy Goodyear Aerospace; Figure 24.20, courtesy EOSAT (Lanham, Md); Figure 24.21, courtesy USGS.

CHAPTER 25

Cartoon, courtesy Newspaper Enterprise Association; Figure 25.1, courtesy *Wis. State Journal*, Madison Newspapers, Inc.; Figure 25.3, after Exxon Corp. advertisement; Figure 25.4, maps plotted by UWCL; Figure 25.6, courtesy National Car Rental Co.; Figure 25.7, after *Time Magazine* maps (May 30, 1977, and June 13, 1977); Figure 25.8, map from *Dells Territory* promotional brochure (1977); Figure 25.9A, after *Time Magazine* map (October 21, 1974); Figure 25.10, courtesy Pan American Airways; quotation from *The New York Times*, reprinted by permission of the New York Times Co., copyright 1972.

APPENDIX B

Figure B.8, courtesy ITT Decca Marine, Inc. (Palm Coast, FL); Figure B.10, courtesy R.J. Doviak, National Severe Storms Laboratory, MOAA; Figure B.11, courtesy Stanford Technology Group; Figure B.12, courtesy Satellite Service Branch, NOAA; Figure B.13, courtesy ERIM (Ann Arbor, MI); Figure B.15, courtesy EROS Data Center; Figure B.16, courtesy USGS and Jet Propulsion Laboratory; Figure B.21, Landsat MSS images (October 11, 1972), courtesy NASA Goddard Space Flight Center; Figure B.22, courtesy EOSAT (Lanham, MD); Figure B.23, Courtesy SPOT Image Corp. (Reston, VA); Figure B.24, courtesy Space Imaging EOSAT (Thornton, CO); Figure B.25, courtesy Optronics International, Inc.; Figure B.26, courtesy Goodyear Aerospace; Figure B.27, courtesy W.A. Davis, Dept. of Computer Science, University of Alberta.

APPENDIX C

Cartoon, courtesy United Feature Syndicate; Figure C.1 (top), from C.H. Deetz and O.S. Adams, *Elements of Map Projection*, Special Publ. No. 68, 5th ed. (Washington, DC: Coast and Geodetic Survey, 1945), p. 21; Figure C.2, after I. Fisher and O.M. Miller, *World Maps and Globes* (New York: Essential Books, 1944), p. 101; Figure C.8, after map in "Life Presents R. Buckminster Fuller's Dymaxion World," *Life*, March 1, 1943; Figure C.9 after E. Raisz, *Principles of Cartography* (New York: McGraw-Hill Book Co., 1962), p. 168; Figure C.16, after Deetz and Adams, pp. 44-45 (see Figure C.1 above); Figure C.18, courtesy UWCL (Madison, WI); Figure C.21, courtesy J.P. Snyder.

APPENDIX D

Figure D.1, courtesy the Brunton Co. (Riverton, WY); Figure D.2, courtesy Silva Co. (LaPorte, IN), Taylor Instrument (Arden, NC), E.S. Ritchie & Sons, Inc. (Pembroke, MA), unknown company (photo courtesy Jeffrey Sledge), Keuffel & Esser Co. (Morristown, NJ), and Olsen Knife Co. (photo courtesy Jeffrey Sledge); Figure D.6A, taken from Figure 4-14 in *Flight Training: Air Navigation*, AFM 51-40 (Washington, DC: U.S. Dept. of the Air Force and Navy, 1973); Figure D.6B, courtesy Gyration, Inc. (Saratoga, CA); Figure D.7, courtesy National Ocean Survey, NOAA; Figure D.8B, courtesy Magellan Systems Corp. (San Dimas, CA); Figure D.10, courtesy Omnistar, Inc. (Houston, TX).

APPENDIX E

Tables E.6 and E.7, courtesy U.S. Coast and Geodetic Survey; Table E.9, from Smithsonian Geographical Tables.

INDEX